Introduction to Public Librarianship

SECOND EDITION

Kathleen de la Peña McCook

Neal-Schuman Publishers, Inc.

New York   London

Published by Neal-Schuman Publishers, Inc.
100 William St., Suite 2004
New York, NY 10038

Printed and bound in the United States of America.

The paper used in this publication meets the minimum requirements of American National Standard for Information Sciences—Permanence of Paper for Printed Library Materials, ANSI Z39.48-1992.

Library of Congress Cataloging-in-Publication Data

McCook, Kathleen de la Peña.
    Introduction to public librarianship / Kathleen de la Peña McCook. — 2nd ed.
       p. cm.
    Includes bibliographical references and index.
    ISBN 978-1-55570-697-5 (alk. paper)
    1. Public libraries—United States. I. Title.

Z731.M355 2011
027.473—dc22

                                      2011004985

Dedication

To three women whose values have affected the development of public librarianship in the twenty-first century:

Anna Eleanor Roosevelt
   Human Rights
   The Human Rights Years, 1945–1948 (Thomson Gale, 2007)

Hillary Rodham Clinton
   Democracy and Global Affairs
   It Takes a Village (Simon and Schuster, 1996)

Laura Welch Bush
   Laura Bush Foundation for America's Libraries
   Laura Bush 21st Century Librarian Program (U.S. Institute of Museum
   and Library Services)

Contents

List of Figures

Foreword

Public libraries today operate in a perpetually changing environment and many managers, staff, and board members feel overwhelmed by the dual pressures of rapidly expanding technologies and limited budgets. Dr. Carl Sagan said, "You have to know the past to understand the present." *Introduction to Public Librarianship* provides a framework and context that will help both current staff and the next generation of librarians know more about the past. This in turn will help them to better understand the present and to plan more effectively for the future.

As I read *Introduction to Public Librarianship*, I realized how long it has been since I thought about the roots of the services that public libraries offer and the evolution of our values and principles. If Melvil Dewey walked into a modern public library, he would probably be astonished at the transformations that have occurred in the institution he so strongly influenced. Today's public libraries, with their open and friendly public spaces, programs and services for all ages, multiple types of media, advanced technology, and emphasis on meeting community needs would appear to be completely different from the venerable public libraries of the nineteenth century. However, if Mr. Dewey spent some time talking to the people who manage and staff modern public libraries, he would discover that the libraries of today are built on the foundations that were established 150 years ago.

The significant changes in the past 100 years have been in the values and principles that support the services provided by public libraries. *Introduction to Public Librarianship* traces the increasing acceptance of the principles of equal access for all ages, races, and ethnicities; intellectual freedom and the Library Bill of Rights; human rights; and support for democracy. It is easy for those of us who work in libraries today to take these principles for granted and to forget how hard previous generations of librarians and library advocates fought for them. *Introduction to Public Librarianship* provides an important reminder that the values which we share must be sustained and that there is more work to be done to ensure that everyone receives the public library services they need and want.

When I work with library staff on identifying priorities, developing new services, measuring the library's success, or creating advocacy plans, I find that many lack the context they need to be able to effectively translate theory into practice. Dr. McCook is an academic whose work is grounded in the real world of librarianship. There is nothing theoretical about her discussions of library statistics and standards, infrastructure and funding, administration and staff, and advocacy and politics. All current and potential librarians need to understand how these issues affect their libraries and their jobs.

Not surprisingly, the chapters that describe the evolution of the library planning process and the current models of service for adults and youth were of great interest to me. Dr. McCook makes a clear distinction between the functions of state public library standards and the purpose of a community-based public library planning process. She underscores the importance of public library planning and the value of the Public Library Association's *Strategic Planning for Results* process.

Strategic Planning for Results includes eighteen public library service responses, defined as "what a library does for, or offers to, the public in an effort to meet a well-defined set of community needs" (Himmel and Wilson, 1998: 54). The current service responses were identified through an open process that I facilitated with June Garcia in 2007. The process involved several hundred library staff members from across the country who participated in open hearings and in discussions on the PLA blog. The final service responses reflect a consensus about the range of possible service priorities a public library might select to meet community needs. Libraries using *Strategic Planning for Results* are encouraged to match the possible service responses with the needs of their communities and to select only those that will most benefit the community as priorities.

Strategic Planning for Results provides detailed information about each service response, including a general description, suggested target audiences, typical services and programs offered by libraries that select the service response as a priority, potential community partners, library policy implications, critical resources, and possible measures (Nelson, 2008: 143–217). The descriptions do not provide any information about the historical context of each service response, and that is what Dr. McCook has done so well in this book.

Dr. McCook has written two chapters on library services, one that discusses adult services and a second that discusses youth services. In each of these chapters, she has organized the service responses into four groups "to reflect a broader vision of the public library's centrality to its community" (p. 206): public sphere, cultural heritage, education, and information. In doing so, she has helped her readers understand not only *what* the service entails but *why* the service is important and *how* it fits into the broader issues of public librarianship.

Last, but by no means least, I want to acknowledge the detailed notes, citations, and bibliographic references that are provided throughout the text. As I read the book, I found myself stopping to look up an article that was referenced or to check a website that provided more information on the topic being presented. This book is a treasure trove of information for any serious student of public librarianship, and I include myself in that category. I have been a practicing librarian for 40 years and I am still fascinated with the profession—its past, its present, and all of its potential futures. *Introduction to Public Librarianship* added to my knowledge and has provided me with new avenues to explore. That is all any could ask of a book such as this—and far more than one usually gets.

Sandra Nelson

References

Himmel, Ethel, and William James Wilson. 1998. *Planning for Results: A Public Library Transformation Process.* Chicago: American Library Association.

Nelson, Sandra. 2008. *Strategic Planning for Results.* Chicago: American Library Association.

Sandra Nelson is a consultant, speaker, trainer, and writer specializing in public library planning and management issues. She is a leader in the development of planning and management tools for public librarians and is the Senior Editor of the Public Library Association (PLA) Results series, an integrated library of planning and resource allocation manuals.

Sandra is the author or co-author of six of the books in Results series, including *Strategic Planning for Results*, the foundation of the series, and the recently published *Implementing for Results*. She has used her planning expertise to help library managers, staff, and board members to develop strategic plans in dozens of public libraries of all sizes.

Preface

Public libraries in the United States of America are in their third century of service as the heart of communities throughout the nation. Our public libraries are our public sphere open to all who desire to use their services—both as cultural spaces and as virtual services. The literature of public librarianship is extensive, but it is also dispersed among many specializations such as management, information technology, youth services, and community planning. In truth, public librarianship incorporates all of these specializations, just as public librarians work to serve all people—all backgrounds, all ethnicities, all ages, all religions or no religion, all abilities, all economic means. This universality of mission and responsibilities presents a grand challenge. The public library of the twenty-first century is more complex than its nineteenth-century predecessor with multiple formats, mobile access, and the mandate to provide equity of access to all. The larger community is made stronger by a vibrant public library and the library remains a positive indicator of the quality of life in every community.

Purpose

Introduction to Public Librarianship, Second Edition, provides the historical, sociological, and cultural background of the public library in the United States. Full understanding is necessary for the future inheritors of this fundamental institution of democracy. This volume is a guide to the extensive literature of the field's various areas of specialization. This book was written for students, new librarians, library trustees and friends, and the general public who wish to understand the historical and sociological foundations of different aspects of public librarianship. Readers of *Introduction to Public Librarianship* will gain a greater understanding of the following key areas:

- The history of public librarianship within the broader historical and cultural movements of the times
- The landmark literature of the field's development
- The evolution of standards and planning for public library service
- The role of the political process in the growth of libraries and library services

- Public libraries' adult and youth services as reflections of changing societal trends in the context of the Public Library Association Strategic Planning model
- The overarching ideas, principles, and goals that drive public librarianship and the necessity of continuing to work toward these goals
- Human rights and human capabilities as the lodestars that will guide public library service in the twenty-first century

Organization

Each chapter provides a holistic approach to its subject. I have provided a historical background to the subject, an organizational context, and discussion about the development of public libraries.

Each chapter is keyed to Selected Readings in Appendix A to help readers better understand the wealth of information available in public libraries and to help them explore topics in greater detail.

Chapter 1, "The Landscape of Public Libraries in the Twenty-First Century," provides readers with a context for understanding where we are today. The scope and range of public librarianship is defined and summarized. This chapter also includes background information about services to Native Americans, a population that is increasingly seeing new service and support from the Institute of Museum and Library Services. This presentation will help readers understand the progress and development outlined in the rest of the book.

Chapter 2, "Brahmins, Bequests, and Determined Women: The Beginnings to 1918," reviews the historical antecedents and the legal basis for establishing tax-supported public libraries. It explores and discusses the fundamental *Report of the Trustees of the Public Library of the City of Boston, 1852*, one of the key documents of U.S. librarianship. This chapter pays special attention to the important role played by women in the establishment of public library service across the United States.

Chapter 3, "Public Library Growth and Values: 1918–Today" covers the history of public libraries from 1918 to the present. It focuses on efforts to equalize opportunity through the growing role assumed by the American Library Association, the enactment of federal legislation (LSA, LSCA, LSTA), and an expanded scope of activity for the public library. It also discusses the work of national and state library associations and the role of state library agencies, as the growing voice of advocacy for libraries that resulted from these actions.

Chapter 4, "Statistics, Standards, Planning, Results, and Quality of Life" explores public library statistics and reviews the development of standards for public library service developed by the American Library Association. It analyzes the evolution of a planning process to replace standards and explores the role of the public library as a quality-of-life indicator in local communities.

Chapter 5, "Organization, Law, Advocacy, Funding, and Politics," reviews the political and economic context in which the public library functions. This chapter pays due attention to the organizational, legal, and funding basis of the public library, noting the parallels to municipal government structure and the move to larger units of service. The importance of advocacy at all levels is emphasized.

Chapter 6, "Administration and Staffing," surveys the structure of governance including model-enabling legislation. It presents the changing role of the library board over time. This chapter also introduces typical position descriptions and describes the need to recruit a diverse staff.

Chapter 7, "Structure and Infrastructure," looks at the history of public library buildings (including the symbolism of the public library building), as well as the influence of the Library Services and Construction Act (LSCA) over construction during the last third of the twentieth century and the shift in federal funding from construction (structure) to support for technology (infrastructure). This chapter also summarizes design standards including accessibility. The need for security and disaster planning are presented.

Chapters 8 and 9, "Adult Services" and "Youth Services," review the history and current status of these two distinct areas of service. In both chapters the service responses enumerated in the Public Library Association *Strategic Planning for Results* (Nelson, 2008) are reorganized under four categories to reflect a different way of looking at the public library's importance to its communities:

1. Public sphere
2. Cultural heritage
3. Education
4. Information

Chapter 9 is coauthored with me by Alicia K. Long, research associate, teacher, Spectrum Scholar, and community volunteer. A list of recommended websites for libraries serving youth is provided.

Chapter 10, "The Interconnective Nature of the Public Library," examines the importance of networking in public librarianship—the role of professional organizations, state library agencies, library consortia, and social networking. The boundary-spanning nature of public librarianship is defined and the importance of this to future development noted.

Barbara J. Ford, distinguished professor of international librarianship and director of the Mortenson Center for International Library Programs at the University of Illinois at Urbana-Champaign, wrote Chapter 11, "Global Perspectives on Public Libraries."

This chapter analyzes the importance of the "IFLA/UNESCO Public Library Manifesto" (UNESCO, 1994), offers points of interest on public library development around the globe, and characterizes international library development initiatives.

Chapter 12, "The Future of Public Libraries in the Twenty-First Century: Human Rights and Human Capabilities," is coauthored with me by Katharine J. Phenix. Ms. Phenix is the Adult Services Librarian (aka Experience Guide) at the Huron Street branch of the Rangeview Library District, Thornton, Colorado. This chapter presents the millennium development goals in service of a human capabilities approach. We note that the path will be clear to achieving universal human rights with the support and commitment of public librarians.

Appendixes

There are four appendixes at the end of the book. Appendix A, "Selected Readings," is an extensive list of readings keyed to each chapter, selected from 150 years of books, articles, and government reports, addressing topics related to the history and development of public libraries. Although I have also included websites, I have taken much care to review and assess salient items, especially those predating 1985. My rationale in this is gauged from a review of much current literature, which seems, increasingly, to rely upon bibliographic citations from online databases. It is my judgment that by providing this selected bibliography at the outset of the twenty-first century, I am helping to connect the public librarians of tomorrow with those from the past, who have written so much and so well for the good of librarianship.

The welcoming remarks from the 21st Century Learner Conference on November 7, 2001, by the first librarian to be director of the Institute of Museum and Library Services, Robert S. Martin, are presented as Appendix B. After the events of September 11, 2001, the nation was in mourning. I felt that this conference would be momentous in the history of librarianship. It was about the convergence of cultural heritage institutions and free-choice learning. My husband, Bill McCook, and my friend the Louisiana state librarian for computing services, Sara M. Taffae, drove with me from Tampa, Florida, to the conference. Dr. Martin's remarks were initially posted at the IMLS website, but they were taken down after 2008. I reproduce his remarks here because I believe that this historic conference, which took place at such a turning point in the history of the United States, was also a turning point in public library development.

Appendix C, "Community Foundations and the Public Library: Libraries for the Future," is an important document that defined the role of foundations in supporting public libraries. It was written by Diantha Dow Schull and William Zeisel for Libraries for the Future (LFF), a national nonprofit organization that championed the role of libraries in American life. LFF ceased operations in March 2009.

Appendix D is "Bibliography of National Statistics on Public Libraries." Beginning with the first federal report on public libraries, completed in 1850, I present in chronological order the record of publications that track statistics about a wide array of aspects of public libraries, such as their numbers, activities, uses, physical features, management, programs, and holdings. The reports by Herbert Goldhor (1983), "U.S. Public Library Statistics in Series: A Bibliography and Subject Index" and Robert V. Williams and Mittie Kristina McLean (2008), *A Bibliographical Guide to a Chronological Record of Statistics of National Scope on Libraries in the United States*, were key to the development of this bibliography.

Introduction to Public Librarianship, Second Edition, provides essential information for future library workers to inherit the future of public libraries as developed by their past and to continue to follow the ideas, principles, and goals that have shaped over 150 years of public librarianship in the United States.

References

Goldhor, Herbert. 1983. "U.S. Public Library Statistics in Series: A Bibliography and Subject Index." In *Bowker Annual of Library & Book Trade Information*. 28th ed., pp. 327–335. New York: R.R. Bowker.

Nelson, Sandra. 2008. *Strategic Planning for Results*. Chicago: American Library Association.

UNESCO. 1994. "The IFLA/UNESCO Public Library Manifesto." http://www.ifla.org/en/publications/iflaunesco-public-library-manifesto-1994.

Williams, Robert V., and Mittie Kristina McLean. 2008. *A Bibliographical Guide to a Chronological Record of Statistics of National Scope on Libraries in the United States*. Columbia, SC: University of South Carolina, School of Library and Information Science.

Acknowledgments

Special gratitude is due to Charles Harmon, Vice President and Director of Publishing at Neal-Schuman, for patience and counsel, and to Amy Knauer for assistance throughout the production process; Alicia K. Long, research associate at the University of South Florida, School of Information, for her review of websites; Loriene Roy, past president of the American Library Association and professor at the University of Texas for her many helpful suggestions, especially regarding Native American library services; and Sara M. Taffae, former director of computer services at the State Library of Louisiana for her observations on the national computing infrastructure and the role of the Gates Foundation.

I am most grateful to Gary O. Rolstad, who passed away April 7, 2005. Gary was director of library development at the State Library of Louisiana and his wisdom on the role of trustees was fundamental to observations on citizen involvement. Also thanks to Susan Dillinger, director of the New Port Richey (Florida) Library, for her thoughts on advocacy issues and to Kathleen Weibel, former director of staff development at the Chicago Public Library, for her abiding practice of the library faith.

On a personal level I extend much gratitude and love to my family of public library patrons—my husband, William W. McCook; my daughter, Margaret H. Christ, and son-in-law, John W. Christ; and to the future, my new grandson, Adam P. Christ.

1

The Landscape of Public Libraries in the Twenty-First Century

The public library is an excellent model of government at its best. A locally controlled public good, it serves every individual freely, in as much or as little depth as he or she wants.

—John N. Berry III, "A Model for the Public Sector," 2001

Public Libraries Today

The public library in cities and towns and rural areas across the United States is a community center for books, media, and information access. In any community, the local public library provides a sense of place, a refuge, and a still point; it is a commons, a vital part of the public sphere and an incubator of ideas. The public library supports family literacy, fosters lifelong learning, helps immigrants find a place, and gives a place to those for whom there is no other place to be. The public library provides a wide-open door to knowledge and information to people of all ages, abilities, ethnicities, and economic status. The public library is a haven in times of disaster, like the aftermath of Hurricane Katrina (Dawson and McCook, 2006).

People who use the public library will fight to maintain it even in hard budget times. People who do not use the public library support it. Individuals afraid of the influence of ideas may attack the public library. But philanthropists and average citizens donate money to support the public library. Politicians make proclamations about the public library as the heart of the community. In the United States, the public library exists in cities and towns and rural counties due to many factors, many advocates, and many dreams.

Today throughout the United States, after over a century and a half of tax-supported public library service, the variety of manifestations of the public library is astounding. Stand-alone libraries serve small towns; systems with dozens of branches meet the needs of large cities; and county libraries and multicounty systems reach even wider areas. The Peterborough Town Library, New Hampshire, is accorded the distinction of being the first public library to be established from the start as a publicly supported institution in 1833. However, through an act of the Massachusetts General Court in 1848, the Boston Public Library was the first municipal library to be authorized by a state law.

If we look at three major assessments of the status of public libraries in the United States, conducted over the last 125, years we observe changing definitions of libraries. These three assessments were published in 1876, 1935, and 2010:

- U.S. Department of the Interior report, *Public Libraries in the United States of America* (1876)
- Carleton Bruns Joeckel's study, *The Government of the American Public Library* (1935)
- U.S. Institute of Museum and Library Services, *Public Libraries Survey: Fiscal Year 2008* (Henderson et al., 2010)

In the 1876 report, *Public Libraries in the United States of America*, the term "free public library" was used to describe tax-supported libraries, while the report covered and combined information on these, plus society libraries, historical societies, mercantile libraries, and government libraries. In 1935 Joeckel commented that the definition of a "public library" is surprisingly difficult. He was referring to the varied methods of funding and governance that characterized libraries officially charged with the responsibility of providing free library service of a general nature to a particular community. Today, the 2010 report, *Public Libraries Survey*, compiled through the voluntary Federal-State Cooperative System (FSCS), defines a public library more precisely:

> Public library (FSCS definition). A public library is an entity that is established under state enabling laws or regulations to serve a community, district, or region, and that provides at least the following: 1) An organized collection of printed or other library materials, or a combination thereof; 2) Paid staff; 3) An established schedule in which services of the staff are available to the public; 4) The facilities necessary to support such a collection, staff, and schedule; and 5) Is supported in whole or in part with public funds. (Henderson et al., 2010: 2)

Yet even with more precision in the definition that we use today, is there a typical public library in the United States? The answer is so complex that general characterization is practically impossible. Great urban libraries in New York, Chicago, and Los Angeles serve millions of people in dozens of branches with many hundreds of librarians and library workers, and millions of books, while scattered rural libraries may stay open a few hours a week based on volunteer availability. Tax support, sometimes generous and sometimes modest, is the glue that holds this continuum together, from a belief in the "library faith" that this institution makes a difference in peoples' lives (Garceau, 1949: 50–52).

Today, 9,221 public libraries (administrative entities) operate in the 50 states and the District of Columbia, functioning with 16,671 stationary service points and 797 bookmobiles. Public libraries in the United States have a combined operating income of $10.7 billion, spending an average of $36.36 per capita. The nation's public library collection numbers 816.1 million print items, 49.6 million audio materials, and 49.2 million video materials. These libraries employ 145,244 staff to provide services. Nationwide circulation is 2.28 billion items, of which 786.4 million are to children. There are 1.5 billion visits per year to U.S. public libraries—five visits per capita. Patrons can access the Internet at 219,736 public use terminals (Henderson et al., 2010). Each public library operates within the context of community norms and support—in a municipal, district, or county structure subject to local politics and the local economy. Figure 1.1 (pp. 4–6) presents these factors.

For oversight and support, each state has a library agency that distributes federal funds, which is charged by state law with the extension and development of public library services throughout the state. This agency administers state plans in accordance with the provisions of the Library Services and Technology Act. The agency collects statistics, coordinates library planning and research, and reviews technology plans for e-rate discounts (Henderson et al., 2010). Within the states, cooperatives facilitate and promote library operations—often with a multitype focus. Additionally, cooperatives such as Lyrasis (http://www.lyrasis.org/) provide multistate services.

Librarians join together for continuing education and advocacy, through national associations such as the American Library Association, regional multistate associations such as the Southeastern Library Association (http://selaonline.org/) or Pacific Northwest Library Association (http://www.pnla.org/), state associations, or even county or city associations. Each of these organizations and associations has contributed to the enhancement of library services through the development of guidelines, standards, benchmarks, and best practices.

Increasingly, public libraries work in partnership with other community agencies, such as museums, historical societies, botanical gardens, art centers, and social service agencies. These partnerships have increased since the creation of the Institute of Museum and Library Services in 1996, as the federal agency responsible for administering the Library Services and Technology Act. The ongoing development of active interaction with other cultural heritage institutions and social service agencies is transforming the public library in the twenty-first century.

As an institution, the public library does not stand alone. This book situates the library within its historical context for each aspect of service. Modern librarians must perceive the public library in connection with the print (or media) culture of its times,

Figure 1.1. Number of Public Libraries, Population of Legal Service Area, Unduplicated Population of Legal Service Area, and Official State Population Estimate by State: Fiscal Year 2008

State	Number of public libraries[1]	Population of legal service area[2]		Unduplicated population of legal service area[3]		State population estimate[4]	
		Total (in thousands)	Response rate[5]	Total (in thousands)	Response rate[5]	Total (in thousands)	Response rate[5]
Total	9,221	298,390	100.0	294,936	100.0	302,864	100.0
Alabama	210	4,438	100.0	4,438	100.0	4,438	100.0
Alaska	86	680	100.0	680	100.0	680	100.0
Arizona	86	6,489	100.0	6,489	100.0	6,500	100.0
Arkansas	51	2,704	100.0	2,656	100.0	2,776	100.0
California	181	38,049	100.0	38,049	100.0	38,049	100.0
Colorado	115	4,861	100.0	4,861	100.0	4,920	100.0
Connecticut	195	4,307	100.0	3,511	100.0	3,511	100.0
Delaware	21	790	100.0	790	100.0	873	100.0
District of Columbia	1	588	100.0	588	100.0	588	100.0
Florida	80	18,982	100.0	18,776	100.0	18,807	100.0
Georgia	59	9,320	100.0	9,320	100.0	9,320	100.0
Hawaii	1	1,283	100.0	1,283	100.0	1,283	100.0
Idaho	104	1,352	100.0	1,332	100.0	1,524	100.0
Illinois	634	11,681	100.0	11,684	100.0	12,902	100.0
Indiana	238	5,822	100.0	5,700	100.0	6,080	100.0
Iowa	539	2,964	100.0	2,964	100.0	3,003	100.0
Kansas	327	2,367	100.0	2,365	100.0	2,776	100.0
Kentucky	116	4,204	100.0	4,204	100.0	4,241	100.0
Louisiana	68	4,433	100.0	4,411	100.0	4,411	100.0
Maine	272	1,375	100.0	1,212	100.0	1,315	100.0

(Continued)

Figure 1.1 (Continued)

State	Number of public libraries[1]	Population of legal service area[2] Total (in thousands)	Response rate[5]	Unduplicated population of legal service area[3] Total (in thousands)	Response rate[5]	State population estimate[4] Total (in thousands)	Response rate[5]
Maryland	24	5,600	100.0	5,600	100.0	5,600	100.0
Massachusetts	370	6,475	100.0	6,449	100.0	6,450	100.0
Michigan	384	9,952	100.0	9,932	100.0	9,953	100.0
Minnesota	138	5,642	100.0	5,263	100.0	5,263	100.0
Mississippi	50	2,960	100.0	2,939	100.0	2,939	100.0
Missouri	152	5,121	100.0	5,121	100.0	5,912	100.0
Montana	80	900	100.0	900	100.0	900	100.0
Nebraska	270	1,388	100.0	1,299	100.0	1,775	100.0
Nevada	22	2,739	100.0	2,739	100.0	2,739	100.0
New Hampshire	231	1,442	100.0	1,311	100.0	1,315	100.0
New Jersey	303	9,030	100.0	8,336	100.0	8,414	100.0
New Mexico	91	1,555	100.0	1,555	100.0	1,955	100.0
New York	755	19,079	100.0	18,928	100.0	18,928	100.0
North Carolina	77	9,068	100.0	9,069	100.0	9,069	100.0
North Dakota	81	571	100.0	571	100.0	641	100.0
Ohio	251	11,511	100.0	11,511	100.0	11,511	100.0
Oklahoma	115	2,979	100.0	2,979	100.0	3,642	100.0
Oregon	126	3,351	100.0	3,351	100.0	3,745	100.0
Pennsylvania	457	12,060	100.0	11,971	100.0	12,284	100.0
Rhode Island	48	1,298	100.0	1,058	100.0	1,058	100.0
South Carolina	42	4,414	100.0	4,414	100.0	4,414	100.0
South Dakota	114	717	100.0	699	100.0	804	100.0
Tennessee	187	6,082	100.0	6,082	100.0	6,107	100.0

(Continued)

Figure 1.1. Number of Public Libraries, Population of Legal Service Area, Unduplicated Population of Legal Service Area, and Official State Population Estimate by State: Fiscal Year 2008 (Continued)

State	Number of public libraries[1]	Population of legal service area[2]		Unduplicated population of legal service area[3]		State population estimate[4]	
		Total (in thousands)	Response rate[5]	Total (in thousands)	Response rate[5]	Total (in thousands)	Response rate[5]
Texas	561	22,262	100.0	22,262	100.0	23,904	100.0
Utah	69	2,636	100.0	2,616	100.0	2,616	100.0
Vermont	183	731	100.0	604	100.0	621	100.0
Virginia	91	7,661	100.0	7,599	100.0	7,712	100.0
Washington	64	6,458	100.0	6,458	100.0	6,588	100.0
West Virginia	97	1,808	100.0	1,808	100.0	1,808	100.0
Wisconsin	381	5,674	100.0	5,674	100.0	5,674	100.0
Wyoming	23	523	100.0	523	100.0	523	100.0
Outlying areas							
Guam	1	26	100.0	26	100.0	155	100.0
Puerto Rico	35	2,710	100.0	1,895	100.0	3,954	100.0

[1]A public library is an administrative entity, the agency that is legally established under local or state law to provide public library service to the population of a local jurisdiction. The administrative entity may have a single public library service outlet, or it may have more than one outlet. The types of administrative structures for public libraries are reported in table 2. See table 3 for additional information.

[2]The number of people in the geographic area for which a public library has been established to offer services and from which (or on behalf of which) the library derives revenue, plus any areas served under contract for which the library is the primary service provider. The determination of this figure is the responsibility of the state library agency and should be based on the most recent official state population figures for jurisdictions in the state available from the State Data Center or other official state sources.

[3]This is the total unduplicated population of those areas in the state that receive library services. The determination of this figure is the responsibility of the state library agency and should be based on the most recent official state population figures for jurisdictions in the state. The population of unserved areas is not included in this figure.

[4]This is the most recent official total population figure for the state that matches the local population figures that are submitted to IMLS. The state data coordinator for the state library agency is instructed to obtain the figure annually from the State Data Center or other official state sources.

[5]Response rate is calculated as the number of libraries that reported the item, divided by the total number of libraries in the survey frame.

NOTE: A state's total *population of legal service area* may be larger than the state's total *unduplicated population of legal service area* or the *official state population estimate* because some public libraries have overlapping service areas. Detail may not sum to totals because of rounding. Data were not reported by the following outlying areas (American Samoa, Northern Marianas, and Virgin Islands). Missing data were not imputed for nonresponding outlying areas.

Source: Institute of Museum and Library Services, Survey of Public Libraries in the United States, Fiscal Year 2008.

Source: U.S. Institute of Museum and Library Services. 2010. *Public Libraries Survey: Fiscal Year 2008.* Washington, DC: U.S. Institute of Museum and Library Services, pp. 25–26.

and in concert with broader social concerns, such as universal education and progressivism. Traditionally, the public has viewed libraries as broad collections of resources, but the process of selecting and gathering books has become a challenge with consolidation of media producers. Librarians today must develop an understanding of publishing and sources able to provide and build diverse collections both physical and digital. The increase in multiple sources of media requires more attention to these issues, coupled with the challenges of providing electronic access. The collection has become dispersed, but the costs of items in the deep Internet still require review and evaluation for payment. Access to the free web through portals and links and the creation of appropriate community-based ideas are important aspects of public librarianship. Especially in times of economic crisis, such as the 2009 recession, the value placed on libraries has increased as people looked for cost-effective resources (American Library Association, 2009), but also for a living place (Christensen and Levinson, 2007). The Public Agenda (2006) report on attitudes of the public toward libraries in the twenty-first century and the characterization of the library as the heart of the nation's communities demonstrate the central role public libraries play in the U.S. panorama (Senville, 2009).

Before turning to the history of the establishment of public libraries in the United States, we should first ponder a very different type of library service—services for and with indigenous peoples of the Americas. When the National Museum of the American Indian opened in September 2004, a resource for the entire world to learn about Native American culture and life became available. While traditional cultural expressions have existed for millennia, those lives and cultures have been sustained by formally established tribal community libraries only since the 1950s. Because it is outside my expertise to address tribal community libraries, I have interviewed and sought the wisdom of Professor Loriene Roy, past president of the American Library Association, to provide a brief introduction to library service to indigenous people (see the following sidebar).

Libraries Services for and with Indigenous Peoples of the Americas: Tribal Community Libraries

This book does not address libraries for the more than 500 tribal nations residing within the geographical boundaries of the United States. There are about 500 recognized tribes and more than 10 unrecognized tribes. Not every tribe has a reservation. Indigenous peoples have a parallel history of knowledge and wisdom that must be considered in its own context. For a broader understanding of this alternative tradition, read *Tribal Libraries, Archives and Museums: Preserving our Language, Memory and Lifeways* (Roy et al., in press).

(Continued)

The U.S. government has addressed the heritage of "knowledge seekers" and "wisdom keepers," who live within Native American tribes and maintain links with traditional tribal knowledge and history; see the official report *Pathways to Excellence* (U.S. National Commission on Libraries and Information Science, 1992). Targeted federal funding is provided through the Native American Library Services Program. The Institute of Museum and Library Services (IMLS) provides basic funds, assistance grants, and enhancement grants to serve the range of needs of Indian tribes and Alaskan Native villages. Separate IMLS funding is also available for Native Hawaiian library development. Loriene Roy (2000) has summarized these programs.

Research and projects such as TRAILS and Four Directions, conducted by Native American library scholars Lotsee Patterson and Loriene Roy, have supported tribal community libraries serving indigenous people. To understand the holistic approach to service development, you can review the papers presented at the biennial International Indigenous Librarians' Forum (Roy and Smith, 2002), participate in meetings of the American Indian Library Association, follow the work of the ALA Committee on Rural, Native and Tribal Libraries of All Kinds (http://www.ala.org/ala/aboutala/offices/olos/rntloakcttee.cfm), and view work done at the National Museum of the American Indian. Roy (2000) makes the following observations about libraries serving American Indians:

> Indians are rediscovering or retaining their culture by establishing genealogy, reading and inventing literature, reclaiming their Native languages, and becoming involved with political and social issues such as natural resource management, reclamation and reburial of human remains, and protection of treaty rights. This renaissance is built partially by the work of the American Indian library community, which has labored for many years to find support for Native American educational needs.

Sources and Further Reading

American Library Association. American Indian Library Association (AILA). http://www.ailanet.org/.

Grounds, Richard A., George E. Tinker, and David E. Wilkins. 2003. *Native Voices: American Indian Identity and Resistance*. Lawrence, KS: University Press of Kansas.

Hills, Gordon H. 1997. *Native Libraries: Cross-Cultural Conditions in the Circumpolar Countries*. Lanham, MD: Scarecrow Press.

Huhndorf, Shari M. 2009. *Mapping the Americas: The Transnational Politics of Contemporary Native Culture*. Ithaca, NY: Cornell University Press.

Patterson, Lotsee. 2000. "History and Status of Native Americans in Librarianship." *Library Trends* 49, no. 1 (Summer): 182–193.

———. 2001. History and Development of Libraries on American Indian Reservations. In *International Indigenous Librarians' Forum Proceedings*, ed. Robert Sullivan, 38–44. Auckland, New Zealand: Te Ropu Whakahau.

———. 2008. "Exploring the World of American Indian Libraries." *Rural Libraries* 28: 7–12.

Roy, Loriene. 2000. "To Support and Model Native American Library Services." *Texas Library Journal* 76 (Spring): 32–35.

———. 2006. "Honoring Generations: Recruiting Native Students into Careers in Librarianship." *Public Libraries* 45 (Jan./Feb.): 48–52.

———. 2009. "If I Can Read, I Can Do Anything." School of Information, University of Texas at Austin. http://www.ischool.utexas.edu/ ~ ifican.

Roy, Loriene, and A. Arro Smith. 2002. "Supporting, Documenting and Preserving Tribal Cultural Lifeways: Library Services for Tribal Communities in the United States." *World Libraries* 12 (Spring): 28–31.

Roy, Loriene, et al. In press. *Tribal Libraries, Archives and Museums: Preserving Our Language, Memory and Lifeways*. Lanham, MD: Scarecrow Press.

U.S. Institute of Museum and Library Services. Native American/Native Hawaiian Museum Services. http://www.imls.gov/applicants/grants/nativeservices.shtm.

U.S. National Commission on Libraries and Information Science. 1992. *Pathways to Excellence: A Report on Improving Library and Information Services for Native American Peoples*. http://www.ncli.gov/libraries/nata.html.

References

American Library Association. 2009. *State of America's Libraries, 2009.* http://www.ala.org/.

Christensen, Karen, and David Levinson. 2007. *The Libraries We Love.* Great Barrington, MA: Berkshire.

Dawson, Alma, and Kathleen de la Peña McCook. 2006. "Rebuilding Community in Louisiana after the Hurricanes of 2005." *Reference and User Services Quarterly* 45 (Summer): 292–296.

Garceau, Oliver. 1949. *The Public Library in the Political Process: A Report of the Public Library Inquiry.* New York: Columbia University Press.

Henderson, E., K. Miller, T. Craig, S. Dorinski, M. Freeman, N. Isaac, J. Keng, P. O'Shea, and P. Schilling. 2010. *Data File Documentation: Public Libraries Survey: Fiscal Year 2008* (IMLS- 2010–PLS-01). Washington, DC: Institute of Museum and Library Services.

Joeckel, Carleton B. 1935. *The Government of the American Public Library.* Chicago: University of Chicago Press.

Public Agenda. 2006. *Long Overdue: A Fresh Look at Public and Leadership Attitudes about Libraries in the 21st Century.* ERIC. ED 493642. http://www.eric.ed.gov/.

Senville, Wayne. 2009. "Libraries at the Heart of Our Communities." *Planning Commissioners Journal* 75 (Summer): 12–18.

U.S. Department of the Interior, Bureau of Education. 1876. *Public Libraries in the United States of America: Their History, Condition, and Management. Special Report.* Washington, DC: U.S. Government Printing Office. Repr., as Monograph Series, no. 4, Champaign, IL: University of Illinois, Graduate School of Library Science.

2

Brahmins, Bequests, and Determined Women: The Beginnings to 1918

And yet there can be no doubt that such reading [for the diffusion of knowledge] ought to be furnished to all, as a matter of public policy and duty, on the same principle that we furnish free education, and in fact, as a part, and a most important part, of the education of all.

—*Report of the Trustees of the Public Library to the City of Boston, 1852*

In public records and published books and articles, we often find the history of public libraries in the United States treated narrowly as the story of New England settlers bringing their values to bear on the development of a new kind of institution—tax-supported public libraries. Standard histories of libraries succinctly recount the received chronology of bookmen and Boston Brahmins. Likewise, readers can find consolidated versions of the comprehensive cultural and historical literature that we must survey to gain a broad picture of this history.

Parts played by men such as George Ticknor, Edward Everett, and Alexandre Vattemare contribute a great deal to our understanding of what led to the establishment of the Boston Public Library. To follow the mainstream development of public libraries in the United States, we must relate what happened in Boston, under the guidance of these men, to later history. However, at the very outset I want readers to note that women such as Elizabeth Putnam Sohier also expanded public library service throughout the nation.

Books were important to the development and stability of the seventeenth-century colonies, particularly in what would one day be Massachusetts, and were viewed as a means to provide a continuity of values. Many of the New England colonists had private libraries. Both men and women were readers.

Europeans grasped the printed page as one of the surest ways to guarantee the safe transport of their ideas, knowledge and philosophies into the New World. As the carrier of inspiration, instructions, memories, and enjoyments, published material outlasted the long and dangerous voyage across

11

> the Atlantic to arrive unscathed on the other side. There was something concrete and unchanging about the printed word, and thus it was a rock in the courageous effort to carve out colonial Europe on the new continent. (Williams, 1999: 2)

The best-documented example of books brought to the New World as the "carrier of inspiration" is the effort of English Anglican clergyman Thomas Bray, whose Society for Promoting Christian Knowledge established parish libraries along the Eastern seaboard in Maryland, Virginia, and South Carolina between 1695 and 1704. Bray initiated three types of libraries: provincial, parochial, and layman's libraries. These also functioned as lending libraries for the public at large (Laugher, 1973). According to library historian Michael Harris (1995: 183), a few volumes from the original Bray libraries have survived in public or church collections, which serves as a reminder of a library venture that preceded the rise of the modern public library by two centuries.

The work of library historians reinforces the importance of New England in the development of tax-supported public libraries, because much of the synthetic literature about the founding of public libraries is based upon accounts written by New Englanders. Charles Coffin Jewett's (1851) *Notices of Public Libraries in the United States of America* provided the foundation for many later studies. Until 1876 the term *public library* meant any library not privately owned, while the term *free public library* was used to indicate libraries that were most like the tax-supported public library of today. Yet in the years prior to laws enabling tax-supported public libraries in the mid-1800s, tens of thousands of libraries open to various publics were established in the United States. While New England's first colonists brought books with them in 1620, and Governor John Winthrop of Connecticut had over 1,000 volumes as early as 1640, the gradual acceptance and support of the tax-supported public library throughout the United States is far more complicated than the story of New England and its influence.

Print Culture and Precursors Influencing the Establishment of Tax-Supported Public Libraries

Ten Thousand Stories

In 1876, the centennial year marking the independence of the United States, the federal Bureau of Education issued the landmark report, *Public Libraries in the United States of America: Their History, Condition, and Management, Special Report* (U.S. Department of the Interior, Bureau of Education, 1876). It included the exhibit, "Table of Public Libraries Numbering 300 Volumes or Upwards," which was the catalyst for McMullen's (2000) study of the library past of the United States, *American Libraries before 1876.* In his analysis, McMullen discusses over 80 types of libraries made available to various publics from the beginning of the colonial period to 1876. These included agricultural societies, apprentices' libraries, asylum libraries, athenaeums, church libraries, circulating libraries (commercial and society), government libraries, historical societies, ladies' libraries, lyceums, mechanics' libraries, mercantile libraries, social libraries, subscription libraries, and workingmen's libraries, as well as libraries affiliated with schools, seminaries, and colleges. McMullen's list calls to mind ten thousand stories that if known would help us to gain a fuller understanding of why communities throughout the United States organized and voted beginning in the mid-1850s to tax themselves to establish public libraries. Each collection helped to create the social and intellectual context that evoked a desire for books among its users.

Print Culture

Social historians help us trace the transformation of society into a widespread reading community.[1] To some degree the secularization of reading accounts for the diffusion of reading, but we should keep in mind that many types of reading—religious/devotional and secular—coexisted during the colonial period. People read out loud to each other, shared reading material, and read a variety of publications—devotional, secular, sensational, and serious. In the 250 or so years prior to the 1876 *Special Report*, reading and sharing books and other printed materials played a vital role in the lives of those living in the colonies and the new nation.

In the colonies, reading took place in quite diverse settings. When Benjamin Harris added a coffee shop to his Boston bookstore in 1690, the reading room in a coffeehouse became a happy consolidation that spread throughout the colonies—sometimes in connection with taverns and printers (Kaser, 1978). A variety of studies cover the world of reading in the colonies, examining religious reading, popular secular reading, the growing idea that reading was a necessity, and the development of the reading public.[2]

Reviewing the history of print culture during colonial times makes the backdrop against which the tax-supported public library was established and flourished more meaningful. But missionaries also viewed reading as a tool to convert Native Americans (Wyss, 2000), and we must remember that, in many parts of what would become the United States, African slaves were forbidden to read at all. In the antebellum South reading was seen as an act of defiance, and slaves were threatened with whipping or hanging for learning to read or write (Cornelius, 1991; Battles, 2009). By reviewing the growth of literacy and the role of reading in daily life, we come to understand more clearly the importance of the founding of the public library.

Difficult as it may be to fashion for ourselves an accurate sense of the scope of reading in the early days of the United States, taking the time to do so helps us to comprehend the social history that contributed to the eventual taxation of the community for this public good. After all, at the heart of the public library movement was an abiding belief that the provision of reading material was important to the progress of democracy.

The two major forerunners of the tax-supported public library were the *social library* and the *circulating library*. Early examples of each were in existence by the early 1700s. Social library collections emphasized literature, history, science, and theology, while circulating library collections reflected popular reading with an emphasis on fiction (as distinguished from literature). The discussions and debates about the book stock of each, almost from their beginnings, reflect the ongoing debates on book selection that persist today.

The Social Library

The social library traces its roots to English gentlemen's libraries and book clubs of the early 1700s. The Library Company of Philadelphia was established in 1731 by Benjamin Franklin as a joint- stock company or proprietary library, and has long been deemed the best known of this early form of library. This type of organization spread through the colonies. Further south, the establishment of the Charleston Library Society in South Carolina in 1748 demonstrates that the social library also existed far from New England.

Social libraries were voluntary societies whose members owned books in common from pooled funds. These included athenaeums, mercantile libraries, and mechanics' and apprentices' libraries— mainly for young men. Each of these various libraries involved the coming together of individuals to fund and develop collections based on their interests. Athenaeums emphasized more scholarly collections and cultural programs. Mercantile and mechanics' libraries, often supported by wealthy businessmen, were intended to promote virtuous habits and diffuse knowledge among workers (Harris, 1995: 185–186; Raven, 2007).

While historians recount in their studies the story of some social libraries, enabling us to imagine the intellectual and pragmatic pursuits of members, we know of many others from the barest of records. Founding dates and locations of a sample provide an indication of the scope of social libraries prior to the advent of tax- supported public libraries. Mechanics' and apprentices' libraries were established in Newport, Rhode Island (1791), Detroit, Michigan, and Portland, Maine (1820), Lowell, Massachusetts (1825), and thirty years later in San Francisco, California (1855). Athenaeums were founded in Boston (1807), Philadelphia (1814), Providence, Rhode Island (1836), Zanesville, Ohio (1828), and Minneapolis (1859). Mercantile libraries included Boston and New York (1820), Philadelphia (1822), Albany, New York, and Detroit (1833), Cincinnati (1835), St. Louis (1846), Milwaukee (1847), San Francisco (1853), Peoria,

Illinois (1855), and Dubuque, Iowa (1866). These were not founded solely by those of British heritage, for newly emigrated Germans, as well, opened reading rooms as early as 1792 in Philadelphia.[3]

Studies of individual libraries and societies outside of New England, such as the Virginia Historical Society (Todd, 2001), or the St. Augustine, Florida, Library Association in the oldest city in the United States (Blazek, 1979) provide a clearer picture of particular places. Broader studies, such as "Women and the Founding of Social Libraries in California, 1859–1910" (Musmann, 1982), or Hoyt's (1999) *Libraries in the German-American Turner Movement*, give us a more sweeping look at the growth of social libraries. From the beginning social libraries existed not only in New England, but also throughout the growing nation, with audiences that included women, new immigrants, and diverse other publics.

The Circulating Library

Circulating libraries of popular books for rent were business enterprises that originated in Germany, France, and England in the mid-1700s. The first circulating library in the colonies was founded in 1762 in Annapolis, Maryland—an enterprise that failed, though it was copied in Boston in 1765 (where it also failed). The Boston Circulating Library, established in 1784, continued to 1787. Concurrently Benjamin Guild began a circulating library, in connection with the Boston Bookstore in 1785, which seems to have been profitable (Shera, 1949: 138–139).

Some circulating libraries were affiliated with bookstores, others with less likely enterprises such as millinery shops (catering mainly to women readers), and still others were freestanding enterprises. The institution spread through Massachusetts with circulating libraries established in Salem (1789) and Newburyport (ca. 1794) and elsewhere in New England: New London, Connecticut (1793); Keene, New Hampshire (1805); Providence, Rhode Island (1820); and Woodstock, Vermont (1821). Profits followed the fiction market and analyses of collections based on catalogs of the time show that fiction dominating the holdings.

Meanwhile, reading rooms continued to thrive in places like Lexington, Kentucky, described by a visitor in 1807 as subscribing to forty-two newspapers from all over the United States. Other locations were as different as a milliner's shop in Wadsworth, Ohio (1820), and rooms in manufacturing towns established for factory workers (1844) or New England mill girls (Kaser, 1978, 1980; McCauley, 1971). While the standard histories of the development of public libraries tend to leave women out, a fuller understanding is provided by Hildenbrand's (1996) monograph, *Reclaiming the American Library Past: Writing the Women In*.

School District Libraries

School district libraries and arguments for their creation provided additional impetus for the foundation of tax-supported public libraries. The Common School movement of the 1830s, which ensured that every child would have a basic tax-supported education, has been described as the product of social reform in an age of perceived social decline. Conceived as a bulwark of traditional values against the tide of immigrants, public schools with the addition of district libraries were viewed as the means to forge a new moral order by educating children properly (Fain, 1978). "The bridge between free schools and free libraries was omnipresent in the early documents of the public library movement," states Ditzion (1947: 22) in his history of public libraries.

In 1812, New York's governor addressed the legislature on the good that might come from providing books to the young; and in 1815, Jesse Torrey, a founder of New York's Juvenile Society for the Acquisition of Knowledge, urged that governments use their money to establish free circulating libraries accessible to all classes and both sexes. Torrey was concerned that social libraries were too limited in their audience and did not provide for the education of women. His ideas—especially that the interdependence of public opinion and government demanded that all be educated, not just the privileged few—were used extensively as arguments for developing public libraries (Ditzion, 1940). The advocacy of New York governor De Witt Clinton (1835) for collections attached to common schools as the basis of a tax on each district for a school library really marks the first state law for tax-supported (though school- based) free library service (Joeckel, 1935: 9).

The support for school district libraries must be reviewed in the context of the work of universal education advocates such as Horace Mann, leader of the common school movement and first secretary of the Massachusetts Board of Education (1837), whose annual reports and other writings formed the intellectual basis for secular, universal education. Mann's efforts to provide access to education included strong pronouncements about the importance of books and reading.

By 1847 there were 8,070 school district libraries (Jewett, 1851: 104). Although the school district as a unit of governance was too small, staffing and location were volatile, and book procurement uneven, the significance to future public library development was of some consequence. The school district system did much to establish certain principles that formed the basis for public libraries, including taxation and state aid to libraries. Support for libraries affiliated with school districts was critical in recognizing the library as an educational agency, an extension of the system of public education beyond the formal instruction offered by schools (Joeckel, 1935: 12). The story of Harper and Brothers' development of collections for these libraries, as told by Freeman (2003), includes title lists that illustrate the scope of reading deemed appropriate for schools.

The U.S. Bureau of Education's *Special Report* (U.S. Department of the Interior, Bureau of Education, 1876: 38–69) provides a summary of how far school district libraries had spread across the United States. Following the first such law enacted in New York in 1835, Massachusetts passed legislation providing for school district libraries in 1837, owing in large part to the eloquence and earnestness of Horace Mann. Eight other states enacted laws by 1848. Before the first law for tax-supported public libraries, ten states had already identified the importance of tax support for school district libraries. A study by Held (1959: 79) of school district libraries in California notes, "Although generally unsuccessful, the attempt to organize popular library service upon the governmental basis of the school district played a distinct role in the evolution of American libraries." Held's study gives a picture of early library development far away from the common patterns of New England.

Although most discussions of the history of public libraries include the school district library, many considerations of the development of libraries in the United States largely dismiss the school district library, because it was not particularly successful in actual delivery. However, the spread of this concept in connection with tax-supported schools across the nation certainly was a factor in creating a fertile opportunity for governments to establish public libraries in the following years. To understand the ongoing research in this area, see the 2007 article by Wayne Wiegand, "The Rich Potential of American Public School Library History: Research Needs and Opportunities for Historians of Education and Librarianship."

Tax-Supported Public Libraries

Factors Leading to Their Establishment

The phrase "free public library," as used by McMullen (2000) in his study of the library past of the United States, most reflects the public library of today. McMullen (2000: 121) identifies two types: (1) ordinary libraries established by local governments, and (2) township libraries established by state governments, but intended for at least partial support and control by local officials. Ordinary libraries resembled social libraries (and in fact were often converted from social libraries) in that support came from users in the form of taxes paid to the local government. Public libraries as tax-supported community agencies enabled by law have existed since the mid- nineteenth century. While by consensus, the establishment of the Boston Public Library (state law enacted in 1848; opened in 1854) marks the beginning of the public library movement, we can point to earlier examples of free public libraries, such as the Peterborough Town Library in New Hampshire, which was granted support in 1833 from a general state fund. Nevertheless, because of the well- documented discussions about its establishment, by and large most historians consider the Boston Public Library to be the wellspring from which the key principles for tax-supported public libraries flowed.

Historians have attempted to determine what social and economic factors came together in New England to create the proper context in which people could visualize the idea and gather support for public libraries. Shera's book, *Foundations of the Public Library*, provides a social history covering 1629–1855. He concludes, "Complex social agencies do not arise in response to a single influence; the dogma of simple causation is an easy and ever threatening fallacy. It cannot be said that the public library began on a specific date, at a certain town, as the result of a particular cause. A multiplicity of forces, accumulating over a long period of time, converged to shape this new library form" (Shera, 1949: 200). In all, he identifies seven diverse factors that contributed to the emergence of tax-supported public libraries:

1. Economic resources in the community
2. Scholarship, historical research, and the urge for conservation
3. Local pride
4. Social importance of universal public education
5. Self-education and the lyceum movement
6. Vocational influence
7. Religion, morality, and the church

Economic Resources

The personal philanthropy of wealthy individuals and the growing wealth of New England provided the financial basis for library development. Examples of the generosity of individuals toward the establishment of libraries abound. Caleb Bingham, a Boston publisher, donated books for a children's library to Salisbury, Connecticut, in 1803 and the town later supplemented this donation with tax monies. Francis Wayland, president of Brown University, donated $500 to the town of Wayland, Massachusetts, in 1847 to establish a public library providing the town matched the donation—a donation that, Ditzion (1947: 44) notes, was instrumental in getting the principle of tax support under way. Contributors donated much larger amounts to establish the Boston Public Library, including $50,000 from Joshua Bates and $10,000 from Abbott Lawrence.

Scholarship

The inadequacy of libraries in the United States to support research and scholarship, and the desire to preserve the documents of the nation further motivated public funding of libraries. Various groups established historical societies and other social libraries devoted to history in the eighteenth century (e.g., Massachusetts Historical

Society, 1791), and these organizations focused much attention on preserving and building scholarly collections. Throughout New England individuals expended a great deal of energy on building libraries out of private collections. Isaiah Thomas, founder of the American Antiquarian Society in 1812, donated his personal collection of 8,000 books and acquired the collection of 1,400 books of Increase, Cotton, and Richard Mather for the society. The many other private libraries being gathered helped to enhance the idea of the need to develop scholarly resources and preserve the past.

Local Pride

The motivation of local pride came to the fore when Boston learned that John Jacob Astor had drawn up a will donating $400,000 to establish a public library in New York. Former Harvard professor and scholar George Ticknor, one of the key supporters of the Boston Public Library and the primary author of the 1852 *Report of the Trustees of the Public Library to the City of Boston*, used the competition between the two cities as a factor to argue for a public library. Shera observes, "It is difficult to envision an agency more characteristic of this period [ca. 1800–1850] than the emerging public library. America, proud of her economic growth, but confronted by the ancient tradition of European culture, sought eagerly to demonstrate her awareness of the necessity for preserving her own heritage" (1949: 216).

Universal Education

The acceptance of universal education as a public responsibility was evidenced in taxation for schools and school district libraries. This concept added strength to the argument for a tax-supported public library. Edward Everett, former governor and congressman of Massachusetts (and future secretary of state and senator) was, with Ticknor, a driving force in establishing the Boston Public Library. Everett had appointed Horace Mann as secretary of the Massachusetts Board of Education and oversaw the improvement of common schools and the extension of education throughout the state. He argued for extending the process of education beyond formal schooling through a tax-supported public library. Ticknor, who felt that the preservation of the republic must be based on the foundation of an educated population, enforced Everett's arguments (Ditzion, 1947: 13–18).

Self-Education

A fully developed plan for adult education through an educational society that would reach every part of the nation was set forth in 1826 by Josiah Holbrook of Derby, Connecticut. He based this plan on the idea of the lyceum, a local association formed for weekly lectures and discussion, which often included small libraries of books and periodicals. From the first lyceum in 1826 the idea expanded to over 3,000 in towns, counties, and states by 1835. The National American Lyceum, an organization of individual lyceums, adopted as its purpose "the advancement of education, especially in the common schools, and the general diffusion of knowledge" (Knowles, 1977: 16–18). The support and popularity for the lyceum idea provided additional receptivity to the support of agencies for self-improvement.

Vocational Influence

Vocational education in New England was a complex mixture of organizations and societies. The Mechanics Institute movement, which originated in England, grew in response to the Industrial Revolution and provided education and training to working men, often with support from manufacturers and factory owners. These institutes usually incorporated libraries to support the education of students. Mercantile libraries, initially a type of social library for men in business, also added lectures and courses. Of these institutions open to working people, Shera remarks:

> If the working classes of the nineteenth century achieved only temporary success in founding libraries planned to meet their needs, the importance of the vocational motive in public library encouragement is not thereby discredited; for as the wage-earning portion of the population increased and it became correspondingly more difficult for the uneducated individual to compete successfully with his highly trained fellows, there developed an increasing pressure for any agency that would raise the apprentice out of the ranks of the day laborer and into the middle-class. (1949: 237)

Religion and Morality

The religious tenor of New England was based on a high degree of reading widely. From the days of the parish libraries founded by Thomas Bray to the time of the establishment of the Boston Public Library, church members valued reading and relied upon parish libraries. The American Sunday School Union, founded in 1817, had as one of its goals to provide communities with libraries for religious instruction (Boylan, 1988).

Legislation

The various types of social libraries discussed above were entities with state charters and governance by trustees or boards of directors elected by shareholders. The trustees or directors were responsible for personnel, budgets, and drafting of rules of use. Thus long before the enactment of laws and legislation for tax-supported public libraries, models were in place for the oversight of library organizations. The steps to legislation that made it possible for communities to tax themselves for public library service are not unlike the process of policy development today. As we have seen, the spirit of the times established the intellectual and societal justification to tax people for universal education. New York enacted a state law in 1835 providing for the funding of school district libraries. A year later, New York also offered matching grants to school districts for the support of libraries using federal monies from the Deposit Act of 1836. Similar laws in the states of New England resulted in library service based on school districts, especially through the efforts of Horace Mann in Massachusetts and Henry Barnard in Rhode Island.

But it is to New Hampshire that we owe the honor of being the first state to enact a law to provide for public libraries, in 1849— "An Act Providing for the Establishment of Public Libraries." Whether this was due to the successful town library in Peterborough (1833), funded initially from a state fund but continued by local monies, or perhaps the persuasion of French ventriloquist M. Nicholas- Marie Alexandre Vattemare, who had addressed the New Hampshire state legislature the day before on the importance of international exchanges of books, the precise reasons for the introduction of the Act at this time we cannot deduce.[4] Nevertheless, this was the watershed event in U.S. public library history.

On Friday, June 28, 1849, Josiah C. Eastman introduced the Act Providing for the Establishment of Public Libraries, and the New Hampshire legislature passed the Act into law on July 7, 1849. It provided:

1. that towns might appropriate funds for the establishment, housing, and maintenance of libraries;
2. that such libraries would be free to all;
3. that the town might receive, hold, and dispose of gifts or behests made to the library; and
4. that libraries established under the law would annually receive works published by the state (Shera, 1949: 186–189).

The Massachusetts law enacted in 1851 came about somewhat differently. Brown University president Francis Wayland had long been a vocal advocate in favor of libraries as a means by which "the man denied the aristocracy of property, is welcomed into the prouder and nobler aristocracy of talent."[5] Wayland's donation in 1847 to the town of Wayland, Massachusetts, to establish a library came up against the dilemma that the town had no authority to contribute to the library's upkeep from municipal funds. Although the library was established in 1850, its right to operate without state authority was the subject of some concern. The representative from Wayland to the Massachusetts legislature, Rev. John Burt Wight, eventually drafted a bill that authorized towns to establish libraries. His remarks to the House were published in Horace

Mann's *Common School Journal* and are important as an early example of policy on public library objectives. Wight described the anticipated social benefits and emphasized the fact that the new law would inspire the establishment of libraries throughout Massachusetts. These libraries would supplement the public school system, provide utilitarian information, support moral and intellectual advance, preserve public documents, encourage creative writing, and increase the effectiveness of public instruction. After the Act passed, Wight sent a circular throughout Massachusetts to encourage the creation of town libraries. In the circular Wight noted, "The universal establishment of such libraries in this Commonwealth—and may I not say in the new England states, in the United States, and throughout the entire civilized world—is a question only of time."[6] Thus, Wayland's gift was the catalyst behind universal establishment.

The Boston Public Library

The Boston Public Library opened to readers on May 2, 1854. Although we have reviewed the New Hampshire and Massachusetts actions that preceded the Boston Public Library, the impetus to establish tax-supported public library service in the United States received its main fuel from this single event. The decision of a major city to enact taxes for the support of a public library was of tremendous import.

In addition to the general factors in New England that created the climate for acceptance of the idea of a tax-supported public library, specific factors in Boston fell in line. It was in Boston that the concentration of social libraries had created recognition of the value of library resources among those of influence in the city. It was at a meeting at the Boston Mercantile Library in 1841 that M. Nicholas-Marie Alexandre Vattemare had proposed the unification of Boston's major social libraries and a committee to investigate this idea appointed by the mayor, Josiah Quincy. Vattemare pursued the idea with the mayor and it continued as a front-burner concern for the city through the 1840s. As a city geared to oversee functions related to the community's well-being (fire protection, education, health), Boston considered it to be a proper function of city government to support a public library; there was little question about the matter.

The authorization to establish the Boston Public Library predated the 1851 Massachusetts state law by three years. A joint special committee of the City Council presented a proposal to the General Court of the state in 1848 that approved a special act permitting the city of Boston to establish a public library.[7] The special act is of great importance to the history of the public library in the United States, for it is the first legal recognition by a state of tax-supported municipal library service.

> The City of Boston is hereby authorized to establish and maintain a public library, for the use of the inhabitants of the said city: and the city council

of the said city may, from time to time, make such rules and regulations, for the care and maintenance thereof, as they may deem proper; provided, however, that no such appropriation for the said library shall exceed the sum of five thousand dollars in any one year. (General Court of Massachusetts, 1848)

In 1851 Mayor Benjamin Seaver declared that time had passed since the enactment of the act and that the city should hold an election to create a board of trustees to move the idea forward.

The trustees submitted the *Report of the Trustees of the Public Library to the City of Boston* (see Figure 2.1, pp. 24–32) in 1852, written by a subcommittee of trustees, mainly driven by George Ticknor and Edward Everett—a seminal document in the history of public librarianship in the United States.[8] The report begins with a compelling justification for the library as an institution, describing how opportunity ends after public education is complete and noting that there is no provision to put books within the reach of young men and women. The report throws down the gauntlet in the form of a question: "Why should not this prosperous and liberal city extend some reasonable amount of aid to the foundation and support of a noble public library, to which the young of both sexes, when they leave the schools, can resort for those works which pertain to general culture, or which are needed for research into any branch of useful knowledge?" (Boston Public Library, 1852: 8).

Tying the argument firmly to support of public education, the trustees summarize the current status of libraries in Boston (athenaeums, mercantile libraries, mechanics' libraries, apprentices' libraries, social libraries, circulating libraries, Sunday school libraries), which do not satisfy the demands for healthy, nourishing reading, "by the great masses of people, who cannot be expected to purchase such reading for themselves." The proposed library would fall into four classes: (1) books that could not be taken out of the library; (2) books that few persons wish to read; (3) books that would be often asked for; and (4) periodical publications. The report goes on to lay out steps to establish the library, including a building and selection and accession of books that would be wanted—trusting that, in the long run, the collection would include most books that could reasonably be wanted. The public library is conceived as the "crowning glory of our system of City schools."

A Boston city ordinance was passed in October 1852 stating that the method of governance was to be a board of trustees with the librarian to be appointed annually by the city council. The impact of this choice of structure laid the foundation for libraries throughout the United States to adopt the board plan of administrative management. So, in the course of the establishment of the Boston Public Library we find the basic structure of U.S. library governance (board plan), the justification for the establish-

(continued p. 33)

Figure 2.1. Report of the Trustees of the Public Library of the City of Boston, 1852

City Document—No. 37.
REPORT
OF
THE TRUSTEES OF THE PUBLIC LIBRARY OF THE CITY OF BOSTON
JULY, 1852.
BOSTON:
1852.
J.H. EASTBURN, CITY PRINTER.
CITY OF BOSTON.

In Board of Mayor and Aldermen, June 30, 1852.

Ordered, That the Trustees of the City Library be requested to report to the City Council upon the objects to be attained by the establishment of a Public Library, and the best mode of effecting them; and that they be authorized to report in print.

Passed. Sent down for concurrence.

BENJAMIN SEAVER, Mayor.
In Common Council, July 1, 1852.

Concurred.

HENRY J. GARDNER, President.

A true Copy. Attest:

S. F. McCLEARY, JR., City Clerk.

REPORT.

The Trustees of the public library, in compliance with the order of the two branches of the City Council, submit the following report on the objects to be attained by the establishment of a public library and the best mode of effecting them : –

Of all human arts that of writing, as it was one of the earliest invented, is also one of the most important. Perhaps it would be safe to pronounce it, without exception the most useful and important. It is the great medium of communication between mind and mind, as respects different individuals, countries, and periods of time. We know from history that only those portions of the human family have made any considerable and permanent progress in civilization, which have possessed and used this great instrument of improvement.

It is principally in the form of books that the art of writing, though useful in many other ways, has exerted its influence on human progress. It is almost exclusively by books that a permanent record has been made of word and deed, of thought and feeling; that history, philosophy and poetry, that literature and science in their full comprehension, have been called into being, by the co-operation of intellects acting in concert with each other, though living in different countries and at different periods, and often using different languages.

Till the middle of the fifteenth century of our era, it was literally the art of writing by which these effects were produced. No means of multiplying books was known but the tedious process of transcription. This of course rendered them comparatively scarce and dear, and thus greatly limited their usefulness. It was a chief cause also of the loss of some of the most valuable literary productions. However much this loss may be regretted, we cannot but reflect with wonder and gratitude on the number of invaluable works which have been handed down to us from antiquity, notwithstanding the cost and labor attending their multiplication.

The same cause would necessarily operate to some extent against the formation of public and private libraries. Still however, valuable collections of books were made in all the cultivated states of antiquity, both by governments and individuals. The library formed by the Ptolemies at Alexandria in Egypt was probably the direct means by which the most valuable works of ancient literature have been preserved to us. At a later period, the collections of books in the religious houses contributed efficaciously toward the same end.

(Continued)

Figure 2.1 *(Continued)*

The invention of printing in the fifteenth century increased the efficiency of the art of writing, as the chief instrument of improvement, beyond all former example or conception. It became more than ever the great medium of communication and transmission. It immediately began to operate, in a thousand ways and with a power which it would be impossible to overstate, in producing the great intellectual revival of the modern world. One of the most obvious effects of the newly invented art was of course greatly to facilitate the formation of libraries.

An astonishing degree of excellence in the art of printing was reached at once. The typography of the first edition of the whole Bible is nearly equal to that of any subsequent edition. But the farther improvements which have taken place in four hundred years in cutting and casting types and solid pages, in the construction of presses and their movement by water, steam, and other power, in the manufacture of paper, and in the materials and mode of binding, have perhaps done as much to make books cheap and consequently abundant, as the art of printing as originally invented.

It is scarcely necessary to add that these causes have led to a great multiplication of libraries in Europe and America. In nearly all the capitals of Europe large collections of books have been made and supported at the public expense. They form a part of the apparatus of all the higher institutions for education, and latterly of many schools; they are found in most scientific and literary societies; and they are possessed by innumerable individuals in all countries.

In proportion as books have become more abundant, they have become the principal instrument of instruction in places of education. It may be doubted whether their employment for this purpose is not, particularly in this country, carried too far. The organization of modern schools, in which very large numbers of pupils are taught by a small number of instructors, tends to make the use of books, rather than the living voice of the teacher, the main dependence. Still however, this is but an abuse of that which in itself is not only useful but indispensable; and no one can doubt that books will ever continue to be, as they now are, the great vehicle of imparting and acquiring knowledge and carrying on the work of education. As far as instruction is concerned, it will no doubt ever continue to be, as it now is, the work of the teacher to direct, encourage, and aid the learner in the use of his books.

In this respect the system of public education in Boston may probably sustain a comparison with any in the world. Without asserting that the schools are perfect, it may truly be said that the general principle and plan on which they are founded, are as nearly so as the nature of the case admits. They compose a great system of instruction, administered in schools rising in gradation from the most elementary to those of a highly advanced character, open to the whole population, and supported by a most liberal public expenditure. The schools themselves may admit improvement, and the utmost care should be taken, that they keep pace with the progress of improvement in other things; but the system itself, in the great features just indicated, seems perfect; that is, in a word, to give a first rate school education, at the public expense, to the entire rising generation.

But when this object is attained, and it is certainly one of the highest importance, our system of public instruction stops. Although the school and even the college and the university are, as all thoughtful persons are well aware, but the first stages in education, the public makes no provision for carrying on the great work. It imparts, with a noble equality of privilege, a knowledge of the elements of learning to all its children, but it affords them no aid in going beyond the elements. It awakens a taste for reading, but it furnishes to the public nothing to be read. It conducts our young men and women to that point, where they are qualified to acquire from books the various knowledge in the arts and sciences which books contain; but it does nothing to put those books within their reach. As matters now stand, and speaking with general reference to the mass of the community, the public makes no provision whatever, by which the hundreds of young persons annually educated, as far as the elements of learning are concerned, at the public expense, can carry on their education and bring it to practical results by private study.

(Continued)

Figure 2.1. Report of the Trustees of the Public Library of the City of Boston, 1852 *(Continued)*

We do not wish to exaggerate in either part of this statement, although we wish to call attention to the point as one of great importance and not yet, as we think, enough considered. We are far from intimating that school education is not important because it is elementary; it is, on the contrary, of the utmost value. Neither do we say, on the other hand, because there are no libraries which in the strict sense of the word are public, that therefore there is absolutely no way by which persons of limited means can get access to books. There are several libraries of the kind usually called public, belonging however to private corporations; and there are numerous private libraries from which books are liberally loaned to those wishing to borrow them.

It will however be readily conceded that this falls far short of the aid and encouragement which would be afforded to the reading community, (in which we include all persons desirous of obtaining knowledge or an agreeable employment of their time from the perusal of books), by a well supplied public library. If we had no free schools, we should not be a community without education. Large numbers of children would be educated at private schools at the expense of parents able to afford it, and considerable numbers in narrow circumstances would, by the aid of the affluent and liberal, obtain the same advantages. We all feel however that such a state of things would be a poor substitute for our system of public schools, of which it is the best feature that it is a public provision for all; affording equal advantages to poor and rich; furnishing at the public expense an education so good, as to make it an object with all classes to send their children to the public schools.

It needs no argument to prove that, in a republican government, these are features of the system, quite as valuable as the direct benefit of the instruction which it imparts. But it is plain that the same principles apply to the farther progress of education, in which each one must he mainly his own teacher. Why should not this prosperous and liberal city extend some reasonable amount of aid to the foundation and support of a noble public library, to which the young people of both sexes, when they leave the schools, can resort for those works which pertain to general culture, or which are needful for research into any branch of useful knowledge? At present, if the young machinist, engineer, architect, chemist, engraver, painter, instrument-maker, musician (or student of any branch of science or literature,) wishes to consult a valuable and especially a rare and costly work, he must buy it, often import it at an expense he can ill afford, or he must be indebted for its use to the liberality of private corporations or individuals. The trustees submit, that all the reasons which exist for furnishing the means of elementary education, at the public expense, apply in an equal degree to a reasonable provision to aid and encourage the acquisition of the knowledge required to complete a preparation for active life or to perform its duties.

We are aware that it may be said and truly, that knowledge acquired under hardships is often more thorough, than that to which the learner is invited without effort on his part; that the studious young man who makes sacrifices and resorts to expedients to get books, values them the more and reads them to greater profit. This however is equally true of school education and of every other privilege in life. But the city of Boston has never deemed this a reason for withholding the most munificent appropriations for the public education. It has not forborne to support an expensive system of free schools, because without such a system a few individuals would have acquired an education for themselves, under every possible discouragement and disadvantage, and because knowledge so acquired is usually thorough, well-digested and available, beyond what is got in an easier way. The question is not what will be brought about by a few individuals of indomitable will and an ardent thirst for improvement, but what is most for the advantage of the mass of the community. In this point of view we consider that a large public library is of the utmost importance as the means of completing our system of public education.

There is another point of view in which the subject may be regarded,—a point of view, we mean, in which a free public library is not only seen to be demanded by the wants of the city at this time, but also seen to be the next natural step to be taken for the intellectual advancement of this whole community and for which this whole community is peculiarly fitted and prepared.

Libraries were originally intended for only a very small portion of the community in which they were established, because few persons could read, and fewer still desired to make inquires that involved the

(Continued)

Figure 2.1 *(Continued)*

consultation of many books. Even for a long time after the invention of printing, they were anxiously shut up from general use; and, down to the present day, a large proportion of the best libraries in the world forbid anything like a free circulation of their books ;—many of them forbidding any circulation at all.

For all this, there were at first, good reasons, and for some of it good reasons exist still. When only manuscripts were known, those in public libraries were, no doubt, generally too precious to be trusted from their usual places of deposit; and the most remarkable, if not the most valuable, of all such collections now in existence—the Laurentian in Florence— still retains, and perhaps wisely, its eight or nine thousand manuscripts chained to the desks on which they lie. So too, when printed books first began to take the place of manuscripts, the editions of them were small and their circulation limited. When, therefore, copies of such books now occur, they are often regarded rightfully as hardly less curious and valuable than manuscripts, and as demanding hardly less care in their preservation. And finally, even of books more recently published, some,—like Dictionaries and Cyclopædias,— are not intended for circulation by means of public libraries, and others are too large, too costly, or otherwise too important to be trusted abroad, except in rare cases.

But while there are some classes of books that should be kept within the precincts of a public library, there are others to which as wide a circulation as possible should be given; books which, in fact, are especially intended for it, and the end of whose existence is defeated, just in proportion as they are shut up and restrained from general use. It was, however, long after this class was known, before it became a large one, and still longer before means were found fitted to give to the community a tolerably free use of it. At first it consisted almost exclusively of practical, religious books. Gradually the more popular forms of history, books of travel, and books chiefly or entirely intended for entertainment followed. At last, these books became so numerous, and were in such demand, that the larger public libraries,—most of which had grown more or less out of the religious establishments of the middle ages, and had always regarded with little interest this more popular literature,—could not, it was plain, continue to be looked upon as the only or as the chief resource for those who were unable to buy for themselves the reading they wanted. Other resources and other modes of supply have, therefore, been at different times devised.

The first, as might naturally have been anticipated, was suggested by the personal interest of a sagacious individual. Allan Ramsay, who, after being bred a wig-maker, had become a poet of the people, and set up a small bookseller's shop, was led to eke out an income, too inconsiderable for the wants of his family, by lending his books on hire to those who were not able or not willing to buy them of him. This is the oldest of all the numberless "Circulating Libraries;" and it sprang up naturally in Edinburg, where in proportion to the population, it is believed there were then more readers than there were in any other city in the world. This was in 1725; and, twenty years ago, the same establishment was not only in existence—as it probably is still—but it was the largest and best of its class in all Scotland. The example was speedily followed. Such libraries were set up everywhere, or almost everywhere in Christendom, but especially in Germany and in Great Britain, where they are thus far more numerous than they are in any other countries; the most important being now in London, where (for at least one of them) from fifty to two hundred copies of every good new work, are purchased in order to satisfy the demands of its multitudinous subscribers and patrons.

All "Circulating Libraries," technically so called, are however, to be regarded as adventures and speculations for private profit. On this account, they were early felt to be somewhat unsatisfactory in their very nature, and other libraries were contrived that were founded on the more generous principle of a mutual and common interest in those who wished to use the books they contained. This principle had, in fact, been recognized somewhat earlier than the time of Allan Ramsay, but for very limited purposes and not at all for the circulation of books. Thus the lawyers of Edinburg, London, and Paris, respectively had already been associated together for the purpose of collecting consulting Law Libraries for their own use, and so it is believed, had some other bodies, which had collected consulting libraries for their own exclusive especial purposes. But the first Social Library of common or popular books for popular use, in the sense we now give the appellation, was probably that of the "Library Company," as it was called, in Philadelphia, founded at the suggestion of Dr. Franklin in

(Continued)

Figure 2.1. Report of the Trustees of the Public Library of the City of Boston, 1852 *(Continued)*

1731, by the young mechanics of that city, where he was then a young printer. The idea was no doubt a fortunate one; particularly characteristic of Franklin's shrewd good sense, and adapted to the practical wants of our own country. The library of these young men, therefore, succeeded and was imitated in other places. Even before the Revolutionary war, such libraries were established elsewhere in the colonies, and, after its conclusion, many sprang up on all sides. New England, in this way, has come to possess a great number of them, and especially Massachusetts; two-thirds of whose towns are said at this time, to possess "Social Libraries," each owned by a moderate number of proprietors.

That these popular "Social Libraries" have done great good, and that many of them are still doing great good, cannot be reasonably doubted. But many of them,—perhaps the majority in this Commonwealth,—are now languishing. For this, there are two reasons. In the first place, such libraries are accessible only to their proprietors, who are not always the persons most anxious to use them, or, in some cases, but not many, they are accessible to other persons on payment of a small sum for each book borrowed. And, in the second place, they rarely contain more than one copy of a book, so that if it be a new book, or one in much demand, many are obliged to wait too long for their turn to read it; so long that their desire for the book is lost, and their interest in the library diminished. Efforts, therefore, have been for some time making, to remedy these deficiencies, and to render books of different kinds more accessible to all, whether they can pay for them or hire them, or not.

Thus, within thirty years, Sunday School Libraries have been everywhere established; but their influence—great and valuable as it is—does not extend much beyond the youngest portions of society and their particular religious teachers. And, within a shorter period than thirty years, District or Public School Libraries have been scattered all over the great State of New York, and all over New England, in such abundance, that five years ago, (1847) the aggregate number of their books in the State of New York was above a million three hundred thousand volumes, and fast increasing; but neither do these school libraries generally contain more than one copy of any one book, nor is their character often such as to reach and satisfy the mass of adult readers.

Strong intimations, therefore, are already given, that ampler means and means better adapted to our peculiar condition and wants, are demanded, in order to diffuse through our society that knowledge without which we have no right to hope, that the condition of those who are to come after us will be as happy and prosperous as our own. The old roads, so to speak, are admitted to be no longer sufficient. Even the more modern turnpikes do not satisfy our wants. We ask for rail-cars and steamboats, in which many more persons— even multitudes—may advance together to the great end of life, and go faster, further and better, by the means thus furnished to them, than they have ever been able to do before.

Nowhere are the intimations of this demand more decisive than in our own city, nor, it is believed, is there any city of equal size in the world, where added means for general popular instruction and self-culture,—if wisely adapted to their great ends,—will be so promptly seized upon or so effectually used, as they will be here. One plain proof of this is, the large number of good libraries we already possess, which are constantly resorted to by those who have the right, and which yet—it is well known,—fail to supply the demand for popular reading. For we have respectable libraries of almost every class, beginning with those of the Athenæum, of the American Academy, of the Historical Society, and of the General Court,—the Social Library of 1792, the Mercantile Library, the Mechanics Apprentices' Library, the Libraries of the Natural History Society, of the Bar, of the Statistical Association, of the Genealogical Society, of the Medical Society, and of other collective and corporate bodies; and coming down to the "Circulating Libraries" strictly so called; the Sunday School Libraries, and the collections of children's books found occasionally in our Primary Schools. Now all these are important and excellent means for the diffusion of knowledge. They are felt to be such, and they are used as such, and the trustees would be especially careful not to diminish the resources or the influence of any one of them. They are sure that no public library can do it. But it is admitted,—or else another and more general library would not now be urged,—that these valuable libraries do not, either individually or in the aggregate, reach the great want of this city, considered as a body politic bound to train up its members in the knowledge which will best fit them for the positions in life to which they may have been born, or any others to which they may justly

(Continued)

Figure 2.1 *(Continued)*

aspire through increased intelligence and personal worthiness. For multitudes among us have no right of access to any one of the more considerable and important of these libraries; and, except in rare instances, no library among us seeks to keep more than a single copy of any book on its shelves, so that no one of them, nor indeed, all of them taken together, can do even a tolerable amount of what ought to be done towards satisfying the demands for healthy, nourishing reading made by the great masses of our people, who cannot be expected to purchase such reading for themselves.

And yet there can be no doubt that such reading ought to be furnished to all, as a matter of public policy and duty, on the same principle that we furnish free education, and in fact, as a part, and a most important part, of the education of all. For it has been rightly judged that,—under political, social and religious institutions like ours,—it is of paramount importance that the means of general information should be so diffused that the largest possible number of persons should be induced to read and understand questions going down to the very foundations of social order, which are constantly presenting themselves, and which we, as a people, are constantly required to decide, and do decide, either ignorantly or wisely. That this can be done,—that is, that such libraries can be collected, and that they will be used to a much wider extent than libraries have ever been used before, and with much more important results, there can be no doubt; and if it can be done anywhere, it can be done here in Boston; for no population of one hundred and fifty thousand souls, lying so compactly together as to be able, with tolerable convenience, to resort to one library, was ever before so well fitted to become a reading, self-cultivating population, as the population of our own city is at this moment.

To accomplish this object, however,—which has never yet been attempted,—we must use means which have never before been used; otherwise the library we propose to establish, will not be adjusted to its especial purposes. Above all, while the rightful claims of no class,—however highly educated already,—should be overlooked, the first regard should be shown, as in the case of our Free Schools, to the wants of those, who can, in no other way supply themselves with the interesting and healthy reading necessary for their farther education. What precise plan should be adopted for such a library, it is not, perhaps, possible to settle beforehand. It is a new thing, a new step forward in general education; and we must feel our way as we advance. Still, certain points seem to rise up with so much prominence, that without deciding on any formal arrangement, until experience shall show what is practically useful, we may perhaps foresee that such a library as is contemplated would naturally fall into four classes, viz:

I. Books that cannot be taken out of the Library, such as Cyclopædias, Dictionaries, important public documents, and books, which, from their rarity or costliness, cannot be easily replaced. Perhaps others should be specifically added to this list, but after all, the Trustees would be sorry to exclude any book whatever so absolutely from circulation that, by permission of the highest authority having control of the library, it could not, in special cases, and with sufficient pledges for its safe and proper return, be taken out. For a book, it should be remembered, is never so much in the way of its duty as it is when it is in hand to be read or consulted.

II. Books that few persons will wish to read, and of which, therefore, only one copy will be kept, but which should be permitted to circulate freely, and if this copy should, contrary to expectation, be so often asked for, as to be rarely on the shelves, another copy should then be bought,—or if needful, more than one other copy,—so as to keep one generally at home, especially if it be such a book as is often wanted for use there.

III. Books that will be often asked for, (we mean, the more respectable of the popular books of the time,) of which copies should be provided in such numbers, that many persons, if they desire it, can be reading the same work at the same moment, and so render the pleasant and healthy literature of the day accessible to the whole people at the only time they care for it,—that is, when it is living, fresh and new. Additional copies, therefore, of any book of this class should continue to be bought almost as long as they are urgently demanded, and thus, by following the popular taste,—unless it should ask for something unhealthy,—we may hope to create a real desire for general reading; and, by permitting the freest circulation of the books that is consistent with their safety, cultivate this desire among the young, and in the families and at the firesides of the greatest possible number of persons in the city.

(Continued)

An appetite like this, when formed, will, we fully believe, provide wisely and well for its own wants. The popular, current literature of the day can occupy but a small portion of the leisure even of the more laborious parts of our population, provided there should exist among them a love for reading as great, for instance, as the love for public lecturing, or for the public schools; and when such a taste for books has once been formed by these lighter publications, then the older and more settled works in Biography, in History, and in the graver departments of knowledge will be demanded. That such a taste can be excited by such means, is proved from the course taken in obedience to the dictates of their own interests, by the publishers of the popular literature of the time during the last twenty or thirty years. The Harpers and others began chiefly with new novels and other books of little value. What they printed, however, was eagerly bought and read, because it was cheap and agreeable, if nothing else. A habit of reading was thus formed. Better books were soon demanded, and gradually the general taste has risen in its requisitions, until now the country abounds with respectable works of all sorts,—such as compose the three hundred volumes of the Harpers' School Library and the two hundred of their Family Library—which are read by great numbers of our people everywhere, especially in New England and in the Middle States. This taste, therefore, once excited will, we are persuaded, go on of itself from year to year, demanding better and better books, and, can as we believe, by a little judicious help in the selections for a Free City Library, rather than by any direct control, restraint, or solicitation, be carried much higher than has been commonly deemed possible; preventing at the same time, a great deal of the mischievous, poor reading now indulged in, which is bought and paid for, by offering good reading, without pay, which will be attractive.

Nor would the process by which this result is to be reached a costly one; certainly not costly compared with its benefits. Nearly all the most popular books are, from the circumstance of their popularity, cheap,—most of them very cheap,—because large editions of them are printed that are suited to the wants of those who cannot afford to buy dear books. It may, indeed, sometimes be necessary to purchase many copies of one of these books, and so the first outlay, in some cases, may seem considerable. But such a passion for any given book does not last long, and, as it subsides, the extra copies may be sold for something, until only a few are left in the library, or perhaps, only a single one, while the money received from the sale of the rest,—which, at a reduced price, would, no doubt often be bought of the Librarian by those who had been most interested in reading them,—will serve to increase the general means for purchasing others of the same sort. The plan, therefore, it is believed, is a practicable one, so far as expense is concerned, and will, we think, be found on trial, much cheaper and much easier of execution than at the first suggestion, it may seem to be.

IV. The last class of books to be kept in such a library, consists, we suppose, of periodical publications, probably excluding newspapers, except such as may be given by their proprietors. Like the first class, they should not be taken out at all, or only in rare and peculiar cases, but they should be kept in a Reading Room accessible to everybody; open as many hours of the day as possible, and always in the evening; and in which all the books on the shelves of every part of the Library should be furnished for perusal or for consultation to all who may ask for them, except to such persons as may, from their disorderly conduct or unseemly condition, interfere with the occupations and comfort of others who may be in the room.

In the establishment of such a library, a beginning should be made, we think, without any sharply defined or settled plan, so as to be governed by circumstances as they may arise. The commencement should be made, of preference, in a very unpretending manner; erecting no new building and making no show; but spending such moneys as may be appropriated for the purpose, chiefly on books that are known to be really wanted, rather than on such as will make an imposing, a scientific or a learned collection; trusting, however, most confidently, that such a library, in the long run, will contain all that anybody can reasonably ask of it. For, to begin by making it a really useful library; by awakening a general interest in it as a City Institution, important to the whole people, a part of their education, and an element of their happiness and prosperity, is the surest way to make it at last, a great and rich library for men of science, statesmen and scholars, as well as for the great body of the people, many of whom are always successfully struggling up to honorable distinctions and all of whom should be encouraged and helped to do it. Certainly this has proved to be the case with some of the best

(Continued)

Figure 2.1 *(Continued)*

libraries yet formed in the United States, and especially with the Philadelphia Library, whose means were at first extremely humble and trifling, compared with those we can command at the outset. Such libraries have in fact enjoyed the public favor, and become large, learned, and scientific collections of books, exactly in proportion as they have been found generally useful.

As to the terms on which access should be had to a City Library, the Trustees can only say, that they would place no restrictions on its use, except such as the nature of individual books, or their safety may demand; regarding it as a great matter to carry as many of them as possible into the home of the young; into poor families; into cheap boarding houses; in short, wherever they will be most likely to affect life and raise personal character and condition. To many classes of persons the doors of such a library may, we conceive, be at once opened wide. All officers of the City Government, therefore, including the police, all clergymen settled among us, all city missionaries, all teachers of our public schools, all members of normal schools, all young persons who may have received medals or other honorary distinctions on leaving our Grammar and higher schools, and, in fact, as many classes, as can safely be entrusted with it as classes, might enjoy, on the mere names and personal responsibility of the individuals composing them, the right of taking out freely all books that are permitted to circulate, receiving one volume at a time. To all other persons, women as well as men—living in the City, the same privilege might be granted on depositing the value of the volume or of the set to which it may belong; believing that the pledge of a single dollar or even less, may thus insure pleasant and profitable reading to any family among us.

In this way the Trustees would endeavor to make the Public Library of the City, as far as possible, the crowning glory of our system of City Schools; or in other words, they would make it an institution, fitted to continue and increase the best effects of that system, by opening to all the means of self culture through books, for which these schools have been specially qualifying them.

Such are the views entertained by the Trustees, with reference to the objects to be attained by the foundation of a public library and the mode of effecting them.

It remains to be considered briefly what steps should be adopted toward the accomplishment of such a design.

If it were probable that the City Council would deem it expedient at once to make a large appropriation for the erection of a building and the purchase of an ample library, and that the citizens at large would approve such an expenditure, the Trustees would of course feel great satisfaction in the prompt achievement of an object of such high public utility. But in the present state of the finances of the city, and in reference to an object on which the public mind is not yet enlightened by experience, the Trustees regard any such appropriation and expenditure as entirely out of the question. They conceive even that there are advantages in a more gradual course of measures. They look, therefore, only to the continuance of such moderate and frugal expenditure, on the part of the city, as has been already authorized and commenced, for the purchase of books and the compensation of the librarian; and for the assignment of a room or rooms in some one of the public buildings belonging to the city for the reception of the books already on hand, or which the Trustees have the means of procuring. With aid to this extent on the part of the city, the Trustees believe that all else may be left to the public spirit and liberality of individuals. They are inclined to think that, from time to time, considerable collections of books will be presented to the library by citizens of Boston, who will take pleasure in requiting in this way the advantages which they have received from its public institutions, or who for any other reason are desirous of increasing the means of public improvement. Besides the collections of magnitude and value, which can hardly fail in the lapse of years to be received in this way, it may with equal confidence be expected, that constant accessions will be made to the public library by the donation of single volumes or of small numbers of books, which, however inconsiderable in the single case, become in the course of time, an important source of increase to all public libraries. A free city library, being an object of interest to the entire population, would in this respect have an advantage over institutions which belong to private corporations. Authors and editors belonging to Boston would generally deem it a privilege to place a copy of their works on the shelves of a public library; and

(Continued)

Figure 2.1. Report of the Trustees of the Public Library of the City of Boston, 1852 *(Continued)*

the liberal publishers of the city, to whose intelligence and enterprise the cause of literature and science has at all times owed so much, would unquestionably show themselves efficient friends and benefactors.

In fact, we know of no undertaking more likely, when once brought into promising operation, to enlist in its favor the whole strength of that feeling, which, in so eminent a degree, binds the citizens of Boston to the place of their birth or adoption. In particular the Trustees are disposed to think that there is not a parent in easy circumstances who has had a boy or a girl educated at a public school, nor an individual who has himself enjoyed that privilege, who will not regard it at once as a duty and a pleasure to do something, in this way, to render more complete the provision for public education.

In order to put the library into operation with the least possible delay, the Trustees would propose to the city government to appropriate for this purpose the ground floor of the Adams school house in Mason street. They are led to believe that it will not be needed for the use of the Normal School proposed to be established in this building. It may be made, at a small expense, to afford ample accommodation for four or five thousand volumes, with an adjoining room for reading and consulting books, and it will admit of easy enlargement to twice its present dimensions. Such an apartment would enable the Trustees at once to open the library with five thousand volumes, a collection of sufficient magnitude to afford a fair specimen of the benefits of such an establishment to the city.

Should it win the public favor, as the Trustees cannot but anticipate, it will soon reach a size, which will require enlarged premises. These, as we have said, can be easily provided by the extension of the present room on the ground floor; and it will be time enough, when the space at command is filled up, to consider what further provision need be made for the accommodation of the library. Should the expectation of the Trustees be realized, and should it be found to supply an existing defect in our otherwise admirable system of public education, its future condition may be safely left to the judicious liberality of the city government and the public spirit of the community.

BENJAMIN SEAVER,
SAMPSON REED,
LYMAN PERRY,
JAMES LAWRENCE,
EDWARD S. ERVING,
JAMES B. ALLEN,
GEORGE W.WARREN,
GEORGE WILSON,
EDWARD EVERETT,
GEORGE TICKNOR,
JOHN P. BIGELOW,
NATHANIEL B. SHURTLEFF,
THOMAS G. APPLETON.

Boston, July 26, 1852.

At a meeting of the Trustees of the Public Library held on the 6th instant, the foregoing Report was submitted by a SubCommittee previously appointed for that purpose, consisting of EDWARD EVERETT, GEORGE TICKNOR, SAMPSON REED, and NATHANIEL B. SHURTLEFF, and was unanimously accepted and ordered to be printed.

GEORGE WILSON, Secretary.

ment of tax-supported public libraries, and in its first years the selection of librarians, like Justin Winsor, who would become national leaders in the emergent profession of librarianship.[9]

Truth or Myth?

The rather detailed discussion thus far provides a narrative and chronology of the founding events in U.S. librarianship. In an interesting 1973 revisionist essay, Michael Harris looks at the events that led to the founding of the Boston Public Library from a different perspective. He describes additional discussions by the standing committee of the Boston Public Library not usually described in general histories, notably expressions of concern by committee members about the increase in foreign populations—generally viewed as unlettered and ignorant. Harris asserts that George Ticknor, the intellectual Boston Brahmin who was the main author of the *Report of the Trustees of the Public Library to the City of Boston*, was motivated to a large degree by the idea that in establishing a public library Boston would uplift the masses so they would be sober, righteous, conservative, and devout. To do this, Harris contends, the trustees selected to oversee the nation's libraries after the enactment of library legislation in the mid-1850s were drawn mainly from the white, male, Protestant, wealthy business and professional class.

Extending the Harris thesis in her 1979 monograph, *Apostles of Culture: The Public Librarian and American Society, 1876–1920*, Garrison describes the first leaders of the American Library Association (ALA)—Justin Winsor (Boston Public Library, Harvard), William Poole (Boston Athenaeum, Cincinnati Public Library, Chicago Public Library, Newberry Library), and Charles Ammi Cutter (Harvard, Boston Athenaeum)—as well as most others assuming positions of responsibility for libraries just after the initial enabling legislation, as from the gentry elite. These individuals placed great emphasis on moral norms as a way of shaping the moral values of a society. Their response to political upheaval and labor unrest after the Civil War was to impose on others their middle-class values of "thrift, self-reliance, industriousness, and sensual control," seeing themselves as the saviors of society.

Francis Miksa, writing in 1982, compared the standard histories of the development of librarianship in the United States—Shera's (1949) *Foundations of the Public Library* and Ditzion's (1947) *Arsenals of a Democratic Culture*—with Harris's and Garrison's revisionist views, and analyzed the challenges of writing library history. Miksa noted that Ditzion, Harris, and Garrison focused on the human element and that such efforts must be viewed as somewhat lacking in their extrapolation of the parts to the whole. Miksa suggests studies of individual librarians would do much to enhance our knowledge of public library history.

Because dominant groups manage memory and myths and because women have largely been invisible in membership, women have been written out of traditional public library history, as Suzanne Hildenbrand contends in her 1996 edited volume, *Reclaiming the Library Past: Writing the Women In*. Since 1982, the addition of research examining the importance of women in the founding and growth of the U.S. public library system has enhanced our understanding of public library history to a great degree.[10] Battles (2009) and Pawley (2003) have explored the history of public librarianship against the backdrop of race, gender, and class. The public librarian concerned with a deeper approach to our history will necessarily supplement the classic texts with these broader analyses.

Developments from 1876 through 1918

1876, the Annus Mirabilis

The United States held its first World's Fair, popularly known as the Centennial Exhibition (formally titled the International Exhibition of Arts, Manufactures and Products of the Soil and Mine), during 1876 in Philadelphia's Fairmount Park overlooking the Schuylkill River. That same year Philadelphia was host to a conference of librarians for U.S. librarianship.

Histories mark 1876 as an annus mirabilis for modern librarianship in the United States, because in that year:

1. the ALA was founded;
2. *Library Journal* (then the *American Library Journal*) began publication;
3. Dewey's *A Classification and Subject Index, for Cataloguing and Arranging the Books and Pamphlets of a Library* (decimal classification) was published; and
4. the first major government report on libraries, *Public Libraries in the United States of America: Their History, Condition, and Management, Special Report*, was issued.

The formation of the ALA gave a voice to those working in libraries, as well as a forum to discuss professional issues. Papers presented at early ALA meetings addressed the proper role of public libraries and the "fiction question." Opinions ranged from a desire for the total exclusion of fiction, because of its dubious effect on readers, to a more liberal selection policy. Most librarians agreed that "the mass reading public was generally incapable of choosing its own reading material judiciously," and that "libraries should intervene for the benefit of society by acquiring and prescribing the best reading materials for the reading public's consumption" (Wiegand, 1986b: 9–10). Studying the journals and articles written during these formative years of public librarianship provides an understanding of the long distance librarians have come in developing a philosophy of service.

Years of Expansion

After 1876 the number of public libraries in the United States grew steadily, with states rapidly enacting library legislation and forming many state library commissions. By 1896 nearly 1,000 public libraries dotted the landscape. Each public library established in a town or county is a story in itself. Some of the stories are grand and well documented, while others will never be told.[11] Many factors account for the growth in the number of public libraries established between 1876 and World War I, but four factors bear special mention: (1) the contribution of women's organizations, (2) philanthropy, (3) the establishment of state commissions and traveling libraries, and (4) the professionalization of librarianship.

Women's Role in the Expansion of Public Libraries

Throughout the United States, as state and local bodies enacted laws enabling tax support for public libraries, women's efforts were central to the passage of these laws and the establishment of new libraries. The role of women in U.S. public library development is barely mentioned by twentieth-century library historians Shera and Ditzion, since women were usually left out of the received history of public library origins. Yet women's clubs that formed after the Civil War were a major force in the spread of libraries. Women's club history, including the growth of women's clubs for self-education and community service, bears review to gain understanding of the sociological context in which public libraries developed.

The General Federation of Women's Clubs notes in its chronology that by 1904 women's clubs had established 474 free libraries and 4,655 traveling libraries. Paula D. Watson has identified and summarized key work of women in organizing libraries throughout the United States. She observes that many women's clubs were organized expressly to found public libraries (see Watson, 1994, 1996, 2003).

The work of women in Michigan, preserved in *Historical Sketches of the Ladies' Libraries Associations of Michigan* (Bixby and Howell, 1876) prepared for the 1876 Centennial Exhibition—the same event where the ALA was formed—is indicative of the grassroots efforts made by women throughout the nation to expand the limits of women's lives and open new possibilities. Children's services played a large role in many of these Michigan libraries long before the ALA addressed the issue. The case studies detailed by Watson (1994, 1996, 2003) provide on-the-ground accounts of women's contribution to the spread of public libraries throughout the period following 1876. In fact, women's efforts also figure prominently when we examine the remaining factors accounting for the growth of public libraries in general.

Philanthropy

Donations from individuals were often the impetus for the establishment of public libraries, not only as the means to purchase buildings and books, but also as an opportunity for the donor to express personal philosophies of the common good. By the mid-1800s the habit of philanthropy was deemed a proper manifestation of the stewardship of wealth.[12] Motivation for donations to libraries may have been a conservative defense by the wealthy to educate the population to be more orderly and submissive or "shrewd policy on the part of millionaires to expend a trifle of the gains which they made off the people in giving them public libraries" (Ditzion, 1947: 136–137). Then again, part of the motivation was likely the manifestation of the ideals of the social obligations of the wealthy.

After the Civil War, with no income tax or corporate tax, vast fortunes were accumulated by industrialists, merchants, and financiers. From 1880 to 1889, $36,000,000 was donated to libraries, including large donations by Astor, Lennox, and Tilden to New York. Smaller donations also made it possible for towns across the United States to establish libraries. However, no single donor made more of an impact on the development of U.S. public libraries than Andrew Carnegie.

Andrew Carnegie donated over $41,000,000 for the erection of 1,679 libraries in 1,412 communities across the United States between 1898 and 1919. Many of them were built in the classical revival style and over time have become architectural landmarks. They are the largest single group of buildings nominated to the National Register of Historic Places. Much has been written about Carnegie, a poor boy from Scotland who became one of the most ruthless capitalists in the United States. The Homestead Strike of June 1892 still stands as one of the bloodiest incidents in U.S. labor history, as Pinkerton guards sent to break the strike killed steel workers who worked at Carnegie's plants.

The motivation behind Carnegie's selection of libraries as a focus of his philanthropy has been widely discussed. His father, a weaver in Dunfermline, Scotland, had led his fellow workers to pool their funds to purchase books for reading out loud—a fact Carnegie often mentioned. As a young clerk in Pittsburgh he had been allowed to use the workingman's library of a Colonel Anderson in Allegheny, which helped convince Carnegie of the importance of access to books to educate and inspire workers. Carnegie wrote essays on his philosophy of wealth and stewardship and made observations that wealthy men should live modestly and use their wealth to help those who would help themselves. He was a product of Scotch Presbyterianism and felt that the concentration of wealth in the hands of a few was a part of life described by evolution. The rich should act as trustees for the poor. Thus, felt Carnegie, the best focus of philanthropy would be universities, libraries, medical centers, public parks, meeting and concert halls, and churches. His philosophy is well known because of his writing (especially his famous essay "Gospel of Wealth"; Carnegie, 1900).

Bobinski (1969) undertook a comprehensive study of the scope of Carnegie's library philanthropy, analyzing Carnegie's approach of giving funds for library building, but also requiring that the communities furnish the site and pledge ongoing support for the library. Although Carnegie initially (1886–1896) gave buildings with endowments—the "retail period"—to communities in which his industries were located, he changed to a "wholesale" approach from 1896–1919, requiring community support (Bobinski, 1969: 13–23).

Carnegie hired James Bertram as a private secretary to handle most of the correspondence relating to the library program, and grants were limited to English-speaking countries. Communities requesting a library were sent a short questionnaire (reproduced in Bobinski, 1969: 203–206). If their response was satisfactory they were asked to supply a letter describing the site and vouching that it was purchased and paid in full. Finally, each community was required to pledge at least 10 percent of the amount of the grant for annual maintenance. In this way, 1,679 communities from forty-six states were able to build libraries. Indiana received the most—164 in all—although the Northeast received the most money due to large gifts to single cities (often for multiple branch libraries).

The first library to serve African Americans was the Western Branch Library in Louisville, which opened in 1905. Responding to the concerns of Albert Ernest Meyzeek, the plan for Carnegie to fund the public library system of Louisville included a branch for "colored" citizens. The Reverend Thomas Fountain Blue was appointed director—the first African American to head a public library (Louisville Free Public Library, 2011).

The grants were generally well received and much sought after. Watson has detailed the efforts of women's clubs to organize for the purpose of obtaining Carnegie grants for their communities. She observes, "the awakening of public sentiment in favor of libraries was the chosen work of state federations of women's clubs and individual clubs throughout the United States" (Watson, 1994: 262). The work of women in securing Carnegie libraries in western states has also been noted by Passet (1994) in *Cultural Crusaders: Women Librarians in the American West*, and in Held's (1973) study of the rise of public libraries in California.

However, some communities refused the money as tainted by Carnegie's repressive labor policies, while others could not meet the financial obligation of the annual pledge. In the volume *Carnegie Denied* (Martin, 1993), a number of scholars have analyzed those communities that applied for building grants but did not complete the project. In their study of Carnegie libraries in New York, Stielow and Corsaro (1993) examined the work of the Progressives, including Melvil Dewey, to promote the library cause, thus melding the pseudo-aristocratic robber barons with the ideals of a new social awareness.

Ditzion's assessment of Carnegie's contribution as a stimulant, not an initiator, is astute. While the public library as an entity began on firm footing in New England, growth might have slowed as communities waited for big donors. Carnegie's great contribution to the idea of the public library was that it needed to be supported by the people of a community through taxation. "Popular initiative, participation and control were the desired aims" (Ditzion, 1947: 150). Philanthropy and the growing involvement of women in the political process were the fuel that moved the public library idea to catch fire.

State Library Commissions and Traveling Libraries

Another great impetus to the growth of public libraries occurred in 1890 with the passage of the Massachusetts Law creating a state Board of Library Commissioners charged to help communities establish and improve public libraries. The law included a grant of $100 to begin collections in towns where none existed. Elizabeth Putnam Sohier, a driving force in the legislative process, was appointed to the first Massachusetts Free Library commission and is representative of the tenacity of women and women's clubs in the spread of library legislation (Watson, 2003: 75). The state soon became more than a passive agent vis-à-vis the development of public libraries. Similar laws were quickly passed in New York (1892), Maine, New Hampshire, and Connecticut (1893).

The New York state law, promoted by Melvil Dewey, accelerated the rate of public library development. Dewey devised a system of traveling libraries for New York in 1893 to provide 100-volume collections that were sent to areas of the state that had no access to a library. The traveling library idea was also put into action by women's clubs in Delaware and Maryland before those states established state library commissions. In 1901 a report by Dewey on traveling libraries gave prominent notice to the activities of women's clubs. The New York system worked closely with the state federation of women's clubs to establish libraries where none existed and to improve and encourage small libraries. A network of women workers was formed and assigned to specific areas of the state to encourage reading and library development (Watson, 1994: 238–241).

In some states women developed and supported traveling libraries for many years before the state provided support. In Illinois, between 1898 and 1905, 300 traveling libraries were maintained before state legislation passed. By 1904, 34 states with women's federations were overseeing over 300,000 volumes in 4,655 traveling collections. Watson (2003: 89–93) provides comparative data on the establishment of traveling libraries by state in her insightful article, "Valleys Without Sunsets: Women's Clubs and Traveling Libraries." For an excellent case study of the influence of women and their work in traveling libraries, see Christine Pawley's 2000 article, "Advocate of Access: Lutie Stearns and the Traveling Libraries of the Wisconsin Free Library Commission: 1895–1914."

The traveling library projects were closely tied to efforts across the country to establish state library commissions. Watson (1994: 244) notes, "There is little doubt that the state federation of women's clubs can claim credit for the passage of legislation in many states to establish library commissions" and then details the efforts of women in Kentucky, Georgia, Illinois, Indiana, Maine, and Wisconsin. From this came appointment of women as commissioners or trustees to these commissions. In his assessment of library law and legislation, Alex Ladenson (1982: 55–57) views the major expansion of public libraries after 1890 as attributable to the passage of legislation for the state library commissions.

The Professionalization of Librarianship

During the period 1876–1918, the founding and growth of the ALA plus the entry of women into the profession contributed to an increase in the number of public librarians, who in turn were active in helping to expand the numbers of libraries. The founders of the ALA are well known to us due to the thoughtful analyses by Wiegand in several studies, including *The Politics of an Emerging Profession*, which paints a picture of an organization led by a highly homogeneous group of men who, in the words of Wiegand (1986b: 230), "shared a relatively closed definition of reality and believed a rational, informed electorate was essential to democracy." The ALA members developed recommended reading lists and collection guides so that libraries might support "best reading" that would induce society to reduce social conflict and ensure social order. In Thomas Augst's (2001: 12) opinion, "Just as the blighted social and economic landscape of industrial capitalism was putting the power of the individual in question, this liberal ideology was propagated with missionary zeal by a new cadre of professional librarians and educators. As they spread the gospel of public culture to small towns across the United States, public libraries would acquire the status as a public good, worthy of tax support."

Public library historians of the 1940s, such as Shera (1949) and Ditzion (1947), failed to treat comprehensively the role of women and their entry into librarianship as paid employees, as we see in their classic studies of the founding of U.S. public libraries. While the 1979 study by Garrison, *Apostles of Culture*, examined the entrance of women into the profession, it tended to view early women librarians as sustainers of the moral views of their male counterparts. Hildenbrand (2000) questions this view, arguing rather for a history of librarianship that looks at the interrelatedness of socially constructed categories. Subsequent studies indicate that the addition of women to the ranks of the library profession may have been a strong factor in the shift from library service shaped for cultural uplift to community-based service. The shift included the opening of stacks, the foundation of youth services, and the development of services to immigrants.

Progressive movement ideals after the 1890s were internalized in librarianship as the field was more open to women and with the establishment of formal educational programs. The first education program, the School of Library Economy, opened by Melvil Dewey in 1886 at Columbia University, included women as students and proved to be controversial as unauthorized coeducation. When Dewey moved to Albany as the secretary of the University of the State of New York and director of the state library in 1888, the program went with him. Programs began throughout the nation (some in large libraries, some affiliated with higher education, some as summer training programs) and the creation of these programs made the profession more accessible to women (Rayward, 1968; Churchwell, 1975; Davis and Dain, 1986; Grotzinger, Carmichael, and Maack, 1994).

The ALA's practice of moving annual conferences about the nation stimulated interest in library matters. Certainly, discussions and programs held by the association made an impact on the way librarians thought about the services they were providing. By the early 1900s, progressive library leader John Cotton Dana observed that the public could forge its own use of the library in ways that it determined, an observation substantiated by the work of Lutie Stearns in Wisconsin on more democratic provision of library services (Mattson, 2000; Pawley, 2000).

As public libraries were established throughout the nation, the attitude toward collection development and users gradually shifted. Wiegand (1986b: 235) points out that by the time of American entry into World War I, the "reforming spirit of the Progressive era had identified the 'problem' groups in American society—the immigrants, the urban indigent, and criminal and insane, the remote rural dweller, the impressionable child, to name but a few—and the historical record shows that the ALA had sponsored some activity or group which sought to address the socialization needs of each." In Jones's (1999: 30) study of libraries and the immigrant experience, he notes that the ALA Committee on Work with the Foreign-Born in the first quarter of the century had an effect on library service: "Ironically, then, as immigrants were being transformed into Americans, librarians were also being transformed through their contacts with immigrants. . . . In the process they, too, were changed, metamorphosed into more tolerant Americanizers, more progressive citizens, and more responsive professionals." From its founding to World War I, the internal debates and personal beliefs of U.S. librarians within the ALA demonstrated a slow but concerted evolution toward a greater commitment to access as needs of immigrants, working people, and children began to receive focus and attention.

World War I marked a turning point for librarians in the United States. In his study of librarians during World War I, *An Active Instrument for Propaganda*, Wiegand (1989) described how, prior to the war, thousands of local libraries were scattered across the United States, staffed by women and men who developed high-quality collections but who longed for a consolidation of their position within the community. The entrance of the United States into World War I gave these librarians the opportunity for connection to other community agencies through cooperation with the war effort—characterized by Wiegand (1989: 133) as "an exhilarating experience that constituted a capstone to the public library movement in Progressive America." Yet this experience was one of the most reprehensible periods of U.S. library history, inasmuch as public librarians put service to the state before democratic principles— censoring German-language material and pacifist and antiwar literature.

At the close of the war, the U.S. public library had achieved integration into the fabric of the life of the commonwealth. The close association with the war effort both at the local level and through the ALA provided the profession with long- sought credibility. By 1918 public libraries were generally accepted as a standard component of municipal services. Yet in spite of the patriotic rush to a place on Main Street, progressive ideas and values were gaining strength among many librarians. In the next chapter we survey the continuing development of public librarianship in the United States as it moves toward greater acceptance and support as an institution, while struggling to define values beyond the mainstream of life in the United States.

Notes

1. See Amory and Hall (2000). For background on the concept of the reading revolution, see Wittmann (1999).

2. Lehmann-Haupt, Wroth, and Silver (1952); Brown (1989); Gilmore (1989); Lehuu (2000); Zboray (1993); Hall (1989; N.B., this volume does not address the history of books or reading in those parts of North America colonized by Spain; Elliott, 2006: 205– 207).

3. The single most enlightening document on a variety of social libraries is the U.S. Bureau of Education's "Public Libraries of Ten Principal Cities" (U.S. Department of the Interior, Bureau of Education, 1876: 837–1009). This article includes sketches on the founding and development of diverse social libraries such as the New York Historical Society Library (1804), Boston Athenaeum (1807), Cincinnati Circulating Library (1811), Apprentices' Library of Brooklyn (1823), Young Men's Association Library of Chicago (1841), Baltimore Mercantile Library Association (1842), Mercantile Library of San Francisco (1853), and Portland, Oregon Library Association (1864). Included for many of the libraries highlighted are membership rolls, budgets, and collection descriptions.

4. French ventriloquist M. Nicholas-Marie Alexandre Vattemare is one of the most interesting personalities in U.S. library history. He was indefatigable in his efforts to establish an international system of exchanges of books and documents. From 1839 to 1849 he campaigned for this idea and was successful in creating an exchange system with the Library of Congress, as well as many states. We can only imagine, looking back, how much influence a persuasive idealist like Vattemare had on the public library idea. Sometimes a charismatic individual can

successfully promote an ideal. Vattemare could be comparable to U2's singer Bono fighting to reduce the debt of poor nations. For background on the connections of ventriloquism and the ideas of the enlightenment see Schmidt (1998). On the idea of international exchanges, Richards (1940).

5. Francis Wayland, in his influential 1838 speech "Discourse at the Opening of the Providence Athenaeum," argues this point. Wayland had been arguing for an athenaeum that would be open to all. While this would not come about until laws were enacted over a decade later, Wayland's discourse provides additional insight into the idea of a free public library. His donation to the town of Wayland was the catalyst that laid the groundwork for free public libraries throughout Massachusetts.

6. Shera (1949: 199) quotes Wight's circular letter. The summary of the Massachusetts legislation is also in Shera (1949: 189–199). The full text of Wight's speech appeared as "Public Libraries," *Common School Journal* 13 (1851): 257–264.

7. "The Report of the Joint Special Committee to the Boston City Council of December 6, 1847" is reprinted in Wadlin (1911: 8–9). See also Shera (1949/1965: 170–181); Joeckel (1935: 18); Ladenson (1982: 7–8); Ditzion (1947: 18–19).

8. Boston Public Library, *Report of the Trustees of the Public Library to the City of Boston*, 1852, is reproduced in Shera (1949/1965: 267–290). The specific steps that led to the establishment of the Boston Public Library have been detailed in various histories of the library, including the intriguing role of the French ventriloquist M. Nicholas-Marie Alexandre Vattemare (see note 4 supra), whose 1841 presentation to Boston society of his plan for an international exchange of books caused recognition that Boston, at that time, had no great library to receive such an exchange. For more extensive background see U.S. Department of the Interior, Bureau of Education (1876: 863–872); Shera (1949/1965: 170–199); Ditzion (1947: 5–7); Joeckel (1935: 16–22); Ladenson (1982: 7–9); as well as many articles and books. See, for example: Wadlin (1911); Whitehill (1956); Knight (2000); Davis (2002).

9. From 1847, "Report of the Joint Special Committee to the Boston City Council" is reprinted in Wadlin (1911: 8–9); from 1851, John B. Wight's speech to the Massachusetts Legislature is reprinted in "Public Libraries," *Common School Journal* 13 (1851): 257–264. The state law enacted in Massachusetts in 1851 resulted in the establishment of ten town libraries by 1854: New Bedford, Beverley, Winchendon, (1851); Fay Library in Southborough (1852); Lenox (1853); Newburyport, Framingham, Groton, Woburn, and West Springfield (1854). "Report of the Trustees of the Public Library to the City of Boston," 1852, is reproduced in Shera (1949/1965: 267–290). Ditzion (1947: 19) adds several more early sources to this list, including an 1852 special library committee report to the trustees of Concord, New Hampshire; speeches delivered at the Librarians' Convention of 1853; speeches at the laying of the cornerstone of the Boston Public Library; and the Boston Public Library memorial to the philanthropist Joshua Bates.

10. Women are largely ignored in Shera (1949), Ditzion (1947), and Harris (1995). Garrison's (1979) treatment of women was, as Francis Miksa (1982) demonstrates, somewhat speculative. For comprehensive bibliographic treatment see the following series: Weibel, McCook, and Ellsworth (1979); McCook and Phenix (1984); Phenix and McCook (1989); later years by Goetsch and Watstein (1993); Kruger and Larson (2000); Kruger and Larson (2006).

11. The grand include Dain (1972). Dozens of books, theses, journal articles, and celebratory histories for most states and a good many individual libraries are listed in Davis and Tucker (1989) and updated in the journal *Libraries and Culture*.

12. The religious and moral underpinnings of library philanthropists may be of interest. Suggested background: Hammer (1998); de Tocqueville (1952); McNeil (1967); Hopkins (1940).

References

Amory, Hugh, and David D. Hall, eds. 2000. *A History of the Book in America*. Vol. 1 of *The Colonial Book in the Atlantic World*. Cambridge, MA: Cambridge University Press.

Augst, Thomas. 2001. "American Libraries and Agencies of Culture." *American Studies* 42 (Fall): 12.

Battles, David M. 2009. *The History of Public Library Access for African Americans in the South: Or, Leaving Behind the Plow*. Lanham, MD: Scarecrow Press.

Bixby, A. F., and A. Howell. 1876. *Historical Sketches of the Ladies' Library Associations of the State of Michigan, 1876*. Adrian, MI: Times and Expositor Steam Print. Reprinted in Kathleen Weibel, Kathleen Heim (de la Peña McCook), and Dianne J. Ellsworth, *The Status of Women in Librarianship, 1876–1976*, pp. 3–4. Phoenix, AZ: Oryx Press, 1979.

Blazek, R. 1979. "The Development of Library Service in the Nation's Oldest City: The St. Augustine Library Association, 1874–1880." *Journal of Library History* 14: 160–182.

Bobinski, George S. 1969. *Carnegie Libraries: Their History and Impact on American Library Development*. Chicago: American Library Association.

Boston Public Library. 1852. *Report of the Trustees of the Public Library to the City of Boston*. Reproduced in Jesse H. Shera, *Foundations of the Public Library: The Origins of the Public Library Movement in New England, 1629–1855*. Chicago: University of Chicago Press, 1949; repr., Hamden, CT: Shoestring Press, 1965, 267–290.

Boylan, Anne M. 1988. *Sunday School: The Formation of an American Institution, 1790–1880*. New Haven, CT: Yale University Press.

Brown, Richard D. 1989. *Knowledge Is Power: The Diffusion of Information in Early America, 1700–1865*. New York: Oxford University Press.

Carnegie, Andrew. 1900. *The Gospel of Wealth and Other Timely Essays*. New York: The Century Co. Repr., ed. Edward C. Kirkland. Cambridge, MA: Harvard University Press, 1962.

Churchwell, Charles D. 1975. *The Shaping of American Library Education*. Chicago: American Library Association.

Cornelius, Janet Duitsman. 1991. *When I Can Read My Title Clear: Literacy, Slavery and Religion in the Antebellum South*. Columbia: University of South Carolina Press.

Dain, Phyllis P. 1972. *The New York Public Library: A History of Its Founding and Early Years*. New York: New York Public Library.

Davis, Donald G., Jr. 2002. *Winsor, Dewey, and Putnam: The Boston Experience*. Champaign: Graduate School of Library and Information Science, University of Illinois at Urbana-Champaign.

Davis, Donald G., Jr., and Phyllis Dain. 1986. "History of Library and Information Science Education." *Library Trends* 34 (Winter).

Davis, Donald G., Jr., and John Mark Tucker. 1989. *American Library History: A Comprehensive Guide to the Literature.* Santa Barbara, CA: ABC-CLIO.

de Tocqueville, Alexis. *Democracy in America.* London: Oxford University Press, 1952.

Ditzion, Sidney H. 1940. "The District School Library, 1835– 1855." *Library Quarterly* 10: 545–547.

———. 1947. *Arsenals of a Democratic Culture: A Social History of the American Public Library Movement in New England and the Middle States from 1850–1900.* Chicago: American Library Association.

Elliott, J. H. 2006. *Empires of the Atlantic World: Britain and Spain in America 1492–1830.* New Haven: Yale University Press.

Fain, Elaine. 1978. "The Library and American Education: Education through Secondary School." *Library Trends* (Winter): 327– 352.

Freeman, Robert S. 2003. "Harper & Brothers' Family and School District Libraries, 1830–1846." In *Libraries to the People: Histories of Outreach*, ed. Robert S. Freeman and David M. Hovde. Jefferson, NC: McFarland.

Garrison, Dee. 1979. *Apostles of Culture: The Public Librarian and American Society, 1876–1920.* New York: Free Press. Repr., University of Wisconsin Press, 2003.

General Court of Massachusetts. 1848. *Massachusetts Acts and Resolves*, Chapter 52. Boston: State of Massachusetts.

Gilmore, William J. 1989. *Reading Becomes a Necessity: Material and Cultural Life in Rural New England, 1780–1835.* Knoxville, TN: University of Tennessee Press.

Goetsch, Lori A., and Sarah B. Watstein. 1993. *On Account of Sex: An Annotated Bibliography on the History of Women in Librarianship, 1987–1992.* Metuchen, NJ: Scarecrow Press.

Grotzinger, Laurel Ann, James Vinson Carmichael, and Mary Niles Maack. 1994. *Women's Work: Vision and Change in Librarianship.* Champaign: University of Illinois.

Hall, David D. 1989. *Worlds of Wonder, Days of Judgment: Popular Religious Belief in Early New England.* New York: Alfred A. Knopf.

Hammer, John H. 1998. "Money and the Moral Order in Late Nineteenth and Early-Twentieth Century American Capitalism." *Anthropological Quarterly* 71 (July): 138–149.

Harris, Michael H. 1973. "The Purpose of the American Public Library: A Revisionist Interpretation of History." *Library Journal* 98 (September 15): 2509–2514.

———. 1995. *History of Libraries in the Western World*, 4th ed. Lanham, MD: Scarecrow Press.

Held, Ray E. 1959. "The Early School District Library in California." *Library Quarterly* 29: 79.

———. 1973. *The Rise of the Public Library in California.* Chicago: American Library Association.

Hildenbrand, Suzanne, ed. 1996. *Reclaiming the American Library Past: Writing the Women In.* Norwood, NJ: Ablex.

———. 2000. "Library Feminism and Library Women's History: Activism and Scholarship: Equity and Culture." *Libraries and Culture* 35 (Winter): 51–63.

Hopkins, C. Howard. 1940. *The Rise of the Social Gospel in American Protestantism, 1865–1915.* New Haven, CT: Yale University Press.

Hoyt, Dolores J. 1999. *A Strong Mind in a Strong Body: Libraries in the German-American Turner Movement*. New York: Peter Lang.

Jewett, Charles Coffin. 1851. "Report on the Public Libraries of the United States of America, January 1, 1850." In *Report of the Board of Regents of the Smithsonian Institution*. Washington, DC: Smithsonian Institution.

Joeckel, Carleton Bruns. 1935. *The Government of the American Public Library*. Chicago: University of Chicago Press.

Jones, Plummer Alston, Jr. 1999. *Libraries, Immigrants, and the American Experience*. Westport, CT: Greenwood Press.

Kaser, David. 1978. "Coffee House to Stock Exchange: A Natural History of the Reading Room." In *Milestones to the Present: Papers from Library History Seminar V*, edited by Harold Goldstein, 238–254. Syracuse, NY: Gaylord Professional Publications.

———. 1980. *A Book for a Six Pence: The Circulating Library in America*. Pittsburgh, PA: Beta Phi Mu.

Knight, Frances R. 2000. "A Palace for the People: The Relationships That Built the Boston Public Library." PhD diss., University of Oxford.

Knowles, Malcolm S. 1977. *A History of the Adult Education Movement in the United States: Includes Adult Education Institutions through 1976*. Huntington, NY: Robert E. Krieger.

Kruger, Betsy, and Cathy Larson. 2000. *On Account of Sex: An Annotated Bibliography on the Status of Women in Librarianship, 1993–1997*. Lanham, MD: Scarecrow Press.

———, eds. 2006. *On Account of Sex: An Annotated Bibliography on the Status of Women in Librarianship, 1998–2002*. Lanham, MD: Scarecrow Press.

Ladenson, Alex. 1982. *Library Law and Legislation in the United States*. Metuchen, NJ: Scarecrow Press.

Laugher, C. T. 1973. *Thomas Bray's Grand Design*. Chicago: American Library Association.

Lehmann-Haupt, Hellmut, Lawrence Wroth, and Rollo G. Silver. 1952. *The Book in America: A History of the Making and Selling of Books in the United States*. New York: R. R. Bowker.

Lehuu, Isabel. 2000. *Carnival on the Page: Popular Print Media in Antebellum America*. Chapel Hill: University of North Carolina Press.

Louisville Free Public Library. 2011. "A Separate Flame—Western Branch: The First African-American Public Library." Louisville Free Public Library. Accessed January 13. http://lfpl.org/ western/htms/welcome.htm.

Martin, Robert Sidney, ed. 1993. *Carnegie Denied: Communities Rejecting Carnegie Library Construction Grants, 1898–1925*. Westport, CT: Greenwood Press.

Mattson, Kevin. 2000. "The Librarian as Secular Minister to Democracy: The Life and Ideas of John Cotton Dana." *Libraries and Culture* 35 (Fall): 514–534.

McCauley, Elfrieda B. 1971. "The New England Mill Girls: Feminine Influence in the Development of Public Libraries in New England, 1820–1860." PhD diss., Columbia University.

McCook, Kathleen de la Peña, and Katharine Phenix. 1984. *On Account of Sex: An Annotated Bibliography on the History of Women in Librarianship, 1977–1981*. Chicago: American Library Association.

McMullen, H. 2000. *American Libraries before 1876*. Beta Phi Mu Monograph Series, no. 6. Westport, CT: Greenwood Press.

McNeil, J. 1967. *The History and Character of Calvinism.* Oxford: Oxford University Press.

Miksa, Francis. 1982. "The Interpretation of American Public Library History." In *Public Librarianship: A Reader*, edited by Jane Robbins-Carter, 73–90. Littleton, CO: Libraries Unlimited.

Musmann, V. K. 1982. "Women and the Founding of Social Libraries in California, 1859–1910." PhD diss., University of Southern California.

Passet, Joanne E. 1994. *Cultural Crusaders: Women Librarians in the American West, 1900–1917.* Albuquerque: University of New Mexico Press.

Pawley, Christine. 2000. "Advocate of Access: Lutie Stearns and the Traveling Libraries of the Wisconsin Free Library Commission: 1895–1914." *Libraries and Culture* 35 (Summer): 434–458.

———. 2003. "Reading *Apostles of Culture*: The Politics and Historiography of Library History." Foreword to reprint of Dee Garrison, *Apostles of Culture.* Madison: University of Wisconsin Press.

Phenix, Katharine, and Kathleen de la Peña McCook. 1989. *On Account of Sex: An Annotated Bibliography on the History of Women in Librarianship, 1982–1986.* Chicago: American Library Association.

Raven, James. 2007. "Social Libraries and Library Societies in Eighteenth-Century North America." In *Institutions of Reading: The Social Life of Libraries in the United States*, edited by Thomas Augst and Kenneth Carpenter, 24–52. Amherst: University of Massachusetts Press.

Rayward, W. Boyd. 1968. "Melvil Dewey and Education for Librarianship." *Journal of Library History* 3: 297–313.

Richards, E. M. 1940. "Alexandre Vattemare and His System of International Exchanges." *Bulletin of the Medical Library Association* 32: 413–448.

Schmidt, Leigh Eric. 1998. "From Demon Possession to Magic Show: Ventriloquism, Religion, and the Enlightenment." *Church History* 67 (June): 274–304.

Shera, Jesse H. 1949. *Foundations of the Public Library: The Origins of the Public Library Movement in New England, 1629– 1855.* Chicago: University of Chicago Press. Repr., Hamden, CT: Shoestring Press, 1965.

Stielow, Frederick J., and James Corsaro. 1993. "The Carnegie Question and the Public Library Movement in Progressive Era New York." In *Carnegie Denied: Communities Rejecting Carnegie Library Construction Grants, 1898–1925*, edited by Robert Sidney Martin, 35–51. Westport, CT: Greenwood Press.

Todd, Emily B. 2001. "Antebellum Libraries in Richmond and New Orleans and the Search for the Practices and Preferences of Real Readers." *American Studies* 42 (Fall): 195–209.

U.S. Department of the Interior, Bureau of Education. 1876. *Public Libraries in the United States of America: Their History, Condition, and Management. Special Report.* Washington, DC: U.S. Government Printing Office. Repr., as Monograph Series, no. 4, Champaign: University of Illinois, Graduate School of Library Science.

Wadlin, Horace Greeley. 1911. *The Public Library of the City of Boston: A History.* Boston: The Trustees.

Watson, Paula D. 1994. "Founding Mothers: The Contribution of Women's Organizations to Public Library Development in the United States." *Library Quarterly* 64 (July): 237.

———. 1996. "Carnegie Ladies, Lady Carnegies: Women and the Building of Libraries." *Libraries and Culture* 31 (Winter): 159–196.

———. 2003. "Valleys Without Sunsets: Women's Clubs and Traveling Libraries." In *Libraries to the People: Histories of Outreach*, edited by Robert S. Freeman and David M. Hovde, 73–95. Jefferson, NC: McFarland.

Wayland, Francis. 1838. *Discourse at the Opening of the Providence Athenaeum*. Providence, RI: Knowles, Vose.

Weibel, Kathleen, Kathleen Heim (de la Peña McCook), and Dianne J. Ellsworth. 1979. *The Status of Women in Librarianship, 1876–1976*. Phoenix, AZ: Oryx Press.

Whitehill, Walter Muir. 1956. *Boston Public Library: A Centennial History*. Cambridge, MA: Harvard University Press.

Wiegand, Wayne A. 1986a. "The Historical Development of State Library Agencies." In *State Library Services and Issues: Facing Future Challenges*, edited by Charles R. McClure, 1–16. Norwood, NJ: Ablex.

———. 1986b. *The Politics of an Emerging Profession: The American Library Association, 1876–1917*. New York: Greenwood Press.

———. 1989. *An Active Instrument for Propaganda: The American Public Library during World War I*. Westport, CT: Greenwood Press.

———. 2007. "The Rich Potential of American Public School Library History: Research Needs and Opportunities for Historians of Education and Librarianship." *Libraries and the Cultural Record* 42, no. 1: 57–74.

Williams, Julie Hedgepeth. 1999. *The Significance of the Printed Word in Early America*. Westport, CT: Greenwood Press.

Wittmann, Reinhard. 1999. "Was There a Reading Revolution at the End of the Eighteenth Century?" In *A History of Reading in the West*, edited by Guglielmo Cavallo and Roger Chartier, 284–312. Amherst, MA: University of Massachusetts Press, 1999.

Wyss, Hilary E. 2000. *Writing Indians: Literacy, Christianity and Native Community in Early America*. Amherst, MA: University of Massachusetts Press.

Zboray, Ronald J. 1993. *A Fictive People: Antebellum Economic Development and the Reading Public*. New York: Oxford University Press.

3

Public Library Growth and Values: 1918–Today

At a time when our public is challenged on multiple fronts, we need to re-commit ourselves to the ideal of providing equal access to everyone, any-where, anytime, and in any format. . . . By finally embracing equity of access we will be affirming our core values, recognizing realities, and as-suring our future.

—Carla D. Hayden, ALA President, 2003–2004

From 1918 to the present, U.S. public libraries have continued to expand outlets, ex-tend service areas, and define broad goals in the context of equity of access, lifelong learning, and intellectual freedom. This chapter summarizes the growth of the library idea from a largely state and local initiative to its acceptance by the nation as a vital and necessary community agency. Today 9,221 public libraries (administrative enti-ties) serve communities in the 50 states and the District of Columbia with 16,671 points of service (e.g., central libraries, branches, bookmobiles). Also in this chapter, I delineate the role of librarians in developing a national planning initiative. Here read-ers can examine for themselves the changing philosophies regarding service to all pa-trons through lifelong learning, support for democracy, intellectual freedom, and Internet access.

Equalizing Library Opportunity: Toward a National Role

During World War I librarians greatly expanded their scope of service and visibility by work on the home front and overseas. The American Library Association's (ALA's) Library War Service in training camps and Europe broadened the general public's ap-preciation for library service (Kelly, 2003). This active engagement positioned librari-ans as more active participants in their communities. Whether municipally or county based, the establishment of state commissions that promoted the library idea coupled with the success of the library in the war effort ensured that in 1918 citizens widely embraced the public library as an appropriate community agency. After World War I the history of public libraries in the United States and the ALA as a factor in the development of public libraries became even more intertwined with the actions of local and state governments.

ALA historian Dennis Thomison (1978: 70–71) has observed that ALA, enlivened by the success of its Library War Service, planned for an Enlarged Program that would include a fundraising campaign to "encourage and promote the development of library service for all Americans." After much effort and discussion the Enlarged Program was dropped, but the planning and work that went into the program shaped the thinking of association leaders after 1918. In 1919 ALA supported the Smith-Towner bill that proposed federal funds to extend public libraries for educational purposes and a bureau of libraries at the federal level. Although the bill was not enacted, the idea to extend access with federal support was in the air (Molz, 1984: 75).

The ALA's Enlarged Program concept, the experience of a national role for libraries during World War I, and the ALA Council's ongoing discussion of federal support for libraries expanded the scope of discussion about the role of public libraries during the 1920s. Of special note were the association's focus on adult education and extension. The 1924 report to the Carnegie Corporation, *The American Public Library and the Diffusion of Knowledge*, included the observation that "the free public library is already an accepted and cherished figure in American intellectual life," and put forth the suggestion that the ALA should provide support for the growth and expansion of smaller libraries (Learned, 1924: 75–80; Latham, 2010). In 1926 the ALA study *Libraries and Adult Education* was published and the association established the Board on Library and Adult Education (later the Adult Education Board) with reports in the *ALA Bulletin*.[1] The concept of the library as an agency of ongoing education for adults became firmly established in U.S. society.

It should be pointed out that library services for youth had been gaining acceptance as a specialization in U.S. libraries and this movement, enlivened by the efforts of Anne Carroll Moore of the New York Public Library (where she served from 1906 to 1941), created even more broad-based support for libraries in communities. As children's literature found a growing appreciative audience, it followed that public libraries offering services for children would be viewed as important to community life (Fenwick, 1976; Jenkins, 2000).

The ALA Committee on Library Extension (established in 1925) worked to extend library services to unserved areas in the United States and appointed a regional field agent for the South, Tommie Dora Barker (1936), with funding from a Carnegie Corporation Grant. The League of Library Commissions (established in 1904 and affiliated with ALA, eventually becoming the State Library Agency of the Extension Division in 1942), worked on rural issues before and during the Depression-era New Deal. The citizens' library movement, especially in North Carolina, demonstrated a grassroots desire for library service ("Library Projects," 1933). During the 1920s and 1930s,

ALA embraced the idea of libraries as a means to provide adult educational opportunities and combined this idea with many efforts to extend library service to unserved areas.[2]

Libraries at the Federal Level

The idea that there should be a federal role for libraries began under the aegis of Carl H. Milam, executive secretary of ALA from 1920 to 1948, with his 1929 memorandum to the ALA Council, "What Should Be the Federal Government's Relation to Libraries?" (Sullivan, 1976: 165). Milam's service on the U.S. National Advisory Committee on Education provided him an opportunity to consider issues, such as federal aid to libraries, in the larger context of the reform ideals of Roosevelt's New Deal planning based in Progressive Era reform and policy development.

The ALA executive board appointed its own National Planning Committee in 1934, which developed a National Plan to examine the inequity of tax support for public libraries and sought provision of financial support so that library materials might be available throughout the nation (Sullivan, 1976: 165; Milam, 1934). The National Plan was discussed at ALA Council during the 1934 annual conference and while a sticking point was the locus of control (federal versus state and local), the committee made revisions affirming state and local responsibility and continuance and increase of local support. The National Plan was approved ("A National Plan for Libraries," 1935). Molz (1984: 37) notes, "the issuance of the *National Plan* was the first time that the Association itself entered the national political arena to state a plank as a public policy actor."

The work done by ALA's Library Extension Board laid much groundwork for a national vision of library service driven by a clearer idea of equity of financial support. Beginning in 1929, the Library Extension Board's occasional mimeographed newsletter, *Library Extension News*, was subtitled *Equalizing Library Opportunities*. The idea of equalization was clearly addressed in a 1936 ALA publication issued jointly by the Library Extension Board and the Committee on Planning, *The Equal Chance: Books Help to Make It*. Using line drawings and charts, *The Equal Chance* compared per capita income to public library availability and declared, "It is increasingly true in our modern world that knowledge is power and that the uninformed man not only is handicapped in making a living, but is a liability as a citizen, for whose ignorance we all pay" (ALA, 1936: 15). This simple pamphlet urged people to get involved in state and national planning for library support to achieve "equalizing of library opportunity."

Due to the work of ALA leaders, the U.S. Department of Education authorized funds in 1937 for a Library Services Division.

The creation in 1937 of a Library Service Division in the United States Office of Education was an event of great significance in the history of Federal relations to libraries. . . . Prior to the establishment of this Division, there was no Federal office directly responsible for leadership in a Nation-wide program of library development. The new unit will serve as a Federal library headquarters and will provide a national focus for library interests. (Joeckel, 1938, quoted in Knight and Nourse, 1969: 468)

Carlton B. Joeckel was appointed chair of a new ALA Committee on Post-Defense Planning (later changed to Post-War Planning) by the executive board in October 1941, which issued *Post-War Standards for Public Libraries* in 1943. Part of a national effort to help make the world a better place in which to live, the *Post-War Standards* asserted the importance of the public library and recommended that public library service should be universally available in the United States and its territories.[3]

A National Plan for Public Library Service was published in 1948 by the American Library Association. The chapter reporting an inventory and evaluation of service noted:

- total national public library income is less than one-third of the amount required to provide minimum service;
- there are very great inequalities among the states in per capita expenditures;
- there are serious inequalities in library expenditures *within* each of the states; large proportions of the American public are served by libraries weak in total income or in income per capita. (Joeckel and Winslow, 1948: 30–31)

Essential features of a national library plan were defined with the role of the state library agency delineated as central to achieving adequate, purposeful public library service. *A National Plan for Public Library Service* proposed "a nation-wide minimum standard of service and support below which no library should fall" (Joeckel and Winslow, 1948: 160). The national plan included a strong call for equalization of financial support: "Very great inequalities among the states in per capita expenditures for public libraries are a dominant characteristic of American library development. . . . Some degree of national equalization of these great differences between the states in library support must be a major concern in library planning" (Joeckel and Winslow, 1948: 30).

ALA established a Washington office in 1945 to clarify the role of librarians in federal research programs, to form a closer relationship with the Office of Education and other library-related agencies, and to strengthen influence with Congress (Thomison, 1978: 162–164).

The Public Library after World War II

Concurrent with the completion of *A National Plan for Public Library Service*, the ALA membership addressed the question of the role of the public library in the postwar world. The ALA leadership developed plans for a study "to define legitimate library activity by adapting the traditional educational purposes of libraries to new social conditions and the public's willingness to pay for such services" (Raber, 1997: 43). Robert D. Leigh of the University of Chicago was selected to carry out, between 1947 and 1952, the multipart project that would be called the Public Library Inquiry.[4]

At a forum on the inquiry held in 1949, Bernard Berelson, author of the inquiry volume *The Library's Public*, responded to concern about his findings that the library reached only a minority of the population—the better educated. He noted a split between the professed and practiced objectives for the public library. "Just as many lawyers will tell you that their objective is to see justice done, whereas they are actually out to win cases, so many librarians will tell you that education is their objective, when they are busy trying to increase circulation" (Asheim, 1950: 62). The inquiry contributed to the reformulation of the public library's service mission during the 1950s by acting as one of many catalysts that stimulated the innovative outreach efforts of the late 1960s and early 1970s (Maack, 1994). Librarians worked with the new ALA Washington office for national-level legislation. Central to the effort was Julia Bennett Armistead, director of the ALA Washington office from 1952 to 1957, who worked with Senator Lister Hill (Holley and Schremser, 1983) and Congressman John F. Fogarty. The story of this legislative effort has been recounted in James Healey's study of Rhode Island Congressman Fogarty, who championed the effort. Healey (1974: 79–80) credits Rhode Island state librarian Elizabeth G. Meyer for finding the touchstone and having a profound effect on Fogarty by taking him on a bookmobile ride.

The passage of the Library Services Act (LSA) in 1956 was the result of 35 years of concerted effort on the part of the ALA. Designed to assist in the establishment of library service in areas unserved, especially in rural parts of the country, the LSA required that each state submit a plan for library development before it was eligible to receive federal aid (Casey, 1975). Although this chapter has not focused on the activities of state library agencies, we must note that the work of the state library agencies, usually in collaboration with the ALA state chapters, has been central to overall national public library development. The 1966 report *The Library Functions of the States* (based on a 1960 survey) recognized the importance of state library agencies in their intermediary role between the federal government and local libraries, and recommended that state library agencies strengthen their role (Monypenny, 1966).

In 1964 the LSA was amended and expanded to include urban libraries and construction and retitled the Library Services and Construction Act (LSCA). In 1966 library cooperation was added to the scope of the LSCA, as well as services to the institutionalized, the blind, and people with physical disabilities. The LSCA stimulated a wide variety of innovative library development. States were given considerable flexibility to adapt to their own needs within federal priorities, which included public library construction and renovation; interlibrary cooperation and resource sharing; adaptation of new technologies for library services; and outreach to special segments of the population—such as the disadvantaged, those with disabilities, the elderly and homebound, those in institutions, those with limited English-speaking ability, those who needed literacy services, residents of Indian reservations, children in child care centers, and latchkey children.

An important assessment of the role of the LSCA in one state—Illinois—provides a substantive case study of the impact of this federal legislation. In her introduction to a special report on the history of the LSCA in Illinois, state librarian Bridget L. Lamont (1998: 93) wrote, "During the LSCA years . . . countless LSCA projects of exceptional merit were undertaken, including expansion of public library services to underserved areas, special library services to nursing homes and other special populations, automation/ technology initiatives and training grants."

Civil Rights and Public Libraries

General public library histories prior to civil rights legislation in the 1960s barely mention the "ugly side of librarianship"—the segregation that prevailed in libraries throughout much of the United States in the first 65 years of the twentieth century (Mussman, 1998; Cresswell, 1996). From *Plessy v. Ferguson* (1896) through *Brown v. Board of Education* (1954), many public libraries had separate and unequal facilities for African Americans—if they had any at all. Eliza Atkins Gleason (1941) in *The Southern Negro and the Public Library* provides a careful history of the treatment of African Americans by libraries up to World War II. Writers such as E. J. Josey (1970), Alma Dawson (2000), John Mark Tucker (1998), Patterson Toby Graham (2002), and David Battles (2009) have constructed histories of the manifestation of segregation in various states and regions. In 1936 Stanley Kunitz wrote an editorial in the *Wilson Library Bulletin* titled "The Spectre at Richmond," criticizing segregation of participants at the ALA conference. Kunitz challenged the entire ALA:

> If you permit this organized insult to pass unchallenged, there is but one conclusion to be made: that American librarians do not, in their hearts, care for democracy or for the foundation principles of decent and enlightened institutions. No elegant platform phrases of devotion to the idea of a

free and equal society or to the theory of liberty can be sufficient to obviate that conclusion. (Kunitz, 1936: 592)

Howard Zinn (1997) has written of the desegregation of the Atlanta Public Library in 1959 led by Irene Dobbs Jackson. The national library press faced the issue at long last in 1960, with *Library Journal* editor Eric Moon engaging Rice Estes, who characterized segregation as the most pressing problem facing the nation and criticized librarians for their failure to face the issue (Estes, 1960; Kister, 2002: 152–164). Moon's efforts were the catalyst for the ALA policy passed at the 1962 annual conference to "urge libraries which are institutional members not to discriminate among users on the basis of race, religion, or personal belief and if such discrimination now exists to bring it to an end as speedily as possible." The policy also contained a provision to obtain accurate information about segregation.

The resulting ALA study, Access to Public Libraries (1963), found direct discrimination (complete exclusion), but also "indirect" discrimination practiced by branch libraries in northern cities that were so differentiated in terms of quantity and quality that one group was more limited in its access to the library resources of a community than another. Of these findings, Virginia Lacy Jones commented, "No one should have been surprised that branch libraries discriminate against Negroes, since all public institutions in the United States had discrimination against Negroes built into them. This fact is well known in the South; it is time the North woke up to it" (Jones, 1963: 744).

One of the last cases addressing segregation in libraries was *Brown v. Louisiana* (1966), a U.S. Supreme Court case based on the First Amendment to the U.S. Constitution. Four African American men had requested a book from the Audubon Regional Library, sat down when told it was not available, and were arrested. The decision held that protesters have a First and Fourteenth Amendment right to engage in a peaceful sit-in at a public library.

The Nation's Library Structure

In 1966 President Lyndon B. Johnson appointed a National Advisory Commission on Libraries (NACL) charged with the task of considering the nation's library structure, the nature of the present and the wisest possible future of federal support in the development of national library and informational resources, and the most effective shaping of those resources to the nation's common need over the next decade (Knight and Nourse, 1969). Among the recommendations of the NACL was the establishment of the National Commission on Libraries and Information Science (NCLIS). At its initial meetings NCLIS developed this goal: "To eventually provide every individual in the United States with equal opportunity of access to that part of the total information resource which will satisfy the individual's educational, working, cultural and leisure-time needs and interests, regardless of the individual's location, social or physical condition or level of intellectual achievement" (U.S. NCLIS, 1975).

NCLIS released its action plan, *Toward a National Program for Library and Information Services: Goals for Action* in 1975. This program set forth eight objectives:

1. ensure that basic minimums of library and information services adequate to meet the needs of all local communities are satisfied;
2. provide adequate special services to special constituencies, including the underserved;
3. strengthen existing statewide services and systems;
4. ensure basic and continuing education of personnel essential to the implementation of a National Program;
5. coordinate existing federal programs of library and information service;
6. encourage the private sector (comprising organizations which are not directly tax supported) to become an active partner in the development of the National Program;
7. establish a locus of federal responsibility charged with implementing the national network and coordinating the National Program under the policy guidance of the National Commission; and
8. plan, develop, and implement a nationwide network of library and information service.

In one sense, as Molz (1984, 120) points out, the National Program was the lineal descendant of the National Plan of 1934. It was widely distributed and formed a critical part of the policy framework for thinking about national public library planning for the last quarter of the twentieth century.

During its initial years as a federal agency, NCLIS prepared for the first White House Conference on Library and Information Services (WHCLIS) in November 1979, which was preceded by 57 preconferences in states and territories and six special national preconferences. The ALA, state chapters, and state library agencies collaborated intensively on this national WHCLIS effort. Delegates approved resolutions urging an increased library role in literacy training, improved access to information for all, the free flow of information among nations, and the idea of a library as a total community information center and an independent learning center. Criticized by some for the unwieldy process, the WHCLIS nevertheless positioned libraries as having continuing importance to the nation's well-being. The sheer enormity of the preconference activity and postconference publications gave librarians a broad visibility among policymakers.

The second White House Conference on Library and Information Services convened in July 1991, with three themes: library and information services for literacy, democracy, and productivity. Following this second Conference, task forces from ALA, the Urban Libraries Council, and Chief Officers of State Library Agencies identified two major goals: improvement of information access through technology and the educational empowerment of those who still live outside the mainstream of quality library service (McCook, 1994). This thinking undergirded new library legislation in 1996, the Library Services and Technology Act (LSTA). The LSTA was a section of the Museum and Library Services Act that moved the administration of federal aid to public libraries from the Department of Education to a new agency, the Institute of Museum and Library Services (IMLS). LSTA built on the strengths of previous federal library programs, but included some major differences. While it retained the state-based approach from previous legislation, it sharpened the focus to two key priorities for libraries—information access through technology and information empowerment through special services. By locating federal support for libraries within the IMLS, since 1996, the government has emphasized the community-based role of libraries, and it includes lifelong learning in the mission of the public library. In this new agency, libraries and museums have converged as cultural heritage institutions with a renewed commitment to collaborative engagement within local and world communities (McCook and Jones, 2002).

The reauthorization of the Museum and Library Services Act in 2003 updated the LSTA to promote improvements in all types of libraries; to facilitate access to, and sharing of, resources; and to achieve economical and efficient delivery of service for the purpose of cultivating an educated and informed citizenry. The act authorized a doubling of the minimum state allotment under the Grants to State Library Agencies program. It helps to coordinate statewide library services and supports a wide array of programs from family literacy to providing broad access to sophisticated databases. It also develops the role of libraries as information brokers helping to make resources and services, which are often prohibitively expensive, more readily available (U.S. IMLS, 1996).

The major features of the LSTA are (1) to promote improvements in library services in all types of libraries in order to better serve the people of the United States; (2) to facilitate access to resources and in all types of libraries for the purpose of cultivating an educated and informed citizenry; and (3) to encourage resource sharing among all types of libraries for the purpose of achieving economical and efficient delivery of library services to the public (U.S. IMLS, 2009).

In 2008 NCLIS was incorporated into the IMLS. Its final report, *Meeting the Information Needs of the American People: Past Actions and Future Initiatives*, provides a history of NCLIS since its establishment in 1970 (Davenport and Russell, 2008). John Berry (2007) has provided insight into the politics of NCLIS.

Achievement of a national voice for public libraries resulted from ongoing collaboration among librarians organized in national and state library associations and through state library agencies. Advocacy for library support at local, state, and national levels since World War II and into the twenty-first century has been orchestrated by the ALA and state chapters with countless hours contributed by members of associations and the concerned public.

The Evolution of the Public Library Message

Librarians worked to achieve federal support to provide for more equal public library service from World War I to the passage of the LSA in 1956. They continued this progress with the LSCA in 1964 and the LSTA in 1996, 2003, and subsequent years. Today librarians have organized with the help of the Office for Library Advocacy of the ALA, which supports the efforts of advocates seeking to improve libraries of all types by developing resources, a peer-to-peer advocacy network, and training for advocates at the local, state, and national level. While federal funding has yet to ensure that all people can experience equal access, it has done much to expand access to library services. We have seen how astute leaders connected library issues to federal programs during the New Deal to gain a place for libraries in postwar planning efforts. The library community has continued to hold this place at the federal level with the evolution of funding, through a series of acts and legislation. Today's library leaders take advantage of social networking to deliver declarations about the importance of libraries. For example, Jim Rettig (2008), ALA president in 2008–2009, wrote an entry in the *Huffington Post* blog, "Libraries Stand Ready to Help in Tough Economic Times." What remains is to identify the overarching issues that librarians have used to help shape public policy, which has resulted in successful legislation to support libraries at federal, state, and local levels.

Lifelong Learning and Literacy as Public Library Functions

The idea of lifelong learning provided much of the impetus throughout the 1920s and 1930s for librarians and communities to develop enthusiasm for the establishment of library service where none existed. In his history of the adult education movement in the United States, Malcolm S. Knowles (1977: 115) observed that by the 1920s, "the library moved from the status of an adult education resource toward that of an adult education operating agency. . . . It moved from perceiving its constituency as consisting of individuals toward perceiving it as a total community, and . . . it moved from regarding its function as custodial toward regarding it as educational." In her historical review of libraries and adult education, Margaret E. Monroe (1963: 6) identified a variety of library services provided by libraries to adults during the first half of the twentieth century that incorporated aspects of adult education. Librarians produced a steady, thoughtful commentary on literacy, reading, and lifelong learning, developed programmatic responses, and conducted research on these topics throughout the twentieth century. This work provides a robust history of librarians working with adult educators and funders to forge alliances that will enhance the lives of adult learners and new readers, and it provides library advocates with a strong argument to take to sources of funding at local, state, and national levels (McCook and Barber, 2002).

At the national level in 2010, two units within the ALA support adult literacy and lifelong learning: (1) the ALA Office for Literacy and Outreach Services (OLOS), which focuses attention on services that include traditionally underserved populations, including new readers and nonreaders; and (2) the ALA Public Programs Office, with the mission to foster cultural programming as an integral part of library service. An example of a public library supporting adult literacy today is the READ/ San Diego program (San Diego Public Library, 2009)—a free literacy, English as a second language, and family literacy instruction service for adults 18 years and older. An example of a lifelong learning program is the Big Read, which encourages and celebrates the reading of great American literature (Price, 2008).

Justifying Policy: Libraries as the Cornerstone of Democracy

Public libraries were characterized in founding documents as providing the resources for citizens to become informed about events and thus be able to participate in the democratic process with greater knowledge. The Public Library Inquiry, carried out and published between 1947 and 1952, has been characterized by Raber (1997: 3) as a professional legitimating project that "constituted an exercise in identity creation that relied heavily on the role of the public library as a sustaining contributor to American democracy."[4] The concept of libraries as supporting the democratic process provided librarians with an ongoing rationale useful in promoting support for libraries and tied closely to the idea of adult lifelong learning. Much of the advocacy that provided input to policymakers for the passage of the LSA rested on these premises.

A structural change occurred within the ALA in 1950 when several units merged (Division of Public Libraries, Library Extension Division, and the Trustees Division), creating the Public Library Division (changed in 1959 to the Public Library Association—PLA). The PLA began to assume increasing responsibility for setting public library standards, issuing documents in 1956 and 1966. In the 1970s another shift took place from a national approach to standards to a local planning process (Pungitore, 1995: 71–74).

"The Public Library: Democracy's Resource, a Statement of Principles" (1985) was issued amid the adoption of the new PLA planning process. This one-page document identified the public library as offering access freely to all members of the community "without regard to race, citizenship, age, education level, economic status, or any other qualification or condition."

When the PLA began to move to a planning process in place of national standards, the effort to establish a national mission for public libraries was no longer part of the PLA agenda, although, as noted above, the 1979 Mission Statement (PLA, Goals, Guidelines and Standards Committee, 1979) and the 1982 "Democracy's Resource" statement surely represent such efforts. While the PLA pulled back from broad mission definition in the 1990s, the ALA and the NCLIS continued to provide general statements of direction. In 1995 the ALA's journal, *American Libraries*, listed "12 Ways Libraries Are Good for the Country," which included the statement, "Libraries safeguard our freedom and keep democracy healthy." With a photograph of the Statue of Liberty in the background, the first of the 12 ways listed was "to inform citizens," because democracy and libraries have a symbiotic relationship.

The 1999 ALA Council adopted the statement "Libraries: An American Value" (ALA, 1999), included it as an official public policy statement (Policy 53.8), and printed it on the cover of the association's 1999–2000 handbook. This statement noted, "we preserve our democratic society by making available the widest possible range of viewpoints, opinions and ideas." The same year, the ALA sponsored a Congress on Professional Education that resulted in an effort to develop a statement on core values, and the NCLIS passed a resolution adopting *Principles for Public Library Service* based on the *UNESCO Public Library Manifesto*. These principles include the key mission that the public library will be a "gateway to knowledge," and that "Freedom, Prosperity and the Development of Society and of individuals are fundamental human values. They will be attained through the ability of well-informed citizens to exercise their democratic rights and to play an active role in society" (U.S. NCLIS, 1999). The millennium president of ALA, Nancy Kranich (2001), reaffirmed the commitment of libraries to the democratic process, editing a monograph of essays on the role libraries play in democracy, *Libraries and Democracy: The Cornerstones of Liberty*.

Libraries are the foundation of a learning society. The long identification of public libraries in the United States with the principles of a democratic government has been central to their support. Initially this support came as libraries characterized themselves as helping to maintain social order and education. Over time, however, the adherence to the ideals of intellectual freedom—sometimes at odds with larger governmental actions during World War I, the cold war, and the war on terror—has come to define the core of the profession's ethical stance ("Resolution on the USA PATRIOT Act," 2003: 93).

Public libraries are a vital component of the public sphere where people learn about complex issues and practice deliberative democracy (Willingham, 2008). New responsibilities include e-government, the provision of government information services through the online environment (Jaeger and Bertot, 2009).

In the years to come I believe that librarians will adopt a comprehensive human rights perspective and function as the keystone for equity and access for all people (McCook and Phenix, 2008).

Public Librarians as Defenders of Intellectual Freedom

Today the defense of intellectual freedom is a central value of public librarians. This commitment to intellectual freedom went all the way to the Supreme Court in 2003 when the ALA challenged the Children's Internet Protection Act (CIPA). CIPA placed restrictions on funding available through the LSTA and the Universal Discount Rate by requiring filters or blocks on Internet access in schools and public libraries. The ALA successfully argued that adult library patrons must have the ability to disable Internet filters to ensure access to constitutionally protected information (Jaeger and Yan, 2009).

The 2010 *Intellectual Freedom Manual* includes expanded interpretations of the Library Bill of Rights including that challenged materials should stay in the collection during the review process; restricted access violates the basic tenets of the Library Bill of Rights; and the use of the principles of universal design to ensure that library facilities, policies, services, and resources meet the needs of all users (ALA, 2009; ALA, Office for Intellectual Freedom, 2010).

How did U.S. public librarians move from their initial somewhat censorious stance of selecting and providing the "right books" and sometimes banning the "wrong books" to become staunch defenders of the First Amendment and intellectual freedom today?

The involvement in censorship and book banning by public librarians at the end of World War I has been characterized in chilling terms: "Librarians willingly but quietly pulled from their shelves any title that might raise suspicions of disloyalty. Some librarians burned these titles, many of which were classic works of German philosophy, books advocating American pacifism, and simple German language texts" (Wiegand, 1989: 6). Recognizing that in less than a century librarians have progressed from participation in censorship to fighting it in the Supreme Court, we see that a change in philosophy regarding intellectual freedom between the end of World War I and the years following World War II marks the growth of U.S. public librarianship as a profession (Robbins, 1996).

The public library gradually made a transition from being an agent of social stability to supporting all points of view. Geller (1984), in *Forbidden Books in American Public Libraries*, characterizes 1923–1930 as the period of a critical shift by public librarians toward a more expansive philosophy of collection development. In 1931

George F. Bowerman, director of the Washington, DC, public library, addressed the issue of censorship and reminded librarians that classics like Eliot's *Adam Bede*, Hardy's *Jude the Obscure*, or Whitman's *Leaves of Grass* were once deemed worthy of condemnation. He characterized censorship as repugnant to public librarians and noted that the public library is "not an institution for the inculcation of standardized ideas. . . . It stands for free opinion and to that end it supplies material on both or all sides of every controversial question of human interest" (Bowerman, 1931: 5–6).

In his study of propaganda and the public library from the 1930s to World War II, Lincove (1994) describes discussions in the field that addressed fascist propaganda as a threat to democracy and capitalism. The core of debate was whether the library should censor based on moralism and control versus a philosophy that would provide access to mainstream and controversial ideas, especially foreign and domestic political propaganda.

> In 1936 the Chicago Public Library issued the first formal intellectual freedom policy to be published by a library in the United States in response to challenges from the local Polish and Russian communities that the collection included works by Marx and Lenin. "The Public Library asserts its right and duty to keep on its shelves a representative selection of books on all subjects of interest to its readers and not prohibited by law, including books on all sides of controversial questions. (Latham, 2007: 15)

The man who would later be named poet laureate of the United States, Stanley J. Kunitz, editor of the *Wilson Bulletin for Libraries* from 1928 to 1943, provided unyielding defense of the freedom to read. In his ongoing column, "The Roving Eye," Kunitz was critical of librarians who did nothing to oppose censorship. While cherishing democracy, Kunitz (1939) opposed intolerance, intellectual provincialism, and protection of the status quo. His editorials are a legacy to the community of public librarians striving to define intellectual freedom as a professional ethic. The social control exercised by boards of trustees has been characterized as crucial in the debate over propaganda. Librarians became increasingly concerned that the oversight of boards created an atmosphere of censorship and caused librarians to select on the safe side. This seemed especially confounding as the library was coming to be viewed as an important vehicle for adult education.

After reading Bernard Berelson's 1938 essay, "The Myth of Library Impartiality" in the *Wilson Library Bulletin*, Forrest Spaulding, director at the public library of Des Moines, Iowa, which had a strong adult education program, worked with his own board of trustees to develop a Library Bill of Rights. This was adapted and adopted by the ALA at the 1939 San Francisco conference. *The Grapes of Wrath*, by John Steinbeck, was published in March 1939 and immediately banned at some libraries because of its social criticism (Lingo, 2003). After passage of the Library Bill of Rights, the ALA Adult Education Board distributed copies to help libraries fight against requests to censor. Because of the rash of book banning across the nation, the ALA appointed a committee to study censorship and recommend policy. In 1940 that committee reported that intellectual freedom and professionalism were linked and recommended a permanent committee, which was established as the Committee on Intellectual Freedom to Safeguard the Right of Library Users to Freedom of Inquiry (changed in 1947 to the Committee on Intellectual Freedom).

Following World War II, the loyalty programs implemented by President Truman, the establishment of the House Un-American Activities Committee, and the general cold war atmosphere presented new threats to intellectual freedom. Librarians responded with a renewed commitment to fight censorship activities. A revised Library Bill of Rights was issued in 1948 with a far stronger statement of the librarian's responsibility to defend freedom of inquiry (Berninghausen, 1948). State intellectual freedom committees were formed, the "Statement on Labeling" was adopted (1951), and a national conference was held in 1952.[5] Events that brought about the "Freedom to Read Statement" (1953) included the overseas library controversy and attacks on the International Information Administration's libraries. Robbins (2001) views the adoption of the "Freedom to Read Statement" and the ALA's commitment to overseas libraries as instrumental in the identification of librarians as defenders of intellectual freedom.

Since the adoption of the "Freedom to Read Statement" in 1953, library workers have continued to face and cope with many challenges. New interpretations of the Library Bill of Rights have been issued, including "Access to Electronic Information Services and Networks" (1996); "Access to Library Resources and Services Regardless of Gender or Sexual Orientation" (2000), and "Importance of Education to Intellectual Freedom" (2009). These and other amplifications of the basic tenets of intellectual freedom define the "active advocacy" that librarians accept when they join the profession (Conable, 2002: 43).

The internalization by public librarians of the principle of defending intellectual freedom, carried on through the Office of Intellectual Freedom and the Freedom to Read Foundation of the ALA, has been fundamental in establishing librarians' "jurisdiction as providers of free access to diverse ideas to all" (Robbins, 1996: 163). This principle was demonstrated by four courageous librarians—the Connecticut Four—who were aware of the principles of privacy and of intellectual freedom in the context of the USA PATRIOT Act (Uniting and Strengthening America by Providing Appropriate Tools Required to Intercept and Obstruct Terrorism), which was passed October 26, 2001, shortly after the attack on the United States on September 11, 2001.

In 2005, Library Connection, a nonprofit consortium of 27 libraries in Connecticut, received a National Security Letter (NSL) from the FBI, along with its accompanying perpetual gag order, demanding library patrons' records. George Christian, executive director of Library Connection, and three members of the executive committee of the board engaged the ACLU to file suit to challenge the constitutional validity of the NSL. Because Section 505 of the USA PATRIOT Act, which authorizes the FBI to demand records without prior court approval, also forbids, or gags, anyone who receives an NSL from telling anyone else about receiving it, they also challenged the validity of the gag order.

For almost a year the ACLU fought to lift the gag order, challenging the government's power under Section 505 to silence four citizens who wished to contribute to public debate on the PATRIOT Act. In May 2006, the government finally gave up its legal battle to maintain the gag order. On June 26, 2006, the ACLU announced that, after dropping its defense of the gag provision accompanying the NSL request, the FBI abandoned the lawsuit entirely.

The Connecticut Four were honored by the ALA with the 2007 Paul Howard Award for Courage for their challenge to the National Security Letter and gag order provision of the USA PATRIOT Act. The Connecticut Four are:

1. George Christian, executive director of Library Connection
2. Peter Chase, vice president of Library Connection, director of the Plainville (CT) Public Library, and chairman of the Connecticut Library Association's Intellectual Freedom Committee
3. Barbara Bailey, president of Library Connection and director of the Welles-Turner Memorial Library in Glastonbury, Connecticut
4. Jan Nocek, secretary of Library Connection and director of the Portland (CT) Library

In a summary of the actions of the Connecticut Four and their challenge to the USA PATRIOT Act, Jones (2009: 223) notes: "Librarians need to understand their country's legal balance between the protection of freedom of expression and the protection of national security. Many librarians believe that the interests of national security, important as they are, have become an excuse for chilling the freedom to read."

U.S. Public Libraries in Their Third Century

Established in the mid-1850s, U.S. public librarianship faces its third century of service and can look back on a history based on commitment to democratic ideals, life-long learning, and facilitation of access to the world's cultural heritage and knowledge for all. See especially the editorial writing of John N. Berry in the pages *of Library Journal* for a synthesis of issues over the past several decades.[6]

In the earlier edition of this book (McCook, 2004: 293–302), written in the first years of the century, I noted trends that would characterize the period from 2000 to 2010. These, I believe continue to be important in the decade to come and so I revisit the topics here.

Sense of Place and the Public Library as Public Sphere

A sense of place (SoP) is the sum total of all perceptions—aesthetic, emotional, historical, supernal—that a physical location and its associated activities and emotional responses invoke in people. The public library provides a sense of place that can transcend new development, big-box stores, and malls, to help a community retain its distinct character. The growing emphasis on sustainable and livable communities encourages creation of public spaces that are true community places. In their edited volume, *The Library as Place: History, Community, and Culture*, John Buschman and Gloria J. Leckie (2007) have explored this idea and extended the concept to address the impact of technology.

The importance of the public library as a commons is part of the larger metaphor of the public sphere in democratic societies. The idea of the public sphere has been developed using the work of philosopher Jürgen Habermas, who has described the significance of people connecting ideas through broad discussion. A vibrant public sphere provides an opportunity for discourse that will enliven democracy. Public libraries that recognize the importance of sustaining the public sphere will respond to their community's desire for a place to address critical issues in their lives.

Responsible public library collection development requires that librarians ensure that materials are available to meet the needs and interests of all segments of their communities, and this is an important way that the public sphere can be enhanced (Budd and Wyatt, 2002). However, real threats to the availability of information for public discourse exist. In *Dismantling the Public Sphere*, Buschman (2003) provides a critique of librarianship in light of increasing commercialization of information and the broad reach of authoritarian populism. Taken together, the provision of a commons, materials in all formats to support exploration of important issues, and offering opportunity for communities to come together are important public library contributions to a rich public sphere. If discourse becomes more democratic through consensus building, it is partly because authentic discourse enables people to move from personal opinions to informed ideas (McCook, 2001).

Convergence of Cultural Heritage Institutions

The convergence of cultural heritage institutions—libraries, museums, archives, historical societies—is not only a manifestation of technological possibilities, but also the result of a new way of looking at lifelong learning. In the overviews of goals at the IMLS website, it is noted:

> As stewards of cultural heritage, information and ideas, museums and libraries have traditionally played a vital role in helping us experience, explore, discover and make sense of the world. That role is now more essential than ever. Through building technological infrastructure and strengthening community relationships, libraries and museums can offer the public unprecedented access and expertise in transforming information overload into knowledge. (U.S. IMLS, 2011)

Public library programs that bring communities together to explore one book or discuss history, literature, or science are increasingly collaborating with other cultural heritage institutions to deepen understanding. The provision of books, music, DVDs, downloads, access to the Internet, and other digital and electronic resources sustains and deepens each learner's journey. David Carr (2003: 172) muses on the responsibilities of libraries in *The Promise of Cultural Institutions*:

> It is our common trust to serve and assist the American journey, fearless, in this transformed century. We are perhaps at the edge of understanding that our institutions, like all of our culture, are about the energies of dream, and courage, solace and renewal. And at that edge, perhaps we can assist others (and ourselves) to understand that what we want most deeply to know as true, we must craft for ourselves.

Inclusive Service Mandates and Commitment to Human Rights and Social Justice

Public libraries have a long history of moving toward inclusive service to all community residents. The goal of equity of access, long advocated by the ALA, is simple in concept, yet complex in implementation (McCook, 2002). As reported by the U.S. Census Bureau in 2010, the U.S. population presents many challenges to the goal of equity of access: there are over 50 million people in the United States with some sort of disability that must be accommodated; 20 percent of the population speaks a language other than English in the home (19.8 percent are foreign born); and 14.3 percent of the population lives below the poverty level (43.6 million people).

Each of these groups presents a set of special service requirements if the public library is to provide equity of access. The public library has a strong intellectual and philosophical commitment to equity of access, as manifested in national policy statements approved by the ALA, such as "Library Services for People with Disabilities Policy," "Library Services for the Poor," and the work of associations that focus on the special reading and information needs of people from diverse cultures. It becomes part of the task of librarians in different communities to identify the demographic composition of the population and develop responsive services.

Social justice is activated as librarians work to provide all community members with inclusive services regardless of age, ethnicity, language, physical or mental challenges, or economic class. Whether ensuring that there is online access in rural public libraries or bringing bookmobiles to urban centers, public librarians contribute to human development and enrichment. The respect that librarians give to all members of their public is a rare yet precious mode of daily work. Social justice in librarianship has been addressed by Kevin Rioux (2010) and this is extended to a human rights model in the last chapter of this volume.

Public libraries and the library workers who are committed to the continuation of this most democratic of all institutions face the future with the charge of maintaining a sense of place and commitment to the sustainability of an open public sphere; being mindful of the convergence of cultural institutions; and being sensitive to the effort that is required to extend inclusion in the spirit of social justice and human rights. The convergence of cultural institutions and the consilience of science and the humanities predicted by Gould (2003) portend a future in which public libraries will play an important part. The public library is endowed with a history of grassroots support for its development, the ongoing commitment of friends and users, and staffs comprised of thoughtful and engaged individuals who tend to its future.

This book has been revised at a time of economic stress in the United States when libraries are seeing budget reductions and declines in tax revenues, but this is also a time when library use has increased over 30 percent (Miller, 2010; Fitzpatrick, 2009; Fiels, 2009). Public librarians work with passion to establish the public library as an essential community agency and to defend the ideals of free inquiry. In the chapters that follow, I examine the component parts that comprise public librarianship in the United States.

Notes

1. ALA, Commission on the Library and Adult Education (1926). For additional background on the Adult Education Board meetings and minutes through its history, see ALA archives under Reference and User Services Association.

2. National leaders, such as Louis R. Wilson based in North Carolina, were able to speak out for citizen involvement. Connected to ALA's extension efforts, see Graham (1932). For an overview of this effort in North Carolina, South Carolina, Georgia, Kentucky, Mississippi, Tennessee, and Virginia, see Anders (1958: 69–80). For an in-depth study of the North Carolina Citizens' Library Movement, see Eury (1951).

3. Molz (1984: 39–63). The work of Joeckel (1935), the ALA Committee on Post-War Planning, and the New Deal National Resources Planning Board is viewed as laying the groundwork for federal legislation for library funding. Molz's (1984: 95–96) characterization of Joeckel's rational planning approach and Milam's pragmatic incremental approach provide insight into the evolution of federal support. See also Sullivan (1976: 135–140); records in the ALA Archives: Post-War Planning Committee File, 1941–1948, including correspondence, reports, drafts, minutes, budgets, statistics, surveys, lists, proposals, and plans concerning a restatement of public library standards—*Post-War Standards for Public Libraries* (Joeckel, 1943), undertaken by the ALA at the request of the National Resources Planning Board (NRPB); a comparison of existing library services with the standards; the formulation of the detailed *National Plan for Public Library Service* (1948) including a Plan for Public Library Service in America; and postwar planning for school, college, and university libraries. Adequate provision for library service had been recognized in the *National Resources Development Report for 1943*, issued by the NRPB in the section "Equal Access to Education," in which it was stated:

> Public libraries deserve support that will enable them adequately to fulfill their functions as major instruments of adult education. Thirty-five million Americans, most of whom reside in rural areas, have no library service. Those to whom libraries are available receive service costing, on the average, little more than a third of the $1.50 per capita estimated to be required to maintain a reasonably good library. (U.S. NRPB, 1943: 70)

4. Raber (1997), "The Public Library and the Postwar World," 23–36, and "The Beginnings of the Public Library Inquiry," 37–49. The Public Library Inquiry consisted of seven volumes all published by Columbia University Press: Bernard Berelson, *The Library's Public* (1949); Alice I. Bryan, *The Public Librarian* (1952); Oliver Garceau, *The Public Library in the Political Process* (1949); Robert D. Leigh, *The Public Library in the United States*, 1950; James L. McCamy, *Government Publications for the Citizen* (1949); William Miller, *The Book Industry* (1949); and Gloria Waldren, *The Information Film* (1949). Supplementary reports were issued on library finance, public use of the library, and effects of the mass media, music materials, and work measurement. For complete list, see Raber (1997: 82).

5. Robbins (1996), Appendix C, "State Intellectual Freedom Committees," 181–183; ALA, Office for Intellectual Freedom (2010: 186–192); Dix and Bixler (1954).

6. For an impassioned assessment and overview of librarianship over the last 50 years, see the work of John N. Berry III, former editor in chief of *Library Journal*, who joined *Library Journal*'s staff in April 1964 and retired in 2009. He wrote 1,016 articles in *Library Journal* and 50 for other journals and books— over 1,060 items. His strong commitment to the ideal of public service has been a soaring voice of encouragement and guidance bridging the twentieth and twenty-first centuries.

References

American Library Association. 1936. *The Equal Chance: Books Help to Make It*. Chicago: American Library Association.

———. 1999. "Libraries: An American Value." American Library Association. http://www.ala .org/ala/aboutala/offices/oif/statementspols/americanvalue/librariesamerican.cfm.

———. 2009. *Intellectual Freedom Manual*. IFC Report to Council. January 28. Chicago: American Library Association.

American Library Association, Commission on the Library and Adult Education. 1926. *Libraries and Adult Education*. Chicago: American Library Association.

———. 2010. *Intellectual Freedom Manual*. 8th ed. Chicago: American Library Association.

Anders, Mary Edna. 1958. "The Development of Public Library Service in the Southeastern States, 1895–1950." PhD diss., Columbia University.

Asheim, Lester. 1950. *A Forum on the Public Library Inquiry*. New York: Columbia University Press. Repr., Westport, CT: Greenwood Press, 1970.

Barker, Tommie Dora. 1936. *Libraries of the South: A Report on Development*. Chicago: American Library Association.

Battles, David M. 2009. *The History of Public Library Access for African Americans in the South or Leaving Behind the Plow*. Latham, MD: Scarecrow Press.

Berelson, Bernard. 1938. "The Myth of Library Impartiality." *Wilson Library Bulletin* 13 (October): 87–90.

Berninghausen, David K. 1948. "Library Bill of Rights." *ALA Bulletin* 42 (July/August): 285.

Berry, John N. 2007. "The Politics of NCLIS." *Library Journal* 132 (March): 10.

Bowerman, George F. 1931. *Censorship and the Public Library*. New York: H. W. Wilson.

Brown v. Louisiana. 1966. 383 U.S. 131 (1966).

Budd, John M., and Cynthia Wyatt. 2002. "'Do You Have Any Books On—': An Examination of Public Library Holdings." *Public Libraries* 41 (March/April): 107–112.

Buschman, John E. 2003. *Dismantling the Public Sphere: Situating and Sustaining Librarianship in the Age of the New Public Philosophy*. Westport, CT: Libraries Unlimited.

Buschman, John, and Gloria J. Leckie, eds. 2007. *The Library as Place: History, Community, and Culture*. Westport, CT: Libraries Unlimited.

Carr, David. 2003. *The Promise of Cultural Institutions*. Lanham, MD: Rowman and Littlefield.

Casey, Genevieve M., ed. 1975. "Federal Aid to Libraries: Its History, Impact, Future." *Library Trends* 24 (July).

Conable, Gordon. 2002. "Public Libraries and Intellectual Freedom." In *Intellectual Freedom Manual*. 6th ed. Chicago: American Library Association.

Cresswell, Stephen. 1996. "The Last Days of Jim Crow in Southern Libraries." *Libraries and Culture* 31 (Summer/Fall): 557–573.

Davenport, Nancy, and Judith Russell. 2008. *Meeting the Information Needs of the American People: Past Actions and Future Initiatives*. Washington, DC: U.S. National Commission on Libraries and Information Science. ERIC 500878.

Dawson, Alma. 2000. "Celebrating African-American Librarians and Librarianship." *Library Trends* 49 (Summer): 49–87.

Dix, William S., and Paul Bixler. 1954. *Freedom of Communications: Proceedings of the First Conference on Intellectual Freedom, New York City, June 28–29, 1952*. Chicago: American Library Association.

Estes, Rice. 1960. "Segregated Libraries." *Library Journal* (December 15): 4418–4421.

Eury, William. 1951. "The Citizens' Library Movement in North Carolina." MA thesis, George Peabody College for Teachers, August.

Fenwick, Sara Innis. 1976. "Library Services to Children and Young People." *Library Trends* 25: 329–360.

Fiels, Keith Michael. 2009. "In Tough Economic Times." *American Libraries* (March): 8.

Fitzpatrick, S. 2009. "Budget Cuts Continue to Loom over U.S. Libraries." *American Libraries* (May): 17–18.

Geller, Evelyn. 1984. *Forbidden Books in American Public Libraries, 1876–1939: A Study in Cultural Change*. Westport, CT: Greenwood Press.

Gleason, Eliza Atkins. 1941. *The Southern Negro and the Public Library: A Study of Government and Administration of Public Library Service to Negroes in the South*. Chicago: University of Chicago Press.

Gould, Stephen Jay. 2003. *The Hedgehog, the Fox and the Magister's Pox: Mending the Gap between Science and the Humanities*. New York: Harmony Books.

Graham, Frank P. 1932. "Citizen's Library Movements." *Library Extension News* 14 (May): 2.

Graham, Patterson Toby. 2002. *A Right to Read: Segregation and Civil Rights in Alabama's Public Libraries, 1900–1965*. Tuscaloosa: University of Alabama Press.

Healey, James Stewart. 1974. *John E. Fogarty: Political Leadership for Library Development*. Metuchen, NJ: Scarecrow Press.

Holley, Edward G., and Robert F. Schremser. 1983. *The Library Servies and Construction Act*. Greenwich, CT: JAI Press.

Jaeger, Paul T., and John Carlo Bertot. 2009. "E-government Education in Public Libraries." *Journal of Education for Library and Information Science* 50 (Winter): 39–49.

Jaeger, Paul T., and Zheng Yan. 2009. "One Law with Two Outcomes: Comparing the Implementation of CIPA in Public Libraries and Schools." *Information Technology and Libraries* 28 (March): 6–14.

Jenkins, Christine. 2000. "The History of Youth Services Librarianship: A Review of the Research Literature." *Libraries and Culture* 35 (Winter): 103–140.

Joeckel, Carleton Bruns. 1935. *The Government of the American Public Library*. Chicago: University of Chicago Press.

———. 1943. *Post-War Standards for Public Libraries*. Chicago: American Library Association.

Joeckel, Carleton B., and Amy Winslow. 1948. *A National Plan for Public Library Service*. Chicago: American Library Association.

Jones, Barbara M. 2009. "Librarians Shushed No More: The USA Patriot Act, the 'Connecticut Four,' and Professional Ethics." *Newsletter on Intellectual Freedom* 58, no. 6: 195, 221–223.

Jones, Virginia Lacy. 1963. "The Access to Public Libraries Study." *ALA Bulletin* 57 (September): 742–745.

Josey, E. J. 1970. *The Black Librarian in America*. Metuchen, NJ: Scarecrow Press.

Kelly, Melody S. 2003. "Revisiting C. H. Milam's 'What Libraries Learned from the War' and Rediscovering the Library Faith." *Libraries and Culture* 38 (Fall): 378–388.

Kister, Kenneth F. 2002. *Eric Moon: The Life and Library Times*. Jefferson, NC: McFarland.

Knight, Douglas M., and E. Shepley Nourse, eds. 1969. *Libraries at Large: Traditions, Innovations and the National Interest; The Resource Book Based on the Materials of the National Advisory Commission on Libraries*. New York: R. R. Bowker.

Knowles, Malcolm S. 1977. *A History of the Adult Education Movement in the United States: Includes Adult Education Institutions Through 1976*. Huntington, NY: Robert E. Krieger.

Kranich, Nancy, ed. 2001. *Libraries and Democracy: The Cornerstones of Liberty*. Chicago: American Library Association.

Kunitz, Stanley. 1936. "The Spectre at Richmond." *Wilson Library Bulletin* 10 (May): 592–593.

———. 1939. "That Library Serves Best." *Wilson Library Bulletin* (December): 314.

Lamont, Bridget L. 1998. "The Legacy of the Library Services and Construction Act in Illinois." *Illinois Libraries* 80 (Summer): 93–184.

Latham, Joyce M. 2007. "White Collar Read: The American Public Library and the Left-Led CIO: A Case Study of the Chicago Public Library, 1929–1952." Unpublished PhD dissertation, University of Illinois at Urbana-Champaign.

———. 2010. "Clergy of the Mind: Alvin S. Johnson, William S. Learned, the Carnegie Corporations and the American Library Association." *Library Quarterly* 80 (July): 249–265.

Learned, William S. 1924. *The American Public Library and the Diffusion of Knowledge*. New York: Harcourt.

"Library Projects Under Public Works, Civil Works and Relief Administrations." 1933. *ALA Bulletin* 27 (December): 539.

Lincove, David A. 1994. "Propaganda and the American Public Library from the 1930s to the Eve of World War II." *RQ* 33 (Summer): 510–523.

Lingo, Marci. 2003. "Forbidden Fruit: The Banning of *The Grapes of Wrath* in the Kern County Free Library." *Libraries and Culture* 38 (Fall): 351–377.

Maack, Mary Niles. 1994. "Public Libraries in Transition: Ideals, Strategies and Research." *Libraries and Culture* 29 (Winter): 79.

McCook, Kathleen de la Peña. 1994. *Toward a Just and Productive Society: An Analysis of the Recommendations of the White House Conference on Library and Information Services*. Washington, DC: National Commission on Libraries and Information Science.

———. 2001. "Authentic Discourse as a Means of Connection Between Public Library Service Responses and Community Building Initiatives." *Reference and User Services Quarterly* 40 (Winter): 127–133.

———. 2002. "Rocks in the Whirlpool: Equity of Access and the American Library Association." ERIC database, ED462981, p. 4.

———. 2004. *Introduction to Public Librarianship*. New York: Neal-Schuman.

McCook, Kathleen de la Peña, and Peggy Barber. 2002. "Public Policy as a Factor Influencing Adult Lifelong Learning, Adult Literacy and Public Libraries." *Reference and User Services Quarterly* 42 (Fall): 66–75.

McCook, Kathleen de la Peña, and Maria A. Jones. 2002. "Cultural Heritage Institutions and Community Building." *Reference and User Services Quarterly* 41 (Summer): 326–329.

McCook, Kathleen de la Peña, and Katharine J. Phenix. 2008. "Human Rights, Democracy and Librarians." In *The Portable MLIS*, edited by Ken Haycock and Brooke E. Sheldon, 23–34. Westport, CT: Greenwood Press.

Milam, Carl H. 1934. "National Planning for Libraries." *ALA Bulletin* 28 (February): 60–62.

Miller, Rebecca. 2010. "Losing Libraries/Saving Libraries." *Library Journal* 135 (August): 20–21.

Molz, Redmond Kathleen. 1984. *National Planning for Library Service: 1935–1975*. Chicago: American Library Association.

Monroe, Margaret E. 1963. *Library Adult Education: The Biography of an Idea*. New York: Scarecrow Press.

Monypenny, Phillip. 1966. *The Library Functions of the States*. Chicago: American Library Association.

Mussman, Klaus. 1998. "The Ugly Side of Librarianship: Segregation in Library Services from 1900–1950." In *Untold Stories: Civil Rights, Libraries and Black Librarianship*, 78–92. Champaign: University of Illinois, Graduate School of Library and Information Science.

"A National Plan for Libraries." 1935. *ALA Bulletin* 29 (February): 91–98.

Price, Lee. 2008. "Libraries Take the Big Read Challenge." *Public Libraries* 47 (January/February): 42–45.

Public Library Association, Goals, Guidelines and Standards Committee. 1979. *The Public Library Mission Statement and Its Imperatives for Service*. Chicago: American Library Association.

"The Public Library: Democracy's Resource, a Statement of Principles." 1985. *Public Libraries* 24 (Winter): 153.

Pungitore, Verna L. 1995. *Innovation and the Library: The Adoption of New Ideas in Public Libraries*. Westport, CT: Greenwood Press.

Raber, Douglas. 1997. *Librarianship and Legitimacy: The Ideology of the Public Library Inquiry*. Westport, CT: Greenwood Press.

"Resolution on the USA PATRIOT Act and Related Measures That Infringe on the Rights of Library Users." 2003. *Newsletter on Intellectual Freedom* 52 (May): 93.

Rettig, Jim. 2008. "Libraries Stand Ready to Help in Tough Economic Times." *Huffington Post*, December 11. http://www.huffingtonpost.com/jim-rettig/libraries-stand-ready-to_b_150268.html.

Rioux, Kevin. 2010. "Metatheory in Library and Information Science: A Nascent Social Justice Approach." *Journal of Education for Library and Information Science* 51 (Winter): 9–17.

Robbins, Louise S. 1996. *Censorship and the American Library: The American Library Association's Response to Threats to Intellectual Freedom: 1939–1969*. Westport, CT: Greenwood Press.

———. 2001. "The Overseas Library Controversy and the Freedom to Read: U.S. Librarians and Publishers Confront Joseph McCarthy." *Libraries and Culture* 36 (Winter): 27–39.

San Diego Public Library. 2009. Read/San Diego. http://www.sandiego.gov/publiclibrary/services/read.shtml.

Sullivan, Peggy. 1976. *Carl H. Milam and the American Library Association*. New York: H. W. Wilson.

Thomison, Dennis. 1978. *A History of the American Library Association, 1876–1972*. Chicago: American Library Association.

Tucker, Harold W. 1963. "The Access to Public Libraries Study." *ALA Bulletin* 57 (September): 742–745.

Tucker, John M. 1998. *Untold Stories: Civil Rights, Libraries and Black Librarianship*. Champaign: University of Illinois, Graduate School of Library and Information Science.

"12 Ways Libraries Are Good for the Country." 1995. *American Libraries* 26 (December): 1113–1119. http://www.ala.org/ala/alonline/selectedarticles/12wayslibraries.htm.

U.S. Census Bureau. 2010. "2010 Census Data—2010 Census." U.S. Census Bureau. http://2010.census.gov/2010census/data/.

U.S. Institute of Museum and Library Services. 1996. "Museum and Library Services Act of 1996." http://www.imls.gov/about/abt_1996.htm.

———. 2009. "Mission." http://www.imls.gov/about/about.shtm.

———. 2011. "IMLS—About Us." Institute of Museum and Library Services. Accessed January 13. http://www.imls.gov/ about/about.shtm.

U.S. National Commission on Libraries and Information Science. 1975. *Toward a National Program for Library and Information Services: Goals for Action*. Washington, DC: U.S. Government Printing Office.

———. 1999. "NCLIS Adopts 'Principles for Public Service.'" http://www.nclis.gov/news/pressrelease/pr99/ppls99.html.

U.S. National Resources Planning Board. 1943. *National Resources Development Report for 1943*. Washington, DC: U.S. Government Printing Office.

Wiegand, Wayne A. 1989. *An Active Instrument for Propaganda: The American Public Library During World War I*. Westport, CT: Greenwood Press.

Willingham, Taylor L. 2008. "Libraries as Civic Agents." *Public Library Quarterly* 27: 97–110.

Zinn, Howard. 1997. "A Quiet Case of Social Change." In *The Zinn Reader: Writings on Disobedience and Democracy*, 31–39. New York: Seven Stories Press.

4
Statistics, Standards, Planning, Results, and Quality of Life

This book can change the course of the Public Library Movement in North America. In particular, it can hasten the day when there will be no millions without good local public library service. But the book will not do it unaided. From here on the success of this planning effort will rest primarily with the state library organizations and library extension agencies.

—Carl H. Milam, executive secretary, American Library Association, foreword to *A National Plan for Public Library Service* (1948)

Making the Case: From Faith to Fact

Making the case for public library support persists as a central task of the library profession. The "library faith"—the belief that libraries support reading and the democratic process—grew and flourished as public libraries were founded throughout the United States (Garceau, 1949: 50–52). Once the idea of the public library as an agency worthy of community funding was broadly established during the nineteenth and early twentieth centuries, the profession sought ways to identify norms and guidelines that would ensure quality service.

Initially librarians relied upon statistics and checklists to establish models that could be used when defining local service. In 1933 the American Library Association (ALA) developed and released the first standards for public libraries. These national standards were revised and reissued in 1943, 1956, and 1966, which implied that meeting numerical goals would establish quality. After 1966 the Public Library Association changed its approach, no longer developing standards, and initiated a planning process that encouraged each library to develop its own goals to reflect community needs. At the state level, however, data and statistics have often been used to create standards in collaboration with the planning process and to establish the case for library support at the local level.

Some efforts have been made to link outcomes from library input data to demonstrate that libraries contribute to the quality of life in a community. Linking library outcomes to community indicators is one way to accomplish this. The Community Indicators Consortium (2010), organized around the belief that information sharing across areas of interest is a key element in successful work to benefit people and their concerns about their communities, has identified the Georgia Family Connection Partnership as one program that connects library use as a benchmark for quality of life. Demonstrating in as compelling a way as possible that strong public libraries enhance the lives of people and their communities is essential to future funding, and the U.S. Institute of Museum and Library Services (IMLS) advocates this outcomes-based approach.

In this chapter we will summarize how public librarians attempt to measure services and their impact—the necessary prelude to inclusion as a key variable when quality of life studies and projects take place. We discuss library statistics and their standardization, the history of standards development in public libraries, the change from the use of national standards to a planning process noting the current status of state library standards and their articulation with the planning process, and the growing use of outcome measures to develop research that can be used by policymakers to advance library support.

Statistics for Public Libraries

Today public libraries report budget and use statistics electronically to the data coordinator at their state library agency—a fairly straightforward activity using the Federal-State Cooperative System (FSCS) for Public Library Data. The results are published electronically by the U.S. IMLS (2010). However, we should all understand that implementation of the current national reporting system required great persistence, determination, and the overcoming of multiple obstacles. Mary Jo Lynch, director of the ALA's Office for Research and Statistics (1978–2003) was a major force in the establishment of the federal-state cooperative system for public library data and served on its steering committee for 20 years ("LPN Talks," 2004).

The history of public library statistics development falls into five periods: exploratory (1870–1937); developmental (1938–1956); broadening responsibility (1956–1965); diversified responsibility (1965–1989); and the current era, which began in 1989 when the National Center for Education Statistics (NCES) initiated a formal library statistics program (Schick, 1971; Chute, 2003; Library Research Service, 2009). See Appendix D for a bibliography of national statistics gathered and reported for U.S. public libraries from 1853 to the present. See also the work of Herbert Goldhor (1983) and Robert V. Williams (1991; Williams and McLean, 2008), who have identified, described, and provided bibliographic information on compilations of statistical information about libraries in the United States.

It was not until 1968 that the gathering of public library statistics was codified. Standardization in the United States is coordinated by the American National Standards Institute (ANSI; www.ansi.org), founded in 1918 to promote and facilitate national consensus standards across all fields and occupations. ANSI's guiding principles are consensus, due process, and openness. Over 175 entities are accredited by ANSI, each issuing American National Standards (ANSs). The entity most closely allied with libraries is the National Information Standards Organization (NISO; http://www.niso.org/index.html), founded in 1939 and accredited by ANSI to identify, develop, maintain, and publish technical standards to manage information in the changing and ever more digital environment. NISO standards apply both traditional and new technologies to the full range of information-related needs, including retrieval, repurposing, storage, metadata, and preservation. NISO has issued many ANSs, including *Standardized Usage Statistics Harvesting Initiative, Guidelines for Abstracts, Permanence of Paper for Publications and Documents in Libraries and Archives, Durable Hardcover Binding for Books,* and, of most interest to this discussion, *Information Services and Use: Metrics and Statistics for Libraries and Information Providers—Data Dictionary* (Z39.7), formerly called *Library Statistics* (NISO, 2004).

The Z39.7 standard identifies and defines the basic data collection categories used to collect library statistical data at the national level. It is intended to provide valid and comparable data on library services, staff, users, and collections. It identifies categories for basic library statistical data at the national level and provides associated definitions of terms. In doing so it deals with the following areas of library operation:

- Reporting unit and target population
- Human resources
- Collection resources
- Infrastructure
- Finances
- Services

Z39.7 is not intended to be comprehensive in scope. Instead, it presents a framework for comparable library data by describing common elements pertaining to libraries of various types in the United States. It does not address detailed statistics for specific areas where it seems more appropriate for experts to make recommendations (e.g., music, government documents, maps). The standard also integrates metrics for electronic network use (e-metrics) into each section as appropriate.[1] It also assists the community in collecting the data necessary to support research and analysis to help libraries improve services and guidance to others interested in information about statistical measures related to library services. The American Library Association, Office for Research and Statistics is the maintenance agency for the Z39.7 standard.

The IMLS administers the Public Library Survey using the Z39.7 standard. From its inception in 1989 though 2007 the survey was administered by the NCES. The Public Libraries Survey, conducted annually beginning in 1988, collects data electronically using the FSCS for Public Library Data.[2] Beginning in 2007 the survey has been administered and published by the IMLS.

Each state has a designated data coordinator to whom each library submits data using Bibliostat Collect (http://www.btol.com/ps_details.cfm?id=222). The Oregon State Library provides an informative behind-the-scenes look at what happens to the public library data sets after they are submitted from the local library to the state data coordinator (Figure 4.1).

To comprehend how statistics have been used to assist in the development of public libraries, readers must understand the adoption of library standards—a history that began during the exploratory period of library statistics development in the 1930s.

National Standards for Public Library Service: 1933–1966

As seen in Chapter 2, the move to develop public library standards in the 1930s occurred at the same time that the library profession began efforts to develop a national plan for public library service. The 1933 "Standards for Public Libraries" was a simple document with a short introduction defining the rationale for the public library: "in order that every man, woman and child may have the means of self-education and recreational reading" (ALA, 1933). Recommended numbers of books for each public library collection were:

- 3 per capita for cities under 10,000
- 2 per capita for cities of 10,000 to 200,000
- 1.5 per capita for cities over 200,000

Recommended standards for lending and library registration were to be measured statistically:

- 50 percent registration and 10 books per capita for cities under 10,000
- 40 percent registration and 9 books per capita for cities 10,000–100,000
- 35 percent registration and 8 books per capita for cities 100,000–200,000
- 30 percent registration and 7 books per capita for cities 200,000–1,000,000
- 25 percent registration and 5 books per capita for cities over 1,000,000

Figure 4.1. Oregon State Library, Library Development Services: The Statistics Process—What Happens to Your Data

The Federal-State Cooperative System (FSCS) for public library data was established by Congress in 1988 under the National Center for Education Statistics. Each state has a Data Coordinator that works with the Federal government to produce quality statistics for all the public libraries in the country. In 2007, the project was moved to the Institute of Museum and Library Services (IMLS) and renamed the Public Library Statistical Cooperative (PLSC). The process remains basically the same as it was in 1988.

After statistics are turned in to the State Library, they go through a detailed examination process. We examine data against previous years, looking for outliers, that is, data values exceeding expected changes. The program, Bibliostat Collect, does the same thing through the edit check process. We look particularly at staffing, income, and expenditures. Data may need to be verified by the library at this point, if there is not a clear analytical note attached to the item in Bibliostat Collect. We also examine certain elements against certain others for logical consistency.

The State then electronically transmits the data for libraries meeting the Federal definition of a public library to the U.S. Census Bureau, a contractor for the Institute of Museum and Library Services. Not all respondents of the state's survey will be included in the national data set. The IMLS works closely with the Chief Officers of State Library Agencies (COSLA), the American Library Association (ALA), researchers, and State Data Coordinators (SDCs) to design and conduct the survey.

After the data has been transmitted, Census compiles the data and checks it for values outside the norm. When a figure is an outlier, most of the same edit checks that you see in Bibliostat Collect are raised. If there is no "federal" note attached to the data that verifies a figure's accuracy, the Census contacts the State Data Coordinator for clarification. In the past, the Oregon State Library has been asked to verify branch library addresses, revenue, number of children's programs, and other information about Oregon's libraries.

After the Census has checked the data, Census delivers preliminary tables to the PLSC Steering Committee and IMLS for review for data quality. Census contacts the State Data Coordinator for clarification of any additional questionable data and data corrections, if necessary, based on this review.

When the data file is approved, the Census will go back and use standard formulas to impute the data, that is, provide estimates for missing data. Approved data is then produced in the First Look reports, and the database is is published. Shortly afterwards, it is available through the public library locator and peer comparison tools. This process takes at least a year.

Source: Ann Reed, Oregon State Library. 2010. "The Statistics Process—What Happens to Your Data." Oregon .gov.http://oregon.gov/OSL/LD/statsreportpublib.shtml#The_Statistics_Process_What_Happens_to_Your_ Data. Reprinted by permission of Ann Reed, State Data Coordinator, Oregon State Library.

Income was recommended at \$1.00 per capita and at least \$25,000 total, though it was recognized that smaller towns would usually need to spend more or enlarge the unit of service (ALA, 1933).

Much of the professional discussion in the 1930s focused on the size of the governmental unit required to support library service (Fair, 1934). This discussion was consolidated in Joeckel's landmark 1935 study, *The Government of the American Public Library*, which summarized the various types of county library systems and characterized them as predominantly emphasizing rural library service. Joeckel argued for larger units of library service—ideally regional—to sustain quality service. Many of the ideas he presented in his analysis have influenced cooperative library projects right to the present. The establishment of the Library Services Division in the U.S. Office of Education in 1938 provided a federal vantage point for national-level planning in collaboration with the National Resources Planning Board. The ALA, anticipating the postwar period in which public library service would be seen as a responsibility of democratic government, appointed Joeckel chair of its Committee on Postwar Planning to (1) oversee the development of postwar standards, (2) coordinate data collection on the status of the U.S. public library, and (3) develop a national plan for public library service.

The result was *Post-War Standards for Public Libraries*, issued in 1943, based on the assumption that "public library service should be available without exception to all people and in all political jurisdictions throughout the nation" (Joeckel, 1943: 15). The lengthy and detailed *Post-War Standards* document included discussion of the rationale for standards in eight areas:

1. Service
2. Government and administration
3. Size and area
4. Finance
5. Buildings
6. Book collection
7. Personnel
8. Technical processes (ALA, 1948)

Covered were items such as recommended percentages of registered borrowers, number of books that should circulate each year for children and adults, hours of service, and collection size as a function of community served. Financial standards were addressed in terms of "limited," "reasonably good," and "superior" service with much attention to the need of a minimum of $25,000 to maintain basic service.

The second phase of the Post-War Planning Committee's work was a report of the inventory and evaluation of selected public libraries in 1943, titled "Taking Stock of the American Public Library." This was the basis for the third phase, which resulted in the publication of *A National Plan for Public Library Service* (Joeckel and Winslow, 1948). At the close of World War II, national per capita public library support was $0.72; and 35 million people were still unserved by any library. The *National Plan for Public Library Service* is of particular importance in the discussion of standards, because it used the standards in place at the time to characterize library service in general as mediocre, and further, it provided a platform from which to argue for the strengthening of library services throughout the United States in support of the goal "to bring into the life of every American an adequate, purposeful public library . . . only to be achieved by the joint efforts of local, state and federal governments"

(Joeckel and Winslow, 1948: 152). In hindsight, as Carl Milam observed in the foreword to the *National Plan*, this book changed the direction of the public library movement in North America.

Acceptance of the idea of larger units of service, support from the state, and even support from the federal government gained traction in discussions during the early 1950s. At the behest of the ALA, the Social Science Research Council carried out the Public Library Inquiry, "an appraisal in sociological, cultural and human terms of the extent to which librarians are achieving their objectives," and "an assessment of the public library's actual and potential contributions to American society." The Public Library Inquiry reports, especially Leigh's (1950) general report, *The Public Library in the United States*, set forth much of the philosophical justification for developing standards in the context of systems.

Early in the 1950s the Public Library Division of the ALA was formed and immediately sought funding to revise and restate the 1943 standards. A Coordinating Committee on Revision of Public Library Standards was appointed and convened in 1954. By 1956, after several meetings and solicitation of profession-wide comment, the committee issued its recommendations, *Public Library Service: A Guide to Evaluation with Minimum Standards* (ALA, Coordinating Committee, 1956). These standards incorporated ideals from the 1943 *Post-War Standards* and the *National Plan*, but went further to emphasize the educational function of the public library, the quality of service, and the organization of service. The concept of library systems was defined, taking note of the fact that while some large cities could provide excellent library services, smaller jurisdictions could not generate enough fiscal support to do so. Thus the 1956 standards advocated that "libraries working together, sharing their services and materials, can meet the full needs of their users and stated forcefully: This cooperative approach on the part of libraries is the most important single recommendation of this document" (ALA, Coordinating Committee, 1956: xv). Data on costs were issued as a supplement that was updated periodically.

Direct aid to public libraries in rural communities and small towns came with the passage of the Library Services Act in 1956 and extended to urban areas and construction in 1964 (Library Services and Construction Act). Other federal legislation, such as Operation Headstart, part of the Economic Opportunity Act, funded library projects in response to the War on Poverty of the 1960s. This federal aspect of funding for public libraries and recognition of the changing context of service was very much in the minds of the Standards Committee of the Public Library Association at the time of the issuance of the *Minimum Standards for Public Library Systems, 1966* (ALA, PLA, Standards Committee, 1967).

The 1966 standards built on the 1956 standards, with the intent that the library profession would frequently revise its standards. An addendum, "Statistical Standards," identified quantitative statements such as hours of service, quantities of materials recommended by size of library, recommended salaries, and ratio of staff to population. Given how rapidly the United States was changing in 1966, it was realized by the public library community that these standards reflected the past instead of anticipating the future. In retrospect, the 1966 standards themselves announced the end of the "standards" phase of U.S. librarianship, though none of those who worked on the 1966 document realized it at the time.

Planning for Public Library Service: 1966–Present

Phase I: Developing the Context for Public Library Transformation

The 1966 standards were issued at a time of great change both in the United States and within the ALA. The ALA had received the results of the report *Access to Public Libraries* in 1964 (ALA, 1963)—a self-audit on the restriction of freedom of access to public libraries based on race—and was digesting this report's implications at the time the 1966 standards were released. The growing societal recognition that the United States was split into a nation of rich and poor, and that there was indeed an "other America," galvanized ALA members to establish the group that became the Social Responsibilities Round Table and to appoint a Coordinating Committee on Library Service to the Disadvantaged.[3]

It became clear to the public library community that the 1966 standards did not address the needs of all the people public libraries purported to serve; that is, all residents of the United States. The Public Library Association, concerned about a lack of momentum and clear sense of direction for the profession, launched a Goals Feasibility Study that resulted in the 1972 publication that would launch a transformation in thinking about public library service, *A Strategy for Public Library Change* (A. B. Martin, 1972).

The ALA identified several responsibilities for public libraries, including supporting formal and continuing education, facilitating acceptance of a changing society, motivating the dispossessed and disorganized, and provision of service alternatives at the neighborhood level. The focus on community-based planning helped shift the profession's discourse to the idea of local planning models (Lynch, 1981).

Additionally, librarians increasingly recognized that the extant standards were not scientific and could not provide a basis for evaluating library service. The Standards Committee of the Public Library Association, which had already begun to consider revision of the 1966 standards, decided to collaborate with Ernest R. De Prospo of Rutgers University to seek funding from the U.S. Office of Education for a study, Measurement of the Effectiveness of Public Libraries, which was reported in the volume *Performance Measures for Public Libraries* (De Prospo, Altman, and Beasley, 1973).

Mary Jo Lynch of ALA's Office for Research characterized the performance measures study as focusing the library profession on output rather than input (Pungitore, 1995: 75–76).

In her brilliant analysis of the shift from standards to a planning model, *Innovation and the Library*, Verna L. Pungitore described the profession's response to this move. Combined with working papers of the PLA's Goals, Guidelines, and Standards Committee (GGSC—a change from simply the Standards Committee), the goals feasibility and performance measures studies caused some furor in the library press, arising from the notion of discontinuing standards in favor of community planning (PLA, Goals, Guidelines, and Standards Committee, 1973). The new direction, "Design for Diversity," focused on planning for the future rather than reporting on the past, managing rather than comparing, and a new concern for output (Blasingame and Lynch, 1974). In 1975 the GGSC consolidated its working papers into "Goals and Guidelines for Community Library Service," to be used while the ALA developed new tools to enable librarians to analyze, set objectives, make decisions, and evaluate achievements.

Between the time when funding for the planning process was awarded and the manuals were published, the Public Library Association issued one additional document, *The Public Library Mission Statement and Its Imperatives for Service* (PLA, GGSC, 1979). The GGSC, chaired by Peter Hiatt, meant for this project to serve as an interim document or bridge, from the 1966 standards to the 1975 "Goals and Guidelines for Community Library Service," as well as planning manuals scheduled for release in the early 1980s. However, the tone and spirit of the mission statement demonstrated that even as the planning model was in the works to replace a national standards model, many public librarians still hoped for the Public Library Association to develop an overall statement of purpose for the U.S. public library. The mission statement identified factors in U.S. society that called for a radical shift in emphasis of the public library: runaway social change, exponential increase in the human record, total egalitarianism, and depletion of natural resources. The report identified ten actions that public libraries would have to undertake to respond adequately to these factors:

1. Provide access to the human record through collections and networking.
2. Organize the human record from a myriad of directions.
3. Collect, translate, and organize the human record on all intellectual levels in print and nonprint packages.
4. Dramatize the relevance of the human record with public information, guidance, and group activities.
5. Develop policies for preserving the record.
6. Take leadership in defining a new statement of ethics.
7. Coordinate acquisition policies.
8. Create a network for access to the record regardless of location.

9. Develop procedures for all to use the record.
10. Ensure that all will have access regardless of education, language, ethnic or cultural background, age, physical ability, or apathy.

This mission statement focused on the entire community as the target audience for public library service. While tension would continue over the need for a broad mission for public libraries, the profession's move to a planning model and local definitions of service characterized public librarianship for the rest of the twentieth century (Pungitore, 1995: 92–94).

Phase II: Planning and Role Setting for Public Libraries

In 1977, with funding from the U.S. Department of Education, the Public Library Association developed manuals for local planning, which resulted in the publication of *A Planning Process for Public Libraries* (Palmour, Bellassi, and DeWath, 1980). The *Planning Process*, a manual outlining methods for community analysis and planning for services, was the new innovation that replaced national public library standards. A companion volume, *Output Measures for Public Libraries*, describing data collection and the use of quantitative measures, was released in 1982 (Zweizig and Rodger, 1982).

The Public Library Association executive board endorsed the move from national standards to local community-based planning in 1981. The result, *A Planning Process for Public Libraries*, was identified as a new strategy for enabling local libraries and library systems to determine their own goals. A series of programs and workshops sponsored by PLA took place in the early 1980s to disseminate the process. Consequently, the Public Library Association revised its "Statement of Principles" in 1982, with reference to planning. Inexorably the change in the way of developing goals and plans for libraries was moving from national standards to local planning (PLA, Public Library Principles Task Force, 1982).

The next stage in the move toward adoption of the planning model was the introduction of the Public Library Development Program (PLDP), announced in 1986 (Balcom, 1986). The initial component of PLDP was *Planning and Role Setting for Public Libraries: A Manual of Options and Procedures* (McClure, 1987), which identified eight potential roles for public libraries and a choice of level of effort for the process, a revision of the output measures manual, and a data service (PLA, Public Library Data Service, 1992–present). The eight roles selected formed the basis of much library planning that followed and reflected a range of library activities:

1. Community activities center
2. Community information center

3. Formal education support center
4. Independent learning center
5. Popular materials library
6. Preschoolers' door to learning
7. Reference library
8. Research center

The association launched the PLDP with plans for facilitating the adoption of the process, including a trainer's manual, output measures for children and young adults, and an annual data service report. The broad acceptance among public librarians of the PLDP was reported in a 1993 survey of state agency use of the process (Smith, 1994). Douglas Raber (1995) has characterized the process as a conflict of cultures moving from tradition to planning. In her study of the profession's move from standards to the adoption of the PLDP, Pungitore (1995: 180) concluded that innovation can be facilitated and that public libraries can be "revitalized and reinvigorated" to assume a significant role.[4]

Phase III: New Planning for Results, 1996–Present

The Public Library Association evaluated the effectiveness of the PLDP in 1995 with a national survey, interviews, and an invitational conference, which concluded that the planning model was working and that its use had done much to include the community and staff in planning (Johnson, 1995). Refinements were suggested and to this end the Public Library Association appointed a ReVision Committee in 1996 to update *Planning and Role Setting for Public Libraries*. The outcome was the 1998 publication, *Planning for Results: A Public Library Transformation Process*, issued in two parts: a guidebook and a how-to manual (Himmel and Wilson, 1998). The eight roles for public libraries that had been identified in 1986 were expanded to thirteen "library service responses." These service responses were defined as what a library does for, or offers to, the public in an effort to meet a set of well-defined community needs (Himmel and Wilson, 1998: 54).

1. Basic literacy
2. Business and career information
3. Commons
4. Community referral
5. Consumer information
6. Cultural awareness
7. Current topics and titles
8. Formal learning support

9. General information
10. Government information
11. Information literacy
12. Lifelong learning
13. Local history and genealogy

Planning for Results also placed a greater focus on resource allocation. Training and workshops were held at state conferences and sponsored by state library agencies to assist in adoption of procedures. A companion volume, *Managing for Results*, was issued in 2000 to help turn plans into reality (Nelson, Altman, and Mayo, 2000).

Refining and modifying the planning process has been a sustained priority for the Public Library Association. A streamlined approach to the planning process was published in 2001, *The New Planning for Results* (Nelson, 2001). Three assumptions guided this efficient manual: (1) excellence must be defined locally—it results when library services match community needs, interests, and priorities; (2) excellence is possible for both small and large libraries—it rests more on commitment than on unlimited resources; and (3) excellence is a moving target—even when it is achieved, it must be continually maintained.

To support the implementation of the planning process, the Public Library Association launched a series of volumes, the *Results* series, offering a consistent set of themes.[5]

Strategic Planning for Results

In 2006 the Public Library Association launched a process to review the 1998 service responses. Meetings were held at the ALA conference and online comments taken at the PLA blog (http://plablog.org/). In 2007 drafts of 18 proposed service responses were posted at the PLAblog for review and discussion. An open meeting was held in 2007 for final input. The deliberations were used for a new planning guide (Nelson, 2008: 144).

Moving from a long-range approach to a more flexible strategic approach, the Public Library Association issued the companion volumes *Strategic Planning for Results* in 2008 and *Implementing for Results* in 2009 (Nelson, 2008, 2009). Both volumes emphasize change and give guidance for transforming strategic plans into reality. *Strategic Planning for Results* reduces the recommended planning timeline and the number of tasks from those in the earlier planning guides and increases the service responses to 18 (Nelson, 2008: 143–217):

1. Be an informed citizen: local, national, and world affairs
2. Build successful enterprises: business and nonprofit support

3. Celebrate diversity: cultural awareness
4. Connect to the online world: public Internet access
5. Create young readers: early literacy
6. Discover your roots: genealogy and local history
7. Express creativity: create and share content
8. Get facts fast: ready reference
9. Know your community: community resources and services
10. Learn to read and write: adults, teens, and family literature
11. Make career choices: job and career development
12. Make informed decisions: health, wealth, and other life choices
13. Satisfy curiosity: lifelong learning
14. Stimulate imagination: reading, viewing, and listening for pleasure
15. Succeed in school: homework help
16. Understand how to find, evaluate, and use information: information fluency
17. Visit a comfortable place: physical and virtual spaces
18. Welcome to the United States: services for new immigrants

We will discuss the way these service responses are reflected in practice in the chapters on youth and adult services.

Today the Public Library Association makes a clear distinction between the Planning and Role Setting for Public Libraries (PRSPL) model (which began about 1980 and continued until 1995) and the New Planning for Results (NPFR) model, which began in 1996 and continues today. The PRSPL model separated the development of planning goals and service goals and indicated they could be developed separately. The NPFR approach is based on the premise that resource allocation decisions must be subordinate to and driven by the library's service priorities as reflected in the service goals and objectives. Additionally, the PRSPL model was used as a process to develop new services and programs with the assumption that they would be funded with new resources. By way of contrast, NPFR makes the assumption that library planners will use the NPFR process to identify library priorities and reallocate extant resources to fund them. The Public Library Association holds annual workshops to develop librarians' capacity to use the NPFR model. "At its core NPFR is about managing change" (Public Library Association, 2003: 29–30) and this philosophy of planning informs the practice of librarianship in the twenty-first century. *Implementing for Results: Your Strategic Plan in Action* (Nelson, 2009) provides the tools to transform vision to reality.

It should be noted that an important new volume that addresses the impact of the Internet, *Public Libraries and Internet Service Roles: Measuring and Maximizing Internet Services* (McClure and Jaeger, 2009), provides insight into the great changes in the social roles of libraries. The authors examine the way in which the Internet is changing the roles, expectations, and effects of the public library in society.

State Standards, Ratings, and Peer Comparison

State Standards

The Public Library Association's decision to move away from the model of national standards after 1966 has not meant that the profession at large has rejected the idea of standards for public library service. Although planning for results may be more effective for the actual development and delivery of library service, pragmatism at the state and local level has also necessitated that quantitative standards continue to be developed. Librarians recognize that it is more compelling to make their case to city councils, county commissions, and regional boards with quantitative standards in hand. Thus many states have continued to develop and publish state-level standards for public libraries. It should also be noted that actions of the Public Library Association and the ALA, which tend to be the narrative thread that is followed in this discussion, are by no means the entire story of the development of public library mission and direction. State library agencies through their own long-range planning, state library associations, federal entities such as the Department of Education's Office of Library Programs, the National Commission on Libraries and Information Science, and today the IMLS, private foundations, multitype library consortia, library systems, and local libraries and their boards are all participants in the constant process of deliberating on the goals and standards of public libraries.

States with published standards include Colorado, Florida, Georgia, Indiana, Iowa, Kansas, Kentucky, Louisiana, Maine, Michigan, Minnesota, Montana, New York, Oregon, Rhode Island, South Carolina, Texas, Utah, Vermont, Virginia, and Wisconsin (WebJunction; http://ct.webjunction.org/tech-security/articles/content/436213). Some states, like Texas, incorporate standards in the state administrative code (Texas State Library and Archives Commission, 2011). At this writing, the Indiana Public Library Association in partnership with the Indiana Trustee Association and the Indiana State Library was developing new standards and sharing planning documents at WebJunction (2009).

A study posted at the Chief Officers of State Library Agencies (COSLA) website (http://www.cosla.org) by Hamilton-Pennell (2010) reviewed the standards of all 50 states and identified the key reasons that state-level standards continue to be developed:

1. Assist in planning efforts
2. Provide an evaluation and mechanism tool for public accountability

3. Provide a philosophical context for quality public library service
4. Serve as a library development tool by stimulating growth and development
5. Serve as a tool to identify strengths and select areas for improvement
6. Provide a shared vision for library service
7. Assist in determining whether resources are sufficient
8. Set minimum guidelines for receipt of state aid

Moorman (1997) has described the way that many states have developed their own quantitative measures of resource-based library effectiveness to use when building the case for library funding. The best place to start to gain an overview of state standards development is at the COSLA website. Each state is listed with links to statistics and other descriptive data. Although states submit data through the FSCS for Public Library Data, many states continue to provide access to their own statistics, continuing traditions of regular publication.[6]

Ratings and Rankings: Hennen's American Public Library Ratings and America's Star Libraries

Other methods for comparing libraries are Hennen's American Public Library Ratings (HALPR) Index and *Library Journal*'s America's Star Libraries. The backstory on the development of these two comparative ratings methods provides much insight into issues of statistical validity, robust data, and interpretation. A discussion of these concerns can be reviewed at the *American Libraries* website.[7]

The HALPR index was developed by Thomas J. Hennen Jr. His reports appeared for several years in *American Libraries* and are now posted at the HALPR website (Hennen, 1999b, 2000a, 2002b, 2003a, 2003b, 2004a, 2005, 2006, 2008, 2010; Kniffel, 2008). Hennen uses input and output measures to devise a weighted score for public libraries to rate library performance by population. The HALPR index is widely cited. In his assessment of the tenth anniversary edition, Hennen (2009) summarized the impact of the index and identified those libraries that had scored highly in all ten years (see Figure 4.2, p. 90).

For some high-scoring libraries, the HAPLR ratings have been used in press releases and noted on library websites. Hennen's methodology has been questioned by Lance and Cox (2000), who use a bivariate correlation to demonstrate the lack of validity of the HAPLR. Nevertheless, the Hennen ratings get broad visibility.

In 2009 the annual *LJ* Index of Public Library Service was launched—America's Star Libraries. This assessment tool for public libraries scrutinizes library service output statistics such as visits, circulation, public Internet computer usage, and program attendance. It excludes resource inputs, such as staffing levels, collection size, and revenues and expenditures. The complete report, America's Star Libraries, organizes

Figure 4.2. Libraries in All Editions of Hennen's American Public Library Rankings	
Library	**State**
Bridgeport Public Library	WV
Carmel Clay Public Library	IN
Columbus Metropolitan Library	OH
Denver Public Library	CO
Hennepin County Library	MN
Johnson County Library	KS
Naperville Public Library	IL
Saint Charles City-County Library District	MO
Santa Clara County Library	CA
Twinsburg Public Library	OH
Washington-Centerville Public Library	OH

Source: Hennen, Thomas J., Jr. 2009. "HALPR 2009: 10th Anniversary Edition." HALPR-Index.com. http://www.haplr-index.com/haplr_2009_10thAnniv_AmerLibrArticle.htm.

libraries into star tiers, much like the Michelin guide. It groups public libraries by total operating expenditures rather than population of legal service area. This rating provides data for more in-depth assessment and improvement-oriented planning. The 2010 report identified 258 star libraries based on 2008 data from the IMLS. The authors note, "The top libraries in each group get five, four, or three stars. All included libraries, stars or not, can use their scores to learn from their peers, expand service to their communities, and advocate for support" (Lyons and Lance, 2010: 24).

Peer Comparisons

The Public Library Data Service (PLDS) survey is published annually by the Public Library Association (Varvel and Lei, 2009). In 2010 over 800 libraries responded. The PLDS identifies top-performing libraries, compares service levels and technology usage, and provides documentation for funding requests. Categories include financial information, library resources and per capita measures, annual use figures, and technology in public libraries. Special surveys are included in different years such as library facilities, finance, or young adult services.

The Public Library Association now offers the PLDS Online Database in a dynamic, web-based format with searchable data exportable into Excel/CSV file formats, and linked data from other report sections. Summary tables can be accessed in interactive charts (breakdown by legal service area as well as by state, and legal services within each state). Subscribers can create customized PLDS data sets with user-defined data, calculations, charts, and other analysis.

The Compare Public Libraries tool at the IMLS website provides access to over 9,000 libraries from the annually collected Public Library Survey FSCS data, *Public Libraries in the United States*. Compare Public Libraries allows users to compare one library (the library of interest) with similar libraries (the comparison group). For example, a user may wish to compare one library's total circulation with that of a group of libraries with similar total expenditures. Statistics on variables including income, operating expenditures, staffing, size of collection, and circulation can be compared among libraries of similar size.

Yan and Zweizig (2000) surveyed public library directors to determine their use of statistics from the PLDS and the Federal-State Cooperative System for Public Library Data. Comparison ranked high among respondents' reasons for accessing peer data. In her discussion of the PLDS and the IMLS data sets, Denise M. Davis (2008) made a cross-comparison of these two rich sources of public library data. They are both reliable for identifying trends and the complexity of library funding.

Bibliostat Connect (http://www.btol.com/ps_details.cfm?id=222), a service of Baker and Taylor, offers FSCS data, information from the PLDS, state, and other data to assess public library quality by conducting graphical peer comparisons using national (FSCS), proprietary (PLDS), and local (state) data sets. The peer comparison output helps libraries identify strengths and weaknesses. The New York State Library (2011) website provides a clear example of the way Bibliostat Connect can be configured for a state to provide easy access and manipulation of public library-specific data and quick creation of rank-order tables, averages, and percentiles. Data can be organized alphabetically, by peers and by benchmarking. As data reporting and gathering is refined and information used for peer comparison available more quickly, librarians will have another tool for decision making and policymaking.

Evaluation, Outcomes, and Quality of Life

The challenge in the new millennium is to connect public libraries to broader value systems such as quality of life and social capital. The statistics and rankings we have reviewed provide data to make the case for the importance of libraries. Factors critical to a public library's success in advocating for resources have been described by McClure (2006) using research conducted by researchers at the Information Use Management and Policy Institute. The IMLS has funded an evaluation portal developed by the Institute at Florida State University (McClure, 2005–2009). This portal, the Evaluation Decision-Making System, provides centralized public access to information related to evaluation of a library's services and resources for management and advocacy purposes. Information provided includes:

- types of evaluation methods typically used to assess the use of services and resources;
- data each type of evaluation can provide;
- how to plan for data collection efforts and tips on how to analyze the data; and
- strategies on how to apply the results of evaluation efforts for management and advocacy purposes.

The American Library Association's "Advocating in a Tough Economy Toolkit" (ALA, 2009) is an example of the way that data can be used to make the case for the way that public libraries help communities in times of financial stress. Public libraries create value, which in turn advances the economic status of communities and neighborhoods. One effective approach is to discuss return on investment. John Pecoraro (2009), who develops reports for 43 public libraries in the Big Country Library System (Texas) that detail the value of the services they provide, reminds librarians:

- "Stories speak louder than statistics."
- Whenever possible, use personal anecdotes. Identify witnesses who will testify, "This is how the library helped me find a job; earn my GED; graduate from college; find my family."
- The crucial question you are attempting to answer for your community is this, "What difference does the library make?"

The value of public libraries in peoples' lives was the focus of a monograph by Joan Durrance and Karen E. Fisher (2005), *How Libraries and Librarians Help*, which provides a model for the evaluation of public library programs and services based on qualitative outcomes. The model demonstrates how librarians can prove their value to communities using outcome assessments. A recent book by Chrystie Hill (2009), *Inside, Outside and Online*, includes "Iterate," a chapter in which she provides examples of measurement tools to demonstrate how libraries change lives. In an essay in the *Planning Commissioners Journal*, Wayne Senville (2009) discusses libraries as important "economic engines" of downtowns and neighborhood districts.

Quality of life projects represent a means by which to monitor progress on a regular basis using selected representative quantitative indicators, which could include library circulation or library card registration. The decision about which indicators to use to measure quality of life by a state or community is the result of neighborhood meetings or visioning processes that provide a consensus about important variables that contribute to that community's definition of well-being. A number of organizations provide background on the use of community indicators, notably Redefining Progress, which recognizes the national movement to use community indicators to change community outcomes. Through their Community Indicators Project, existing and emerging initiatives using community indicators have been linked. Redefining Progress and the International Institute for Sustainable Development merged their online databases on indicator initiatives as the Compendium of Sustainable Development Indicator Initiatives. The Compendium provides a comprehensive and up-to-date information base of sustainable development indicator initiatives being carried out at the international, national, and provincial, territorial, or state levels. With a searchable source so readily available, it is fairly easy to assess which variables and values communities have selected to provide indicators of progress.

Efforts to include libraries in the indicator movement will ensure that library-related outcomes will be viewed as key variables in future initiatives (McCook and Brand, 2001).

It is far more compelling, however, for library indicators—whether used by the profession or by larger quality of life initiatives—to be outcomes rather than inputs. Several recent research projects demonstrate this approach to the evaluation of public library services.

There are two main reasons for considering the importance of libraries in the context of community indicator development. The first is the most pragmatic. When public libraries are included as indicators contributing to a better quality of life for a community, they can attract better support and additional resources from funding entities. If the service is missing from the list of indicators a community has deemed important enough to rank, then the service is far less likely to gain adequate support to execute its mission and goals. Libraries are often included among services that community leaders suggest contribute to the quality of life of a community, but they are seldom identified as important enough to be included as an indicator.

The second reason that should compel librarians to strive to have their services counted as indicators of genuine progress has been explored in a *Public Libraries* "Perspectives" column on libraries and sustainability. Jeffrey L. Brown (2001: 24) observes, "Libraries have a reputation as one of our society's most trusted institutions; librarians can offer their facilities as neutral ground where community or economic groups that have been in conflict can meet to mediate their differences." It is Brown's characterization of the reputation of libraries that provides the strongest motivation for librarians to assert the importance of their work. What other agency has received such trust? By working to establish libraries and library services as vital community indicators, librarians will broaden the influence of an important institution and in so doing strengthen the influence of a trusted institution.

In years to come public libraries should be included in quality of life studies as part of the community movement. Johnson (2010) has explored the connection between public library use and social capital. The global recognition of the importance of information and cultural heritage as preserved by libraries in a sustainable manner will be achieved by the careful use of data to make the case for the contribution of libraries to the development of human capabilities (Møller and Huschka, 2009).

Notes

1. Initially published in 1968 as the *Library Statistics* standard, Z39.7 was affirmed in 1974 and revised in 1983, 1995, and 2004 (NISO, 2004). See also reports of the Information Use Management and Policy Institute (2002). NISO held a Forum on Performance Measures and Statistics for Libraries in 2001 that recommended moving beyond defining data elements to providing methodologies for qualitative and quantitative measures of library service. It was also recommended that NISO take a leadership role in supporting the development of surveys and measurements to gauge service quality and outcomes. For a detailed report, see article on the 2002 revision of the Standard for Library Statistics (Davis, 2004).

2. The IMLS and NCES reports are listed in Appendix D, "Bibliography of National Statistics on Public Libraries."

3. Harrington (1962); American Library Association, Committee on Economic Opportunity Programs (1969); Samek (2001); McCook (2002).

4. The Public Library Association, Public Library Development Program documents:

- Charles R. McClure, *Planning and Role Setting for Public Libraries: A Manual of Options and Procedures* (Chicago: American Library Association, 1987).
- Nancy Van House, Mary Jo Lynch, Charles R. McClure, Douglas L. Zweizig, and Eleanor Jo Rodger, *Output Measures for Public Libraries: A Manual of Standardized Procedures* (Chicago: American Library Association, 1987).
- Public Library Association, Public Library Data Service, *Statistical Report* (Chicago: Public Library Association, annual, 1992–present) continues *Public Library Data Service Statistical Report* (Chicago: Public Library Association, 1988–1991).
- Peggy O'Donnell, *Public Library Development Program: Manual for Trainers* (Chicago: American Library Association, 1988).
- Virginia A. Walter, *Output Measures for Public Library Service to Children: A Manual of Standardized Procedures* (Chicago: Association for Library Service to Children, Public Library Association, American Library Association, 1992).
- Virginia A. Walter, *Output Measures and More: Planning and Evaluating Public Library Services for Young Adults* (Chicago: Young Adult Library Services Association, Public Library Association, American Library Association, 1995).

5. The Public Library Association, *Results* series:

- Ethel Himmel and William James Wilson, *Planning for Results: A Public Library Transformation Process* (Chicago: American Library Association, 1998).
- Diane Mayo and Sandra Nelson, *Wired for the Future: Developing Your Library Technology Plan* (Chicago: American Library Association, 1999).
- Sandra Nelson, Ellen Altman, and Diane Mayo, *Managing for Results: Effective Resource Allocation for Public Libraries* (Chicago: American Library Association, 2000).
- Sandra Nelson, *The New Planning for Results: A Streamlined Approach* (Chicago: American Library Association, 2001).

- Diane Mayo and Jeanne Goodrich, *Staffing for Results: A Guide to Working Smarter* (Chicago: American Library Association, 2002).
- Sandra Nelson and June Garcia, *Creating Policies for Results: From Chaos to Clarity* (Chicago: American Library Association, 2003).
- Rhea Joyce Rubin, *Demonstrating Results: Using Outcome Measurement in Your Library* (Chicago: American Library Association, 2005).
- Diane Mayo, *Technology for Results: Developing Service-Based Plans* (Chicago: American Library Association, 2005).
- Cheryl Bryan, *Managing Facilities for Results: Optimizing Space for Services* (Chicago: American Library Association, 2007).
- Sandra Nelson, *Strategic Planning for Results* (Chicago: American Library Association, 2008).
- Sandra Nelson, *Implementing for Results: Your Strategic Plan in Action* (Chicago: American Library Association, 2009).

6. Although states submit data through the FSCS for Public Library Data, many states continue to provide access to their own statistics, continuing traditions of regular publication. For examples, see the following state library websites, reviewed in October 2010:

- Alaska: http://www.library.state.ak.us/dev/plstats/plstats.html
- Connecticut: http://ct.webjunction.org/ct/stats/articles/content/33911593
- Florida: http://dlis.dos.state.fl.us/bld/research_office/2008LibraryDirectory/index.cfm
- Maryland: http://www.sailor.lib.md.us/MD_topics/lib/_sta.html
- Massachusetts: http://mblc.state.ma.us/advisory/statistics/public/index.php
- Nebraska: http://www.nlc.state.ne.us/Statistics/statlist.html
- New Hampshire: http://www.nh.gov/nhsl/lds/public_library_stats.html
- Ohio: http://www.library.ohio.gov/LPD/LibraryStats
- Oregon: http://oregon.gov/OSL/LD/statsmain.shtml
- Texas: http://www.tsl.state.tx.us/ld/pubs/pls/index.html
- Utah: http://library.utah.gov/programs/development/statistics/index.html

7. Kniffel (2009). Back in January 1999, *American Libraries* published the first installment of Tom Hennen's HAPLR Index, ranking America's public libraries using statistics collected by the FSCS. We made the decision to publish Hennen's study based on our assessment of his research and the conclusion that the rankings would be useful to the libraries that came out on top. We were careful to characterize the rankings as the work of an independent researcher, and the article was replete with caveats about the shortcomings of the FSCS data. "Data measurement cannot capture a friendly smile and warm greeting at the circulation desk," Hennen said at the time, "nor can data alone measure the excitement of a child at story time or a senior surfing the Internet for the first time." At the 1999 Midwinter Meeting, John N. Berry, then *Library Journal* editor in chief, joked with me that he was wildly jealous that *American Libraries* had published the HAPLR Index, and wondered how we had pulled it off. He knew, of course, that opposition from ALA's Office for Research and Statistics (and just about everyone else in the building) would be strong to publishing anything that sent even the hint of ALA rating libraries, no matter how many times I insisted that the rankings were Hennen's work and Hennen's alone (something we now call a branding issue). That said, we expected libraries to be able to use

their rankings as a publicity hook for local media. And use them they did. This discussion continues with comments from multiple perspectives. For those interested in the use of statistics in comparing libraries, Kniffel (2009) is important reading.

References

American Library Association. 1933. "Standards for Public Libraries." *ALA Bulletin* 27 (November): 513–514.

———. 1948. "Post-War Planning Committee File, 1941–1948 / The American Library Association Archives." The University of Illinois at Urbana-Champaign. http://www.library. illinois.edu/archives/ala/holdings/?p=collections/controlcard&id=7857.

———. 1963. *Access to Public Libraries Study*. Chicago: American Library Association.

———. 2009. "Advocating in a Tough Economy Toolkit." http://www.ala.org/ala/ issuesadvocacy/advocacy/advocacyuniversity/toolkit/index.cfm.

American Library Association, Committee on Economic Opportunity Programs. 1969. *Library Service to the Disadvantaged: A Study Based on Responses to Questionnaires from Public Libraries Serving Populations Over 15,000*. Chicago: American Library Association.

American Library Association, Coordinating Committee on Revision of Public Library Standards. 1956. *Public Library Service: A Guide to Evaluation with Minimum Standards*. Chicago: American Library Association.

American Library Association, Public Library Association, Standards Committee. 1967. *Minimum Standards for Public Library Systems, 1966*. Chicago: American Library Association.

Balcom, Kathleen Mehaffey. 1986. "To Concentrate and Strengthen: The Promise of the Public Library Development Program." *Library Journal* 111 (June 15): 36–40. http://nces.ed .gov/pubs98/98310.pdf.

Blasingame, Ralph, Jr., and Mary Jo Lynch. 1974. "Design for Diversity: Alternatives to Standards for Public Libraries." *PLA Newsletter* 13: 4–22.

Brown, Jeffrey L. 2001. "Making a Huge Difference in So Many Little Ways." *Public Libraries* 40 (January/February): 24.

Chute, Adrienne. 2003. "National Center for Education Statistics Library Statistics Program." In *The Bowker Annual Library and Book Trade Almanac*, 95–102. New York: R. R. Bowker.

Community Indicators Consortium. 2010. "Georgia Indicators for Child, Family and Community Well-Being." http://www.communityindicators.net/.

Davis, Denise M. 2004. "NISO Standard Z39.7—The Evolution to a Data Dictionary for Library Metrics and Assessment Methods." *Serials Review* 30, no. 1: 15–24.

———. 2008. "A Comparison of Public Library Data PLDS in Context." *Public Libraries* 47 (September/October): 20–25.

De Prospo, Ernest R., Ellen Altman, and Kenneth Beasley. 1973. *Performance Measures for Public Libraries*. Chicago: American Library Association.

Durrance, Joan C., and Karen E. Fisher. 2005. *How Libraries and Librarians Help: Assessing Outcomes in Your Library*. Chicago: American Library Association.

Fair, E. M. 1934. *Countywide Library Service*. Chicago: American Library Association.

Garceau, Oliver. 1949. *The Public Library in the Political Process: A Report of the Public Library Inquiry*. New York: Columbia University Press.

"Goals and Guidelines for Community Library Service." 1975. *PLA Newsletter* 14: 9–13.

Goldhor, Herbert. 1983. "U.S. Public Library Statistics in Series: A Bibliography and Subject Index." In *Bowker Annual of Library and Book Trade Information*. 28th ed., 327–335. New York: R. R. Bowker.

Hamilton-Pennell, Christine. 2010. "Public Library Standards: A Review of Standards and Guidelines from the Fifty States of the U.S. for the Colorado, Mississippi, and Hawaii State Libraries." Mosaic Knowledge Works. Chief Officers of State Library Agencies. http://www.cosla.org.

Harrington, Michael. 1962. *The Other America: Poverty in the United States*. New York: Macmillan.

Hennen, Thomas J., Jr. 1999a. "Go Ahead, Name Them: America's Best Public Libraries." *American Libraries* 30 (January): 72–76.

———. 1999b. "Great American Public Libraries: HAPLR Ratings: Round Two." *American Libraries* 30 (September): 64–68.

———. 2000a. "Great American Public Libraries: HAPLR Ratings: 2000." *American Libraries* 31 (November): 50–54.

———. 2000b. "Why We Should Establish a National System of Standards." *American Libraries* 31 (March): 43–45.

———. 2002a. "Are Wider Library Units Wiser?" *American Libraries* 33 (June/July): 65–70. www.haplr-index.com/wider_and_wiser_units.htm.

———. 2002b. "Great American Public Libraries: HAPLR Ratings: 2002." *American Libraries* 33 (October): 64–68.

———. 2003a. "Great American Public Libraries: HAPLR Ratings: 2003." *American Libraries* 34 (October): 44–49.

———. 2003b. "Hennen's American Public Library Ratings." March. www.haplr-index.com/index.html.

———. 2004a. "Great American Public Libraries: HAPLR Ratings: 2004." *American Libraries* 35 (October): 54–59.

———. 2004b. *Hennen's Public Library Planner: A Manual and Interactive CD-ROM*. New York: Neal-Schuman.

———. 2005. "Great American Public Libraries: HAPLR Ratings: 2005." *American Libraries* 36 (October): 42–48.

———. 2006. "Hennen's American Public Library Ratings 2006." *American Libraries* 37 (November): 40–42.

———. 2008. "Hennen's American Public Library Ratings 2008." *American Libraries* 39 (October): 56–61.

———. 2009. "HALPR 2009: 10th Anniversary Edition." http://www.haplr-index.com/haplr_2009_10thAnniv_AmerLibrArticle.htm.

———. 2010. "HALPR 2010." http://www.haplr-index.com/2010_haplr_edition.htm.

Hill, Chrystie. *Inside, Outside and Online: Building Your Library Community*. Chicago: American Library Association, 2009.

Himmel, Ethel, and William James Wilson, with the ReVision Committee of the Public Library Association. 1998. *Planning for Results: A Public Library Transformation Process.* Chicago: American Library Association.

Information Use Management and Policy Institute. 2002. *Developing National Data Collection Models for Public Library Network Statistics and Performance Measures.* Florida State University. http://www.ii.fsu.edu/content/view/full/14845.

Joeckel, Carleton Bruns. 1935. *The Government of the American Public Library.* Chicago: University of Chicago Press.

———. 1943. *Post-War Standards for Public Libraries.* Chicago: American Library Association.

Joeckel, Carleton B., and Amy Winslow. 1948. *A National Plan for Public Library Service.* Chicago: American Library Association.

Johnson, Catherine A. 2010. "Do Public Libraries Contribute to Social Capital? A Preliminary Investigation into the Relationship." *Library and Information Science Research* 32: 147–155.

Johnson, Debra Wilcox. 1995. "An Evaluation of the Public Library Development Program." Unpublished report for the Public Library Association.

Kniffel, Leonard. 2008. "Public Library Ratings Corrected." *American Libraries* 39 (November): 54–55.

———. 2009. "LJ Index: Too Much Too Late." American Libraries online. March 3. http://americanlibrariesmagazine.org/2009/03/03/lj-index-too-much-too-late.

Lance, Keith Curry, and Marti A. Cox. 2000. "Lies, Damn Lies and Indexes." *American Libraries* 31 (June/July): 82–87.

Leigh, Robert D. 1950. *The Public Library in the United States: The General Report of the Public Library Inquiry.* New York: Columbia University Press.

Library Research Service. 2009. National Public Library Statistics. http://www.lrs.org/public/national.php.

"LPN Talks with Retiring ORS Director Mary Jo Lynch." 2004. *Library Personnel News* 16 (Winter): 2–3.

Lynch, Mary Jo. 1981. "The Public Library Association and Public Library Planning." *Journal of Library Administration* 2 (Summer/Fall/Winter): 29–41.

Lyons, Ray, and Keith Curry Lance. 2010. "America's Star Libraries: The 'LJ' Index of Public Library Service, 2010." *Library Journal* 35 (October 1): 22–27.

Martin, Allie Beth. 1972. *A Strategy for Public Library Change: Proposed Public Library Goals—Feasibility Study.* Chicago: American Library Association.

McClure, Charles R. 1987. *Planning and Role Setting for Public Libraries: A Manual of Options and Procedures.* Chicago: American Library Association.

———. 2005–2009. "Increasing the Effectiveness of Evaluation for Improved Public Library Decision Making." Information Use Management and Policy Institute, Florida State University. http://www.libevaluation.com/edms/.

McClure, Charles R. 2006. "Politics and Advocacy: The Role of Networking in Selling the Library to Your Community." *Public Library Quarterly* 25, no. 1.2: 137–154.

McClure, Charles R., and Paul T. Jaeger. 2009. *Public Libraries and Internet Service Roles: Measuring and Maximizing Internet Services.* Chicago: American Library Association.

McCook, Kathleen de la Peña. 2002. *Rocks in the Whirlpool: Equity of Access and the American Library Association.* ERIC. ED462981: 25–43.

McCook, Kathleen de la Peña, and Kristin Brand. 2001. "Community Indicators, Genuine Progress, and the Golden Billion." *Reference and User Services Quarterly* 40 (Summer): 337–340.

Møller, Valerie, and Dennis Huschka. 2009. *Quality of Life and the Millennium Challenge.* New York: Springer.

Moorman, John A. 1997. "Standards for Public Libraries: A Study in Quantitative Measures of Library Performance as Found in State Public Library Documents." *Public Libraries* 36 (January/February): 32–39.

National Information Standards Organization. 2004. *Information Services and Use: Metrics and Statistics for Libraries and Information Providers—Data Dictionary.* NISO Z39.7- 2004. http://www.niso.org/dictionary/toc.

Nelson, Sandra. 2001. *The New Planning for Results: A Streamlined Approach.* Chicago: American Library Association.

———. 2008. *Strategic Planning for Results.* Chicago: American Library Association.

Nelson, Sandra. 2009. *Implementing for Results: Your Strategic Plan in Action.* Chicago: American Library Association.

Nelson, Sandra, Ellen Altman, and Diane Mayo. 2000. "Managing Your Library's Staff." In *Managing for Results: Effective Resource Allocation for Public Libraries*, 29–110. Chicago: American Library Association.

New York State Library. 2011. "Bibliostat Connect: Easy Online Access to Public Library Statistics from Your State Library." New York State Library. Accessed January 13. http://www .nysl.nysed.gov/libdev/libs/biblcnct.htm.

Palmour, Vernon E., Marcia C. Bellassi, and Nancy V. DeWath. 1980. *A Planning Process for Public Libraries.* Chicago: American Library Association.

Pecoraro, John. 2009. "What's It Worth? The Value of Library Services as an Advocacy Tool." *Texas Library Journal* 85 (Spring): 8–9.

Public Library Association. 2003. "Everything You Want to Know about the *Results* Series." http://www.pla.org/ala/pla/pla.htm.

Public Library Association, Goals, Guidelines and Standards Committee. 1973. "Community Library Services: Working Papers on Goals and Guidelines." *Library Journal* 96: 2603–2609.

———. 1979. *The Public Library Mission Statement and Its Imperatives for Service.* Chicago: American Library Association.

Public Library Association, Public Library Data Service. 1992–present. *Statistical Report* (annual). Chicago: Public Library Association. http://cirss.lis.illinois.edu/Surveys/plds .html. Continues *Public Library Data Service Statistical Report.* Chicago: Public Library Association, 1988–1991.

Public Library Association, Public Library Principles Task Force. 1982. "The Public Library: Democracy's Resource, A Statement of Principles." *Public Libraries* 21 (Fall): 92.

Pungitore, Verna L. 1995. *Innovation and the Library: The Adoption of New Ideas in Public Libraries.* Westport, CT: Greenwood Press.

Raber, Douglas. 1995. "A Conflict of Cultures: Planning vs. Tradition in Public Libraries." *RQ* 35 (Fall): 50-63.

Samek, Toni. 2001. *Intellectual Freedom and Social Responsibility in American Librarianship, 1967–1974.* Chicago: American Library Association.

Schick, Frank L. 1971. "Library Statistics: A Century Plus." *American Libraries* 2: 727–741.

Senville, Wayne. 2009. "Libraries at the Heart of Our Communities." *Planning Commissioners Journal* 75 (Summer): 12–18.

Smith, Nancy Milner. 1994. "State Library Agency Use of Planning and Role Setting for Public Libraries and Output Measures for Public Libraries." *Public Libraries* 33 (July/August): 211–212.

Texas State Library and Archives Commission. 2011. "Texas Public Library Standards." Texas State Library and Archives Commission. Accessed January 13. http://www.tsl.state.tx.us/plstandards/.

U.S. Institute of Museum and Library Services. 2010. *Public Libraries Survey: Fiscal Year 2008.* IMLS-2010–PLS-02. Washington, DC: Institute of Museum and Library Services. http://harvester.census.gov/imls/pubs/Publications/pls2008.pdf.

Varvel, V. E., Jr., and X. Lei. 2009. "Characteristics and Trends: In the *Public Library Data Service* 2008 Report." *Public Libraries* 48 (March/April): 6–12.

WebJunction. 2009. Public Library Standards. Indiana. http://in.webjunction.org/in/plstandards/-/resources/overview.

Williams, Robert V. 1991. "The Making of Statistics of National Scope on American Libraries, 1836–1986: Purposes, Problems, and Issues." *Libraries and Culture* 26 (Spring): 464–485.

Williams, Robert V., and Mittie Kristina McLean. 2008. *A Bibliographical Guide to a Chronological Record of Statistics of National Scope on Libraries in the United States.* [S.l.]: University of South Carolina, School of Library and Information Science. http://www.libsci.sc.edu/bob/LibraryStatistics/LibraryStatisticsGuide.html.

Yan, Quan Liu, and Douglas L. Zweizig. 2000. "Public Library Use of Statistics: A Survey Report." *Public Libraries* 39 (March/April): 98–105.

Zweizig, Douglas L., and Eleanor Jo Rodger. 1982. *Output Measures for Public Libraries.* Chicago: American Library Association.

5

Organization, Law, Advocacy, Funding, and Politics

We who believe in the democratic mission of libraries must speak up and fight for information equity for all. Otherwise, we will endanger our most precious rights in a democratic society—the rights of free speech, inquiry, and self-governance.

—Nancy C. Kranich, ALA President 2000–2001,
in "Libraries, the New Media, and the Political Process"

Operating a public library requires an awareness of the social, political, and economic factors that impact the delivery of library services. This chapter treats the multiple contexts in which the public library functions, paying particular attention to the organizational, legal, and funding systems. To understand these contexts fully it is critical that librarians scan and understand the national, state, regional, and local political environment, because public policy and legislation at all these levels influences each library's funding and governance.

Over 50 years ago, in his work *The Public Library in the Political Process*, Garceau (1949: 239) clearly defined this important duty: "Public librarians are inescapably a part of government and involved in 'politics.'" Today public librarians should stay apprised of overarching concerns by reviewing policy issues addressed by organizations such as the National Governors Association (http://www.nga.org), the National Association of Counties (http://www.naco.org), the Alliance for Regional Stewardship (http://www.regionalstewardship.org), and the U.S. Conference of Mayors (http://www.usmayors.org). The governance of each public library today takes place within the interlocking contexts of local, regional, state, and national political jurisdictions. As stated at a congressional hearing in 2009, libraries are anchor institutions in their communities ("ALA Calls on House Subcommittee," 2009).

The Organizational Basis of the Public Library

When governing bodies established the first tax-supported public libraries over 160 years ago as a community service, they had no models of governance to follow, and the structure we have today was crafted within the framework of local situations. For the first 50 years of the public library's existence, the city, or in some cases the school district, was the basis of library service. Smaller communities and rural areas generally remained unserved.

The first two periods in the governmental history of the library movement in the United States roughly track the development of municipal government. The first period (1850–1890) was the rise of the "board plan" of administration, as municipalities established boards to oversee new functions and services. As communities established public libraries, they commonly adopted this type of structure. During this period state library laws were passed rapidly. Though differing from state to state, these laws generally outlined the roles and responsibilities of trustees, authorized taxation for library support, and maintained independence for the library board.

The second period of governmental history (1890–1934) witnessed the development of municipal home rule and a commission form of government. At the state level, the establishment of library agencies served to generate support for the founding of new libraries (Joeckel, 1935). A third period can be identified with the initiation of the American Library Association's (ALA's) active promotion of the extension of library service to unserved rural areas beginning in the 1930s. The national plan of service issued by ALA in 1939 provided a national vision for comprehensive service that would culminate in federal funds for rural library services in the 1950s through the Library Services Act of 1956 ("A National Plan for Libraries, 1935, 1939).

The county as a basis for library service emerged as state legislation provided legal means for a broader tax base. In 1898 Ohio (Cincinnati and Hamilton County) and Maryland (Hagerstown and Washington County) authorized taxes by the city and county for library service. Wisconsin and California passed similar legislation in 1901. While each state has a singular experience in the development of library services beyond the municipal level, California's story serves as the prototype for the county library movement. Ray Held (1973) recounts the California story in his comprehensive history, *The Rise of the Public Library in California*, which provides—for those interested—a detailed analysis of steps toward county service.

The inception of larger units of library service as another basis for the organization of libraries was suggested by Joeckel in 1935, to address the needs of regions where municipal or even county organization did not offer economy of scale. These include library districts—authorized by state law to provide library service—and multi-jurisdictional libraries comprising two or more government entities providing service through an intergovernmental agreement.

While the predominant legal basis of the public library in the United States continues to be municipal government, upon reflection, some conclude that the multicounty and library district units can provide more resources. Hennen (2002, 2005) has developed arguments that demonstrate advantages of wider units of service, including reallocation of administrative costs, equalization of tax rates, and a recognition of the impact of devolution. In fact in 2008 two of Minnesota's largest public library systems, Minneapolis and Hennepin County, merged—the largest public library consolidation in North America since the 1997 amalgamation of five systems into Toronto Public Library (Landgraf, 2008). Data for assessing new geographic service models is available through GEOLIB (http://www.geolib.org), a digital geographic information system for library planning. GEOLIB is a nationwide public library database system funded by the Institute for Museum and Library Services (IMLS; http://www.imls.gov/index.htm) and linked to a digital base map, which includes data sets from the U.S. Census, IMLS, and the National Center for Educational Statistics.

Figure 5.1 (pp. 104–106) shows that, of the 9,214 public libraries (administrative entities) in the United States, the majority are based in municipal government (52.8 percent), followed by nonprofit associations or agencies (14.8 percent), county or parish (9.9 percent), library districts (14.5 percent), multijurisdictions (3.4 percent), school districts (2.4 percent), and city or county (1.2 percent). The remaining libraries are under the aegis of Native American tribal government and combined public and school libraries. States vary greatly: Indiana's 239 libraries are wholly district based, while 98.5 percent of Iowa's 539 libraries are based in municipalities.

The Legal Basis of the Public Library

The legal basis for public libraries resides in state laws that grant a city, town, village, or district the right to establish a library, authorize the power to levy taxes, and determine the structure and powers of the library board that will oversee operation. *Library Law and Legislation in the United States* is a concise introduction to the three basic areas of law that relate to libraries—constitutional, statutory, and administrative (Ladenson, 1970, 1982). Constitutional law emanates from the people; statutory law consists of the compilations and codes of law enacted by a legislative body (Congress, state legislatures, county commissions, city councils); and administrative law governs functions of administrative agencies.

Figure 5.1. Percentage Distribution of Public Libraries, by Type of Legal Basis and State: Fiscal Year 2008

State	Number of public libraries	Type of legal basis[1]								Response rate[10]
		Municipal government[2]	County/parish[3]	City/county[4]	Multi-jurisdictional[5]	Nonprofit association or agency libraries[6]	School district[7]	Library district[8]	Other[9]	
		Percentage distribution								
Total	9,221	52.9	9.8	1.0	3.4	14.9	2.0	14.6	1.5	100.0
Alabama	210	74.8	7.6	0.5	17.1	0	0	0	0	100.0
Alaska	86	40.7	17.4	0	7.0	24.4	0	0	10.5	100.0
Arizona	86	53.5	9.3	10.5	1.2	7.0	1.2	3.5	14.0	100.0
Arkansas	51	19.6	41.2	2.0	31.4	0	0	0	5.9	100.0
California	181	64.1	24.3	2.2	2.8	0	1.7	5.0	0	100.0
Colorado	115	35.7	12.2	0	7.0	0	0.9	44.3	0	100.0
Connecticut	195	51.8	0	0	0	48.2	0	0	0	100.0
Delaware	21	14.3	28.6	4.8	0	0	0	52.4	0	100.0
District of Columbia	1	100.0	0	0	0	0	0	0	0	100.0
Florida	80	37.5	43.8	1.3	15.0	0	0	2.5	0	100.0
Georgia	59	0	44.1	0	55.9	0	0	0	0	100.0
Hawaii	1	0	0	0	0	0	0	0	100.0	100.0
Idaho	104	48.1	0	0	0	0	0	51.9	0	100.0
Illinois	634	49.2	0	0	0	0	0	50.8	0	100.0
Indiana	238	0	0	0	0	0	0	100.0	0	100.0
Iowa	539	99.1	0.6	0	0	0	0	0	0.4	100.0
Kansas	327	91.4	4.3	0	0.9	0	0	2.8	0.6	100.0
Kentucky	116	0	9.5	0	0.9	0	0	89.7	0	100.0
Louisiana	68	5.9	88.2	1.5	2.9	0	1.5	0	0	100.0
Maine	272	37.9	0	0	0	62.1	0	0	0	100.0
Maryland	24	4.2	95.8	0	0	0	0	0	0	100.0

(Continued)

Figure 5.1 (Continued)

State	Number of public libraries	Type of legal basis[1] (Percentage distribution)								Response rate[10]
		Municipal government[2]	County/parish[3]	City/county[4]	Multi-jurisdictional[5]	Nonprofit association or agency libraries[6]	School district[7]	Library district[8]	Other[9]	
Massachusetts	370	93.2	0	0	0.3	6.5	0	0	0	100.0
Michigan	384	50.8	4.9	0	0	0	4.9	39.3	0	100.0
Minnesota	138	75.4	9.4	7.2	8.0	0	0	0	0	100.0
Mississippi	50	4.0	34.0	26.0	34.0	2.0	0	0	0	100.0
Missouri	152	13.2	0	0	0	1.3	0	85.5	0	100.0
Montana	80	36.3	33.8	16.3	13.8	0	0	0	0	100.0
Nebraska	270	95.9	3.7	0	0.4	0	0	0	0	100.0
Nevada	22	4.5	50.0	0	4.5	0	0	40.9	0	100.0
New Hampshire	231	91.8	0	0	0.4	6.9	0	0	0.9	100.0
New Jersey	303	76.9	4.6	0	2.0	16.5	0	0	0	100.0
New Mexico	91	62.6	1.1	2.2	0	14.3	0	0	19.8	100.0
New York	755	26.1	0.8	0	0	47.3	0.1	25.2	0.5	100.0
North Carolina	77	14.3	54.5	1.3	19.5	6.5	0	0	3.9	100.0
North Dakota	81	65.4	1.1	8.6	14.8	0	0	0	0	100.0
Ohio	251	8.8	22.7	0	0	7.6	59.8	0.4	0.8	100.0
Oklahoma	115	87.8	5.2	0.9	6.1	0	0	0	0	100.0
Oregon	126	68.3	1.1	0	0	3.2	3.2	14.3	0	100.0
Pennsylvania	457	0	0.2	0	0	85.1	0	0	14.7	100.0
Rhode Island	48	47.9	0	0	0	52.1	0	0	0	100.0
South Carolina	42	2.4	92.9	0	4.8	0	0	0	0	100.0
South Dakota	114	65.8	0.5	5.3	13.2	0.9	0	0	4.4	100.0
Tennessee	187	56.1	0.1	3.7	0	0	0	0	0	100.0

(Continued)

Figure 5.1. Percentage Distribution of Public Libraries, by Type of Legal Basis and State: Fiscal Year 2008 (Continued)

State	Number of public libraries	Type of legal basis[1] Percentage distribution								Response rate[10]
		Municipal government[2]	County/ parish[3]	City/ county[4]	Multi-jurisdictional[5]	Nonprofit association or agency libraries[6]	School district[7]	Library district[8]	Other[9]	
Texas	561	56.7	20.0	2.0	1.8	16.4	0.2	2.5	0.5	100.0
Utah	69	60.9	37.7	1.4	0	0	0	0	0	100.0
Vermont	183	54.1	0	0	5.5	39.9	0	0.5	0	100.0
Virginia	91	25.3	39.6	0	25.3	9.9	0	0	0	100.0
Washington	64	59.4	1.6	0	0	0	0	39.1	0	100.0
West Virginia	97	49.5	33.0	0	17.5	0	0	0	0	100.0
Wisconsin	381	88.5	2.1	0.8	7.1	0	0.3	0	1.3	100.0
Wyoming	23	0	100.0	0	0	0	0	0	0	100.0
Outlying areas										
Guam	1	0	0	0	0	0	0	0	100.0	100.0
Puerto Rico	35	34.3	0	0	0	5.7	0	0	60.0	100.0

[1] Type of legal basis refers to the type of local government structure within which the library functions.

[2] An organized local government authorized in a state's constitution and statutes and established to provide general government for a specific concentration of population in a defined area.

[3] An organized local government authorized in a state's constitution and statutes and established to provide general government.

[4] A multi-jurisdictional entity that is operated jointly by a county and a city.

[5] A public library that is operated jointly by two or more units of local government under an intergovernmental agreement.

[6] A public library that is privately controlled but meets the statutory definition of a public library in a given state.

[7] A public library that is under the legal basis of a school district.

[8] A local entity other than a county, municipality, township, or school district is authorized by state law to establish and operate a public library.

[9] This includes libraries under the legal basis of Native American Tribal Government and combined public/school libraries.

[10] Response rate is calculated as the number of libraries that reported type of legal basis, divided by the total number of libraries in the survey frame. For item(s) with response rate below 100 percent, data for nonrespondents were imputed. Data were not imputed for the outlying areas.

NOTE: Detail may not sum to totals because of rounding. Data were not reported by the following outlying areas (American Samoa, Northern Marianas, and Virgin Islands). Missing data were not imputed for nonresponding outlying areas.

SOURCE: Institute of Museum and Library Services, Survey of Public Libraries in the United States, Fiscal Year 2008.

Source: U.S. Institute of Museum and Library Services. 2010. *Public Libraries Survey: Fiscal Year 2008.* Washington, DC: U.S. Institute of Museum and Library Services, pp. 43–44. http://harvester.census.gov/imls/ pubs/Publications/pls2008.pdf.

State Law and Legislation

Library laws were compiled by the American Library Association, culminating in the series *American Library Laws*, which ceased publication in 1983. Current access to the library statutes of most states can be found on the website for Chief Officers of State Library Agencies (COSLA; http://www.cosla.org), which lists a profile of each state library agency including the current website and links to the legislation for li braries currently in force for the state.[1]

Public library directors in each state need to be knowledgeable about their respective laws. Here are examples of a few state declaratory mandates that provide justification and preface these laws:

- **Colorado**. Legislative declaration. The general assembly hereby declares that it is the policy of this state, as a part of its provision for public education, to promote the establishment and development of all types of publicly-supported free library service throughout the state to ensure equal access to information without regard to age, physical or mental health, place of residence, or economic status, to aid in the establishment and improvement of library programs, to improve and update the skills of persons employed in libraries through continuing education activities, and to promote and coordinate the sharing of resources among libraries in Colorado and the dissemination of information regarding the availability of library services. (Colorado Library Law, 24-90-102)
- **Montana**. It is the purpose of this part to encourage the establishment, adequate financing, and effective administration of free public libraries in this state to give the people of Montana the fullest opportunity to enrich and inform themselves through reading. (Montana Code Annotated, 22-1-302)
- **Vermont**. The general assembly declares it to be the policy of the state of Vermont that free public libraries are essential to the general enlightenment of citizens in a democracy and that every citizen of the state of Vermont should have access to the educational, cultural, recreational, informational and research benefits of a free public library. (Vermont Statutes, 22 VSA 67a)
- **Wisconsin**. The legislature recognizes:
  (a) The importance of free access to knowledge, information and diversity of ideas by all residents of the state;
  (b) The critical role played by public, school, special and academic libraries in providing that access;
  (c) The major educational, cultural and economic asset is represented in the collective knowledge and information resources of a state's libraries;
  (d) The importance of public libraries to the democratic process; and

(e) That the most effective use of a library resources in this state can occur only through interlibrary cooperation among all types of libraries and the effective use of technology. (Wisconsin Statutes, 43.001)

These declarations are tangible manifestations of states' commitment to the value of libraries in the lives of their residents. They are the result of the efforts of many people working together over many years to incorporate the library as a public good in law. By way of example, Figure 5.2 is that portion of the Colorado legislation that outlines steps in the method for establishing public libraries.

Figure 5.2. Colorado Revised Statutes, Office of Legislative Legal Services, Colorado General Assembly

ARTICLE 90—LIBRARIES
24-90-107. Method of Establishment.

(1) A municipal or county library may be established for a governmental unit either by the legislative body of said governmental unit on its own initiative, by adoption of a resolution or ordinance to that effect, or upon petition of one hundred registered electors residing in the proposed library's legal service area. A joint library may be established by the legislative bodies of two or more governmental units, and a library district by the legislative bodies of one or more governmental units, each proceeding to adopt a resolution or an ordinance to that effect. A library district may also be formed by petition of one hundred registered electors residing within the proposed library district addressed to the boards of county commissioners in each county in the proposed library district.

(2) If establishment of a municipal, county, or joint library or a library district is to be by resolution or ordinance, the following procedures shall be followed:

(a) Public hearings following notice shall be held by those governmental units forming the public library. Such notice shall set forth the matters to be included in the resolution or ordinance and shall fix a date for the hearing which shall be not less than thirty nor more than sixty days after the date of first publication of such notice.

(b) Such public hearings shall include discussion of the purposes of the library to be formed and, where more than one governmental unit is involved, the powers, rights, obligations, and responsibilities, financial and otherwise, of each governmental unit.

(c) The resolution or ordinance shall describe the proposed library's legal service area, identifying any excluded areas, shall specify the mill levy and property tax dollars to be imposed or other type and amount of funding, and shall state that the electors of the governmental unit or library district must approve any amount of tax levy not previously established by resolution or ordinance nor previously approved by the electors before the library can be established.

(d) Upon the adoption of the resolution or ordinance, the legislative body or bodies shall establish the public library and provide for its financial support beginning on or before January 1 of the year following the adoption of the resolution or ordinance by all those legislative bodies effecting the establishment or, if any amount of tax levy not previously established by resolution or ordinance nor previously approved by the electors is to provide the financial support, following elector approval of that levy.

(e) Upon establishment of a joint library or library district, and after appointment of the library board of trustees, a written agreement between the legislative body of each participating governmental unit and the library board of trustees shall be effected within ninety days and shall set forth fully the rights, obligations, and responsibilities, financial and otherwise, of all parties to the agreement.

(Continued)

Figure 5.2 *(Continued)*

(3) If establishment of a county or municipal library or a library district is by petition of registered electors, the following procedures shall be followed:

(a) The petition shall set forth:

(I) A request for the establishment of the library;

(II) The name or names of the governmental unit or units establishing the library;

(III) The name of the proposed library, and for a library district, the chosen name preceding the words "library district";

(IV) A general description of the legal service area of the proposed public library with such certainty as to enable a property owner to determine whether or not such property owner's property is within the proposed library's legal service area; and

(V) Specification of the mill levy to be imposed or other type and amount of funding and that the electors must approve any amount of tax levy not previously established by resolution or ordinance nor previously approved by the electors before the county or municipal library or library district can be established.

(b) Petitions shall be addressed to the legislative body of the county or municipality, or, in the case of a library district, to the boards of county commissioners of each county having territory within the legal service area of the proposed district.

(c) (I) Except as otherwise provided in subparagraphs (II) and (III) of this paragraph (c), at the time of filing the petition for the establishment of a library district, a bond shall be filed with the county or counties sufficient to pay all expenses connected with the organization of the library district if such organization is not affected.

(II) Except as otherwise provided in subparagraph (III) of this paragraph (c), the board of county commissioners of each county having territory within the legal service area of the proposed library district may:

(A) Waive the bonding requirement; and

(D) With the consent of the board of trustees of an existing library, pay for the costs of the election for the proposed library district. If the legal service area of a proposed library district includes two or more counties, the costs of election for such library district to be paid by any county pursuant to this sub-subparagraph (B) shall not exceed a percentage of said costs equal to the percentage that the population of the county within the boundaries of the legal service area bears to the total population within the boundaries of such service area.

(III) (A) Subject to the provisions of sub-subparagraphs (B) and (C) of this subparagraph (III), the board of county commissioners of each county having territory within the legal service area of the proposed library district shall pay no less than fifty percent of the costs of the election for such library district if the petition submitted pursuant to subsection (1) of this section contains signatures by registered electors residing in the proposed library district in an amount equal to at least five percent of the total number of votes cast in every precinct in the proposed library district for all candidates for the office of secretary of state at the previous general election.

(B) Payment of election costs for any library district shall not be required of any county under this subparagraph (III) more than once every four years.

(C) In the case where the legal service area of a proposed library district includes two or more counties, the costs of the election for the library district shall be paid on a prorated basis with each county within the boundaries of the proposed library's legal service area paying a percentage of said costs equal to the percentage that the population of the county within the boundaries of the library's legal service area bears to the total population of such service area.

(c.5) Notwithstanding any other provision of this section, the costs of the election of a proposed library district may be assumed by an existing library where the assumption of the costs has been approved by the board of trustees of said library.

(Continued)

Figure 5.2. Colorado Revised Statutes, Office of Legislative Legal Services, Colorado General Assembly *(Continued)*

(d) Upon receipt of such petition, the legislative body or bodies shall either establish the library by resolution or ordinance, in accordance with subsection (2) of this section, or shall submit the question of the establishment of a public library to a vote of the registered electors residing in the proposed library's legal service area in accordance with the following provisions:

(I) In the case of a municipal library, such election shall be held in accordance with article 10 of title 31, C.R.S., and section 20 of article X of the state constitution, and shall be held on the date of the state biennial general election, the first Tuesday in November in odd-numbered years, or the municipal regular election, whichever is earliest; except that such petition shall be filed at least ninety days before such election.

(II) In the case of a library district or county library, such election shall be held in accordance with articles 1 to 13 of title 1, C.R.S., and section 20 of article X of the state constitution, and shall be held on the date of the state biennial general election or the first Tuesday in November in odd-numbered years, whichever is earliest; except that such petition shall be filed at least ninety days before such election.

(III) Public hearings shall be conducted by such legislative body or bodies prior to an election and shall include a discussion of the purposes of the library to be formed and, where more than one governmental unit is involved, the powers, rights, obligations, and responsibilities, financial and otherwise, of each governmental unit.

(e) and (f) (Deleted by amendment, L. 97, p. 411, § 1, effective April 24, 1997.)

(g) If a majority of the electors voting on the question vote in favor of the establishment of a library, the legislative body of each establishing governmental unit shall forthwith establish such library and provide for its financial support beginning on or before January 1 of the year following the election.

(h) Upon establishment of a library district, and after appointment of the library board of trustees, a written agreement between the legislative body of each participating governmental unit and the library board of trustees shall be effected within ninety days and shall set forth fully the rights, obligations, and responsibilities, financial and otherwise, of all parties to the agreement.

(i) If organization of a library district is effected, the district shall reimburse the legislative bodies holding the election for expenses incurred in holding the election.

Source: L. 79: Entire article R&RE, p. 986, § 1, effective July 1. L. 87: (1) and (2) amended, p. 319, § 60, effective July 1. L. 90: Entire section R&RE, p. 1295, § 3, effective July 1. L. 93: (1) amended, p. 1462, § 8, effective June 6. L. 94: (2)(c), (2)(d), and (3)(a)(V) amended, p. 736, § 2, effective July 1. L. 97: (3)(c) to (3)(f) amended, p. 411, § 1, effective April 24. L. 98: (3)(c)(III)(A) amended, p. 831, § 59, effective August 5. L. 2003: (1), (2)(c), (3)(a)(IV), (3)(b), IP(3)(c)(II), (3)(c)(II)(B), (3)(c)(III)(A), (3)(c)(III)(C), and IP(3)(d) amended and (3)(c.5) added, p. 2447, § 8, effective August 15.

Editor's note: (1) This section was contained in an article that was repealed and reenacted in 1979. Provisions of this section, as it existed in 1979, are similar to those contained in 24-90-110 and 24-90-111 as said sections existed in 1978, the year prior to the repeal and reenactment of this article.

(2) Subsections (1), (2)(c), (3)(a)(IV), and (3)(b), the introductory portion to subsection (3)(c)(II), subsections (3)(c)(II)(B), (3)(c)(III)(A), (3)(c)(III)(C), and (3)(c.5), and the introductory portion to subsection (3)(d) were contained in a 2003 act that was passed without a safety clause. The act establishes an effective date of August 15, 2003, for these provisions. For further explanation concerning the effective date, see page vii of this volume.

ANNOTATION

Applied in Ramos v. Lamm, 485 F. Supp. 122 (D. Colo. 1979).

Local Ordinances

In addition to state law, many municipalities and counties have passed local ordinances that enhance or identify local policies relating to library governance. Home rule is the principle or practice of self-government in the internal affairs of a dependent country or other political unit. Powers granted under home rule vary in each state by government functions and regarding the ability of local governments to raise taxes or impose regulations. To put home rule in context for each state, review *Home Rule in America* (Krane, Rigos, and Hill, 2001).

A few examples of local ordinances that provide for public library regulations give an idea of specific instances of local regulation supplementing state legislation.

- **Cedar Falls, Iowa**. Annual report. The board of library trustees shall make a report to the city council immediately after the close of the municipal fiscal year. This report shall contain statements of the condition of the library, the number of books added thereto, the number of books circulated, the amount of fines collected and the amount of money expended in the maintenance of the library during the year, together with such further information as required by the council. (Cedar Falls, Iowa, Code, Sec. 2-286)
- **Ypsilanti Township, Michigan**. Larceny from libraries. It shall be unlawful for any person, within the township to procure or take in any way from any public library . . . any book, pamphlet, map, chart, painting, picture, photograph, periodical, newspaper, magazine, manuscript or exhibit or any part thereof with intent to convert the same to his own use or with intent to defraud the owner thereof. (Ypsilanti Township, Washtenaw Co., Michigan, Code of Ordinances, Sec. 42-142)
- **New Port Richey Public Library, Florida**. Sale of books by public library. The New Port Richey Public Library may conduct a sale of books on city owned property upon receiving the prior approval of the city manager. In addition, the Friends of the Library, upon the city manager's prior approval, may conduct a public sale of books on city owned property on behalf of the New Port Richey Public Library. All income, monies, and other proceeds collected from any sale conducted without the assistance of the Friends of the Library shall be deposited in the New Port Richey Public Library Special Revenue Fund. All income, monies, and other proceeds collected from any sale conducted by or with the assistance of the Friends of the Library shall be retained by the Friends of the Library. Notwithstanding the foregoing, all revenue, monies and other proceeds retained by the Friends of the Library shall be used solely for the providing, enhancement of library services offered by the New Port Richey Public Library. (New Port Richey, Florida, Code of Ordinances, 2-166)

- **Park Ridge, Illinois.** Public Gatherings and Crowds: Conduct in Public Library. It shall be unlawful for any person using the Park Ridge Public Library or its facilities to:
  1. Disturb the peace in said library building.
  2. Cause disturbing speech or noise within the reading rooms.
  3. Damage property of the library including buildings, furniture, fixtures or grounds. This subsection shall apply whether or not the person doing such damage is using the Park Ridge Public Library at the time of doing such damage.
  4. Fail to return books or other loaned material within the grace period provided by the rules and regulations of said library.
  5. Disobey or violate any rules or regulations established by the Board of Directors of said library, providing said rules and regulations have been posted in a conspicuous place within said library building. (Municipal Code of Park Ridge, 14-1-7)

Multitype laws and legislation are often a collaboration among local governments with state regulation. See, for example, the Massachusetts Regulations for Regional Library Systems (http://mblc.state.ma.us/mblc/laws/code/605cmr7.php), which establish minimum eligibility standards for regional reference and research centers relating to strength of resources, accessibility to resources, use of resources, and level of performance. Another example is the definition for Nebraska Library Systems, which are regional multitype library systems organized as nonprofit corporations to foster and conduct regional cooperative library programs and services (Nebraska Library Commission, 2011). One of the best-documented case studies of multitype collaboration are the regional library systems of Illinois, known for advocacy and cooperation (Byrnes, 2005).

State Library Agencies

The federal government is also important for governance. The federal program that provides funding to libraries is the Library Services and Technology Act (LSTA), a title of the Museum and Library Services Act of 2003 (P.L. 108-81). Other federal programs have an impact on various aspects of library service. Federal laws that relate to library issues such as privacy, copyright, and Internet filtering are examples. The ALA Legislative Action Center (http://capwiz.com/ala/home/) helps librarians to track and take action on legislation that will affect library service.

The LSTA, administered through IMLS, is the piece of federal legislation that impacts local public library funding most directly.

IMLS and State Libraries

The LSTA, the major source of federal funds for public libraries, first became law in 1996, and built upon previous federal library legislation (the Library Services Act of 1956 and the Library Services and Construction Act of 1964–1996). The LSTA takes a state-based approach to strengthening library services.[2] The 2003 reauthorization of Museum and Library Services Act (Public Law 108-81) updated the LSTA with three overall purposes:

- to promote improvements in library services in all types of libraries in order to better serve the people of the United States;
- to facilitate access to resources in all types of libraries for the purpose of cultivating an educated and informed citizenry; and
- to encourage resource sharing among all types of libraries to achieve economical and efficient delivery of service.

The LSTA authorizes the IMLS to administer several grant programs including Grants to States, National Leadership Grants, Library Services for Native Americans and Native Hawaiians, and contracts and Cooperative Agreements (see "Grants to State Library Agencies," http://www.imls.gov/grants/library/lib_gsla .asp).

The Grants to States program adheres to six priorities:

1. expanding services for learning and access to information and educational resources in a variety of formats, in all types of libraries, for individuals of all ages;
2. developing library services that provide all users access to information through local, state, regional, national, and international electronic networks;
3. providing electronic and other linkages among and between all types of libraries;
4. developing public and private partnerships with other agencies and community-based organizations;
5. targeting library services to individuals of diverse geographic, cultural, and socioeconomic background, to individuals with disabilities, and to individuals with limited functional literacy or information skills; and
6. targeting library and information services to persons having difficulty using a library and to underserved urban and rural communities, including children (from birth through age 17) from families with incomes below the poverty line. (Manjarrez, Langa, and Miller, 2009: 6)

The Grants to States program, a federal-state partnership, is the IMLS's largest program. It uses a population-based formula with each state receiving a base award with additional funds based on population size. Figure 5.3 (pp. 114–115) shows state allocations from 2003 to 2009.

State	FY 2003	FY 2004	FY 2005	FY 2006	FY2007	FY 2008	FY 2009
AK	$631,170	$769,497	$828,563	$887,453	$888,213	$833,016	$982,953
AL	$2,369,145	$2,507,472	$2,556,671	$2,610,549	$2,602,935	$2,545,491	$2,731,303
AR	$1,568,332	$1,704,034	$1,760,329	$1,820,073	$1,819,735	$1,766,109	$1,936,529
AZ	$2,961,981	$2,946,156	$3,041,222	$3,150,258	$3,211,248	$3,228,606	$3,489,664
CA	$16,222,180	$16,360,507	$16,457,012	$16,557,920	$16,506,165	$16,431,277	$16,882,275
CO	$2,378,206	$2,516,533	$2,579,074	$2,642,220	$2,650,213	$2,612,765	$2,834,875
CT	$1,905,106	$2,043,433	$2,100,240	$2,154,030	$2,141,681	$2,068,566	$2,232,404
DC	$598,204	$736,531	$790,234	$842,132	$838,393	$794,432	$940,761
DE	$704,320	$843,489	$904,235	$965,243	$967,412	$912,962	$1,063,308
FL	$7,898,120	$8,037,303	$8,172,813	$8,332,483	$8,429,449	$8,425,588	$8,769,895
GA	$4,225,196	$4,349,960	$4,433,740	$4,522,400	$4,590,936	$4,622,315	$4,910,727
HI	$903,039	$1,041,366	$1,101,687	$1,157,565	$1,157,491	$1,101,262	$1,248,864
IA	$1,668,229	$1,806,556	$1,858,287	$1,909,822	$1,902,157	$1,840,733	$2,004,457
ID	$946,563	$1,084,890	$1,150,464	$1,215,563	$1,225,259	$1,180,138	$1,344,613
IL	$6,035,999	$6,177,300	$6,214,291	$6,249,722	$6,216,116	$6,133,883	$6,376,914
IN	$3,084,585	$3,263,933	$3,317,057	$3,369,822	$3,357,739	$3,292,765	$3,492,560
KS	$1,565,707	$1,706,659	$1,759,339	$1,812,456	$1,804,558	$1,745,712	$1,910,465
KY	$2,191,121	$2,329,448	$2,384,878	$2,439,668	$2,433,669	$2,374,218	$2,560,041
LA	$2,191,708	$2,505,725	$2,554,689	$2,604,141	$2,587,884	$2,409,825	$2,582,970
MA	$3,247,148	$3,385,475	$3,423,733	$3,449,395	$3,413,560	$3,346,669	$3,538,865
MD	$2,807,829	$2,946,918	$3,008,965	$3,067,643	$3,062,016	$2,988,627	$3,170,341
ME	$925,456	$1,063,783	$1,123,275	$1,181,762	$1,177,883	$1,116,986	$1,263,854
MI	$4,875,315	$5,023,914	$5,059,705	$5,093,053	$5,052,531	$4,941,233	$5,144,352
MN	$2,610,305	$2,748,632	$2,807,289	$2,864,372	$2,856,123	$2,793,089	$2,983,854
MO	$2,808,591	$3,043,905	$3,096,707	$3,155,054	$3,150,050	$3,087,560	$3,285,618
MS	$1,638,841	$1,777,168	$1,830,121	$1,886,927	$1,882,233	$1,809,550	$1,973,756
MT	$751,325	$889,652	$949,157	$1,008,157	$1,007,986	$952,693	$1,104,574
NC	$4,211,633	$4,241,339	$4,309,258	$4,394,254	$4,419,501	$4,401,145	$4,696,318
ND	$626,793	$765,120	$821,842	$878,082	$876,330	$818,116	$963,555
NE	$1,122,069	$1,260,396	$1,317,786	$1,372,965	$1,370,433	$1,311,709	$1,466,582
NH	$916,679	$1,055,006	$1,115,181	$1,173,868	$1,172,791	$1,114,075	$1,263,243
NJ	$4,103,012	$4,363,523	$4,412,959	$4,464,364	$4,434,773	$4,343,636	$4,530,049
NM	$1,179,001	$1,317,328	$1,378,496	$1,442,371	$1,445,113	$1,392,895	$1,553,168
NV	$1,323,020	$1,461,347	$1,542,939	$1,634,252	$1,659,300	$1,628,664	$1,817,110
NY	$9,004,514	$9,142,841	$9,146,819	$9,146,249	$9,074,434	$8,955,719	$9,233,751
OH	$5,505,038	$5,643,905	$5,667,969	$5,691,792	$5,643,980	$5,543,747	$5,762,731
OK	$1,920,127	$2,058,454	$2,112,874	$2,162,902	$2,158,232	$2,100,996	$2,283,382
OR	$1,932,701	$2,071,028	$2,134,437	$2,194,490	$2,199,259	$2,153,972	$2,341,066
PA	$5,917,510	$6,057,207	$6,085,045	$6,075,494	$6,034,092	$5,963,310	$6,190,856
PR	$2,096,742	$2,235,820	$2,277,522	$2,296,792	$2,318,588	$2,252,920	$2,427,058
RI	$823,812	$962,139	$1,020,285	$1,076,537	$1,069,862	$1,006,294	$1,148,886
SC	$2,367,398	$2,335,912	$2,398,034	$2,462,858	$2,469,636	$2,424,418	$2,633,725

Figure 5.3. Grants to States Program Allocation by State, FY 2003–2009

(Continued)

			Figure 5.3 *(Continued)*			
SD	$684,211	$822,538	$880,376	$938,791	$937,650	$881,774	$1,032,923
TN	$2,903,168	$3,100,308	$3,158,288	$3,220,133	$3,221,670	$3,173,028	$3,408,976
TX	$10,183,839	$10,328,875	$10,460,595	$10,597,273	$10,661,984	$10,787,020	$11,275,657
UT	$1,387,588	$1,525,917	$1,592,429	$1,658,384	$1,683,421	$1,652,433	$1,852,547
VA	$3,638,702	$3,777,029	$3,851,240	$3,913,359	$3,928,187	$3,872,179	$4,098,398
VT	$618,870	$757,197	$815,233	$872,315	$870,330	$812,903	$955,372
WA	$3,125,806	$3,223,195	$3,288,255	$3,354,800	$3,364,690	$3,328,627	$3,547,140
WI	$2,800,929	$2,939,256	$2,992,540	$3,010,271	$3,033,754	$2,962,815	$3,162,937
WV	$1,154,946	$1,293,273	$1,349,667	$1,394,138	$1,396,003	$1,333,562	$1,483,188
WY	$565,552	$703,879	$762,355	$821,234	$820,240	$765,437	$911,745
TOTAL	$126,351,149	$132,504,450	$135,043,887	$137,576,077	$137,439,279	$134,822,488	$166,028,386

Source: Manjarrez, C., L. Langa, and K. Miller. 2009. A Catalyst for Change: LSTA Grants to States Program Activities and the Transformation of Library Services to the Public (IMLS-2009-RES-01). Washington, DC: Institute of Museum and Library Services, pp. 27–28. http://www.imls.gov/pdf/CatalystForChange.pdf.

Eligibility for LSTA funds requires that state library agencies submit five-year plans to IMLS. It is through the states' administration of LSTA funds that local plans are developed to conform to LSTA goals.

State library agencies coordinate the development of state plans in collaboration with their state's library community and other contextual factors such as the state's library infrastructure to determine use of LSTA funds (LSTA Five-Year Plans, http://www.cosla.org/content.cfm/id/lsta_five_year_plans). For example, the California plan for 2008–2012 identified four themes:

- All Californians have access to information and learning opportunities that help them be successful.
- Libraries have the resources to develop programs and services that are responsive to changing needs of Californians.
- Libraries are able to create and support digital preservation projects that enable long-term access to California information.
- Libraries provide access to a wide variety of electronic resources and training for users, and are a resource for patrons for learning about and using new information technologies. (California State Library, 2008)

The Georgia plan for 2008–2012 developed by the Georgia Public Library Service (GPLS, 2007) reported on an environmental scan along with three SWOT (Strengths, Weaknesses, Opportunities, and Threats) analyses of the state library agency (by the GPLS staff, the GPLS strategic planning team, and the 59 public library directors). Five common themes emerged from the information and feedback collected: (1) library funding, (2) training, (3) technology issues, (4) marketing, and (5) collaboration.

A review of state library plans provides a rich understanding of the variation of missions and goals configured to the needs of each state's people gained through a broad participatory approach. Plans include a description of stakeholder involvement, monitoring, and evaluation. The COSLA website (http://www.cosla.org) provides links to most current state plans. States configure their plans taking into account their respective regulations and context. Figure 5.4 demonstrates how state planning factors make an impact on state plans.

Advocacy and Federal Legislation

All federal legislation that impacts libraries is closely followed by the ALA Washington Office of Government Relations. The office works to ensure that libraries are consistently involved in the legislative and policy decision-making processes by:

1. informing government of the needs and concerns of the library community;
2. providing library supporters with up-to-date information on government actions or proposals;
3. building coalitions with Washington-based representatives of other groups with similar concerns; and
4. developing grassroots networks to lobby legislators and further library interests.

At the direction of the ALA Committee on Legislation, the Office of Government Relations covers a broad range of issues including, but not limited to copyright, appropriations, library programs, government information, and telecommunications.

Grassroots networks of librarians who will speak with lawmakers about library issues are fostered by events such as National Library Legislative Day, held each May in Washington, DC, to bring librarians, library board members, and library friends to advocate on behalf of libraries. A Virtual Library Advocacy Day is held at the same time. This national event is the culmination of similar events at each state legislature.

Working with direction from the ALA Committee on Legislation, the Office of Government Relations monitors issues and develops strategies. The ALA Federal Library Legislative and Advocacy Network (http://www.ala.org/ala/aboutala/offices/wo/getting involved/fllan/fllan.cfm) provides another level of grassroots support.

The ALA Office for Library Advocacy (http://www.ala.org/ala/aboutala/offices/ ola/index.cfm) supports the efforts of advocates seeking to improve libraries of all types by developing resources, a peer-to-peer advocacy network, and training for advocates at the local, state, and national levels. Areas of national concern include support to fund LSTA at $300 million in 2011, inclusion of school libraries in the

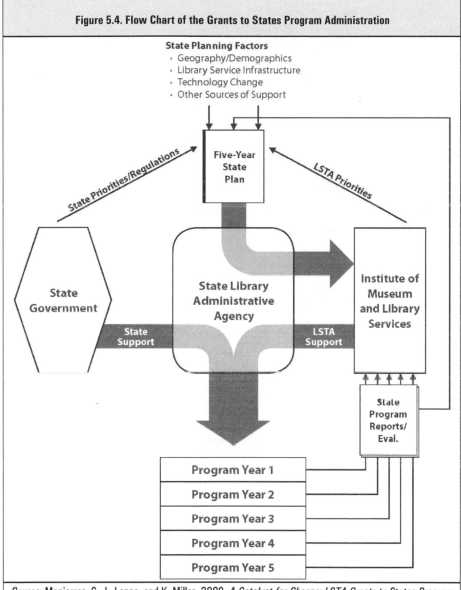

Figure 5.4. Flow Chart of the Grants to States Program Administration

State Planning Factors
- Geography/Demographics
- Library Service Infrastructure
- Technology Change
- Other Sources of Support

Five-Year State Plan

State Priorities/Regulations

LSTA Priorities

State Government

State Library Administrative Agency

Institute of Museum and Library Services

State Support

LSTA Support

State Program Reports/Eval.

Program Year 1
Program Year 2
Program Year 3
Program Year 4
Program Year 5

Source: Manjarrez, C., L. Langa, and K. Miller. 2009. *A Catalyst for Change: LSTA Grants to States Program Activities and the Transformation of Library Services to the Public* (IMLS-2009-RES-01). Washington, DC: Institute of Museum and Library Services, p. 8. http://www.imls.gov/pdf/CatalystForChange.pdf.

reauthorization of the Elementary and Secondary Education Act, strengthening of the Whistleblower Protection Act, support for e-rate discounts, intellectual freedom, copyright, information technologies, and preservation.

A highly publicized involvement of libraries at the level of federal law was the ALA's effort to prevent the linkage of universal service (e-rate) funding to Internet filtering. The Telecommunications Act of 1996 provided discounts in telecommunication costs to schools and libraries. However, passage of the Children's Internet Protection Act (CIPA) and the Neighborhood Children's Internet Protection Act required libraries receiving federal funds to filter Internet access. The ALA challenged CIPA in federal court as unconstitutional, but the decision was upheld by the Supreme Court. In 2008, 31.6 percent of public libraries refused to apply for e-rate to avoid CIPA requirements. Jaeger and Yan (2009) observe that libraries that defend the patron's right to free access are being forced to turn down the chance for funding.

Another case that won national attention was *Doe v. Gonzales*, in which Connecticut librarians challenged the constitutionality of the nondisclosure provisions of National Security Letters issued by the government under the USA PATRIOT Act ("Straight Answers," 2006).

From 2000 to 2008 First Lady Laura Bush, married to President George W. Bush, supported funding for the recruitment of librarians via the IMLS Laura Bush 21st Century Librarian Education Program, and increases for federal library support (Kniffel, 2008).

These examples of federal advocacy, legal actions by ALA, and policy decisions in local libraries demonstrate the library profession's commitment to advocacy for all aspects of government policy that affect library service.

Articulation of Legal Considerations

Understanding the expansion of the legal basis of the U.S. public library over the past 160 years requires grounding in the continuum of government from the local to the federal levels. Librarians interact most closely with the government of the community served, and state library agencies act as the link between local activity and the federal government through the collaborative development of state library plans. Through state library associations, programs sponsored by state library agencies, and efforts by the ALA, support for public libraries is integrated across all levels of government. The activation involves citizens, who oversee the policies and growth of the library, through their collaborative service on library boards (Minow and Lipinski, 2003; Miller and Fisher, 2007).

Library Funding

Public libraries' primary funding comes from local tax dollars. State aid, federal monies, and support from grants, local fundraising, and development efforts also contribute to the total budget (Figure 5.5, pp. 120–122). In 2008, the most recent year for which statistics have been published by IMLS, average public library per capita support was $38.62. Of this $31.94 was local, $3.35 state, $0.17 federal, and $3.16 from other sources such as monetary gifts and donations received in the current year, interest, library fines, fees for library services, or grants. The range among states varied from a high of $63.47 per capita in Ohio to a low of $16.43 per capita in Mississippi (U.S. IMLS, 2010).

While some of the difference in level of per capita support for libraries lies in variations of the income of residents, this does not account for all the differences. Looking at American Community Survey Median Family Income for 2010 (U.S. Census Bureau, 2010):

- Texas had a median family income of $47,106 but ranked 48th in total library operating revenue;
- Florida had a median family income of $45,887 and ranked 27th in library support; and
- Louisiana, with a far lower median income of $42,528, ranked 17th (U.S. IMLS, 2010: 152; U.S. Census Bureau, 2009).

No obvious correlation exists between a state's income and its level of funding for libraries. These disparate statistics are the result of attitudes over time, zeal of trustees and advocates, and general governmental philosophy. Libraries have begun to assert their economic worth with valuation studies that demonstrate the return on investment and social return on investment of funds used for libraries (Imholz and Arns, 2007).

Local Funding

Local support comes in the form of taxation, which is either appropriated from a general fund, accrues from tax levies, or accrues from special earmarked tax revenues. The level of assessment that a property tax can generate is usually set forth in state law. The millage rate is the total number of mills (1 mill = 1/1,000 of $1) being levied by each taxing authority. The property tax is, in the main, the primary support for public libraries. Thus, it is the work of the library board in collaboration with the library director and staff that—over time—provides the majority of funds for library operations. Successful strategies for tax campaigns for the support of public libraries are described by Turner (2000) and regular reports in *American Libraries* (Goldberg, 2008).

Library board members and friends of libraries also enhance local budgets through a variety of initiatives. These include fundraising through library endowment development, book sales, and other philanthropic efforts (Dowlin, 2008).

Figure 5.5. Total Per Capita Operating Revenue of Public Libraries, by Source of Revenue and State: Fiscal Year 2008

State	Number of public libraries	Total per capita operating revenue[1]									
		Total		Federal[2]		State		Local		Other[3]	
		Total	Response rate[4]	Total	Response rate[4]	Total	Response rate[4]	Total	Response rate[4]	Total	Response rate[4]
Total	9,221	$38.62	97.9	$0.17	97.7	$3.35	97.7	$31.94	97.7	$3.16	97.7
Alabama	210	22.21	100.0	0.31	100.0	1.15	100.0	18.42	100.0	2.33	100.0
Alaska	86	46.85	100.0	1.48	100.0	1.37	100.0	41.73	100.0	2.27	100.0
Arizona	86	30.77	94.2	0.16	95.3	0.10	94.2	28.61	95.3	1.90	95.3
Arkansas	51	23.57	96.1	0.04	96.1	1.73	96.1	20.31	96.1	1.50	96.1
California	181	34.85	98.9	0.11	99.4	0.90	99.4	31.38	99.4	2.46	98.9
Colorado	115	53.22	100.0	0.06	100.0	0.03	100.0	48.77	100.0	4.37	100.0
Connecticut	195	50.78	92.8	0.04	92.8	0.55	92.8	42.99	92.8	7.20	92.8
Delaware	21	32.90	100.0	#	100.0	4.01	100.0	26.91	100.0	1.98	100.0
District of Columbia	1	77.91	100.0	1.57	100.0	0	100.0	75.75	100.0	0.59	100.0
Florida	80	35.23	96.3	0.03	96.3	1.67	96.3	31.96	96.3	1.57	96.3
Georgia	59	22.35	100.0	0.04	100.0	3.78	100.0	17.29	100.0	1.23	100.0
Hawaii	1	27.59	100.0	0.97	100.0	24.43	100.0	0	100.0	2.19	100.0
Idaho	104	32.24	98.1	0.14	98.1	0.85	98.1	28.29	98.1	2.97	98.1
Illinois	634	61.15	98.4	0.27	98.6	2.95	98.7	52.91	98.4	5.03	98.4
Indiana	238	50.60	100.0	0.12	100.0	3.25	100.0	43.71	100.0	3.52	100.0
Iowa	539	33.44	96.7	0.19	96.8	0.93	96.7	29.37	96.7	2.95	96.7
Kansas	327	45.83	98.8	0.13	98.8	1.69	98.8	39.91	98.8	4.11	98.8
Kentucky	116	36.08	100.0	0.17	100.0	1.79	100.0	31.25	100.0	2.87	100.0
Louisiana	68	41.98	100.0	1.23	100.0	1.91	100.0	36.09	100.0	2.74	100.0
Maine	272	32.77	95.6	0.01	95.6	0.31	95.6	24.13	95.6	8.33	95.2

(Continued)

Figure 5.5 *(Continued)*

| | Number of public libraries | Total per capita operating revenue[1] | | | | | | | | | |
| | | Total | | Federal[2] | | State | | Local | | Other[3] | |
State		Total	Response rate[4]	Total	Response rate[4]	Total	Response rate[4]	Total	Response rate[4]	Total	Response rate[4]
Maryland	24	$48.21	100.0	$0.50	100.0	$6.06	100.0	$33.96	100.0	$7.69	100.0
Massachusetts	370	40.63	98.1	0.36	98.1	1.42	98.1	35.24	98.1	3.66	98.1
Michigan	384	44.72	97.7	0.02	90.6	1.02	90.6	40.63	90.6	3.05	90.6
Minnesota	138	37.73	100.0	0.09	100.0	1.47	100.0	32.92	100.0	3.25	100.0
Mississippi	50	16.43	100.0	0.15	100.0	3.37	100.0	11.08	100.0	1.84	100.0
Missouri	152	41.27	100.0	0.36	100.0	0.84	100.0	36.54	100.0	3.53	100.0
Montana	80	24.90	100.0	0.04	100.0	0.42	100.0	21.90	100.0	2.54	100.0
Nebraska	270	36.93	82.2	0.18	82.2	0.44	82.2	33.78	82.2	2.58	82.2
Nevada	22	37.12	100.0	0.45	100.0	1.34	100.0	26.68	100.0	8.64	100.0
New Hampshire	231	39.45	98.3	f	97.8	0.02	97.8	36.48	98.3	2.94	98.3
New Jersey	303	59.42	92.4	0.12	92.4	0.98	92.4	55.83	92.4	2.49	92.4
New Mexico	91	30.43	100.0	0.22	100.0	1.64	100.0	27.11	100.0	1.51	100.0
New York	755	60.00	100.0	0.28	100.0	3.08	100.0	49.30	100.0	7.34	100.0
North Carolina	77	23.14	100.0	0.16	100.0	1.87	100.0	19.46	100.0	1.66	100.0
North Dakota	81	22.49	100.0	f	100.0	1.26	100.0	18.75	100.0	2.47	100.0
Ohio	251	63.47	100.0	0	100.0	39.08	100.0	17.74	100.0	6.64	100.0
Oklahoma	115	30.91	100.0	0.09	100.0	0.93	100.0	28.08	100.0	1.81	100.0
Oregon	126	50.61	99.2	0.20	100.0	0.21	99.2	47.18	99.2	3.01	99.2
Pennsylvania	457	28.87	99.6	0.37	99.6	7.07	99.6	17.27	99.6	4.16	99.6
Rhode Island	48	45.00	97.9	0.30	97.9	8.26	97.9	30.97	97.9	5.47	97.9

(Continued)

Figure 5.5. Total Per Capita Operating Revenue of Public Libraries, by Source of Revenue and State: Fiscal Year 2008 (Continued)

State	Number of public libraries	Total per capita operating revenue[1]									
		Total		Federal[2]		State		Local		Other[3]	
		Total	Response rate[4]	Total	Response rate[4]	Total	Response rate[4]	Total	Response rate[4]	Total	Response rate[4]
South Carolina	42	$25.92	100.0	$0.12	100.0	$2.22	100.0	$22.30	100.0	$1.28	100.0
South Dakota	114	31.00	92.1	0.04	92.1	0.01	92.1	29.26	92.1	1.66	92.1
Tennessee	187	17.08	100.0	0.06	100.0	0.07	100.0	15.57	100.0	1.38	100.0
Texas	561	20.21	100.0	0.05	100.0	0.23	100.0	19.07	100.0	0.86	100.0
Utah	69	32.63	98.6	0.13	98.6	0.32	98.6	30.44	98.6	1.73	98.6
Vermont	183	34.18	92.3	0.06	92.3	0.14	92.3	24.26	93.4	9.73	93.4
Virginia	91	36.48	100.0	0.07	100.0	2.27	100.0	32.38	100.0	1.75	100.0
Washington	64	52.05	100.0	0.09	100.0	0.17	100.0	49.91	100.0	1.88	100.0
West Virginia	97	18.47	100.0	0.14	100.0	4.95	100.0	11.63	100.0	1.75	100.0
Wisconsin	381	37.53	100.0	0.17	100.0	0.76	100.0	34.60	100.0	1.99	100.0
Wyoming	23	53.51	100.0	0.11	100.0	0.21	100.0	48.88	100.0	4.31	100.0
Outlying areas											
Guam	1	56.58	100.0	0	0	0	0	55.26	100.0	1.31	100.0
Puerto Rico	35	2.94	51.4	0.01	80.0	0.36	82.9	2.14	65.7	0.24	74.3

\# Rounds to zero.

[1] Per capita is based on the total unduplicated population of legal service areas.

[2] This includes federal funds, such as Library Services and Technology Act (LSTA) funds, that are distributed to public libraries through state library agencies. Other federal funds that are used by state library agencies or library cooperatives to provide services that benefit local public libraries are not included in the table because they are not received as income.

[3] This includes monetary gifts and donations received in the current year, interest, library fines, fees for library services, or grants.

[4] Response rate is calculated as the number of libraries that reported the item, divided by the total number of libraries in the survey frame. For item(s) with response rates below 100 percent, data for nonrespondents were imputed and are included in the table. Data were not imputed for the outlying areas.

NOTE: Detail may not sum to totals because of rounding. Data were not reported by the following outlying areas (American Samoa, Northern Marianas, and Virgin Islands). Missing data were not imputed for nonresponding outlying areas.

SOURCE: Institute of Museum and Library Services, Survey of Public Libraries in the United States, Fiscal Year 2008.

Source: U.S. Institute of Museum and Library Services. 2010. *Public Libraries Survey: Fiscal Year 2008.* Washington, DC: U.S. Institute of Museum and Library Services, pp. 99–100. http://harvester.census.gov/imls/ pubs/Publications/pls2008.pdf.

Friends of Libraries USA (http://www.folusa.org) and the Association of Library Trustees and Advocates of the ALA merged in 2009 to become the Association for Library Trustees, Advocates, Friends and Foundations, a new division of the ALA. These citizen voices have often been the determining factor in passing bonds and referenda (Reed, 2009).

State Funding

State funding varies greatly. Among the variety of methods are equalization grants, funding incentives, per capita support for direct service, materials grants, or lump sum grants. Some states provide funding for competitive grants, interlibrary loan, or construction. Multitype services supporting collaborative or cooperative projects that will extend and support services are also funded. No one has written a straightforward overview of methods used by state library agencies to distribute state funds (Himmel, Wilson, and DeCandido, 2000: 13–14). Schaefer made this point clearly in a 2001 study about funds distribution among state libraries. Most state library agencies require that public libraries meet compliance requirements (e.g., hours of service, paid employees, submission of annual reports and statistical data) and then generally distribute state aid funds based on level of compliance. This process establishes minimum levels of public library service within a state.

Federal Funding

Federal funds for local public libraries are primarily administered through state library agencies as LSTA funds, as described above. In 2009 the level of federal funding reached the level requested by library advocates. The FY09 Omnibus Appropriations Bill included $171.5 million for grants to state library agencies within the LSTA. This was a $10 million increase over 2008 and allowed for full implementation of a 2003 law that ensures equitable distribution of grants ("State Library Agencies," 2009). There are two overriding priorities: information access through technology and the provision of information access through empowerment.

The 2009 IMLS report, *A Catalyst for Change: LSTA Grants to States Program Activities and the Transformation of Library Services to the Public*, underscored the value of the LSTA grants to state programs in helping libraries embrace technology, establish new service models, and engage the public (Manjarrez, Langa, and Miller, 2009).

Foundation Funding

Many libraries have established foundations to support their work. These may be very large and well-funded, such as the Chicago Public Library Foundation (2011), "established in 1986 as an independent, nonprofit educational organization dedicated to working with the City of Chicago in a true public/private partnership to enrich the collections and programs of the Chicago Public Library" with $3.6 million in revenue in 2008. Foundations are also effective in smaller communities such as Brevard County, Florida, where the Brevard Library Foundation (http://www .brevardlibraryfoundation .org/index.html) raised $15,432 in the summer of 2009 to keep the mobile library on the road. At this writing there is no comprehensive directory of public library foundations, but a Google search will provide a rich set of results. On September 15, 2009, the first page of results listed websites for the Austin Public Library (Texas); Library Foundation of Los Angeles; Chicago Public Library Foundation; Fort Worth Public Library Foundation; Berkeley, CA, Public Library Foundation; DC Public Library Foundation; Salem, OR, Public Library Foundation; San Jose Public Library Foundation; New Orleans Public Library Foundation; and the Seattle Public Library Foundation. The sites are inspired examples of communities and libraries working together to develop programs and provide resources.

Public and private foundations also provide funding for public libraries. Private foundations generally award grants for special projects or demonstrations. The Bill and Melinda Gates Foundation's U.S. Library Program (http://www.gatesfoundation .org/topics/Pages/libraries.aspx), the largest foundation award to public libraries since the Carnegie building grants in the early twentieth century, brought 40,000 computers to libraries in all 50 states, increasing computer access for all U.S. residents, with a focus on the most impoverished, between 1997 and 2003. The Gates Program continued this with Opportunity Online in three rounds after the initial program, totaling over $350 million in U.S. library support. Other Gates support has included funding for advocacy training, notably Prosper with Passion, Purpose and Persuasion: A PLA Toolkit for Success.[3] Siobhan Stevenson's (2006/2007) assessment of the impact of this philanthropy examines how Gates, like Carnegie, has played a powerful role in shaping the public library policy agenda.

Public libraries can benefit from grants made directly to them from specific foundations or through foundation-supported projects of broader scope. One source of information on foundation opportunities is accessible to readers at the Foundation Center (http://www.foundationcenter.org/), which promotes public understanding of the field and helps grant seekers succeed.

Community foundations are public charities that are nonprofit, tax-exempt, publicly supported, grant-making organizations. They develop broad support from many unrelated donors with a wide range of charitable interests in a specific community. The Council on Foundations (http://www.cof.org) provides resources for working with local community foundations. In the United States, community foundations serve tens of thousands of donors, administer more than $31 billion in charitable funds, and address the core concerns of nearly 700 communities and regions. A Libraries for the Future report noted that 75 percent of community foundations support public library initiatives.[4]

Libraries and the Political Process

Public libraries exist within a nested and overlapping structure of local, regional, state, and national political entities. At each level libraries must work hard to educate policymakers about the fiscal and legal needs of libraries. From the enactment of the first laws for tax-supported libraries in the 1850s to the testimony for reauthorization of the LSTA in 2009, the political process has been central to the progress of public library development.

E. J. Josey (ALA president, 1984–1985) edited a series of classic books on the library and the political process that laid out the intricate and interlocking effort that librarians must make to ensure that politicians understand the needs of libraries (Josey, 1980, 1987; Josey and Shearer, 1990). ALA presidents Patricia Schuman (1991–1992) and Carol Brey-Casiano (2004–2005) made advocacy the centerpiece of their presidential years and wrote compellingly about the librarian's role in the political process (Schuman, 1999; Brey-Casiano, 2005). Camila Alire (ALA president 2009–2010) was elected after chairing the ALA's Committee on Legislation. Her 2009–2010 presidential initiative was Front Line Advocacy—to educate and train librarians to seize opportunities at all levels and especially from the front lines to promote the value of libraries.

The ALA Office for Library Advocacy works closely with its Washington Office for Governmental Relations, the Chapter Relations Office, and the Public Information Office. Briefings on key topics are prepared to assist in explaining library issues to policymakers. The national legislative day is held each year in May to bring librarians, library trustees, board members, and other library friends to Washington, DC, to talk with their representatives and senators about issues of concern to the library community. The Office for Library Advocacy, in partnership with *American Libraries*, the Public Information Office, and the Chapter Relations Office monitor issues that arise around the country. This group worked with 2008–2009 ALA resident Jim Rettig on the 2009 funding crisis in Ohio. Figure 5.6 is the press release from that effort that demonstrates the strong stand ALA takes on behalf of public library support.

The complex funding and political environment in which librarians must work to gain support for their libraries has been well described by John N. Berry, who has observed that library leaders have been reluctant to condemn politicians who oppose library funding but quick to cheer those who find new funds or push for restoration. His counsel is to reposition libraries as basic to the economic and social health of the community and the nation (Berry, 2009).

Figure 5.6. ALA Press Release: Statement on Proposed Ohio Library Budget Cuts

NEWS
For Immediate Release
June 23, 2009

ALA president Jim Rettig releases statement on proposed Ohio library budget cuts

Proposed library cuts largest on record

CHICAGO—Since January 2009, Ohio public libraries have lost approximately 20 percent of their state funding. Currently Governor Ted Strickland has proposed an additional 30 percent reduction. The following statement was released by American Library Association (ALA) President Jim Rettig in response to Gov. Strickland's proposed library budget cuts.

"A projected 50 percent reduction in funding for Ohio's libraries would result in unprecedented national disaster," said ALA President Jim Rettig. "We understand that in a recession difficult choices must be made, but libraries are part of the solution when a community is struggling economically, and are a necessity in efforts to get Americans back on their feet.

"From coast to coast, libraries have been first responders to the national economic crisis. They have been inundated by job seekers and users looking to better their lives through education. This also is the case in Ohio, as Ohioans are depending on their local libraries for free Internet access, employment services, personal finance resources, small business development and education and cultural programs.

"What will happen to the people of Ohio if their right to free access to information is taken away? The Governor's drastic proposed library budget cuts are the largest in history and will impact more than 8 million registered library card holders. Every one of Ohio's 251 public library systems could experience limited hours, program and staffing reductions or, worse yet, closures.

"Libraries are so much more than bricks and mortar. They are places where everyone—regardless of age, race or income—can come together, whether it's for information, self-help or to find their place in the community.

"I encourage all Ohioans to contact the Governor's office to express their opposition to his proposal to cut library funding and urge Ohio legislators to reject the Governor's plan."

The Ohio Library Council offers its libraries resources to prevent this proposal from moving forward. They can be found at http://www.olc.org or http://www.saveohiolibraries.com.

Source: American Library Association. 2009. "ALA President Jim Rettig Releases Statement on Proposed Ohio Library Budget Cuts." American Library Association. http://www.ala.org/ala/newspresscenter/news/pressreleases2009/june2009/ohiostatement_pio.cfm.

The ALA Public Awareness Committee oversees National Library Week and coordinates the ALA Public Relations Assembly. Each state chapter holds advocacy workshops and a state legislative day.

Public libraries have been effective in maintaining funding and support at the local, state, and federal levels. In the stressful and dark economic days of the late-2000s recession, with severe budget reductions all over the United States (Holland and Verploeg, 2009), initiatives such as the Campaign for America's Libraries, which integrates various public relations initiatives such as "Advocacy Grows @Your Library," "Step Up to the Plate@Your Library," and the website ilovelibraries.org, which reaches out to people who use and care about libraries (Burger, 2007), provide inspiration and support. Across the United States in towns and villages and cities, especially in times of economic stress, public libraries are viewed as the heart of the community (Christensen, 2007).

Notes

1. Public Library Association (1940); Library Extension Board (1942); American Library Association (1930, 1943, 1962; supplements 1965–1970, 1972–1978, 1983). For current legislation, see Chief Officers of State Library Agencies (http://www.cosla.org). See also the Library Law blog (http://blog.librarylaw.com/). Some states, such as New York, have compiled statutes and regulations. See Carter (1999); see also Minow and Lipinski (2003); Torrans (2004); Carson (2007).

2. The historical development of federal legislation is important to public libraries. For analysis of the LSA and LSCA, see Fry (1975); Mersel (1969); Holley (1983).

3. Several sources provide information on the role and impact of the Gates Foundation on public libraries. See *The Public Library Funding and Access Study.* (http://www.ala.org/ala/research/initiatives/plftas/index.cfm); Andrew C. Gordon, Margaret T. Gordon, Elizabeth Moore, and Linda Heuertz, "The Gates Legacy," *Library Journal* (March 1, 2003): 44–48; Lynn Blumenstein, "Gates Grant Funds Spanish Outreach," *Library Journal* 130 (December 2005): 26; "PLA Gets $7.7M from Gates for Advocacy," *Library Journal* 132 (August 2007): 22; "Gates Gives WebJunction $12.6 Million," *American Libraries* 38 (August 2007): 36; "Gates: $6.5M for Computers," *Library Journal* 132 (August 2009): 10; "ALA to Share $6.9 Million Gates Foundation Grant," *American Libraries* 40 (March 2009): 12; and the Bill and Melinda Gates Foundation website (http://www.gatesfoundation.org).

4. The organization Libraries for the Future ceased operations in March 2009 (*American Libraries*, 2009, http://www.ala.org/ala/alonline/currentnews/newsarchive/2009/march2009/lffcloses .cfm). Their excellent report, *Community Foundations and the Public Library*, is not available as it was only posted at their website, which is now shut down. I have included the report as Appendix C, "Community Foundations and the Public Library."

References

"ALA Calls on House Subcommittee to Use Libraries, Other Anchor Institutions to Promote Universal Broadband." 2009. *District Dispatch.* http://www.wo.ala.org/districtdispatch/?p=3644.

American Library Association. 1930. *American Library Laws.* Chicago: American Library Association). Also 1943; 1962; supplements 1965–1970, 1972–1978, 1983.

Berry, John N. 2009. "No Villains: Threatened Cuts and Partial Restorations Point Out the Ambiguous Politics of Library Funding." *Library Journal* (September 15): 24–25.

Brey-Casiano, Carol. 2005. "Grassroots Advocacy Works." *American Libraries* 36 (June/ July): 5.

Burger, Leslie. 2007. "I Love Libraries." *American Libraries* 38 (January): 6.

Byrnes, Shirley M. 2005. "Advocacy and Illinois Regional Library Systems." *Illinois Libraries* 86 (December): 80–81.

California State Library. 2008. *LSTA Five-Year Plan 2008–2012*. http://www.library.ca.gov/ grants/lsta/docs/STATE_PLAN_08_12.pdf.

Carson, Bryan M. 2007. *The Law of Libraries and Archives*. Lanham, MD: Scarecrow Press.

Carter, Robert Allen. 1999. *Public Library Law in New York State*. New York: New York State Library.

Chicago Public Library Foundation. 2011. "About." Chicago Public Library Foundation. Accessed January 13. http://www.chicagopubliclibraryfoundation.org/about/.

Christensen, Karen. 2007. *Heart of the Community: The Libraries We Love*. Great Barrington, MA: Berkshire.

Dowlin, Ken. 2008. *Getting the Money: How to Succeed in Fundraising for Public and Nonprofit Libraries*. Westport, CT: Libraries Unlimited.

Fry, James W. 1975. "LSA and LSCA, 1956–1973: A Legislative History." *Library Trends* 24 (July): 7–28.

Garceau, Oliver. 1949. *The Public Library in the Political Process: A Report of the Public Library Inquiry*. New York: Columbia University Press.

Georgia Public Library Service. 2007. *Library Services and Technology Act Five Year Plan for Georgia's Libraries 2008–2012*. http://www.georgialibraries.org/lib/lsta/5yr_plan2008_12 .pdf.

Goldberg, B. 2008. "Voters Buck Gloomy Economic Outlook to Fund Libraries." *American Libraries* 39 (December): 23.

Gordon, Andrew C., Margaret T. Gordon, Elizabeth Moore, and Linda Heuertz. 2003. "The Gates Legacy." *Library Journal* (March 1): 44–48.

Held, Ray E. 1973. *The Rise of the Public Library in California*. Chicago: American Library Association.

Hennen, Thomas J., Jr. 2002. "Are Wider Library Units Wiser?" *American Libraries* 33 (June/July): 65–70. http://www.haplr-index.com/wider_and_wiser_units.htm.

———. 2005. "Is There a Library Consolidation in Your Future?" *American Libraries* 36 (October): 49–51.

Himmel, Ethel E., William J. Wilson, and GraceAnne DeCandido. 2000. *The Functions and Roles of State Library Agencies*. Chicago: American Library Association.

Holland, Suzann, and Amanda Verploeg. 2009. "No Easy Targets: Six Libraries in the Economy's Dark Days." *Public Libraries* 48 (July/August): 27–38.

Holley, Edward Gailon. 1983. *The Library Services and Construction Act: An Historical Overview from the Viewpoint of Major Participants*. Greenwich, CT: JAI Press.

Imholz, Susan, and Jennifer Weil Arns. 2007. *Worth Their Weight: An Assessment of the Evolving Field of Library Valuation*. New York: Americans for Libraries Council.

Jaeger, Paul T., and Zheng Yan. 2009. "One Law with Two Outcomes: Comparing Implementation of CIPA in Public Libraries and Schools." *Information Technology and Libraries* 28 (March): 6–14.

Joeckel, Carleton Bruns. 1935. *The Government of the American Public Library*. Chicago: University of Chicago Press.

Josey, E. J. 1980. *Libraries and the Political Process*. New York: Neal-Schuman.

———. 1987. *Libraries, Coalitions and the Public Good*. New York: Neal-Schuman.

Josey, E. J., and Kenneth D. Shearer. 1990. *Politics and the Support of Libraries*. New York: Neal-Schuman.

Kniffel, Leonard. 2008. "8 Years Later: Laura Bush, Librarian in the White House." *American Libraries* 39 (December): 42–47.

Krane, Dale, Platon N. Rigos, and Melvin Hill Jr. 2001. *Home Rule in America: A Fifty State Handbook*. Washington, DC: CQ Press.

Ladenson, Alex. 1970. "Library Legislation: Some General Considerations." *Library Trends* 19 (October): 175–181.

———. 1982. *Library Law and Legislation in the United States*. Metuchen, NJ: Scarecrow Press.

Landgraf, G. 2008. "Minneapolis Public Library Merges with Hennepin County Library." *American Libraries* 39 (March): 19.

Library Extension Board. 1942. *Regional and District Laws*. Chicago: American Library Association.

Manjarrez, C., L. Langa, and K. Miller. 2009. *A Catalyst for Change: LSTA Grants to States Program Activities and the Transformation of Library Services to the Public*. IMLS-2009-RES-01. Washington, DC: Institute of Museum and Library Services. http://www.imls .gov/pdf/CatalystForChange.pdf.

Mersel, Jules. 1969. *An Overview of the Library Services and Construction Act, Title 1*. New York: R. R. Bowker.

Miller, Ellin G., and Patricia H. Fisher. 2007. *Library Board Strategic Guide*. Lanham, MD: Scarecrow Press.

Minow, Mary, and Tomas A. Lipinski. 2003. *The Library's Legal Answer Book*. Chicago: American Library Association.

"A National Plan for Libraries." 1935. *ALA Bulletin* 29 (February): 91–98.

"A National Plan for Libraries." 1939. *ALA Bulletin* 33 (February): 136–150.

Nebraska Library Commission. 2011. "Rules and Regulations of the Nebraska Library Commission: Title 236," Chapter 2.002.07. Nebraska Library Commission. Accessed January 13. http://www.nlc.state.ne.us/mission/rules.html#General%20Information.

Public Library Association. 1940. *Library Extension Legislation*. Chicago: American Library Association.

Reed, Sally Gardner. 2009. "Amalgamating for Advocacy." *American Libraries* 40 (March): 34–36.

Schaefer, Steve W. 2001. "Going for the Green: How Public Libraries Get State Money." *Public Libraries* 40 (September/October): 298–304.

Schuman, Patricia. 1999. "Speaking Up and Speaking Out: Ensuring Equity Through Advocacy." *American Libraries* 30 (October): 50–53.

"State Library Agencies Get Requested Fed Funding." 2009. *Library Journal* 134 (April 1): 13.

Stevenson, Siobhan. 2006/2007. "Philanthropy's Unintended Consequences: Public Libraries and the Struggle Over Free Versus Proprietary Software." *Progressive Librarian* 28 (Winter): 64-77.

"Straight Answers from George Christian and Peter Chase." 2006. *American Libraries* 37 (August): 22.

Torrans, Lee Ann. 2004. *Law and Libraries: The Public Library*. Westport, CT: Libraries Unlimited.

Turner, Anne M. 2000. *Vote Yes for Libraries: A Guide to Winning Ballot Measure Campaigns for Library Funding*. Jefferson, NC: McFarland.

U.S. Census Bureau. 2009. State and County Quick Facts. http://quickfacts.census.gov/qfd/states/00000.html.

————. 2010. American Community Survey, 2010. http://www.census.gov/hhes/www/income/statemedfaminc.html.

U.S. Institute of Museum and Library Services. 2010. *Public Libraries Survey: Fiscal Year 2008*. Washington, DC: U.S. Institute of Museum and Library Services, pp. 43–44. http://harvester.census.gov/imls/pubs/Publications/pls2008.pdf.

6
Administration and Staffing

Each public library must have a regular, paid, qualified staff of one or more persons, including a properly certified library director who is responsible to a library board. The public library staff should project an image of competence and friendliness to all members of the public. Public library staff members should understand the service goals of the library, should be aware of all library policies, and should be well trained in the practices and procedures required by their individual positions.

—*Wisconsin Public Library Standards* (2010: 23)

Library workers activate the mission of the public library. The use of collections, community partnerships, and one-on-one service that supports lifelong learning to people of all ages is facilitated by a qualified and committed staff. Many people—the library board, library workers, and volunteers—working together shape a library that functions as the heart of the twenty-first-century community.

This chapter presents model organizational charts. It pays attention to the composition and responsibilities of the library board, with consideration of the need to achieve greater diversity. It also provides details about the characteristics of the library director. The chapter addresses the organization of the library staff based on aggregated national data. In addition, it describes recruitment, staff development, and the role of unions. Finally, it identifies the importance of library volunteers.

Organizational Structures

Public librarians must conceive of the administration and staffing of public libraries in the context of the overall organizational structure, which exists as a function of municipal, county, or district governance. Public service and civil service structures specify the particular conditions of employment, and due to their local nature, they differ from community to community. The library director most often reports to a library board that is authorized by state statute. There are many variations on the organizational structure of public libraries. We provide three examples: Akron–Summit County, Ohio (population 542,562); Bedford Free Public Library, Massachusetts (population 12,600); and Denver Public Library (population 598,707). These demonstrate the variety of U.S. public library organization.

The Akron–Summit County Public Library provides a very clear example of organization and governance consisting of a central library, eighteen branches, and bookmobile/van services. Figure 6.1a depicts the Akron–Summit County Public Library organization chart with the line of authority to the board of trustees. Figure 6.1b (p. 134) shows the Town of Bedford, Massachusetts, organization chart. The Bedford Free Public Library reports to the Library Trustees. The chart shows how the library fits as compared to other town services. Figure 6.3c (p. 135) shows the Denver Public Library and a cluster structure for public service.

Library Boards

Community oversight of public libraries in the United States is by citizens—usually called a board of trustees or directors, but characterized here simply as the library board. This citizen body has its roots in the structure of the Boston Public Library and parallels the school board in many ways. The enabling legislation for public libraries in each state generally specifies the composition and method of appointment of the library board. Commonly appointed by a governing body, but sometimes elected, the library board has responsibility for a range of functions:

- Analysis of community needs
- Hiring, recommending, and evaluating the public library director
- Acting in an advocacy role to develop community support for bond issues and taxation
- Budget review and approval
- Policy review and approval
- Commitment to freedom of inquiry and expression
- Formulation of long-range planning

In her handbook for successful trustees, Moore (2009) has outlined what it means to be a trustee with a focus on advocacy, policy development, director hiring and evaluation, strategic planning, budgeting, and fundraising. Miller and Fisher (2007) have developed a strategic guide that demonstrates how the director-board relationship fulfills a social contract with the community.

Trustees face many challenges. A study by Jennifer Arns (2007) examined three contentious censorship controversies at the Medina, Ohio Public Library, the Metropolitan Library System of Oklahoma County, and the Cumberland County Public Library and Information Center of North Carolina. In these case studies the library

Figure 6.1a. Akron–Summit County (OH) Public Library Organization Chart

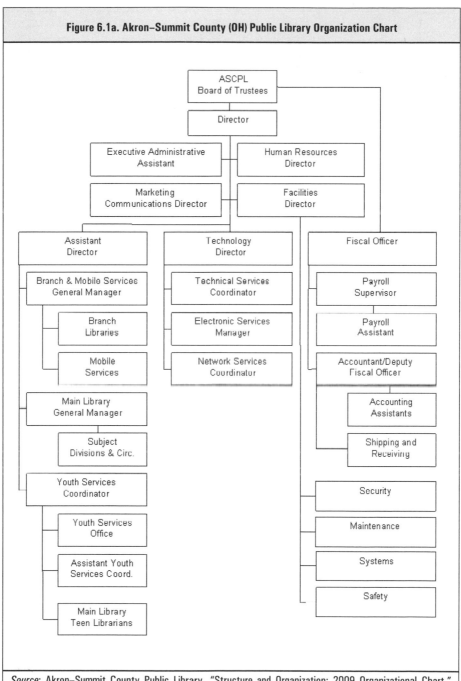

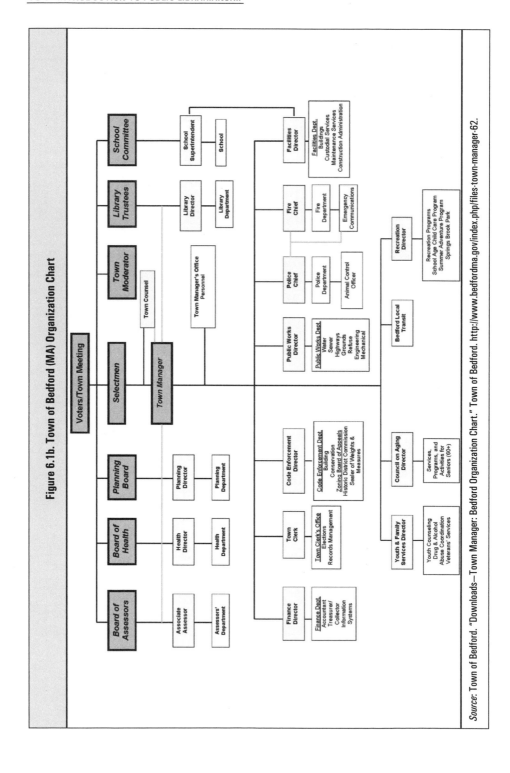

Figure 6.1b. Town of Bedford (MA) Organization Chart

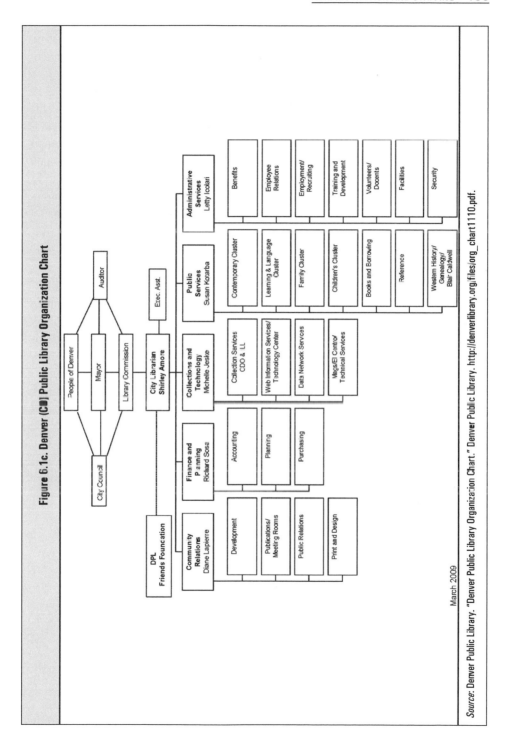

Figure 6.1c. Denver (CO) Public Library Organization Chart

March 2009

Source: Denver Public Library. "Denver Public Library Organization Chart." Denver Public Library. http://denverlibrary.org/files/org_chart1110.pdf.

system weathered the storm of community dissension and stood for an open public sphere. Arns analyzed leadership characteristics among trustees that enabled them to work constructively with the community.

Library board members are supported by national and state-level associations in developing intellectual and philosophical aspects of service. The Association of Library Trustees, Advocates, Friends and Foundations (ALTAFF; http://www.ala.org/ala/mgrps/divs/altaff/index.cfm) of the American Library Association (ALA) was formed in 2009 by a merger of the Association of Library Trustees and Advocates and Friends of Libraries USA (FOLUSA). Sally Gardner Reed (2009), executive director of ALTAFF, sees the combination of ALTA and FOLUSA into ALTAFF as a bold step to expand the voice of America's libraries. The Trustee Section of the ALTAFF website includes a model ethics statement for trustees, sample mission statements, and relationships with Friends of the Library organizations (http://www.ala.org/ala/mgrps/divs/altaff/trustees/orgtools/index.cfm).

State library associations and state library agencies also provide programs for library board members, which focus on state issues and organize programs, produce handbooks, and provide other means of support for the work of shared governance. The members of the library board articulate the importance of the library to the general public; therefore, board members' recognition of local and state issues is essential. Each state develops support that reflects its context. For instance, the *Georgia Public Library Trustees Manual* by Lyn Hopper (2008) of the Georgia Public Library Service outlines the legal and fiduciary responsibilities of trustees and provides a focused and effective discussion of the meaning of public libraries.

The New York State Association of Library Boards, a statewide organization that represents, assists, educates, and honors public library boards and their trustees as providers of free and universal library service, distributes the *Handbook for Library Trustees of New York State*. The 2010 Welcome section sets the tone:

> In the complicated and always challenging world of library finances and policy, we as library trustees, must be vigilant in our fiduciary role; mindful of our responsibility to develop libraries of excellence through our attention to library policies; and embrace an active commitment to on-going trustee education and training. This handbook provides you with a solid foundation to start your tenure as an educated library trustee. (Nichols, 2010: iv)

The Wisconsin Division for Libraries, Technology, and Community Learning publishes *Trustee Essentials* (2009), a handbook that includes a job description that succinctly defines the library board member's function: "Participate as a member of a team (the library board) to protect and advance the interests of the broader community by effectively governing the operations and promoting the development of the local public library."

The Michigan Library Association's Trustees and Advocates Division (2006) has produced a DVD that covers authorizing statutes, funding, legal requirements, and trustee responsibilities regarding resources, budget, finance, and library technology. The division posts a Powerpoint slide show on its website that is part of the Quality Service Audit Checklist certification process.

The demographic composition of library boards has tended to be fairly homogeneous over time. In his classic 1949 study of boards for the *Public Library Inquiry*, Garceau observed that boards were generally comprised of older, middle-class members of the community. A half-century later, Kelley's (1999) study of library trustees in Illinois, sent to 4,800 trustees, found that 70 percent were women, 50 percent were over 55, and occupations were primarily professional (e.g., accounting, banking, education, public service). Applegate, Gibbs, Cowser, and Scarbrough (2007) surveyed trustees in Indiana, 60 percent of whom were women between 55 and 64. She studied continuing education needs of trustees and noted that the trustees were more educated than the average member of the communities represented.

Clearly, in a United States that has an increasingly diverse population there is a need to recruit and retain trustees who reflect the population served. This is a challenge faced by advisory boards across the United States and bears deliberation at state and national policy forums (Gardyn, 2003).

It is the persistence and advocacy of library boards that create the community support for building programs, increased taxes, or even new operational structures. An Illinois survey found that the state's trustees contributed over 250,000 hours of time in a single year. The role of trustees in new public library construction has been detailed by Ames and Heid (2009: 9), who note the library board of trustees is the owner of the construction program and represent the community—as necessary to the design and construction as the library director, staff, architect, and contractor.

We can identify various examples of the dynamic nature of trustee efforts, often through their firsthand accounts. Shirley Lang (2008), of the Syosset, New York, board of trustees and a longtime member of ALTA, has written insightfully on the relationship between directors and trustees. The story of a county rural district formed in Stevens County in Washington State (Hague, 1999); a trustee's views of a campaign to pass a library bond issue (Glennon, 1997), and Louisiana trustee Jeanne T. Kreamer's (1990) credo on trustee activism all provide an understanding of the complex political environment in which trustees work to forge policy and support for service. These library board members' contagious enthusiasm and hope are emblematic of the committed, dedicated citizen, who has worked side by side with librarians to establish, develop, and strengthen library services. Libraries are not mandated by law; they are enabled and voluntary—the roots are nurtured and rise from the people. In addition to the focus on trustee support by the state library agencies and professional state and national library associations, there are many resources that help librarians and trustees develop service, as shown in Figure 6.2, "Examples of Trustee and Board Materials Developed by States."

The Library Director

In 2008 the U.S. economic crisis and weak economy caused great fiscal distress throughout the nation (Center on Budget and Policy Priorities, 2009). Public libraries were faced with tighter budgets and lower tax revenues. Recognizing the challenges, Washington, DC, public library director Ginnie Cooper stressed that leaders set the mood for the staff. Her strategy for leading through times of crisis is "don't panic" (Thomas, 2009).

What are the skills, knowledge, and personal style of a successful library director?

The library director works closely with the library board to realize the public library mission, develop long-range plans, and implement policies for the library's operations. The director works at the nexus of community and staff. Directors are expected to handle numerous responsibilities, such as the following:

Figure 6.2. Examples of Trustee and Board Materials Developed by States

Hopper, Lyn. 2006, 2008. *Georgia Public Library Trustee Manual*. Georgia Public Library Service. http://www.georgialibraries.org/lib/publications/trusteemanual/.

Library Trustees Association of New York State. 2010. *Handbook for Library Trustees of New York State*. Prominence Solutions. http://www.librarytrustees.org/.

Michigan Library Association, Trustee and Advocates Division. 2006. *Basic Training for Trustees*. http://www.mla.lib.mi.us/tad. *See also* Michigan Department of Education. 2011. "Quality Services Audit Checklist (QSAC." Michigan Department of Education. Accessed January 14. http://www.michigan.gov/hal/0,1607,7-160-17451_45510—,00.html.

Mississippi Library Commission. 2011. "Services for Libraries: Library Advocacy—Library Boards of Trustees." Mississippi Library Commission. Accessed January 14. http://www.mlc.lib.ms.us/ServicesToLibraries/ladv_board.html.

State of Rhode Island, Office of Library and Information Services. 2011. *Rhode Island Public Library Trustees Handbook*. Office of Library and Information Services. Accessed January 14. http://www.olis.state.ri.us/pubs/trustees/section1.pdf.

Wisconsin Department of Public Instruction. 2002, 2009. *Trustee Essentials: A Handbook for Wisconsin Public Library Trustees*. Wisconsin Department of Public Instruction. http://dpi.state.wi.us/pld/handbook.html.

- Lead the planning cycles
- Organize human resources
- Represent the library in the community
- Oversee financial operations
- Interact with local, state, and national library entities
- Develop the library's fiscal base through development and fundraising
- Manage facilities and technology
- Plan, design, and evaluate services

Don Sager (2001), who has directed major public libraries and served as president of an executive search and management firm, summarized the knowledge and skills required by public library directors in a classic article:

- **People skills**: Participation in a wide range of community, social, and professional organizations. Experience with collaborative activities and team-centered projects and proficiency in working successfully with diverse groups.
- **Vision**: Insight into the role the library will play in the future and ability to lead the organization in that direction.
- **Marketing ability**: Someone who can sell a new vision of library service to the community.
- **Communication**: The ability to articulate vision to governance, staff, the public, and funding authorities. Superior writing and public speaking ability and effective use of new technology, as well as creative promotional techniques including representation of the institution in the broadcast media.
- **Collaborative skills**: Strength and experience in partnering with a variety of different institutions and groups; skill in forging coalitions with other influential groups in the community; political savvy in gaining the trust of elected officials; team-building talent in marshaling the support of boards, staff, and users; and results-oriented collaborations.
- **Technical skills**: Skill in recommending policies for effective use of computers, the Internet, and other, newer resources such as e-books. How to evaluate the impact of new information formats, how to train staff and the public in the latest hardware and software, and how to fund and prepare for the next generation of technology.
- **Customer service skills**: Listening to library users and potential users and seeking feedback.
- **Problem-solving ability**: Faced with challenges to Internet access, diminishing budgets, and an increasingly diverse service base, public library directors with a track record of tackling difficult issues will be sought.

- **Risk taking**: Integrity, courage, and a thick skin are required for the director, who must be increasingly innovative.
- **Self-renewal**: Astute candidates recognize that the demands of leadership require a personal plan for professional growth. Those who acknowledge this are likely to endure.

Analysis of announcements for library director positions demonstrates that library boards value experience with multicultural communities, knowledge of current and developing technologies, and understanding of the importance of community involvement, as well as experience working with an advisory board and community groups and elected officials. Figure 6.3 is a 2010 announcement from the Marion Public Library (Iowa) and is a representative example of a director position announcement. Library directors are expected to be leaders with strong interpersonal, communication, staff development, and collaborative skills.

Organization of the Public Library Staff

Public library staffing is structured in response to community needs. Libraries bridge traditional divisions between technical and public services positions by changing technologies, modify divisions through access to external databases, and reconfigure divisions depending on the local situation. For a directory of public library job descriptions, see Brumley (2005). The ALA accredits master's-level graduate programs that educate librarians using the 2008 *Standards for Accreditation* to serve as a mechanism for quality assessment and quality enhancement. "Library and Information Studies and Human Resource Utilization," policy 54.1 of the ALA, provides guidance as to education and articulation of positions within libraries.

Issues relating to interests of public library support staff are addressed by the ALA within the Library Support Staff Interests Round Table (http://www.ala.org/ala/ mgrps/ rts/lssirt/index.cfm). The Library Support Staff Certification Program began in 2010—a national certification program that allows library support staff to demonstrate their competencies and be certified by the ALA (ALA-APA, 2010).

While announcements for public library employment still reflect the need for positions that are managerial, including branch administration, public service (information services, readers' advisory services, children's and youth services), or technical service (cataloging, acquisitions, network systems), in substance, the on-the-job expectations are more often for a convergence of administrative, public service, and technical infrastructure. New positions such as digital services librarian, web librarian, and electronic resources librarians have emerged in the 2000s in the Internet era. See Figure 6.4 (pp. 142–143) for examples of public library job postings in 2009–2010.

Figure 6.3. Library Director Job Announcement, Marion (IA) Public Library

Library Director

Marion (IA) Public Library

One of Iowa's Great Places needs a new Library Director! The Board of Trustees of the Marion Public Library—serving a city population of over 33,000 (874,000 annual circulation) — seeks an innovative and creative library director. The library is a partner in the Metro Library Network along with the Cedar Rapids and Hiawatha public libraries. The network serves a metro area population of over 256,000.

The Marion community is undertaking a major redevelopment project that will reinvigorate its historical uptown. The library is in the heart of this district. Marion is adjacent to Cedar Rapids and has a friendly small-town feel with the advantages of a large metro area.

With a dedicated staff (18 FTE) and Library Board, a $1.6 million annual budget, and successful Library Foundation and Friends groups—the Marion Library has an exciting future.

Responsibilities. The Director of the Marion Public Library reports to a nine-member Library Board of Trustees—appointed by the Mayor and confirmed by City Council—and partners with city officials to achieve the Library's mission, goals, and objectives within the context of community needs and priorities. Overall responsibilities include fostering effective internal and external communications with community, city officials, the Library Board, the Library Foundation, Friends of the Library, and library staff. The Director proposes recommendations and implements Board policies and operating procedures. The Director develops the library staff as a strong team through leadership, mentoring, and providing staff development opportunities; provides sound fiscal management while seeking additional revenue sources (including working with the Library Foundation); and explores and develops collaborative relationships with a variety of local, regional, and statewide organizations and agencies. Additional information about the library and the city can be found at http://marionpubliclibrary.org and http://cityofmarion.org.

Minimum Qualifications. A master's degree in library science from an ALA-accredited program and a minimum of 6 years progressively responsible public library experience (including at least 4 years in a supervisory and/or administrative position), strong personnel management skills, grant writing experience, strong communication and public relations skills, and experience with/knowledge of computer technologies. Essential attributes include energy and enthusiasm, personal integrity and excellent interpersonal skills, thorough knowledge of financial management and budgeting, collaboration and consensus-building skills, sensitivity, flexibility, creativity, and a solid understanding of trends and "best practices" in the library and information technology fields. Experience reporting to a governing board is highly desirable.

Compensation. Starting salary range of $75,852–$107,085 (dependent upon experience and qualifications) with excellent benefits.

Apply via e-mail with a cover letter and your résumé as attachments by November 30, 2010. Please include three professional references.

The Marion Public Library is a community gathering place that offers everyone easy access to information, recreation, and cultural resources. The library provides programs and services in an atmosphere that is friendly and comfortable. Equal Opportunity Employer.

Source: Posted October 4, 2010. Reprinted with permission from the Marion Public Library.

There are no national standards that govern staffing patterns for public libraries. The Workload Measures and Staffing Patterns Committee of the Public Library Association conducted a survey in 2003 and determined "if excellence is defined by meeting locally identified and defined needs, then there can be no 'one size fits all' answers or externally defined standards" (Goodrich, 2005: 280).

Figure 6.4. Sampling of Library Position Announcements

Assistant Director of Community Library Services
Queens (NY) Library

If you have the ability to set and achieve goals, lead by example, inspire managers and staff, promote enthusiastic teamwork, and have fun doing it, then this position is for you!

Queens Library is currently seeking an Assistant Director of Community Library Services to lead and develop 20 community libraries (branches). If you have what it takes to be part of our team, let us know about yourself.

As a part of our team, you will develop and implement service goals to deliver quality public library services. Plan, organize, direct, evaluate, and continuously improve the individual effectiveness of services and programs for community libraries; direct the professional development, evaluation, and use of staff and other resources to ensure that customers receive high-quality responsive customer service. Coach, supervise, and manage performance for 20 community library managers.

An MLS from an ALA-accredited library school and eligibility for NYS librarian certification required. A minimum of five years of demonstrated library management experience required. At least two years experience with responsibility for multiple public libraries highly preferred. Experience in a large library system, consortium, or state library preferred. Demonstrated experience in collection development required. Ability to set and effectively manage performance. Excellent communication skills (written and oral) with exceptional interpersonal skills and creative problem-solving ability required. Must have a valid driver's license. At least 50 percent of time will be spent in the field—this is not a desk job. EOE.

Senior Librarian—Family and Youth Services
Newport News (VA) Public Library System

The City of Newport News, located in the Virginia Tidewater area, is seeking a Librarian for Family and Youth Services. Under the direction of the branch manager and with the direction/guidance of the Family and Youth Services Coordinator, this position works collaboratively with other branch staff and as part of the Library System's Youth Services Committee to plan and conduct children's and young adult programs throughout the year and for special events. The Librarian will work with families and children from preschool through young adult. Applicants should be knowledgeable of youth literature and collection development philosophies and methods. Responsibilities include planning and implementing branch-specific preschool, children, young adult, and family programs. Candidates should have knowledge of and display a strong interest in working with children and teenagers as well as knowledge of computers and information services.

Candidates must be creative, motivated, and have a sense of humor. Newport News Public Library System is recognized for our youth leadership programs. We wish to continue to deliver excellence in services to children and teens by giving them the tools they need to achieve success in education and to think creatively and independently. We are dedicated to giving our coworkers the latitude to grow and make the best use of their talents within a highly developed team environment.

REQUIREMENTS: Requires a Master's Degree in Library Science from an accredited ALA library school and 3–5 years experience as a professional librarian with some lead or supervisory experience or an equivalent combination of education and experience. Requires certification as a professional librarian by the Library of Virginia within 6 months of employment.

Web Programmer
Kansas City (KS) Public Library

Under the supervision of the Digital and Web Manager, the Web Programmer provides support to the Kansas City Public Library by performing a variety of technical tasks in the development and maintenance of the Library's web presence. Responsibilities include applying advanced technologies to support new models for integrating physical and digital collections and services; designing, coding, and testing web applications using PHP, Drupal customization, XML/XSLT, JavaScript, and Linux/Apache; participating in after-hours and

(Continued)

Figure 6.4 *(Continued)*

weekend on-call support rotation cycle; and assisting in training Library employees in the use of web development tools; responding to voice calls and e-mail requests and logging requests into tracking system; and communicating status information to customers. Minimum qualifications include a BS/BA degree; 3 or more years experience in website development, preferably with open source technologies, or equivalent combination of education and related experience. Must have direct experience with PHP and Linux/Apache and working knowledge of the Drupal content management system; ability to build content entry forms; excellent verbal and written communication skills; outstanding customer service skills; ability to pay attention to detail; and excellent time management and organizational skills. The successful candidate will be a self-motivated, independent worker and strong team player with the ability to effectively handle multiple tasks and the ability to learn new skills and systems quickly.

Full-Time Shared Youth Services Librarian
Cedar Falls and Waterloo (IA) Public Libraries

Position is salaried and supervises the Youth Departments at both the Cedar Falls and Waterloo Public Libraries. Some evening and weekend work required. Qualifications include understanding of child/adolescent development; strong knowledge of children's literature and print/electronic reference sources appropriate for children; familiarity with children's electronic media and general technology; strong written and oral communication skills; the ability to plan and develop children's programming relevant to two diverse communities; the ability to lead two departments with humor, integrity, fairness, and support a team-oriented constantly changing environment; possess a philosophy of youth services, and a management philosophy/model; possess grant-writing skills, the courage to try new approaches, energy, and creativity; have knowledge of assessment and determining effective outreach venues. Spanish language preferred, but not required. ALA-accredited master's or comparable postgraduate degree required. Four years of increasingly responsible experience in a library setting, including two years of lead or supervisory experience. Position also requires the physical condition necessary for standing, sitting, or walking for prolonged periods of time; adequate speech, hearing, and eyesight required; may be required to lift moderately heavy objects. Post offer, pre-employment physical and drug screen required.

Deputy County Librarian
Alameda County (CA) Library

The Alameda County Library is a progressive department recognized by the community and professional organizations as a leader in innovation, service delivery, and employee excellence. The Deputy County Librarian is a key member of the Library's executive staff, responsible for the effective daily operation of the Library. The ideal candidate will have the ability to develop, refine, and drive the realization of initiatives in collaboration with key stakeholders while facilitating innovative approaches to the implementation and acceptance of change in order to achieve the vision of the department. The Deputy County Librarian is the highest management level position reporting to the County Librarian and is responsible for the effective daily operation of the Library.

In this position, the Principal Librarian for Branch Services and the Principal Librarian for Collections and Community Relations will be accountable to the Deputy County Librarian. The Deputy will also supervise the Coordinators for Children's, Teen, and Older Adult Services. The Deputy is a key member of the Executive Council and serves as the County Librarian in her absence.

Established in 1910, the Library has a staff of 218 and a budget of $24 million. The County Library provides service to the cities of Albany, Dublin, Fremont, Newark, and Union City. The unincorporated area is served by the Castro Valley and San Lorenzo libraries. Outreach services are provided through the Bookmobile, the Literacy Program, Senior Outreach, as well as service to the County Jails and juvenile facilities.

Note: These announcements were provided on employer websites and submitted to joblines in 2009–2010. The examples here are intended to demonstrate the variety of positions available. All are reprinted with permission of the respective libraries.

National public library statistics show that in 2008 (Figure 6.5) libraries averaged 12.31 FTE (full-time equivalent staff) per 25,000 population. When the number of staff is reviewed by state, Ohio ranks at the top with 21.24 and Tennessee at the bottom with 7.56.

Figure 6.5. Number of Paid Full-Time Equivalent (FTE) Staff and Paid FTE Librarians per 25,000 Population of Public Libraries by State: Fiscal Year 2008

State	Ranking	Total paid FTE staff per 25,000 population[1]	State	Ranking	Total paid FTE staff per 25,000 population[1]
Total	†	12.31	Total	†	4.06
Ohio	1	21.24	Kansas	1	9.87
Wyoming	2	20.85	New Hampshire	2	8.80
Indiana	3	20.07	Wyoming	3	8.43
Kansas	4	19.36	Vermont	4	8.02
District of Columbia[2]	5	18.92	Iowa	5	7.85
Illinois	6	18.03	Connecticut	6	7.41
New York	7	17.47	Maine	7	7.12
Connecticut	8	17.17	Nebraska	8	6.91
New Hampshire	9	16.32	Massachusetts	9	6.75
Maryland	10	15.63	Indiana	10	6.29
Nebraska	11	15.61	Ohio	11	6.25
New Jersey	12	15.60	Kentucky	12	6.17
Missouri	13	15.52	Illinois	13	6.07
Colorado	14	14.95	Maryland	14	5.86
Massachusetts	15	14.80	New York	15	5.75
Rhode Island	16	14.76	Rhode Island	16	5.66
Maine	17	14.74	District of Columbia[2]	17	5.24
Washington	18	14.10	Oklahoma	18	5.18
Iowa	19	14.10	Montana	19	5.11
Wisconsin	20	13.53	South Dakota	20	5.09
Vermont	21	13.48	Wisconsin	21	5.08
Virginia	22	13.08	North Dakota	22	5.07
Idaho	23	13.04	Mississippi	23	5.02
Louisiana	24	13.01	Michigan	24	4.91
Michigan	25	12.96	Louisiana	25	4.81
South Dakota	26	12.88	New Mexico	26	4.77
Oregon	27	12.80	Colorado	27	4.69
Kentucky	28	12.56	West Virginia	28	4.42
New Mexico	29	11.64	New Jersey	29	4.39
Alaska	30	11.60	Alaska	30	4.02
Minnesota	31	11.28	Delaware	31	3.92
Utah	32	11.07	Alabama	32	3.91
Hawaii[3]	33	10.82	Minnesota	33	3.84
Oklahoma	34	10.77	Missouri	34	3.77
South Carolina	35	10.62	Oregon	35	3.73
Mississippi	36	10.57	Idaho	36	3.70
Pennsylvania	37	10.34	Hawaii[3]	37	3.39
Delaware	38	10.25	Virginia	38	3.37

(Continued)

Figure 6.5 *(Continued)*					
State	Ranking	Total paid FTE staff per 25,000 population[1]	State	Ranking	Total paid FTE staff per 25,000 population[1]
Alabama	39	9.89	Washington	39	3.36
Arkansas	40	9.78	South Carolina	40	3.29
Florida	41	9.72	Pennsylvania	41	3.19
North Dakota	42	9.71	Utah	42	3.14
Montana	43	9.63	Arkansas	43	2.92
Nevada	44	9.09	Florida	44	2.86
North Carolina	45	8.77	Texas	45	2.55
Arizona	46	8.74	Arizona	46	2.48
West Virginia	47	8.65	California	47	2.38
California	48	8.36	Tennessee	48	2.31
Georgia	49	8.34	Nevada	49	2.14
Texas	50	8.16	North Carolina	50	2.05
Tennessee	51	7.56	Georgia	51	1.90

† Not applicable.
[1] Per 25,000 population is based on the total unduplicated population of legal service areas.
[2] The District of Columbia, while not a state, is included in the state rankings. Special care should be used in comparing its data to state data.
[3] Caution should be used in making comparisons with the state of Hawaii, as Hawaii reports only one public library for the entire state.
SOURCE: Institute of Museum and Library Services, Survey of Public Libraries in the United States, Fiscal Year 2008.

Source: U.S. Institute of Museum and Library Services. 2010. *Public Libraries Survey: Fiscal Year 2008*. Washington, DC: U.S. Institute of Museum and Library Services, p. 163. http://harvester.census.gov/imls/pubs/Publications/pls2008.pdf.

Some state standards include staffing recommendations. Wisconsin uses population served as a basis for defining staff size. For a population of 25,000 using the Wisconsin algorithm, the public library staff would be 15 for basic service and 25 for excellent service. Illinois has a similar approach, suggesting population as a basis for staff size. The percentage of public library staff with degrees accredited by the ALA is 22.4 percent nationwide. Libraries serving populations of 1 million or more report that 25.6 percent of staff hold the ALA-accredited degree, but that percentage decreases by population size. At populations served from 10,000 to 24,999, 21.4 percent of staff have the ALA-accredited degree (U.S. IMLS, 2010: 90). Figure 6.6 (pp. 146–147) displays the number of FTE librarians with the ALA-accredited degree per 25,000 population.

There is a wide variation of staffing patterns throughout the United States. Figure 6.7 (pp. 148–150) shows that the states with the highest percentage of staff with the ALA-accredited degree are Rhode Island (34 percent), Hawaii (31.3 percent), and Connecticut (31.1 percent). The states with the lowest percentages are Idaho (10.5 percent), Wyoming (10.1 percent), and Mississippi (8.6 percent).

The variation in staffing—both total FTE and percentage that hold the ALA-accredited degree—is the result of different states' long-term approaches to lifelong learning and education. The Campaign for America's Librarians initiated by Mitch Freedman (2003) developed a toolkit to assist libraries in demonstrating the value of library staff to the community (ALA-APA, 2007).

Figure 6.6. Number of Paid Full-Time Equivalent (FTE) Librarians with an "ALA-MLS" and Other Paid FTE Staff of Public Libraries per 25,000 Population, by State: Fiscal Year 2008

State	Ranking	Paid FTE librarians with "ALA-MLS" per 25,000 population[1]	State	Ranking	Other paid FTE staff per 25,000 population[1]
Total	†	2.76	Total	†	8.25
Connecticut	1	5.34	Ohio	1	14.98
District of Columbia[2]	2	5.24	Indiana	2	13.78
Rhode Island	3	5.02	District of Columbia[2]	3	13.68
New York	4	4.90	Wyoming	4	12.42
Ohio	5	4.46	Illinois	5	11.96
Massachusetts	6	4.40	Missouri	6	11.75
New Jersey	7	4.36	New York	7	11.72
Indiana	8	3.97	New Jersey	8	11.21
Illinois	9	3.75	Washington	9	10.73
New Hampshire	10	3.67	Colorado	10	10.27
Hawaii[3]	11	3.39	Maryland	11	9.77
Michigan	12	3.39	Connecticut	12	9.76
Maine	13	3.31	Virginia	13	9.71
Washington	14	3.22	Kansas	14	9.49
Colorado	15	3.04	Idaho	15	9.34
Maryland	16	3.03	Rhode Island	16	9.10
Oregon	17	2.95	Oregon	17	9.07
Virginia	18	2.95	Nebraska	18	8.70
Kansas	19	2.90	Wisconsin	19	8.46
Wisconsin	20	2.83	Louisiana	20	8.20
Minnesota	21	2.59	Massachusetts	21	8.05
South Carolina	22	2.54	Michigan	22	8.05
Florida	23	2.45	Utah	23	7.93
New Mexico	24	2.34	South Dakota	24	7.78
Pennsylvania	25	2.26	Maine	25	7.62
Alaska	26	2.23	Alaska	26	7.57
California	27	2.19	New Hampshire	27	7.52
Nebraska	28	2.15	Minnesota	28	7.44
Wyoming	29	2.11	Hawaii[3]	29	7.43
Vermont	30	2.11	South Carolina	30	7.33
Louisiana	31	2.05	Pennsylvania	31	7.15
Iowa	32	1.99	Nevada	32	6.95
Arizona	33	1.97	New Mexico	33	6.87
North Carolina	34	1.96	Florida	34	6.86
Missouri	35	1.95	Arkansas	35	6.85
Delaware	36	1.91	North Carolina	36	6.72
Oklahoma	37	1.90	Georgia	37	6.44
Texas	38	1.86	Kentucky	38	6.39

(Continued)

Figure 6.6 *(Continued)*					
State	Ranking	Paid FTE librarians with "ALA-MLS" per 25,000 population[1]	State	Ranking	Other paid FTE staff per 25,000 population[1]
Georgia	39	1.84	Delaware	39	6.33
Kentucky	40	1.81	Arizona	40	6.26
Utah	41	1.67	Iowa	41	6.24
South Dakota	42	1.65	California	42	6.00
Alabama	43	1.63	Alabama	43	5.99
Nevada	44	1.62	Texas	44	5.61
North Dakota	45	1.55	Oklahoma	45	5.59
Montana	46	1.39	Mississippi	46	5.55
Idaho	47	1.37	Vermont	47	5.45
West Virginia	48	1.31	Tennessee	48	5.24
Tennessee	49	1.28	North Dakota	49	4.64
Arkansas	50	1.09	Montana	50	4.53
Mississippi	51	0.91	West Virginia	51	4.24

† Not applicable.
[1] An "ALA-MLS" is a master's degree from a program of library and information studies accredited by the American Library Association. Per 25,000 population is based on the total unduplicated population of legal service areas.
[2] The District of Columbia, while not a state, is included in the state rankings. Special care should be used in comparing its data to state data.
[3] Caution should be used in making comparisons with the state of Hawaii, as Hawaii reports only one public library for the entire state.
SOURCE: Institute of Museum and Library Services, Survey of Public Libraries in the United States, Fiscal Year 2008.

Source: U.S. Institute of Museum and Library Services. 2010. *Public Libraries Survey: Fiscal Year 2008.* Washington, DC: U.S. Institute of Museum and Library Services, p. 164. http://harvester.census.gov/imls/pubs/Publications/pls2008.pdf.

Today the "results model" is the mechanism recommended by the Public Library Association (PLA) to develop staffing patterns, as outlined in *Managing for Results* (Nelson, Altman, and Mayo, 2000). The model is tied to the integrated approach to planning and resource allocation developed by PLA. Staff is viewed as a resource to be used as efficiently and effectively as possible and engaged in activities that are most important to a library's mission, goals, and objectives. The aspects of staffing considered in the results model are:

1. identifying activities and when and where they will be performed;
2. identifying abilities needed to accomplish activities;
3. determining the number of staff in relation to patron use and staff workload;
4. understanding how staff currently use their time; and
5. determining how to find staff to accomplish the library's priorities.

To accomplish these actions the book provides work forms, which assist in gathering data to analyze the number and classification of staff required to achieve the li-

Figure 6.7. Number of Paid Full-Time Equivalent (FTE) Staff in Public Libraries, by Type of Position; Percentage of Total Librarians and Total Staff with "ALA-MLS" Degrees; and Number of Libraries with "ALA-MLS" Librarians, by State: Fiscal Year 2008

State	Number of public libraries	Total		Paid FTE staff[4]						Percentage of total FTE librarians with "ALA-MLS"	Percentage of total FTE staff with "ALA-MLS"	Number of public libraries with "ALA-MLS" librarians
				Librarians		Librarians with "ALA-MLS"[2]		Other				
		Total	Response rate[3]	Total	Response rate[3]	Total	Response rate[3]	Total	Response rate[3]			
Total	9,221	145,243.5	98.1	47,925.6	98.1	32,561.9	98.1	97,317.9	98.1	67.9	22.4	4,463
Alabama	210	1,756.4	100.0	694.0	100.0	288.9	100.0	1,062.4	100.0	41.6	16.4	75
Alaska	86	315.3	100.0	109.4	100.0	60.5	100.0	205.9	100.0	55.3	19.2	19
Arizona	86	2,268.3	95.3	644.6	95.3	512.3	95.3	1,623.7	95.3	79.5	22.6	43
Arkansas	51	1,038.8	96.1	310.7	98.0	115.6	98.0	728.2	96.1	37.2	11.1	35
California	181	12,725.2	98.9	3,592.7	98.9	3,336.4	98.9	9,132.5	98.9	92.9	26.2	170
Colorado	115	2,907.8	100.0	911.8	100.0	590.8	99.1	1,996.0	100.0	64.8	20.3	66
Connecticut	195	2,411.4	92.8	1,041.2	92.8	749.8	92.8	1,370.2	92.8	72.0	31.1	155
Delaware	21	323.8	100.0	123.9	100.0	60.2	81.0	199.9	100.0	48.6	18.6	12
District of Columbia	1	445.3	100.0	123.3	100.0	123.3	100.0	322.0	100.0	100.0	27.7	1
Florida	80	7,303.0	95.0	2,148.0	96.3	1,836.7	96.3	5,155.0	95.0	85.5	25.1	76
Georgia	59	3,108.1	100.0	708.2	100.0	687.6	100.0	2,399.9	100.0	97.1	22.1	59
Hawaii	1	555.6	100.0	174.0	100.0	174.0	100.0	381.6	100.0	100.0	31.3	1
Idaho	104	694.9	98.1	197.2	98.1	73.1	98.1	497.7	98.1	37.1	10.5	28
Illinois	634	8,427.1	98.7	2,838.31	98.7	1,751.4	98.7	5,588.8	98.7	61.7	20.8	348
Indiana	238	4,577.2	100.0	1,434.4	100.0	905.5	100.0	3,142.8	100.0	63.1	19.8	141
Iowa	539	1,671.4	96.7	930.9	96.7	236.4	100.0	740.5	96.7	25.4	14.1	80
Kansas	327	1,831.4	98.8	933.5	98.5	274.1	98.5	897.8	98.5	29.4	15.0	55
Kentucky	116	2,112.5	100.0	1,037.2	100.0	305.2	100.0	1,075.3	100.0	29.4	14.4	43
Louisiana	68	2,296.2	100.0	849.2	100.0	361.9	100.0	1,447.0	100.0	42.6	15.8	53
Maine	272	714.9	95.6	345.3	95.6	160.4	95.6	369.6	95.6	46.4	22.4	91

(Continued)

Figure 6.7 (Continued)

State	Number of public libraries	Paid FTE staff[4] Total — Total	Total — Response rate[3]	Librarians — Total	Librarians — Response rate[3]	Librarians with "ALA-MLS"[2] — Total	Librarians with "ALA-MLS"[2] — Response rate[3]	Other — Total	Other — Response rate[3]	Percentage of total FTE librarians with "ALA-MLS"	Percentage of total FTE staff with "ALA-MLS"	Number of public libraries with "ALA-MLS" librarians
Maryland	24	3,502.4	100.0	1,313.2	100.0	678.2	100.0	2,189.2	100.0	51.6	19.4	24
Massachusetts	370	3,818.2	99.2	1,741.2	99.2	1,135.0	99.2	2,077.0	99.2	65.2	29.7	262
Michigan	384	5,147.4	99.5	1,950.4	99.5	1,345.7	99.5	3,197.0	99.5	69.0	26.1	220
Minnesota	138	2,375.0	100.0	808.4	100.0	546.1	100.0	1,566.6	100.0	67.6	23.0	60
Mississippi	50	1,242.0	100.0	590.0	100.0	107.0	100.0	652.0	100.0	18.1	8.6	40
Missouri	152	3,179.7	100.0	772.7	100.0	399.1	100.0	2,407.0	100.0	51.7	12.6	57
Montana	80	347.0	100.0	183.9	100.0	50.1	100.0	163.1	100.0	27.3	14.4	22
Nebraska	270	811.1	82.2	359.3	82.2	111.5	82.2	451.9	82.2	31.0	13.7	29
Nevada	22	996.1	100.0	235.0	100.0	178.0	100.0	761.1	100.0	75.7	17.9	11
New Hampshire	231	855.8	97.4	461.5	97.4	192.3	94.8	394.3	97.4	41.7	22.5	95
New Jersey[4]	303	5,200.5	92.7	1,464.0	92.7	1,453.0	92.7	3,736.5	92.7	99.2	27.9	250
New Mexico	91	723.9	100.0	296.8	100.0	145.3	100.0	427.1	100.0	48.9	20.1	26
New York	755	13,228.4	100.0	4,355.0	100.0	3,705.5	100.0	8,873.4	100.0	85.1	28.0	407
North Carolina	77	3,181.8	100.0	745.0	100.0	709.8	100.0	2,436.8	100.0	95.3	22.3	75
North Dakota	81	221.6	100.0	115.7	100.0	35.5	95.1	105.9	100.0	30.6	16.0	11
Ohio	251	9,778.3	100.0	2,879.9	100.0	2,051.7	100.0	6,898.4	100.0	71.2	21.0	190
Oklahoma	115	1,283.4	100.0	616.8	100.0	226.5	100.0	666.5	100.0	36.7	17.6	35
Oregon	126	1,715.9	100.0	499.7	100.0	395.6	100.0	1,216.1	100.0	79.2	23.1	72
Pennsylvania	457	4,950.2	99.6	1,525.6	99.6	1,083.9	99.6	3,424.6	99.6	71.0	21.9	261
Rhode Island	48	624.6	97.9	239.4	97.9	212.6	97.9	385.2	97.9	88.8	34.0	47
South Carolina	42	1,875.4	100.0	581.6	100.0	448.5	100.0	1,293.8	100.0	77.1	23.9	41
South Dakota	114	359.9	92.1	142.3	92.1	46.0	87.7	217.6	92.1	32.3	12.8	19
Tennessee	187	1,838.5	100.0	562.5	100.0	312.1	100.0	1,276.0	100.0	55.5	17.0	42

(Continued)

Figure 6.7. Number of Paid Full-Time Equivalent (FTE) Staff in Public Libraries, by Type of Position; Percentage of Total Librarians and Total Staff with "ALA-MLS" Degrees; and Number of Libraries with "ALA-MLS" Librarians, by State: Fiscal Year 2008 (Continued)

State	Number of public libraries	Paid FTE staff[4]								Percentage of total FTE librarians with "ALA-MLS"	Percentage of total FTE staff with "ALA-MLS"	Number of public libraries with "ALA-MLS" librarians
		Total		Librarians		Librarians with "ALA-MLS"[2]		Other				
		Total	Response rate[3]	Total	Response rate[3]	Total	Response rate[3]	Total	Response rate[3]			
Texas	561	7,267.2	100.0	2,273.6	100.0	1,654.2	99.8	4,993.6	100.0	72.8	22.8	209
Utah	69	1,158.3	98.6	328.3	98.6	174.7	98.6	830.1	98.6	53.2	15.1	20
Vermont	183	325.5	93.4	193.8	94.0	50.9	94.0	131.7	93.4	26.3	15.6	41
Virginia	91	3,975.8	100.0	1,025.1	100.0	895.6	100.0	2,950.7	100.0	87.4	22.5	83
Washington	64	3,641.3	100.0	869.2	100.0	831.0	100.0	2,772.1	100.0	95.6	22.8	47
West Virginia	97	626.0	100.0	319.4	100.0	94.6	100.0	306.6	100.0	29.6	15.1	36
Wisconsin	381	3,071.9	100.0	1,152.3	100.0	642.7	100.0	1,919.7	100.0	55.8	20.9	167
Wyoming	23	436.1	100.0	176.3	100.0	44.1	100.0	259.8	100.0	25.0	10.1	13
Outlying areas												
Guam	1	32.0	100.0	0	100.0	0	100.0	32.0	100.0	0	0	0
Puerto Rico	35	301.0	100.0	84.0	85.7	18.0	100.0	217.0	100.0	21.4	6.0	12

[1] Paid staff were reported in FTEs. To ensure comparable data, 40 hours was set as the measure of full-time employment (for example, 60 hours per week of part-time work by employees in a staff category divided by the 40-hour measure equals 1.50 FTEs). FTE data were reported to two decimal places but rounded to one decimal place in the table. Paid staff is one of four criteria used in the Public Libraries Survey to define a public library. Some states report public libraries that do not have paid staff but meet the definition of a public library under state law.

[2] "ALA-MLS": A Master's degree from a graduate library education program accredited by the American Library Association (ALA). Librarians with an "ALA-MLS" are also included in total librarians.

[3] Response rate is calculated as the number of libraries that reported the item, divided by the total number of libraries in the survey frame. For item(s) with response rates below 100 percent, data for nonrespondents were imputed and are included in the table. Data were not imputed for the outlying areas.

[4] The number of "certified" librarians was reported in the Librarians with "ALA-MLS" column, as the state does not distinguish between Master's degrees from programs of library and information studies accredited by the American Library Association (ALA) and all other Master's degrees in library science awarded by institutions of higher education. Nationally, 7162 Master's degrees in library science were awarded by institutions of higher education in 2007-08 (Digest of Education Statistics, 2009, [NCES 2010013], Table 272. U.S. Department of Education, National Center for Education Statistics. Washington, DC: Government Printing Office.) Data for Master's degrees from ALA-accredited programs were not available yet. However, the 4-year average was 87 percent, which is an estimated 5,887 graduates in 2006–2007. (ALA, Office for Human Resource Development and Recruitment, Degrees and Certificates Awarded by U.S. Library and Information Studies Education Programs).

NOTE: Detail may not sum to totals because of rounding. Data were not reported by the following outlying areas (American Samoa, Northern Marianas, and Virgin islands). Missing data were not imputed for nonresponding outlying areas.

SOURCE: Institute of Museum and Library Services, Survey of Public Libraries in the United States, Fiscal Year 2008.

Source: U.S. Institute of Museum and Library Services. 2010. *Public Libraries Survey: Fiscal Year 2008.* Washington, DC: U.S. Institute of Museum and Library Services, pp. 87–88. http://harvester.census.gov/imls/pubs/Publications/pls2008.pdf.

brary's goals and objectives. The companion volume, *Staffing for Results* (Mayo and Goodrich, 2002) begins at the activity level—a set of tasks that results in a measurable output of things done or services delivered—and supports analysis of work at the task level—the series of sequential actions that converts inputs to outputs. By applying numeric analysis for diagnostic purposes and prescriptive analyses to determine direction reasonable adjustments in assignments can be made.

Broad-Based Issues Relating to Staffing

Recruitment

Careers in public librarianship are advanced by the PLA and the ALA through its service LibraryCareers.org (http://www.ala.org/ala/educationcareers/careers/). The need for funds to educate new librarians led to over $100 million dollars in grants through the Laura Bush 21st Century Librarian program, funded by the Institute of Museum and Library Services (IMLS) beginning in 2003 and continuing at this writing in 2010 (Oder, 2008). The program recognizes the key role of libraries and librarians in maintaining the flow of information critical to support formal education and to create a climate for democratic discourse. Support to educate the next generation of librarians has focused on public librarians, certification of rural librarians, recruitment of people of color, and youth services librarians. In 2009–2010 the Laura Bush 21st Century Librarian grants included the following:

- "Preparing Librarians to Serve Diverse Communities Along Our Nation's Borders" (San Jose State University)
- "Sharing Success: Training Education Leaders for Youth Services Librarianship" (University of Illinois)
- "Librarians Build Communities" program, which will prepare 45 students to be public librarians and provide them with expertise in community building (Valdosta State University and Georgia Public Library Service)
- "Project Recovery," for libraries in southern Louisiana that continue to experience staffing shortages as a result of the damage caused to local communities by Hurricane Katrina (Louisiana State University)
- Accessible Libraries for All (ALFA) Universal Information Access (University of Alabama, University of South Florida, the Alabama Public Library Service, and the Florida Department of Education Bureau of Braille and Talking Book Library Services) (U.S. IMLS, 2009)

Public librarians and their associations continue to work to broaden the diversity of staff at all levels to reflect the diversity of the U.S. population. Scholarships and mentoring for people of color are provided by the ethnic affiliate organizations of the ALA:

- American Indian Library Association (AILA, http://www.ailanet.org/)
- Asian/Pacific American Librarians Association (APALA, http://www.apalaweb .org)
- Black Caucus of the ALA (BCALA, http://www.bcala.org)
- Chinese American Librarians Association (CALA, http://www.cala-web.org)
- REFORMA—National Association to Promote Library and Information Services to Latinos and the Spanish-Speaking (http://www.reforma.org)

The ALA Office for Diversity oversees the Spectrum scholarship program to recruit new librarians of color (http://ala.org/diversity). The Spectrum Scholarship Program was established by the ALA in 1997 to address the issue of underrepresentation of critically needed ethnic librarians within the profession while serving as a model for ways to bring attention to larger diversity issues in the future (Hill, 2009). These efforts have yet to provide a profession-wide profile that reflects the changing U.S. population at large, but have reversed the sentiment that diversity issues have been deferred (Roy, 2006).

Staff Development, Continuing Education, ALA-APA, and Certification

> After January 1, 2010, individuals certified as public librarians in New York State must be able to demonstrate completion of continuing education and training equal to or greater than 60 hours within each five-year period to maintain their certification. (New York State Library, 2010)

Continuing education is critical to the development of excellent library service. There are multiple options to fulfill the mandate for staff to develop their knowledge, skills, and abilities throughout their careers. The PLA provides ongoing staff development and continuing education for public librarians through national conferences, meetings, and publications. In 2010, for example, the national PLA conference held in Portland featured the programs Self-Directed Learning Environments, Technology Trends, Building Local History Collections, and Regional Library Cooperation.

Staff development and continuing education for library staff are central to positive performance. Opportunities are made available in a variety of formats, both internal and external to the employing library depending on the library's size and structure. Library-based staff development programs include curricula targeted to new knowledge or skills generally planned by a staff development committee. Ideally, a coordinator provides leadership. Other aspects of staff development include funding for travel to conferences such as the national PLA event mentioned above, state and regional meetings, staff institute days, continuing education events both face to face and virtual, and tuition reimbursement (Webjunction, 2009).

Education and continuous learning is one of the Key Action Areas of the ALA (http://www.ala.org/ala/aboutala/missionhistory/keyactionareas/index.cfm). The association fosters profession-wide commitment to continuing education and staff development through its Human Resource Development and Recruitment Office (http://www.ala.org/ala/aboutala/offices/hrdr/index.cfm) and its Learning Round Table (http://www.ala.org/ala/mgrps/rts/clenert/index.cfm).

The American Library Association-Allied Professional Association (ALA-APA) was authorized in 2001 as a companion organization to ALA to promote the mutual professional interests of librarians and other library workers. This new organization focuses on certification of individuals in specializations. The certification program for the certified public library manager is intended to provide managerial knowledge in budgeting and finance, building planning and maintenance, serving diverse populations, fundraising and grantsmanship, organization and personnel, politics and networking, marketing, and technology. The Library Support Staff Certification funded by an IMLS grant provides education for competency sets including foundations, technology, and teamwork (ALA-APA, 2010).

Certification can also take place at the state level. Many states have certification requirements for library directors and other staff. For example, Kentucky has a state board for the certification of librarians that requires directors, assistant directors, department heads, branch librarians, bookmobile librarians, and other full-time staff who provide information service to be examined (http://www.kdla.ky.gov/libsupport/certification.htm). The rationale behind the examination is the board's belief that librarians must increase their skills and knowledge to keep abreast of developments in the information age, and that effort enriches the individual librarian and promotes quality library service. State library agencies have different requirements regarding certification and, as one might expect, each state is different. See other examples of public librarian certification for Georgia (http://gla.georgialibraries.org/certification.htm), New York (http://www.nysl.nysed.gov/libdev/cert/), or Washington (http://www.secstate.wa.gov/library/libraries/training/certification.aspx).

Unions and Better Salaries and Working Conditions

Unions contribute to a stable, productive workforce—where workers have a say in improving their jobs. Library workers have organized in unions for better wages, working conditions, and benefits (McCook, 2010). Union members earn more money, have more benefits, and have more say about the best way to get work done. The historical paternalism of the library workplace has sometimes allowed libraries to keep salaries below market value, permitted movement of employees from locations at the will of the administration, and sustained a hierarchical workplace. Unions clarify work rules, working conditions, and salaries. In a *Public Libraries* forum, Cameron Johnson (2002) observed, "unions can help make libraries better by offering a collaborative model for employee relations that management might want to emulate. . . . Union leadership consists of grassroots workplace politics: talking to employees at all levels, building consensus, discussing, persuading, and acting democratically."

ALA has taken action to advocate for librarians' working conditions and pay within the ALA-APA, which provides direct support of comparable worth and pay equity initiatives, and other activities designed to improve the salaries and status of librarians and other library workers. Salary structure information to enable library workers to make a case for better pay is provided in the online publication *Advocating for Better Salaries and Pay Equity Toolkit* (ALA-APA, 2007). This instrument was developed as a project of the Campaign for America's Librarians, by the Better Salaries and Pay Equity for Library Workers Task Force, initiated by Mitch Freedman during his tenure as ALA president. Diane Fay (2008) has written in *Library Worklife* about the benefits of union membership for public library workers. The ALA has issued a statement in support of the Employee Free Choice Act (Sheketoff, 2009).

Volunteers

The United States has long fostered a culture of engagement and volunteering. The Corporation for National and Community Service (http://www.nationalservice.gov) was established in 1993 and has the goal to improve lives, strengthen communities, and foster civic engagement through service and volunteering. In this spirit, libraries actively solicit the support of volunteers for library operations. For instance, the Los Angeles Public Library (2011) states on its website: "Volunteering at the Los Angeles Public Library connects you with the world of literacy, cultural diversity, and learning. Rewarding opportunities exist at the Central Library and branch facilities. In all cases, excellent training is provided to ensure that your volunteer experience is both enjoyable and fruitful."

While many volunteers come to the library from organized Friends of the Library groups, library websites provide online applications for volunteers and report thousands of hours contributed to basic library services. A statewide study for Florida reported volunteers contributed time equivalent to 722 full-time staff (nearly 29,000 hours per week) serving in all areas of the state's public libraries—shelving books, checking material in and out, staffing reference and information desks, and providing behind-the-scenes support. In many libraries, coordinators are assigned to organize and make the best use of these community-minded volunteers (Driggers and Dumas, 2002). See Reed and Nawalinski (2008) for expanded ideas for Friends and volunteer actions.

The Seattle Public Library lists adult and teen volunteer opportunities (http://www .spl.org/default.asp?pageID=about_support_volunteering_opportunities). For adults: book groups, computers for English tutors, Talk Time volunteers to help patrons with English, computer instructors, homework helpers, Welcome Desk volunteers, and Center for the Book Volunteers. For teens, help librarians plan and host programs and events, including programs celebrating Teen Read Week, Banned Books Week, National Poetry Month, and African-American History Month; encourage children for summer reading; design posters.

The future of volunteerism by young adults in public libraries has been assessed by Bernier (2009), who observed that the degree of public value may frequently be underappreciated by libraries, supervisors, and administrators. He suggests that library staff may benefit from better volunteer administration skills and planning and points out that volunteering is a mechanism to more powerfully connect young people with their libraries and communities.

Perhaps the best way to define the potential of volunteers is in the words of John J. Roberts (2010: 6), an active public library volunteer in, Georgia.

> My life has been enriched and influenced by libraries, librarians, library staffs and, of course, books. . . . We realized the importance of our public libraries in serving communities in a multitude of ways. We joined The Friends of The Libraries of Towns County, hoping to help by volunteering to work on fundraising projects and perhaps repay in some measure for the years of support provided by the many libraries that have touched our lives.

References

American Library Association. "Library and Information Studies and Human Resource Utilization: Policy Statement." Policy 54.1. http://www.ala.org/ala/aboutala/governance/policymanual/index.cfm.

———. 2008. *Standards for Accreditation of Master's Programs in Library and Information Studies.* Chicago: American Library Association. http://www.ala.org/ala/educationcareers/education/accreditedprograms/standards/index.cfm.

American Library Association-Allied Professional Association. 2007. *Advocating for Better Salaries and Pay Equity Toolkit.* 3rd ed. Chicago: American Library Association-Allied Professional Association. http://www.ala-apa.org/toolkit.pdf.

————. 2010. Certification News. http://ala-apa.org/certification.

Ames, Kathyrn S., and Greg Heid. 2009. "The Role of the Library Board of Trustees in the Construction of a Public Library." *Georgia Library Quarterly* 46 (Winter): 9–14.

Applegate, Rachel, Paulette Gibbs, Catherine Sue Cowser, Jill Scarbrough. 2007. "Public Library Trustees: Characteristics and Educational Preferences." *Public Library Quarterly* 26 (October): 21–43.

Arns, Jennifer. 2007. "Challenges in Governance: The Leadership Characteristics and Behaviors Valued by Public Library Trustees in Times of Conflict and Contention." *Library Quarterly* 77: 287–310.

Bernier, Anthony. 2009. "Young Adult Volunteering in Public Libraries: Managerial Implications." *Library Leadership and Management* 23 (Summer): 133–139.

Brumley, Rebecca. 2005. *The Neal-Schuman Directory of Public Library Job Descriptions.* New York: Neal-Schuman.

Center on Budget and Policy Priorities. 2009. "New Fiscal Year Brings Continued Trouble for States Due to Economic Downturn." http://www.cbpp.org.

Driggers, Preston F., and Eileen Dumas. 2002. *Managing Library Volunteers: A Practical Toolkit.* Chicago: American Library Association.

Fay, Diane. 2008. "Joining a Union." *Library Worklife* 5 (July).

Freedman, Maurice (Mitch) J. 2003. "For the People Who Work in Libraries." *Library Journal* 128 (April 2): 46.

Garceau, Oliver. 1949. "The Governing Authority of the Public Library." In *The Public Library in the Political Process: A Report of the Public Library Inquiry*, 53–110. New York: Columbia University Press.

Gardyn, R. 2003. "Building Board Diversity." *The Chronicle of Philanthropy.* (December 11). http://philanthropy.com/free/articles/v16/i05/05002501.htm.

Glennon, Michael. 1997. "Developing and Passing a Bond Issue: A Trustee's View." *Public Libraries* 36 (January/February): 24–28.

Goodrich, Jeanne. 2005. "Staffing Public Libraries: Are There Models or Best Practices?" *Public Libraries* 44 (September/October): 277–281.

Hague, Rodger. 1999. "A Short History of the Stevens County Rural Library District." *Alki* 15 (July): 22–23.

Hill, Nanci Milone. 2009. "Across the Spectrum." *Public Libraries* 48 (March/April): 15.

Hopper, Lyn. 2008. *Georgia Public Library Trustee Manual.* http://www.georgialibraries.org/lib/publications/trusteemanual/.

Johnson, Cameron. 2002. "Professionalism, Not Paternalism." *Public Libraries* 41 (May/June): 139–140.

Kelley, H. Neil. 1999. "Portrait of the Illinois Trustee Community." *Illinois Libraries* 81 (Fall): 222–225.

Kreamer, Jean T. 1990. "The Library Trustee as a Library Activist." *Public Libraries* 29 (July/August): 220–223.

Lang, Shirley. 2008. "From the Other Side." *Public Libraries* 47 (September/October): 28–29.

Los Angeles Public Library. 2011. "Volunteer Opportunities Available at the Los Angeles Public Library." Accessed February 22. http://www.lapl.org/about/volunteer.html.

Mayo, Diane, and Jeanne Goodrich. 2002. *Staffing for Results*. Chicago: American Library Association.

McCook, Kathleen de la Peña. 2010. "Unions in Public and Academic Libraries." In *Encyclopedia of Library and Information*. London: Taylor and Rutledge.

Michigan Library Association, Trustee and Advocates Division. 2006. *Basic Training for Trustees*. http://www.mla.lib.mi.us/tad.

Miller, Ellen G., and Patricia H. Fisher. 2007. *Library Board: Strategic Guide*. Lanham, MD: Scarecrow Press.

Moore, Mary Y. 2009. *The Successful Library Trustee Handbook*. 2nd ed. Chicago: American Library Association.

Nelson, Sandra, Ellen Altman, and Diane Mayo. 2000. "Managing Your Library's Staff." In *Managing for Results: Effective Resource Allocation for Public Libraries*, 29–110. Chicago: American Library Association.

New York State Library. 2010. "Continuing Education for Public Librarian Certification." New York State Library. http://www.nysl.nysed.gov/libdev/cert/conted.htm.

Nichols, Jerry. 2010. *Handbook for Library Trustees of New York State*. Bellport, NY: Suffolk Cooperative Library System.

Oder, Norman. 2008. "IMLS: $20.3M for Recruitment." *Library Journal* 133 (August): 16.

Reed, Sally Gardner. 2009. "Amalgamating for Advocacy." *American Libraries* 40 (March): 34–36.

Reed, Sally Gardner, and Beth Nawalinski. 2008. *Even More Great Ideas for Libraries and Friends*. New York: Neal-Schuman.

Roberts, John J. 2010. "Volunteering with Friends Groups Is Rewarding Experience." *Georgia Library Quarterly* 47 (Winter): 6.

Roy, Loriene. 2006. *Bridging Boundaries to Create a New Workforce: A Survey of SPECTRUM Scholarship Recipients, 1998–2003*. Chicago: American Library Association.

Sager, Donald J. 2001. "Evolving Virtues: Public Library Administrative Skills." *Public Libraries* 40 (September/October): 268–272.

Sheketoff, Emily. 2009. "Employee Free Choice Act." *Progressive Librarian* 32 (Winter/Spring): 76.

Thomas, Mary Augusta. 2009. "Interview with Ginnie Cooper." *Library Leadership and Management* 23 (Fall): 177–178.

U.S. Institute of Museum and Library Services. 2009. "Laura Bush 21st Century Librarian Program: June 2009 Grant Recipients." http://www.imls.gov/news/2009/061709b_list.shtm.

———. 2010. *Public Libraries Survey: Fiscal Year 2008*. IMLS-2010–PLS-02. Washington, DC: Institute of Museum and Library Services. http://harvester.census.gov/imls/pubs/Publications/pls2008.pdf.

Webjunction. 2009. "Libraries as Learning Organizations." http://www.webjunction.org/learning-organization/-/articles/content/61714988.

Wisconsin Department of Public Instruction. 2009. *Trustee Essentials: A Handbook for Wisconsin Public Library Trustees*. http://dpi.state.wi.us/pld/handbook.html.

Wisconsin Public Library. 2010. *Wisconsin Public Library Standards*, Fifth Edition. Wisconsin Department of Public Instruction. http://dpi.wi.gov/pld/standard.html.

7
Structure and Infrastructure

I have always imagined that Paradise will be a kind of library.

—Jorge Luis Borges, "Poema de los Dones," from *El Hacedor*

The library is a beacon of hope.

—Cedar Rapids, Iowa, city councilor Monica Vernon
after the flood of 2008 (Berry, 2009)

This chapter considers the symbolism of the public library building. It summarizes the history of public library buildings in the United States, reviews the role of the Library Services and Construction Act (LSCA) in construction during the last third of the twentieth century, and outlines design standards including accessibility. The move from federal support of structures through LSCA to federal support for infrastructure through the Library Services and Technology Act affects all public libraries. The need for security and planning for disaster is addressed.

The Symbolism of the Public Library Building

In *The New Downtown Library*, Shannon Mattern (2007) investigates how libraries serve as multiuse public spaces, anchors in urban redevelopment, civic icons, and showcases of renowned architects. The public library building is an emblem of the past, a source of educational and cultural sustenance for the present, and a hopeful vision for the future. Public library buildings are at once a symbol of cultural heritage and a testimony to a shared community vision of the commons. The public library can be a factor in community sustainability and redevelopment. It is vital for those working in public libraries to understand the importance of the library to the community's sense of self-identity. Through its structure and infrastructure, the library is simultaneously a tangible representation of humanity's ideals and an active system for electronic access and communication. The library can be a public space that inspires, sustains, and anchors a community's educational and cultural self-perception.

In library systems with multiple branches, each branch can act as a neighborhood center responding over time to changes in the community or reflecting the community's heritage (Rivers, 2004). In Mount Prospect, Illinois, a Community Connections Center to serve immigrant communities was added as a branch (Blumenstein, 2010). The architecture of the Atkins Branch of the Shreve Memorial Library System in Caddo Parish, Louisiana reflects the nautical history of Shreveport (Duggar, 2009).

The Chicago Public Library, with more than 75 branches, reflects neighborhood diversity in architecture, as well as collections and services. The Rudy Lozano branch, housing the library's largest Spanish materials collection, features an Olmec pre-Columbian design and art by Latino artists. The involvement of people who will use the facility in the design of public library buildings provides a sense of shared ownership and has come to be an important aspect of community building. In *Better Together*, Putnam and Feldstein (2003) characterize the branches of the Chicago Public Library as "third places," neither work nor home, where people can spend time together. Their case study of the Near North Branch Library, which bridges the wealthy, mainly white Gold Coast and the African American Cabrini-Green community, details the library's role as the heartbeat of the community.

The framework for understanding the library as place has been studied in the context of the Seattle Public Library (see Figure 7.1; Fisher et al., 2007). In May 2004, the new Seattle Public Library, designed by Rem Koolhaas, opened. The building's angled, soaring architecture captures water views and cityscapes from every floor of

---

Excerpts from a Speech by Carnegie Corporation President Vartan Gregorian to the Kansas City Club

October 17, 2002

Libraries contain the heritage of humanity, the record of its triumphs and failures, its intellectual, scientific and artistic achievements and its collective memory. They are a source of knowledge, scholarship and wisdom. They are an institution, withal, where the left and the right, God and the Devil, are together classified and retained, in order to teach us what to emulate and what not to repeat.

But libraries are more than repositories of past human endeavor, they are instruments of civilization. They are a laboratory of human aspiration, a window to the future and a wellspring of action. They are a source of intellectual growth, and hope. In this land and everywhere on earth, they are a medium of progress, autonomy, empowerment, independence and self-determination. They have always provided—and I would suggest, always will provide—a place and space for imaginative recreation, for imaginative rebirth. That is because the library is a transcendent institution, being able to surpass the limitations of time and space. The library is an oasis, a place for reflection, for contemplation, for privacy, for the renewal of one's imagination and the development of one's mind.

Source: Gregorian, Vartan. 2002. "Libraries as Acts of Civic Renewal" (Speech). Kansas City Public Library. http://www.kclibrary.org/support/central/index.cfm (no longer available). Used with permission of Carnegie Corporation of New York.

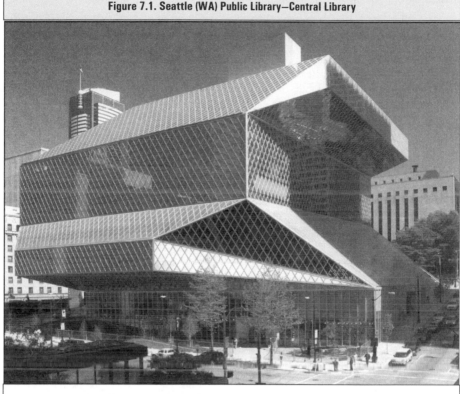

Figure 7.1. Seattle (WA) Public Library—Central Library

Source: Reprinted by permission of Seattle Public Library.

its transparent facade. It provides a quantum leap in technology, five main platforms, or levels, that are pushed and pulled out. Between these platforms are four "floating layers." Koolhaas had observed that existing libraries face a "Sisyphean fight against disorder," so the design aims to incorporate storage for digital information, as well as expandable space for books (Goldberger, 2004). Fisher and colleagues (2007: 152) found that the library was regarded as a societal good in terms of political role, habit of association, and recreational spirit.

The role of the library as the single most important institution in America today was explored by Wayne Senville (2009) in the *Planning Commissioners Journal*, where he characterized libraries as the cornerstone of new downtowns in dozens of cities. Commitment to a new library has been described as an act of civic renewal by Vartan Gregorian (2002; see also the sidebar on p. 160), who said of the Kansas City Public Library, "the new library will grace the city, help stimulate a downtown renaissance and—most importantly—be better able to play its central role in the cultural, intellectual and democratic life of the entire metropolitan community." In Minneapolis the new central library designed by Cesar Pelli was conceived as "a dynamic, resource-rich, downtown destination—an essential gathering place that inspires learning, invites interaction, and improves access to information and knowledge for everyone" (Kenney, 2001: 12).

Public Library Buildings in the Beginning

Early public libraries in the United States were housed in a variety of settings. Individual benefactors provided funds for buildings or libraries shared space with other civic agencies, clubs, storefronts, even fire departments. The most influential architect of library buildings in the mid-nineteenth century was Henry Hobson Richardson, who had enormous influence on the architectural vocabulary of the institution. Of special note was his design of the Crane Memorial Library in Quincy, Massachusetts, built 1879–1881 (Breisch, 2003).

A more focused approach to the development of library facilities came about during the period of Carnegie library philanthropy (1886–1919). Initially each community receiving a Carnegie building grant was able to develop its own library architecture, and these buildings were emblems of civic pride.

Midway through the program of grants for library buildings (1911), the Carnegie Corporation issued "Notes on Library Buildings" that provided suggested guidelines for libraries built with Carnegie funds. The variety of architectural styles for the 1,689 Carnegie-funded libraries included Italian renaissance, Beaux-Arts, classical revival, Spanish revival, prairie, Tudor revival, and Carnegie classical (Bobinski, 1969). Communities in the United States initially tended to think of public libraries as a civic landmark and a matter of community pride with perhaps less attention to functionality. Carnegie's gifts focused communities on the idea of a public library as a logical community service with some basic standardization of structure. Figure 7.2 depicts a Carnegie branch of the New York Public Library.

The American Library Association's *National Plan for Public Library Service* assessed the status of the nation's public library buildings in a general fashion, noting, "The present [physical plant of the public library] is barely 50 percent adequate for existing public library services. And for the extension of library service to the 35 million people now entirely without public libraries, a great new building program must be undertaken" (Joeckel and Winslow, 1948: 29). While specifics were not given as to design, general statements of accessibility, functionality, and the idea of the public library as a "modern educational center" with meeting rooms, film viewing space, and listening areas were set forth.

Figure 7.2. New York (NY) Public Library—Muhlenberg Branch

Source: Photo courtesy of Miguel A. Figueroa.

Setting National Standards for Facilities and Federal Funds for Construction

The Federal Library Services Act (LSA) and LSCA programs provided support for public library extension, construction, and renovation from 1956 to 1996. The ALA responded to this financial support with attention to facilities and buildings in national public library standards. The "Physical Facilities" section of *Public Library Service: A Guide to Evaluation with Minimum Standards* noted, "The public library building should serve as a symbol of library service. It should offer to the community a compelling invitation to enter, read, look, listen and learn" (ALA, 1956: 56). This document also provided general specifications for the public library building, such as good signage, a flexible structure that would allow expansion, workrooms, standards for lighting, sound control, and meeting rooms. A decade later, the *Minimum Standards for Public Library Systems, 1966* were somewhat more detailed about accommodating additional services such as typewriters for public use, vertical transportation, and study carrels (Public Library Association, 1967: 56–64).

From 1965 to 1997 LSCA funds provided monies for the construction of new library buildings; the acquisition, expansion, remodeling, and alteration of existing buildings; remodeling to conserve energy; retrofitting to meet standards set by the Americans with Disabilities Act; purchasing historic buildings for conversion to public libraries; and the acquisition, installation, maintenance, or replacement of equipment necessary to provide access to information and communication technologies.[1] This infusion of over $300 million in construction support encouraged state and local governments to match and enhance funding for public library construction. Annual appropriations from 1965–1996 are shown in Figure 7.3.

Figure 7.3. Fiscal Appropriations for Library Construction, 1965–1996

**Public Library Construction and Technology
Enhancement Grants to State Library Agencies
(CFDA No. 84.154)**

I. Legislation

Library Services and Construction Act (LSCA), Title II, as amended (20 U.S.C. 351 et seq.) (expires September 30, 1997).

II. Funding History[1]

Fiscal Year	Appropriation	Fiscal Year	Appropriation
1965	$30,000,000	1987	$22,050,000
1970	7,807,250	1988	22,143,100
1975	0	1989	21,877,520
1980	0	1990	18,572,036
1981	0	1991	18,833,395
1982	0	1992	16,383,640
1983	50,000,000	1993	16,252,571
1984	0	1994	17,436,160
1985	24,500,000	1995	17,436,160
1986	21,102,000	1996	16,041,620

[1] There is no time limit for the expenditure of these funds.

Source: U.S. Department of Education, Office of Educational Research and Improvement. 2011. *Biennial Evaluation Report, 1995–1996: Public Library Construction and Technology Enhancement Grants to State Library Agencies* (CFDA No. 84-154). Accessed January 17. http://www2.ed.gov/pubs/Biennial/95-96/eval/603-97.pdf.

The passion for library building during this period is illustrated by the best-documented event in public library building history—the design and building competition for the central Chicago Public Library announced in 1987. The problem of building a civic monument for Chicago was viewed as a clear choice between two distinct alternatives. One option was to build a static tranquil space conducive to the search for knowledge that would project an image of solidity and permanence, a structure that would express civic dignity and monumentality. A second option was to create an image that would reflect the dynamism of the city, symbolizing the active collection of information rather than the contemplation of knowledge. The video "Design Wars" follows the architects and builders in competition for the Chicago Public Library as they tried to accommodate issues of functionality, safety, public appeal, and expression of a vision of Chicago (MARZ Associates, in association with WGBH, Boston, 1989).

The design selected in 1988, a Beaux-Arts building by Hammond, Beeby, and Babka, Inc., has been characterized as fitting aesthetically and architecturally into the city like a glove, with a monumental, decorative, yet profoundly public, innovative, and urban-appropriate form. As hoped, the central library, named the Harold Washington Library Center (Figure 7.4) after the city's first African American mayor,

Figure 7.4. Chicago (IL) Public Library—Harold Washington Library Center

Source: Reprinted by permission of Chicago Public Library.

who died in 1987, sparked a revitalization of Chicago's South Loop District after it opened in 1991 ("Six Chicago Architects," 1989; Lane, 1989).

The story of community-wide engagement in the selection of the design for the Chicago Public Library is emblematic of the importance of the library as a great public space (Kent and Myrick, 2003). Public libraries that reach into the heart of a community may be monumental central libraries or small intimate branches. During the LSCA construction grant period, many communities found an opportunity to build public libraries that not only provided educational and recreational needs but also gave them a great public space during a time of expansive suburbanization and growth in edge cities.

The end of period of LSCA funds for construction in 1996–1997 did not halt the period of public library building expansion. In 2010, for example, $100 million was set aside for rural libraries including construction (ALA, 2010d).

Public Library Buildings for the Twenty-First Century

The Variety of Public Library Buildings

> Whether new or reconditioned, historic Carnegie or more contemporary, shooting for LEED certification or not, this year's library projects have one thing in common: establishing themselves as the flagship, hub, oasis, crossroads, anchor, intersection, civic presence, fabric, destination, living room, to the constituents of their communities and institutions while meeting the needs and sensibilities of 21st-century library service. (Fox, 2009)

Over $1.1 billion were spent on public library buildings in 2009. The annual *Library Journal* series on public library buildings reported 80 new facilities completed between July 1, 2008, and June 30, 2009, in communities throughout the United States at a cost of $656,020,880. Another 90 buildings had additions, renovations, or remodeling costing $482,214,848. Funding for this construction came predominantly from local sources ($911,114,613), followed by state funds ($103,865,294), gifts, and donations ($100,989,602). Federal funds accounted for $24,923,188.

To illustrate the variety of building taking at the beginning of a new decade, the best sources are the annual features with full-color photographs on new public library buildings that appear in the journals *American Libraries* and *Library Journal*.

The integration of information technology in a service environment is a central feature of most new buildings. While every public library strives to reflect the needs and spirit of its community, outstanding examples provide a spectrum of ideas and an annual review of these winners creates ongoing awareness of trends in library architecture and design. Each year *American Libraries*'s April issue features articles and photographs spotlighting new, expanded, and renovated library buildings. The 2010 issue included these libraries:

- **Brentwood, Tennessee, Public Library.** The expansion of Brentwood Public Library increased the size of the children's library considerably. Styled as a park, the themes include trees, nature murals, woodland animals, and a fantasy-land of books. An animated owl in one of the trees greets visitors, and a flat screen adjacent to the story room tells the story of the area's Native Americans.
- **Cambridge, Massachusetts, Public Library.** The renovation and expansion of Cambridge Public Library consists of three components: the historic main library built in 1889 and newly restored to its original appearance; the transparent New Building; and a newly landscaped city park made possible by locating the 70-space parking garage underground. The addition features a double-skin glass curtain wall with three feet of space between glass surfaces that insulates against heat gain or loss, reduces glare, and improves ventilation.
- **San Francisco Public Library, Portola branch.** The Portola branch's open-book motif is represented in sunshades along the building's southern wall that modulate light and reduce heat gain. The shape is echoed in an art installation of revolving stained glass panels by artist Dana Zed placed in the front windows, while skylights provide additional natural light.
- **Houston Public Library, Morris Frank branch.** The branch focuses on technology offerings, including free wireless, 21 public access desktop computers, 20 laptops, an LCD monitor for event and information postings, bilingual early literacy stations, and a range of electronic gaming opportunities for teens ("2010 Library Design Showcase," 2010).

Public library buildings also provide the opportunity for adaptive reuse of older buildings, while retaining historic features. In New York an 1886 candy factory was renovated to be the Mulberry Street branch of the New York City Public Library (Murdock, 2008). The Gentry Public Library in Gentry, Arkansas, home of Little Debbie Snack Cakes, is a restored hardware store and since 2007 has become a beacon for Gentry's hardscrabble downtown district (Kolleeny, 2008).

The Kansas City Public Library completed remodeling the First National Bank Building, which was built in 1906 for $450,000. The remodeling cost over 100 times that amount, $46,000,000, in 2004. Tompkins County, New York, renovated a Woolworth store in downtown Ithaca in 2002 (http://www.tcpl.org/index.html); Denton, Texas, converted a grocery store into a branch library in 2003. These projects involve multiple partners and preserve the character of a community. Rabun (2000) discusses factors to consider in adaptive reuse. It is interesting to note that reuse can go the other way. Older library buildings, especially Carnegie buildings, have been converted to new uses: the Fulbright Building in Fayetteville, Arkansas (Broome, 2009); the Arizona Hall of Fame Museum in Phoenix; and police facilities in Colusa, California (Jones, 1997).

Green building principles began to be incorporated into library building plans with great attention during the first decade of the twenty-first century. The ALA Social Responsibilities Round Table Task Force on the Environment (http://www.ala.org/ala/mgrps/rts/srrt/tfoe/taskforceenvironment.cfm) addressed sustainability issues in 2001 with the Libraries Build Sustainable Communities project. In her assessment of the green library movement, Antonelli (2008) sees 2003 as the point when green principles began to gain widespread commitment among librarians. Under the criteria of the U.S. Green Building Council's LEED (Leadership in Energy and Environmental Design) performance system, a green building is one that is built incorporating the following design elements:

- Sustainable site selection and development
- Water conservation
- Energy efficiency
- Local resources, material conservation, and waste reduction
- Indoor environmental quality
- Innovation in design (Green Libraries, http://www.greenlibraries.org/)

Facilities experts view the green library as a basis for developing a culture of sustainability at the community level (Bryan, 2009; Urbanska, 2009). Darien Public Library in Connecticut was planned to be sustainable inside and out and achieved LEED Gold Certification (see Figures 7.5a and 7.5b). The Darien Library was envisioned, designed, and constructed with the idea that life cycle costs are more important than initial savings. It is a beacon of sustainable design, serving as both an educational tool for the community and an inspiration for all (Gisolfi, 2009).

The Green Libraries website documents libraries that are green and sustainable. Highlighted public libraries include the Ballard branch of the Seattle Public Library (picked by the American Institute of Architects Committee on the Environment as one of the Top Ten Green Projects in 2006); Blair Library, Fayetteville, Arkansas (one of the first public libraries in the United States to register with the U.S. Green Building Council, in 2006); and the Santa Monica Public Library, which won a Gold LEED rating in 2006.

The first carbon-positive library in the United States—thanks to solar panels, a geothermal heating and cooling system, and a gift of carbon-offset credits—is Range-

Figure 7.5a. Darien (CT) Public Library Courtyard

Source: Robert Mintzes, Peter Grisolfi Associates; used with permission.

Figure 7.5b. Darien (CT) Public Library Main Entrance

Source: Robert Mintzes, Peter Grisolfi Associates; used with permission.

view Library District's new Anythink Brighton, Colorado, branch, which opened in September 2009 and offsets 167,620 pounds of carbon dioxide—16 percent more than it is anticipated to use annually (Figure 7.6). Environmentally friendly features include geothermal heating and cooling (a closed system of pipes carries fluid through the floors to wells 500 feet below the parking lot); solar tubes that capture natural light outside and deliver it through reflective tubes to illuminate interior spaces, even if there is no window or skylight; lighting controls, including motion sensors and stepped ballasts, to regulate the amount of artificial lighting needed; and south-facing facades ("New Colorado Facility," 2009).

At the national level, professional support for planning and building library facilities is within the purview of the ALA, Library Leadership and Management Association, Building and Equipment Section (LLAMA BES). LLAMA BES exercises responsibility for matters relating to library structures for all types of libraries, including site selection, design, construction, alteration, interior design, furnishings, and equipment. Programs held at the 2009 annual AL A conference demonstrate the scope of LLAMA BES: Library 2.0 Buildings: Creating Zones with Heart; Budget Conscious

Figure 7.6. Rangeview's Anythink Branch in Brighton, Colorado

Source: Marcus Farr Studio; used with permission.

Library Space Designs; and Small Scale Green: Techniques for Environmentally Conscious Renovation and Restoration Projects (Mosley and Arant-Kaspar, 2009).

The Library Building Awards program at the ALA conference showcases the joint biennial awards made by ALA and the American Institute of Architects for outstanding, recently completed library building projects. In 2009 public library awards were given to the Arabian Library, Scottsdale Public Library, Scottsdale, Arizona; New York Public Library, Francis Martin Library, Bronx, New York; Gentry Public Library, Gentry, Arkansas; Minneapolis Central Library, Minneapolis; and the Palo Verde Library/Maryvale Community Center, Phoenix (American Institute of Architects, 2009).

Publications that provide support to those planning buildings produced by LLAMA BES include the *Checklist of Building Design Considerations* (Sannwald, 2008) and *Libraries Designed for Users: A 21st Century Guide* (Lushington, 2002). LLAMA BES also maintains a list of building consultants (http://www.ala.org/ala/mgrps/divs/llama-roster.cfm?committee=lam-beslbcl).

State libraries provide additional specific information about public library building requirements. One extraordinarily important document is *Public Library Space Needs: A Planning Outline/2009* by Anders C. Dahlgren, issued by the Wisconsin Department of Public Instruction, Public Library Development office. The outline introduces the concept of the "design population," which takes into consideration the actual scope of use as contrasted with the defined geographical service area of the library. By using the outline librarians and trustees can estimate space needs based on a library's service goals.[2] The space requirements are organized in six categories with formulas for estimating needs. A few examples follow.

- **Collection space:** books, periodicals, nonprint resources, and digital resources. A general average for books housed in different environments is ten volumes per square foot. This is predicated on housing a normal variety of adult trade books on full-height shelving 84 inches or 90 inches tall installed with a three-foot aisle, and leaving the top and bottom shelves vacant for future expansion (Dahlgren, 2009: 10).
- **Reader seating space:** varies depending on type of use (general reading, intensive use by youth doing schoolwork) and size of population. This space should have at least 30 square feet per seat.
- **Staff work space:** work stations needed to support a library's service program. This space should feature between 125 and 150 square feet for each work station.
- **Meeting space:** several types of meeting space to be considered: (1) general program room space with theater or lecture hall seating; (2) conference room space; (3) children's storytime space; and (4) computer lab space. In a general

meeting room, a library should allow 10 square feet per audience seat, plus another 100 square feet for a speaker's podium or presentation area at the front of the room (p. 19). In a computer training lab, allow 50 square feet per station, plus another 80 square feet at the front of the room for the trainer (an allowance of 50 square feet reserves the option of seating two per station) (p. 20).

- **Special use space:** usually about 10 percent of the library's overall space for index tables, photocopiers, exhibits.
- **Nonassignable space:** This space—about 25 percent—would be for heating and cooling equipment, storage, corridors, and custodial space.

The categories assessed by Dahlgren provide a convenient overview of the library spaces that need to be considered in building design.

Libris Design software is a library facility planning information system and downloadable database that was developed for California Public Library planners and funded by the Institute of Museum and Library Services. It permits users to tailor generic library models into building programs and to project estimated costs. It was designed as an expert system to facilitate the creation of generic models that could be tailored to a specific community. The Libris Design software is free on the website (http://librisdesign.org/), which includes technical information and supporting documentation.

Accessibility and Humane Design

In the future, public libraries will need to be bigger, since no services are going away. Beyond traditional functions there needs to be more humane design (accessibility), space for more computers, wireless hotspots for use of laptops, space for the information technology staff to work and repair computers, and a more people-centered orientation with coffee bars and lounge areas. Library redesigns will need to take into account the fact that workstations require space for more than a computer and keyboard, as well as ergonomic support, the need for acoustical barriers to limit computer white noise, and enhanced electrical capacity (Forrest, 2002).

The *Wisconsin Public Library Standards*, Fifth Edition, emphasizes access. The chapter "Access and Facilities" provides a good overview of current requirements relating to public library buildings. Echoing the enduring aspects of national standards set forth in the 1950s, the introduction notes:

> The *physical* library facility also has a direct effect on access. All public library buildings should be easily accessible and offer a compelling invitation to the community. Library buildings should be flexible enough to respond to changing use and new technologies. Buildings should be ex-

pandable to accommodate growing collections and new services. Buildings should be designed for user efficiency. Building designs also should support staff efficiency, because staff costs are the major expense in library operation. (Wisconsin Department of Public Instruction, 2010: 33)

The following key criteria in the chapter "Access and Facilities" define the goal of accessibility (Wisconsin Department of Public Instruction, 2010: 33–35):

- The library takes action to reach all population groups in the community. Appropriate services may include home delivery services; deposit collections for childcare facilities, institutions, and agencies; books-by-mail service; bookmobile service; programs held outside the library; and remote access to the library online catalog and other resources. (Standard 8-3)
- The library ensures access to its resources and services for patrons with disabilities through the provision of assistive technology and alternative formats, in compliance with the Americans with Disabilities Act. (Standard 8-4)
- The library's online catalog and other electronic resources are accessible to persons with disabilities through the use of adaptive and assistive technology. (Standard 8-13)
- The library authorizes and maintains (or jointly maintains) an up-to-date uni-versally-accessible web page that includes library hours, phone numbers, ser-vices, and other basic information. (Standard 8-16)
- The library has allocated space for child and family use, with all materials readily available, and provides furniture and equipment designed for children and persons with disabilities. (Standard 8-25)
- The library building and furnishings meet state and federal requirements for physical accessibility, including the *ADA Accessibility Guidelines for Buildings and Facilities (ADAAG)* (2002). (Standard 8-27)
- In compliance with the ADAAG, the library provides directional signs and instructions for the use of the collection, the catalog, and other library services, in print, Braille, and alternate formats, as appropriate. (Standard 8-28)
- The library's accessible features, such as entrance doors and parking spaces, display the International Symbol of Accessibility. (Standard 8-29)

ADAAG is the basis of design requirements of the ADA (U.S. Access Board, 2010). The *Wisconsin Standards* are a model response and are in accord with the ALA policy "Library Services for People with Disabilities," which states, "Libraries play a catalytic role in the lives of people with disabilities by facilitating their full participation in society. Libraries should use strategies based upon the principles of universal design to ensure that library policy, resources and services meet the needs of all people" (ALA, 2010c). A portion of the ALA policy appears in Figure 7.7. Public library service must also incorporate state laws relating to library services for people with disabilities as identified in the Library of Congress (2009) Guide to State Laws. Burke's (2009) study of people with disabilities' use of public libraries found that use was a predictor of positive opinion.

Figure 7.7. ALA's Policy on Library Services for People with Disabilities

ALA 54.3.2 *Library Services for People with Disabilities*

The American Library Association recognizes that people with disabilities are a large and neglected minority in the community and are severely under represented in the library profession. Disabilities cause many personal challenges. In addition, many people with disabilities face economic inequity, illiteracy, cultural isolation, and discrimination in education, employment and the broad range of societal activities.

Libraries play a catalytic role in the lives of people with disabilities by facilitating their full participation in society. Libraries should use strategies based upon the principles of universal design to ensure that library policy, resources and services meet the needs of all people.

ALA, through its divisions, offices and units and through collaborations with outside associations and agencies, is dedicated to eradicating inequities and improving attitudes toward and services and opportunities for people with disabilities.

For the purposes of this policy, "must" means "mandated by law and/or within ALA's control" and "should" means "it is strongly recommended that libraries make every effort to . . ." Please see http://www .ala.org/ascla/accesspolicy.html for the complete text of the policy, which includes explanatory examples.

1) The Scope of Disability Law. Providing equitable access for persons with disabilities to library facilities and services is required by Section 504 of the Rehabilitation Act of 1973, applicable state and local statutes, and the Americans with Disabilities Act of 1990 (ADA).

2) Library Services. Libraries must not discriminate against individuals with disabilities and shall ensure that individuals with disabilities have equal access to library resources. Libraries should include persons with disabilities as participants in the planning, implementing, and evaluating of library services, programs, and facilities.

3) Facilities. The ADA requires that both architectural barriers in existing facilities and communication barriers that are structural in nature be removed as long as such removal is "readily achievable." (i.e., easily accomplished and able to be carried out without much difficulty or expense.)

4) Collections. Library materials must be accessible to all patrons including people with disabilities. Materials must be available to individuals with disabilities in a variety of formats and with accommodations, as long as the modified formats and accommodations are "reasonable," do not "fundamentally alter" the library's services, and do not place an "undue burden" on the library. Within the framework of the library's mission and collection policies, public, school, and academic library collections should include materials with accurate and up-to-date information on the spectrum of disabilities, disability issues, and services for people with disabilities, their families, and other concerned persons.

5) Assistive Technology. Well-planned technological solutions and access points, based on the concepts of universal design, are essential for effective use of information and other library services by all people. Libraries

(Continued)

Figure 7.7 *(Continued)*
should work with people with disabilities, agencies, organizations and vendors to integrate assistive technology into their facilities and services to meet the needs of people with a broad range of disabilities, including learning, mobility, sensory and developmental disabilities. Library staff should be aware of how available technologies address disabilities and know how to assist all users with library technology.
6) Employment. ALA must work with employers in the public and private sectors to recruit people with disabilities into the library profession, first into library schools and then into employment at all levels within the profession. Libraries must provide reasonable accommodations for qualified individuals with disabilities unless the library can show that the accommodations would impose an "undue hardship" on its operations. Libraries must also ensure that their policies and procedures are consistent with the ADA and other laws.
7) Library Education, Training and Professional Development. All graduate programs in library and information studies should require students to learn about accessibility issues, assistive technology, the needs of people with disabilities both as users and employees, and laws applicable to the rights of people with disabilities as they impact library services. Libraries should provide training opportunities for all library employees and volunteers in order to sensitize them to issues affecting people with disabilities and to teach effective techniques for providing services for users with disabilities and for working with colleagues with disabilities.
Source: American Library Association. Annually revised. "Library Services for People with Disabilities." In *ALA Policy Manual,* 54.3.2. Chicago: American Library Association. http://www.ala.org/ala/aboutala/governance/policymanual.

Branches Both Physical and Digital, Bookmobiles, Joint-Use Libraries, and M-libraries

Many public libraries extend services beyond the central library by developing branch systems or digital electronic branches, providing bookmobile services, collaborating through joint-use libraries, and facilitating access by mobile devices. Beginning with the fiscal year 2008 IMLS Public Libraries Survey (U.S. IMLS, 2010), locale codes have been added to the outlet and administrative entity-level data sets. These locale codes allow users to identify which library outlets and administrative entities are located in cities, suburbs, towns, or rural areas. The locale code system classifies territory into four major types: city, suburban, town, and rural. The coding methodology was developed by the Census Bureau as a way to identify the location of public schools in the National Center for Education Statistics' Common Core of Data. As of 2008, each library outlet and administrative entity survey has one of the 12 locale codes assigned to it. Bookmobiles and books-by-mail-only outlets were not assigned locale codes (U.S. IMLS, 2010: 18). The 2010 survey reported 9,221 public libraries with 7,629 branches for a total of 16,671 stationary outlets. There were 797 bookmobiles in service. Figure 7.8 (pp. 176–178) shows the distribution of branches and bookmobiles in the United States.

Figure 7.8. Number of Public Libraries with Branches and Bookmobiles, and Number of Service Outlets, by Type of Outlet and State: Fiscal Year 2008

State	Number of public libraries	Number of libraries with		Number of outlets						
		Branches	Bookmobiles	Total[2]	Stationary outlets				Bookmobiles[1]	
					Central libraries		Branches			
					Total	Response rate[3]	Total	Response rate[3]	Total	Response rate[3]
Total	9,221	1,559	670	16,671	9,042	100.0	7,629	100.0	797	100.0
Alabama	210	21	13	288	209	100.0	79	100.0	16	100.0
Alaska	86	6	2	102	86	100.0	16	100.0	2	100.0
Arizona	86	24	8	207	81	100.0	126	100.0	10	100.0
Arkansas	51	36	3	216	46	100.0	170	100.0	3	100.0
California	181	118	42	1,117	167	100.0	950	100.0	63	100.0
Colorado	115	36	9	250	101	100.0	149	100.0	10	100.0
Connecticut	195	26	9	242	195	100.0	47	100.0	9	100.0
Delaware	21	3	2	33	19	100.0	14	100.0	2	100.0
District of Columbia	1	1	1	27	1	100.0	26	100.0	1	100.0
Florida	80	51	23	518	60	100.0	458	100.0	29	100.0
Georgia	59	53	16	387	59	100.0	328	100.0	17	100.0
Hawaii	1	1	1	51	1	100.0	50	100.0	2	100.0
Idaho	104	17	9	140	102	100.0	38	100.0	10	100.0
Illinois	634	43	21	791	634	100.0	157	100.0	24	100.0
Indiana	238	72	30	434	238	100.0	196	100.0	35	100.0
Iowa	539	8	4	559	539	100.0	20	100.0	4	100.0
Kansas	327	12	3	376	327	100.0	49	100.0	5	100.0
Kentucky	116	33	83	196	116	100.0	80	100.0	87	100.0
Louisiana	68	50	24	332	68	100.0	264	100.0	28	100.0
Maine	272	2	0	278	272	100.0	6	100.0	0	100.0

(Continued)

Figure 7.8 (Continued)

State	Number of public libraries	Number of libraries with		Total	Number of outlets					
		Branches	Bookmobiles		Stationary outlets				Bookmobiles[1]	
					Central libraries		Branches			
					Total	Response rate[3]	Total	Response rate[3]	Total	Response rate[3]
Maryland	24	24	13	18□	15	100.0	168	100.0	18	100.0
Massachusetts	370	40	4	47□	370	100.0	104	100.0	4	100.0
Michigan	384	64	14	65□	379	100.0	278	100.0	14	100.0
Minnesota	138	25	12	36□	128	100.0	232	100.0	13	100.0
Mississippi	50	39	2	23□	47	100.0	190	100.0	2	100.0
Missouri	152	43	17	35□	140	100.0	219	100.0	29	100.0
Montana	80	15	2	11□	80	100.0	30	100.0	2	100.0
Nebraska	270	2	8	23□	270	100.0	17	100.0	8	100.0
Nevada	22	14	5	3□	19	100.0	66	100.0	5	100.0
New Hampshire	231	5	0	23□	231	100.0	5	100.0	0	100.0
New Jersey	303	40	12	45□	303	100.0	151	100.0	12	100.0
New Mexico	91	10	3	11□	91	100.0	27	100.0	3	100.0
New York	755	57	7	1,06□	753	100.0	316	100.0	8	100.0
North Carolina	77	64	32	33□	66	100.0	323	100.0	35	100.0
North Dakota	81	6	13	9□	80	100.0	10	100.0	13	100.0
Ohio	251	101	48	72□	241	100.0	484	100.0	64	100.0
Oklahoma	115	9	4	20□	115	100.0	91	100.0	5	100.0
Oregon	126	22	10	21□	123	100.0	89	100.0	11	100.0
Pennsylvania	457	49	27	62□	452	100.0	177	100.0	34	100.0
Rhode Island	48	7	2	7□	48	100.0	24	100.0	2	100.0
South Carolina	42	34	31	18□	41	100.0	148	100.0	33	100.0

(Continued)

Figure 7.8. Number of Public Libraries with Branches and Bookmobiles, and Number of Service Outlets, by Type of Outlet and State: Fiscal Year 2008 *(Continued)*

State	Number of public libraries	Number of libraries with		Number of outlets						
		Branches	Bookmobiles	Total[2]	Stationary outlets				Bookmobiles[1]	
					Central libraries		Branches			
					Total	Response rate[3]	Total	Response rate[3]	Total	Response rate[3]
South Dakota	114	11	7	150	114	100.0	36	100.0	8	100.0
Tennessee	187	28	5	289	187	100.0	102	100.0	6	100.0
Texas	561	68	9	864	561	100.0	303	100.0	12	100.0
Utah	69	18	17	116	55	100.0	61	100.0	18	100.0
Vermont	183	3	7	183	180	100.0	3	100.0	7	100.0
Virginia	91	60	29	343	79	100.0	264	100.0	31	100.0
Washington	64	23	12	334	55	100.0	279	100.0	26	100.0
West Virginia	97	27	6	173	97	100.0	76	100.0	7	100.0
Wisconsin	381	18	7	458	378	100.0	80	100.0	8	100.0
Wyoming	23	20	2	76	23	100.0	53	100.0	2	100.0
Outlying areas										
Guam	1	1		6	1	100.0	5	100.0	1	100.0
Puerto Rico	35	5	0	44	35	100.0	9	100.0	0	100.0

[1] A bookmobile is a traveling branch library. It consists of at least one of the following: (1) A truck or van that carries an organized collection of library materials; (2) paid staff; and (3) regularly scheduled hours (bookmobile stops) for being open to the public.

[2] Total stationary outlets is the sum of central and branch libraries.

[3] Response rate is calculated as the number of libraries that reported the item, divided by the total number of libraries in the survey frame.

[4] Of the 9,221 public libraries in the 50 States and DC, 7,469 were single-outlet libraries and 1,752 were multiple-outlet libraries. Single-outlet libraries are a central library, bookmobile, or books-by-mail-only outlet. Multiple-outlet libraries have two or more direct service outlets, including some combination of one central library, branch(es), bookmobile(s), and/or books-by-mail-only outlets.

NOTE: Data were not reported by the following outlying areas (American Samoa, Northern Marianas, and Virgin Islands). Missing data were not imputed for nonresponding outlying areas.
SOURCE: Institute of Museum and Library Services, Survey of Public Libraries in the United States, Fiscal Year 2008.

Source: U.S. Institute of Museum and Library Services. 2010. *Public Libraries Survey: Fiscal Year 2008.* Washington, DC: U.S. Institute of Museum and Library Services, pp. 35–36. http://harvester.census.gov/imls/pubs/Publications/pls2008.pdf.

Branches: Physical and Digital

Branch libraries serve their communities by providing convenient locations and access to materials and information as a link to the wider world of what libraries have to offer. In her discussion of the branches at nine locations of the Wichita Public Library, with a focus on the Alford Regional Branch Library, Jean Hatfield (2008) characterizes the branch library service as a community center.

In *The Branch Librarian's Handbook* (Rivers, 2004), the variety of branch services are described to support branch management. The type of innovation that can arise in branches is manifested in such programs as the Library Partnership—A Neighborhood Resource Center at the Alachua County Library District in Gainesville, Florida, that merges branch and social services ("Florida Library," 2009) or the showcasing of green public art at the Pearl Avenue branch of the San Jose Public Library (Blumenstein, 2009). Putnam and Feldstein (2003) have famously characterized branch libraries as the heartbeat of the community.

Library functions can be increasingly virtual. The digital branch has been defined by David King (2009a: 43) as "a branch library, delivered digitally, on the web. It offers much more than a traditional library website in many ways, because a digital branch has real staff, a real building, a real collection, and a real community happening on and around it." Virtual branches in the Orange County Public Library, Florida (Sampson, 2009), and in Idaho (Persichini, Samuelson, and Zeiter, 2008) demonstrate the range of services that can be offered without ties to time or space. Another example from Pawtucket Public Library, Rhode Island, is facilitation of the library website for social networking, including homework help (Jeffers, 2009).

Bookmobiles

Nearly 800 bookmobiles are in use in the United States. The ALA parade of bookmobiles includes history, photographs, and links to bookmobiles (ALA, Office for Literacy and Outreach Services, 2010). The Association of Bookmobile and Outreach Services (ABOS; http://www.abos-outreach.org), the Service to Bookmobile Communities, and the *Handbook for Mobile Library Staff* (ALA, Office for Literacy and Outreach Services, 2008) are resources that provide public libraries with a range of cultural and technical support to extend service to meet diverse programming and outreach needs—especially for rural communities.

In 2008, national guidelines were adopted that provided criteria for management, staffing, collection development, funding, vehicle construction, and maintenance—from chassis to tires (ABOS, 2008). The annual bookmobile conference sponsored by ABOS includes many case studies and exemplary programs for mutual support and service development of bookmobile librarians.

Joint-Use Libraries

The joint-use library has been defined as libraries of two or more different types amalgamating to offer collections and services that neither could have afforded to offer individually (Miller, 2001). Examples include the public library system in Broward County, Florida, and Nova Southeastern University (Quinlan and Tuñón, 2004) and Seminole Community Library and St. Petersburg College (Olliver and Anderson, 2001).

The Gale/*Library Journal* 2004 Library of the Year Award was conferred on the Dr. Martin Luther King, Jr. Library in San Jose, California (Berry, 2004). The project demonstrated that two existing libraries (San Jose Public Library and San Jose State University Library), with different missions, clients, and bureaucracies, not only could share a building but also successfully integrate operations (Brevik, Budd, and Woods, 2005). This joint-use library serves over a million people.

Another approach to public libraries cooperating with academic libraries has been successful in New Hampshire, with Keene State College and Keene Public Library sharing an automation system. This led to increased interaction between the two libraries' communities and was the catalyst for a new approach to cultural heritage in the Monadnock region of southwestern New Hampshire (Halverson and Plotas, 2006). School-public library partnerships, as explored by Henderson (2007), provide new opportunities for focus on lifelong learning and information literacy.

Mobile Devices and M-libraries

If the library is to be a part of the lives of on-the-go users, the library must come to them—not just by making scheduled visits in a bookmobile, but by being accessible at all hours through the mobile devices they carry with them (Balas, 2009). In 2010 WorldCat piloted the service WorldCat Mobile, which provides library searches, WorldCat library locations, links to library phones, and maps (http://www.worldcat .org/wcpa/content/mobile/). A 2009 Pew Internet and American Life report found over half the U.S. population using mobile devices (Horrigan, 2009). For many users, broadband mobile devices like the iPhone have already begun to assume many tasks that were once the exclusive province of portable computers (Johnson, Levine, and Smith, 2009). Libraries have been quick to respond to the evolving technology. Just as e-libraries characterized the period 2000–2009, m-libraries and the use of mobile devices will characterize the next decade of library technology development. SMS (short message services) will be increasingly used for information service (Krabrill, 2009).

New York Public Library has a redesigned mobile interface that provides access to its LEO and CATNYP catalogs, and information about exhibits and events as well as branch map locations and hours (Hadro, 2009; NYPL Labs, http://labs.nypl.org/).

Washington, DC, Public Library has added an iPhone app that provides catalog access and hold service (Distant Librarian, 2009).

Looking ahead at the impact of mobile devices on library services, Lorcan Dempsey observed in 2009: "We can see the impact of mobile communication on services in two ways. First, services may be made mobile-ready, as with special mobile interfaces for library services, alerting services, and so on. Second, mobilization continues the restructuring of services, organizations and attention that networking has brought about."

The 2010 Office for Information Technology Policy Brief, "There's an App for That! Libraries and Mobile Technology: An Introduction to Public Policy Considerations" (Vollmer, 2010) identifies key challenges about mobile technology: content and ownership, privacy, digital rights management, and accessibility. "The relationships between librarians and their users are changing as patrons access content and services online. The continued evolution from primarily physical, in-person interaction with patrons and content to increasingly virtual, digital, and mobile interaction creates unique challenges for libraries" (Vollmer, 2010: 3).

In 2010 millions of e-book, audiobook, music, and video titles were downloaded from libraries. Public library websites provide instructions for access. An outstanding example is the Downloads to Go website of the Buffalo and Erie County Public Library (http://buffalo.lib.overdrive.com/8FA99691-6BC2-42D6-B5DB-C53F1325CEC9/10/400/en/Help-QuickStartGuide.htm).

Planning the Infrastructure: LSTA, Public Access Computing, and Broadband USA

The importance of public libraries to public access computing has been assessed in a series of reports called the Public Library Funding Technology and Access Studies, issued by the ALA.[3] The most recent study, *2009–2010 Public Library Funding and Technology Access Survey*, reported that public libraries offer their communities a substantial array of public access technologies and Internet-enabled services:

- **Infrastructure:** Libraries reported an average of 14.2 public access workstations, up from 11.0 in 2008–2009, and 82.2 percent of public library branches offer wireless Internet access, up from 76.4 percent reported in 2008–2009.
- **Broadband:** Libraries reported increased connectivity speeds, with 51.8 percent of libraries reporting connectivity speeds of greater than 1.5 mbps, as compared to 44.5 percent in 2008–2009.

- **Wireless:** Libraries reported an increase in providing wireless (Wi-Fi) access to the Internet, with 82.2 percent of public library branches offering wireless Internet access, up from 76.4 percent reported in 2008–2009.
- **Content:** Libraries reported offering access to a number of resources, including licensed databases (95.0 percent, up from 89.6 percent in 2008–2009); homework resources (88.2 percent, up from 79.6 percent in 2008–2009); audio content, such as podcasts and audiobooks (82.5 percent, up from 72.9 percent in 2008–2009); digital reference (72.3 percent, up from 62.4 percent in 2008–2009); and e-books (65.9 percent, up from 55.4 percent in 2008–2009).
- **Employment support:** 88.2 percent of libraries reported providing access to jobs databases and other job opportunity resources, and 67.1 percent of those libraries also reported providing patrons with assistance in completing online job applications.
- **E-government:** 78.7 percent of libraries reported providing patrons assistance in applying for or accessing e-government services, and 63.3 percent of those reported that staff provide assistance to patrons for completing government forms. (Bertot et al., 2010)

How did public libraries become the anchor institutions providing public access computing in so many communities? In 1993 the ALA held a forum, Telecommunications and Information Infrastructure Policy Issues, to provide a mechanism for the library community to identify national policy issues, questions, and principles in the areas of telecommunications and information infrastructure. Public librarians proved to be highly capable environmental scanners and moved quickly to implement new technologies into their daily work.

Public librarians were among the first community service workers to apply for a series of grants for model programs that demonstrated innovative use of network technology in 1994.[4] At Newark Public Library, funds were used to support the Newark Electronic Information Infrastructure Demonstration Project; New York Public Library, working with the Literacy Assistance Center of New York City, tested networked information resources at 30 neighborhood branches for people with limited literacy skills; Danbury Public Library developed a model community Freenet planning process for the state of Connecticut; three counties in southeast Florida (Broward, Dade, and Palm Beach) developed a Free-Net training infrastructure coordinated by the South East Florida Information Network; and Salem (Oregon) Public Library developed OPEN (Oregon Public Electronic Network) to enhance the exchange of information between governments and citizens (McCook, 2000: 71–72).

Recognizing the complexity of issues relating to information policy, ALA created the Office for Information Technology Policy in 1995 (http://www.ala.org/ala/

aboutala/offices/oitp/index.cfm#). This office focuses on enhancing the ability of ALA's Washington office to follow and influence national issues relating to electronic access to information as a means to ensure the public's right to a free and open information society. The Library Services and Technology Act (LSTA) of 1996 (a title under the Museum and Library Services Act), which replaced the LSCA, emphasizes technology in its grants to libraries. The LSTA has helped libraries to create the technological infrastructure required to obtain and use electronic resources through funding based on required state plans (McCook, 2002; Gregory, 1999).

The establishment of the LSTA is testimony to the vision of the Clinton-Gore administration's recognition of the need for broad access to the information superhighway and the library community's readiness to work with government to put new projects in place. The rapid adoption of telecommunication technologies and the support to activate them for communities demonstrates the capacity of the nation's public libraries to respond with alacrity to change.

The Telecommunications Act of 1996 made possible an annual subsidy of $65 million for discounted telecommunication rates to libraries and schools. Through the E-Rate (Schools and Libraries Universal Service Support Mechanism), libraries have been able to add telecommunications infrastructure (Federal Communications Commission, 2010).[5] The Schools and Libraries Program of the Universal Service Fund makes discounts available to eligible schools and libraries for telecommunication services, Internet access, and internal connections. The program is intended to ensure that schools and libraries have access to affordable telecommunications and information services. Investments by public libraries in Internet terminals increased by more than 600 percent in the decade of 1998–2008 and investments in hardware and software, telecommunications, and technology vendor services, which account for 57.3 percent of a public library technology operating budget on average, now help local libraries provide access to more media and documents than they could physically house in their library building (Manjarrez, Langa, and Miller, 2009: 4).

The Bill and Melinda Gates Foundation recognized the public library as a partial solution to the "digital divide" between people with and people without computer access. To assist in overcoming this divide, the foundation brought computer packages into all 50 states by 2003. The Gates donations—the largest gift to U.S. public libraries since Carnegie—amounted to $250 million for 40,000 computers in 10,000 libraries from 1997 to 2003. The focus was low-income communities where 10 percent of the population were below the federal poverty line (Gordon et al., 2003; Bill and Melinda Gates Foundation, 2010). In an interview with the *American Libraries* editor, who called Gates a "latter-day Andrew Carnegie," the philanthropist observed:

> I didn't really realize that librarians are often working without much acknowledgment of the important role they play. The program was valuable

in terms of adding this new tool to the library, but also giving the librarians a chance to remind people of the central role that the library has in the community and the fact that staying up-to-date requires a sustained commitment from people in the community for the library to play that role. (Kniffel, 2003)

Other Gates initiatives include the Native American Access to Technology Program, which provided computers to tribal libraries in New Mexico, Arizona, Colorado, and Utah (Dorr and Akeroyd, 2001); the Staying Connected program to sustain access and provide technology training (Stone, 2005); extended funding support to enhance computer and Internet services and training for U.S. public libraries serving low-income communities (Oder, 2007); funding to help states organize broadband summits and to provide some states with funds to bring their Internet connections up to speed with a new pilot program that ensures low-income individuals have access to online job applications and other opportunities (Greenwood, 2009); and in 2010 the Opportunity Online Program to provide technical and consulting assistance to help libraries compete for federal broadband stimulus funds. The scope of the Gates contribution in Louisiana is characterized by a librarian involved in the implementation beginning with the Gates grants in the 1990s:

> The initial grant from the Gates Foundation allowed the State Library of Louisiana to spend money on establishing T-1 Internet access at every headquarters library in the state. Until the grant came along that money was earmarked for buying computers for all of the libraries. The Gates money provided the computers and routers and the state library paid for not only T-1 access at headquarters but Internet connectivity to each of the 300-plus public libraries in the state. . . . Additional grants from the Gates Foundation (Staying Connected and PACHUG) provided assistance with public computer hardware upgrades, training for library staffs, expansion of broadband coverage and technical support.[6]

The convergence of support from LSTA, Universal Service through E-Rate, and the Gates Foundation philanthropy provided U.S. public libraries with the means to incorporate new technologies and integrate electronic services as enhanced performance standards for public libraries throughout the nation. These new standards became generally accepted through the LSTA planning process.

Each state library agency undergoes a five-year evaluation of its results in meeting the goals and objectives of its LSTA plans submitted to the IMLS. A review of the 50 state evaluations demonstrates technology progress. For example, in its 2002–2007 five-year plan, the Texas State Library and Archives Commission identified this goal:

"Encourage and assist libraries to use technology to serve the information needs of Texans." This was evaluated in 2007: "On average, libraries increased the number of their public access/patron computers by 38.5 percent from the beginning of 2003 to 2006 and by 57.7 percent from 2003 to 2007" (U.S. IMLS, 2007: 57–67). In its 2008–2012 five-year plan, Texas determined: "Texans need technology based library services to help them achieve economic, educational, and other personal goals" (U.S. IMLS, 2008h: 12–14). Using the five-year evaluations and five-year plans as submitted for each state library agency and its constituent public libraries, which are available at the IMLS website (http://www.imls.gov/programs/5yearplans.shtm) provides us with a unified sense of the methods and means by which technology was incorporated into public library service at the outset of the twenty-first century.

McClure and Jaeger (2009) have identified Internet-enabled service roles that public libraries fulfill, including public access to the Internet, e-government services provider, emergency and disaster relief provider, Internet and technology trainer, and youth educational support provider. These roles will become increasingly central to public library service as the broadband infrastructure grows.

The 2009 American Recovery and Reinvestment Act (ARRA) funded the National Telecommunications and Information Administration's Broadband Technology Opportunity Program (BTOP, http://www2.ntia.doc.gov//), targeted at enhancing America's broadband infrastructure—of which a minimum of $200 million was set aside for public access centers, including public libraries ("Gates Foundation," 2010: 31; Ball, 2009: 552).

Libraries in six states were among the beneficiaries of the first round of awards from the ARRA broadband grants, including the following:

- $1.5 million sustainable broadband adoption grant (with an additional $591,000 in matching funds) to the New Mexico State Library to increase broadband adoption and promote computer literacy and Internet use statewide
- $1.3 million public computing grant (with matching funds of $320,000) to the Arizona State Library, Archives, and Public Records to enhance existing facilities in more than 80 public libraries throughout the state
- $1.9 million public computing grant (with matching funds of $477,000) to the city of Boston to expand computer and Internet capacity at the main library and 25 branches, 16 community centers, and 11 public housing sites

Changes made to the second round of funding for BTOP and the USDA's Rural Utilities Service (RUS) Broadband Initiatives Program (BIP) expanded the opportunities for libraries and other community anchor institutions to apply and receive additional funding. Through the Commerce Department's National Telecommunications and Information Administration (NTIA), libraries have benefited from over $749.7 million in grants disturbed by BTOP. These funds—awarded directly, in partnership with, or indirectly to libraries—are being used for broadband infrastructure, public computer centers, and broadband adoption projects to expand the availability and use of broadband. An up-to-date list of grants awarded is available at the NTIA's BroadbandUSA website (http://broadbandusa.sc.egov.usda.gov/).[7]

A discussion of issues relating to broadband by Mandel and colleagues (2010) addresses the fact that public libraries are the only free Internet access in the majority of U.S. communities and thus their role as Internet service providers is crucial. Public libraries are vital community institutions, and numerous studies of broadband penetration have determined that community-based efforts are a key element for successful adoption. Noting the complex challenges relating to broadband provision, the authors observe:

> Amidst this fluid policy environment, public libraries would benefit from a national-level telecommunications policy containing clear objectives. Because libraries are internet providers to millions of Americans, broadband policymakers may benefit from partnering with public librarians to spread the deployment of broadband internet across U.S. communities and help the FCC meet their charged goal of universal broadband. Still, if public libraries hope to obtain a deserved seat at the table, they will need to demonstrate more clearly and frequently to other stakeholders their valuable roles as centers that provide internet access and resources, which are staffed by information providers retaining expertise, and facilitate internet-enabled services in almost every U.S. community. (Mandel et al., 2010: 289)

Protecting the Public and the Public Library: Security and Disaster Planning

Safety, Security, and Patron Interaction

Safety and security in public space have been studied from legal, design, and policy vantage points by community planners. Németh and Schmidt (2007: 283) have observed: "Although security is necessary for creating spaces the public will use, making it a top priority is often criticized for restricting social interaction, constraining individual liberties, and unjustly excluding certain populations." In the monograph *Library Security and Safety Guide to Prevention, Planning, and Response*, Kahn (2008) provides security tools and strategies so libraries can be better prepared to protect patrons, staff, and collections.

Trapskin (2008: 69) has discussed security in the context of changing patterns of library use:

> Libraries are no longer passive repositories of information but lively commons where people can share ideas in person or online. This shift brings with it not only an all-time record of high library visits but also increasing security incidents. Today's library administrators need to address security threats proactively. Two basic proactive solutions are to pay greater attention to the design of collaborative and other spaces and to actively promote positive interactions between staff and patrons.

"Problem situations, not problem patrons," is how Slavick (2009) characterizes difficult interactions with users who might be homeless, inflicted with mental, emotional, or physical illness, or suffering from substance abuse. He suggests active listening, empathizing, staying on topic, and maintaining an impersonal but flexible approach to diffuse problem situations.

Another positive approach to difficult patrons has been described by staff members of the Fairfax County, Virginia, Public Library, who state they do not have a problem behavior philosophy; they have a customer service philosophy:

1. Every customer who uses our libraries should feel welcomed, valued, and respected.
2. All our rules are applied humanely, courteously, and fairly to all.
3. Every day is a new beginning. Except in extreme cases, we should not presume that a problem will occur because of past experience.
4. Every customer is entitled to their individual style of use of the library as long as it does not interfere with the rights of others.
5. Not all behaviors are problem behaviors.
6. Actions should be taken in a calm, reasonable fashion only after obtaining sufficient evidence that a problem really exists. (Waller and Bangs, 2007)

Disaster Planning

In June 2008 the Cedar River in Iowa crested at 31 feet. Despite heroic efforts by the staff to move everything out of danger to 26-feet-high shelves, the Cedar Rapids Public Library (CRPL) lost 160,000 items, including large parts of its adult and youth collections, magazines, newspapers, reference materials, CDs, and DVDs. Most of its public access computers were destroyed as was its computer lab and microfilm equipment. The automatic circulation and security systems were ruined. The work of the CRPL management team to restore service and embrace the recovery is an inspiration for Cedar Rapids and for all librarians. In 2009 the CRPL staff was named Librarian of the Year by *Library Journal*—"For their courage, their indomitable optimism, and their deep and strong commitment to uninterrupted library service to the people of Cedar Rapids" (Berry, 2009).

Disasters beset many public libraries in the first decade of the twenty-first century. In addition to the Cedar River flood in 2008, Hurricane Ike devastated libraries in Texas and Louisiana ("Narratives from the Storm," 2008; Oder, 2008); Hurricane Gustav caused massive evacuations throughout the southeast (Bracquet, 2009); Hurricane Katrina and Hurricane Rita destroyed libraries in Mississippi and Louisiana (Ellis and Shambra, 2008; Dawson and McCook, 2006). Fifty-one hurricanes or other severe storm systems have impacted the state of Florida since the year 2000, resulting in over $64 billion in damage and 149 related fatalities (McClure et al., 2009).

Resources that help public libraries prepare for disasters include Todaro's (2009) *Emergency Preparedness for Libraries* and Alire's (2000) *Library Disaster Planning and Recovery Handbook*. Additional resources include the following:

- The web portal at Florida State University, Information Use Management and Policy Institute: "Hurricane Preparedness and Response for Florida's Public Libraries" (McClure et al., 2009)
- IMLS-supported research, "Investigating Library and Information Services During Community-Based Disasters: Preparing Information Professionals to Plan for the Worst" (Zach and McKnight, 2010b)
- Disaster Preparedness and Recovery website (ALA, 2010a; Disaster Planning Resources, Collection Valuation, Collection Preservation and Recovery)

Yet, as Reita Fackerell (2008: 15) of the Seaside, Oregon, Public Library wrote after a fearsome storm had caused massive power outages, the emergency that happens may not be the emergency you expected:

> Because we were one more dark building in a county of dark buildings, we made an "Open" sign and put it out on the library lawn. We did not really expect any patrons. After all, who would leave the safety of home, drive around downed power lines, under trees leaning over the road and through knee deep water to come to a library?
>
> Lots of people, it turned out. We had our regular readers, but then, we got a whole new set, because when you have no cable, no Internet, no video games, and no phone service, what do you want to do? Read!

Keeping Up

Public librarians face a continuous need to incorporate new technologies into our daily work. The LSTA plans submitted to IMLS contain state library agency goals to support the continuing education of public library staff. For example, the Oklahoma Department of Libraries Five-Year Plan 2008–2012 identified the goal, "Lead statewide library technology planning. Assist libraries in creatively adapting to societal changes through innovation and technology adoption" (U.S. IMLS, 2008a: 20–21).

The public library technology environment requires a high level of engagement to stay aware of new developments. Several online services provide current information. WebJunction, a public library portal, is an online community of libraries and other agencies sharing knowledge and experience to provide the broadest public access to information technology (http://www.webjunction.org/about). The portal is funded by the Online Computer Library Center (OCLC), the world's largest library cooperative, with additional grants from the Bill and Melinda Gates Foundation and library service partners. These groups established WebJunction to provide the best possible public access to information technology. The Webjunction Technology Portal provides training on the integration of technology in library services. OCLC (2010) also provides online training and support for its many technological services.

The Library and Information Technology Association of the ALA provides overviews of technology trends, which are widely disseminated including sessions at the Public Library Association national conference (Hadro, 2010). The ALATechSource website on library technology (http://www.techsource.ala.org), and the *Library Technology Guides* (http://www.librarytechnology.org/?SID=20101217433959960) provide comprehensive information on library automation, including bibliographies and information on automation companies.

Other options for in-service technology training include programs offered by LYRASIS, the nation's largest regional membership organization serving libraries and information professionals. The education services statement at LYRASIS reads: "New technologies and the inevitability of change are a constant challenge for the library and information services community. LYRASIS strives to provide staff of both member and nonmember institutions with a balance of hands-on training, continuing education opportunities, and general staff development" (http://www.lyrasis.org/).

Finally, laws and legislation regarding technology that affects public libraries must be monitored at all levels of government. Examples of work done by the ALA Office for Information Technology Policy in 2010 include filings with the FCC on the connection between economic development and broadband, public access to information in a digital environment, and the political and legal aspects of networks.

At the state level, each state library association works to review and provide information to state governments, generally with the collaboration of the respective state library agency. Many states have Internet filtering laws that apply to public libraries. Some states also require publicly funded institutions to install filtering software on library terminals (National Conference of State Legislatures, 2009). The state library agencies work together through Chief Officers of State Library Agencies (COSLA, http://www.cosla.org/) a continuing mechanism for dealing with the problems and challenges faced by the agencies responsible for statewide library development.

The metaphors of the library as the community's heart, its nerve center, its beacon of hope, and our shared paradise prevail in even these digital times. Through capable oversight, the public library communities at local, state, regional, and national levels have collaborated to secure the role of the library in the twenty-first century. The convergence of infrastructure challenges with the freedom to read requires ongoing effort to safeguard a robust commons for those who use public libraries. The public library in the United States is physical and virtual; it is mobile and Web 2.0. The structure and infrastructure of the public library have evolved and stayed viable and secure over three centuries due to the diligent work of public librarians to respond to their communities' changing needs and modes of access.

Notes

1. For background on overall public library construction funded by the LSCA from 1965 to 1997, examine the archived report of the U.S. Department of Education, Office of Educational Research and Improvement (1996). Other sources of information include ERIC reports and state library agency reports. For example, Rhode Island has provided a well-done state funding history of public library construction beginning in 1965 that documents the distribution of local, state, and federal funds (http://www.olis.ri.gov/grants/construction/planning/funding.php). State library association journals are another source for summaries of the impact of LSCA construction funds (e.g., Lamont, 1998; Fredericksen, 1999).

2. Anders C. Dahlgren, author of *Public Library Space Needs: A Planning Outline*, has written an author's note to the 2009 edition that modestly summarizes the history of this important work: "With extensive support from Wisconsin, Department of Public Instruction's editors, Publication No. 8210, *Public Library Space Needs: A Planning Outline* appeared in 1988. A revision was published online in 1998. Since that original publication, a number of state library agencies and state library associations have modeled similar recommended processes on *Public Library Space Needs: A Planning Outline*, including Connecticut, Iowa, Illinois, and Texas. . . . In 2007, the Library Buildings and Equipment Section of the International Federation of Library Associations published *IFLA Library Building Guidelines: Developments & Reflections*, which includes a variation on the *Outline* as its recommended method for establishing a library's space need. It's gratifying to see that the Outline has legs, given its modest beginnings. This update reflects the essential facility concerns of public libraries in the early part of the twenty-first

century and with a little luck will continue to be a useful tool for librarians across Wisconsin and beyond."

3. Since 2006, the Center for Library and Information Innovation at the University of Maryland, the Information Institute at Florida State University, and the ALA, with funding from the Bill and Melinda Gates Foundation, have partnered to conduct the Public Library Internet surveys as part of the larger *Public Library Funding and Technology Access Study* (ALA, 2007–2009). The Center for Library and Information Innovation, under the direction of John Carlo Bertot, led the survey component of the study for the 2009–2012 survey series. In their most recent report the study team recognized the significant efforts of the state librarians, state data coordinators, other state library staff members, and all the public librarians who completed the survey and participated in the focus groups and site visits (Bertot et al., 2010). See also the series *Public Library and the Internet*, posted at the website of the Center for Library and Information Innovation (http://www.liicenter.org).

4. This was the Telecommunications and Information Infrastructure Assistance Program, Technology Opportunities Program, funded by the U.S. Department of Commerce, NTIA (http://www.ntia.doc.gov/).

5. The Universal Service Administrative Company (USAC, http://www.universalservice.org/sl/) is an independent, not-for-profit corporation designated as the administrator of the federal Universal Service Fund by the FCC. USAC administers Universal Service Fund programs for high-cost companies serving rural areas, low-income consumers, rural health care providers, and schools and libraries. The Universal Service Fund helps provide communities across the country with affordable telecommunications services. The Schools and Libraries Program reimburses telecommunications, Internet access, and internal connections providers for discounts on eligible services provided to schools and libraries. While schools and libraries apply for these discounts, USAC works in conjunction with service providers to make sure these discounts are passed on to program participants.

6. Interview with Sara M. Taffae, computing consultant, State Library of Louisiana, Baton Rouge, 2010. Sara coordinated the team that implemented the Gates grants in Louisiana through the state library. Sara's work throughout Louisiana to create the public library computing infrastructure from the 1980s through 2010 has been recognized for her capacity to adapt to change—from laser discs to mobile devices. Sara is truly a model library innovator whose career paralleled the automation of public libraries. She learned computing from the ground up in service of information equity. Thank you, Sara for all you did. Sara retired in the summer of 2010.

7. The NTIA issued a Notice of Funds Availability (NOFA) and solicitation of applications on July 1, 2009, announcing the availability of funds and providing guidelines for the State Broadband Data and Development Program pursuant to the American Recovery and Reinvestment Act of 2009 and the Broadband Data Improvement Act. [Pub. L. No. 111-5, 123 Stat. 115 (2009); Title I of Public L. No. 110-385, 122 Stat. 4096 (2008). See the NOFA on the State Broadband Data and Development Program for all application requirements.] The State Broadband Data and Development Program is a competitive, merit-based matching grant program to fund projects that collect comprehensive and accurate state-level broadband mapping data, develop state level broadband maps, assist in the development and maintenance of a national

broadband map, and fund statewide initiatives directed at broadband planning. See State Broadband Data and Development Program Notice of Funds Availability (Broadband USA: Connecting America's Communities, http://www2.ntia.doc.gov/rules)—the Recovery Act appropriated $7.2 billion and directed the Department of Agriculture's RUS and NTIA to expand broadband access to unserved and underserved communities across the United States, increase jobs, spur investments in technology and infrastructure, and provide long-term economic benefits. The result is the RUS BIP and the NTIA BTOP. BIP will make loans and grants for broadband infrastructure projects in rural areas. BTOP will provide grants to fund broadband infrastructure, public computer centers, and sustainable broadband adoption projects (http://broadbandusa.gov/index.htm).

References

ADA Accessibility Guidelines for Buildings and Facilities. 2002. U.S. Access Board. http://www.access-board.gov/adaag/html/adaag.htm.

Alire, Camila A. 2000. *Library Disaster Planning and Recovery Handbook*. New York: Neal-Schuman.

American Institute of Architects. 2009. "2009 AIA/ALA Building Awards." http://www.aia.org/press/AIAB061549.

American Library Association. 1956. *Public Library Service: A Guide to Evaluation with Minimum Standards*. Chicago: American Library Association.

American Library Association. 2007–2009. *Public Library Funding and Technology Access Study*. American Library Association. http://www.ala.org/ala/research/initiatives/plftas/2008_2009/index.cfm.

American Library Association. 2010a. "Disaster Preparedness and Recovery." http://www.ala.org/ala/issuesadvocacy/advocacy/federallegislation/govinfo/disasterpreparedness/index.cfm.

American Library Association. 2010b. "Know Your Stimulus." http://www.ala.org/ala/issuesadvocacy/advocacy/knowstimulus/index.cfm.

American Library Association. 2010c. "Library Services for People with Disabilities." In *ALA Policy Manual*, 54.3.2. Chicago: American Library Association. http://www.ala.org/ala/aboutala/governance/policymanual.

American Library Association. 2010d. "U.S. Department of Agriculture Designates $100 Million for Rural Libraries." *District Dispatch*. http://www.wo.ala.org/districtdispatch/?p=4314.

American Library Association, Office for Literacy and Outreach Services. 2008. *Handbook for Mobile Library Staff*. http://www.ala.org/ala/aboutala/offices/olos/bookmobiles/mobileservices.cfm.

American Library Association, Office for Literacy and Outreach Services. 2010. "Services to Bookmobile Communities." http://www.ala.org/ala/aboutala/offices/olos/bookmobiles.cfm.

American Recovery and Reinvestment Act of 2009. P.L. 111-5, 123 Stat, 115 (2009).

Antonelli, Monika. 2008. "The Green Library Movement: An Overview of Green Library Literature from 1979 to the Future of Green Libraries." *Electronic Green Journal* 27 (Fall). http://escholarship.org/uc/item/39d3v236.

Association of Bookmobile and Outreach Services. 2008. *National Bookmobile Guidelines.* http://www.abos-outreach.org/2008BookmobileGuidelines.pdf.

Balas, Janet L. 2009. "The Library for the Mobile Patron." *Computers in Libraries* 29 (May): 33.

Ball, Mary Alice. 2009. "Aggregating Broadband Demand: Surveying the Benefits and Challenges for Public Libraries." *Government Information Quarterly* 26 (October): 551–558.

Berry, John N. 2004. "The San Jose Model: Gale/*Library Journal* Library of the Year 2004: San Jose Public Library and San Jose State University Library." *Library Journal* 129 (June 15): 34.

———. 2009. "Team Cedar Rapids." *Library Journal* 134 (January 1): 28—30.

Bertot, J. C., Lesley A. Langa, Juston M. Grimes, Kathryn Sigler, and Shannon N. Simmons. 2010. *2009–2010 Public Library Funding and Access Survey.* American Library Association. http://www.plinternetsurvey.org/?q=node/13.

Bill and Melinda Gates Foundation. 2010. "Libraries." http://www.gatesfoundation.org/Libraries.

Blumenstein, Lynn. 2009. "San Jose's Green Art." *Library Journal Library by Design* (Spring): 24–25.

———. 2010. "Small Footprint with Big Impact." *Library Journal Library by Design* 30 (Spring): 30.

Bobinski, George S. 1969. "Carnegie Library Architecture." In *Carnegie Libraries: Their History and Impact on American Library Development*, 57–75. Chicago: American Library Association.

Bracquet, Donna. 2009. "Information Needs in a Hurricane Gustav Evacuation Shelter: Reflections on a Librarian's Volunteer Experience." *Southeastern Librarian* 57 (Fall): 16–28.

Breisch, Kenneth A. 2003. *Henry Hobson Richardson and the Small Public Library in America: A Study in Typology.* Cambridge: MIT Press.

Brevik, Patricia Senn, Luann Budd, and Richard F. Woods. 2005. "We're Married! The Rewards and Challenges of Joint Libraries." *Journal of Academic Librarianship* 31 (September): 401–408.

Broome, Beth. 2009. "Marlon Blackwell Renews the Dignity of the Aging Fulbright Building." *Architectural Record* 197 (June): 86–90.

Bryan, Cheryl. 2009. "Beginning Your Green Building." *Library Journal* (Fall): 31.

Burke, Susan K. 2009. "Perceptions of Public Library Accessibility for People with Disabilities." *The Reference Librarian* 50, no. 1: 43–54.

Dahlgren, Anders C. 2009. *Public Library Space Needs: A Planning Outline/2009.* Wisconsin Department of Public Instruction, Public Library Development. http://dpi.wi.gov/pld/pdf/plspace.pdf#page=5.

Dawson, Alma, and Kathleen de la Peña McCook. 2006. "Rebuilding Community in Louisiana after the Hurricanes of 2005." *Reference and User Services Quarterly* 45 (Summer): 292–296.

Dempsey, Lorcan. 2009. "Always on: Libraries in a World of Permanent Connectivity." *First Monday* 14 (January). http://firstmonday.org/htbin/cgiwrap/bin/ojs/index.php/fm/article/viewArticle/2291/2070.

Distant Librarian. 2009. "DC Public Library Announces iPhone App for Their Catalog." http://distlib.blogs.com/distlib/2009/01/dc-public-libra.html..

Dorr, Jessica, and Richard Akeroyd. 2001. "New Mexico Tribal Libraries: Bridging the Digital Divide." *Computers in Libraries* 21, no. 8 (October): 36–43. http://www.infotoday.com/cilmag/oct01/dorr&akeroyd.htm.

Duggar, David. 2009. "Atkins Branch: Shreveport's Seaport." *Louisiana Libraries* 71 (Winter): 21–24.

Ellis, Jamie Bounds, and Jane Shambra. 2008. "Reshaping Public Services after a Disaster." *Mississippi Libraries* 72 (Fall): 51–53.

Fackerell, Reita. 2008. "So You Think You Are Ready for a Disaster? Don't Be So Sure . . . Learning from the Seaside Public Library Experience." *OLA Quarterly* 14 (Winter): 15–16.

Federal Communications Commission. 2010. "Universal Service." http://www.fcc.gov/wcb/tapd/universal_service/.

Fisher, Karen, M. L. Saxton, P. M. Edwards, and J.-E. Mai. 2007. "Seattle Public Library as Place: Reconceptualizing Space, Community, and Information at the Central Library." In *Library as Place: History, Community and Culture*, edited by G. J. Leckie & J. Buschman, 135–160. Westport, CT: Libraries Unlimited.

"Florida Library Merges Branch, Social Services." 2009. *Library Journal* 134 (August): 10.

Forrest, Charles. 2002. "Building Libraries and Library Building Awards—Twenty Years of Change: An Interview with Anders C. Dahlgren." *Library Administration and Management Journal* 16 (Summer): 120–125.

Fox, Bette-Lee. 2009. "Library Buildings 2009: The Constant Library." *Library Journal* (December 15).

Fredericksen, L. 1999. "To House the Books and the Readers: LSCA Title II Grants in Washington." *Alki* 15 (December 15): 14–15.

"Gates Foundation Commits $3.4 Million to Better Broadband Access." 2010. *American Libraries* 41 (January/February): 31.

Gisolfi, Peter. 2009. "A Green Library Inside and Out." *Library Journal: Library by Design* (Spring): 8.

Goldberger, Paul. 2004. "High-Tech Bibliophilia." *The New Yorker* 80 (May 24): 90–92.

Gordon, Andrew C., Margaret T. Gordon, Elizabeth Moore, and Linda Heuertz. 2003. "The Gates Legacy." *Library Journal* 128 (March 1): 44–48.

Greenwood, Bill. 2009. "Bill and Melinda Gates Foundation Targets Library Internet Speeds." *Computers in Libraries* 29 (March): 32.

Gregorian, Vartan. 2002. "Libraries as Acts of Civic Renewal" (Speech). Kansas City Public Library. http://www.kclibrary.org/support/central/index.cfm (no longer available).

Gregory, Gwen. 1999. "The Library Services and Technology Act: How Changes from LSCA Are Affecting Libraries." *Public Libraries* 38 (November/December): 378–382.

Hadro, Josh. 2009. "Interfaces Galore for Mobile Devices." *Library Journal* 134 (March 1): 19–20.

———. 2010. "Top Tech Trends Panel Focuses on End Users and E-Books." *Library Journal* (January).

Halverson, Kathleen, and Jean Plotas. 2006. "Creating and Capitalizing on the Town/Gown Relationship: An Academic Library and a Public Library Form a Community Partnership." *Journal of Academic Librarianship* 32 (November): 624–629.

Hatfield, Jean. 2008. "Doing What We Do Best." *Public Libraries* 47 (July/August): 19–20.

Henderson, Jill. 2007. "Exploring the Combined Public/School Library." *Knowledge Quest* 35 (January/February): 34–37.

Horrigan, John. 2009. *Wireless Internet Use.* Pew Internet and American Life Project. http://pewinternet.org/Reports/2009/12-Wireless-Internet-Use.aspx.

Jeffers, Eugene J. 2009. "Electronic Outreach and Our Internet Patrons." *Public Libraries* 48 (January/February): 21–22.

Joeckel, Carleton B., and Amy Winslow. 1948. *A National Plan for Public Library Service.* Chicago: American Library Association.

Johnson, L., A. Levine, and R. Smith. 2009. The 2009 Horizon Report. Austin, TX: New Media Consortium. http://wp.nmc.org/horizon2009/.

Jones, Theodore. 1997. *Carnegie Libraries Across America: A Public Legacy.* New York: John Wiley.

Kahn, Miriam B. 2008. *The Library Security and Safety Guide to Prevention, Planning, and Response.* Chicago: American Library Association.

Kenney, Brian. 2001. "Minneapolis PL to Revitalize Its Downtown." *Library Journal* 126 (June 15): 12.

Kent, Fred, and Phil Myrick. 2003. "How to Become a Great Public Space." *American Libraries* 34 (April): 72–76.

King, David Lee. 2009a. "Building a Digital Branch." *American Libraries.* (October). 40.

———. 2009b. "Building the Digital Branch: Guidelines for Transforming Your Library Website." *Library Technology Reports* 45 (August/September).

Kniffel, Leonard. 2003. "Bill Gates: Why He Did It." *American Libraries* 34 (December): 48–53.

Kolleeny, Jane F. 2008. "Gentry Public Library." *Architectural Record* 196 (October): 138.

Krabrill, Britta. 2009. "Tweeting in the Stacks: Why Public Libraries Should Embrace Twitter." *Florida Libraries* 52 (Fall): 14–15.

Lamont, Bridget L. 1998. "The Legacy of the Library Services and Construction Act in Illinois." *Illinois Libraries* 80, no. 3 (Summer): 93–184.

Lane, Christian K. 1989. "Chicago Public Library Competition." *Chicago Architectural Journal* 7: 6–27.

Library of Congress, National Library Service for the Blind and Physically Handicapped. 2009. *Guide to State Laws Relating to Library Services for Blind and Physically Handicapped Individuals.* Washington, DC: Library of Congress.

Lushington, Nolan. 2002. *Libraries Designed for Users: A 21st Century Guide.* New York: Neal-Schuman.

Mandel, Lauren H., Bradley Wade Bishop, Charles R. McClure, John Carlo Bertot, and Paul T. Jaeger. 2010. "Broadband for Public Libraries: Importance, Issues, and Research Needs." *Government Information Quarterly* 27 (July): 280–291.

Manjarrez, C., L. Langa, and K. Miller. 2009. *A Catalyst for Change: LSTA Grants to States Program Activities and the Transformation of Library Services to the Public*. IMLS-2009-RES-01. Washington, DC: Institute of Museum and Library Services. http://www.imls.gov/pdf/ CatalystForChange.pdf.

MARZ Associates, in association with WGBH, Boston. 1989. "Design Wars." *Nova*. VHS. Boston: WGBH Educational Foundation.

Mattern, Shannon. 2007. *The New Downtown Library*. Minneapolis: University of Minnesota Press.

McClure, Charles R., and Paul T. Jaeger. 2009. *Public Libraries and Internet Service Roles: Measuring and Maximizing Internet Services*. Chicago: American Library Association.

McClure, Charles R., J. Ryan, L. H. Mandel, J. Brobst, C. C. Hinnant, J. Andrade, and J. T. Snead. 2009. "Hurricane Preparedness and Response for Florida Public Libraries: Best Practices and Strategies." *Florida Libraries* 52 (Spring): 4–7.

McCook, Kathleen de la Peña. 2000. *A Place at the Table: Participating in Community Building*. Chicago: American Library Association.

———. 2002. *Rocks in the Whirlpool: The American Library Association and Equity of Access*. ERIC ED462981. Chicago: American Library Association.

Miller, William. 2001. "Joint-Use Libraries: Introduction." *Resource Sharing and Information Networks* 15: 131–150.

Mosley, Pixey Anne, and Wendi Arant-Kaspar. 2009. "LLAMA News Section." *Library Leadership & Management* 23 (Summer): 152–155.

Murdock, James. 2008. "Mulberry Street Branch, New York City." *Architectural Record* 196 (February): 148–151.

"Narratives from the Storm." 2008. *Texas Library Journal* 84, no. 4 (Winter): 162, 164–166.

National Conference of State Legislatures. 2009. *Children and the Internet: Laws Relating to Filtering, Blocking and Usage Policies in Schools and Libraries*. http://www.ncsl.org/IssuesResearch/TelecommunicationsInformationTechnology/StateInternetFilteringLaws/tabid/13491/Default.aspx.

Németh, Jeremy, and Stephan Schmidt. 2007. "Toward a Methodology for Measuring the Security of Publicly Accessible Spaces." *Journal of the American Planning Association* 73 (Summer): 283–297.

"New Colorado Facility Becomes First Carbon-Positive Library." 2009. *American Libraries Online* (December 12). http://www.americanlibrariesmagazine.org/.

OCLC. 2010. "Support and Training." http://www.oclc.org/us/en/supportandtraining/default.htm.

Oder, Norman. 2007. "Gates Offers New Grant Program." *Library Journal* 132 (February 15): 16–17.

———. 2008. "Hurricanes Hurt Gulf Coast PLs." *Library Journal* 133 (October): 15.

Olliver, James, and Susan Anderson. 2001. "Seminole Community Library: Joint-Use Library Services for Community and the College." *Resource Sharing and Information Networks* 15: 89–102.

Persichini, Gina, Michael Samuelson, and Lisa Bowman Zeiter. 2008. "E-Branch in a Box: How Idaho Libraries Created an Easy and Sustainable Web Presence." *PNLA Quarterly* 72 (Winter): 18–19.

Public Library Association. 1967. *Minimum Standards for Public Library Systems, 1966*. Chicago: American Library Association.

Putnam, Robert D., and Lewis M. Feldstein. 2003. "Branch Libraries: The Heartbeat of the Community." In *Better Together: Restoring the American Community*, 34–54. New York: Simon and Schuster.

Quinlan, Nora J., and Johanna Tuñón. 2004. "Providing Reference in a Joint-Use Library." *Internet Reference Services Quarterly* 9, no. 1/2: 111–128.

Rabun, J. Stanley. 2000. *Structural Analysis of Historic Buildings: Restoration, Preservation and Adaptive Reuse Applications for Architects and Engineers*. New York: Wiley.

Rivers, Vickie. 2004. *The Branch Librarians' Handbook*. Jefferson, NC: McFarland.

Sampson, Joann. 2009. "Outreach as Virtual Branch." *Public Libraries* 48 (January/February): 23–24.

Sannwald, William W. 2008. *Checklist of Building Design Considerations*. 5th ed. Chicago: American Library Association.

Senville, Wayne. 2009. "Libraries: The Hubs of Our Communities." *Planning Commissioners Journal* 75 (Summer): 12–18.

"Six Chicago Architects: Impressions of the Chicago Public Library Competition." 1989. *Chicago Architectural Journal* 7: 28–37.

Slavick, Steven. 2009. "Problem Situations, Not Problem Patrons." *Public Libraries* 48 (November/December): 38–42.

Stone, Amy. 2005. "Gates Foundation Gives Away $10.9 Million." *American Libraries* 36 (February): 12, 14.

Todaro, Julie Beth. 2009. *Emergency Preparedness for Libraries*. Lanham, MD: Government Institutes.

Trapskin, Ben. 2008. "A Changing of the Guard: Emerging Trends in Public Library Security." *Library and Archival Security* 21 (September): 69–76.

"2010 Library Design Showcase." 2010. *American Libraries* 41 (April): 38–45.

Urbanska, Wanda. 2009. "A Greener Library, A Greener You." *American Libraries* 40 (April): 52–55.

U.S. Access Board. 2010. "Accessibility Guidelines and Standards." http://www.access-board.gov/index.htm.

U.S. Department of Education, Office of Educational Research and Improvement. 1996. *Biennial Evaluation Report, 1995–1996: Public Library Construction and Technology Enhancement Grants to State Library Agencies* (CFDA No. 84-154). http://www.ed.gov/pubs/Biennial/95-96/eval/603-97.pdf.

U.S. Institute of Museum and Library Services. 2007. "State Programs: 5 Year Plans." Institute of Museum and Library Services. http://www.imls.gov/programs/5yearplans.shtm.

———. 2008a. "Library Services and Technology Act (LSTA) Five Year Plan, 2008–2012: Oklahoma Department of Libraries." Institute of Museum and Library Services. http://www.imls.gov/pdf/5yrplans/OKplan2012.pdf.

———. 2008b. "Library Services and Technology Act (LSTA) Five Year Plan for Texas, 2008–2012. Institute of Museum and Library Services. http://www.imls.gov/pdf/5yrplans/TXplan2012.pdf.

————. 2010. *Public Libraries Survey: Fiscal Year 2008.* IMLS-2010–PLS-02. Washington, DC; Institute of Museum and Library Services. http://harvester.census.gov/imls/pubs/Publications/pls2008.pdf.

Vollmer, Timothy. 2010. "There's an App for That! Libraries and Mobile Technology: An Introduction to Public Policy Considerations." Washington, DC: ALA Office for Information Technology Policy. http://www.ala.org/ala/aboutala/offices/oitp/publications/policybriefs/mobiledevices.pdf.

Waller, Elizabeth, and Patricia Bangs. 2007. "Embracing the Problem Customer." *Public Libraries* 46 (September/October): 27–28.

Wisconsin Department of Public Instruction. 2010. *Wisconsin Public Library Standards.* 5th ed. http://dpi.state.wi.us/pld/standard/html.

Zach, Lisl, and Michelynn McKnight. 2010a. "Innovative Services Improvised During Disasters: Evidence-Based Education Modules to Prepare Students and Practitioners for Shifts in Community Information Needs." *Journal of Education for Library and Information Science* 51 (Spring): 76–85.

————. 2010b. "Special Services in Special Times: Responding to Changed Information Needs During and After Community-Based Disasters." *Public Libraries* 49 (March/April): 37–43.

8

Adult Services

Knowing which services public libraries provide for adults, including special groups of adults, and how these services are selected, is vital to determining and publicizing the valuable contributions public libraries make to their communities.

—A. Stephens

The scope of public library services for adults has expanded, from the initial provision and oversight of collections organized mainly for serious adult reading beginning in the nineteenth century to cultural enrichment and adult education taking hold in the twentieth century, and to a far broader set of services relating to the public sphere, cultural heritage, education, and information today. During the twentieth century more active services were added to collection development such as reference and information, adult education, readers' advisory, community programming, career support, genealogy, and local history. Librarians worked thoughtfully as a profession during the twentieth century to define and measure the ideal configuration of public library adult services, especially since the 1980s when the planning process model replaced national standards for public libraries.

In the twenty-first century, public libraries are characterized not only by the services developed by librarians in collaboration with community assessment and planning, but by society's recognition of public libraries as anchor institutions—centers of community reinvention (Birch, 2007). Adult services have added new dimensions in the twenty-first century in response to changing technologies, notably mobile access and digital services.

Each public library determines the structure of its adult services. The difficulty in characterizing adult services derives from their variety and also from the changing organization within the American Library Association (ALA), which does not place coordinated emphasis on adult services as an area of practice. The focus for development of adult service standards resides primarily within three divisions of the ALA—the Reference and User Services Association (RUSA), the Public Library Association (PLA), and the Association of Specialized and Cooperative Library Agencies (ASCLA)—as well as under the aegis of the Office for Literacy and Outreach Services and the Ethnic and Multicultural Information Exchange Round Table. Adult services are not addressed as a whole in the same way as library services to children or young adults. Services for adults are addressed as individual services, which makes it a challenge to convey adult services as a unified focus for public librarians. This chapter provides a brief history of the development of adult services in public libraries and then an overview of the current status of the most common adult services, using the services responses developed by the PLA (Nelson, 2008).

Definitions and Milestones

Adult services is an inclusive term designating all services provided to adults in the public library, including the following:

- Selection of resources for the library's collection including print, digital, audio, and visual media
- Providing physical, electronic, and mobile access to the collection, including services to facilitate access such as instruction, readers' advisory, and guidance
- Reference and information services
- Activation of use of the library's resources for individuals and community groups

From the time of their founding, public libraries have provided support to adults seeking self-education. This included reading guidance, service to community organizations, and adaptation of service for people with special needs. The conflict between librarians who felt libraries should only develop collections as their central purpose—evident in the ALA presidential address of Hiller C. Wellman (1915)—and those who felt that educational services were most important—evident in the presidential address of Walter L. Brown (1917) two years later—continued for decades.

Formalization of the public library's commitment to adult services became clearer in the 1920s with the publication of several major studies relating to adult education. *The American Public Library and the Diffusion of Knowledge*, by William S. Learned (1924), resonated among librarians already involved in a variety of adult services. Adult services scholar Margaret Monroe (1963: 29) characterized Learned's book as "a perceptive synthesis and orderly summation of significant services already envisioned and initiated in public libraries." It also provided the intellectual justification for ALA to take action with the appointment of a Commission on the Library and Adult Education. The commission's report, *Libraries and Adult Education* (1926), studied the role of adult education and became the foundation of the subsequent expansion of adult services in public libraries. ALA then established a Board on Library and Adult

Education, which reported activities in the journal *Adult Education and the Library* (1924–1930) and later the ALA *Bulletin*. These included reading studies, the Reading with a Purpose Project, and ongoing work with the American Association for Adult Education. The work of Julia Wright Merrill on behalf of ALA's Library Extension Board was informed by progressive ideals and contributed to empowerment of adults through the extension of education as a public library goal.[1]

In 1934 John Chancellor was appointed to the ALA headquarters staff to initiate a ten-year assessment of adult education development in public libraries. Libraries were viewed as deeply conscious that they were an adult education agency; readers' advisory services gained acceptance; and librarians interacted with other adult education agencies. Alvin Johnson developed the argument that the public library can be a vibrant provider of knowledge in his 1938 study, *The Public Library—A People's University*. Johnson's motivations have been questioned by Latham (2010), who points to his early engagement with social power brokers who viewed the public library as an avenue of social control.[2] Even so, library professionals appropriated Johnson's catchphrase, "the people's university," and used it to cement the role of the public library in American society. Swain (1995) has documented the expansion of readers' services during the New Deal, including supervised reading rooms, bookmobiles, and rural library services.

By the late 1930s, librarians began to use the broader term *adult services* but projects within the ALA under the rubric *adult education* continued. These included the establishment of the Adult Education Section within the Public Library Division in 1946; the American Heritage Project, funded by the Ford Foundation Fund for Adult Education, 1951–1954 (Preer, 1993); and the creation of the Office of Adult Education at ALA, which awarded subgrants of $1.5 million to libraries to stimulate adult education activities (1951–1961). Funds were provided for Great Books and political education, emphasizing discussion groups. A national survey of 1,692 public libraries conducted by Helen Lyman, *Adult Education Activities in Public Libraries*, was published in 1954—the first effort to describe the scope of adult services across the United States.

In 1957 after these landmark efforts, the organization of services to adults within ALA had outgrown its place within the Public Library Division and was granted division status as the Adult Services Division (ASD). At its founding ASD identified five aspects of adult services:

- Indirect guidance (displays, reading lists)
- Advisory services (informed and planned reading)
- Services to organizations and groups (exhibits, readings lists, book talks, program planning support)

- Library-sponsored programs (films, discussion groups, radio, television)
- Community advisory services

The Notable Books Council and other bibliographic projects relating to adult materials also fell under ASD. The division published the *ASD Newsletter*, which incorporated the *Library Services to Labor Newsletter* in 1964. Projects carried out included the Library-Community Project, the Reading for an Age of Change series, and work with adult new readers (Heim, 1990; Phinney, 1967).

In 1970 the ASD jointly adopted the policy, "Library Rights of Adults: A Call for Action," with the Reference Services Division, which stated that each adult should have the right to a library that seeks to understand both his needs and his wants and that uses every means to satisfy them. Given the common goals of the two divisions, a merger took place in 1972 to form the Reference and Adult Services Division (RASD). Adult services within RASD were the focus of several committees, including the Service to Adults Committee (Hansen, 1995).

During the late 1960s and 1970s, U.S. libraries made a renewed stronger commitment to equal service for all and adult services expanded in focus. Libraries in the South desegregated and libraries throughout the nation focused on outreach (Tucker, 1998; Josey, 1994; Weibel, 1982). In 1970 ALA established the Office for Library Service to the Disadvantaged, now the Office for Literacy and Outreach Services, under the direction of Jean E. Coleman. The purposes of the office were (1) to promote the provision of library service to the urban and rural poor, of all ages, and to those people who are discriminated against because they belong to minority groups; (2) to encourage the development of user-oriented informational and educational library services to meet the needs of the urban and rural poor, ethnic minorities, the underemployed, school dropouts, the semiliterate and illiterate, and those isolated by cultural differences; and (3) to ensure that librarians and others have information and access to technical assistance and continuing education opportunities to assist them in developing effective outreach programs (McCook, 2001b).

In *The Service Imperative for Libraries* (Schlachter, 1982), the adult services paradigm for public libraries was presented in a series of essays in honor of adult services scholar Margaret E. Monroe. The four basic adult services functions identified were information, guidance, instruction, and stimulation. Monroe viewed stimulation as a library's response to community needs along a continuum from highly innovative to extensions of existing services.

In 1983 the Services to Adults Committee of RASD won an ALA Goal Award to conduct a national survey of adult services among 1,758 libraries serving populations of 25,000 or more. This survey, which extended the work done by Helen Lyman 30 years earlier, was titled the Adult Services in the Eighties Project. Results appeared in the monograph, *Adult Services: An Enduring Focus for Public Libraries* (Heim and

Wallace, 1990), with essays focusing on key services: lifelong learning; services to minorities, job seekers, labor, parents, older adults, people with disabilities, and genealogists; support for economic development; and public access microcomputers. Analysis conducted by Wallace included comparison of regional differences in service provision and demographic differences (Heim and Wallace, 1990).[3]

RASD became the Reference and User Services Association (RUSA) in 1996, at which time the designation "adult services" disappeared from the divisional organizational structure of the ALA. No longer the specific focus of a particular ALA unit, adult services as an area of library practice are now addressed by various smaller subsets. These include sections of RUSA:

1. CODES, the Collection Development and Evaluation Section
2. History Section, which represents the subject interests of reference librarians, archivists, bibliographers, genealogists, historians, and others engaged in historical reference or research
3. Machine-Assisted Reference Section (MARS), which represents the interests of those concerned with all forms of computer-based reference information services
4. BRASS, Business Reference and Services Section
5. RSS, Reference Services Section, for librarians and support staff involved with frontline reference, and for those providing library services to special populations of users such as the aging and Spanish –speakers; includes a committee on services to adults with the charge: to identify the library and program interests of adults; to collect and disseminate information on existing library programs and services; to develop guidelines for programs and services to meet specific interests and needs of adults; to serve as a consultant for libraries with adult programming and/or services problems; and to create ad hoc subcommittees as needed to accomplish the above goals
6. STARS, Sharing and Transforming Access to Resources Section, dedicated to resource-sharing activities (RUSA, http://www.ala.org/RUSA)

The PLA includes aspects of adult services in its Communities of Practice—groups of people who continuously come together to share their knowledge and enthusiasm for a specific subject. Adult services Communities of Practice as listed at the PLA website in 2010 include audiovisual services, readers' advisory, services to Spanish speakers, and service to urban populations (Public Library Association, Communities of Practice, http://www.ala.org/ala/mgrps/divs/pla/plagroups/placops/index.cfm).

The Libraries Serving Special Populations Section of ASCLA works to improve the quality of library service for people with special needs, including people who have vision, mobility, hearing, and developmental differences, people who are elderly, and people in prisons, health care facilities, and other types of institutions; to improve library service for families and professionals working with these people; and to foster awareness of these populations and their needs in the library community and among the general public.

The ALA Office for Literacy and Outreach Services (OLOS) also focuses attention on services that are inclusive of traditionally underserved populations, including new readers and nonreaders, geographically isolated people, people with disabilities, rural and urban poor people, and people generally discriminated against based on race, ethnicity, sexual orientation, age, language, and social class. The office ensures that training, information resources, and technical assistance are available to help libraries and librarians develop effective strategies to develop programs and service for new users (OLOS, http://www.ala.org/ala/aboutala/offices/olos/index.cfm).

The ALA Ethnic and Multicultural Information Exchange Round Table (EMIERT, http://www.ala.org/ala/mgrps/rts/emiert/aboutemiert/aboutemiert.cfm) serves as a source of information on recommended ethnic collections, services, and programs. It maintains a liaison with OLOS and cooperates with other ALA units, including the ethnic caucuses, in joint projects for the betterment of outreach services. The ethnic caucuses are the American Indian Library Association, Asian/Pacific American Librarians Association, Black Caucus of the American Library Association, Chinese American Librarians Association, and REFORMA—National Association to Promote Library and Information Services to Latinos and the Spanish-Speaking.

Thus, while there is no single national access point for the public librarian desiring information about adult services that parallels the youth services associations of the ALA (Association for Library Service to Children and the Young Adult Services Association), an overarching commitment to adult services is embedded in the fabric of the work librarians do. One way to view these evolving services is in the context of the planning process as defined by the PLA.

After the widespread adoption of the PLA planning process for public libraries in the 1980s, services in public libraries were characterized as aspects of eight public library roles:

1. Community activities center
2. Community information center
3. Formal education support center
4. Independent learning center
5. Popular materials library
6. Preschoolers Door to Learning
7. Reference library
8. Research center (McClure, 1987)

When the planning process changed the terminology "library roles" to "service responses" in the 1990s, the various functions were delineated as thirteen service responses:

1. Basic literacy
2. Business and career information
3. Commons
4. Community referral
5. Consumer information
6. Cultural awareness
7. Current topics and titles
8. Formal learning centers
9. General information
10. Government information
11. Information literacy
12. Lifelong learning
13. Local history and genealogy (Nelson, 2001)

In 2008 the PLA planning guide, *Strategic Planning for Results*, expanded the number of service responses from 13 to 18:

1. "Be an Informed Citizen: Local, National and World Affairs"
2. "Build Successful Enterprises: Business and Nonprofit Support"
3. "Celebrate Diversity: Cultural Awareness"
4. "Connect to the Online World: Public Internet Access"
5. "Create Young Readers: Early Literacy"
6. "Discover Your Roots: Genealogy and Local History"
7. "Express Creativity: Create and Share Content"
8. "Get Facts Fast: Ready Reference"
9. "Know Your Community: Community Resources and Services"
10. "Learn to Read and Write: Adults, Teens and Family Literature"
11. "Make Career Choices: Job and Career Development"
12. "Make Informed Decisions: Health, Wealth and Other Life Choices"
13. "Satisfy Curiosity: Lifelong Learning"
14. "Stimulate Imagination: Reading, Viewing and Listening for Pleasure"
15. "Succeed in School: Homework Help"
16. "Understand How to Find, Evaluate, and Use Information: Information Fluency"
17. "Visit a Comfortable Place: Physical and Virtual Spaces"
18. "Welcome to the United States: Services for New Immigrants" (Nelson, 2008: 143–217)

In 2009 McClure and Jaeger proposed an alternative to the 18 service responses. They presented the concept of "Internet-enabled" service roles based on a 2007 Pew Internet and American Life report (Estabrook, Witt, and Rainie, 2007). In the discussion of service roles below we identify those that may also be Internet-enabled.

Functions of Adult Services as Reflections of Service Responses

It is one of the aims of this book to tie together the various resources that support public librarianship within the context of current practice by addressing adult services as components of the 18 discrete service responses delineated in *Strategic Planning for Results* (Nelson, 2008: 143–217). The variety of adult services in relationship to the service responses is organized here to reflect a broader vision of the public library's centrality to its communities. Additionally, we will refer to the Internet-enabled roles and responses addressed by McClure and Jaeger (2009). To structure the discussion, the services are presented in four categories (and youth services are similarly characterized in the next chapter) as follows:

- Public sphere
- Cultural heritage
- Education
- Information

Public Sphere

The public library's most expansive role is to be a central component of a community's public sphere. John Buschman (2005: 1) has observed, "Libraries help make possible the democratic public sphere ideal in the form of rational organization of human cultural production and they embody an essential element of democracy: a place where the ideal of unfettered communication and investigation exists in rudimentary form, hosting the turbulent discourse of a democracy and its culture." In this capacity librarians can support the community's links to the daily reality and discourse of those it serves. The theory of information worlds formulated by Jaeger and Burnett (2010) and the social elements that interrelate and interact will be central to public library service development in the decades to come. It is through enhancement of the public sphere that the library builds community and encourages authentic dialogue.

The service responses from *Strategic Planning for Results* that reflect enhancement of the public sphere are "Be an Informed Citizen: Local, National and World Affairs"; "Know Your Community: Community Resources and Services"w; and "Visit a Comfortable Place: Physical and Virtual Spaces."[4]

Be an Informed Citizen: Local, National and World Affairs

The information needed to promote democracy, fulfill civic responsibilities, and participate in community decision making is supported by this service response (Nelson, 2008: 149). The public library is an important part of the public sphere and functions as a commons where community voices come together. Libraries provide the means to foster authentic dialogue, and librarians have long worked to ground the discussion of the public library's service in justice (Preer, 2008; McCook, 2001a). The 2009 Knight Commission report, *Informing Communities: Sustaining Democracy in the Digital Age*, recommended enhanced funding for public libraries as key centers for community dialogue (p. 25). Kranich (2010: 20) has observed: "Extending library programming into the realm of deliberation offers citizens a chance to learn together, frame issues of common concern, weigh choices for solving problems, deepen understanding about others' opinions, and connect across the spectrum of thought."

The importance of the public library in providing a place for engaged citizenship was the topic of several books published at the beginning of the twenty-first century that explored the role of the public library in connection to civil society: *Inside, Outside, and Online* (Hill, 2009); *Libraries and Democracy: The Cornerstones of Liberty* (Kranich, 2001); *Civic Librarianship* (McCabe, 2001); *A Place at the Table: Participating in Community Building* (McCook, 2000b); and *Civic Space/Cyberspace* (Molz and Dain, 1999). Extensive testimony to the public library response of informed citizenship appears in the *Encyclopedia of Community* (Christensen and Levinson, 2003), which characterizes the public library as the starting point for a wide range of community projects. Ristau (2010) has discussed civic engagement programs in California's public libraries.

This service response is also supported by the work of the Government Documents Round Table (GODORT, http://ala.org/ala/mgrps/rts/godort/index.cfm) of the ALA. See, for example, Morrison (2008) on ways to support library users with e-government resources at the local, state, and national levels and especially the GODORT quarterly publication *Documents to the People* (http://ala.org/ala/mgrps/rts/godort/dttp/aboutdttp .cfm).

Public library programs expose the community to new ideas and viewpoints. At the national level, the Public Programs Office of the ALA develops programs that contribute to the intellectual foundation of the library as providing stimulus for civic engagement (http://www.ala.org/ala/aboutala/offices/ppo/index.cfm).

In the tradition of the American Heritage Project of the 1950s (Preer, 1993) the Public Programs Office has promoted reading and viewing discussion programs in the new century, often in partnership with the National Endowment for the Humanities. Hundreds of public libraries have fostered informed citizens with programs such as Picturing America for Public Libraries; One Community, One Book; End of the World or World Without End; Long Gone: The Literature and Culture of African American Migration; and One Vision, Many Voices: Latino Literature in the U.S. (Programming Librarian, 2010).

Know Your Community: Community Resources and Services

Provision of information about the wide variety of programs, services, and activities offered by community agencies and organizations define this service (Nelson, 2008: 180). Public libraries have a long history of providing community information.

The 1970s were the defining period for information and referral (I&R). The Detroit Public Library's Information Place was a model library organized to provide community information, as conceptualized by its director, Clara S. Jones (1978). In a visionary article written for *American Libraries* in 1979, Arthur Curley discussed information and referral as a revolution that would bring information from the people to the people. The classic work covering practical case studies and the actual delivery of library-based I&R, *Information and Referral in Public Libraries*, provided an intellectual and philosophical analysis of the profession's work to develop I&R in the 1970s (Childers, 1984). The appropriate role of libraries in I&R and community information was defined at the national level in the 1983 U.S. National Commission on Libraries and Information Science report, which recommended that community information and I&R are best accomplished with an interdisciplinary coordination of social service agencies and libraries.

I&R and community information services were formally put into action by the Community Information Section of the PLA beginning in 1979. The section developed standards for information and referral for over 25 years, producing four editions of *Guidelines for Establishing Community Information and Referral Services in Public Libraries* (Maas and Manikowski, 1997).

With the advent of the Internet, community networking emerged as a complement to I&R systems (whether library based or not). Librarians were well represented among early rounds of grantees from the Telecommunications and Information Infrastructure Assistance Program (McCook, 2000c). Committed community information librarians utilized new technologies to serve community information needs. In 1999 the possibilities of yoking I&R and electronic web-based information as the Internet exploded were addressed in *The Community Networking Handbook* (Bajjaly, 1999).

In 2000, the Federal Communications Commission assigned 2-1-1 to serve as the three-digit number for access to information and referral services. Involvement by librarians in the implementation of the 2-1-1 initiative is a natural evolution of the profession's long activity in community information services (McCook, 2000c; Chepesiuk, 2001). An outstanding example is LINC, the Library Information Center at the Memphis Public Library (http://www.memphislibrary.org/linc/211.htm). LINC, in conjunction with United Way of the Mid-South, is the local source for community re-

sources. The center maintains a large, comprehensive database of human services organizations, government agencies, and volunteer groups, which can be accessed by
dialing 2-1-1.

Durrance and Pettigrew (2002) identified the contributions libraries make as providers of community information. They view the library and its staff as uniquely qualified to coordinate the provision of community information in local communities,
especially as it becomes widely available in digital formats and distributed by multiple agencies. This service model has grown in importance as e-government has expanded. As pointed out by Jaeger and Bertot (2009), patrons now seek assistance from
public librarians for a range of government services. The roles of e-government service provider and digital ombudsman find librarians providing advice and specific
techniques for applying and integrating various digital and Internet-enabled services
(McClure and Jaeger, 2009: 50–51).

Visit a Comfortable Place: Physical and Virtual Spaces

This service response calls for the library to be a safe and welcoming physical place
where people can meet and interact, read quietly, and have open and accessible virtual spaces that support networking (Nelson, 2008: 210).

The library as place has been the focus of intense analysis in the twenty-first century. The Buschman and Leckie (2007) collection of essays analyzes the public library
as a physical entity, as cultural space, and as a locus of intellectual meaning. Ari
Kelman (2001) has explored the historical meaning of reading at the New York Public
Library, which provides a thoughtful counterpoint to writers like Ron McCabe (2001),
who traces the evolution from silence to a robust commons at the McMillan Memorial
Library in Wisconsin Rapids.

Meeting rooms continue to be an important service, with 225,000 people coming
together in public libraries every day (OCLC, 2010; Hill, 2009). Article VI of the ALA
Library Bill of Rights states that meeting facilities should be made available to members of a community on "an equitable basis, regardless of the beliefs or affiliations of
individuals or groups requesting their use."

Enhanced aspects of the physical space include exhibitions by local artists, traveling displays, and exhibits (Price, 2009a; Swisher, 2007). The addition of cafés to public libraries has been reviewed by Wise (2005), who discusses successful integration
of cafés at the Everett Public Library in Seattle. A case study of librarians developing
new ways to serve the homeless community at the Free Library of Philadelphia provides an illustration of the library as a change agent combining innovative solutions to
meet community challenges with a café, a restroom staffer, and interagency cooperation (Price, 2009b).

The Internet-enabled role of the public library as a "connector of friends, families,
and others" in the networked environment is a means for people to stay connected in

regular times and during disasters. In their monograph on Internet-enabled service roles for the public library, McClure and Jaeger (2009) extend the idea of visiting a comfortable place to a function that ensures family and community sustainability.

Cultural Heritage

Libraries are agencies for the holding and keeping of records and artifacts that help us overcome the limits of insularity (Carr, 2006: 131). Public libraries have long played an important role in preserving and activating cultural heritage and often include museum-like collections (Dilevko and Gottlieb, 2004). Reading discussion groups, lectures, film series, exhibits, and celebrations of different cultures are central adult services that are the basis for partnerships that have expanded the library's involvement in local communities. Additionally, attention to cultural heritage connects the library to state and national organizations that have cognate missions. Three especially come to mind: the Institute of Museum and Library Services (IMLS), the National Endowment for the Humanities (NEH), and the Center for the Book and its affiliates (http://www.read.gov/cfb/affiliates.html).

The IMLS (http://www.imls.gov/index.htm) was established in 1996 as an independent federal grant-making agency that fosters innovation, leadership, and a lifetime of learning by supporting the nation's museums and libraries. Grants and programs supported by IMLS have strengthened the ties between libraries and other cultural heritage institutions—especially museums. The IMLS focus on the learner in a changing world through collaborative partnerships strengthens public library ties to cultural heritage values. IMLS is the primary source of federal support for the nation's libraries and museums. The institute's mission is to create strong libraries and museums that connect people to information and ideas. The institute works at the national level and in coordination with state and local organizations to sustain heritage, culture, and knowledge; enhance learning and innovation; and support professional development.

The NEH has supported opportunities for the public to explore the humanities and culture through activities such as exhibitions, reading and film discussion series, catalogs, lectures, symposia, and websites since 1979 (http://www.neh.gov/index.html). State humanities councils affiliated with NEH have strengthened cultural heritage presence with a regional focus (http://www.neh.gov/whoweare/statecouncils.html). The ALA, most often through its Public Programs Office, has collaborated with NEH to develop library-based humanities programming underscoring the integral role libraries play in providing a forum for cultural exploration.[5] The Public Programs Office fosters cultural programming as an essential component part of library service.

The cultural heritage mission is further enhanced through public libraries' connection to the Center for the Book at the Library of Congress (http://www.read.gov/cfb/), established in 1977 under the aegis of then Librarian of Congress Daniel J. Boorstin, who saw great value in the Library of Congress actively promoting books and reading. The National Book Committee (1954–1974) and the U.S. Governmental Advisory Committee on International Books and Library Programs (1962–1977), supported by the State Department, merged to became the first Advisory Committee for the Center for the Book. The Center for the Book and its state affiliates work closely with libraries to promote national reading campaigns (Lamolinara, 2010). In 2010 a special issue of *Libraries and the Cultural Record* was dedicated to the director of the Center for the Book: "John Y. Cole: Librarian, Bookman, and Scholar" (Maack, 2010). That same year the National Book Festival (http://www.loc.gov/bookfest/), initiated by First Lady Laura Bush in 2001, celebrated its first decade ("A Decade of Words and Wonder," 2010).

The service responses from *Strategic Planning for Results* (Nelson, 2008) that reflect enhancement of the cultural heritage category are "Celebrate Diversity: Cultural Awareness"; "Discover Your Roots: Genealogy and Local History"; "Express Creativity: Create and Share Content"; "Satisfy Curiosity: Lifelong Learning"; and "Stimulate Imagination: Reading, Viewing and Listening for Pleasure."[6]

Celebrate Diversity: Cultural Awareness

This response identifies the need for librarians to provide programs and services that promote appreciation and understanding of the community's various heritages (Nelson, 2008: 158). Cultural competence is required for librarians to meet the needs of a diverse user population (Overall, 2009). Helping users to understand and appreciate the culture of others is an important aspect of adult services; however, identifying resources and evaluating them can be difficult without specific expertise. EMIERT is a source of information on ethnic collections, services, and programs.

The ALA Office for Diversity (http://www.ala.org/ala/aboutala/offices/diversity/index.cfm) serves as a clearinghouse for diversity resources. Librarians of color have formed separate organizations to focus more clearly on service to people from different cultures. These include the American Indian Library Association, Asian/Pacific American Librarians Association, Black Caucus of the American Library Association, Chinese American Librarians Association, and REFORMA—National Association to Promote Library and Information Services to Latinos and the Spanish-Speaking.

The ALA works closely with these affiliates through its Offices of Diversity and the Office for Literacy and Outreach Services, which sponsors the annual Jean E. Coleman lecture on outreach.[7] By working in collaboration with organizations of librarians of color, public librarians will find the resources and support to develop services that honor and respect the cultural heritage of the many people who comprise the diverse population of the United States (McCook, 2000a). In 2006 the first Joint Conference of Librarians of Color was held in Dallas (Goodes, 2006; Proceedings, 2009). A second conference is set for 2012.

The ALA's Gay, Lesbian, Bisexual, and Transgendered Round Table works to develop service models. Carmichael (1998), in *Daring to Find Our Names: The Search for Lesbigay Library History* (1998), describes how the energies of the round table have been devoted to service concerns for lesbigay patrons through subject headings that are not pejorative and the promotion of gay literature. Joyce (2000) has reviewed the literature for public librarians and described the challenges of developing fully inclusive service for the gay, lesbian, and transgendered community. Rothbauer (2007) has explored the challenges that persist in providing a space that can be claimed.

Discover Your Roots: Genealogy and Local History

This service response will help residents and visitors connect the past with the present through family and community histories (Nelson, 2008: 169). For many communities the public library provides access to community memory through the development of local history collections and genealogy services.

The RUSA (2006) Local History Committee has issued "Guidelines for Establishing Local History Collections," which state at the outset that libraries should connect with other community agencies. A key partnership for librarians who work to serve local history needs is the American Association for State and Local History, which provides leadership and support to preserve and interpret state and local history to make the past more meaningful to all Americans. Preserving and safeguarding local history is a central contribution that librarians can make to build local communities. Given and McTavish (2010) have observed a reconvergence of libraries, archives, and museums in the digital age. For example, the Charlotte County, Florida, Library System and the Charlotte County Historical Center collaborated on an IMLS grant after Hurricane Charley to craft a comprehensive digital initiatives plan to preserve and make available online archival and genealogical resources (Jones, 2010).

The Orange County Library System Orlando Memory Project in Florida is another example of a library building community memories by capturing local people's stories and images using innovative technologies (Bachowski, 2009). Indiana's statewide digital history project is a case study of a local history collaborative (Rendfeld, 2008).

The responsibility of public libraries to serve the needs of patrons interested in genealogical research is addressed by the RUSA Genealogical Committee (1999), which has issued "Guidelines for Developing Beginning Genealogical Collections and Services." Services to genealogists are an important aspect of cultural heritage service that connects cultural awareness and local history concerns. Paul Kaplan (2007), an Illinois adult services librarian, has provided an anecdotal introduction to the role public libraries can play in assisting patrons with genealogy and connections to resources outside the local level.

Express Creativity: Create and Share Content

Support for community groups and individual artists and writers is described in this service response (Nelson, 2008: 173). Examples include the following:

- Poetry contests in connection with an Emily Dickinson garden at the Bettendorf, Iowa, Public Library (Hustedde, 2005)
- The Greensboro Public Library partnership with the Green Hill Center for North Carolina Art (Favreau, 2007)
- The Zine Library Group at the Multnomah, Oregon, Public Library, which works in collaboration with the Independent Publishing Resource Center (Nelson, 2007)

Anythink, a "Revolution of Rangeview Libraries" in Adams County, Colorado, has used the creativity response to celebrate imagination, play, and interactivity (http://www.anythinklibraries.org/). The public library as a place for social networking and creative interaction has been explored by Cohen (2009).

Satisfy Curiosity: Lifelong Learning

Resources needed by library patrons to explore topics of personal interest to support their learning throughout life are provided by this service response (Nelson, 2008: 195). Lifelong learners have been defined as adults involved in learning activities other than compulsory (K–12) education. According to Jarvis (2010), new attention will need to be paid to the way technologies affect the way people learn and changing approaches to knowledge and its acquisition and assessment. Lifelong learners include those involved in voluntary learning, as well as in activities that are required for legal, professional, or other reasons (U.S. Department of Education, 2000). Elmborg (2010) has explored the multiple literacies adult learners bring to the learning process within libraries, the changing narratives of libraries, and the importance of helping learners develop skills in critical information literacy.

Public librarians can call upon a long tradition of commitment to the development of human capabilities to provide continuing emphasis on the humanistic aspects of adult learning (Lee, 1966; Monroe, 1963; Van Fleet, 1990; Van Fleet and Raber, 1990). Guides to adult programming provide libraries with methods to integrate programming and lifelong learning (Lear, 2002; Mates, 2003; Rubin, 1997). An outstanding example of lifelong learning facilitated at the Salinas, Kansas, Public Library is the Community Learning and Skill Sharing program (Brack and McKenzie, 2007). An overview of the capability approach to education has been presented by Hinchcliffe and Terzi (2009).

Stimulate Imagination: Reading, Viewing and Listening for Pleasure

Reading and services for the general reader—what most people think of as the central purpose of the public library—are addressed in *Strategic Planning for Results* under the service response of stimulating imagination (Nelson, 2008: 199).

Reading, viewing, and listening for pleasure are a central focus for most public libraries, and acquiring, organizing, and making available current collections is a primary function in the twenty-first century.

The role of recreational reading material in the public library collection provides an interesting history of this primary activity. A substantive summary of the discussions appears in two volumes by Esther Carrier (1965, 1985), *Fiction in Public Libraries, 1876–1900* and *Fiction in Public Libraries, 1900–1950*, which provide a comprehensive analysis of the debate between adherents of "quality" fiction and those who feel that fiction of all types should be included in collections.

Librarians responsible for collection development and readers' advisory services are most effective when they are aware of the history and sociology of reading and its role in the lives of library users. Karetzky's (1982) summary of the history of reading research provides an intellectual guide to the work of early reading theorists. Knowledge of the investigations of reading provides an intellectual basis for public library collection development. Key works like *The Reading Interests and Habits of Adults* (Gray and Munroe, 1929), *What People Want to Read About* (Waples and Tyler, 1931), *Living with Books* (Haines, 1935), and *The Geography of Reading* (Wilson, 1938) are classic studies that help provide an appreciation of the historical role of librarians in the promotion and support of reading.

Understanding reading in the life of adults is beneficial to librarians whose role is to select and promote books. Several analyses provide excellent context:

- Maatta (2010), *A Few Good Books*
- Manguel (2010), *A Reader on Reading*
- Kaestle and Radway (2009), *Print in Motion: The Expansion of Publishing and Reading in the United States, 1880–1940*
- Beam (2008), *A Great Idea at the Time: The Rise, Fall and Curious Afterlife of the Great Books*
- Ross (2006), *Reading Matters: What the Research Reveals about Reading, Libraries and Community*
- Farr (2004), *Reading Oprah: How Oprah's Book Club Changed the Way America Reads*
- Korda (2001), *Making the List: A Cultural History of the American Best Seller*

These works examine reading and try to distill the meaning of the act of reading—what McCook has characterized as "the first virtual reality" or, as Manguel (1996: 303) has observed, trying to describe the variety of moods in reading:

> We read in slow, long motions, as if drifting in space, weightless. We read full of prejudice, malignantly. We read generously, making excuses for the text, filling gaps, mending faults. And sometimes, when the stars are kind, we read with an intake of breath, with a shudder, as if someone or something had "walked over our grave," as if a memory had suddenly been rescued from a place deep within us—the recognition of something we never knew was there, or of something we vaguely felt as a flicker or a shadow, whose ghostly form rises and passes back into us before we can see what it is, leaving us older and wiser.

The shaping of collections that will cause this intake of breath, this rescued memory, is a trust that the public grants librarians. In the early 1990s the profession moved so far from the idea of shaping the collection that librarians such as Charles Robinson advocated, "Give 'Em What They Want"—and selection began to be viewed by some as primarily a reaction to demand (Rawlinson, 1990: 77). This abdication of responsibility has been tempered by leaders such as Sarah Ann Long (2001: viii), who has noted, "We were fitting in with a tide of stylish opinion that was sweeping the country that was both anti-intellectual and antiauthority." The public has also shown an appreciation for some clarity in book selection, as expressed by Vivian Gornick (1998: 40) in a now-classic article in the *New York Times* about books that matter: "I cannot help thinking, 50 years ago in the Bronx, if the library had responded to my needs instead of shaping my needs, what sort of reader would I have become?"

Public librarians serving adults should know the history of reading and reading culture to be able to strike a balance between popular books and the classic and meaningful books that lead to introspection and understanding. This has been discussed by Ross (2009) in her two models of leisure reading in public libraries: "Reading with a Purpose" and "Only the Best" (2009). The Notable Books Council of the ALA produces an annual list of recommended books that demonstrate this balance (http://ala .org/ala/mgrps/divs/rusa/awards/notablebooks/index.cfm).

In addition to philosophical and sociological grounding in book culture, the public sphere is enhanced by librarians' stimulation of reading current topics and titles. A local example with national impact is the Adult Reading Round Table, founded in 1984 and based in concern over the profession's lack of attention to readers' advisory services for adults (Saricks, 2009a). A renaissance of interest in readers' advisory services took place during the 1990s—the same years when so much of the profession's focus was on technology, the Internet, and digitization (Wyatt, 2008; Balcom, 2002).

In the twenty-first century the use of websites and social networking has burgeoned as readers' advisory resources and strategies (Wyatt, 2008; Stover, 2009).

Audiobook and video/DVD collections are important aspects of this service response (Lesesne, 2009; "Notable Videos for Adults," 2010). As Walt Crawford (2003: 59) has astutely characterized the role of complex media in libraries:

> Video tells stories differently than books, which tell stories differently than songs; all have their roles. It's a lot more complicated to make a good video or film than to write a good book. Fortunately, in a world of many media, we—librarians and users—can appreciate, collect, and preserve many different forms of storytelling.

Examples of specific activities librarians can undertake to stimulate imagination include the following:

- Author programs (Langemack, 2007)
- Book talks (Booktalking: Quick and Simple, http://nancykeane.com/book talks/)
- Library programs online (Peters, 2009)
- *One Book, One Community Planning Guide* (Programming Librarian, 2010); see model program from Chicago Public Library (2010): One Book: One Chicago
- Readers' advisory services[8]

The Center for the Book at the Library of Congress and State Center Affiliates for the Book (http://www.read.gov/cfb/state-affiliates.php) develop activities that promote each state's book culture and literary heritage. Book festivals at the national, state, and local level emerged during the 1990s as a new focus for celebrating reading (http://www.imls.gov/pubs/bookfest.htm). First Lady Laura Bush (2001–2009), who initiated the Texas Book Festival in 1995 when she was first lady of Texas, worked with the Library of Congress to begin the Washington, DC, National Book Festival in 2001 (Kniffel, 2001). The National Book Festival continues at this writing, with President and Mrs. Obama cochairing the 2010 festival ("A Decade of Words and Wonder," 2010; Merola, 2009).[9]

The NEH and state humanities councils support research, education, preservation, and public programs. By working closely with these entities, public librarians can extend community dialogue based on reading to topics of current importance.

Library historians seeking to capture the library experience from the users' viewpoint and that of others involved with libraries can clarify the role of libraries in the life of the individual and in the intellectual, cultural, and social life of those who live in the United States. For instance, examining the library experience will further increase understanding of the extent to which librarians have attempted to mediate between the reader and the book to lead the reader to "high" culture (Carpenter, 1996). Herein may be the heart of the librarian's role in the transcendence of the public sphere. The meaning of carefully developed library collections, expert readers' advisory service, and the importance of books in our society is reinforced by musing upon the power of the humanities. In *Riches for the Poor*, Earl Shorris (2000) tells the story of the poor in the United States; shows that the difference between a comfortable life and a life of poverty is often the failure of the poor to enter political life—a life that requires reflection. The power of reading to change lives through cultivation of the public sphere in libraries is mighty.

Education

The 21st Century Learner Conference, a major national event for librarianship held at the beginning of the twenty-first century in November 2001, reaffirmed the role of the public library as an educational institution. Robert S. Martin (2001; see Appendix B), director of the IMLS, stated:

> There is a difference between information and knowledge, and the most important role of the library is not providing access to information, it is supporting, enhancing, and facilitating the transfer of knowledge—in other words, education.

The history of the educational role of the public library has been described by Johnson (1938), Monroe (1981), Blayney (1977), McCook (2002), and Taylor (2010).

The service responses from *Strategic Planning for Results* (Nelson, 2008) that support education are "Create Young Readers: Early Literacy"; "Learn to Read and Write: Adults, Teens and Family Literacy"; "Make Career Choices: Job and Career Development"; "Succeed in School: Homework Help"; and "Understand How to Find, Evaluate, and Use Information: Information Fluency."[10]

Create Young Readers: Early Literacy

Strategic Planning for Results addresses the service response to provide children from birth to age five with programs and services designed to ensure they will enter school ready to learn to read, write, and learn (Nelson, 2008: 165). In the twenty-first century public librarians have emphasized the partnership between parents, caregivers, and children's librarians.

Public librarians' commitment to young readers has been manifested in the "Every Child Ready to Read @ Your Library" program, which was initiated in 2002 as a joint project of the PLA and the Association of Library Services to Children. Ash and Meyers (2009) have observed that the project firmly established public libraries as partners in the educational continuum and strengthened the link between library activities and relevant research on early literacy.

In a study of the availability of library storytimes to working parents, researchers reported that both the children and the adults who accompany them are learners in any program. Parents and caregivers learn strategies for sharing literature with their children, activities and tips to support literacy development, ways to select age-appropriate literature, and parenting skills (Hughes-Hassell and Agosto, 2007). A model connection to the community in Douglas County, Colorado, has been described by Priscilla Queen (2008) who worked with the Early Childhood Council to extend the impact of early childhood library programs.

Learn to Read and Write: Adults, Teens and Family Literacy

Adult, youth, and family literacy are addressed in *Strategic Planning for Results* (Nelson, 2008: 184). This service response will support adults and teens to meet their personal goals and fulfill their responsibilities as parents, citizens, and workers.

The ALA OLOS serves as liaison to national literacy organizations such as the National Coalition for Literacy (http://www.national-coalition-literacy.org/) and provides policy input at the national level.[11] Dale Lipschultz, ALA literacy officer, served as the National Coalition for Literacy president in 2005. Historical examples of public library literacy services are included in studies by founding OLOS director Jean E. Coleman (1996) and the OLOS volume *Literacy and Libraries: Learning from Case Studies* (DeCandido, 2001). Currently ProLiteracy (http://www.proliteracy.org) is an ALA affiliate organization.

Fundamental questions about the focus of public libraries and the provision of adult literacy services were addressed in 2001 when the ALA Committee on Literacy was established. Discussion at this time contended that librarians should incorporate adult lifelong learning theory with literacy to make a broad commitment to "learning for life" (McCook and Barber, 2002). George Demetrion (2005) has examined the role of adult literacy in the life of the United States in his monograph *Conflicting Paradigms in Adult Literacy Education: In Quest of a U.S. Democratic Politics of Literacy*. His historical review provides a convincing argument for a stronger commitment to adult literacy by librarians.

BuildLiteracy, an OLOS project, is an interactive how-to website for building and sustaining literacy coalitions, collaborations, and partnerships (www.buildliteracy .org/index.htm). "Libraries, Literacy and Learning in the 21st Century" (2005) was an article about a Literacy Toolkit produced by the ALA to challenge, inspire, and support public library literacy efforts. This project was updated for immigrants by the American Dream Starts @ Your Library toolkit (2008; go to http://www.american

dreamtoolkit.org/). Baer, Kutner, and Sabatini (2009) have reported on the ongoing demand for public libraries to support adult literacy.[12]

The Literacy Assembly of the ALA (http://connect.ala.org/node/71957) is a focal point that emphasizes the association's continuing commitment to literacy beyond divisional and unit membership committees, provides an opportunity for broad representation of the membership and affiliated groups to exchange information and share ideas, identifies concerns and omissions, coordinates programming, and develops and promotes strategies for increased literacy activity within the ALA.

The connection between public libraries and adult literacy and education organizations has ebbed and flowed over the years. This is partly due to changing adult education policies within the federal government. The shift to an emphasis on workforce training from adult education and adult literacy has grown since the passage of the 1998 Workforce Investment Act. Conflicts over participants' roles, the interpretation of the legislation, and ambiguity about the process of implementation emerged (Hopkins, Monaghan, and Hansman, 2009). The challenges are defined in *Reach Higher, America*, the National Commission on Adult Literacy (2008) report, which presented powerful evidence that failure to address U.S. adult education and workforce skill needs puts our country in great jeopardy and threatens the national standard of living and economic viability. In the lead-up to reauthorization of the Workforce Investment Act, changes that should be made to provide greater support from the federal government for adult education were addressed at a Council for the Advancement of Literacy Round Table (Chisman, 2010). Librarians must be aware of the "learn to earn" movement and recognize that our traditions of "learn to live" are also a rich motivation for adult literacy.

At the state and local levels there are many exemplary public library adult literacy programs. Of critical importance is the partnership with other community literacy agencies exemplified by such programs, for example:

- Los Angeles Public Library, Help with Reading program (http://www.lapl
  .org/literacy/main.html)
- Miami-Dade Public Library System, Project L.E.A.D. (Literacy for Every Adult in Dade, http://www.mdpls.org/services/outreach/lead.asp)
- New York State Adult Literacy Library Services grants (http://www.nysl.nysed
  .gov/libdev/literacy/)
- Tulsa City County Library, Ruth G. Hardman Adult Literacy Service (http://
  www.tulsalibrary.org/literacy/)

In 2010 ALA President Camila Alire showed the power of the ALA presidency by her support for the Family Literacy Focus program to develop and implement innovative family literacy models in libraries serving Native American, Asian American, Pacific American, African American, Chinese American, and Latino communities. Activities supported included family reading nights, intergenerational storytelling, and take-home literacy activities ("New Family Literacy Focus," 2010).

Make Career Choices: Job and Career Development

Skills and resources to help adults and young adults identify career opportunities that suit their individual strengths and interests are supported by this service response in *Strategic Planning for Results* (Nelson, 2008: 188).

The Office for Research and Statistics of the ALA (2009) found great use of library technology for job seeking and e-government in public libraries. In every state visited by the research team, library staff and users reported library computers and Internet access are used to search for employment, prepare résumés, and file for unemployment benefits. Aiding job seekers was increasingly viewed as a critical role for public libraries, with 66 percent of libraries reporting this service as critical to the library's mission, up from 44 percent two years earlier.

An outstanding example of state library–initiated support for job seekers is the Job Search Toolkit developed by the State Library of North Carolina with ongoing contributions from library staff across the state (http://statelibrary.ncdcr.gov/ld/jobsearchtoolkit.html). The toolkit provides resources that help library staff respond to the increasing needs of job seekers in their communities. It was developed to support job search workshops presented in nine public libraries across North Carolina in March 2009.

The ALA publication *Crisis in Employment: A Librarian's Guide to Helping Job Seekers* (Jerrard, 2009) included case studies from the Dwight Foster Public Library, Fort Atkinson, Wisconsin; Fresno County Library, California; Nappanee Public Library, Indiana; and the Nashville Public Library. Many public libraries provide websites with job information such as the New York Public Library Job Search Central (http://www.nypl.org/locations/tid/65/node/40820); Milwaukee Public Library Job Seeker Help (http://www.mpl.org/FILE/jobs_index.ht); and the Tacoma Public Library Education and Job Center (http://www.tpl.lib.wa.us/Page.aspx?nid=216).

Succeed in School: Homework Help

Services to help students succeed in school are addressed in *Strategic Planning for Results* (Nelson, 2008: 203). This response includes services for students enrolled in public, private, and charter schools as well as homeschooling families. Many families that homeschool their children rely on the public library to provide them with resources to use in their educational endeavors and with services such as library tours, story programs, and computer instruction (Davis, 2008). For more information, see Succeed in School in Chapter 9.

Understand How to Find, Evaluate, and Use Information: Information Fluency

Residents will know when they need information to resolve an issue and have the skills to search for, locate, evaluate, and effectively use information to meet their needs (Nelson, 2008: 207).

While much of the research and writing on information literacy has focused on academic settings, the findings are applicable to public library development of information literacy services. The National Forum on Information Literacy was created as an ongoing response to the recommendations of the ALA's Presidential Committee on Information Literacy (Breivik, Hancock, and Senn, 1998). The forum leaders stated that no other change in American society has offered greater challenges than the emergence of the information age.

In 2009, heeding the advocacy of the National Forum, President Barack Obama proclaimed October National Literacy Awareness Month:

> This month, we dedicate ourselves to increasing information literacy awareness so that all citizens understand its vital importance. An informed and educated citizenry is essential to the functioning of our modern democratic society, and I encourage educational and community institutions across the country to help Americans find and evaluate the information they seek, in all its forms. (White House, 2009)

The Information Literacy Toolkit issued by the Association of College and Research Libraries states that information literacy "forms the basis for lifelong learning. . . . It enables users to master content and extend their investigations, become more self-directed, and assume greater control over their learning . . . [and] develop a metacognitive approach to learning, making them conscious of the explicit actions required for gathering, analyzing, and using information" (http://www.ala.org/acrl). The toolkit provides a basis for developing information literacy tools for all adults. Information literacy is related to information technology skills but has broader implications for the individual, the educational system, and society. Information technology skills enable an individual to use computers, software applications, databases, and other technologies to achieve a wide variety of academic, work-related, and personal goals. Information-literate individuals necessarily develop some technology skills.

Webjunction (2010), in collaboration with the San Francisco Public Library, was awarded a National Leadership Grant to look at online patron instruction in public libraries. In January 2010 a survey was sent to 650 large and medium libraries in the United States to get a snapshot of patron instruction programs. The results will determine and document the most urgent patron needs. The findings will provide information to design and launch a pilot online course at the San Francisco Public Library.

Once tested, the course creation details and the actual course will be available for download via WebJunction.org.

Information

The landmark study by Bernard Berelson (1949) marks the real start of writing and research about the information needs of public library users. In their bibliographic review of understanding information seeking in the public library context, Leckie and Given (1995) identify trends in the information-seeking literature that apply across user populations:

- People's information needs are grounded in the contexts of a person's life.
- Individuals' information needs change over time.
- People often use interpersonal sources first.
- People use a range of sources and formats.
- People seek information actively and passively.
- There is no one-size-fits-all model of information seeking. (Leckie and Given, 1995: 6–7)

Information provision in public libraries is supported by RUSA's standards and guidelines. In 2008 the Reference Services Section of RUSA defined *reference transactions* as information consultations in which library staff recommend, interpret, evaluate, or use information resources to help others meet particular information needs. Reference work includes reference transactions and other activities that involve the creation, management, and assessment of information or research resources, tools, and services. "Professional Competencies for Reference and User Services Librarians" (RUSA, 2003) outlines the characteristics of information services librarians, who are responsive to user needs, carefully analyze sources and services, keep current with developments in the field, utilize new knowledge to enhance service, and communicate the nature of the services provided to users. Information services should be effectively designed and organized to meet the needs of the primary community, promoted to users, and evaluated and assessed on an ongoing basis.

"Guidelines for Behavioral Performance of Reference and Information Service Providers" has been revised to provide guidance in serving remote as well as in-person users (RUSA, 2004). "Guidelines for the Introduction of Electronic Information Resources to Users" (RUSA, 2006b) offers practical guidance to library staff concerned with strategies for implementation, policy, procedure, education, or direct provision of electronic information resources, as does "Guidelines for Implementing and Maintaining Virtual Reference Services" (RUSA, 2010).

Five public library responses from *Strategic Planning for Results* (Nelson, 2008) are organized around the broad category of information. These are "Build Successful Enterprises: Business and Nonprofit Support," "Connect to the Online World: Public Internet Access," "Get Facts Fast: Ready Reference," "Make Informed Decisions: Health, Wealth and Other Life Choices," and "Welcome to the United States: Service to New Immigrants."[13]

Build Successful Enterprises: Business and Nonprofit Support

Business owners and nonprofit organizations are provided the resources they need to develop and maintain strong, viable organizations through this service response in *Strategic Planning for Results* (Nelson, 2008: 153).

Public libraries are an important source of information for economic development for the community. Business and nonprofit support includes services for community economic development and services for the individual. The Business Reference and Services Section (BRASS) of RUSA provides extensive resources that address the needs of the business community and includes committees that focus on service to public libraries. BRASS publishes the "Public Libraries Briefcase," an online column on topics that support business reference such as using local business resources in a challenging economy, the top ten best business reference sources for nonbusiness librarians, and building business connections.

- Boston Public Library (http://www.bpl.org/research/kbb/kbbhome.htm) offers an extensive array of business resources including directories of public and private companies, weekly and daily financial publications, investment advisory newsletters, statistics, and other listings and databases. The Kirstein Business Library also offers programming on topics such as strategic job searches and business planning.
- Brooklyn Public Library (http://www.brooklynpubliclibrary.org/business), the Business Library, supports the needs of businesses and individuals by providing free access to business and investment resources. Corporations, small business owners, investors, employees, students, and entrepreneurs turn to the Business Library for up-to-date information.
- Los Angeles Public Library, Business and Economics Department, contains 172,000 books, 230 current periodical titles, and hundreds of trade and association directories. The department's resources are particularly popular with small business owners and operators, entrepreneurs, importers and exporters, investors, analysts, industry researchers, job hunters, students, and marketing personnel.

- New York Public Library, Science, Industry and Business Library is a premier public business library with comprehensive print materials, e-resources, and services for startups and established businesses seeking expansion, and for job seekers from entry to executive levels. Library staff provide roving assistance and consultations, and advisory services are offered on-site by experienced business owners, career coaches, and a financial specialist.

In Indiana, the Bartholomew County Public Library developed a program for business and nonprofits that made participation at local business events part of the outreach plan. The step-by-step overview of the project demonstrates how this service response can build partnerships (Hatton, Wirrig, and Miller, 2008). Graham and Sparks (2010) have discussed a summit in San Antonio, Texas, that identified the library as a resource for economic development, workforce development, and education.

Connect to the Online World: Public Internet Access

Provision of high-speed access to the digital world to ensure that everyone can take advantage of the ever-growing resources available on the Internet is addressed in this service response (Nelson, 2008: 162), which supports adults and teens to meet their personal goals and fulfill their responsibilities as parents, citizens, and workers.

In their book *Public Libraries and Internet Service Roles*, McClure and Jaeger (2009: 50) identify the related Internet service role for the public library as the "place for public access to the Internet": "For a majority of communities, the public library is the only place where free access to the Internet is available. This service response requires staff who are trained in assisting users to locate the services/resources available and requires that the library have a high-quality technology infrastructure, e.g., adequate workstations, bandwidth, and up-to-date equipment and software."

Adequacy of broadband is being addressed by American Recovery and Reinvestment Act, administered by the National Telecommunications and Information Administration and the Rural Utilities Service. In the broadband provision, $250 million is targeted for innovative projects that encourage sustainable broadband service. Public libraries are eligible to submit project proposals for these funds—in particular for large broadband build-out and deployment projects that will deliver high-speed (fiber-optic cable) broadband to libraries. Although the public computer center capacity provision explicitly specifies public libraries, the act does not preclude libraries from applying for all of the other funding areas (Sheketoff, 2009).

Changes public libraries have made to address patron needs in an increasingly Internet-centric environment were explored in the IMLS study Service Trends in U.S. Public Libraries, 1997–2007, which defines service differences in urban and rural communities (Henderson, 2009). The funding that supports this service response at the national, state, and local levels requires libraries to compete for funds and develop staffs prepared to assist users.

A study for the ALA Office for Information Technology Policy reported:

> Libraries can better serve their users by embracing the growing capabilities of mobile technology. They can promote and expand their existing services by offering mobile access to their websites and online public access catalogs; by supplying on-the-go mobile reference services; and by providing mobile access to e-books, journals, video, audio books, and multimedia content. (Vollmer, 2010)

Get Facts Fast: Ready Reference

In *Strategic Planning for Results*, this service response is to the point: someone will be available to answer residents' questions on a wide array of topics of personal interest (Nelson, 2008: 177).

Information services take a variety of forms—direct individual assistance, signs, directories, website links, telephone, e-mail, and 24-7 chat-based services. "Guidelines for Information Services," developed by RUSA (2000), addresses six categories:

- **Services**—stressing accuracy, accessibility, instruction, publicity, community information, adding value to information, and referral.
- **Resources**—the information collection should be current and reflect the spectrum of the population served; when necessary, external reference sources should be consulted.
- **Access**—information services should be well configured with attention to the needs of people with disabilities, state-of-the art communications methods, and services available to meet the community's needs.
- **Personnel**—staff should have knowledge and preparation to meet information needs of the library's clientele, effective interpersonal communication skills, and competency in using information technology.
- **Evaluation**—services should be evaluated for response time, accessibility, effectiveness for various groups among the population served, effectiveness in meeting the community's needs, and statistical data for comparison with national norms.
- **Ethics**—the ALA Code of Ethics governs conduct of those providing information services.

General information services are undergoing continuous change as information services evolve to accommodate an increasingly digital world. "Professional Competencies for Reference and User Services Librarians" (RUSA, 2003) outlines the information services librarian's responsibilities to maintain currency and engagement with these changes, and "Guidelines for Behavioral Performance of Reference and Information Service Providers" provides strategies regardless of format (RUSA, 2004). "Guidelines for Implementing and Maintaining Virtual Reference Services" were revised in 2010 (RUSA, 2010).

Internet-enabled roles identified in *Public Libraries and Internet Service Roles* (McClure and Jaeger, 2009: 50–51) that expand this service response include "Anyplace Anywhere Anytime Individualized Information Provision." For example, the ask-a-librarian service might be available by mobile device. Another is "Virtual, Seamless, and Endless Electronic Information Provider." Fast facts can be provided by statewide and nationally developed electronic resource-sharing networks that are virtual, seamless, extensive and almost instantaneous.

Make Informed Decisions: Health, Wealth and Other Life Choices

Providing residents with the resources they need to identify and analyze risks, benefits, and alternatives before making decisions that affect their lives is a key information service response in *Strategic Planning for Results* (Nelson, 2008: 191). Aspects of delivering this set of services are affirmed in "Guidelines for Medical, Legal and Business Responses" (RUSA, 2001), which state: "A library's information services staff must have the knowledge and preparation appropriate to meet the routine legal, medical, or business information needs of their clientele."

The 2010 report on the state of U.S. public libraries noted that every day 300,000 people receive job-seeking assistance at public libraries and that more libraries provide career assistance than U.S. Department of Labor One-Stop Centers (OCLC, 2010). Financial literacy is an important library service (Bell et al., 2009).

Welcome to the United States: Services for New Immigrants

New immigrants will receive information on citizenship, English language learning, employment, public schooling, health and safety, and available social services, as described in this service response from *Strategic Planning for Results* (Nelson, 2008: 214).

REFORMA, the National Association to Promote Library and Information Services to Latinos and the Spanish-Speaking, advocates for Latinos' rights to library service. REFORMA (2006) has issued the "Librarian's Toolkit for Responding Effectively to Anti-Immigrant Sentiment," for use by library administrators and workers to enlighten, inform, and expand their knowledge of immigrants and their rights to free public library access.

RUSA (2007) has established "Guidelines for the Development and Promotion of Multilingual Collections and Services," which assert it is the responsibility of libraries to provide an equitable level of service to all members of their communities regardless of ethnic, cultural, or linguistic background. Libraries should establish goals, objectives, and policies that integrate multilingual services into their overall work plan.

In the monograph *Serving New Immigrant Communities in the Library*, Cuban (2007) has identified how the American public library system plays a key role in helping immigrants adapt to their new lives by providing relevant information, materials, referrals, and programs. Taken together, books, toolkits, and articles by librarians on serving immigrant populations are important components that assist library workers in protecting the human rights of immigrants (Naficy, 2009; Burke, 2008; Koontz and Jue, 2008; Roy, 2007). To be an "advocate for the education of undocumented immigrants about their human rights it is the responsibility of library workers to provide current and up-to-date information about the legislative progress of bills and laws that will have an impact on the lives of immigrants and to develop tools that enable immigrants to realize full human rights" (McCook, 2007).

Service for All

Adult services configured to respond to community needs must take into consideration the needs of individual adults and the challenges to provide access for everyone in the community.

Implementation of the goal to provide service for all has many aspects, including usability for people with disabilities; linguistic diversity, through materials and services for people speaking different languages; helping communities overcome economic barriers, such as bandwidth needs; and helping people who face the most serious of economic challenges, such as the homeless or ex-offenders (MacCreaigh, 2010).

> Various association initiatives such as the "Library Services for People with Disabilities Policy" (ALA, 2010a) extend this commitment: "Libraries play a catalytic role in the lives of people with disabilities by facilitating their full participation in society. Libraries should use strategies based upon the principles of universal design to ensure that library policy, resources and services meet the needs of all people."

Similarly, RUSA's (2008b) "Guidelines for Library Services to Older Adults" demonstrate the multifaceted approach that must be taken to develop equitable service for any special category of users. The guidelines consider accessibility, respect, communication, programming, materials, and community partnerships. They provide an overall structural approach that parallels specific service responses.

For U.S. residents who speak a language other than English at home, public libraries must provide resources to assist in learning English as a second language and access to materials in native languages (EMIERT). The challenges in serving the population that do not speak English are great, especially since many come from countries where public library services do not exist; they may not be literate in their spoken language; and library signage and forms may be only in English.

The ALA (2010b) policy "Library Services for the Poor" states, "it is crucial that libraries recognize their role in enabling poor people to participate fully in a democratic society." Librarians need to study communities to determine the best configuration of services. Serving communities that are at once poor and represent a different culture requires a commitment by librarians for social justice and equity. Librarians configuring adult services must consider all aspects of the human condition (Gieskes, 2009). The ALA Office for Literacy and Outreach Services sponsors the annual Jean E. Coleman lecture, which focuses on equity of access.[14]

In her assessment of the status of adult services at the outset of the twenty-first century, Stephens (2006: 233) called for continuing research:

> Knowing which services public libraries provide for adults, including special groups of adults, and how these services are selected, is vital to determining and publicizing the valuable contributions public libraries make to their communities. It will also provide a valuable knowledge base for future research on use and evaluation of services and numerous other aspects of public library management. Such a knowledge base should prove beneficial for local and state library budget requests and for local, state-level and national library planning.

Notes

1. Interview with Joyce M. Latham, 2010. Dr. Latham's historical scholarship on the philosophies of John M. Chancellor and Julia Wright Merrill contributes to our understanding of the importance of progressive ideals to the goal of empowering adults through the extension of education in libraries.

2. See ALA Archives for Minutes of the Library Extension Committee (1925–1930) and Board (1931–1940) containing material on cooperation with the Commission for Adult Education, Carnegie Corporation grants, book funds, budgets, regional field work (especially in the South), library services during the Depression, state surveys of library services, Rosenwald Fund, state library agencies and associations, publications, publicity, and reports. http://www.library.illinois.edu/archives/ala/.

3. For additional background on the organizational history of adult services within the ALA, see articles by Hansen (1995), McCook (1992), and Heim (1986).

4. "Public Sphere" service responses as defined by McCook based on Nelson (2008), chapters: "Be an Informed Citizen: Local, National and World Affairs" (149–152); "Know Your Community: Community Resources and Services" (180–183); and "Visit a Comfortable Place: Physical and Virtual Spaces" (210–213).

5. In 1965 the National Foundation on the Arts and Humanities Act was passed, creating the NEH. In 1979 a program to support humanities programs in public libraries was established (National Endowment for the Humanities, 1998; National Endowment for the Humanities, "Who We Are—Timeline." http://www.neh.gov/whoweare/timeline.html.

6. Cultural heritage service responses as defined by McCook based on Nelson (2008), chapters: "Celebrate Diversity: Cultural Awareness" (158–161); "Discover Your Roots: Genealogy and Local History" (169–172); "Express Creativity: Create and Share Content" (173–176); "Satisfy Curiosity: Lifelong Learning" (195–198); and "Stimulate Imagination: Reading, Viewing and Listening for Pleasure" (199–202).

7. Websites:
- American Library Association. Office for Diversity. http://www.ala.org/diversity. American Library Association. Office for Literacy and Outreach Services. http://www.ala.org/ala/aboutala/offices/olos/index.cfm.
- American Indian Library Association (AILA). Established 1979. http://www.ailanet.org/.
- Asian/Pacific American Librarians Association (APALA). Established 1980. http://www.apalaweb.org/.
- Black Caucus of the American Library Association (BCALA). Established 1970. http://www.bcala.org.
- Chinese American Librarians Association (CALA). Established 1983. http://www.cala-web.org.
- REFORMA: The National Association to Promote Library and Information Service to Latinos and the Spanish Speaking. Established 1971. http://www.reforma.org.

8. Moyer and Stover (2010), Trott (2008), Saricks (2005), Shearer and Burgin (2002), Nordmeyer (2001), Smith (2000). There are many guides and resources for specific types of readers' advisory, for example, Saricks (2009b), and Herald (2005), as well as the other books in the Libraries Unlimited Genreflecting series.

9. The Library of Congress, National Book Festival. http://www.loc.gov/bookfest/. Many states and local communities also hold book festivals. The Center for the Book lists these at its website: http://www.read.gov/resources/statefairs.html. See for instance:
- Arizona Book Festival, http://www.azbookfestival.org/.
- Border Book Festival, http://www.borderbookfestival.org/.
- Louisiana Book Festival, http://www.louisianabookfestival.org/.
- *St. Petersburg Times* Festival of Reading, http://www.festivalofreading.com/.
- Texas Book Festival, http://www.texasbookfestival.org/.
- Utah Humanities Book Festival, http://www.utahhumanities.org/BookFestival.htm.
- Virginia Festival of the Book, http://www.vabook.org.festival.org/overview.

10. Education service responses as defined by McCook based on Nelson (2008), chapters: "Create Young Readers: Early Literacy" (165–168); "Learn to Read and Write: Adults, Teens and Family Literacy" (184–187); "Make Career Choices: Job and Career Development" (188–190); "Succeed in School: Homework Help" (203–206); and "Understand How to Find, Evaluate, and Use Information: Information Fluency" (207–209).

11. The National Institute for Literacy (NIFL, http://www.nifl.gov), founded in 1991, served as a catalyst for improving opportunities for adults, youth, and children to thrive in a progressively more literate world. At the institute, literacy was broadly viewed as more than just an individual's ability to read; it was the ability to read, write, speak in English, compute, and solve problems at levels of proficiency necessary to function on the job, in the family, and in society. NIFL was established by the National Literacy Act and reauthorized in 1998 by the Workforce Investment Act. NIFL was not funded by the Obama administration and ended operation in fall 2010. At this writing (2010) it is not clear what federal agency will take an interest in adult literacy issues. The result will flow from the fate of the Workforce Investment Act.

12. Historical note: Prior to the reorganization of the PLA in 2008 (Sanders, 2008), two PLA committees supported literacy services. The Basic Education and Literacy Services committee identified resources useful in developing, implementing, and maintaining literacy activities and worked to make librarians aware of the value of cooperation with others. The Resources for the Adult New Reader committee informed publishers of librarian support for the development of professional and learning materials in areas of adult education, literacy, GED, and career information. The committee also compiled the list of "Best Books for the Adult New Reader" that continued earlier ALA projects by Helen H. Lyman: *Library Materials in Service to the Adult New Reader* (Chicago: ALA, 1973); *Reading and the Adult New Reader* (Chicago: ALA, 1976); *Literacy and the Nation's Libraries* (Chicago: ALA, 1977).

13. Information service responses as defined by McCook based on Nelson (2008), chapters: "Build Successful Enterprises: Business and Nonprofit Support" (153–157); "Connect to the Online World: Public Internet Access" (162–164); "Get Facts Fast: Ready Reference" (177–179); "Make Informed Decisions: Health, Wealth and Other Life Choices " (191–194); and "Welcome to the United States: Service to New Immigrants" (214–217).

14. Dr. Jean E. Coleman was the first director of OLOS. This lecture series commemorates her work to ensure that all citizens, particularly Native Americans and adult learners, have access to quality library services. Sponsored by OLOS, the Jean E. Coleman Library Outreach Lecture is presented each year during the ALA's annual conference. Here are the speakers and lectures since 2000:

- 2010: Kathleen de la Peña McCook, "Librarians and Human Rights"
- 2009: Kathleen Mayo, "The Challenges and Opportunities of Serving America's Elders"
- 2008: Clara Chu, "Dislocations of Multicultural Librarianship"
- 2007: Anne Moore, "Lies in the Libraries: Changing the Image of Gay and Lesbian from Abnormal to Acceptance"
- 2006: Carla Hayden, "Access Agenda for All Libraries"
- 2005: Sanford Berman, "Classism in the Stacks: Libraries and Poverty"

- 2004: Richard Chabrán, "Answering the Call: How the FCC's Definition of Information Service Threatens the Future of Universal Service"
- 2003: Thelma H. Tate, "Unserved and Underserved Populations: Empowering People for Productivity in the 21st Century"
- 2002: Lotsee Patterson, "Indigenous Librarianship: A Global Perspective"
- 2001: Gary E. Strong, "Reading . . . Still Cool? Libraries, Literacy and Leadership"
- 2000: Barbara J. Ford, "Libraries, Literacy, Outreach and the Digital Divide"

References

American Library Association. 2010a. "Library Services for People with Disabilities." In *ALA Handbook of Organization.* http://www.ala.org/ala/aboutala/governance/policymanual/index.cfm.

American Library Association. 2010b. "Library Services for the Poor." In *ALA Handbook of Organization.* Chicago: American Library Association. http://www.ala.org/ala/aboutala/governance/policymanual/index.cfm.

American Library Association, Office for Research and Statistics. 2009. *Job-Seeking in U.S. Public Libraries.* http://www.ala.org/ala/research/initiatives/plftas/issuesbriefs/ JobBrief 2009_2F.pdf.

Ash, Viki, and Elaine Meyers. 2009. "Every Child Ready to Read @Your Library." *Children and Libraries* 7 (Spring): 3–7.

Association of Specialized and Cooperative Library Agencies. "Guidelines for Distance Learning Library Services." ALA, Libraries Serving Special Populations Section. http://www.ala .org/ala/mgrps/divs/ascla/asclaourassoc/asclasections/lssps/lssps.cfm.

Bachowski, Donna. 2009. "Orlando Memory: Capturing Community Memories." *Florida Libraries* 52 (Fall): 8–9.

Baer, J., M. Kutner, and J. Sabatini. 2009. *Basic Reading Skills and the Literacy of America's Least Literate Adults: Results from the 2003 National Assessment of Adult Literacy (NAAL) Supplemental Studies* (NCES 2009-481). Washington, DC: National Center for Education Statistics, Institute of Education Sciences, U.S. Department of Education. http://nces.ed .gov/pubs2009/2009481.pdf.

Bajjaly, Stephen T. 1999. *The Community Networking Handbook.* Chicago: ALA Editions.

Balcom, Ted. 2002. "The Adult Reading Round Table." *Reference and User Services Quarterly* 41 (Spring): 238–243.

Beam, Alex. 2008. *A Great Idea at the Time: The Rise, Fall, and Curious Afterlife of the Great Books.* New York: Public Affairs.

Bell, Lori, Tom Peters, Margaret Monsour, and Kitty Pope. 2009. "Financial Information Literacy Services at Your Library." *Searcher* 17 (June): 18–21, 53.

Berelson, Bernard. 1949. *The Library's Public.* New York: Columbia University Press.

Birch, Eugenie. 2007. "Special Report: Anchor Institutions." *Next American City* (Summer). http://americancity.org/magazine/article/special-report-anchor-institutions-birch/.

Blayney, M. S. 1977. "Libraries for the Millions." *Journal of Library History* 12: 235–249.

Brack, Lori, and Joe McKenzie. 2007. "CLASS: The Future of Adult Programming in the Public Library." *Public Libraries* 46 (May/June): 40–44.

Breivik, Patricia Senn, Vicki Hancock, and J. A. Senn. 1998. *A Progress Report on Information Literacy: An Update on the American Library Association Presidential Committee on Information Literacy: Final Report.* Chicago: Association of College and Research Libraries. http://www.ala.org/ala/mgrps/divs/acrl/publications/whitepapers/progressreport.cfm.

Brown, Walter L. 1917. "The Changing Public." *ALA Bulletin* 11 (July): 91–95.

Burke, Susan K. 2008. "Use of Public Libraries by Immigrants." *Reference & User Services Quarterly* 48 (Winter): 164–174.

Buschman, John. 2005. "Libraries and the Decline of Public Purpose." *Public Library Quarterly* 24: 1–12.

Buschman, John, and Gloria J. Leckie, eds. 2007. *Library as Place: History, Community and Culture.* Westport, CT: Libraries Unlimited.

Carmichael, James V., Jr. 1998. *Daring to Find Our Names: The Search for Lesbigay Library History.* Westport, CT: Greenwood Press.

Carpenter, Kenneth E. 1996. *Toward a History of Libraries and Culture in America.* Washington, DC: Library of Congress.

Carr, David. 2006. *A Place Not a Place: Reflection and Possibility in Museums and Libraries.* Lanham, MD: Altamira Press.

Carrier, Esther Jane. 1965. *Fiction in Public Libraries, 1876–1900.* New York: Scarecrow Press.

———. 1985. *Fiction in Public Libraries, 1900–1950.* Littleton, CO: Libraries Unlimited.

Chepesiuk, Ronald. 2001. "Dial 211: Libraries Get Involved with a New Social Service Initiative." *American Libraries* 32 (December) 11: 44–46.

Chicago Public Library. 2010. *One Book: One Chicago.* http://www.chipublib.org/eventsprog/programs/onebook_onechgo.php.

Childers, Thomas. 1984. *Information and Referral: Public Libraries.* Norwood, NJ: Ablex.

Chisman, Forrest P. 2010. *Local Perspectives on WIA Reauthorization from a CAAL Roundtable.* Council for the Advancement of Adult Literacy. http://www.caalusa.org/LPP.pdf.

Christensen, Karen, and David Levinson, eds. 2003. *Encyclopedia of Community.* Thousand Oaks, CA: Sage. See especially the articles, Information Communities, 657–660; Public Libraries, 1114–1117; and Libraries Build Community, Appendix 2, 1533–1551.

Cohen, Alex. 2009. "Learning Spaces in Public Libraries." *Public Library Quarterly* 28 (July/September): 227–233.

Coleman, Jean Ellen. 1996. "Literacy Education Programs in Public Libraries as a Response to a Socio-educational Need: Four Case Studies." PhD diss., Rutgers, the State University of New Jersey.

Crawford, Walt. 2003. "Thinking about Complex Media." *American Libraries* 34 (December): 59.

Cuban, Sondra. 2007. *Serving New Immigrant Communities in the Library.* Westport, CT: Libraries Unlimited.

Curley, Arthur. 1979. "Information from the People to the People." *American Libraries* 10 (July): 316–320.

Davis, Elizabeth. 2008. "Homeschooling @ Your Library." *Public Libraries* 47 (May/June): 20–21.

"A Decade of Words and Wonder." 2010. *Library of Congress Information Bulletin* 69, no. 6 (June): 116–117.

DeCandido, GraceAnne, ed. 2001. *Literacy and Libraries: Learning from Case Studies*. Chicago: American Library Association.

Demetrion, George. 2005. *Conflicting Paradigms in Adult Literacy Education: In Quest of a U.S. Democratic Politics of Literacy*. Mahwah, NJ: Erlbaum.

Dilevko, Juris, and Lisa Gottlieb. 2004. *The Evolution of Library and Museum Partnerships: Historical Antecedents, Contemporary Manifestations and Future Directions*. Westport, CT: Libraries Unlimited.

Durrance, Joan C., and Karen E. Pettigrew. 2002. *Online Community Information: Creating a Nexus at Your Library*. Chicago: American Library Association.

Elmborg, Jim. 2010. "Literacies, Narratives, and Adult Learning in Libraries." *New Directions for Adult and Continuing Education* 127 (Fall): 67–76.

Estabrook, Leigh S., Evans Witt, and Lee Rainie. 2007. *Information Searches That Solve Problems: How People Use the Internet, Libraries, and Government Agencies When They Need Help*. Washington, DC: Pew Internet and American Life Project. http://www.pewinternet.org/~/media//Files/Reports/2007/Pew_UI_LibrariesReport.pdf.pdf.

Farr, Cecilia K. 2004. *Reading Oprah: How Oprah's Book Club Changed the Way America Reads*. Albany: State University of New York Press.

Favreau, Karen. 2007. "A Library and an Art Center." *American Libraries* 38 (February): 38–40.

Gieskes, Lisa. 2009. "Library Services for the Poor" ALA Task Force Member Survey on Policy 61. *Progressive Librarian* 32 (Winter/Spring): 82–87.

Given, Lisa M., and LiAnne McTavish. 2010. "What Are Old Is New Again: The Reconvergence of Libraries, Archives and Museums in the Digital Age." *Library Quarterly* 80 (January): 7–32.

Goodes, Pamela A. 2006. "Historic Gathering Draws Hundred to Dallas." *American Libraries* 37 (November): 20–21.

Gornick, Vivian. 1998. "Apostles of the Faith That Books Matter." *The New York Times* (February 1998): B40.

Graham, Elizabeth, and Roberta Sparks. 2010. "Libraries as a Catalyst for Economic Growth and Community Development: A Mayor's Summit on Public Libraries." *Texas Library Journal* 86 (Spring): 30–31.

Gray, William S., and Ruth Munroe. 1929. *The Reading Interests and Habits of Adults*. New York: Macmillan.

Haines, Helen E. 1935. *Living with Books: The Art of Book Selection*. New York: Columbia University Press.

Hansen, Andrew M. 1995. "RASD: Serving Those Who Serve the Public." *RQ* 34 (Spring): 314–338.

Hatton, Jason, Denise Wirrig, and Dave Miller. 2008. "Making the Library Visible to the Business and Nonprofit Communities." *Indiana Libraries* 27: 33–34.

Heim, Kathleen M. 1986. "Adult Services as Reflective of the Changing Role of the Public Library," *RQ* 26 (Winter): 180–187.

———. 1990. "Adult Services: An Enduring Focus." In *Adult Services: An Enduring Focus for Public Libraries*, edited by Kathleen M. Heim (de la Peña McCook) and Danny P. Wallace, 11–26. Chicago: American Library Association.

Heim, Kathleen M., and Danny P. Wallace, eds. 1990. *Adult Services: An Enduring Focus for Public Libraries*. Chicago: American Library Association.

Henderson, E. 2009. *Service Trends in U.S. Public Libraries, 1997-2007*. Research Brief series, no. 1 (IMLS-2010-RB-01). Washington, DC: Institute of Museum and Library Services. http://www.imls.gov/pdf/Brief2010_01.pdf.

Herald, Diana Tixier. 2005. *Genreflecting: A Guide to Reading Interests in Genre Fiction*. 6th ed. Englewood, CO: Libraries Unlimited.

Hill, Chrystie. 2009. *Inside, Outside, and Online*. Chicago: American Library Association.

Hinchcliffe, Geoffrey, and Lorella Terzi. 2009. "Capabilities and Education." *Studies in Philosophy and Education* 28 (September): 387–390.

Hopkins, John L., Catherine H. Monaghan, and Catherine A. Hansman. 2009. "Conflict and Collaboration: Providers and Planners Implementing the Workforce Investment Act (WIA)." *Adult Education Quarterly* 59 (May): 208–226.

Hughes-Hassell, Sandra, and D. E. Agosto. 2007. "Making Storytime Available to Children of Working Parents: Public Libraries and the Scheduling of Children's Literacy Programs." *Children and Libraries* 5 (Summer/Fall): 43–48.

Hustedde, Hedy N. R. 2005. "Emily Dickinson Lives! @ the Bettendorf Public Library." *Public Libraries* 44 (September/October): 287–291.

Jaeger, Paul T., and John Carlo Bertot. 2009. "E-government Education in Public Libraries: New Service Roles and Expanding Social Responsibilities." *Journal of Education for Library and Information Science* 50 (Winter): 39–49.

Jaeger, Paul T., and Gary Burnett. 2010. *Information Worlds: Behavior, Technology and Social Context in the World of the Internet*. London: Routledge.

Jarvis, Peter. 2010. *Adult Education and Lifelong Learning*. London: Routledge.

Jerrard, J. 2009. *Crisis in Employment: A Librarian's Guide to Helping Job Seekers*. Chicago: American Library Association.

Johnson, Alvin. 1938. *The Public Library—A People's University*. New York: American Association for Adult Education.

Jones, Christopher. 2010. "Preserving History in Charlotte County." *Florida Libraries* 53 (Spring): 4–5.

Jones, Clara S. 1978. *Public Library Information and Referral Service*. Syracuse, NY: Gaylord Professional Publications.

Josey, E. J. 1994. "Race Issues in Library History." In *Encyclopedia of Library History*, edited by W. A. Wiegand and D. G. Davis, 533–537. New York: Garland.

Joyce, Steven. 2000. "Lesbian, Gay and Bisexual Library Service: A Review of the Literature." *Public Libraries* 39 (September/October): 270–279.

Kaestle, Carl F., and Janice A. Radway. 2009. *Print in Motion: The Expansion of Reading in the United States, 1880–1940*. Chapel Hill: University of North Carolina Press.

Kaplan, Paul. 2007. "How Public Libraries Can Provide Basic Genealogy Instruction." *Illinois Libraries* 86 (Spring): 16–20.

Karetzky, Stephen. 1982. *Reading Research and Librarianship: A History and Analysis.* Westport, CT: Greenwood Press.

Kelman, Ari. 2001. "The Sound of the Civic: Reading Noise at the New York Public Library." *American Studies* 42 (Fall): 23–41.

Kniffel, Leonard. 2001. "Authors Take Center Stage at First National Book Festival." *American Libraries* 32 (October): 16–17.

Knight Commission on the Information Needs of Communities in a Democracy. 2009. *Informing Communities: Sustaining Democracy in the Digital Age.* Washington, DC: Aspen Institute.

Koontz, Christine M., and Dean K. Jue. 2008. *Serving Non-English Speakers in U.S. Public Libraries: 2007 Analysis of Library Demographics, Services and Programs, a Report.* Chicago: American Library Association.

Korda, Michael. 2001. *Making the List: A Cultural History of the American Best Seller, 1900–1999.* New York: Barnes and Noble.

Kranich, Nancy, ed. 2001. *Libraries and Democracy: The Cornerstones of Liberty.* Chicago: American Library Association.

———. 2010. "Promoting Adult Learning Through Civil Discourse in the Public Library." *New Directions for Adult and Continuing Education* no. 127 (Fall): 15–24.

Lamolinara, Guy. 2010. "The National and International Roles of the Center for the Book." *Libraries and the Cultural Record* 45, no. 1: 37–55.

Langemack, Chapple. 2007. *The Author Event Primer.* Westport, CT: Libraries Unlimited.

Latham, Joyce M. 2010. "Clergy of the Mind: Alvin S. Johnson, William S. Learned, the Carnegie Corporations, and the American Library Association. *Library Quarterly* 80 (July): 249–265.

Lear, Brett W. 2002. *Adult Programs in the Library.* Chicago: American Library Association.

Learned, William S. 1924. *The American Public Library and the Diffusion of Knowledge.* New York: Harcourt.

Leckie, Gloria J., and Lisa M. Given. 2005. "Understanding Information-Seeking: The Public Library Context." In *Advances in Librarianship* 29, edited by Anne Woodsworth, 1–72. New York: Emerald Group.

Lee, Robert Ellis. 1966. *Continuing Education for Adults through the American Public Library 1833–1966.* Chicago: American Library Association.

Lesesne, Teri S. 2009. "Reading with Your Ears or with Your Eyes: Does It Matter?" *Voice of Youth Advocates* 32 (April): 44–46.

"Libraries, Literacy and Learning in the 21st Century." (2005). *American Libraries* 36 (August): supplement.

Long, Sarah Ann. 2001. "Foreword." In *Civic Librarianship: Renewing the Social Mission of the Public Library*, edited by Ronald B. McCabe, vii–ix. Lanham, MD: Scarecrow Press.

Lyman, Helen. 1954. *Adult Education Activities in Public Libraries.* Chicago: American Library Association.

Maack, Mary Niles. 2010. "John Y. Cole: Librarian, Bookman, and Scholar." *Libraries and the Cultural Record* 45, no. 1: 1–4.

Maas, Norman L., and Dick Manikowski. 1997. *Guidelines for Establishing Community Information and Referral Services in Public Libraries.* 4th ed. Chicago: American Library Association.

Maatta, Stephanie L. 2010. *A Few Good Books: Using Contemporary Readers' Advisory Strategies to Connect Readers with Books.* New York: Neal-Schuman.

MacCreaigh, Erica. 2010. "Tough Times After Hard Times: How Public Libraries Can Ease the Reentry Process for Ex-offenders." *Interface* (Winter): http://ascla.ala.org/interface/.

Manguel, Alberto. 1996. *A History of Reading.* New York: Penguin.

———. 2010. *A Reader on Reading.* New Haven, CT: Yale University Press.

Martin, Robert K. 2001. 21st Century Learners Conference. Institute of Museum and Library Services. November 7.

Mates, Barbara T. 2003. *5-Star Programming and Services for Your 55+ Customers.* Chicago: American Library Association.

McCabe, Ronald B. 2001. *Civic Librarianship: Renewing the Social Mission of the Public Library.* Lanham, MD: Scarecrow Press.

McClure, Charles R. 1987. *Planning and Role Setting for Public Libraries: A Manual of Options and Procedures.* Chicago: American Library Association.

McClure, Charles R., and Paul T. Jaeger. 2009. *Public Libraries and Internet Service Roles: Measuring and Maximizing Internet Services.* Chicago: American Library Association.

McCook, Kathleen de la Peña. 1992. "Where Would We Be without Them? Libraries and Adult Education Activities: 1966–1991." *RQ* 32 (Winter): 245–253.

———, ed. 2000a. "Ethnic Diversity in Library and Information Science." *Library Trends* 49 (Summer): 1–214.

———. 2000b. *A Place at the Table: Participating in Community Building.* Chicago: American Library Association.

———. 2000c. "Service Integration and Libraries." *Reference and User Services Quarterly* 40 (Winter): 22–25.

———. 2001a. "Authentic Discourse as a Means of Connection between Public Library Service Responses and Community Building Initiatives." *Reference and User Services Quarterly* 40 (Winter): 127–133.

———. 2001b. "Poverty, Democracy, and Public Libraries." In *Libraries and Democracy: The Cornerstones of Liberty*, edited by Nancy Kranich, 28–46. Chicago: American Library Association.

———. 2002. *Rocks in the Whirlpool: The American Library Association and Equity of Access.* ERIC ED462981. Chicago: American Library Association. www.ala.org/ala/ourassociation/governingdocs/keyactionareas/equityaction/rockswhirlpool.htm.

McCook, Kathleen de la Peña. 2007. "Librarians as Advocates for the Human Rights of Immigrants." *Progressive Librarian* 29 (Summer): 51–54.

McCook, Kathleen de la Peña, and Peggy Barber. 2002. "Public Policy as a Factor Influencing Adult Lifelong Learning, Adult Literacy and Public Libraries." *Reference and User Services Quarterly* 42, no. 1 (Fall): 66–75.

Merola, Marci. 2009. "Book Festival Draws Record Crowd." *American Libraries* 40 (November): 19.

Molz, Redmond Kathleen, and Phyllis Dain. 1999. *Civic Space/Cyberspace: The American Public Library in the Information Age.* Cambridge, MA: MIT Press.

Monroe, Margaret E. 1963. *Library Adult Education: The Biography of an Idea.* New York: Scarecrow Press.

———. 1981. "The Cultural Role of the Public Library." *Advances in Librarianship* 11: 1–49.

Morrison, Andrea M. 2008. *Managing Electronic Government Information in Libraries.* Chicago: American Library Association.

Moyer, Jessica E., and Kaite Mediatore Stover. 2010. *The Readers' Advisor Handbook.* Chicago: American Library Association.

Naficy, Homa. 2009. "Centering Essential Immigrants Help on the Library Web Site: The American Place (TAP) at Hartford Public Library." *Public Library Quarterly* 28 (April/June): 162–175.

National Commission on Adult Literacy and Council for Advancement of Adult Literacy. 2008. *Reach Higher, America: Overcoming Crisis in the U.S. Workforce: Report of the National Commission on Adult Literacy.* New York: Council for Advancement of Adult Literacy.

National Endowment for the Humanities. 1998. *NEH and America's Libraries.* Washington, DC: NEH.

Nelson, Sandra. 2001. *The New Planning for Results: A Streamlined Approach.* Chicago: American Library Association.

———. 2008. *Strategic Planning for Results.* Chicago: American Library Association.

Nelson, Sarah. 2007. "Multnomah County Library Champions Portland Zine Scene." *OLA Quarterly* 17 (Summer): 17–19.

"New Family Literacy Focus Initiative Begins." 2010. *American Libraries* 41 (March): 13.

Nordmeyer, Ricki. 2001. "Readers' Advisory Websites." *Reference and User Services Quarterly* 41 (Winter): 139–143.

"Notable Videos for Adults." 2010. *Booklist* 106 (March): 32.

OCLC. 2010. *How Libraries Stack Up: 2010.* http://www.oclc.org/reports/pdfs/214109usf_how_libraries_stack_up_gray.pdf.

Overall, Patricia Montile. 2009. "Cultural Competence: A Conceptual Framework for Library and Information Science Professionals." *Library Quarterly* 79 (April): 175–204.

Peters, Thomas A. 2009. *Library Programs Online.* Westport, CT: Libraries Unlimited.

Phinney, Eleanor. 1967. "Ten Years from the Vantage Point of the Executive Secretary." *AD Newsletter* 4 (Summer): 11–14.

Preer, Jean L. 1993. "The American Heritage Project: Librarians and the Democratic Tradition in the Early Cold War." *Libraries and Culture* 28 (Spring): 165–88.

———. 2008. "Promoting Citizenship: How Librarians Helped Get Out the Vote in the 1952 Presidential Election." *Libraries and the Cultural Record* 43, no. 1: 1–28.

Price, Lee. 2009a. "Celebrating the Humanities." *Public Libraries* 48 (May/June): 23–25.

———. 2009b. "The Story of the H.O.M.E. Page Café." *Public Libraries* 48 (January/February): 32–34. Programming Librarian. http://programminglibrarian.org/.

Proceedings of the First National Joint Conference of Librarians of Color. 2009. *Gathering at the Waters: Embracing Our Spirits, Telling Our Stories.* http://www.nxtbook.com/ nxtbooks/hall-erickson/jclc_2006conf/.

Programming Librarian. 2010. *One Book, One Community Planning Guide.* http://www .programminglibrarian.org/library/programs/discussion-programs/book-discussion-programs/ one-book.html.

Queen, Priscilla. 2008. "Libraries Wanted: Boosting Our Role in Early Childhood Communities." *Colorado Libraries* 34, no. 4: 12–16.

Rawlinson, Nora K.. 1990. "Give 'Em What They Want!" *Library Journal* (June)115: 77–79.

Reference and User Services Association. 1999. "Guidelines for Developing Beginning Genealogical Collections and Services." http://www.ala.org/ala/rusa/rusaprotools/referenceguide/ guidelinesdeveloping.htm.

———. 2000. "Guidelines for Information Services." http://www.ala.org/ala/mgrps/divs/rusa/ resources/guidelines/guidelinesinformation.cfm.

———. 2001. "Guidelines for Medical, Legal and Business Responses." http://www.ala .org/ala/mgrps/divs/rusa/resources/guidelines/guidelinesmedical.cfm.

———. 2003. "Professional Competencies for Reference and User Services Librarians." http://www.ala.org/ala/mgrps/divs/rusa/resources/guidelines/professional.cfm.

———. 2004. "Guidelines for Behavioral Performance of Reference and Information Service Providers." http://www.ala.org/ala/mgrps/divs/rusa/resources/guidelines/guidelinesbehavioral .cfm.

———. 2006a. "Guidelines for Establishing Local History Collections." History Section. Local History Committee. http://www.ala.org/ala/mgrps/divs/rusa/resources/guidelines/ guidelinesestablishing.cfm.

———. 2006b. "Guidelines for the Introduction of Electronic Information Resources to Users." http://www.ala.org/ala/mgrps/divs/rusa/resources/guidelines/guidelinesintroduction .cfm.

———. 2007. "Guidelines for the Development and Promotion of Multilingual Collections and Services." http://www.ala.org/ala/mgrps/divs/rusa/resources/guidelines/guidemultilingual .cfm.

———. 2008a. "Definitions of Reference." http://www.ala.org/ala/mgrps/divs/rusa/resources/ guidelines/definitionsreference.cfm.

———. 2008b. "Guidelines for Library Services to Older Adults." http://www.ala.org/ala/ mgrps/divs/rusa/resources/guidelines/libraryservices.cfm.

———. 2010. "Guidelines for Implementing and Maintaining Virtual Reference Services." *Reference and User Services Quarterly* 50 (Fall): 92–96.

REFORMA. 2006. "Librarian's Toolkit for Responding Effectively to Anti-Immigrant Sentiment." http://www.reforma.org/ToolkitPartI.pdf.

Rendfeld, Connie. 2008. "Indiana Memory: The Making of a Statewide Digital Library." *Indiana Libraries* 27, no. 2: 23–25.

Ristau, Stephen. 2010. "Get Involved: Promoting Civic Engagement through California Public Libraries." *California State Library Foundation Bulletin* 12–14.

Ross, Catherine Sheldrick. 2009. "Public Libraries, Pleasure Reading and Models of Reading." *Library Trends* 57 (Spring): 632–656.

Ross, Catherine Sheldrick. 2006. *Reading Matters: What the Research Reveals about Reading, Libraries and Community*. Westport, CT: Libraries Unlimited.

Roy, Loriene. 2007. "Circle of Community." *American Libraries* 38 (November): 6.

Rothbauer, Paulette. 2007. "Locating the Library as Place among Lesbian, Gay, Bisexual, and Queer Patrons." In *Library as Place: History, Community and Culture*, edited by John Buschman and Gloria J. Leckie, 101–115. Westport, CT: Libraries Unlimited.

Rubin, Rhea Joyce. 1997. *Humanities Programming: A How-to-Do-It Manual*. New York: Neal-Schuman.

Sanders, Jan. 2008. "Bylaws Changes Will Create a More Inclusive PLA." *Public Libraries* 47 (January/February): 7–8.

Saricks, Joyce G. 2005. *Readers' Advisory Services in the Public Library*. 3rd ed. Chicago: American Library Association.

———. 2009a. "Celebrate ARRT." *Booklist* 105: 24.

———. 2009b. *The Readers' Advisory Guide to Genre Fiction*. Rev. ed. Chicago: American Library Association.

Schlachter, Gail A. 1982. *The Service Imperative for Libraries: Essays in Honor of Margaret E. Monroe*. Littleton, CO: Libraries Unlimited.

Shearer, Kenneth D., and Robert Burgin. 2002. *Readers' Advisor's Companion*. Littleton, CO: Libraries Unlimited.

Sheketoff, Emily. 2009. "Public Libraries and the American Recovery and Reinvestment Act." *Public Libraries* 48 (July/August): 44–51.

Shorris, Earl. 2000. *Riches for the Poor*. New York: Norton.

Smith, Duncan. 2000. "Talking with Readers: A Competency Based Approach to Readers' Advisory Services." *Reference and User Services Quarterly* 40 (Winter): 135–142.

Stephens, Annabel K. 2006. "Twenty-First Century Public Library Adult Services." *Reference and User Services Quarterly* 45 (Spring): 223–235.

Stover, Kaite Mediatore. 2009. "Stalking the Wild Appeal Factor." *Reference and User Services Quarterly* 48 (Spring): 243–246, 269.

Swain, Martha H. 1995. "A New Deal in Libraries: Federal Relief Work and Library Service, 1933–1943." *Libraries and Culture* 30: 265–283.

Swisher, Susan Herrick. 2007. "'A' Is for Art, Not Age: The Hammond Public Library's Annual Senior Art Exhibit." *Indiana Libraries* 26, no. 2: 38–39.

Taylor, Edward W. 2010. "Cultural Institutions and Adult Education." *New Directions for Adult and Continuing Education* 127 (Fall): 5–14.

Trott, Barry. 2008. "Building on a Firm Foundation: Readers' Advisory over the Next Twenty-Five Years." *Reference and User Services Quarterly* 48 (Winter): 132–135.

Tucker, John Mark. 1998. *Untold Stories: Civil Rights, Libraries, and Black Librarianship*. Champaign, IL: Publications Office, Graduate School of Library and Information Science.

U.S. Department of Education. 2000. *Lifelong Learning NCES Task Force: Final Report, Volume II, Working Paper No. 2000-16b*. Washington, DC: U.S. Department of Education.

U.S. National Commission on Libraries and Information Science. 1983. *Final Report to the National Commission on Libraries and Information Science from the Community Information and Referral Task Force.* ERIC ED241014. Washington, DC: National Commission on Libraries and Information Science.

Van Fleet, Connie. 1990. "Lifelong Learning Theory and the Provision of Adult Services." In *Adult Services: An Enduring Focus for Public Libraries*, edited by Kathleen M. Heim (de la Peña McCook) and Danny P. Wallace, 166–211. Chicago: American Library Association.

Van Fleet, Connie, and Douglas Raber. 1990. "The Public Library as a Social/Cultural Institution: Alternative Perspectives and Changing Contexts." In *Adult Services: An Enduring Focus for Public Libraries*, edited by Kathleen M. Heim (de la Peña McCook) and Danny P. Wallace, 456–500. Chicago: American Library Association.

Vollmer, Timothy. 2010. "There's an App for That! Libraries and Mobile Technology: An Introduction to Public Policy Considerations." Washington, DC: ALA Office for Information Technology Policy. http://www.ala.org/ala/aboutala/offices/oitp/publications/policybriefs/mobiledevices.pdf.

Waples, Douglas, and Ralph W. Tyler. 1931. *What People Want to Read About: A Study of Group Interests and a Survey of Problems in Adult Reading.* Chicago: University of Chicago Press.

WebJunction. 2010. National Leadership Grant. http://www.webjunction.org/patron-training-research.

Weibel, Kathleen. 1982. *The Evolution of Library Outreach 1960–75 and Its Effect on Reader Services: Some Considerations.* Occasional Paper Number 16. Urbana: Graduate School of Library and Information Science. ERIC ED231376.

Wellman, Hiller C. 1915. "The Library's Primary Duty." *ALA Bulletin* 9 (July): 89–93.

White House, Office of the Press Secretary. 2009. "National Information Literacy Awareness Month, 2009: By the President of the United States of America, a Proclamation" (Press release). The White House. http://www.whitehouse.gov/the_press_office/Presidential-Proclamation-National-Information-Literacy-Awareness-Month.

Wilson, Louis R. 1938. *The Geography of Reading: A Study of the Distribution and Status of Libraries in the United States.* Chicago: University of Chicago Press.

Wise, Mary. 2005. "Books, Hot Coffee and a Comfortable Chair." *Alki* 21 (March): 11–12.

Wyatt, Neal. 2008. "RA ToolKit." *Library Journal* 133 (June 15): 42–45.

9

Youth Services

Alicia K. Long and Kathleen de la Peña McCook

The child as reader, the child of the information age, the child in the community, the global child, or the empowered child? Which child will we target as we plan and deliver library services in our communities? Better yet, can we strive to target them all?

—V. Walter, "The Children We Serve"

Youth Services in Public Libraries

For over three centuries, youth services in U.S. public libraries have grown and adapted as youth librarians have worked with commitment and focus to define and develop services appropriate for young people. These services began in the 1800s in public libraries with collections of books for the educational and cultural development of children and broadened to include designated rooms for youth. Library story hours, programs, and outreach were added to the scope of services during the twentieth century. In 2008 circulation of children's materials in public libraries was 786.3 million, or 34.5 percent of total circulation. Attendance at children's programs was 60.1 million (U.S. IMLS, 2010). The use of newly developed technologies has opened up new avenues of participation for children and youth in the beginning of the twenty-first century. This chapter reviews the history of public library services for youth, details national initiatives such as competency statements, and characterizes youth services in the context of the Public Library Association's (PLA's) *Strategic Planning for Results* (Nelson, 2008).

---

*Long and McCook have revised the 2004 chapter by Linda Alexander and Barbara Immroth that appeared in the first edition of *Introduction to Public Librarianship*.

History

Beginnings to 1951

During the nineteenth century, the societal view of children and their needs slowly changed. The growth of cities and industrialization brought the realization that while children could be an economic asset, especially for the poor, they also needed to achieve literacy, which was addressed by the formation of Sunday school libraries for children whose parents could not afford to pay for private school. These libraries primarily contained religious books, but included a broader range of subjects and were a source of free books for many children in the 1820s and 1830s. They probably influenced the inclusion of district libraries in common schools (Walter, 1941).

Wealthy individuals such as Caleb Bingham, a bookseller in Salisbury, Connecticut, donated books for nine- to sixteen-year-olds for a small library in 1803. In 1810 the town appropriated funds to buy additional books, making it "probably the first example of an American municipal government allocating support for a public library" (Fenwick, 1976: 332). Several states passed school district laws incorporating the concept of school libraries in the 1830s to the 1850s, but no appropriations for collections and staff were made. Although these early libraries were not direct forerunners of later public children's and school libraries, their existence demonstrates a growing awareness of the need to provide reading material for children.

The idea of providing library access for children came to national attention with the establishment of public libraries in the mid-1850s, the growth of literature for children, and changing attitudes toward the improvement of child welfare. Fletcher addressed age restrictions on library use and the quality of books being published for children in the 1876 report, *Public Libraries in the United States of America: Their History, Condition, and Management.*

For an extensive analysis of the development of children's services in public libraries from 1876 to 1906, see Thomas (1982), who identifies five conditions that allowed for the emergence of youth services:

1. Specialized collections
2. Specialized space
3. Specialized personnel
4. Specialized programs
5. The existence of organizations and agencies devoted to youth

Jenkins (2000) used Thomas's model to discuss the research literature of youth services librarianship at the outset of the twenty-first century.

Key librarians in the nineteenth and early twentieth centuries who developed the foundation of library services to youth include:

- Caroline Hewins, librarian at the Hartford, Connecticut, Public Library, who published a list of the best children's books available in 1882 and wrote yearly reports called *Reading for the Young*.
- Mary Wright Plummer, librarian at Pratt Institute, who advocated for libraries to take an active role in children's reading; she designed the first public library children's room in 1895 (Lundin, 1996: 840–850).
- Lutie Stearns, Milwaukee Public Library, who wrote *Report on Reading for the Young* and held a general meeting about children's issues at the 1894 American Library Association conference, signifying acceptance of children's services by the library profession (Fenwick, 1976: 337).
- Anne Carroll Moore, superintendent for work with children at Pratt Institute, in 1896 began giving lectures on children's services. She wrote "Special Training for Children's Librarians" (Moore, 1898) and included a children's room in every branch of the New York Public Library, where she worked as a children's librarian from 1906 to 1941.

In the 1890s some public libraries abolished age restrictions and established separate children's rooms that included collections and staff. In the public schools the Progressive movement championed a change from textbook teaching to use of a broader range of resources, and public libraries in some cities began to provide schools with special collections and services. In 1899 the National Education Association published *Report of the Committee on the Relations of Public Libraries to Public Schools*, which recommended cooperation between schools and public libraries and a small library in every elementary school.

Professional education for children's librarianship began in the first decade of the twentieth century. In addition to Hewins's classes at Pratt, Frances Jenkins Olcott started classes for children's librarians at the Carnegie Library in Pittsburgh, which became the Training School for Children's Librarians in 1901 and continued to train children's librarians exclusively until 1917 (Fenwick, 1976: 341). In the public schools, activity-centered learning required numerous resources as students made new demands on library collections. Public libraries responded in several ways. Some provided classroom collections on loan to schools, or opened a branch library in the school; some shared responsibility for library collections with the schools; and in some places the schools began their own libraries. High schools had collections of books earlier than elementary schools.

Other high points in the early development of youth services as a public library specialization included establishment of the American Library Association's (ALA's)

Section for Children's Librarians, organized in 1900; Louise Seaman Bechtel's appointment as the first head of a juvenile department at a publisher, Macmillan (1919); and Children's Book Week, organized in 1919 by Frederick Melcher, chair of the American Booksellers Association. Recognizing the success of publishers, booksellers, and librarians working together, and the dedication and professionalism of children's librarians, Melcher was the driving force in establishing the John Newbery Medal in 1922 for the most distinguished children's book published in the United States each year, which is administered by the Association for Library Service to Children of the ALA.

In the late 1920s, the ALA Board of Education for Librarianship initiated a series of texts for library schools including *Library Work with Children* by Effie L. Power (1930). In a study of her career, Kimball notes that Power's ambitious aim was to present, insofar as was possible in a single textbook, a comprehensive introduction and guide to public youth services librarianship (Kimball, Jenkins, and Hearne, 2004). A comparative reading with the second edition of 1940 provides a prescriptive picture of professional attitudes and practices deemed essential to youth services librarianship from the late 1920s to the early 1940s.

The years 1920–1950 were a time of consolidation, standardization, and broadening horizons for library service to children. McDowell (2007) has assessed the impact of the Progressive era on the development of youth services. During the Depression public library circulation soared and circulation to children was 40–45 percent of the total. Children's librarians continued to provide services that had been established earlier: individual reader guidance, book selection, and provision of reading promotion materials. Storytelling programs provided a literacy experience for older children, and libraries instituted youth and preschool story hours.

The need to bridge the gap between children's and adults' reading was recognized by the opening of special rooms for teens, the first in 1925 at the Cleveland Public Library. In 1930 the Young People's Reading Round Table was established within the ALA. In 1941, children's librarians, young peoples' librarians, and school librarians formed the Division of Libraries for Children and Young People in the ALA, with Mildred Batchelder as the executive secretary. In 1951 when the American Association of School Librarians (AASL) became a separate ALA division, Batchelder remained as executive secretary of the Children's Service Division and the Young People's Services Division. However, as Jenkins (2000) notes, youth services were largely neglected in the landmark Public Library Inquiry of the late 1940s.

Serving Minority Youth

Throughout most of the twentieth century, the story of public library service to youth of color was not told in mainstream narratives. Native American children were often sent to boarding schools—detribalized in institutions like the Carlisle Indian Industrial School. African American children were not provided with equal access to libraries during the first part of the twentieth century due to segregation (Gleason, 1941). Yet there were bright spots. For instance, early children's librarians reached out to immigrant children and provided small neighborhood book collections.

While it is difficult to characterize fully the lack of resources and support devoted to serving African American youth in the first half of the twentieth century (Mussman, 1998), it is important to take note of leaders who did lay the foundation for better days to come. Charlemae Hill Rollins, children's librarian and scholar of African American literature for children, worked at the Chicago Public Library from 1927 to 1963. In 1957 Mrs. Rollins was the first African American to head the ALA Children's Services Division. Augusta Braxton Baker, storyteller, author, and consultant based at the New York Public Library from 1937 to 1974, initiated the series *The Black Experience in Children's Books* and wrote the classic, *Storytelling: Art and Technique*. Fannette H. Thomas (1993) edited a collective biography on African American youth services librarians who protected African American children from racism and discrimination and challenged these social problems in adult society.

Post–World War II to the Present

Following World War II, two major court cases made an impact on the educational opportunities for youth. In 1947 *Mendez v. Westminster School District* held that the segregation of Mexican and Mexican American students into separate "Mexican schools" was unconstitutional. The 1954 court decision *Brown v. Board of Education* declared separate but equal educational facilities inherently unequal and urged desegregation of public schools with all deliberate speed. Public libraries followed at varying rates. Birmingham, Alabama, which had duplicate facilities and collections for African Americans and whites, integrated by 1963. The story of the desegregation of public libraries can be found in disparate regional analyses, but youth services librarians today can be proud that some librarians were active in the desegregation struggle (Cresswell, 1996).

An increasing use of media and resources beyond the book for teaching in schools impacted library services for children and youth during the period 1950–1975. The 1956 Library Services and Construction Act provided federal funding for public libraries to experiment with new outreach programs for the unserved (Walter, 2001: 7). Public libraries also experienced a shift in patrons, with poorer, less educated patrons in the central cities and more affluent families moving to the suburbs. Desegregation presented new challenges. Supporting the teaching of basic reading literacy skills and providing collections that appealed to minorities became more important for central city libraries. Preschool storytimes became more popular, as did storytellers in languages other than English. Jones's (2004) study *Still Struggling for Equality* provides well-documented bibliographic sources to extend the narrative, including work projects carried out under the Library Services Act.

Young adults became a more visible focus of librarians with the establishment of the ALA Young Adult Services Division in 1957. High school students were more than half of the users of public libraries, placing new demands on collections and staff (Fenwick, 1976: 358). In 1963 the Library of Congress named Virginia Haviland the head of the Children's Book Section, later the Children's Literature Center. She was a leader in national and international children's literature activities.

Federal education funding during the 1960s and early 1970s provided money to purchase school library books and to hire librarians. This brought about discussion and research on school–public library cooperation, shared collection building, and other joint ventures that extend to present day (Woolls, 2001). An influential book by Margaret A. Edwards of the Enoch Pratt Library in Baltimore, *The Fair Garden and the Swarm of Beasts: The Library and the Young Adult*, was published in 1969. This book provided a "well-defined philosophy for services for teens and discussions for best practice" (Walter and Meyers, 2003: 10).

Proposition 13 in California in 1978 and similar initiatives in other states led to large local tax cuts, and public library expenditures all over the country declined. During the 1980s funding became a major issue for library services (Walter and Meyers, 2003: 26). Society placed an increased emphasis on social, cultural, and educational growth of youth, urging the passage of state and federal laws requiring public library professionals to provide books and materials to day care centers and parents of preschool children. ALA task forces specified and defined goals, policies, and recommendations to implement these services (ALA, 1984; Rollock, 1988). Circulation statistics, quantitative evaluation methods, and accountability were required to validate effectiveness and justify the use of tax money to administer services and programs. Public libraries wrote mission statements, and strategic planning was a point of convergence for connecting information to libraries. About half of all public library users were under the age of eighteen, with one-fourth being between the ages of twelve and eighteen (U.S. National Center for Education Statistics, 1988).

As a response to the needs of teens, the Young Adult Services Division (YASD) has published such books as *Young Adults Deserve the Best: YALSA's Competencies in Action* (Flowers, 2010). Lists of "Quick Picks" for reluctant readers and "Best Books for Young Adults" became popular with young library patrons. The YASD was reorganized as the Young Adult Library Services Association (YALSA) in 1992.

In 1992 the Association for Library Service to Children (ALSC) of ALA commissioned Virginia Walter to write *Output Measures for Public Library Service to Children*, a companion volume to the 1982 PLA *Output Measures for Public Libraries* (Zweizig and Rodger, 1982). YALSA followed ALSC's lead, and Walter (1995) produced *Output Measures and More: Planning and Evaluating Public Library Services for Young Adults.*

A group of experienced children's librarians created the "Prototype of Public Library Services for Young Children and Their Families" at a U.S. Department of Education–supported conference in Austin, Texas, in 1994. The prototype was based on research in child development and emergent literacy and advocated significant improvements in preschool services in public libraries (Immroth and Ash-Geisler, 1995). ALA President Mary Somerville's theme, "Kids Can't Wait . . . Library Advocacy Now!" in 1996–1997 emphasized a focus on youth services and youth services librarians.

At the outset of the twenty-first century the Urban Libraries Council initiative, Public Libraries as Partners in Youth Development, supported by the DeWitt Wallace Reader's Digest Fund, called for teen-friendly library spaces, more relevant materials and services, increased computer access and instruction, improved customer service, and a review of policies on hours and fines (Meyers, 2001).

The PLA's Early Literacy Project began in 2000 with a partnership with the National Institute of Child Health and Human Development, which released the National Reading Panel's (2000) landmark report, *Teaching Children to Read: An Evidence-Based Assessment of the Scientific Research Literature on Reading and Its Implications for Reading Instruction,* providing research-based findings concerning reading development in America's children. The Every Child Ready to Read @ Your Library (ECRR) initiative based on this work provided research-based findings on how children learn to read, including the importance of early childhood experiences that promote literacy development. PLA contracted with researchers in emergent literacy to develop a model program for parents and caregivers. To broaden the dissemination of these materials and to test their effectiveness, PLA and the ALSC formed a partnership to pilot these materials in public libraries across the country. In October 2001, 20 demonstration sites were selected representing a wide range of library size and demographics.

In 2009 the ALSC and PLA boards of directors received an evaluation on the ECRR initiative that recommended continuation of the ALSC/PLA divisional partnership and support of core values for the ECRR initiative. These core values include:

- Parents/caregivers are the child's first and best teacher.
- Play provides a wide range of benefits and opportunities for the young child.
- Reading is an essential life skill.
- Lifelong learning is a primary role of the public library and this learning begins at birth.

In *Twenty-First Century Kids, Twenty-First Century Librarians*, Walter (2010) reviews the history, assesses the present, and forecasts the future of children's services in public libraries. She describes five aspects of children relative to the library: as readers, as products of the information age, as community members, as global, and as empowered people. She emphasizes multiple literacies.

Professional Associations

Each public library determines the scope of youth services that it provides. Some libraries have children's services staff; some have children's and young adult services staff; and some have youth services staff, who provide services to young people from birth to age 18. Several ALA units focus on youth. Organizational units within ALA addressing the needs of children and young adults were created in 1957 when the Association of Young People's Librarians split into the Children's Services Division (now ALSC) and the Young Adult Services Division (now YALSA). ALSC and YALSA have developed partnerships on the national level, with the Liaison with National Organizations Serving Children and Youth (ALSC) and Partnerships Advocating for Teens (YALSA). They work in collaboration with AASL on public library–school partnerships and with the PLA on issues of common interest.

Regional, state, and local associations parallel national-level associations providing opportunities for active engagement. Examples are the California Library Association, Youth Services Group; Iowa Library Association, Youth Services Subdivision; and the Montana Library Association, Children's and Youth Services Interest Group.

The Association for Library Service to Children

ALSC is the world's largest organization dedicated to the support and enhancement of library service to children. The core purpose of ALSC is creating a better future for children through libraries. In 2010 four major initiatives of ALSC were:

- Born to Read,
- El Día de los Niños/El Día de los Libros (Children's Day/Book Day),
- Every Child Ready to Read, and
- Kids! @ Your Library public awareness campaign.

ALSC advocates for children and children's librarians on a national level. Committees of ALSC determine the major awards including the Caldecott, Newbery, Sibert, Wilder, Carnegie, Batchelder, Belpré, Geisel, and Odyssey awards and the May Hill Arbuthnot Honor Lecture. Other committees compile annual lists of notable books, recordings, videos, and computer software for children. ALSC promotes reading and books through recommendations, compilations of lists, and related services, such as the following:

- Book List for the Service Network for Children of Inmates, October 2009
- Hi-Lo Books for Upper Elementary Grades, February 2009
- Great Early Elementary Reads, May 2008
- Translated Newbery Titles, June 2008
- Translated Caldecott Titles, June 2008

ALSC administers professional awards, including grants and fellowships, to recognize members, support outstanding programming, and aid in continuing education. ALSC committee members advocate for children on the local, state, and national levels on issues including intellectual freedom and legislation. The ALSC journal is *Children and Libraries*. The association also uses social networking to communicate, including a blog, ALA Connect, Facebook, and electronic discussion lists.

Young Adult Library Services Association

The mission statement of YALSA is "to advocate, promote, and strengthen service to young adults as part of the continuum of total library service, and to support those who provide service to this population." The following activities provide the means to fulfill the mission:

- Advocate the young adult's right to free and equal access to materials and services, and assists librarians in handling problems with such access.
- Evaluate and promote materials of interest to adolescents through special services, programs, and publications, except for those materials designed specifically for curriculum use.
- Identify research needs related to young adult service and communicates those needs to the library academic community in order to activate research projects.
- Stimulate and promote the development of librarians and other staff working with young adults through formal and continuing education.
- Stimulate and promote the expansion of young adult service among professional associations and agencies at all levels.
- Represent the interests of librarians and staff working with young adults to all relevant agencies, governmental or private, and industries that serve young adults as clients or consumers.
- Create and maintain communication links with other units of ALA whose developments affect service to young adults.

Young Adult Library Services is the official journal of YALSA. In 2010 YALSA began to publish the online *Journal of Research on Libraries and Young Adults* to serve as a vehicle for disseminating research of interest to librarians, library workers, and academics who focus on library service to young adults, ages 12 through 18.

Competencies

ALSC recommends core competencies to all children's librarians and other staff whose primary duties include delivering and advocating library service for children ages 0–14. Competencies are broadly categorized in nine areas:

1. Knowledge of client group
2. Administrative and management skills
3. Communication skills
4. Knowledge of materials
5. User and reference services
6. Programming skills
7. Advocacy, public relations, and networking skills
8. Professionalism and professional development
9. Technology (ALSC, 2009)

YALSA's competencies for librarians serving young adults, *Young Adults Deserve the Best: Competencies for Librarians Serving Young Adults*, were developed in 1981 and revised in 1998, 2003, and 2010. These competencies are provided for librarians who serve young adults. Library workers who demonstrate the knowledge and skills laid out in thedocument will provide quality library service for and with teenagers. Institutions seeking to improve their overall service capacity and increase public value to their community are encouraged by YALSA (2010) to adopt the competencies: "institutions adopting these competencies will necessarily improve overall service capacities and increase public value to their respective communities."

Youth services librarians will also want to be familiar with materials issued by the AASL that promote the improvement and extension of library media services in elementary and secondary schools as a means of strengthening the total education program. The AASL's (2007) *Standards for the 21st-Century Learner* respond to the changing world of information and technology.

Censorship

Each year, Banned Books Week is a reminder of the vigilance required to guarantee intellectual freedom, especially in libraries serving youth (Petrilli, 2009). Banning books goes back to the time of Plato, who "argued that banishing various poets and dramatists was essential for the moral good of the young" (Nilsen and Donelson, 2001: 395). During the late nineteenth and early twentieth centuries, Anthony Comstock imprisoned "evil" authors, destroyed what he conceived of as bad literature, and published *Traps for the Young* on temptations for youth (Bremmer, 1967). The 1896 ALA conference attendees questioned whether Crane's *Red Badge of Courage* should be on the list of recommended books (Nilsen and Donelson, 2001: 396).

During the twentieth century, librarians discussed what was appropriate for young people to read or view. Court cases document the multitude of challenges to books and other materials and free speech issues throughout the United States. It is imperative that all library professionals be informed on these issues and that they develop policies and procedures to address potential challenges to the accessibility of materials. We cannot emphasize enough that being ready when the censor arrives is part of the responsibility of all personnel working in libraries. *Intellectual Freedom for Children: The Censor Is Coming* (ALSC, 2000) provides guidance; the YALSA and ALSC websites also provide information about dealing with banned and challenged materials and for teaching children about these issues. *Kids, Know Your Rights! A Young Person's Guide to Intellectual Freedom*, created by ALSC's Intellectual Freedom Committee (2007) is a good example. Since materials for children and youth are among the most frequently challenged in library collections, it is especially important for librarians serving these populations to understand the issues and know how to react if items in their collections are challenged.

Internet connections available to children, the fear of danger to children, and the societal upheaval in the wake of 9/11 resulted in sweeping new federal legislation and brought intellectual freedom issues into national prominence at the end of the twentieth and the beginning of the twenty-first centuries. The Children's Internet Protection Act (CIPA) requires "the installation and use by schools and libraries of technology for filtering or blocking material on the Internet on computers with Internet access to be eligible to receive or retain universal service assistance." The implications for youth have been explored by Jaeger and Zheng (2009).

Two especially useful publications are *Protecting Intellectual Freedom in Your School Library: Scenarios from the Front Lines* (Scales, 2009) and the collaborative publication by ALSC and the PLA, *Children and the Internet: Policies That Work*, an electronic publication that compiles the most recent information and guidelines about the issue (Braun, 2010).

Types of Children and Youth Services Today

It is one of the aims of this book to tie together the various resources that support public librarianship within the context of current practice. We organize the variety of youth services in relationship to four categories of the 18 service responses delineated in *Strategic Planning for Results* (Nelson, 2008) to reflect a larger vision of the public library's centrality to communities. Additionally, we refer to the Internet-enabled roles and responses addressed by McClure and Jaeger (2009) in *Public Libraries and Internet Service Roles*. The four categories are:

- Public sphere
- Cultural heritage
- Education
- Information

Public Sphere

The public library in its most expansive role is a central component of a community's public sphere. In this capacity, librarians can support the community's links to the daily reality and discourse of those it serves. It is through enhancement of the public sphere that the library builds community and encourages authentic dialogue. The service responses in *Strategic Planning for Results* (Nelson, 2008) that enhance the public sphere are "Be an Informed Citizen: Local, National and World Affairs," "Know Your Community: Community Resources and Services," and "Visit a Comfortable Space: Physical and Virtual Spaces."[1]

Be an Informed Citizen

The information needed to promote democracy, fulfill civic responsibilities, and participate in community decision making is supported by this service response (Nelson, 2008: 149).

School assignments or other queries often call for information about elected officials and governmental agencies that enable people to learn how to participate in the democratic process. For many reasons, including the need for an educated citizenry, youth need an awareness of the existence of government publications and the ability to access education laws, rules, practices, and information about health, jobs, and their communities. In the United States, government agencies publish reliable and authentic information on almost every field of inquiry on the local, state, and federal levels. The topics in government publications range from gardening and fertilizers to information about railroads, engineering, education, NASA, and the Internet. The various government agencies even publish coloring books and cookbooks for children. Normally, only large public libraries that are designated depository libraries receive the many series of printed documents due to space or other issues. Print collections of documents are not generally housed in such a way as to be good browsing collections and can be difficult to locate for even the most savvy researcher. There are over 1,400 designated government depository libraries in the United States, many of which are part of university or large public library collections.

In a public library, local government-published information can include grassroots campaigns, or locally published brochures on topics of health, education, community meetings, and profiles on neighborhoods in that city. Government information can be a useful resource for adults who work with children, as well as students in middle and high school.

Since the mid-1990s, each agency of the government has begun to provide free public access to much government information via the World Wide Web. Websites for state and federal documents can also be accessed through Internet-connected computer terminals. The website http://www.kids.gov is an excellent portal to all kinds of information prepared by different government agencies, many of which have developed pages exclusively for children and youth. One such example of government websites of interest to youth, teachers, and parents is Ben's Guide to U.S. Government for Kids (http://bensguide.gpo.gov/). This site includes tools for K–12, teaches how the government works, and includes locators for government sites developed for youth. Ben's Guide is an educational component of GPO Access provided by the Superintendent of Documents (Ziegenbein, 2008).

Librarians serving youth can provide assistance in finding relevant electronic sources, whereas print sources may be pamphlets, forms, and other documents provided by the public library as a service to local citizens.

Know Your Community

Provision of information about the wide variety of programs, services, and activities of community agencies and organizations define this service (Nelson, 2008: 180). Public libraries have a long history of providing community information.

Community referral service in public libraries is the provision of information on services offered by community agencies and organizations. Libraries develop databases of available services with phone numbers and web and physical addresses of helping agencies, and provide information about qualifications for receiving specific services. Ready reference for children is a complement to the general reference service. Information about the local community, including services that can be attractive to children and youth, or useful to their families, should be available and displayed on bulletin boards or in other highly visible forms, as well as in electronic form. Services may include responding to walk-ins or providing toll-free phone numbers or easy access to information via the Internet. Referrals to resources such as town directories and maps, lists of elected officials, local institutions and agencies, and other local programs are part of the services that youth librarians should be able to provide.

In *Twenty-First Century Kids, Twenty-First Century Librarians*, Virginia Walter (2010) explores five aspects of service to children. The third of these aspects is the child in the community. Over the history of services to children, the need to consider the child's environment has always been contemplated. Outreach services to remote areas or low-income neighborhoods and programs for at-risk youth and foster children are some examples of types of involvement in the community to which the younger patrons belong (Walter, 2010). Librarians have traditionally accepted their role in social reform, and the challenge to collaborate with other social agencies that seek solutions for at-risk youth is still relevant today (Lukenbill, 2006). Community services for children need to be represented in the library, and the library needs to be aware of the community's needs outside of the library building (Woelfer and Hendry, 2009).

This service model has grown in importance as e-government has expanded. As pointed out by Jaeger and Bertot (2009), patrons now seek assistance from public librarians for a range of government services. The roles of e-government service provider and digital ombudsman find librarians providing advice and specific techniques for applying and integrating various digital and Internet-enabled services (McClure and Jaeger, 2009: 50–51).

Visit a Comfortable Space: Physical and Virtual Spaces

This service response calls for the library to be a safe and welcoming physical place where people can meet and interact, read quietly, and have open and accessible virtual spaces that support networking (Nelson, 2008: 210).

All people, especially youth, have a need to meet and interact with others in the community and to participate in public discourse about community issues. The concept and practice of the commons allows libraries to provide program opportunities that draw the diverse community of youth together. The public library provides meeting spaces, events bulletin boards, access to e-mail accounts, and a common environment as a public place (McCook, 2001).

With the development of digital technologies and social media, public space intentionally designed for children and youth in the library has developed into two spaces: physical and virtual.

It is essential that the public library consider the physical space requirements to provide a welcoming environment for children and youth. In Chapter 7 of *Interior Design for Libraries*, Carol Brown (2002) addresses the main principles that should guide the selection and design of the space destined to be used by children. An intentional design of the children's area shows that libraries consider youth as an integral part of the community, and their value is reflected in their buildings (Bernier, 2009). At a time when many fear the demise of libraries as physical buildings, others try to prove that the public library will still exist, among other reasons, due to its appeal as a "destination place" (Walter, 2010). For this reason, it is important that managers and administrators in public libraries consider (or reconsider) questions such as the amount of space destined for children and youth, the location of those spaces, and their furnishings, materials, aesthetics, and appeal for young patrons and their families. A reevaluation of these spaces includes the assessment of aesthetic value, functionality, and purpose. The space needs to cover several possibilities for isolated and group work, and it needs to provide accommodations for different postures and movements (Cranz and Cha, 2006). In many cases, the first step consists of involving youth, especially teens, in the planning: by participating and making suggestions about the design of their own space, teens will find the way to show their interests and needs (Suellentrop, 2008). Bolan (2006) also recommends their input and participation in the planning as one of the guidelines to ensure the success of a teen area. Many libraries addressing the issue of appealing to youth in their communities have made the effort to research what attracts kids and teens to other places to get inspiration for what the library should offer. Children, and especially adolescents, manifest their interest in having a nice place to hang out, read, and use new technologies. However, libraries also need to differentiate themselves from common, commercially based destinations such as chain bookstores and coffee shops by providing the same attractive atmosphere and customer service, and then something else (Farrelly, 2006a). The public library's traditional mission of providing free information access to all is still at the core of the newly designed spaces for youth. That is where libraries as a destination for children and youth have a unique role to play.

There are many interesting examples of libraries creating specially designed places for the children and youth in their communities. Some of them required complete transformations and others simple redesign projects. Depending on the magnitude and local characteristics of each library, one can benefit from these examples. Two of the most recent and successful projects are the Cerritos Library in California and ImaginOn, a joint venture of Charlotte Mecklenburg Public Library and the Children's Theatre, in Charlotte, North Carolina (Holt, 2008; Walter, 2010). These two projects have attracted a lot of attention as being among the first libraries in the twenty-first century to embark on a new concept of buildings designed for children's exploration and enjoyment. Besides furniture and collections oriented especially toward children and youth, these libraries have themed spaces and architectural features that have the children's experience at their core (Holt, 2008). Magnet boards, manipulable objects, play areas, gaming stations, technology centers, and media production studios are some features found in these carefully designed (and even environmentally friendly, as the case of ImaginOn) buildings. Other libraries have also addressed the needs of the youngest (toddlers and preschoolers) by discovering the benefits of sections appropriate for these little ones and their caregivers (Walter,

2010). The Trove in New York's White Plains Public Library is another excellent example (Kenney, 2006). Preschoolers and school-age kids enjoy the wonders of imaginative places ready for them to explore.

Many scholars, writers, and librarians have analyzed the increasing importance of teen spaces. In "The Beasts Have Arrived," the authors summarize the assistance that YALSA provides for those working in teen services: guidelines and ideas about designing spaces for youth, and successful programs such as Teen Read Week, Teen Tech Week, Teens' Top Ten, and others (Herald and Monnier, 2007). These services have a better outcome when the building is adequate to teens' needs.

No matter the size and scope of a public library, children and youth need a comfortable space where they can interact and benefit from library services. In some cases it would be a Teen Zone or a Young Adults Reading Center; in others it will imply bigger structural projects. The "cyberpool" in the Trove and the "loft" in ImaginOn are good examples (Holt, 2008; Kenney, 2006). By consulting experts' research and guidelines and considering the particular characteristics of the community and the children's needs, each library can reevaluate and develop programs that would make their buildings attractive destinations.

The twenty-first century has added a new dimension to the library as a comfortable space to visit. Children, youth, and families can now visit their library in a virtual way. It is important to devote some consideration to the virtual space provided by the library to its users, especially the young. As King and Brown (2009) pointed out, for many teens, the library's website is the library. John Palfrey and Urs Gasser's (2008) book *Born Digital* provides an overview of the special characteristics and challenges relating to the first generation of digital natives, or those who were born after social digital technologies were developed. These are the young patrons to whom libraries are trying to reach out. Communication with them undeniably needs to include the virtual space. Besides being the main platform for reaching them, the library's presence in cyberspace contributes to the goal of democratizing information by providing a more widespread access to its services (Aiken, 2006).

Web 2.0 in Youth Services

The development of what is known as Web 2.0 technologies has passed from being an emerging trend to a widespread reality. The library's presence can be developed in several platforms that youth and children use. In a presentation for librarians about emerging trends and 2.0 technologies, King and Brown (2009) explained and gave examples of the many ways in which libraries can use these technologies, which are essential in youth services. They recommend ways to connect virtually through the following (not exhaustive) list of applications and platforms.

Blogs, Wikis, Podcasts, and Videocasts

Libraries can use blogs to communicate with young patrons, to start conversations and reach customers, and to promote new books and materials as well as events and library news. Although blogging can be seen as a one-way communication tool, the ability to provide comments and feedback can be managed by the library. Wikis allow for more active participation and can be used in special projects and with regular patrons. Podcasts and videocasts are good ways to promote books and other materials.

Social Networking

There are different trends in the tools used for social networking, with Facebook, Myspace, Flickr, or Twitter being the most widespread at this writing. These and other applications provide attractive ways to promote the library and its programs. These technologies complement traditional methods such as fliers and posters without adding material costs (except the time to develop and maintain them) (Farrelly, 2009). For children and youth who are connected to these programs almost constantly, getting the library's announcements, news, updates, and invitations alongside their other social network activities situates the library as an active participant in their world.

Bookmarking, Instant Messaging, and Expanding the Catalog

Many libraries are experimenting with social bookmarking for specific collections or as a tagging approach, to provide a user-friendly way to put more books in the hands of their young readers. Expanding their catalogs to the online world is also being tried at several libraries. Virtual reference, whether by e-mail or instant messaging, already has a place in many public libraries, and this is undeniably helpful to reach to younger audiences.

Virtual Worlds

Libraries can use alternative worlds such as Second Life to establish a presence in spaces visited by many young adults. The virtual world of Second Life is divided into two grids: one for adults and one for teens. The second one is a secure environment destined for 13–17-year-olds (Hedreen et al., 2008). Some libraries are exploring the possibilities of establishing a presence in this teen grid to reach the thousands of teens that participate in this environment (Hedreen et al., 2008).

Gaming: Where Virtual and Physical Space Meet

An emerging trend in public libraries is the development of gaming programs for teens and youth. YALSA's Teen Tech Week and other programs encourage the development of initiatives that give kids a safe space for gaming in the library. Traditional board games cohabit with electronic consoles in gaming sessions for older children and teens. Gaming sessions at ALA and other professional conferences make sure that librarians are knowledgeable about popular games such as Guitar Hero, Rock Band, Dance, Dance, Revolution, and others (Scordato, 2008). Creating jam sessions, game nights, and other open-door venues is an opportunity for libraries to provide a full spectrum of services and gives teens a chance to socialize, be entertained, and learn in a safe environment (Farrelly, 2008).

The Internet-enabled role of the public library as a connector of friends, families, and others in the networked environment is a means for people to stay connected in ordinary times and during disasters. In their monograph on Internet-enabled service roles for the public library, McClure and Jaeger (2009) extend the idea of "visiting a comfortable place" to a function that ensures family and community sustainability.

Cultural Heritage

Public libraries have long played an important role in preserving and activating cultural heritage. Reading discussion groups, lectures, film series, exhibits, and celebrations of different cultures are central adult services that are the basis for partnerships that have expanded the library's involvement in local communities. Richard Jensen (2000: 10) has noted, "culture is composed of the things that define us, the physical manifestations of what we as a collective people bring to a place." Planning library spaces for the teen culture must "challenge traditions to be authentic" (Weinberg, 2009; Walter and Meyers, 2003: 65; Jensen, 2000: 10). The service responses from *Strategic Planning for Results* (Nelson, 2008) that reflect enhancement of the cultural heritage category are "Celebrate Diversity: Cultural Awareness,"; "Discover Your Roots: Genealogy and Local History," "Express Creativity: Create and Share Content," "Satisfy Curiosity: Lifelong Learning," and "Stimulate Imagination: Reading, Viewing and Listening for Pleasure."[2]

Celebrate Diversity: Cultural Awareness

This response identifies the need for librarians to provide programs and services that promote appreciation and understanding of the community's various heritages (Nelson 2008: 158).

We should not need to be reminded that the public library is here for everyone and everyone should feel welcome (Farrelly, 2007a). However, it takes a conscious effort to embrace diversity and to make sure that services, programs, and collections reflect the diverse population in which the library is immersed. To ensure that youth services are inclusive and respond to differences of race, creed, color, religion, gender, disability, socioeconomic background, language, and national origin, among other factors, the websites and publications of professional organizations provide a good starting point to make diversity a reality in services to children and youth.

Several units of the ALA focus on diversity: the Office for Diversity, the Office for Literacy and Outreach Services, the Ethnic and Multicultural Information Exchange Round Table (EMIERT, http://www.ala.org/ala/mgrps/rts/emiert/index.cfm), and the

Gay, Lesbian, Bisexual, and Transgendered Round Table all provide examples, guidelines, and strategic planning tools to implement measures to diversify services.

A subset of diversity is cultural diversity, or multiculturalism. Affiliate organizations include: American Indian Library Association, Asian Pacific American Librarians Association, Black Caucus of the American Library Association, Chinese American Librarians Association, and REFORMA, the National Association to Promote Library and Information Services to Latinos and the Spanish-Speaking. Each of these organizations provides resources that assist in broadening service implementation.

Examples of programs that provide cultural awareness to youth are author programs, music and drama groups, and workshops on creative writing. Such public library services can help youth gain understanding of their own cultural heritage and that of others. Services can involve providing in-depth collections, multilingual and ethnic resource centers, forums on cultural sensitivity, and library materials in several languages. These service responses can target children in Head Start projects, sponsor Holocaust memorials, or focus on cultures in the community using collections in many languages, programming, outreach, fairs, and performing arts and exhibits.

EMIERT focuses on materials that enhance cultural awareness. Its committees include the Coretta Scott King Book Awards Committee, the Jewish Information Committee, the Armenian Librarians and Libraries Information Committee, and the Multicultural Awards Committee. EMIERT has published *Venture into Cultures: A Resource Book of Multicultural Materials and Programs* (Kuharets, 2001), *Directory of Ethnic and Multicultural Publishers, Distributors and Resource Organizations* (Wertsman, 2003), and bibliographies such as "Contemporary Immigrant Experiences in Children's Books" (EMIERT, 2006), "Those Who Forget the Past," on the Armenian genocide of 1915 (EMIERT, 2005b), and "The Humor in Multicultural Literature" (EMIERT, 2005a). EMIERT also publishes the quarterly *EMIE Bulletin*.

Most of the affiliated ethnic associations compile materials and provide support for services for children and youth that develop an awareness of multiculturalism.

REFORMA promotes an annual national day of observance called El Día de los Niños/El Día de los Libros (Children's Day/Book Day, http://reforma.org/resources/ninos/dia.html). This festival "celebrates children, literacy, language, and books for children of all linguistic and cultural backgrounds."

The El Día de los Niños/El Día de los Libros website lists many ideas and activities from years of festivals all over the nation. Pat Mora, an outstanding children's writer, supports this celebration of children and books. As part of ALA President Camila Alire's Family Literacy Focus Initiative, the ALA and REFORMA launched a new program called Noche de Cuentos in 2010 in conjunction with World Storytelling Day, celebrated every year in March. A multicultural awareness through storytelling is the basis for this program. These types of initiatives provide an excellent space to embrace cultural awareness in youth services.

Multiculturalism implies representation of the majority culture as well as the others, for the benefit of all children. The way these cultures are represented in collections is also of importance. Aspects such as authenticity, balanced perspective, and absence of stereotypes in the representation of Asian Americans in literature, as presented by Yokota (2009) for example, constitute a challenge for the existence of diverse collections. The same applies to every culture or ethnic group.

Several strategies for including teens with special needs in youth library programs, including an analysis of challenges and concerns, are provided by Elsworth Rockefeller (2008). Ann Curry's (2005) research on reference services to gay and lesbian youth reveals that a welcoming and helpful reference librarian can have an impact on a youth who needs information on GLBT topics. Measures to ensure that the library is a safe place to get information about gay and lesbian topics extend from collection development to reference and outreach services (Farrelly, 2007a).

Discover Your Roots

This service response helps residents and visitors connect the past with the present through family and community histories (Nelson, 2008: 169). Libraries that offer services in local history and genealogy do so in response to those in the community, who want to know and understand personal or community heritage. The services may include instruction in research methods, archives, oral histories, and photographs. Although most of these services may be geared to the adult population, family tree assignments in elementary school and lessons about the community from preschool to college are opportunities for young patrons to learn about personal, family, or community history.

An example is the Kentucky Library and Museum in Bowling Green, which offers a vast assortment of Civil War relics and diaries, displays from the Victorian times, opportunities for family tree searches using a card catalog for the historical collection, the Robert Penn Warren collection, artifacts, and archives, all of which are open for touring by school and other groups. On the property sits a fully furnished cabin from the early 1900s, which is accessible during visits by schoolchildren; teachers can arrange to visit the cabin through the educational programs librarian.

The Nashville Public Library's Civil Rights Collection includes photographs, print materials, artifacts, and displays such as an actual counter to sit at and read, evoking the historic sit-ins during the civil rights movement in the city (http://www.library.nashville.org/). These and other libraries that include collections or displays related to their local history are excellent resources for youth services. Numerous online resources are available for children and youth who want to explore their family history. Keeping an updated reference resource with these websites is an invaluable tool for the children's services department. Some of these resources are suggested in Appendix A. These types of services and programs help children find genealogical roots and connect with their family and local histories.

Express Creativity: Create and Share Content

Support for community groups and individual artists and writers is described in this service response (Nelson, 2008: 173).

Traditionally, libraries have been at the end of the information chain, preserving and sharing resources already created by others. However, libraries have started developing a role in helping communities create their own resources (Brophy, 2007). This promotion of the value of creation is even more important in youth services.

Literature and the arts offer numerous opportunities to promote creativity in children and youth. Poetry is an area that helps children discover art put into words in a playful manner, and the benefits of poetry in developing literacy can never be overestimated (Vardell, 2006).

Music is another valuable resource to encourage creativity and develop young minds. Music programs for children can include visits by local musicians or activities in which children create their own instruments or songs. Brown (2009) suggested using the theory of multiple intelligences of Howard Gardner to provide programs that address different learning styles. Music makes a natural connection to children's literature and to the development of listening skills, abstract thinking, memory, and word plays.

Play is an important component of learning, especially for younger children. Psychologists and pedagogues have studied for many years the effects of play in the development of cognitive and linguistic abilities (Bane, 2008). However, the value of playing also resides in the enjoyment of the activity itself. And it is through playing that children create their world. Programs for children that encourage play and pretend activities provide a place for children to express creativity (Bane, 2008). An added value of these types of programs is their low cost. For pretend activities, librarians can use many recycled materials such as boxes, wrapping materials, cartons, and other things that encourage imagination and creativity (Bane, 2008).

Teens can also benefit from activities that develop their creativity, although programs for this age group will be different than those for school-age kids. Creative writing is being explored with teens in public libraries. Prichard's (2008) Write Here, Write Now program is a good example of creating a safe space for teens to explore their creative side in a nonjudgmental and unforced way. The use of technologies is particularly important in creativity-fostering activities. Teen programs can encourage creativity by providing the opportunity of producing finished products that can be shared: documentary shorts, podcasts, blogs, and video clips uploaded to sharing networks such as YouTube will be especially attractive for teens and provide a safe space at the same time (Farrelly, 2006b).

Satisfy Curiosity: Lifelong Learning

Resources needed by library patrons to explore topics of personal interest to support their learning throughout life are provided by this service response (Nelson, 2008: 195). The public library provides a number of services to assist youth in opportunities for self-directed personal growth and development, such as easy access to the circulating collection through the online catalog and programs destined to foster a desire for learning at any age.

A library responding to this need will provide such services for everyone, from Born to Read, or Mommy and Me, to bibliographic instruction, family literacy, homework assistance, tours for schools and homeschoolers, and GED services. The target population includes all ages. Intergenerational programs are an excellent way to spark curiosity and learning at different stages of life. Youth services can expand to provide programs that include children as well as adults and seniors. Rosemary Honnold (2004), who has authored several publications on programming for teens, listed many benefits for teens interacting with older generations, with building developmental assets as one of the principal results. When teens and young adults perform services or interact in different ways with seniors, they receive admiration and respect from adults other than their parents. In addition, intergenerational programs help break barriers and avoid stereotypes (Honnold, 2004). Many possibilities arise when programming for different ages, mixing teens with children, teens with parents, and teens with seniors, including Book Buddies, Reader's Theater, carnivals and festivals, college knowledge, international game nights, computer tutors, poetry or historical discussions, pen pals, mentorships, and many others (Honnold, 2004). One such program in Wheeling, Illinois, reported in a column by former ALA president Sarah Long (2005), matched seniors with fifth graders to be e-mail pen pals. The benefits for the children as well as the seniors were enormous, and the library was at the center of this connection.

Stimulate Imagination: Reading, Viewing, and Listening for Pleasure

Reading and services for the general reader—what most people think of as the central purpose of the public library—are addressed in *Strategic Planning for Results* under the service response of stimulating imagination (Nelson, 2008: 199).

Making collections available for children and young adults is one of the main focuses for collection development in public libraries. Anne Carol Moore, who was one of the first children's librarians in the early 1900s, noted that there were few books published specifically for children. She was challenged to search the adult shelves for materials that might be suitable for youth in order to stock shelves in children's rooms (Walter, 2001: 20). When publishers saw a potential market for juveniles, they began to publish special lines of children's books along with their trade books. Schools and public libraries were the main markets until cuts in library funding and the increase in the number of bookstores made the retail market more significant. Certainly, publishing for children has developed side by side with children's librarianship (Walter, 2010).

Twenty-first-century librarians know about the importance of stimulating the imagination of children and youth through reading, and the new technologies and developments of the century help to reinforce the need for reading in our youth (Walter, 2010). To successfully promote a culture of reading for pleasure, the library needs to provide access to a current collection and readers' advisory to meet individual needs for reader guidance. Readers' Advisory and Reference Services are the mainstays of library services to children and youth.

A broad collection includes best sellers, classic titles, and materials in multiple formats, supported by children's and young adult book talks, bibliographies by subject or author, displays, puppets, author signings, and previews for other media such as video and audio formats and computer resources and games. Collections for youth should reflect popular demand in terms of paperback and hardback books and magazines published specifically for children and young adults. Virtual access to the library's catalog and to other sources of recommendations has helped to expand the possibilities for reader's advisory for youth.

Awards for Books and Materials

A long-standing activity of youth librarians is the evaluation and selection of appropriate books and materials. ALSC and YALSA give a number of awards for outstanding materials each year and prepare lists of recommended titles in numerous formats, all of which would be outstanding additions to collections for children and youth. Beginning with the Newbery Award in 1922 and the Caldecott Award in 1938, children's librarians have a distinct visible record of highlighting excellent books and materials. *Children's Book Awards International, 1990 through 2000* (Smith, 2003) lists 141 children's book awards in the United States. The best-known awards include the following:

- The John Newbery Award, established in 1922, given annually to the author who has made the most distinguished contribution to American literature for children in the preceding year.
- The Randolph Caldecott Award, established in 1938, given to the artist of the most distinguished picture book for children.
- The Mildred Batchelder Award, established in 1968, given to an American publisher for "the most outstanding [children's] book originally published in a for-

eign language in a foreign country and subsequently published in English in the United States" (ALA, 2003: 78).

- The Laura Ingalls Wilder Award, established in 1954, given to an author or illustrator whose books have made a substantial and lasting contribution to literature for children for a period of years.
- The Coretta Scott King Award, established in 1969, given to African American authors and illustrators who have published distinguished books that promote an understanding and appreciation of the culture and contribution of all people for the American dream. This award was initially given under the auspices of ALA SRRT, now EMIERT (Smith, 1994, 1999, 2004, 2009).
- The Pura Belpré Award, established in 1996, given to a Latino/Latina writer and illustrator whose work best portrays, affirms, and celebrates the Latino cultural experience in an outstanding work of literature for children and youth. This award is given by ALSC and REFORMA.
- The Virginia Hamilton Literary Award, created in 1998 to give recognition to authors and illustrators whose work makes a lasting contribution to multicultural literature for children and young adults (ALA, 2010; http://dept.kent .edu/virginiahamiltonconf/litawd1.htm).

YALSA gives the following awards:

- Alex Award, which selects from the previous year's publications ten books written for adults that have special appeal for young adults.
- Margaret A. Edwards Award, established in 1988, given for an author's lifetime achievement for writing books that have been popular with teenagers, published in the United States within the past five years.
- Michael L. Printz Award, established in 2000, given for a book that exemplifies literary excellence in young adult literature published in the United States in the preceding year.
- William C. Morris Award, established in 2009, honors a book written for young adults by a first-time, previously unpublished author.
- Odyssey Award honors the producer of the best audiobook for children or young adults, available in English in the United States. Coadministered with ALSC.
- YALSA Award for Excellence in Nonfiction for Young Adults in 2010 to honor the best nonfiction book for young adults.

Promotion of books and reading takes many forms: summer reading programs, websites, book talks, story hours, puppet shows, author programs, displays, and celebrating Children's Book Week, Teen Read Week, International Children's Book Day, and El Día de los Niños/El Día de los Libros. Walter (2010: 30) reminds us that "the individual child is the primary user of children's services." In this light, the topics of diversity and multiculturalism addressed here have an influence in the space dedicated to multicultural literature. The importance of multicultural books and materials cannot be overestimated in the twenty-first-century society in which children are now growing up. Again, the ethnic professional organizations and the awards that they sponsor are great sources for recommendations and bibliographies for a multicultural selection.

As with the other youth services and programs, reading programs for teens may take on different characteristics than those for younger children. The undeniable success of phenomena like the Harry Potter series have had the consequence of making reading acceptable (and even popular) in the teenage culture. And the world did not end when the seventh and last of Harry's adventures was published (Farrelly, 2007b). However, there are many creative ways to keep teens reading "in the post–Harry Potter world" (Farrelly, 2007b: 48). The "Harry Potter effect" (Cart, 2007) made teens discover the fun in reading for pleasure. Although research on teen reading habits is not clear, libraries have been quick to come to the rescue of reading for fun and are implementing many creative programs directed toward maintaining young adults' interest in reading (Cart, 2007; Snowball, 2008). Besides the already mentioned Teen Read Week, other programs such as the Big Read are targeting youth in different communities (Cart, 2007). Graphic novels, *manga*, and anime are also part of a recent trend that is fueling teens' interest in reading, and libraries are implementing special collections or displays to cater to kids who enjoy them (Mori, 2007; Snowball, 2008).

Education

In the website for ALA's public campaign "@ Your Library there are many testimonies by users that show how libraries play an educational role in today's society. From the immigrant learning a language to the recently unemployed who needs to craft a new résumé or the student needing help to find reliable sources for study, the library has many ways to provide educational opportunity.

In their book *Public Libraries and Internet Service Roles*, McClure and Jaeger (2009: 50) identify the related Internet service role for the public library as "Youth Educational Support Provider," supporting youth in need of assistance in accessing electronic information for formal education and homeschooling educational needs.

In the area of youth services, the educational role of the public library is of vital importance. The service responses from *Strategic Planning for Results* (Nelson, 2008) included in this section are: "Create Young Readers: Early Literacy," "Learn to Read and Write: Adult, Teen, and Family Literacy," "Make Career Choices: Job and Career

Development," Succeed in School: Homework Help," and "Understand How to Find, Evaluate, and Use Information: Information Fluency."[3]

Create Young Readers: Early Literacy

Strategic Planning for Results addresses the service response to provide children from birth to age five with programs and services designed to ensure they will enter school ready to learn to read, write, and learn (Nelson, 2008: 165).

Library programs for infants and toddler, as well as their parents and caregivers are common practice in public libraries, as ways to familiarize them with the library's resources and contribute to early literacy (McKechnie, 2006). Numerous programs at the national level address the need for library-based early literacy initiatives: Family Place and Born to Read are two examples (Walter, 2010). These programs usually teach parents and caregivers the importance of reading to little ones and reinforce the enjoyment of this activity for both parents and children.

An important initiative that resulted from a partnership between the ALSC and the PLA (2010) is the campaign Every Child Ready to Read @ Your Library (ECRR). The program helps public libraries play a key role in their communities by disseminating early literacy information to parents, child care providers, early childhood educators, children's advocates, and political decision makers (ALSC and PLA, 2009, 2010). ECRR assists librarians in providing workshops that train caregivers in the essential skills that babies, toddlers, and preschoolers need to acquire at their young ages. Research supports the basic preliteracy skills that are developed with consistent reading programs like those that a library can implement, such as story hours and other activities (Walter, 2010).

Books for Babies is another literacy program that helps parents of newborns learn the importance of reading for their babies' development. In this program, libraries partner with Friends groups, women's clubs, or other organizations to distribute Books for Babies kits to parents of newborn babies in hospitals. *Babies in the Library*, by Jane Marino (2007), offers insightful advice to create programs for the newborn to two-year-old set. This useful volume provides practical approaches to working with the youngest patrons. In 2010 the Association of Library Trustees, Advocates, Friends and Foundations, in partnership with Nordstrom, awarded grants to libraries to purchase Books for Babies kits.

Learn to Read and Write: Adult, Teen, and Family Literacy

Adult, youth, and family literacy are addressed in *Strategic Planning for Results* (Nelson, 2008: 184). This service response supports adults and teens as they strive to meet their personal goals and fulfill their responsibilities as parents, citizens, and workers. In addition to early literacy, many of the skills needed to deal with information are necessary over the course of a person's lifetime. The public library, and especially its services to children and youth, needs to play an essential role in information literacy. The latest report by the National Endowment for the Arts, *To Read or Not to Read: A Question of National Consequence* (Iyengar and Ball, 2007) describes the current literacy situation with terms such as *alarming* and *disturbing*.

Some of the components of basic literacy services for youth involve family literacy, such as English as a second language programs, tutoring involving multiple generations, teaching parents to read to their kids, and developing language appreciation and skills through spoken and written language activities.

Literacy services include high/low literacy collections; active outreach programs for preschoolers; tutoring students in reading; teen services that focus on study skills, life skills, and positive values; GED preparation programs; family literacy programs that address the needs of parents and caregivers; and English as a second language classes, tutoring, and computer skills instruction. Many libraries are encountering growing literacy and multicultural needs among children, including specific needs for immigrant children and their families (Thiang, 2008). Programs such as bilingual book clubs and bilingual storytime provide a solution to two main problems: illiteracy and parental involvement (Saldana, 2009). Multicultural initiatives such as the already mentioned Noche de Cuentos also provide opportunities to reach out to the whole family, demonstrating the library's role in developing family literacy.

We cannot discuss information literacy services without mentioning the multitude of links on professional organizations' websites, where users can find various links to basic literacy services, information literacy services, and learning support for children and teens.

Make Career Choices: Job and Career Development

Skills and resources to help adults and young adults identify career opportunities that suit their individual strengths and interests are supported by this service response in *Strategic Planning for Results* (Nelson, 2008: 188). Libraries play an important role in business and career services to the public. During difficult economic times, public libraries have found themselves playing a key role in reactivating the economy and job search in their communities.

In the children's services department, providing information and training for young job seekers and future professionals constitutes an important contribution to teens and families. Public libraries can complement high school services in this area, but also can reach other citizens that are not included in formal educational career services.

Services to teens and young adults consist of information about career options, institutions, and plans of study; referrals to counseling and sources of vocational advice; and partnership with social agencies and organizations. The library can also serve as a liaison with outside sources (Fourie, 2009). Special programs that showcase different careers and presentations by professionals and workers in the community are another possibility.

Teens can also benefit from job-specific training programs. A technical training summer program for teens conducted in the Brooklyn Public Library (Today Teens, Tomorrow Techies—T4) served several purposes such as providing technology training, job experience, and services to the community (Cheney, 2006). Other programs help teens enter the world of work by giving them instruction on résumé creation or job interviews, by partnering with outside organizations (Williams, 2004).

Succeed in School: Homework Help

Services to help students succeed in school are addressed in *Strategic Planning for Results* (Nelson, 2008: 203). Learning support helps students enrolled in a formal program of education or who are pursuing their education through homeschooling. Examples of this service include parent education, emergent literacy, school visits and class visits to the library, retaining reading skill levels through summer reading, computer access and instruction in webpage design, easily accessible webpages devoted to sources for children and young adults, GED instruction, and bibliographic instruction.

Youth services librarians view themselves as educators. Danley (2003: 98) describes the role of the children's librarian as being first and foremost an educator, who "guides the children to become independent information gatherers." She refers to the use of constructivist psychological principles by successful children's librarians, who know how to relate to and guide young patrons in meeting their information needs. Using principles of child development and cognition in dynamic ways, librarians can help children become self-directed learners for meeting educational and information needs. Assistance to young students with homework and school projects is one of the most relevant functions of public libraries in support of formal education. Although traditionally the public library has been a destination for after-school hours, this was usually a passive role. More recently, libraries have been actively seeking strategies to assist students (Rua, 2008). Educational programming for after-school hours includes help with homework and tutoring, in addition to enrichment programs such as science clubs, arts and crafts programs, chess clubs, and many other possibilities (Rua, 2008).

Besides the implementation of special programs, public libraries can increase their success in this role by establishing a pattern of collaboration with the area's teachers and school librarians. Although there is some reluctance to form such alliances, the benefits and results experienced by those who have implemented collaboration suggest that it is important to make the effort to pursue these strategies (Katz, 2009). In most communities, families with low income or a minority origin need some sort of support for helping their children with homework and recur to the public library to satisfy this need (Walter, 2010).

Summer provides another important opportunity for the public library to support formal education. Evidence of a loss in achievement and reading levels in children during the summer has prompted educators to provide them with reading lists and projects to turn in when school resumes (Lu, 2009). In an evaluation of a collaborative project between a library and a high school for summer reading, Lu (2009) concluded that students' active participation produced more meaningful learning and better results.

Another important area where the public library can support education is in homeschooling. More than a million children between the ages of 5 and 17 in the United States are homeschooled (Hilyard, 2008). In addition to providing resources and services that homeschooled children and their parents can access in the library, there is much more that libraries can do for these patrons: morning and early afternoon storytime, reading clubs, specific compilations of resources, and special events such as homeschool fairs where organizations can offer their services to homeschooling families are some examples (Hilyard, 2008).

Understand How to Find, Evaluate, and Use Information: Information Fluency

Residents will know when they need information to resolve an issue and have the skills to search for, locate, evaluate, and effectively use information to meet their needs (Nelson, 2008: 207). Information literacy and fluency services address the need to help patrons develop skills for finding, evaluating, and using information effectively.

School librarians are responsible for teaching these skills to children in formal educational settings. The AASL emphasizes information literacy as one of the most important skills, especially for school-age students. In *Information Power: Building Partnerships for Learning* (AASL and Association for Educational Communications and Technology, 1998) and *Standards for the Twenty-first Century Learner* (AASL, 2009), the association compiled the benchmarks and competencies that students need to develop to be effective users of information. However, some may question the role of public libraries in this area: is the job of public librarians to teach these skills? As Walter (2010) pointed out, the context of the public library provides a privileged position to use these skills in an actual case of information seeking. A simple reference question that starts at the public library's reference desk can be a wonderful window of opportunity to teach and apply information literacy skills to an actual problem-solving situation (Walter, 2010). Printed and electronic pathfinders are often used to assist youth with academic projects, such as research papers, as well as real life problem solving. The possibilities that open up thanks to new technologies and digital resources for compiling information complement this traditional function as well.

Gilton (2008) also suggested that public libraries do have a role in teaching information literacy, but in their own terms. Collaboration with schools and help with homework and homeschooling are educational roles of the library that supplement formal schooling, but deliberate programs that teach information skills can be part of children's services programming as well. The difference is that public librarians need to make sure that their programs supplement and support what school media specialists already do (Gilton, 2008). Public libraries can also provide instruction by incorporating it into their written materials and their websites, instructional pages, and displays (Gilton, 2008; Walter, 2010).

Information

Public libraries have played an important role in providing youth with general information, government information, and business, consumer, and career services. Information should be provided and organized to meet the needs of children and youth. Five public library responses from *Strategic Planning for Results* (Nelson, 2008) are organized around the broad category of information: "Build Successful Enterprises: Business and Nonprofit Support," "Connect to the Online World: Public Internet Access," "Get Facts Fast: Ready Reference," "Make Informed Decisions: Health, Wealth and Other Career Development," and "Welcome to the United States: Services for New Immigrants."

Build Successful Enterprises: Business and Nonprofit Support

Business owners and nonprofit organizations are provided the resources they need to develop and maintain strong, viable organizations through this service response (Nelson, 2008: 153).

The importance of the public library's role in community development through its support of businesses and organizations has been discussed in Chapter 8 for Adult Services. Children and youth can benefit from the library's partnerships and solutions for organizations that address their needs.

Teens can participate in library programs involving these partnerships as a way to learn about how these organizations work. Examples of such programs can be health fairs, community preparedness events, job fairs, and other informational events in which teens can volunteer and interact with the community's businesses and nonprofits.

Children and youth learn about business in their educational and recreational endeavors. As explained in the previous section, career guidance for youth can be especially important to groups such as teen parents or those leaving high school before graduation who need to work. Materials for résumé writing can be provided and extensive job listings are available in books, newspapers, and online resources.

Connect to the Online World: Public Internet Access

Provision of high-speed access to the digital world to ensure that everyone can take advantage of the ever-growing resources available on the Internet is addressed in this service response (Nelson, 2008: 162).

In the digital world of the twenty-first century, the Internet has undeniably made access to lots of information possible for everyone . . . or not. In reality, public librarians know that not everyone has access to the Internet or the digital world on a daily basis or in the comfort of their own home. By providing this service to everyone who walks through the library's door, public libraries contribute to bridge the digital gap.

Terminals with broadband connection are becoming a common sight in every public library. In the case of youth services, this trend has been the source of controversy and debate. Unrestricted access to the web for minors is a topic of discussion, as is the need for filters and the repercussions in the field of freedom of information. Controversy over access to social networking sites such as Myspace or Facebook has sprung up in many libraries around the nation. However, as Aiken (2006: 33) has argued, "we need to step back and examine the facts before deciding to censor materials our patrons wish to access." Many libraries provide an invaluable service to teenagers who, for economic or social reasons, do not have access to the digital world at home. Regardless of their economic circumstances, by using the libraries' resources those teens have access to the same information as their more affluent peers (Aiken, 2006).

In their book *Public Libraries and Internet Service Roles*, McClure and Jaeger (2009) identify the related Internet service role for the public library as the "Place for Public Access to the Internet." They note that for a majority of communities, the public library is the only place where free access to the Internet is available. This service response requires staff who are trained in assisting users to locate the services and resources available and requires that the library have a high-quality technology infrastructure, including adequate workstations, bandwidth, and up-to-date equipment and software (McClure and Jaeger, 2009: 50).

Get Facts Fast: Ready Reference

In *Strategic Planning for Results*, this service response is to the point: residents will have someone to answer their questions on a wide array of topics of personal interest (Nelson, 2008: 177).

Youth need information on a broad array of topics related to work, school, and personal life. Library services for youth include teaching or helping children to answer their many questions.

Many of the services already discussed encompass reference and information services for children and youth and for their teachers and caregivers.

Instruction in use of digital resources, electronic databases, and print library resources is discussed under some of the services listed above. Training for staff and volunteers who work with children is necessary for assisting with information-seeking behavior of different age groups.

Children and youth also benefit from ready reference that is accessible by electronic or virtual channels. Texting the librarian with questions, ask-a-librarian services by electronic mail, or library pages in social networks such as Facebook provide opportunities to bring the reference service into their everyday lives. A new trend in digital technologies has been the use of programs such as Twitter to deliver short pieces of information to selected followers fast. Tweeting libraries had an instant appeal for teens, and this tool has been useful in attracting them to other programs and services (Farrelly, 2009; King and Brown, 2009). A library can use Twitter to send random facts to followers as a way to keep them informed and also to keep the library in their minds as a source of information (Farrelly, 2009).

Libraries who develop a presence in virtual worlds such as Second Life will find it useful to establish reference services in their virtual libraries, as a way to build a community to guide youth in the virtual world of information (Czarnecki, 2008). Second Life Library 2.0, a program developed by the Alliance Library System and Online Programming for All Libraries in 2006, promotes the use of a library to residents of Second Life and explores the provision of reference services from strategically located desks or kiosks, and also by having their avatars wear T-shirts that read "Librarian," which attracts the attention of other residents they meet (Hedreen at al., 2008). As explained in the section about virtual space, the teen grid in Second Life is a teen-safe environment (adults that access the island need to pass a background check) where some libraries (like Charlotte Mecklenburg County Public Library) are creating a presence that provides ready reference for teens using Second Life (Czarnecki, 2008).

Make Informed Decisions: Health, Wealth, and Other Career Development

Providing residents with the resources they need to identify and analyze risks, benefits, and alternatives before making decisions that affect their lives is a key information service response (Nelson, 2008: 191).

Services for children and youth also include the family as a consumer of children's services. In this role, the library can offer parents and youth the information needed to make informed decisions regarding health issues, as well as consumer reviews and alerts. Many public libraries have displays with recalls and product alerts. This service can be expanded by offering links to online resources on the library's webpage.

Partnerships with community organizations are a good option to provide information on health services. In 2008 the Laredo Public Library partnered with the University of Texas Health Science Center at San Antonio to develop an outreach program on health information for children. With a grant from the National Network of Libraries of

Medicine and partnerships with other local organizations, the library implemented a summer-long series of activities and a health fair that reached out to Laredo and Webb County residents, most of whom experience a disparity of access to health services (Ren, Cogdill, and Potemkin, 2009). Youth librarians can also have an impact by participating in services that the library offers to the whole population by customizing part of the event for children and youth.

Welcome to the United States: Services for New Immigrants

New immigrants will have information on citizenship, English language learning, employment, public schooling, health and safety, and available social services in this service response (Nelson, 2008: 214).

Today's immigrants to the United States are facing many of the same problems that immigrants faced historically: having to reach a balance between adherence to the civic responsibilities of their new country and still preserving their identities and original culture (Lukenbill, 2006). The role of the public library in this context is invaluable, and children and youth who are immigrants or whose families are immigrants can become active participants in their adopted communities with the help of the public library.

In addition to having a collection that responds to immigrants' needs, with materials about immigration laws and the citizenship process, libraries with significant numbers of immigrants in their population can implement special programs and events to reach out to these newcomers. An important factor to consider when planning services for this sector of the population is that (for a variety of reasons) libraries can encounter a lack of response from new immigrants. The difficulty of bringing them to the library can be overcome with careful planning and ideas. One such program developed in Baltimore's Enoch Pratt Free Library provided library services to Spanish-speaking families and child care providers with young children in the Baltimore area. Buena Casa, Buena Brasa (a rhyme that means "warm home, warm hearth") consisted of a program featuring rhymes and songs in Spanish and a few in English for children from birth to age three and their caregivers (Diamant-Cohen and Calderon, 2009).

Immigrants also can experience hardship adapting to their new country, which can be especially damaging for children and teens. After the events of September 11, 2001, many immigrants from Arabic countries had to deal with exclusion and discrimination (Fredericks, 2005). The library can offer a safe refuge for teenagers who feel threatened and programs especially designed for them, and at the same time provide activities that teach tolerance for all children and youth (Fredericks, 2005).

Looking at the Future of Youth Services

Youth services librarianship faces multiple challenges in the twenty-first century, including mobile applications, intellectual property issues, keeping up with a networked world, and the library's need to be available as a 24/7 learning resource, as well as the general economic downturn that began in 2008 and continues to impact budgets and staffing (Valenza and Johnson, 2009).

In an important essay, "Children and Information Technology," Andrew Large (2009: 198) stated:

> Information technology is but a tool whose ultimate value depends upon the user and the use. . . . The role of information professionals, educators, policy makers and parents, in collaboration with children themselves, is to facilitate the exploitation of IT so as to maximize its potential to enrich the lives of young people while minimizing any harmful effects for this population that seems vulnerable to IT misuse.

Recognition of the complex IT environment is essential for the development of youth services in public libraries.

Youth services librarians will continue to be called upon to work creatively with public library service responses. This includes sharing love of literature, delight in programs, and mastery of technology in the years ahead. *The Dominican Study: Public Library Summer Reading Programs Close the Reading Gap*, found that students who participated in public library summer reading programs scored higher on reading achievement tests at the beginning of the next school year than those who did not (Roman and Fiore, 2010). Public libraries persist as community anchors for youth development, education, recreation, and opportunity—changing and adapting to new technologies.

Notes

1. Public sphere service responses as defined by McCook based on Nelson (2008): "Be an Informed Citizen: Local, National and World Affairs" (149–152); "Know Your Community: Community Resources and Services" (180–183); and "Visit a Comfortable Place: Physical and Virtual Spaces" (210–213).

2. Cultural heritage service responses as defined by McCook based on Nelson (2008): "Celebrate Diversity: Cultural Awareness" (158–161); "Discover Your Roots: Genealogy and Local History" (169–172); "Express Creativity: Create and Share Content" (173–176); "Satisfy Curiosity: Lifelong Learning" (195–198); and "Stimulate Imagination: Reading, Viewing and Listening for Pleasure" (199–202).

3. Education service responses as defined by McCook based on Nelson (2008): "Create Young Readers: Early Literacy" (165–168); "Learn to Read and Write: Adults, Teens and Family Literacy" (184–187); "Make Career Choices: Job and Career Development" (188–190); "Succeed in School: Homework Help" (. 203–206); and "Understand How to Find, Evaluate, and Use Information: Information Fluency" (207–209).

4. Information service responses as defined by McCook based on Nelson (2008): "Build Successful Enterprises: Business and Nonprofit Support" (153–157); "Connect to the Online World: Public Internet Access" (162–164); "Get Facts Fast: Ready Reference" (177–179); "Make Informed Decisions: Health, Wealth and Other Life Choices" (191–194); and "Welcome to the United States: Service to New Immigrants" (214–217).

References

Aiken, Julian. 2006. "Hands Off Myspace." *American Libraries* 37 (August): 33.

American Association of School Librarians. 2007. *Standards for the 21st Century Learner*. Chicago: American Association of School Librarians.

———. 2009. *Standards for the Twenty-first Century Learner in Action*. Chicago: American Association of School Librarians.

American Association of School Librarians and Association for Educational Communications and Technology. 1998. *Information Power: Building Partnerships for Learning*. Chicago: American Library Association.

American Library Association. 1984. *Realities, Educational Reform in a Learning Society*. Chicago: American Library Association.

———. 2003. *ALA Handbook of Organization: 2003–2004*. Chicago: American Library Association.

———. 2010. "Coretta Scott King/Virginia Hamilton Award for Lifetime Achievement." http://www.ala.org/template.cfm?template=/CFApps/awards_info/award_detail_home .cfm&FilePublishTitle=Awards,%20Grants%20and%20Scholarships&uid=82625279E E3B6200.

Association for Library Service to Children. 2000. *Intellectual Freedom for Children: The Censor Is Coming*. Chicago: American Library Association.

———. 2009. *Competencies for Librarians Serving Children in Public Libraries*. http:// www.ala.org/ala/mgrps/divs/alsc/edcareeers/alsccorecomps/corecomps.cfm.

Association for Library Service to Children, Intellectual Freedom Committee. 2007. *Kids, Know Your Rights! A Young Person's Guide to Intellectual Freedom*. http://www.ala.org/ ala/mgrps/divs/alsc/issuesadv/intellectualfreedom/kidsknowyourrights.pdf.

Association for Library Service to Children and Public Library Association. 2009. "Every Child Ready to Read Evaluation Task Force: Evaluation Summary and Recommended Next Steps." American Library Association. http://www.ala.org/ala/mgrps/divs/alsc/ecrr/ecrr eval.cfm.

———. 2010. *Every Child Ready to Read at Your Library Web Site*. http://www.ala.org/ ala/mgrps/divs/alsc/ecrr/index.cfm.

Bane, Rebecca. 2008. "Let's Pretend: Exploring the Value of Play at the Library." *Children and Libraries* 6 (Summer/Fall): 21–23.

Bernier, Anthony. 2009. "A Space for Myself to Go: Early Patterns in Small YA Spaces." *Public Libraries* 48 (September/October): 33–47.

Bolan, Kimberly. 2006. "Looks Like Teen Spirit." *School Library Journal* 52 (November): 44–48.

Braun, Linda W. 2009. "Using Technology to Market Teen Library Programs and Services." *Voice of Youth Advocates* 31 (February): 510–511.

———. 2010. *Children and the Internet: Policies That Work.* Chicago: PLA/ALSC. http://www.ala.org/ala/mgrps/divs/alsc/issuesadv/internettech/childrentheinternetpoliciesthatwork/index.cfm.

Bremmer, Robert. 1967. *Traps for the Young.* Cambridge, MA: Harvard University Press.

Brophy, Peter. 2007. *The Library in the Twenty-first Century.* London: Facet.

Brown, Amy. 2009. "Don't Stop the Music! Creating Tuneful Times at Your Library." *Children and Libraries* 7 (Summer/Fall): 36–42.

Brown, Carol R. 2002. *Interior Design for Libraries: Drawing on Function and Appeal.* Chicago: American Library Association.

Cart, Michael. 2007. "Teens and the Future of Reading." *American Libraries* 38 (October): 53–54.

Cheney, Amy. 2006. "Today's Techie, Training Teens." *Library Journal* 131, no. 5: 18.

Cranz, Galen, and Eunah Cha. 2006. "Body-Conscious Design in a Teen Space." *Public Libraries* 45 (November/December): 48–56.

Cresswell, Stephen. 1996. "The Last Days of Jim Crow in Southern Libraries." *Libraries and Culture* 31 (Summer/Fall): 557–573.

Curry, Ann. 2005. "If I Ask, Will They Answer? Evaluating Public Library Reference Service to Gay and Lesbian Youth." *Reference User Services Quarterly* 45, no. 1: 65–75.

Czarnecki, Kelly. 2008. "Building Community as a Library in a 3D Environment." *Australas Public Libraries Information Services* 21 (March): 25–27.

Danley, Elizabeth. 2003. "The Public Children's Librarian as Educator." *Public Libraries* 42 (March/April): 98–101.

Diamant-Cohen, Betsy, and Anne Calderon. 2009. "Buena Casa Buena Brasa." *American Libraries* 40 (December): 41–43.

Edwards, Margaret A. 1969. *The Fair Garden and the Swarm of Beasts: The Library and the Young Adult.* Chicago: American Library Association.

Ethnic and Multicultural Information Exchange Round Table. 2005a. "The Humor in Multicultural Literature." http://www.ala.org/ala/mgrps/rts/emiert/usefullinks/humorlit.pdf.

———. 2005b. "Those Who Forget the Past." http://www.ala.org/ala/mgrps/rts/emiert/usefullinks/armeniagen.pdf.

———. 2006. "Contemporary Immigrant Experiences in Children's Books." http://www.ala.org/ala/mgrps/rts/emiert/usefullinks/contempimmigrant.pdf.

Farrelly, Michael Garrett. 2006a. "Does Your Space Appeal to Teens?" *Public Libraries* 45 (May/June): 40–41.

―――. 2006b. "The Possibilities of YouTube." *Public Libraries* 45 (September/October): 34–35.

―――. 2007a. "More on Serving Gay Youth." *Public Libraries* 46 (May/June): 38–39.

―――. 2007b. "YA Services in a Post-Harry Potter World." *Public Libraries* 46 (September/October): 48–49.

―――. 2008. "Guitar Hero and Rock Band: Games That Are Fun and Educational." *Public Libraries* 47 (March/April): 40–41.

―――. 2009. "Tweet, Tweet." *Public Libraries* 48 (January/February): 35–36.

Fenwick, Sara Innis. 1976. "Library Services to Children and Young People." *Library Trends* 25 (Summer): 329–360.

Fletcher, William I. 1876. "Public Libraries and the Young." In *Public Libraries in the United States: Their History, Condition and Management*, 412–418. Washington, DC: Department of the Interior, Bureau of Education.

Flowers, Sarah. 2010. *Young Adults Deserve the Best: YALSA's Competencies in Action*. Chicago, IL: ALA Editions. http://www.ala.org/ala/mgrps/divs/yalsa/profdev/yacompetencies 2010.cfm.

Fourie, J. A. 2009. "A Theoretical Model for the Provision of Educational and Career Guidance and Information Services for High School Learners in Public Libraries." *Mousaion* 27, no 1: 1–23.

Fredericks, Nancy. 2005. "Another Day in the Life." *Young Adult Library Services* 3 (Spring): 15–16.

Gilton, Donna L. 2008. "Information Literacy as a Department Store." *Young Adult Library Services* 6 (Winter): 39–44.

Gleason, Eliza Atkins. 1941. *The Southern Negro and the Public Library: A Study of Government and Administration of Public Library Service to Negroes in the South*. Chicago: University of Chicago Press.

Hedreen, Rebecca C., Jennifer L. Johnson, Mack A. Lundy, Peg Burnette, Carol Perryman, Guus Van Den Brekel, J. J. Jacobson, Matt Gullett, and Kelly Czarnecki. 2008. "Exploring Virtual Librarianship: Second Life Library 2.0." *Internet Reference Services Quarterly* 13, nos. 2–3: 167–195.

Herald, Diana Tixier, and Diane P. Monnier. 2007. "The Beasts Have Arrived." *Voice of Youth Advocates* 30 (June): 116–119.

Hilyard, Nann B. 2008. "Welcoming Homeschoolers to the Library." *Public Libraries* 47 (May/June): 17–18.

Holt, Glen E. 2008. "ImanginOn, the First Twenty-first Century Public Library Building in the U.S." *Public Library Quarterly* 27, no. 2: 174–191.

Honnold, Rosemary. 2004. "Connecting Teens with Generations A-Z." *Public Libraries* 43 (September/October): 281–284.

Immroth, Barbara Froling, and Viki Ash-Geisler. 1995. *Achieving School Readiness: Public Libraries and National Education Goal No. 1 with a Prototype of Public Library Services for Young Children and Their Families*. Chicago: American Library Association.

Iyengar, Sunil, and Don Ball. 2007. *To Read or Not to Read: A Question of National Consequence*. Washington, DC: National Endowment for the Arts. http://purl.access.gpo.gov/GPO/LPS92960.

Jaeger, Paul T., and John Carlo Bertot. 2009. "E-government Education in Public Libraries: New Service Roles and Expanding Social Responsibilities." *Journal of Education for Library and Information Science* 50 (Winter): 39–49.

Jaeger, Paul T., and Yan Zheng. 2009. "One Law with Two Outcomes: Comparing the Implementation of CIPA in Public Libraries and Schools." *Information Technology and Libraries* 28 (March): 6–14.

Jenkins, Christine A. 2000. "The History of Youth Services Librarianship: A Review of the Research Literature." *Libraries and Culture* 35 (Winter): 103–139.

Jensen, Richard. 2000. *Clark and Menefee*. New York: Princeton Architectural Press.

Jones, Plummer Alston. 2004. *Still Struggling for Equality: American Public Library Services with Minorities*. Westport, CT: Libraries Unlimited.

Katz, Jeff. 2009. "A Common Purpose: Public/School Library Cooperation and Collaboration." *Public Libraries* 48 (May/June): 28–31.

Kenney, Brian. 2006. "Welcome to the Fun House." *Library Journal* (Spring): 8–13.

Kimball, Melanie A., Christine A. Jenkins, and Betsy Hearne. 2004. "Effie Louise Power: Librarian, Educator, Author." *Library Trends* 52 (Spring): 924–951.

King, David L., and Stephanie W. Brown. 2009. "Emerging Trends, 2.0, and Libraries." *Serials Librarian* 56, no. 1: 32–43.

Kuharets, Olga R., ed. 2001. *Venture into Cultures: A Resource Book of Multicultural Materials and Programs*. 2nd ed. Chicago: American Library Association.

Large, Andrew. 2009. "Children and Information Technology." In *Information Technology in Librarianship: New Critical Approaches*, edited by Gloria J. Leckie and John Buschman, 181–203. Westport, CT: Libraries Unlimited.

Long, Sarah. 2005. "Program Puts Kids, Mentors on Same Page." *Library Mosaics* 16 (July/August): 18.

Lu, Ya-Ling. 2009. "Engaging Students with Summer Reading: An Assessment of a Collaborative High School Summer Reading Program." *Journal of Education for Library and Information Science* 50 (Spring): 90–106.

Lukenbill, W. Bernard. 2006. "Helping Youth at Risk: An Overview of Reformist Movements in American Public Libraries to Youth." *New Review of Children's Literature and Librarianship* 12, no. 2: 197–213.

Lundin, Anne. 1996. "The Pedagogical Context of Women in Children's Services and Literature Scholarship." *Library Trends* 44 (Winter): 840–850.

Marino, Jane. 2007. *Babies in the Library*. Lanham, MD: Scarecrow Press.

McClure, Charles R., and Paul T. Jaeger. 2009. *Public Libraries and Internet Service Roles: Measuring and Maximizing Internet Services*. Chicago: American Library Association.

McCook, Kathleen de la Peña. 2001. "Authentic Discourse as a Means of Connection between Public Library Service Responses and Community-Building Initiatives." *Reference and User Services Quarterly* 41 (Winter): 127–133.

McDowell, Kathleen. 2007. *The Cultural Origins of Youth Services Librarianship, 1876–1900.* PhD thesis. Urbana, IL: University of Illinois at Urbana-Champaign,

McKechnie, Lynne. 2006. "Observations of Babies and Toddlers in Library Settings." *Library Trends* 55 (Summer): 190–201.

Meyers, Elaine. 2001. "The Road to Coolness: Youth Rock the Public Library." *American Libraries* 32 (February): 46–48.

Mori, Maryann. 2007. "Graphic Novels: Leading the Way to Teen Literacy and Leadership." *Indiana Libraries* 26, no. 3: 29–32.

Moore, Anne Carroll. 1898. "Special Training for Children's Librarians." *Library Journal* 12 (August): 81.

Mussman, Klaus. 1998. "The Ugly Side of Librarianship: Segregation in Library Services from 1900–1950." In *Untold Stories: Civil Rights, Libraries and Black Librarianship*, 78–92. Champaign: University of Illinois, Graduate School of Library and Information Science.

National Education Association. 1899. *Report of the Committee on the Relations of Public Libraries to Public Schools*. Washington, DC: National Education Association.

National Reading Panel. 2000. *Report of the National Reading Panel: Teaching Children to Read: An Evidence-Based Assessment of the Scientific Research Literature on Reading and Its Implications for Reading Instruction*. Washington, DC: National Institute of Child Health and Human Development, National Institutes of Health.

Nelson, Sandra. 2008. *Strategic Planning for Results*. Chicago: American Library Association.

Nilsen, Alleen, and Kenneth L. Donelson. 2001. *Literature for Today's Young Adults*. 6th ed. New York: Longman.

Palfrey, John, and Urs Gasser. 2008. *Born Digital: Understanding the First Generation of Digital Natives*. New York: Basic Books.

Petrilli, Ken. 2009. "Banned Books Week: Celebrating Your (and Your Teens!) Freedom to Read." *Young Adult Library Services* 7 (Summer) 4–5.

Power, Effie. 1930. *Library Service for Children: Library Curriculum Studies*. Chicago: American Library Association.

Prichard, Heather. 2008. "Write Here, Write Now." *Young Adult Library Services* 6 (Summer): 19–23.

Ren, Rena, Keith Cogdill, and Alex Potemkin. 2009. "Partnerships for a Healthy Community." *Public Libraries* 48 (January/February): 59–61.

Rockefeller, Elsworth. 2008. "Striving to Serve Diverse Youth." *Public Libraries* 47 (January/February): 50–55.

Rollock, Barbara T. 1988. *Public Library Services for Children*. Hamden, CT: Shoe String Press.

Roman, Susan, Deborah T. Carran, and Carole D. Fiore. 2010. "Public Library Summer Reading Programs Close the Reading Gap." *Illinois Library Association Reporter* 28 (August): 20–22.

Rua, Robert J. 2008. "After-School Success Stories." *American Libraries* 39 (November): 46–48.

Saldana, Rene. 2009. "The Bilingual Book Club: A Family Affair." *Teacher Librarian* 36 (Fall): 27–32.

Scales, Pat. 2009. *Protecting Intellectual Freedom in Your School Library: Scenarios from the Front Lines*. Chicago: American Library Association.

Scordato, Julie. 2008. "Gaming as a Library Service." *Public Libraries* 47 (January/February): 67–73.

Smith, Henrietta M. 1994. *The Coretta Scott King Awards Book: From Visions to Reality*. Chicago: American Library Association.

———. 1999. *The Coretta Scott King Awards Book, 1970–1999*. Chicago: American Library Association.

———. 2004. *The Coretta Scott King Awards Book, 1970–2004*. Chicago: American Library Association.

Smith, Henrietta M. 2009. *The Coretta Scott King Awards, 1970-2009*. Chicago: ALA Editions.

Smith, Laura. 2003. *Children's Book Awards International, 1990 through 2000*. Jefferson, NC: McFarland.

Snowball, Clare. 2008. "Teenagers Talking about Reading and Libraries." *Australian Academic and Research Libraries* 39, no. 2: 106–118.

Suellentrop, Tricia. 2008. "It's Not about You." *School Library Journal* 54 (April): 27.

Thiang, Alicia. 2008. "Alter Ego: An Interactive Public Library Literacy Program for Disadvantaged Children." *Australasian Public Libraries Information Services* 21, no. 3: 106–108.

Thomas, Fannette H. 1982. "The Genesis of Children's Library Services in the American Public Library, 1876–1906." PhD diss., University of Wisconsin– Madison.

———. 1993. "The Black Mother Goose: Collective Biography of African-American Children's Librarians." In *Culture Keepers: Enlightening and Empowering Our Communities: Proceedings of the First National Conference of African American Librarians*, edited by Stanton F. Biddle, 196–200. Newark, NJ: Black Caucus of the American Library Association.

U.S. Institute of Museum and Library Services. 2010. *Public Libraries Survey: Fiscal Year 2008* (IMLS-2010–PLS-02). Washington, DC: Institute of Museum and Library Services.

U.S. National Center for Education Statistics. 1988. *Services and Resources for Young Adults in Public Libraries*. Washington, DC: U.S. Government Printing Office.

Valenza, Joyce Kasman, and Doug Johnson. 2009. "Things That Keep Us Up at Night." *School Library Journal* 55: 29–32.

Vardell, Sylvia M. 2006. "A Place for Poetry: Celebrating the Library in Poetry." *Children and Libraries* 4 (Summer/Fall): 35–41.

Walter, Fran K. 1941. "A Poor but Respectable Relation—the Sunday School Library." *Library Quarterly* 12 (July): 734.

Walter, Virginia A. 1992. *Output Measures for Public Library Service to Children: A Manual of Standardized Measures*. Chicago: American Library Association.

———. 1995. *Output Measures and More: Planning and Evaluating Public Library Services for Young Adults*. Chicago: American Library Association.

———. 2001. *Children and Libraries: Getting It Right*. Chicago: American Library Association.

———. 2009. "The Children We Serve: Five Notions of Childhood Suggest Ways to Think about the Services We Provide." *American Libraries* 40 (October): 52–55.

———. 2010. *Twenty-First Century Kids, Twenty-First Century Librarians*. Chicago: American Library Association.

Walter, Virginia A., and Elaine Meyers. 2003. *Teens and Libraries: Getting It Right*. Chicago: American Library Association.

Wertsman, Vladimir F. 2003. *Directory of Ethnic and Multicultural Publishers, Distributors and Resource Organizations*. 5th ed. Niles, IL: Ethnic and Multicultural Information Exchange Round Table.

Williams, Cynthia. 2004. "Helping Teens Enter the World of Work." *Voice Youth Advocates* 27 (4): 281.

Woelfer, Jill Palzkill, and David G. Hendry. 2009. "Stabilizing Homeless Young People with Information and Place." *Journal of the American Society for Information Science and Technology* 60 (November): 2300–2312.

Woolls, Blanche. 2001. "Public Libraries–School Library Cooperation: A View from the Past with a Predictor for the Future." *Journal of Youth Services in Libraries* 14 (Spring): 8–10.

Yokota, Junko. 2009. "Asian-Americans in Literature for Children and Young Adults." *Teacher Librarian* 36, no. 3: 15–19.

Young Adult Library Services Association. 2010. *YALSA's Competencies for Librarians Serving Youth: Young Adults Deserve the Best*. American Library Association. http://www.ala.org/ala/mgrps/divs/yalsa/profdev/yadeservethebest_201.pdf.

Ziegenbein, Sarah. 2008. "Government Documents and Children." *Arkansas Libraries* 65, no. 2: 6–8.

Zweizig, Douglas L., and Eleanor Jo Rodger. 1982. *Output Measures for Public Libraries*. Chicago: American Library Association.

10

The Interconnective Nature of the Public Library

"Libraries Build Community," means collaborating and forming partnerships and alliances. To be effective, we need to work with other libraries, groups, organizations and individuals who share our goals.

—Sarah Ann Long, ALA's millennial president, 1999–2000,
A Place at the Table: Participating in Community Building, Foreword

Connections

For over three centuries, public librarians have been leaders in collaborating beyond local boundaries to extend and expand library service. Initially these collaborations were through professional affiliations such as the American Library Association (ALA) or state associations that laid the groundwork for more formal cooperation. Today public libraries are connected through a variety of mechanisms including local cooperative agreements, state library agencies, library consortia, multistate regional networks, and national and international cooperatives such as the Online Computer Library Center (OCLC). These entities comprise a creative series of overlapping networks in which public libraries have functioned to expand and extend their services using cutting-edge technologies. Librarians have long worked at the state and national levels to develop policies on all aspects of service from interlibrary loan to cataloging standards. Through state library agencies, librarians have worked on statewide plans, professional development, collaborative grants, cooperative licensing, and massive digitization projects. These collaborations have continuously shifted, with different groups taking on different projects at different times in different places. Oftentimes the same leaders have shaped a plan at different levels. Interlocking collaborative work by thousands of librarians to extend library service is one of the greatest achievements of public librarianship in the United States.

In addition to understanding the local political processes that govern the daily operations of the public library, it is important that librarians recognize the relationships the public library has to larger systems that provide support and connections to additional resources. These various components in the overall network of librarians and libraries provide opportunities to carry on professional connections that enrich careers and strengthen ties to others. The spirit and energy of individual librarians has built the foundation of this network. We turn attention in this chapter to the growth of public library cooperative initiatives in the United States, noting four factors:

1. Professional associations
2. State library agencies
3. Library networks and systems
4. Groupware and collaborative systems

Professional Associations

American Library Association

Librarians were one of the first occupational groups in the United States to organize as a professional association. The ALA, established in 1876, provided an ongoing mechanism for discussing, planning, and developing cooperative initiatives. One of the first committees established by librarians in the United States was a committee on cooperation that sought to provide shared cataloging. The publication of the report *Public Libraries in the United States of America: Their History, Condition, and Management: Special Report* (U.S. Bureau of Education, 1876), which included histories and statistics of libraries, greatly enhanced the collaborative work of librarians. The special report provided a context of growth and development by which libraries could establish goals and future development. The establishment of *Library Journal*, which was the official publication of the ALA until 1908 when the *ALA Bulletin* began, also contributed to the capacity of librarians to work together and share ideas. Thus, in 1876 librarians realized two key elements—baseline data and a mechanism for ongoing communication—that paved the way for collaborative progress.

In the years since U.S. librarians formally organized themselves as the American Library Association, they have focused on the concerns of public libraries, broadly speaking. But under the umbrella of this larger association, special associations, divisions, sections, or committees have paid special attention to public libraries. The Division of Public Libraries was formed within ALA in 1944 and merged with the Library Extension Division in 1950 to become the Public Library Division. In 1958 this division was reorganized as the Public Library Association (PLA), which today is the national overarching professional association for public librarians, with membership of over 11,000 in 2010.

The core purpose of PLA is "to strengthen public libraries and their contribution to the communities they serve." These are PLA core values:

- Provide visionary leadership ever open to new ideas.
- Dedicate to lifelong learning.
- Focus on and be responsive to member needs.
- Commit to a free and open exchange of information and active collaboration.
- Respect diversity of opinion and community needs.
- Commit to excellence and innovation. (PLA, 2011)

Public librarians also participate in other units of the ALA, based upon their primary interests: Association for Library Collections and Technical Services, Association for Library Service to Children, Association of Library Trustees, Advocates, Friends and Foundations, Library Leadership and Management Association, Library Information and Technology Association, Reference and User Services Association, and the Young Adult Library Services Association. Each of these units has, over the years, developed cooperative projects, formulated standards and guidelines, recommended best practices, and provided opportunity for librarians to collaborate to improve and expand the quality of public library services. Twice yearly (at the ALA Annual Conference and Midwinter Meetings) 15,000–20,000 librarians from all over the United States meet to plan, exchange ideas, and learn about new developments in the field. In addition to these two major national conferences, the PLA holds its own biennial national conference to provide continuing education for the nation's public librarians.

In 2010 librarians who could not attend the national conference, Learn, Share, Connect, held in Portland, Oregon, were able to participate virtually. The PLA 2010 Virtual Conference featured panel discussions, poster sessions, interactive workshops, and chats with colleagues. The Virtual Conference included elements of the live conference and aspects targeted to the online venue, including live, interactive webcasts; handouts and other supporting presentation materials; online poster sessions; and discussion boards.

The leadership of public libraries at the national level as represented by the presidents of the PLA from 1945 to 2012 appears in Figure 10.1 (pp. 286–287). These individuals have represented large and small public libraries from every region of the United States. The contributions of these presidents and association activists to the development of public libraries through their focus on advocacy, the political process, strategic planning, and program provision are part of the rich heritage of connections that has laid the groundwork for the enduring institution that is the twenty-first-century public library. Their work has been voluntary and visionary and for the most part unsung. Every time we pass a public library, we should pause a moment to quietly thank the women and men who have selflessly devoted themselves to this cause.

Figure 10.1. Public Library Association Presidents, 1945–2011	
1945–1946	Amy Winslow, Cuyahoga County Library, OH
1946–1947	Carl Vitz, Head, Public Library of Cincinnati and Hamilton County, OH
1947–1948	Forrest Spaulding, Librarian, Des Moines, IA
1948–1949	Louis Nourse, Assistant Librarian, St. Louis, MO
1949–1950	John S. Richards, Librarian, Seattle Public Library, WA
1950–1951	Helen M. Harris, Librarian McGhee Library Knoxville, TN
1951–1952	Harold Brigham, Director, Indiana State Library, IN
1952–1953	Ruth Rutzen, Director, Home Reading Service, Detroit Public Library, MI
1953–1954	Jack B. Spear, Head, Traveling Libraries, New York State Library, NY
1954–1955	Ruth W. Gregory, Head Librarian, Waukegan Public Library, Waukegan, IL
1955–1956	Mildred W. Sandoe, Personnel Director, Cincinnati, OH
1956–1957	John T. Eastlick, City Librarian, Denver, CO
1957–1958	Arthur H. Parsons Jr., Director, Omaha Public Library, NE
1958–1959	Laura Currier, Director, Mississippi Library Commission, MS
1959–1960	James E. Bryan, Director, Newark Public Library, NJ
1960–1961	Elinor Walker, Coordinator of work with young people, Carnegie Library of Pittsburgh, PA
1961–1962	Harold Hamill, City Librarian, Los Angeles Public Library, CA
1962–1963	Clara Breed, City Librarian/Director, San Diego Public Library, CA
1963–1964	Ransom L. Richardson, Director, Flint Public Library, MI
1964–1965	William Chait, Director, Dayton and Montgomery County Public Library, OH
1965–1966	Alta Parks, Assistant Director, Gary Public Library, IN
1966–1967	David M. Stewart, Chief Librarian, Nashville Public Library, TN
1967–1968	Helen E. Fry, Staff Librarian, U.S. Army DCSPER SPEC SERV HQ 4th Army, Ft. Sam Houston, TX
1968–1969	Willard O. Youngs, City Librarian, Seattle Public Library, WA
1969–1970	June E. Bayless, City Librarian, Beverly Hills Public Library, CA
1970–1971	Andrew Geddes, Director, Nassau Library System, NY
1971–1972	Effie Lee Morris, Coordinator, San Francisco Public Library Children's Services, CA
1972–1973	David Henington, Director, Houston Public Library, TX
1973–1974	Lewis C. Naylor, Director, Toledo-Lucas County Library, OH
1974–1976	Dorothy M. Sinclair, Professor of Library Science, Case Western Reserve University, OH
1976–1978	Genevieve M. Casey, Professor of Library Science, Wayne State University, Detroit, MI
1978–1980	Ronald A. Dubberly, Director, Seattle Public Library, WA
1980–1981	Robert Rohlf, Director, Hennepin County Library, MN
1981–1982	Agnes M. Griffen, Director, Montgomery County Department of Public Libraries, MD
1982–1983	Donald J. Sager, Director, Elmhurst Public Library, IL
1983–1984	Nancy M. Bolt, President, JNR Associates, MD
1984–1985	Charles W. Robinson, Director, Baltimore County Public Library, MD
1985–1986	Patrick O'Brien, Director, Dallas Public Library, TX
1986–1987	Kathleen M. Balcom, Director, Downers Grove Public Library, IL
1987–1988	Susan S. Kent, Deputy Library Director, Tucson Public Library, AZ
1988–1989	Melissa Buckingham, Free Library of Philadelphia, PA
1989–1990	Sarah Ann Long, Systems Director, North Suburban Library System, Wheeling, IL
1990–1991	Charles M. Brown, Director of Libraries, Arlington, VA

(Continued)

Figure 10.1 *(Continued)*	
1991–1992	June Garcia, Extension Services Administrator, Phoenix Public Library, AZ
1992–1993	Elliot Shelkrot, Director, Free Library of Philadelphia, PA
1993–1994	Pat A. Woodrum, Executive Director, Tulsa City-County Library System, OK
1994–1995	Judy Drescher, Director, Memphis/Shelby County Public Library, TN
1995–1996	LaDonna Kienitz, City Librarian, Newport Beach, CA
1996–1997	Linda Mielke, Director, Carroll County Public Library, MD
1997–1998	Ginnie Cooper, Director, Multnomah County Library, OR
1998–1999	Christine L. Hage, Director, Rochester Hills Public Library, MI
1999–2000	Harriet Henderson, Director, Louisville Public Library, KY
2000–2001	Kay Runge, Director, Scott County Library System, IA
2001–2002	Toni Garvey, Director, Phoenix Public Library, AZ
2002–2003	Jo Ann Pinder, Director, Gwinnett County Public Library, GA
2003–2004	Luis Herrera, Director, Pasadena Public Library, CA
2004–2005	Clara Nalli Bohrer, Director, West Bloomfield Township Public Library, MI
2005–2006	Daniel L. Walters, Executive Director, Las Vegas-Clark County Library District, NV
2006–2007	Susan Hildreth, State Librarian of California
2007–2008	Jan Sanders, Director, Pasadena Public Library, CA
2008–2009	Carol Sheffer, Director, Round Lake Library, NY
2009–2010	Sari Feldman, Executive Director, Cuyahoga County Public Library, OH
2010–2011	Audra L. Caplan, Director, Harford County Public Library, Belcamp, MD
2011–2012	Marcia A. Warner, Director, Grand Rapids, Public Library, MI

State and Regional Library Associations

For many public librarians, state or regional associations—ALA chapters—provide a parallel, but more local, opportunity to meet and collaborate. Chapters promote general library service and librarianship within their geographic area, provide geographic representation to the Council of the American Library Association, and cooperate in the promotion of general and joint enterprises with the ALA and other library groups. The importance of state library association journals has been studied by Scherlen (2008).

Four recent case histories illustrate the richness of regional and state associations:

1. The Pacific Northwest Library Association (British Columbia, Washington, Oregon, Idaho, Montana, and Utah), founded in 1909, which made cooperation and collaboration a central activity (Frederiksen, 2009)
2. The North Dakota Library Association (2006) centenary history: *Dakota Gold: NDLA Celebrates 100 Years*
3. An essay on the centenary of the Virginia Library Association (Altshuler, 2005)

4. *The History of the Louisiana Library Association, 1925–2000*, by Dawson and Jumonville (2003), which includes Dawson's analysis of the participation of African Americans

Many associations, such as the Florida Library Association and the South Dakota Library Association (http://sdlibraryassociation.org), post histories at their websites.

Fifty-seven state and regional library association chapters are affiliated with the ALA, each including at least a committee or section that addresses public library issues. Generally, these associations hold an annual conference, as well as ongoing workshops and programs. A complete list of state and regional chapters including websites and Facebook page links are posted at the ALA website (http://www.ala .org/ala/mgrps/affiliates/chapters/state/stateregional.cfm).

The tapestry of relationships created by public librarians working at national, state, and regional levels to set policies, develop standards, and provide continuing education opportunities has been and continues to be a great strength of U.S. public librarianship. For three centuries librarians in the United States have gotten to know each other in a sustained and engaged manner, which has provided the foundation for more formalized cooperative relationships. Just like the national association presidents and member activists, librarians work for the greater good at the local, state, and regional levels.

Urban, Rural, Bookmobile, and Outreach Organizations

Public librarians also organize to respond to the needs of the communities they serve. Three major independent organizations stand out. Each holds conferences, provides professional development opportunities, and facilitates communication on issues of common concern.

- Urban Libraries Council (ULC, http://urbanlibraries.org/index.cfm), founded in 1971, is a member organization of North America's leading public library systems. ULC serves as a forum for research widely recognized and used by public and private sector leaders. Its members are dedicated to leadership, innovation, and the continuous transformation of libraries to meet community needs. The ULC offers webinars such as Public Libraries as a Central Driver of Family Literacy and Strategic Role of Building a Fundraising Board. Publications include *Welcome, Stranger—Public Libraries Build the Global Village: Toolkit* (Borrett and Milam, 2008) and *The Engaged Library: Chicago Stories of Community Building* (Kretzmann and Rans, 2005).

- The Association for Rural and Small Libraries (ARSL, http://www.arsl.info/about/) is a network of persons throughout the country dedicated to the positive growth and development of libraries. Its founder was Dr. Bernard Vavrek, director of the Center for the Study of Rural Librarianship at Clarion University in Pennsylvania. ARSL was "at home" there until 2007. ARSL believes in the value of rural and small libraries and strives to create resources and services that address national, state, and local priorities for libraries situated in rural communities. ARSL serves membership and constituents in the following ways: organizes a network of members concerned about the growth and development of useful library services in rural and small libraries; provides opportunities for the continuing education of members and the exchange of ideas and regular meetings; partners with other library and nonlibrary groups and organizations serving rural and small library communities; and advocates for rural and small libraries at the local, state, and national levels.
- The Association of Bookmobile and Outreach Services (ABOS, http://www.abos-outreach.org/) supports and encourages government officials, library administrators, trustees, and staff in the provision of quality bookmobile and outreach services to meet diverse community information and programming needs. ABOS provides a forum for bookmobile and outreach services in libraries; contributes to the education and training of library staff working in the area of bookmobile and outreach services; promotes bookmobile and outreach services as essential services in libraries; and sponsors and annual conference. In 2008 ABOS published guidelines for these services.

Through these associations, public librarians are accorded professional support in many ways that ensure their work is established with best practices and current research. These organizations provide opportunities for education, development, and advocacy.

State Library Agencies

State library agencies have been mentioned in previous chapters, for their role in supporting the establishment of public libraries, but they also stand out as a catalyst for a great deal of the motivation for public library cooperation. Founded beginning in the 1890s to encourage public library development, state library agencies play an important role in enhancing library cooperation, extension, and collaboration. Public library leaders in the early twentieth century recognized that the creation of independent public libraries affiliated with municipal governments could not meet the library needs of the nation. Some communities were too small or distances too great to provide adequate library services based on local taxing districts. Over the years, state library agencies played a major role in encouraging larger units of service to provide library resources. The Library Services Act (LSA, 1956) and the Library Services and Construction Act (LSCA, 1964) were keystones in the goal of providing library service throughout the nation.[1]

State librarians deserve much gratitude for their dedication to cooperation and the extension of service. Seeds of the 1956 LSA were planted by Elizabeth Myer, Rhode Island state librarian. John E. Fogerty, the Congressman who began his political career as president of the Bricklayers and Masons, Local 1, Rhode Island, worked with Senator Lister Hill to establish the LSA. Myer is credited in James Healey's (1974) volume, *John E. Fogarty: Political Leadership for Library Development*, as playing a crucial role in Fogarty's library interest. Healey quotes John Humphry:

> I have little doubt but what he [Fogarty] was greatly impressed with the pioneer work that Betty Myer did in reaching people through bookmobile and other local outlets; her active and aggressive public relations programs; and her ability to relate effectively to legislators, government officials, librarians and the people who benefited from library services. (p. 81)

In the early 1960s, the Association of State Libraries initiated a survey to review the status of state library agencies to make recommendations for their future. The 1966 report *The Library Functions of the States* identified "coordination and cooperation" among each state's libraries as a key function of state library agencies (Monypenny, 1966), a point that was made the following year with strong emphasis in the U.S. National Advisory Commission on Libraries (1969) report, *Libraries at Large: Traditions, Innovations and the National Interest*. This report included the recommendation that the LSCA be amended to strengthen state library agencies and specifically that this be done so that the agencies could "coordinate planning for total library service." This was a watershed event because it set policy for the future of library cooperation as a means by which public libraries could serve the broadest possible range of people.

LSCA and Planning

The ALA worked diligently through its Washington office to see that the National Advisory Commission on Libraries's recommendation that state library agencies be strengthened was implemented through amendments to the LSCA in 1970. State plans were required, but states were given latitude in the way that they expended funds to coordinate and strengthen library services. Each state developed a different pattern of service throughout the LSCA period. The state plans provide a history of the innovation and cooperative efforts made by each state to strengthen the nation's library services.

To provide an overview of the substance of cooperative activities coordinated by state library agencies during the LSCA period (1964–1995), we provide a few illustrative abstracts of model plans from this period in this section. Library development in each state was configured to its own needs. A sample, but by no means all, of state library agency plans and annual reports are available through the U.S. Department of Education, Education Resources Information Center (ERIC), and taken together they provide a detailed history of the manner in which state library agencies encouraged innovation during the LSCA period. The cooperative and collaborative activities of the states relied heavily upon individual libraries participating in the planning process. Libraries worked to forge innovative services to extend library resources to the underserved, enhance personnel development, and build the capacity of libraries to respond to the needs of each state's residents in the manner most suitable for them. In every state the habit of cooperative planning grew among librarians and fostered a climate for working together toward common goals at a state level, while focusing on local service.

The following four examples of state library agency plans submitted to the federal government during the LSCA period show a variety of plans created by each state. Every state has its own variation on the development of services through the state library agencies. The complete documents are available through the ERIC system. Those wishing to compile a historical record of any state's library development will find that the plans submitted to state library agencies are vital primary sources, as demonstrated by these brief selections.

Illinois State Library—Annual Program LSCA, 1974

Brief summaries are provided of 17 library projects being conducted in Illinois in 1974, dealing with the following matters:

1. The development of the Illinois State Library
2. Library manpower training
3. Library research
4. The Illinois State Library Materials Processing Center
5. The professional development of library personnel
6. The demonstration of library services to groups without libraries
7. The provision of services to groups lacking adequate libraries
8. Library resources, research, and references
9. Bibliographic control and access to resources
10. Public library system development
11. A children's book review and examination center

12. Multimedia services
13. Library services to the institutionalized
14. Library services to the blind and the physically handicapped
15. Local public library services
16. Multitype library activities

Each summary provides a brief description of the project, including details about its goals and major activities, the agencies that support it, and the legislation that enables it (ERIC ED089712, 1974).

Wyoming State Library—Five-Year Plan, 1974–1978

An overview of the Wyoming State Library Five-Year Plan is presented. The first major component deals with demographic characteristics, giving data on the state's geographic area, population, and racial characteristics, and the location of minority groups. The second main component provides a brief review of the Wyoming State Library Advisory Council and the means by which it facilitates broader participation in planning library services, while the third component summarizes the methods used to evaluate present services and to develop new programs. These include formal liaison with the Advisory Council, personal contact with library personnel, systems studies of programs, and analyses of demographic and other statistical data. State library publications and financial statements will be used for dissemination purposes. The final component lists the goal of library service as being to provide informational, cultural, and recreational services and materials to all citizens in the state. Specific objectives related to this goal are enumerated, including the provision of: (1) consultant, financial, and reference services to libraries; (2) services to the handicapped, the institutionalized, and the disadvantaged; (3) library services to rural areas; (4) research and library development services; and (5) aid with library construction (ERIC ED089714, 1974).

New York State Library—Long-Range Plan, 1987–1992

The State of New York submitted its long-range plan under the title, "Library Service to the People of New York State. A Long-Range Program, October 1, 1987–September 30, 1992, for the Improvement of Library Services Utilizing Local, State and Federal Resources." This annual report on the comprehensive five-year program for the enhancement of libraries in New York State achieves the following: (1) provides a benchmark for the continuing planning, development, and evaluation of state library services; (2) summarizes the objectives, policies, and programs undertaken for the improvement of those services; (3) serves as a guide to library networks, regional planning groups, and other agencies that wish to participate in the LSCA program; and (4) meets the LSCA requirements. An overview of the state library environment is offered; library systems and networks are profiled; statewide resource sharing and technological change are summarized; constraints on services are outlined; and the program's goals and objectives are discussed. Tables provide summary statistics on public, academic, school, institution, and medical libraries; the New York State Library; public library systems; systems and libraries by region; and state appropriations for higher education. A 23-item bibliography of major documents for the New York State library service program and lists of New York members of the LSCA Advisory Council and the Regents Advisory Council on Libraries are also provided. "LSCA Program Purposes—Needs and Intended Actions" and "Policy Guidelines on the Administration of LSCA Funds 1987–88" are included as supplements (ERIC ED286536, 1987).

The South Carolina Program for Library Development, 1991–1994

This report outlines the long-range program of the LSCA in South Carolina. The first of five chapters presents excerpts of the LSCA that describe its Title I–III programs; explains the evolution of South Carolina's long-range Program for Library Development; discusses the dissemination of publications related to the LSCA programs in South Carolina; and touches on how LSCA programs are coordinated. Focusing on the library public, the second chapter discusses the probable impact of population increases on information needs and library services, and inventories the special needs of the economically disadvantaged, the illiterate, the blind and physically handicapped, persons with limited English-speaking ability, the elderly, and the institutionalized. The third chapter focuses on South Carolina libraries and their needs, including the South Carolina State Library, public libraries, institutional libraries, academic libraries, technical college learning resource centers, school library media centers, and special libraries. Library education programs in South Carolina institutions of higher education are also described, and maps and statistics are provided for public, institutional, and college and university libraries, and the South Carolina Library Network. A copy of the state aid agreement form between the South Carolina State Library and the state's public library systems is included. The adequacy, priorities, and evaluation procedures of Title I, II, and III projects are the focus of the fourth chapter, and the fifth presents the four goals of the state library together with objectives designed to meet those goals (ERIC ED345688, 1992).

LSTA and the Future of State Library Agencies

Looking back on over 50 years of federal support for libraries as embodied in the LSA (1956–1964), the LSCA (1964–1996), and current legislation, the Library Services and Technology Act (LSTA, 1996–present), we can assess library services that have developed over the years to address the act's purposes and priorities. These include a range of services designed to build human capital, expand existing library services, and update the information infrastructure of today's libraries (IMLS, 2009).

The passage of the LSTA in 1996 shifted the manner in which the federal government funded state activities, but the work of state library agencies continued to revolve around the enhancement of library services. In 2000 the Association of Specialized and Cooperative Library Services (ASCLA) and the Chief Officers of State Library Agencies (COSLA) issued *The Functions and Roles of State Library Agencies* (Himmel, Wilson, and DeCandido, 2000), which replaced the earlier series of *Standards for Library Functions at the State Level*. The ASCLA COSLA study described state library agency services in three broad categories:

1. **Services to the public**: reference and interlibrary loan to the public; statewide reference services; virtual and digital libraries; libraries for the blind and physically handicapped; state centers for the book; and state history museums
2. **Services to government**: law collections; reference and interlibrary loan services to state government; state documents collections and depository systems; state archives; state computer center and data operations; preservation for state agencies
3. **Services to libraries**: administration of federal and state aid; certification of librarians; gathering of statistics; consulting services; continuing education programs; database development; Internet access; library legislation preparation and review; library evaluation and research; literacy; statutory responsibility for public libraries and multitype library systems; summer reading programs

The LSTA is part of the Museum and Library Services Act, which created the Institute of Museum and Library Services (IMLS) and established federal programs to help libraries and museums serve the public. The LSTA sets out three overall purposes:

1. Promote improvements in library services in all types of libraries in order to better serve the people of the United States.
2. Facilitate access to resources in all types of libraries for the purpose of cultivating an educated and informed citizenry.
3. Encourage resource sharing among all types of libraries for the purpose of achieving economical and efficient delivery of library services to the public.

The report *A Catalyst for Change: LSTA Grants to States Program Activities and the Transformation of Library Services to the Public* (U.S. IMLS, 2009) describes how the population-based formula grant to each state has been the backbone of federal support for libraries for more than 50 years. It provides a snapshot of the federal-state partnership as manifested by the LSTA Grants to States program. The report reviews the extent to which the LSTA program has been a catalyst for statewide planning and evaluation of library services and underscores the value of the Grants to States program in helping libraries embrace technology, establish new service models, and engage the public. These grants have played an important role in keeping the U.S. public library a treasured, effective, and popular national resource, vital to the educational, economic, and cultural success of communities throughout the nation (U.S. IMLS, 2009: 1).

Of critical importance has been the requirement that each state submit a five-year plan to IMLS at the beginning of a grant cycle. The plans must be based upon the priorities described in LSTA for use of funds under the Grants to States program and identify goals and outcomes that each state will achieve within the five-year cycle. In the context of LSTA priorities, states tailor their plans to take into account state government rules and regulations and other contextual factors such as the characteristics and needs of the state's population, the state's library service infrastructure, the rapid pace of technological change, and the funding environment for related programs and services (U.S. IMLS, 2009: 7). Plans for each state can be viewed at the COSLA website (http://www.cosla.org).[2]

The *State Library Agencies Survey* (Henderson et al., 2009) was the third release of library statistics data from the IMLS. It contains data on state library agencies in the 50 states and the District of Columbia for each fiscal year. The data were collected through the State Library Agencies (StLA) Survey, the product of a cooperative effort between COSLA, IMLS, and the U.S. Census Bureau. This cooperative effort made possible the 100 percent response rate achieved for this survey. The frame or source of the list of respondents for this survey is based on the list of state library agencies that COSLA maintains. The FY 2008 survey is the 15th in the StLA series (Henderson et al., 2009). Prior to IMLS, the National Center for Education Statistics issued these reports.

Survey data demonstrates the range of services, including the following:

- **Collections**: state library holdings of materials in various formats.
- **Service transactions**: library use, such as circulation and reference transactions.
- **Internet access and electronic services**: describes the efforts of agencies to facilitate Internet access among libraries in their states, as well as the availability of statewide electronic services, information, and networks.
- **Staffing and public service hours**: staffing levels and the functions performed by employees of state library agencies, as well as the number of public service hours during a typical week.
- **Expenditures**: describes how state library funds are expended.

- **Revenue**: identifies various sources of revenue.
- **Services to libraries and cooperatives**: identifies activities and programs that support public, academic, school, special libraries, and library cooperatives.

To demonstrate the range of services provided directly or by contract to public libraries by state library agencies, we reprint a key table from the 2008 survey in Figure 10.2. This shows the range of services and the number of agencies. All agencies administer LSTA grants while slightly over half coordinate digital programs.

The evolution of state library agencies in each state has been a journey shared by the public librarians and the people of each state. The state library agency staffs also exchange information and ideas by participation in the State Library Agency Section of ASCLA (http://www.ala.org/ala/mgrps/divs/ascla/ascla.cfm). The purpose of the State Library Agency Section is to develop and strengthen the unique role and functions of state library agencies in providing leadership and services that foster and improve the delivery of library services, and to stimulate the continued professional development of state library agency personnel in discharging their unique functions in such areas as statewide planning and evaluation, services to state governments and legislatures, services to local libraries, services to users with special needs, and so on. Discussion groups are Consultants for Service to Children and Young People, LSTA Coordinators, and State Library Consultants/Library Development.

The breakthrough collaborative nature of projects initiated by state library agencies is demonstrated by Project Compass, a partnership of the State Library of North Carolina and Webjunction funded in 2009–2010 that supported state library agencies in maximizing the effectiveness of local libraries, providing activities, services, and outreach to unemployed residents; fostered successful, ongoing collaboration and knowledge exchange among state library agencies; promoted strategic partnerships with other organizations that serve the unemployed; increased awareness of library services and demonstrated to key decision makers the critical role libraries serve during times of economic crisis; and collected stories and evidence of the impact libraries have on the employment recovery or career advancement of patrons (Webjunction, http://www.webjunction.org/project-compass).

Networks, Systems, and Consortia

A useful definition of libraries working together was formulated by Joseph Becker (1979: 89): "When two or more libraries engage formally in a common pattern of information exchange, through communications, for some functionally interdependent purpose, we have a library network." This definition is manifested a thousandfold in

(continued p. 303)

Figure 10.2. Number of Services Provided Directly or by Contract to Public Libraries by State Library Agencies: Fiscal Year 2008

State	Accreditation of libraries	Administration of LSTA grants[1]	Administration of state aid	Certification of librarians	Collection of library statistics	Consulting services	Continuing education programs	Cooperative purchasing of library materials	Inter-library loan referral services	Library legislation preparation/review	Library planning/evaluation/research	Literacy program support
50 States and DC	14	51	39	22	51	50	50	23	47	47	51	38
Directly	14	51	39	22	51	50	47	16	42	46	51	32
Contract	0	0	0	0	0	0	3	7	5	1	0	6
Alabama	N	D	D	N	D	D	D	N	D	N	D	D
Alaska	N	D	D	N	D	D	D	N	D	D	D	N
Arizona	N	D	D	N	D	D	C	C	D	D	D	C
Arkansas	N	D	D	N	D	D	D	N	D	D	D	D
California	N	D	D	N	D	D	C	C	N	D	D	D
Colorado	N	D	N	N	D	D	D	N	C	C	D	D
Connecticut	N	D	D	N	D	D	D	N	D	D	D	C
Delaware	N	D	N	N	D	D	D	D	D	D	D	N
Dist. of Columbia	N	D	N	N	D	N	N	D	D	D	D	D
Florida	N	D	D	N	D	D	D	N	D	D	D	D
Georgia	N	D	D	N	D	D	D	D	D	D	D	D
Hawaii	N	D	N	N	D	D	D	D	N	D	D	D
Idaho	N	D	N	N	D	D	D	N	D	D	D	D
Illinois	N	D	D	N	D	D	D	N	N	D	D	D
Indiana	D	D	D	D	D	D	D	D	D	D	D	D
Iowa	D	D	D	D	D	D	D	D	D	D	D	D
Kansas	N	D	D	D	D	D	D	C	D	D	D	N

(Continued)

Figure 10.2. Number of Services Provided Directly or by Contract to Public Libraries by State Library Agencies: Fiscal Year 2008 (Continued)

State	Accreditation of libraries	Administration of LSTA grants[1]	Administration of state aid	Certification of librarians	Collection of library statistics	Consulting services	Continuing education programs	Cooperative purchasing of library materials	Inter-library loan referral services	Library legislation preparation/review	Library planning/evaluation/research	Literacy program support
Kentucky	N	D	D	D	D	D	D	N	N	D	D	C
Louisiana	N	D	D	D	D	D	D	N	D	D	D	D
Maine	N	D	N	N	D	D	D	C	D	D	D	D
Maryland	N	D	D	D	D	D	D	D	C	D	D	D
Massachusetts	D	D	D	D	D	D	D	C	C	D	D	D
Michigan	D	D	D	D	D	D	D	N	D	D	D	N
Minnesota	N	D	N	N	D	D	D	N	C	D	D	N
Mississippi	D	D	D	N	D	D	D	N	D	D	D	N
Missouri	N	D	D	N	D	D	D	N	C	D	D	D
Montana	N	D	D	D	D	D	D	C	D	D	D	N
Nebraska	D	D	D	D	D	D	D	D	D	D	D	C
Nevada	N	D	D	D	D	D	D	N	D	D	D	D
New Hampshire	N	D	N	N	D	D	D	N	D	D	D	D
New Jersey	N	D	D	N	D	D	D	N	D	D	D	C
New Mexico	D	D	D	D	D	D	D	N	D	N	D	C
New York	D	D	D	D	D	D	D	D	D	D	D	D
North Carolina	D	D	D	D	D	D	C	C	D	D	D	N
North Dakota	N	D	D	N	D	D	D	N	D	N	D	N
Ohio	N	D	D	N	D	D	D	N	D	D	D	D
Oklahoma	D	D	D	D	D	D	D	N	D	D	D	D
Oregon	N	D	D	N	D	D	D	N	N	D	D	D

(Continued)

Figure 10.2 (Continued)

State	Accreditation of libraries	Administration of LSTA grants[1]	Administration of state aid	Certification of librarians	Collection of library statistics	Consulting services	Continuing education programs	Cooperative purchasing of library materials	Inter-library loan referral services	Library legislation preparation/review	Library planning/evaluation/research	Literacy program support
Pennsylvania	N	D	D	D	D	D	D	N	D	D	D	D
Rhode Island	D	D	D	N	D	D	D	N	D	D	D	D
South Carolina	N	D	D	D	D	D	D	D	D	D	D	D
South Dakota	N	D	N	N	D	D	D	N	D	D	D	D
Tennessee	N	D	D	D	D	D	D	D	D	D	D	D
Texas	D	D	D	N	D	D	D	D	D	D	D	D
Utah	D	D	D	N	D	D	D	N	D	D	D	N
Vermont	D	D	N	D	D	D	D	D	D	D	D	N
Virginia	N	D	D	D	D	D	D	D	D	D	D	D
Washington	N	D	N	D	D	D	D	D	D	D	D	N
West Virginia	N	D	D	N	D	D	D	N	D	D	D	D
Wisconsin	N	D	N	D	D	D	D	D	D	N	D	D
Wyoming	N	D	N	N	D	D	D	D	D	N	D	N

(Continued)

Figure 10.2. Number of Services Provided Directly or by Contract to Public Libraries by State Library Agencies: Fiscal Year 2008 (Continued)

State	OCLC Group Access Capability (GAC)[2]	Preservation/conservation services	Reference referral services	Retrospective conversion of bibliographic records	State standards/guidelines	Statewide coordinated digital program or service	Statewide public relations/library promotion campaigns	Statewide virtual reference service	Summer reading program support	Union list development[3]	Universal Service (E-rate discount) Program review[4]
50 States and DC	33	18	42	17	42	27	35	22	50	36	51
Directly	29	12	38	8	40	21	32	10	47	25	51
Contract	4	6	4	9	2	6	3	12	3	11	0
Alabama	D	N	D	N	D	D	D	D	D	N	D
Alaska	D	N	D	N	D	D	C	N	D	C	D
Arizona	D	N	D	C	D	D	C	N	D	C	D
Arkansas	D	C	D	N	D	N	N	N	C	D	D
California	D	C	D	N	N	C	N	C	C	C	D
Colorado	N	N	D	N	D	C	D	D	D	N	D
Connecticut	N	N	N	D	D	C	N	N	D	D	D
Delaware	N	D	D	N	C	N	D	N	D	D	D
Dist. of Columbia	D	D	D	D	D	N	D	N	D	N	D
Florida	D	D	D	C	C	C	N	C	D	C	D
Georgia	D	N	D	D	D	N	D	N	D	D	D
Hawaii	D	N	D	N	D	D	D	N	D	N	D
Idaho	D	N	D	N	D	N	D	N	D	D	D
Illinois	D	N	D	N	D	D	D	D	D	C	D
Indiana	N	D	D	N	D	D	D	D	D	N	D
Iowa	N	N	D	N	D	D	D	N	D	D	D
Kansas	D	N	D	N	N	D	D	N	D	D	D
Kentucky	D	C	D	N	N	D	D	C	D	C	D
Louisiana	D	N	D	N	N	D	D	D	D	D	D
Maine	N	D	D	N	D	D	D	N	D	D	D

(Continued)

Figure 10.2 (Continued)

State	OCLC Group Access Capability (GAC)[2]	Preservation/conservation services	Reference referral services	Retrospective conversion of bibliographic records	State standards/guidelines	Statewide coordinated digital program or service	Statewide public relations/library promotion campaigns	Statewide virtual reference service	Summer reading program support	Union list development[3]	Universal Service (E-rate discount) Program review[4]
Maryland	C	N	C	N	D	C	D	C	D	N	D
Massachusetts	N	D	D	N	D	N	C	C	D	N	D
Michigan	N	N	D	N	D	D	D	N	D	D	D
Minnesota	N	N	C	N	D	C	N	N	N	N	D
Mississippi	D	N	D	N	D	N	N	N	D	D	D
Missouri	C	N	N	C	D	D	N	N	D	C	D
Montana	C	N	D	N	D	N	D	C	D	C	D
Nebraska	D	N	D	C	D	D	D	N	D	D	D
Nevada	D	D	D	N	D	N	D	N	D	N	D
New Hampshire	N	N	D	C	D	N	N	D	D	D	D
New Jersey	N	C	N	N	D	N	D	C	C	D	D
New Mexico	D	N	D	N	D	N	D	N	D	D	D
New York	N	D	D	N	D	N	D	N	D	N	D
North Carolina	D	N	D	C	D	N	D	C	D	D	D
North Dakota	D	N	D	D	N	N	D	N	D	C	D
Ohio	D	N	D	N	N	N	N	D	D	N	D
Oklahoma	N	D	N	C	D	N	D	D	D	D	D
Oregon	N	N	C	N	N	N	N	C	C	C	D
Pennsylvania	C	C	D	C	D	D	D	C	D	C	D
Rhode Island	N	C	C	N	D	N	D	C	D	N	D
South Carolina	D	D	D	N	D	N	D	N	D	D	D
South Dakota	D	N	D	N	N	N	N	N	D	C	D
Tennessee	D	D	N	D	D	D	D	N	D	D	D

(Continued)

Figure 10.2. Number of Services Provided Directly or by Contract to Public Libraries by State Library Agencies: Fiscal Year 2008 (Continued)

State	OCLC Group Access Capability (GAC)[2]	Preservation/conservation services	Reference referral services	Retrospective conversion of bibliographic records	State standards/guidelines	Statewide coordinated digital program or service	Statewide public relations/library promotion campaigns	Statewide virtual reference service	Summer reading program support	Union list development[3]	Universal Service (E-rate discount) Program review[4]
Texas	D	N	N	N	D	D	N	N	D	D	D
Utah	N	N	N	N	D	N	D	N	D	N	D
Vermont	D	N	D	D	D	N	D	N	D	N	D
Virginia	D	D	D	D	D	D	N	N	D	D	D
Washington	D	N	D	N	N	D	N	N	D	D	D
West Virginia	D	N	D	D	D	D	D	D	D	D	D
Wisconsin	N	N	D	C	D	D	N	C	D	C	D
Wyoming	N	N	D	N	N	D	D	N	D	D	D

D Directly. Services provided directly by the state library agency (StLA) are those provided without any intermediary by the StLA to libraries or library cooperatives.

C Contract. Services provided by contract by the StLA are those provided by a third party or intermediary under legal contract to the StLA.

N Not provided. The state library agency does not provide this service.

[1] LSTA—Library Services and Technology Act (P.L. 104-208).

[2] OCLC Group Access Capability (GAC)—Use of the Online Computer Library Center (OCLC) system, originally the Ohio College Library Center, by a group of libraries for resource sharing and interlibrary lending (ILL). Group Access Capability (GAC) related activities may include coordinating group profiling, establishing group policies, coordinating ILL protocols within the group, and referring requests outside of a GAC group.

[3] Union list development—A union list is a list of titles of works, usually periodicals, and their locations in physically separate library collections.

[4] This program was established by the Federal Communications Commission (FCC) under the Telecommunications Act of 1996 (P.L. 104-104). State library agencies review and approve technology plans for libraries or library cooperatives applying for E-rate discounts under this program.

SOURCE: Institute of Museum and Library Services, State Library Agencies Survey, Fiscal year 2008.

Source: U.S. Institute of Museum and Library Services. 2009. *State Library Agency Survey: Fiscal Year 2008.* Washington, DC: U.S. Institute of Museum and Library Services, pp. 37–40. http://harvester.census.gov/imls/pubs/Publications/StLA2008.pdf.

the work of the world's biggest library network, OCLC. OCLC was founded in 1967 by university presidents in Ohio to share library resources and reduce costs by using computers and technology. Online shared cataloging for libraries was introduced in 1971; interlibrary loan service in 1979; and FirstSearch was introduced as a reference tool in 1991. OCLC is a cooperative venture that gives a library access to WorldCat, the global union catalog, and offers paid access to a wide range of services and databases. OCLC's membership makes it the world's largest library consortium. It exists to further access to the world's information and reduce library costs by offering services for libraries and their users.

The growth of networks in the late twentieth century is viewed by Woodsworth (1991) as a response to the OCLC policy that shared cataloging would take place through networks, rather than individual libraries. In the late twentieth century, 17 regional service providers, such as Amigos (http://www.amigos.org), PALINET, and SOLINET, contracted with OCLC to provide support and training for OCLC services. Public librarians will find inspiration in the history and development of the regional service providers. Though many have merged into larger networks such as LYRASIS, the historical record provides insight into the growth and development of public libraries. Each of these networks had an interesting history, and exploring these histories provides a look at the overlapping efforts among professional associations, government funding, and individual institutional commitment that leads to cooperation.[3]

In 2008, the boards of PALINET and SOLINET recognized the shared mission of both organizations and the unprecedented opportunities to expand education, leadership development, technology, and savings for members, while adding critical new initiatives needed for the future. In February 2009, members of these two well-established regional library networks voted to merge, creating LYRASIS (http://www.lyrasis.org/). LYRASIS fosters collaboration and cooperation among members and facilitates networking and programming, innovative solutions, and significant cost savings through group purchasing for products and services. To some extent LYRASIS is a legacy organization. Both PALINET and SOLINET (Southeastern Library Network) were major multistate multitype networks, PALINET in the mid-Atlantic region and SOLINET in the southeastern region. NELINET, a regional network rooted in the New England region, joined LYRASIS in October 2009 to create the nation's largest regional network serving libraries and information professionals.

The merger became effective on April 1, 2009. In January 2011 the Bibliographic Center for Research (BCR), which provided services to libraries and cultural heritage institutions located in the Rocky Mountain West and Midwest, phased out operations and joined LYRASIS. As the premier technology advisor, LYRASIS offers members cutting-edge education and innovative technology solutions. Preservation and digitization services give members the capability to participate fully in the digital future and safeguard their collections.

Network-level information provides a good opportunity for librarians to change the way users see and make use of descriptive information, customizing it to take fullest advantage of the data. Librarians who understand the metadata that constitutes these bibliographic databases are in a position to help develop and refine tools to take optimal advantage of the underlying descriptive information (Banush, 2010).

Multitype Library Cooperatives

Libraries working regionally in collaborative arrangements are variously called multitype library cooperatives, systems, networks, or consortia. Today the term that has gained the broadest use is the multitype library cooperative (MLC). The MLC has increased in importance to the daily life of public librarians since the 1970s. It is difficult to generalize about MLCs, because even more than state library agencies MLCs have developed directly in response to local needs. They have evolved from the combined efforts of librarians working through professional associations in collaboration with state library agencies. It is most likely, however, that an MLC will be more involved in the daily work of a library than a professional association, state library agency, or regional service provider. Long's (1995: 118) definition of library cooperation marked an evolution in the concept, "an independent library-related entity with an autonomous governing board whose responsibilities include library cooperation and improvement of member libraries."

The MLC was an evolution in the long push for larger units of library service, first described in the 1920s and legitimized in the LSA, which called for state plans to promote service to rural areas. The 1967 addition of Title III to the LSTA specifically promoted multitype library development, and the standards issued by the PLA (1967) were titled *Minimum Standards for Public Library Systems, 1966*. The library system, as discussed in the standards, was intended to provide accessibility through branches, cooperating libraries, and bookmobile stops, plus a pool of resources and services used in common by all the outlets. Nelson Associates' 1969 study provided an overview of the growth of these systems, structures, and institutions, during the height of public library-based system implementation.

The increase in scope of the MLCs in the 1970s and 1980s strongly contributed to public library development and acted as a mechanism to help equalize services for all people. Consulting services and continuing education provided by the MLCs rendered support to small libraries without professional staff. Some MLCs purchased core collections to share among member libraries, established review centers, or coordinated cooperative collection development. By 1990 standards had been established for MLCs and state laws consolidated to support further development (ASCLA, 1990; Fields, Neumann, and Brown, 1991).

Support for librarians working in MLCs or system environments comes from two units of the ALA. The InterLibrary Cooperation and Networking Section of ASCLA provides discussions, programs, and planning activities for the effective delivery of quality library services through multitype library networks (http://www.ala.org/ala/mgrps/divs/ascla/asclaourassoc/asclasections/ican/ican.cfm). The Public Library Systems Community of Practice of the PLA encourages improved library service through the involvement of public libraries in multijurisdictional library systems and the participation of public libraries in multitype library systems.

The ALA has produced key publications guiding the development of MLCs, including *Library Networks in the New Millennium* (Laughlin, 2000).

An analysis of the future of MLCs was initiated by the Light Bulb Group (LBG): five multitype library directors interested in the current status and activities of multitype library systems commissioned a study to develop a snapshot of exemplary library systems in the United States. Of special interest to the LBG were the challenges that systems were addressing, their use of innovation, and successful leadership skills. As one could expect, cooperative planning and developing consensus was viewed (next to funding) as the main challenge (Long, 2004).

The scope of multitype library consortia, systems, and networks can best be assessed by perusing listings in the *American Library Directory: 2010–2011* (Information Today, 2010). Examples include:

- Baynet, a multitype library association (http://www.baynetlibs.org/), has as its mission to strengthen connections among all types of libraries and information centers, and to promote communication, professional development, cooperation, and innovative resource sharing.
- Connecticut Library Consortium (http://www.ctlibrarians.org), a statewide membership collaborative serving all types of Connecticut libraries by initiating and facilitating cost-effective services, creating and supporting educational and professional development, and helping libraries to strengthen their ability to serve their users.
- Tampa Bay Library Consortium (TBLC, http://www.tblc.org/) is a nonprofit multitype library cooperative that assists and empowers libraries of all types, including public, academic, school, and special. Today, 97 libraries are TBLC members, including six community colleges, three state university system libraries, 27 private academic schools, colleges, and universities, four public school systems, and 41 public and 16 special libraries. Together these libraries serve over 4.2 million Floridians, or almost a quarter of Florida's population, in 12 counties.

However, the general economic downturn that began in 2008 has eroded funds to support consortia. One dire example is Illinois, a state whose regional library systems set a model for the nation. Library systems in Illinois were forced to lay off dozens of staff in spring 2010 due to the worst financial crisis in the state's history (Kniffel, 2010). The irony is that these visionary systems had just celebrated nearly a half century of service. The dreams and reality of the multitype achievements in Illinois have been well documented in the journal *Illinois Libraries* (Ison, 2005; Long, 2005).

Reinventing cooperation in the twenty-first century has been addressed by Brenda Bailey-Hainer (2010), ASCLA president, who noted, "cooperation must undergo a metamorphosis that goes beyond existing models and creates new partnerships that cross sectors. It's time to make more of cooperation and focus on the quality of the experience and the results to be gained."

Social Networking, Groupware, and Collaborative Systems

Connections among public librarians in the twenty-first century are enhanced by collaborative systems, groupware, and social networking. In the collaborative systems paradigm, work group members and their mediators work interactively and share operational responsibility (Jank, 2010). Multiple groups working autonomously with central repositories for the storage of necessary information provide the foundation for a habit of virtual communication among librarians.

The first broadly used electronic discussion list for public librarians was PUBLIB, founded in December 1992, by Jean Armour Polly and John Iliff. PUBLIB is managed by volunteers Sara Weissman and Karen G. Schneider and hosted by Webjunction. The PUBLIB electronic discussion list is for the discussion of issues relating to public librarianship. At the turn of the millennium, Donald Sager (2000) used PUBLIB to determine the most significant events in librarianship during the twentieth century.

In a comprehensive essay on the many forms of e-collaboration, Fichter (2005) explored a range of strategies including blogs, wikis, and instant messaging. She noted that some collaboration initiatives are targeted specifically at communities of practice, helping them find information on a topic, share successes, develop best practices, replicate ideas, and identify experts.

Webjunction, an online learning community, provides a portal designed to help library staff make the best use of emerging digital opportunities (Mason, 2009). This portal, funded by the Bill and Melinda Gates Foundation, promotes learning for all library staff by providing open, affordable online communities, and community, collaboration, and support for lifelong learning.

ALA Connect (http://connect.ala.org/about) is a centralized space where official ALA members and groups can work together online and connect with other members around professional interests, issues, and advocacy. It is an online version of what has traditionally taken place in the physical world.

Librarians Ignoring Boundaries

Public librarians serve locally with a strong community focus. They are also motivated by an overarching commitment to preserve the human record and make it accessible to all. These parallel goals have been central to U.S. public librarianship since the first interlibrary loan. Perhaps the most long-standing example of cooperating across boundaries is the National Library Service for the Blind and Physically Handicapped (NLS, http://www.loc.gov/nls), which began with the Pratt-Smoot Act in 1931 and is now a national network of cooperating libraries for Braille and audio books, that "all may read." Each public library in the United States acts as a contact in a national network to provide materials. In addition, NLS has become a center for materials of all types relating to persons with disabilities and serves as a national clearinghouse for information regarding issues related to blindness and physical handicaps. Institutions and agencies whose clientele might be expected to include blind or physically handicapped persons—such as hospitals, retirement homes, nursing homes, and rehabilitation centers—also are eligible to use NLS services (Cylke, Moodie, and Fistick, 2007).

The joint-use library is another example of public librarians spanning boundaries. Libraries such as these serve different user constituencies in one facility:

- Henna Welch and Laura Bush Community Library, El Paso, Texas (El Paso Public Library and El Paso Community College)
- Harmony Library in Fort Collins, Colorado (Front Range Community College and City of Fort Collins)
- Seminole Community Library, Florida (town of Seminole and St. Petersburg College)
- Dr. Martin Luther King, Jr. Library (San Jose, California Public Library and San Jose State University)
- Alvin Sherman Library, Research and Information Technology Center (Nova Southeastern University and Broward County Libraries, Florida)

Characterized as the ultimate form of cooperation, joint-use libraries require intergovernmental agreements, collaborative policies, and a spirit of mutual goal development. Dornseif (an academic librarian) and Draves (a public librarian) have addressed the benefits of a more varied collection, expanded hours of operation, and efficiency (Dornseif and Draves, 2003). Kifer and Light (2010) have assessed the scope of joint-use libraries including public-academic and public-school collaborations.

Public librarians have internalized resource sharing as part of their professional ethos, so new technological advances that transcend geographical perimeters, such as Internet portals, metadata standards, collaborative digitization projects, or 24/7 information services, are simply extensions of the public librarians' ideal of service without boundaries.

The IMLS has recognized the boundary-spanning and resource-sharing capacity of public librarians and has funded a variety of projects that make use of this capacity. These include collaboratives between Salinas Public Library and the National Steinbeck Center to explore the area's cultural past, present, and future; to digitize key documents for online access; and to collect new personal and organizational histories that comprise the untold story of the city. Another example is the Children's Museum of Houston, in partnership with the Houston Public Library, which developed and made available multilingual kits that will increase literacy and family learning. Public libraries and museums brought together through the leadership of IMLS will expand the role of the public library in serving cultural heritage.

Since the establishment of public libraries in the mid-1800s, public librarians have demonstrated a capacity to share information and resources that results in improved and expanded service. From their first meetings in 1876 to the establishment of worldwide electronic systems, librarians have been early adopters of technologies in service of the public library ideal that all may have access to information and preserve cultural heritage.

Notes

1. As of the this writing, a call for submissions has been issued for a special issue of *Libraries and the Cultural Record*, a peer-reviewed journal of history published by the University of Texas Press, to be published in January 2013. The special issue will be devoted to exploring historical perspectives on state library agencies in the United States. Possible themes might include (but are not limited to): the history and evolving role of the state library agency as a type, or of a specific state library agency; biographical sketches of significant individuals, including former state librarians, staff, and relevant government officials; the history of statewide initiatives such as resource sharing, cooperative online catalogs, or technology training and support; state library roles in the certification, organization, or professional development of library staff; state extension of library services to rural or underserved communities; history of the development and implementation of federal programs for supporting library services that are administered by state library agencies; history of interactions between libraries and education, history, museum, or other departments at the state level; history of efforts at the state level to document or preserve regional and local history, or to organize and enhance access to state government information; comparative histories of two or more state libraries; the history of ASCLA, the Col-

laborative Summer Library Program, or the IMLS; and other entities that encourage collaboration between states.

2. The COSLA website (www.cosla.org) includes links to each state library agency homepage, statistics, and five-year plans.

3. Each of these networks had a different history. Taken together, their histories provide great insight into library development throughout the United States. The Union Library Catalogue of Pennsylvania was originally formed in 1936, making it one of the oldest library networks in the United States. Its name was shortened to PALINET in 1975. In November 1995, PALINET merged with the Pittsburgh Regional Library Center to expand services into western Pennsylvania and West Virginia to provide information professionals in those regions with expanded product and service offerings with greater savings. PALINET's original membership was chiefly composed of libraries in the mid-Atlantic region (Pennsylvania, Delaware, New Jersey, Maryland, West Virginia). At the time of merger with LYRASIS, membership had grown to 612 members in 12 states and two other countries.

The Southeastern Library Network (SOLINET) was established in 1973 by the Association of Southeastern Research Libraries with 99 charter members. At the time of the merger with LYRASIS, SOLINET was the largest regional library network in the United States, with over 3,400 members, chiefly from the southeastern region (Alabama, Florida, Georgia, Indiana, Kentucky, Louisiana, Mississippi, North Carolina, South Carolina, Tennessee, Virginia), Puerto Rico, and the U.S. Virgin Islands.

NELINET began in 1955 when the New England Board of Higher Education was established by the six New England states (Connecticut, Maine, Massachusetts, New Hampshire, Rhode Island, and Vermont) to foster interinstitutional cooperation. In 1964, land grant university libraries in the six states agreed to work together in cooperative ventures in technical services and in 1967, the organization adopted the name New England Library Network (NELINET). Since that time, membership has grown steadily to more than 500 academic, public, and special libraries in the six New England states.

BCR was headquartered in Aurora, Colorado, and provided services to libraries and cultural heritage institutions located in the Rocky Mountain West and Midwest. BCR's mission was to bring libraries together for greater success by expanding their knowledge, reach, and power. Starting in 1935, BCR helped libraries learn new skills, reach new customers, increase productivity, and save money. After 75 years of service, BCR phased out its operations and members transitioned to LYRASIS in 2010–2011 (LYRASIS, http://www.lyrasis.org/).

Exploring the history and vision of any of the OCLC regional service providers demonstrates the passion librarians have shown to develop better access for library users. Public librarians will find inspiration in the history and development of the regional service providers. Though many have merged into larger networks such as LYRASIS, the historical record provides insight into the growth and development of public libraries. For additional background on the shared cataloging connection to OCLC, see Jordan (2010).

References

Altshuler, Alyssa. 2005. "The Virginia Library Association: A Retrospective." *Virginia Libraries* 51 (July/August/September): 5–10.

Association of Bookmobiles and Outreach Services. 2008. "Guidelines." http://www.abos-outreach.org/2008BookmobileGuidelines.pdf.

Association of Specialized and Cooperative Library Agencies. 1990. *Standards for Cooperative Multitype Library Organizations*. Chicago: American Library Association.

Bailey-Hainer, Brenda. 2010. "ASCLA President's Column: Reinventing Cooperation Is Our Future." *ASCLA Interface* (blog), March 31. http://ascla.ala.org/interface/2010/03/ascla-president%E2%80%99s-column-reinventing-cooperation-is-our-future/.

Banush, David. 2010. "Cooperative Cataloging at the Intersection of Tradition and Transformation: Possible Futures for the Program for Cooperative Cataloging." *Cataloging and Classification Quarterly* 48, no. 2/3: 247–257.

Becker, Joseph. 1979. "Network Functions." In *The Structure and Governance of Library Networks*, edited by Alan Kent and Thomas J. Galvin. New York: Marcel Dekker.

Borrett, Rochelle M., and Danielle Patrick Milam. 2008. *Welcome, Stranger—Public Libraries Build the Global Village: Toolkit*. Chicago, IL: Urban Libraries Council.

Cylke, Frank Kurt, Michael M. Moodie, and Robert E. Fistick. 2007. "Serving the Blind and Physically Handicapped in the United States of America." *Library Trends* 55, no. 4: 796–808.

Dawson, Alma, and Florence M. Jumonville. 2003. *A History of the Louisiana Library Association, 1925–2000*. Baton Rouge: Louisiana Library Association.

Dornseif, Karen, and Ken Draves. 2003. "The Joint-Use Library: The Ultimate Collaboration." *Colorado Libraries* 29 (Spring): 5–7.

Fichter, D. 2005. "The Many Forms of E-Collaboration: Blogs, Wikis, Portals, Groupware, Discussion Boards, and Instant Messaging." *Online* 29 (July/August): 48–50.

Fiels, Keith Michael, Joan Neumann, and Eva R. Brown. 1991. *Multitype Library Cooperation State Laws, Regulations and Pending Legislation*. Chicago: Association of Specialized and Cooperative Library Agencies.

Frederiksen, Linda. 2009. "A Century of Cooperation: The Pacific Northwest Library Association, 1909–2009." *PNLA Quarterly* 73 (Summer): 5–35.

Healey, James S. 1974. *John E. Fogarty: Political Leadership for Library Development*. Metuchen, NJ: Scarecrow Press.

Henderson, Everett, Kim Miller, Michelle Farrell, Faye Brock, Suzanne Dorinski, Michael Freeman, Lisa Frid, Laura Hardesty, Christopher Music, Patricia O'Shea, and Cindy Sheckells. 2009. *State Library Agencies Survey: Fiscal Year 2008* (IMLS-2010-StLA-01). Washington, DC: Institute of Museum and Library Services.

Himmel, Ethel E., William J. Wilson, and GraceAnne DeCandido. 2000. *The Functions and Roles of State Library Agencies*. Chicago: American Library Association.

Information Today. 2010. *American Library Directory: 2010–2011*. Medford, NJ: Information Today.

Ison, Jan. 2005. "Multitype Cooperation—the Competitive Advantage." *Illinois Libraries* 86 (December): 57–59.

Jank, David. 2010. "Collaborative Systems and Groupware." In *Encyclopedia of Library and Information Sciences*, 3rd ed., 1:1, 1088–1096.

Jordan, Jay. 2010. "OCLC: A Worldwide Library Cooperative." In *Encyclopedia of Library and Information Sciences*. 3rd ed., 1:1, 3924–3937.

Kniffel, Leonard. 2010. "With No Check in the Mail, Illinois Cooperatives Lay Off Dozens." *American Libraries* (May 19). http://americanlibrariesmagazine.org/news/05192010/no-check-mail-illinois-cooperatives-lay-dozens.

Kretzmann, Jody, and Susan Rans. 2005. *The Engaged Library: Chicago Stories of Community Building*. Chicago, IL: Urban Libraries Council.

Laughlin, Sara. 2000. *Library Networks in the New Millennium: Top Ten Trends*. Chicago: American Library Association.

Long, Sarah, 2000. "Foreword." In *A Place at the Table: Participating in Community Building*, edited by Kathleen de la Peña McCook, vii. Chicago: American Library Association.

———. 2005. "Top 10 Reasons Why Regional Library Systems Are Vital in 2005—and Beyond." *Illinois Libraries* 86: 68–69.

Long, Sarah Ann. 1995. "Systems, Quo Vadis? An Examination of the History, Current Status and Future Role of Regional Library Systems." *Advances in Librarianship* 19: 118.

———. 2004. "The Story of the Light Bulb Group." *Interface* 26 (Summer).

Kifer, Ruth E., and Light, Jane F. 2010. "Shared Libraries." *Encyclopedia of Library and Information Sciences*, 3rd ed., 1:1, 4741–4746.

Mason, Marilyn Gell. 2009. "Weblunction: A Community for Library Staff." *Journal of Library Administration* 49 (October): 701–705.

Monypenny, Phillip. 1966. *The Library Functions of the States*. Chicago: American Library Association.

Nelson Associates. 1969. *Public Library Systems in the United States: A Survey of Multi-jurisdictional Systems*. Chicago: American Library Association.

North Dakota Library Association. 2006. *Dakota Gold: NDLA Celebrates 100 Years; Centennial Cookbook and History*. Bismarck, ND: North Dakota Library Association.

Public Library Association. 1967. *Minimum Standards for Public Library Systems, 1966*. Chicago: American Library Association.

———. 2011. "About PLA." American Library Association. Accessed January 18. http://www.ala.org/ala//pla/aboutpla/aboutpla1.cfm.

Sager, Donald J. 2000. "Before the Memory Fades: Public Libraries in the Twentieth Century." *Public Libraries* 39 (March/April): 73–77.

Scherlen, Allan. 2008. "Local to Global: The Importance of State-Level Journals to Library Literature." *Serials Review* 34, no. 2: 129–136.

U.S. Department of the Interior, Bureau of Education. 1876. *Public Libraries in the United States of America: Their History, Condition, and Management. Special Report*. Washington, DC: U.S. Government Printing Office. Repr., as Monograph Series, no. 4, Champaign: University of Illinois, Graduate School of Library Science.

U.S. Institute of Museum and Library Services. 2009. *A Catalyst for Change: LSTA Grants to States Program Activities and the Transformation of Library Services to the Public*. Washington, DC: Institute of Museum and Library Services.

U.S. National Advisory Commission on Libraries. 1969. *Libraries at Large: Traditions, Innovations, and the National Interest*, edited by Douglas M. Knight and E. Shepley Nourse. New York: R. R. Bowker.

Woodsworth, Anne. 1991. "Governance of Library Networks: Structures and Issues." *Advances in Librarianship* 15: 155–174.

11

Global Perspectives on Public Libraries

Barbara J. Ford

The public library, the local gateway to knowledge, provides a basic condition for lifelong learning, independent decisionmaking and cultural development of the individual and social groups.

—IFLA/UNESCO Public Library Manifesto, 1994

In 2010 the United Nations Development Programme (UNDP) published *Beyond the Midpoint: Achieving the Millennium Development Goals* as background to the General Assembly's high level review of advances toward the development goals in September 2010. The report assessed what it will take to accelerate progress toward the goals around the world. The UN Millennium Declaration of 2000 (http://www.un.org/millennium/declaration/ares552e.htm) had committed countries to do all they could to eradicate poverty, promote human dignity and equality, and achieve peace, democracy, and environmental sustainability. The goals that emanated from this declaration include the achievement of universal primary education and an increase in literacy. Librarians have discussed and written about how public libraries can assist with all the development goals (Forsyth, 2005). Additionally, 2010 marks a turning point for assessing progress toward World Summit on the Information Society (WSIS, http://www.itu.int/wsis/implementation/2010/forum/geneva/) implementation and for proposing new strategies to ensure the achievement of the WSIS goals by 2015. The global perspective provided by the UNDP and the WSIS provides context for presenting this chapter's introduction to public libraries from an international viewpoint.

History and Purpose of Public Libraries: A World View

The United Nations Educational, Scientific and Cultural Organization (UNESCO) first issued the "Public Library Manifesto" in 1949, then revised it in 1972, and again in 1994 and 1998. The manifesto was prepared in cooperation with the International Federation of Library Associations and Institutions (IFLA) and can be seen in over 20 languages on the IFLA website. The latest available "Public Library Manifesto" (UNESCO, 1994) has several sections, including mission, funding, legislation, networks, operation, management, and implementation. The manifesto proclaims "UNESCO's belief in the public library as a living force for education, culture and information, and as an essential agent for the fostering of peace and spiritual welfare through the minds of men and women." To supplement the UNESCO manifesto, many countries in all parts of the world have their own declarations, adopted by their library professional or government agencies, about the mission and purpose of public libraries.

The history of public libraries is virtually unique to each country. Each country's public libraries have developed along different lines, with varying degrees of government interest, citizen involvement, mechanisms for financial support, and structure. Changes in public libraries can occur very rapidly as the national situation changes or evolve slowly when resources are limited or there is no impetus for change. The exact number of public libraries in the world today is difficult to assess. Michael Heaney (2009) has reported on the ongoing global library statistics project under the auspices of IFLA in *Library Statistics for the Twenty-first Century World*. He places this in connection within *UNESCO Framework for Cultural Statistics (FCS)* (UNESCO, 2009). The UNESCO Libraries Portal provides an international gateway that is updated for librarians and library users (http://www.unesco-ci.org/cgi-bin/portals/libraries/).

At present there is no single list of the world's public libraries. With wide differences in distribution, financial support, and population characteristics, few general statements can possibly apply universally. However, since the middle of the nineteenth century the tax-supported, open-to-all public library has become a part of the cultural life of many nations.

Public libraries have often been created in communities around the world as part of a societal change process, to become a source of knowledge and a basis for lifelong learning. Periods of turbulence and rapid change often result in renewed focus on what the public library has to offer. The public library can become an informal classroom to ensure that groups are included in governmental processes and have equal access to knowledge and information. Today in some countries, public libraries are seen as a potential line of defense against threats to democracy and social disintegration partly caused by the digital revolution.

Adaptation to changes in technology and digital information has led to discussions of the role of the public library. Public libraries range from those that make use of the latest technology, such as those found in Singapore, to camel delivery services in Africa, and from multimedia- and Internet-based institutions to libraries building on oral traditions in countries with low literacy rates. In recent years many countries have been reviewing public libraries in light of the Internet and digitization. Equal access to information, the need to promote information literacy, and lifelong learning are key concepts for the future of public libraries. Substantial investment in infrastructure has been necessary and is essential to foster the growth of technical skills among the populations served.

Great Britain

The growth of public libraries in Great Britain is one example of how development has taken place in a pattern most like the United States. The Public Libraries Act of Great Britain, passed in 1850, provided for spending for the establishment and maintenance of a public library open to all and supported by taxes. The act was motivated by the instabilities of the time, including the Industrial Revolution, and public libraries were conceived as help for the working class, contributors to economic growth, and cultivators of democracy. New libraries did not reach significant numbers until donations from the Carnegie Corporation began in the 1880s. By the 1960s and 1970s library service became more a matter of national government concern and funds were provided to put up new buildings, expand holdings, and hire more staff. By the 1970s public libraries in the United Kingdom had moved toward larger units of service and the national government was providing some funding. In 1997 the British arts minister announced a fund to bring local public libraries to the forefront of the information technology revolution. The complexity of the role of the public library has been explored by Black (2000: 171), who exhorts librarians "to resurrect the true, radical essence of its philosophy: the enhancement and emancipation of the self within the context of progress and social justice." A 2008 literature review covered the attitudes of public library staff toward social inclusion policy and disadvantaged groups, and found that the concept of social inclusion remains at the core of current public library policy and strategy (Birdi and Wilson, 2008).

Worldwide Snapshot

Global Library and Information Science (Abdullahi, 2009) provides brief overviews of public libraries by region. The *International Dictionary of Library Histories* (Stam, 2001) provides a worldwide survey of public libraries and some important landmarks, giving a global snapshot of public library development.

In Africa the planned development of libraries was rare until after the 1920s. Subscription libraries existed in South Africa as early as 1838 and were later developed into the public library system. Libraries in Lagos, Nigeria, were founded and supported by the British Colonial Office and funded by the Carnegie Corporation. The first national public library service established by statute in sub-Saharan Africa was the Ghana Library Service in 1948. Public library development in Africa escalated in the 1960s and 1970s with local librarians trained abroad.

Public libraries in the areas encompassed by the former British Empire generally followed a similar pattern of development. Originating as institutions such as subscription libraries for the wealthy elite, libraries slowly broadened their scope to include service to all. After independence, the trend toward service to all continued. In the English-speaking Caribbean region, organized public library services were created in the nineteenth century after financial assistance from the Carnegie Corporation and British Council helped set up library services. Provision for public library development in India has been included in its five-year plans since independence from colonial rule, but public library services are available by and large only to urban residents. The Delhi Public Library in India was established as a pilot project in 1951 in cooperation with UNESCO and has become a model public library for South Asian countries. Very slow progress has been made in the development of rural libraries in India, and there is a fundamental challenge in convincing communities that information can be a vital resource for development (Vashishth, 1995).

While private libraries developed quite early in Islamic history, public libraries are a recent development in Islamic countries. New public library buildings and expanded services in countries like the United Arab Emirates are notable in recent years. In nearby Bhutan and the Maldives, public libraries are virtually nonexistent. Public library services in southeast Asia range from initial development in Thailand to a broad-based joint effort in Malaysia, where public library development is the responsibility of state, federal, and local government authorities, to the remarkable development in Singapore, where the National Library operates the public library system. In 1966 public libraries were opened in Nepal with the assistance of the Danish International Development Agency, UNESCO, and the Nepal National Library. Development of public libraries in the Pacific islands dates primarily from after World War II.

In China public libraries did not exist before their introduction through missionaries in the early 1900s. After the communist takeover, however, the government decreed in 1957 that public libraries were to be part of a system to inculcate citizens with patriotism and socialism and make them good Party members. China's Cultural Revolution in 1966 led to the closure or destruction of many public libraries. Since that time certain cities and provinces have slowly reestablished public libraries (Yitai and Gorman, 2000). The pattern was similar in the Balkan countries, where public libraries emerged in the mid-nineteenth century as part of a national emancipation movement. During the post–World War II period, the communist states supported large-scale programs to change their library systems and libraries to political propaganda tools for mass indoctrination with Marxist-Leninist ideology. Poor infrastructures and the absence of national standards and trained personnel have slowed recent attempts to automate library services in the Balkans. In Central and Eastern Europe following the communist era, various organizations (e.g., the Mellon Foundation, Soros Foundation, and the Council of Europe) poured significant funding into automation and infrastructure upgrades.

In Finland, nationalism and the quest for education established public libraries in the 1860s, followed in the 1920s by written standards enforced by library inspectors. Sweden's combination of education and religious movements facilitated the creation of public libraries, originally aimed at the lower classes. In the mid-nineteenth century reading societies in Iceland evolved into public libraries in rural parts of the country. Spain's public library movement, as defined by a 1901 ruling, has led to a service orientation toward the public. The proliferation and growth of Iberian libraries after the 1970s has been remarkable. Both Spain and Portugal have modernized their libraries with the advent of the Internet and web-based digital technology. Spain held its first national conference on public libraries in 2002, with papers and discussions illustrating the innovative programs existing in Spain's public libraries.

Essays by Bukenya (Africa), Yang (Asia), Jones et al. (Australia), Koren (Europe), Leyva (Latin America), and Alyaqou (Middle East) in *Global Library and Information Science*, published by IFLA, provide summaries in the context of globalization (Abdullahi, 2009).

IFLA and UNESCO

IFLA is the leading international body representing the interests of library and information services and their users. It is the global voice of the library and information profession, with 1,700 members from more than 150 countries. The roots of IFLA are in the International Congress of Librarians and Booklovers held at Prague in 1926. It was there that Gabriel Henriot, then president of the Association des bibliothécaires francais and professor at the American Library School in Paris, recommended the creation of a standing international library committee, to be elected by individual national organizations. The impetus was part of the international movement to promote cooperation across national frontiers that followed World War I.

One year later, in 1927, IFLA was founded in Edinburgh during the celebration of the fiftieth anniversary of the Library Association of the United Kingdom. IFLA's first constitution was approved in 1929 at the First World Congress of Librarianship and Bibliography in Rome. Wieder and Campbell (2002) tell the story of IFLA's first 50 years, primarily summarizing early development and pointing out the importance of IFLA's formal agreement with UNESCO. Founded in 1946, UNESCO assumed the goal of assisting libraries and promoting the development of documentation, library, and archival services as part of national information infrastructures. IFLA was officially recognized as the principal nongovernmental organ for UNESCO's cooperation with professional library associations in Oslo in 1947. At the same time, UNESCO promised financial support for the execution of IFLA's program.

In recent years the advent of computer and telecommunications technology that permits the international exchange of information in digital format and the governmental reform movement have brought a renewed interest in public libraries. Eradicating the digital divide has become a major topic of concern for national governments, private foundations, nongovernmental organizations, and the computer industry. A core value of IFLA is the belief that people, communities, and organizations need universal and equitable access to information, ideas, and works of imagination for their social, educational, cultural, democratic, and economic well-being.

Documents developed by IFLA, including the "IFLA Internet Manifesto" and the "Glasgow Declaration on Libraries, Information Services and Intellectual Freedom" (IFLA, 2002; Figure 11.1), illustrate the importance of these issues. IFLA was active in support of the World Summit on the Information Society in Geneva in December 2003 and in the second phase in Tunis in December 2005. The implications of the WSIS declaration of principles are discussed in "Promoting the Global Information Commons" (IFLA, 2005). IFLA developed a Success Stories Database to showcase the value of libraries to society. Advocacy has become a focus of activities for IFLA, and projects like training and guidelines for increasing the effectiveness of library associations are important.

Since the mid-1960s, the objectives of public libraries in many parts of the world have been the subject of regular review to examine whether they respond adequately to the needs of communities. With social changes there have been increased demands for citizens for improved access to information and education while advances in the production and distribution of information have increased expectations. The public library has traditionally responded to such demands and has become a focal point for the aspirations of citizens and vital to many governments. The role of public libraries in communities cannot be overlooked, as they are often the most successful focal point of local democratic life and support continuous lifelong learning.

Public Libraries Section of IFLA; IFLA Standards and Guidelines

Public libraries have important responsibilities in providing the public with access to information. The IFLA Section on Statistics and Evaluation, the UNESCO Institute for

---

Figure 11.1. Glasgow Declaration on Libraries, Information Services, and Intellectual Freedom

Meeting in Glasgow on the occasion of the 75th anniversary of its formation, the International Federation of Library Associations and Institutions (IFLA) declares that:

IFLA proclaims the fundamental right of human beings both to access and to express information without restriction.

IFLA and its worldwide membership support, defend and promote intellectual freedom as expressed in the United Nations Universal Declaration of Human Rights. This intellectual freedom encompasses the wealth of human knowledge, opinion, creative thought and intellectual activity.

IFLA asserts that a commitment to intellectual freedom is a core responsibility of the library and information profession worldwide, expressed through codes of ethics and demonstrated through practice.

IFLA affirms that:

- Libraries and information services provide access to information, ideas and works of imagination in any medium and regardless of frontiers. They serve as gateways to knowledge, thought and culture, offering essential support for independent decision-making, cultural development, research and lifelong learning by both individuals and groups.

- Libraries and information services contribute to the development and maintenance of intellectual freedom and help to safeguard democratic values and universal civil rights. Consequently, they are committed to offering their clients access to relevant resources and services without restriction and to opposing any form of censorship.

- Libraries and information services shall acquire, preserve and make available the widest variety of materials, reflecting the plurality and diversity of society. The selection and availability of library materials and services shall be governed by professional considerations and not by political, moral and religious views.

- Libraries and information services shall make materials, facilities and services equally accessible to all users. There shall be no discrimination for any reason including race, national or ethnic origin, gender or sexual preference, age, disability, religion, or political beliefs.

- Libraries and information services shall protect each user's right to privacy and confidentiality with respect to information sought or received and resources consulted, borrowed, acquired or transmitted.

IFLA therefore calls upon libraries and information services and their staff to uphold and promote the principles of intellectual freedom and to provide uninhibited access to information.

This Declaration was prepared by IFLA/FAIFE.

Approved by the Governing Board of IFLA 27 March 2002, The Hague, Netherlands.

Proclaimed by the Council of IFLA 19 August 2002, Glasgow, Scotland.

Statistics, and the International Organization for Standardization recognize that comparison of statistical results between institutions and countries will never be possible if data and data collection methods have not been defined and fixed carefully (Poll, 2009). A decade ago, UNESCO's (1998) *World Culture Report* showed that the distribution of public libraries in the world can lead to inequity and imbalance. In Finland the proportion of the population who were registered public library users from 1989 to 1994 was 47 percent, compared with 28 percent in Jamaica, 7 percent in Malaysia, and 1 percent in Zimbabwe. The number of books in public libraries per 100 people was 712 for Finland, 47 for Jamaica, 41 for Malaysia, and 10 for Zimbabwe. It appears from the statistics and literature about public libraries that there is a strong relationship between the level of development and the use of public libraries, and that development often increases public library use. As the project for new global library statistics moves forward, there should be progress in identifying the ways in which library support contributes to an improved quality of life for all people (Heaney, 2009).

The IFLA Public Libraries Section provides an international forum and network for the development and promotion of public libraries. The goals, objectives, and strategies of the section are developed within the context of the principles enshrined in the "Public Library Manifesto" and the IFLA Professional Priorities. The Public Libraries Section has over 300 members and many others look to it for professional direction and guidance. Section program goals include the following:

- Promote equal access to all.
- Raise the quality of services in public libraries by defining standards, developing guidelines, and documenting and disseminating best practices.
- Promote the importance of training and professional development for librarians.
- Defend the role of the public library in democratizing access to and using information technology.
- Promote literacy, reading development, and lifelong learning projects.
- Promote networking and cooperation between libraries and other agencies to balance the needs of users with the intellectual property rights of authors.
- Promote the role of libraries in society.

In 1973 IFLA published "Standards for Public Libraries," which was reissued with slight revisions in 1977. In 1986 this document was replaced by "Guidelines for Public Libraries." As their titles suggest, they represent two different approaches to providing practical guidance to librarians. The introduction to the 1973 standards stated that separate standards were not considered desirable, since the general objectives in all countries were the same, the modifying factor being the pace at which development could take place. The 1973 version therefore provided a range of quantitative standards, including the size of collections and administrative units, opening hours, staffing levels, and building standards. The 1986 guidelines took a different view, recognizing that when needs and resources vary so widely there can be no common standards for services. The guidelines offered not rules but advice, based on experience drawn from many different countries and useful for general application. The guidelines recognized that recommendations on desirable levels of library service, based on past experience in quite different circumstances, are bound to be unreliable and misleading.

The next approach to standards took the form of consultative meetings in Amsterdam (1998), Bangkok (1999), and Jerusalem (2000) to develop a set of guidelines for the twenty-first century framed to provide assistance to librarians in any situation to develop an effective public library service related to the requirements of their local community.

The IFLA Public Library Service Guidelines, Second Edition, was published in 2010 updating the 2001 version. The guidelines address following areas:

- The mission and purposes of the public library
- Legal and financial framework
- Meeting the needs of customers
- Collection development
- Human resources
- Management of public libraries
- The marketing of public libraries (Koontz and Cubbin, 2010)

These guidelines and standards can be relevant to any public library at some point in its development. Where public libraries cannot meet all the standards and recommendations immediately, it is hoped that they provide a target for the future.

Around the world, people are becoming aware of the key role of public libraries in providing access to information to help everyone participate in the democratic process and develop their country. Countries are slowly learning the role that information can play in solving problems and advancing national development goals. Some parts of the world still face challenges to gain access to technology that allows public libraries to be linked with networks internationally. Some countries do not have national information policies or a national information infrastructure. Public librarians are collaborating and working beyond traditional boundaries with public information networks for citizens and providing opportunities for lifelong learning. Digitization is providing sets of images to be stored and indexed and made accessible to the public. A good balance between print collections and electronic materials is needed. Networking can transform and revitalize public libraries. In many countries public libraries are working to provide access to new technologies and to make use of the IFLA/UNESCO *Guidelines for Development* (IFLA, 2001).

The IFLA document *Public Libraries and Lifelong Learning* (Häggström, 2004), describes the role of libraries as important prerequisites for an informed democratic knowledge society. "Meeting User Needs: A Checklist for Best Practices" (IFLA, 2008) provides practical guidance for public libraries in understanding their users' and potential users' needs through consultation, survey, and feedback. This objective follows from the general guidance provided in Chapter 3 of *Guidelines for Development 2008* and is a helpful tool that provides examples from around the world.

User Services, Collection Development, and Intellectual Freedom

The range of possible services offered by public libraries varies considerably, since the public library has a very broad charge and serves everyone. Most public libraries offer separate services for children and adults. Students are often the greatest users of public libraries in much of the world, as a quiet place to study or an important source of information for homework or family and personal needs.

Collections are the concrete expressions of the public library's mission; and issues relating to the preservation of intellectual freedom and guaranteeing the right to read are central to collection development. In developing countries, there may be less opportunity to develop balanced collections, since space is valuable and there are many donated books with limited resources for acquiring materials. Libraries often import expensive materials from abroad and in addition to purchase costs and shipping costs, issues related to customs and import duties may present difficulties. In some cases, collections may be largely or wholly dependent on international donations.

The Committee on Multicultural Library Services of the Swedish Library Association (1999) produced *Library at the Centre of the World: Multicultural Library Services* to illustrate the status of public libraries at the close of the twentieth century and to demonstrate the importance of the public library in multicultural integration. Topics included services to users whose first language is different from the majority, to elderly immigrants, and to minorities. Purchasing books at international book fairs and using databases and the Internet to serve multicultural populations are some of the responses suggested by the committee.

Africa has its own unique challenges, since its libraries were often founded to serve educated urban populations and not those with primarily oral traditions. However, Bukenya (in Abdullahi, 2009) sees new initiatives such as reading tents, village reading room programs, and the New Partnership for African Development as catalyzing the utilization of information within African communities. Historically the public library may not have been a notable success in Africa, because it is an imported institution that African governments have never financed at levels that allow it to be effective (Sturges and Neill, 1998). The trend of population growth gives reason to believe that a reading society, which will need library services, is in the process of emerging in Africa. Currently libraries must be stocked to meet the needs of the children and students who are the primary clientele.

Elsewhere in Africa, some rural information and cultural centers have been developed to find new ways to reach the general public with library service. Rural audio libraries have been founded to address the preservation and transmission of oral cultures in Mali, Swaziland, Zimbabwe, and Tanzania. A lending service provided out of a van or truck or by bicycle or camel may serve towns that cannot support a library building or librarian. Box book schemes to remote rural areas are a typical way of responding to needs for materials to read where a room is available and people cannot be served in any other way.

In some parts of the world, community action spontaneously created new public libraries. Senegal's tiny libraries, which can be found as part of community centers in the suburbs of Dakar, funded by local societies and donor organizations, are a case in point. Working with the Soros Foundation, Haitian communities developed community libraries around the country. In Mexico, new presidential leadership has led to the creation of a substantial number of new public libraries in the early part of the twenty-first century.

Article 19 of the Universal Declaration of Human Rights provides the basis for discussion of intellectual freedom and access to information. In 1997 IFLA created a committee focusing on the Freedom of Access to Information and Freedom of Expression (FAIFE) to speak for all libraries on their role regarding intellectual freedom. IFLA's executive board strongly endorsed FAIFE as an essential activity for the federation to support as a priority for libraries and a crucial activity for IFLA. The main task for FAIFE is to promote freedom of speech and emphasize the vital role of the library as the doorway to information and knowledge. In 2001 the first IFLA/FAIFE *World Report on Libraries and Intellectual Freedom* was published. The report and others that followed includes a short, factual summary of the situation in a number of countries, including the general situation concerning libraries, librarianship, and intellectual freedom; specific cases of challenges of censorship or other violations of intellectual freedom; the legislation of libraries and intellectual freedom; and library association positions related to intellectual freedom including professional codes of conduct or ethics.

Training programs and materials that FAIFE has developed on the Internet including access to information on HIV/AIDS through libraries and the "IFLA Manifesto on Transparency, Good Governance, and Freedom from Corruption" are useful as libraries around the world address these important issues. In 2010 the chair of FAIFE and national librarian of Finland, Kai Ekholm, announced the debut of the *FAIFE Newsletter* (http://www.ifla.org/en/publications/faife-newsletter) and a social networking plan.

Because of the important role of information in contemporary society, a new class of people who are information poor has emerged, resulting in what is often referred to as the digital divide. Many cannot buy computers and many who own them cannot use them effectively. Public libraries that have the technology and skills have a responsibility to aid and guide those who do not. By providing access, training, and the chance to experiment, public libraries can help users meet their educational needs. The importance of strong, well-funded public libraries for economic and social development in contemporary society cannot be underestimated.

In the essay "Bridging between Libraries and Information and Communication Technologies for Development," libraries and the information technology field are seen to share an interest in the use of technology to achieve their ultimate goals (Sears and Crandall, 2010). While their contexts come from very different histories and intentions, there are many areas of commonality that are worth exploring as possible collaborative efforts.

Governance and Funding

The public library is generally the responsibility of local and national authorities, supported by specific legislation and financed by national and local governments. Private funds provide important supplements in many locations. International financial support can be of benefit, but strong local government support is necessary for development of new programs and maintenance of existing services. The constraints on libraries often relate to the lack of funds and therefore lack of facilities, materials, and staff salaries. Disruptions, including political and economic conflicts, poverty, war, and disease, can erode the hard work and achievements of libraries.

In many countries, public libraries are faced with diminishing financial resources. At the same time, ways of delivering information are expanding and librarians are convinced that public libraries should provide information in print and nonprint formats. The use of electronic information often causes extra financial pressures. Funding is one of the major challenges for public libraries around the world, and public libraries are reacting in a number of ways to these changes. Recruiting volunteers to reduce personnel costs, raising costs for patrons by initiating annual charges, charging for lending some items, and different rates for different services have been among the strategies used. Promoting the public library in an effective way has become essential, and one strategy to achieve this is through cooperation with social and cultural organizations. Sponsorship of projects for public libraries by the private sector is also becoming more common.

While the UNESCO "Public Library Manifesto" (Figure 11.2) states that the public library shall in principle be free of charge, in libraries there is an ongoing discussion about payment for services. Some argue for equal and easy access to free services, and others insist that fiscal concerns and market mechanisms point to the need for charges and payment. Some libraries are introducing registration or subscription charges for public library membership. These strategies become more common with political and economic changes and reductions in funds.

Figure 11.2. UNESCO Public Library Manifesto

November 1994

Freedom, prosperity and the development of society and of individuals are fundamental human values. They will only be attained through the ability of well informed citizens to exercise their democratic rights and to play an active role in society. Constructive participation and the development of democracy depend on satisfactory education as well as on free and unlimited access to knowledge, thought, culture and information.

The public library, the local gateway to knowledge, provides a basic condition for lifelong learning, independent decision-making and cultural development of the individual and social groups.

This Manifesto proclaims UNESCO's belief in the public library as a living force for education, culture and information, and as an essential agent for the fostering of peace and spiritual welfare through the minds of men and women.

UNESCO therefore encourages national and local governments to support and actively engage in the development of public libraries.

The Public Library

The public library is the local centre of information, making all kinds of knowledge and information readily available to its users.

The services of the public library are provided on the basis of equality of access for all, regardless of age, race, sex, religion, nationality, language or social status. Specific services and materials must be provided for those users who cannot, for whatever reason, use the regular services and materials, for example linguistic minorities, people with disabilities or people in hospital or prison.

All age groups must find material relevant to their needs. Collections and services have to include all types of appropriate media and modern technologies as well as traditional materials. High quality and relevance to local needs and conditions are fundamental. Material must reflect current trends and the evolution of society, as well as the memory of human endeavour and imagination.

Collections and services should not be subject to any form of ideological, political or religious censorship, nor commercial pressures.

Missions of the Public Library

The following key missions which relate to information, literacy, education and culture should be at the core of public library services:

1. creating and strengthening reading habits in children from an early age;

2. supporting both individual and self conducted education as well as formal education at all levels;

3. providing opportunities for personal creative development;

4. stimulating the imagination and creativity of children and young people;

5. promoting awareness of cultural heritage, appreciation of the arts, scientific achievements and innovations;

6. providing access to cultural expressions of all performing arts;

7. fostering inter-cultural dialogue and favouring cultural diversity;

8. supporting the oral tradition;

9. ensuring access for citizens to all sorts of community information;

10. providing adequate information services to local enterprises, associations and interest groups;

11. facilitating the development of information and computer literacy skills;

(Continued)

Figure 11.2. UNESCO Public Library Manifesto *(Continued)*

12. supporting and participating in literacy activities and programmes for all age groups, and initiating such activities if necessary.

Funding, legislation and networks

- The public library shall in principle be free of charge. The public library is the responsibility of local and national authorities. It must be supported by specific legislation and financed by national and local governments. It has to be an essential component of any long-term strategy for culture, information provision, literacy and education.

- To ensure nationwide library coordination and cooperation, legislation and strategic plans must also define and promote a national library network based on agreed standards of service.

- The public library network must be designed in relation to national, regional, research and special libraries as well as libraries in schools, colleges and universities.

Operation and management

- A clear policy must be formulated, defining objectives, priorities and services in relation to the local community needs. The public library has to be organized effectively and professional standards of operation must be maintained.

- Cooperation with relevant partners—for example, user groups and other professionals at local, regional, national as well as international level—has to be ensured.

- Services have to be physically accessible to all members of the community. This requires well situated library buildings, good reading and study facilities, as well as relevant technologies and sufficient opening hours convenient to the users. It equally implies outreach services for those unable to visit the library.

- The library services must be adapted to the different needs of communities in rural and urban areas.

- The librarian is an active intermediary between users and resources. Professional and continuing education of the librarian is indispensable to ensure adequate services.

- Outreach and user education programmes have to be provided to help users benefit from all the resources.

Implementing the Manifesto

Decision makers at national and local levels and the library community at large, around the world, are hereby urged to implement the principles expressed in this Manifesto.

The Manifesto is prepared in cooperation with the International Federation of Library Associations and Institutions (IFLA).

A trend in local government in some parts of the world is to merge libraries into larger units of leisure, culture, or education. The head of the library service may be a librarian who also manages programs outside the library sector, or a nonlibrarian who is responsible for a range of services including libraries. Certain countries in some parts of the world, faced with diminishing governmental resources, have considered radical changes. One option is to contract out the public library service, so that it is provided by an outside company on behalf of a local or central government body. Not many jurisdictions have adopted this course, since most people think it is important that the public library is an independent and impartial institution that provides education, culture, recreation, and information to all.

Networking and resources are particularly essential today. No single library can buy everything its users need. Public libraries are increasingly used for education and personal development and as information resource centers. Economic necessity and the need to increase the effectiveness of individual libraries have spurred cooperative efforts among groups of libraries to achieve equity of access. Many new library networks are multitype and broker remote access to information. With electronic sources of information becoming key to the provision of reference and information services, networks are becoming more common and more essential.

Information about the current state of public libraries in Europe has been facilitated by the creation of the European Union and the European Commission. A green paper on the role of libraries in the information society was issued in 1997 (Thorhauge et al., 1997). Nations in northern Europe were shown to have relatively higher percentages of their population registered as borrowers from public libraries. In 2008 the European Union launched a vast online library, which offers access to millions of books, maps, recordings, photographs, archival documents, paintings, and films from its member states' national libraries and cultural institutions. The site, Europeana.eu, aims to provide new ways for people to explore Europe's heritage.

In countries such as Malaysia and Singapore, public libraries are being built on a planned basis with strong direction by the national library. The role of the public library as a cultural center is key in some countries. In Bulgaria public libraries are housed in cultural centers, and in the United Kingdom most metropolitan public libraries are administered as part of a leisure or cultural directorate. With social, technological, and telecommunications advances, one of the responses of public libraries has been to create large units of administration and to fund coordinating mechanisms. In 2001 Mexico held its first international conference on public libraries, with speakers from Germany, Canada, Spain, the United States, France, Italy, and Mexico. As libraries are expanded, Mexico has benefited from a substantial donation from the Bill and Melinda Gates Foundation (2008) to bring technology to public libraries and librarians working with government officials to enhance the technological infrastructure.

Librarians have in recent years begun to address the issue of the value of the public library, in terms of the ways in which libraries contribute to the economic development of the local community. An Australian management consultant asserts that politicians and librarians underestimate the current and potential economic value of public libraries and suggests that the benefit created is twice as much as the funds spent (Haratsis, 1995). Consultants in New Zealand developed a cost-benefit methodology for assessing the value of library output (New Zealand Library and Information Association, 1996). The role of the library in economic development can involve a wide range of activities, from encouragement of literacy to the provision of specialized business services. With financial constraints and the perceived need to provide new services while maintaining book and multimedia collections and delivering specialized services to minority groups, there are discussions about which services are basic—and therefore should be free of charge—and which might be fee based. Many libraries face stable or diminishing budgets and the need to provide new services and meet increased demands. UNESCO's 2010 global monitoring report on the Education for All initiative, *Reaching the Marginalized*, discusses the scale of deprivation. The report identifies disadvantages in education worldwide and assesses the effectiveness of national policies in combating marginalization. Literacy is an important aspect of the fight against marginalization and public libraries can be a factor.

International Library Development Initiatives

Public libraries around the world have received targeted support from philanthropic organizations, such as the Carnegie Corporation, Bertelsmann Foundation, British Council, Book Aid International, and more recently the Bill and Melinda Gates Foundation, among others. When countries have fewer resources, public libraries may be viewed as a new concept imported from the West. At the beginning of the last century, Andrew Carnegie was instrumental in spreading the influence of libraries through countries that were part of the former British Commonwealth. Carnegie provided funds for over 2,800 public library buildings, most of them in the English-speaking world. Carnegie required that the community donate space for the building and provide for the operating expenses. The Carnegie Corporation (2010) has focused on libraries in Africa and noted on its website: "In a global economy that is increasingly centered on access to knowledge and information, books continue to be a critical key to solving a nation's problems and learning remains a critical element in a nation's arsenal of strategies for survival."

Bill and Melinda Gates Foundation

The Bill and Melinda Gates Foundation International Library Initiative (http://www.gatesfoundation.org) supports libraries throughout the world to help individuals improve their lives through information and technology. The foundation has supported the Abre Tu Mundo (Open Your World) project in Chile, which has given Chilean residents no-cost access to computers and the Internet in Chile's 368 public libraries, as well as training on the use of new information technologies and the generation of local content for the Internet (Biblioredes, http://www.biblioredes.cl).

The Access to Learning Awards funded by the foundation are given annually to a public library or similar organization outside the United States that has shown a commitment to offering the public free access to information technology through an existing innovative program (Council on Library and Information Resources, http://www.clir.org/fellowships/gates/gates.html). Awards have included the following:

- Biblioteca del Congreso, Argentina—one of the few libraries in the country that provides services to the public free of charge, including a computer center that is open around the clock.
- Biblored, Colombia—a network of 19 public libraries in Bogotá that offer no-cost access to digital information in some of the city's poorest neighborhoods.
- Helsinki City Library, Finland—among the first public libraries in the world to offer Internet access to the public. It established the Information Gas Station, a portable unit providing immediate information by phone, fax, or text messages.
- Proyecto Bibliotecas (Probigua), Guatemala—libraries and technology centers in rural communities. These centers include computer training labs that teach new skills to underserved populations.
- Smart Cape Access Project of Cape Town, South Africa—innovative efforts to connect residents, particularly in low-income neighborhoods, with no-cost public access to computers and the Internet. The Access to Learning Award made it possible to install computers in all Cape Town libraries.
- Shidhulai Swanirvar Sangstha, Bangladesh—converts indigenous boats into mobile libraries that provide free computer and Internet stations and training to agricultural communities.
- Rural Education and Development (READ), Nepal—works with villages to build self-supporting libraries funded through community projects that provide free access to the Internet, books, and multimedia tools.
- Northern Territory Library, Australia—in remote underprivileged communities, a technological solution is helping preserve culture and drawing indigenous Australians into local libraries.
- Vasconcelos Program, an innovative mobile technology program, that provides computer access and training to remote, indigenous communities in Mexico's Veracruz state.

The 2010 award went to Veria Central Public Library in Veria, Greece, which realized the power of technology early on. In 1992, the library's catalog was already fully automated. In 1996, the library became the first in the nation to provide its users free access to computers and the Internet. In 1997, it was the first to have its own website.

Veria's library is small, serving the town's 50,000 residents and 130,000 more people in the surrounding areas, but its commitment to innovation and experimentation has made it a model for libraries in Greece and throughout the world. Most importantly, the mission of the Veria Library is to make a real difference in people's lives.

Open Society Institute, Soros Foundation

The Open Society Institute (OSI) is a private operating and grant-making foundation based in New York City that serves as the hub of the Soros Foundation's network, a group of autonomous foundations and organizations in more than 50 countries (http://www.soros.org). OSI and the network implement a range of initiatives that aim to promote open societies by shaping government policy and supporting education, media, public health, and human and women's rights, as well as social, legal, and economic reform. To diminish and prevent the negative consequences of globalization, OSI seeks to foster a global open society by increasing collaboration with other nongovernmental organizations, governments, and international institutions.

OSI's Library Program helped libraries transform themselves into public and service-oriented centers for their communities. The Network Library Program developed model libraries that function as civic information centers. In 1999–2000 15 model libraries were supported in eight countries of Central and Eastern Europe and Russia with support from local government. The Electronic Information for Libraries (eIFLnet, http://www.osi.hu/nlp) consortium, launched in late 1999, provides a structural solution to the digital divide in content access.

The consortium, which serves an estimated 5 million users through several thousand libraries in more than 50 countries, enables low-cost access to 5,000 social science and humanities journals and 3,000 journals in science, technology, and medicine. eIFL is now an independent foundation governed by a board elected by national consortia belonging to the network, which receives some core operating support from OSI but is increasingly supported by its membership.

The OSI Information Program (http://www.soros.org/initiatives/information) promotes the equitable deployment of knowledge and communications resources and is based on three premises. First, human beings are not passive subjects or only economic agents seeking personal gain, but civic beings who share a world, which they have the power to shape. Second, the ability to exchange ideas, knowledge, and information is the lifeblood of citizenship and participation in a shared public sphere. Third, while traditional media remain essential to citizenship, new digital technologies hold potential for enhancing civic life that is still largely untapped.

Bertelsmann Foundation

Since its inception in 1977, the Bertelsmann Foundation has conducted projects in the sphere of public libraries where they emphasize the construction and promotion of model libraries, as well as the development of future-oriented methods of library management. The Bertelsmann Foundation International Network of Public Libraries worked to pool international know-how, to strengthen the exchange of experience among public library experts, to develop concepts for modern library management, and, above all, to promote the transfer of such model solutions into practice (Poustie, 1999). With 16 experts from 10 counties, the network created a forum in which people could share information and expertise to increase the effectiveness and efficiency of libraries. The two modules are international research and preparation of model solutions on issues of modern library management and implementation of these solutions at the practical level to test their suitability for everyday use. Volume 1 of a series of case studies sponsored by the Bertelsmann Foundation International Network of Public Libraries (Windau, 1999) outlines successful solutions. The report of the Canterbury Public Library, serving the city of Christchurch, New Zealand, and the methodology used to evaluate its ability to meet the challenges of the twenty-first century provides guidelines and recommendations on how to implement change in a meaningful way (Windau, 1999). The Bertelsmann Foundation now focuses on model libraries, online continuing education programs, and library comparison to initiate change.

British Council

Since 1934, librarians in the British Council have created an international library network and have helped lay the foundations of public library systems in the developing world (Coombs, 1988). The council maintained its own libraries, administered book aid schemes, encouraged professional interchange and education, and ran courses in librarianship. In 1959 the public library development scheme emerged to sponsor public library systems more or less from scratch. The areas of most intense activity were West and East Africa. By the 1970s the council felt the need to provide integrated and more sophisticated information service. More recently, people have questioned the relevance of the British model, based partly on the fact that appropriate materials were difficult to acquire from indigenous publishers. The focus of the British Council has changed, with less support for this work today.

Mortenson Center for International Library Programs

The Mortenson Center for International Library Programs, at the University of Illinois at Urbana-Champaign, designs programs for working professionals to exchange ideas and upgrade their knowledge and skills, through experiences and internships (http://www.library.uiuc.edu/mortenson). This is achieved through a structured program of skills development, formal coursework, consultation with library and library school faculty, and literature reviews, as well as library tours and conferences. Since 1991 librarians from 90 countries have participated in the program.

Book Donation Programs

Several hundred book donation programs operate throughout the world, which function with varying degrees of success. The key is to be certain that books that are not needed, or dated materials, are not sent at a great financial cost. Book Aid International is a major donor of new and used books. They have teamed with African Books Collective to promote African titles abroad and to ease their distribution internationally within Africa.

The Canadian Organization for Development through Education, the Norwegian Agency for Development Cooperation, and other agencies have provided funding for libraries. A number of useful workshop meetings devoted to the organization of library services have occurred, heavily facilitated by IFLA's Action for Development through Libraries Programme (ALP, http://www.ifla.org/en/alp). In French-speaking Africa, a network of centers was set up to provide access to information media. The cultural center as focus for information activity is a well-established concept in francophone West Africa. Senegal is an example, wherein the Ministry of Culture provides each administrative region of the country with a major cultural center. Cultural promotion and association with a complex of other cultural activities has led to library activity.

In the end, each country and community must decide what kind of public library is needed and develop the local support to ensure its success. International programs can help, but local support and leadership are essential.

Community Outreach and Services

An international comparison of public library services and statistics at the end of the twentieth century revealed that of the wide range of services provided, books, interlibrary lending, and children's services are nearly universal (Hanratty and Sumsion, 1996). The library is for many people the reason for coming to the central city and is considered by people of many cultures to be a safe and nonthreatening environment.

Public Libraries and the Information Society, prepared for the European Commission, proposes a vision for public libraries for the twenty-first century. This report outlines the necessity of developing national policies and strategies for public libraries and the importance of continuing education for librarians (Thorhauge et al., 1997). The report discusses how the public library fulfills a variety of functions, including local cultural center, local learning center, general information center, and social center. Libraries can help all people prosper in an information society and be a key part of the educational system. Public libraries are a key component for a civil society and lifelong learning, education, and democratic process in an open society.

Similar evaluations took place in other parts of the world, including discussions of the barefoot librarian in Africa (Onwubiko, 1996). Access to knowledge and lifelong learning is vital in democracies. Unequal access to information and technology, as well as information illiteracy, may create additional social divisions, but public libraries can help, and changes in government can lead to opportunities to renew public libraries. Administrative reform can lead to changes, but most countries remain committed to financing them by public budgets.

Outreach services such as bookmobiles, providing electronic information, and cooperation with other libraries to improve services are important. Bookmobiles can expand service by reaching out to people who cannot get to a library. Those managing public libraries must find a balance between varied goals, such as using marketing techniques and providing a collection that is not based on commercial interests. The introduction of the Camel Library Service by the Kenya National Library Service is an innovative approach to delivering services to those with a nomadic lifestyle (Atuti, 1999). Rahman (2000) reports on the status of rural and small libraries in Bangladesh, describing the reality of isolation, poor telecommunications infrastructure, and neglect faced by many rural libraries around the world that sometimes serve illiterate populations.

Libraries respond to community needs in ways that are most appropriate to their setting and resources. Camel book boxes, bicycle book carts, donkey-drawn book carts, and other programs illustrate ingenious ways librarians respond to community needs and deliver services. Mali has a library in a railway car that serves ten communities along the railway line. In Zimbabwe a donkey cart is used as a means of conveyance. Pack mules have been used in South America to transport collections of books to remote communities. Bicycles can move information workers and small quantities of materials at low cost over difficult terrain.

From 2010 the ALP will be the primary vehicle for delivering the professional development strand of IFLA's Advocacy Framework through training based on policy and guidelines developed by IFLA's core activities or sections. ALP will be an important mechanism for developing plans to extend library service.

The IFLA (2009) Public Libraries Section has issued "10 Ways to Make a Public Library Work," which suggests ideas for public library development:

1. Develop public library buildings emphasizing community and cultural spaces, not just physical stores of knowledge.
2. Liberate our services using the World Wide Web 2.0 and look toward Web 3.0 and 4.0.
3. Connect with our communities and educate and train people. Librarians and information scientists can act as educators and personal knowledge advisors and not just keepers of keys or Internet gateways.
4. Develop a "worldwide wisdom"—a global knowledge and understanding—by creating international cultural pathways on the web.

5. Work internationally to erode barriers and censorship while respecting all cultures.
6. Support our staff with continued training and encouragement to be proactive.
7. Develop our digitized collections services and knowledge—the hybrid library—knowledge, education, and information in diverse forms.
8. Improve accessibility to our catalogs and databases, especially for users with visual impairments.
9. Establish national and international standards on the Internet environment.
10. Public libraries as cultural storehouses—the live environment alongside the recorded one—archives, museums, libraries and culture combined: a "comby library."

Telecommunication infrastructures vary widely among nations. Donations of computer information systems are increasingly common, but internal funds may not be available for ongoing maintenance and upgrades. Digital and Internet-based projects provide new opportunities for public libraries. In countries without a strong public library tradition, it is difficult to show relevance and need for the Internet and technology. The Internet democratizes information and empowers users, and public libraries can be gateways to information and assist people in learning how to use these resources.

Library cooperation is a major means for providing services today, and libraries throughout the world have become more connected to each other through systems and networks, making it easier to share resources. Systems, networks, and databases make it possible to search for information in other libraries. As the local gateway to information, the public library has to meet the information needs of a community by using not only their collection, but also those of others. The changing financial situation for public libraries and rapidly changing technology mean that skilled leadership and staff are essential.

The world's public librarians learned lessons at the 2010 World Summit on the Information Society with its focus on broadband, social networking, and information and communication technologies for disaster management. Of special significance are future developments and funding recognizing the importance of broadband networks in facilitating progress toward achieving the Millennium Development Goals.

Economic, Social, and Cultural Rights as the Future of World Librarianship

Public librarianship follows a variety of models in different parts of the world, including technology centers, cultural centers, and study centers, among others. The

UNESCO Libraries Portal provides access to over 200 library sites around the world for comparative analysis. As society continues to undergo ideological, political, cultural, social, economic, and technological changes, public libraries must develop policies and strategies that demonstrate their relevance. Libraries are perceived to be at a crossroads in their history. People wonder whether they will have a central place in the electronic society or remain on the margins, and whether they will be able to attract the funds to provide the varied resources and programs needed by the public. Issues of censorship and the wide range of materials available on the Internet, copyright and intellectual property rights, and providing services free at the point of delivery are key for future public library services. Public libraries play an essential role in providing and organizing electronic materials for use and in helping and training users to use digital resources. Users demand that libraries provide not only the software and hardware needed, but also the professional support to help independent learners use resources. Through participation in the ALA International Relations Round Table (http://www.ala.org/irrt) or attendance at IFLA, U.S. librarians can work to be part of world librarianship.

The global library community has many challenges and opportunities ahead, including the right to education as outlined in the International Covenant on Economic, Social and Cultural Rights. The aims and objectives of education have moved toward a growing consensus in international human rights law that education should enable the individual to freely develop her or her own personality and dignity, to participate in a free society, and to respect human rights (Kalantry, Getgen, and Koh, 2010: 262). These goals can be supported by public libraries and the librarians who staff them to provide equal and open access to information for all.

References

Abdullahi, Ismael. 2009. *Global Library and Information Science*. Munich: K. G. Saur.

Atuti, Richard M. 1999. "Camel Library Service to Nomadic Pastoralists: The Kenyan Scenario." *IFLA Journal* 25: 152–158.

Bill and Melinda Gates Foundation. 2008. "Mobile Classrooms Reach Rural Mexico." http://www.gatesfoundation.org/atla/Pages/2008-vasconcelos-program. aspx.

Birdi, Briony, and Kerry Wilson. 2008. "The Public Library, Exclusion and Empathy: A Literature Review." *Library Review* 57, no. 8: 576–592.

Black, Alistair. 2000. *The Public Library in Britain, 1914–2000*. London: British Library.

Carnegie Corporation. 2010. "Higher Education and Libraries in Africa." http://carnegie.org/programs/higher-education-and-libraries-in-africa/.

Coombs, Douglas. 1988. *Spreading the Word: The Library Work of the British Council*. London: Mansell.

Forsyth, Ellen. 2005. "Public Libraries and the Millennium Development Goals." *IFLA Journal* 31, no. 4: 315–323.

Häggström, Britt Marie. 2004. *The Role of Libraries in Lifelong Learning: Final Report of the IFLA Project under the Section for Public Libraries.* International Federation of Library Associations. http://archive.ifla.org/VII/s8/proj/Lifelong-LearningReport.pdf.

Hanratty, Catherine, and John Sumsion. 1996. *International Comparison of Public Library Statistics.* Loughborough, UK: Loughborough University, Library and Information Statistics Unit.

Haratsis, Brian. 1995. "Justifying the Economic Value of Public Libraries in a Turbulent Local Government Environment." *Australasian Public Libraries and Information Services* 8: 164–172.

Heaney, Michael. 2009. *Library Statistics for the Twenty-first Century World: Proceedings of the Conference Held in Montrèal on 18–19 August 2008 Reporting on the Global Library Statistics Project.* Munich: K. G. Saur.

International Federation of Library Associations and Institutions. 2001. *The Public Library Service: IFLA/UNESCO Guidelines for Development.* Munich: K. G. Saur.

———. 2002. "Glasgow Declaration." http://www.ifla.org/en/publications/the-glasgow-declaration-on-libraries-information-services-and-intellectual-freedom.

———. 2005. "Promoting the Global Information Commons: A Statement by IFLA to WSIS Tunis PrepCom2." http://archive.ifla.org/III/wsis/wsis-24Feb05.html.

———. 2008. "Meeting User Needs: A Checklist for Best Practices." http://archive.ifla .org/VII/s8/proj/Mtg_UN-Checklist.pdf.

———. 2009. "10 Ways to Make a Public Library Work." http://www.ifla.org/en/publications /10-ways-to-make-a-public-library-work-update-your-libraries.

International Federation of Library Associations and Institutions and Freedom of Access to Information and Freedom of Expression. 2001. *Libraries and Intellectual Freedom: IFLA/ FAIFE World Report: Denmark.* Denmark: IFLA/FAIFE Office.

Kalantry, Sital, Jocelyn E. Getgen, and Steven Arrigg Koh. 2010. "Enhancing Enforcement of Economic, Social, and Cultural Rights Using Indicators: A Focus on the Right to Education in the ICESCR." *Human Rights Quarterly* 32 (May): 253–310.

Koontz, Christie, and Barbara Gubbin. 2010. *IFLA Public Library Service Guidelines.* Berlin: De Gruyter/Saur.

New Zealand Library and Information Association. 1996. *Valuing the Economic Costs and Benefits of Libraries: A Study Prepared for the N Strategy.* Wellington: New Zealand Library and Information Association.

Onwubiko, Chidi P. C. 1996. "The Practice of Amadi's Barefoot Librarianship in African Public Libraries." *Library Review* 45: 39–47.

Poll, Roswitha. 2009. "Standardisation of Library Statistics." In *Library Statistics for the Twenty-First Century World: Proceedings of the Conference Held in Montrèal on 18–19 August 2008 Reporting on the Global Library Statistics Project,* edited by Michael Heaney, 27–30. Munichen: K. G. Saur.

Poustie, Kay. 1999. "The Bertelsmann International Network of Public Libraries: A Model of Public Library Cooperation on an International Scale." *Asian Libraries* 8, no. 11: 422–430.

Rahman, Faizur. 2000. "Status of Rural and Small Libraries in Bangladesh: Directions for the Future." *Rural Libraries* 20: 52–64.

Sears, Rebecca, and Michael Crandall. 2010. "Bridging between Libraries and Information and Communication Technologies for Development." *IFLA Journal* 36 (March): 70–73.

Stam, David H., ed. 2001. *International Dictionary of Library Histories*. Chicago: Fitzroy Dearborn.

Sturges, Paul, and Richard Neill. 1998. *The Quiet Struggle: Information and Libraries for the People of Africa*. 2nd ed. London: Mansell.

Swedish Library Association. 1999. *Library at the Centre of the World: Multicultural Library Services*. Lund, Sweden: Committee on Multicultural Library Services of the Swedish Library Association.

Thorhauge, J., C. Larsen, H.-P. Thun, and H. Albrechtsen. 1997. *Public Libraries and the Information Society*. Luxembourg: European Commission.

UNESCO. 1994. "The IFLA/UNESCO Public Library Manifesto." http://www.ifla.org/en/publications/iflaunesco-public-library-manifesto-1994.

———. 1998. *World Culture Report 1998: Culture, Creativity and Markets*. France: UNESCO.

———. 2009. *The 2009 UNESCO Framework for Cultural Statistics (FCS)*. Montreal. http://www.uis.unesco.org/template/pdf/cscl/framework/FCS_2009_EN.pdf.

———. 2010. *Education for All Global Monitoring Report—2010. Reaching the Marginalized*. New York: Oxford University Press.

United Nations Development Programme. 2010. *Beyond the Midpoint: Achieving the Millennium Development Goals*. New York: United Nations. http://content.undp.org/go/cms service/stream/asset/?asset_id=2223855.

Vashishth, C. P., ed. 1995. *Libraries as Rural Community Resource Centres: Papers and Proceedings of the Workshop on Rural Community Resource Centres*. Delhi: B. R. Publishing.

Wieder, Joachim, and Harry Campbell. 2002. "IFLA's First Fifty Years." *IFLA Journal* 28: 107–117.

Windau, Bettina, ed. 1999. *International Network of Public Libraries*. 6 vols. Lanham, MD: Scarecrow Press.

Yitai, Gong, and G. E. Gorman. 2000. *Libraries and Information Services in China*. Lanham, MD: Scarecrow Press.

12

The Future of Public Libraries in the Twenty-First Century: Human Rights and Human Capabilities

Kathleen de la Peña McCook and Katharine J. Phenix

Where, after all, do universal human rights begin? In small places, close to home—so close and so small that they cannot be seen on any maps of the world. Yet they are the world of the individual person; the neighborhood he lives in; the school or college he attends; the factory, farm, or office where he works. Such are the places where every man, woman, and child seeks equal justice, equal opportunity, equal dignity without discrimination. Unless these rights have meaning there, they have little meaning anywhere. Without concerted citizen action to uphold them close to home, we shall look in vain for progress in the larger world.

—Eleanor Roosevelt, remarks at the United Nations, March 27, 1953

We believe that the Universal Declaration of Human Rights (United Nations, 1948) will be the lodestar that guides public library service in the twenty-first century. Changing technologies will, of course, drive many aspects of the future of public librarianship, but as Buschman (2009: 287) has pointed out, librarianship must question and critique technologies and the larger socioeconomic technical structures in which they are embedded.

In the twenty-first century, U.S. public librarians will increasingly forge service models and use language that reflects human rights values as the work of the field evolves. For the public librarian, the human capabilities approach, which helps people to function in a variety of areas, provides a road map to extending service in the framework of human rights. Notable among these capabilities and of particular importance to the practice of public librarianship in the twenty-first century is Martha

Nussbaum's (2007: 23) characterization of the "development and expression of senses, imagination, and thought":

> Being able to use the senses, to imagine, think, and to reason—and to do these things in a "truly human" way, a way informed and cultivated by an adequate education, including, but by no means limited to, literacy and basic mathematical and scientific training. Being able to use imagination and thought in connection with experiencing and producing works and events of one's own choice, religious, literary, musical, and so forth. Being able to use one's mind in ways protected by guarantees of freedom of expression with respect to both political and artistic speech, and freedom of religious exercise.

We present highlights of U.S. public library philosophy that lead us to a human rights perspective. From this perspective we take a human capabilities approach that values the development of each person. Discourse about public library services among library workers since the establishment of the public library as a public good in the mid-nineteenth century has evolved along the lines of general progressive thought. This discourse has been framed in a fashion that primarily, and as would be expected, reflects U.S. experience.

Even after the United Nations' adoption of the Universal Declaration of Human Rights in 1948, U.S. public librarianship has largely refrained from describing services using the more universal language of human rights (United Nations, 1948). The reasons for this have much to do with political decisions made outside of librarianship that nevertheless have affected the way U.S. librarians describe and activate services. Thus, while we assert that U.S. public libraries do provide services that embody human rights, we also recognize that the connections for frontline public librarians in the United States to the larger global discourse presented in Chapter 11 have yet to be made clearly. In an increasingly global society this will change.

The work of U.S. librarians has evolved in a manner that incorporates human rights values and precepts without having generally used the language that characterizes the philosophical and ethical goals of human rights and human development. Samek (2005) points this out in her reflections on twenty-first-century information work in support of librarianship's responsibilities for the attainment of human rights in the context of the knowledge society.

The American Library Association (ALA) has long been on record as supporting first- and second-generation human rights since the Library Bill of Rights was adopted on June 18, 1948, six months before the Universal Declaration of Human Rights was signed. One example of long-standing librarian commitment to the modes of service that could be characterized as third-generation human rights (sometimes also known as solidarity rights) is the establishment of the ALA Office for Library Service to the Disadvantaged in 1970 (McCook, 2002).[1] Thus, we assert that human rights have been a long-standing value of U.S. librarians, though not generally recognized in the literature of the field as written by U.S. practitioners (Edwards and Edwards, 2010).

We identify the instruments that provide the foundation for human rights and demonstrate the ways in which U.S. public librarians can begin to describe the work we have been doing in language that enables us to claim our place among nations. We describe the international attention paid to these issues in declarations and statements on social, economic, and cultural rights to help us visualize the structure that upholds our work as librarians bound to support, acknowledge, and inform these rights.[2] We discuss three areas that intersect with the social and cultural aspects of public library service as illuminated by integration of human rights concepts:

1. Access to knowledge is fundamental to human development. The basis of librarians' commitment to human rights and human development as grounded in the Universal Declaration of Human Rights and the Millennium Development Goals.
2. The public library is a living force for culture. Instruments that provide the foundation for librarians' role as primary promoters of the rights detailed in the Universal Declaration of Human Rights and additional international statements and declarations on peoples, regions, situations, and specific rights.
3. Public library service responses in the United States as reflective of the International Federation of Library Associations (IFLA) multicultural library manifesto. The 18 public library service responses used by the Public Library Association (PLA) are presented as a point of activation in the United States informed by a human rights philosophy. These are compared with the IFLA/UNESCO Multicultural Library Manifesto.

It is our intention that by presenting U.S. public library practice in comparison to the goals and guidelines of IFLA that going forward U.S. public librarians will have the context and documentation as reflected by the Universal Declaration of Human Rights for the development of expanded commitment in the service of human capabilities (Comim, Qizilbash, and Alkire, 2008).

Access to Knowledge Is Fundamental to Human Development

Article 19. Everyone has the right to freedom of opinion and expression; this right includes freedom to hold opinions without interference and to seek, receive and impart information and ideas through any media and regardless of frontiers.

—Universal Declaration of Human Rights (United Nations, 1948)

Access to knowledge is fundamental to human development, yet this has not been a generally accepted precept. Worldwide universal literacy, a Millennium Development Goal, is still yet to be achieved. In this section we make the connections between international initiatives on human rights and public library policy in the United States. We believe that the work librarians do in public libraries every day is in service of human rights and that by tracing these connections we provide librarians of the twenty-first century with a summary of policies and documents that give social and historical context.

A brief summary of librarians' connection to human rights is included in the ALA "International Relations Policy Statement" adopted by ALA Council on June 29, 1978:

> The association's involvement since 1936 in the area of human rights and since 1940 with intellectual freedom, as reflected in the Library Bill of Rights, has given the association a maturing sensitivity over the years regarding the importance of human rights. This concept is now expressed in the Universal Declaration of Human Rights adopted and proclaimed by the General Assembly of the United Nations. The association affirms its stance that threats to the freedom of expression of any persons become threats to the freedom of all. (ALA, Governance Office, 2010: 5)

The "International Relations Policy Statement" continues with a list of charges and objectives, one of which is "recognizing and demonstrating support for human rights and intellectual freedom around the world." Public librarians have many supporting materials in our repertoire as we endeavor to promote the principles of human rights in practice. Commitment to the right to expression had been codified in Section 53, "Intellectual Freedom," of the American Library Association *Policy Manual* as 53.1, "The Library Bill of Rights" (ALA, Governance Office, 2010). The *Policy Manual* is a useful source of collected deliberations as duly discussed and voted upon by the ALA's governance body.

These sentiments are further supported by the ALA *Policy Manual* Section 58, "International Relations." Policy objectives cited include encouragement of the exchange, dissemination, and access to information and the unrestricted flow of library materials in all formats throughout the world, and the promotion and support of human rights and intellectual freedom worldwide (ALA, Governance Office, 2010). The association voted and approved the language of the Universal Declaration of Human Rights, Article 19, with the adoption of Policy 58.4 and 58.4.1 in 1991 [Council Document #24].

58.4 Article 19 of the United Nations' Universal Declaration of Human Rights

Everyone has the right to freedom of opinion and expression; this right includes freedom to hold opinions without interference and to seek, receive and impart information and ideas through any media regardless of frontiers.

58.4.1 Human Rights and Freedom of Expression

The ALA shall work with other associations and institutions that belong to IFLA to develop positions and programmatic plans of action in support of human rights and freedom of expression. The president or the member officially representing the Association at IFLA conferences shall be directed to support and carry them out; and, in the absence of such specific direction, the president or the member officially representing the Association at IFLA conferences is empowered to vote on new IFLA resolutions related to human rights and freedom. Their votes shall be guided by ALA's adoption of Article 19 of the Universal Declaration of Human Rights and the good of the Association. (ALA, Governance Office, 2010)

The "Resolution on IFLA, Human Rights, and Freedom of Expression" was passed by ALA Council on July 2, 1997. It highlighted Universal Declaration Article 19 and ALA's endorsement of it. It states, quite simply: "Librarians worldwide made a commitment to promote and defend human rights in relation to information access in 1997 when the International Federation of Library Associations (IFLA) voted to establish the Committee on Free Access to Information and Freedom of Expression (FAIFE)" (ALA, 1997; Byrne, 2007; Falconer, 2007).

The ALA has taken stands on Article 19 incorporating support in its policy manual. It is from the departure point of Article 19 that the way opens to integrate other human rights instruments that can be used to expand library services, especially in cultural contexts.

U.S. librarians have addressed the Universal Declaration of Human Rights via Article 19, which seems to align best with the values of library workers, but Article 19 is simply the first codification that leads to a far more expansive recognition of the connections of the declaration to library services. The Universal Declaration of Human Rights is actually a part of the International Bill of Human Rights (United Nations, High Commissioner for Human Rights [UN-HCHR], 1996), which also contains the International Covenant on Economic, Social, and Cultural Rights (UN-HCHR, 1966a) and the International Covenant on Civil and Political Rights (UN-HCHR, 1966b).

These documents share the same roots, but after the declaration was drafted, the other covenants were considered separately, addressing the two types of rights. As Amnesty International (2005) notes:

> On one side the achievement of economic, social and cultural rights (an adequate standard of living, education, health care, and income protection) was presented as requiring a political commitment to socialism. On the other, civil and political rights (the right to vote, free expression, and legal representation) were portrayed as a luxury that could only be afforded once a certain level of economic development had been achieved.

Moving from the realm of human rights scholarship to a broad U.S. audience, Dr. Martin Luther King Jr. (1967: 2–3) spoke to the Southern Christian Leadership Conference: "I think it is necessary to realize that we have moved from the era of Civil Rights to the era of human rights. When you deal with human rights you are not dealing with something clearly defined in the Constitution. They are rights that are clearly defined by the mandates of a humanitarian concern." To understand King's meaning, we need to review the growing body of conventions and other instruments that were enacted after World War II as a realization of human rights in full.

Some of the major human rights instruments created through the UN and archived at the website of the Office of the United Nations High Commissioner for Human Rights include:

- Convention on the Prevention and Punishment of the Crime of Genocide (UN-HCHR, 1951)
- The Convention on the Elimination of All Forms of Racial Discrimination (UN-HCHR, 1965)
- The Convention on the Elimination of Discrimination against Women (UN-HCHR, 1979)
- The Convention against Torture and Other Cruel, Inhuman or Degrading Treatment or Punishment (UN-HCHR, 1984)
- The Convention on the Rights of the Child (UN-HCHR, 1989)
- The International Convention on the Protection of Migrant Workers and Their Families (UN-HCHR, 1990)

Many of these rights are acknowledged and protected by laws in the United States, but others are not present in American legal jurisprudence, although economic, social, and cultural rights are now recognized as enforceable in the courts (justifiable) under both national and international law. As noted most passionately in *Something Inside So Strong: A Resource Guide on Human Rights in the United States:*

> Human rights conceive of civil, political, economic, social and cultural
> rights as interdependent, transcending the current U.S. rights framework
> that often pits disadvantaged groups against one another. Applying a hu-
> man rights framework puts the power of rights back into the hands of the
> people who possess those rights, whether or not they are recognized in do-
> mestic law. (Cho et al., 2003)

The philosophical aspects of human rights have been made part of the public sphere by various conferences and programs of UNESCO. Since the United States left UNESCO in 1983 and did not rejoin until 2004, the discussion of human rights and their interpretations in this country has been interrupted, which has stunted similar discussions and interpretations in libraries. U.S. citizens have not been kept informed of the interrelatedness of the second and third generations of rights, which have become more prominent since the late 1980s, and U.S. librarians have not used this rich legacy to describe expanding concepts of service.

Another United Nations initiative that bears review since 1990 is the Human Development Approach, intended to enlarge people's choices and enhance human capabilities (United Nations Development Programme [UNDP], 2010). This framing is of interest to librarians because it incorporates the idea that access to knowledge is fundamental to human development. The series of reports issued by the Human Development Programme beginning in 1990 provides a well-documented history of new models for human growth. Among the issues and themes of the human development movement, besides social progress, economic growth, equity in economics, and so forth, is the concept of participation and freedom, including cultural liberty, particularly for marginalized groups defined by urban-rural, sex, age, religion, ethnicity, physical and mental parameters, and so on. As librarians serve the underserved, especially in outreach situations, we contribute to the erasure of margins and celebrate cultural diversity and differences by being accessible and available.

UNESCO's Universal Declaration on Cultural Diversity, adopted November 2001, stated, "Cultural rights are an integral part of human rights, which are universal, indivisible, and independent," Much of the literature connects them, for example: "The [right] to identity entails minority rights (ICCPR 27), freedom in arts and sciences (ICESR 15) and freedoms of thought, religion and opinion (ICCPR 18, 19)" (Kunnemann, 1995, p. 225). Using this connectivity argument, Weeramantry (1997: 253) concluded that "if there is in reality human rights at any level it must necessarily follow that access to the information appropriate to the exercise of that right becomes a right in itself." And as the UNESCO Declaration on Cultural Diversity continues in Article 6:

> While ensuring the free flow of ideas by word and image care should be exercised that all cultures can express themselves and make themselves known. Freedom of expression, media pluralism, multilingualism, equal access to art and to scientific and technological knowledge, including in digital form, and the possibility for all cultures to have access to the means of expression and dissemination are the guarantees of cultural diversity.

The UNESCO Convention on the Protection and Promotion of the Diversity of Cultural Expressions was adopted in 2005. It celebrated the importance of cultural diversity for the full realization of human rights and fundamental freedoms proclaimed in the Universal Declaration of Human Rights and other universally recognized instruments. A guiding principle is that cultural diversity can be protected and promoted only if human rights and fundamental freedoms, such as freedom of expression, information, and communication, as well as the ability of individuals to choose cultural expressions, are guaranteed.

In his essay, "The Declaration of Human Rights in Postmodernity," Jose A. Lindgren Alves (2000) explored the milestone status of the Vienna Declaration for the formalization of the Universal Declaration of Human Rights.[3] He observed that "the acceptance of multiculturalism in place of rational, universalistic humanism is, in fact, if not the 'foundation,' at least the keynote of all brands of postmodern thinking." The publication of *Human Rights and Human Development* by the United Nations Development Programme in 2000 marked a possible convergence of the two approaches—human rights and development:

> Human rights and human development share a common vision and a common purpose—to secure, for every human being, freedom, well-being and dignity. Divided by the Cold War, the rights agenda and development agenda followed parallel tracks. Now converging, their distinct strategies and traditions can bring new strength to the struggle for human freedom. The Human Development Report 2000 looks at human rights as an intrinsic part of development—and at development as a means to realizing human rights. It shows how human rights bring principles of accountability and social justice to the process of human development.

In 2000 a Millennium Summit was held to discuss the role of the United Nations in the new millennium. The United Nations Millennium Declaration that resulted included reaffirmation of the Universal Declaration of Human Rights and establishment of eight Millennium Development Goals for 2015. The principles of the Public Library Manifesto were placed in a public library context by Ellen Forsythe (2005), who wrote that library staffs have expertise to contribute to the global initiative of the Millennium

Development Goals, in partnership with other groups of workers and thinkers. She noted that libraries are integral to community development and provide access to information and works of imagination in a variety of formats and languages contributing to social inclusion. The development goals:

1. eradicate extreme poverty and hunger;
2. achieve universal primary education;
3. promote gender equality and empower women;
4. reduce child mortality;
5. improve maternal health;
6. combat HIV/AIDS, malaria, and other diseases;
7. ensure environmental sustainability; and
8. develop a global partnership for development (United Nations, 2010).

The Millennium Development Goals continue to provide the road map for reducing poverty and hunger, saving children and mothers from premature death, providing sustainable and decent livelihoods, and preserving the environment for future generations. Meeting that commitment not only is a moral imperative, but reflects a mutual interest to live in a stable and prosperous world (UNDP, 2010). Access to knowledge, facilitated by public librarians, is fundamental to human development. Public librarians will review the results of the September 2010 Summit and the Millennium Development Goals to strengthen commitment to universal human rights

The Public Library Is a Living Force for Culture

> This Manifesto proclaims UNESCO's belief in the public library as a living force for education, culture and information, and as an essential agent for the fostering of peace and spiritual welfare through the minds of men and women.
>
> —Public Library Manifesto (UNESCO, 1994)

In the twenty-first century, frontline U.S. public librarians will be engaged with issues of the preservation of culture and memory. We present various aspects of human rights as cultural rights, and point out some of the statements and policies on these issues that inform U.S. public library services.

In "The Right to Take Part in Cultural Life," Stephen Hansen (2006) provides a point of departure to examine the implications of these rights in the context of the U.S. public library in the twenty-first century. His descriptions of rights relating to culture concern creativity, including the visual arts, literature, music, dance, and theater. In Western society, the cultural rights inferred relate to the commercial access to these achievements. Individuals are free to participate, subject, of course, to economic constraints. A symphony, a ballet, a show at the local art museum, or a visiting performer, any one of which might be appealing to us, are all examples of cultural appreciation in a commercial context. This is expressed in the second part of the Universal Declaration, Article 27: "Everyone has the right to the protection of the moral and material interests resulting from any scientific, literary or artistic production of which he is the author" (United Nations, 1948).

In "Where Social Justice Meets Librarianship," Sergio Chaparro-Univazo (2007) suggests, "The increasing wave of privatization, commercialization, global market fundamentalism and how they impact copyright practices on the part of corporate information forces and international bodies make necessary to bring on elements of human rights to the discussion in order to protect, preserve, and guarantee the survival of cultural heritage for those that genuinely own it." The library response to the Google book digitization effort in the form of the Open Book Alliance, founded by librarians, is a good example of this. In a July 2009 letter to the U.S. Department of Justice, librarians wrote, "In the absence of competition for the services it will enable, the settlement could compromise fundamental library values such as equity of access to information, patron privacy, and intellectual freedom" (Open Book Alliance, 2009).

Another approach is rights to a culture, which focuses on the conservation and preservation of culture, as well as the right to have access and participate in it. It is within this context that UNESCO's "Recommendation on the Participation by the People at Large in Cultural Life and Their Contribution to It" states that culture means "opportunities available to everyone, in particular, through the creation of the appropriate socio-economic conditions, for freely obtaining information, training, knowledge and understanding, and for enjoying cultural values and cultural property" (Hansen, 2006: 227; UNESCO, 1976). "Everyone has the right freely to participate in the cultural life of the community, to enjoy the arts and to share in scientific advancement and its benefits" (United Nations, 1948L Article 27, Sec. 1).

What is the stance of policymakers and governing bodies of libraries today in relation to cultural rights? Certainly the work done to ensure access to a culture, by ensuring the civil rights of groups, is visible in the historical effort to pressure libraries to integrate since 1956 when ALA held its first integrated conference in Miami or later in 1961 when the Library Bill of Rights was amended to say, "the rights of an individual to the use of a library should not be denied or abridged because of his race, religion, national origins, or political views" (ALA, 1996). By contrast, today African American collections are held at public libraries and many cultural organizations are dedicated to preserving black history (Davis, 2008).

Further, "access to a culture" is documented in the *ALA Policy Manual*, which is a useful source of codified deliberations. By working to eliminate barriers such as language, library workers in the United States have proactively declared inclusiveness by including all populations in the library's community. The people's right "freely to participate in the cultural life of the community, to enjoy the arts and to share in scientific advancement and its benefits" means access to library services in their most basic form (ALA, Governance Office, 2010).

The *Policy Manual* provides detail regarding proactive policies and reactive rights of library users. For instance, in the Services and Responsibilities of Libraries, subsection 52.4.3, "Immigrants' Rights of Free Public Library Access," the ALA recognizes that there are barriers to use (in this case, proof of ID for library usage and the bureaucratic barrier this may represent to the foreign born). In 2005, REFORMA, the National Association to Promote Library and Information Services to Latinos and the Spanish-Speaking, and the ALA Council passed a resolution against the REAL I.D. Act as a violation of human rights and resolved to inform and educate public libraries and member constituents on ways a patron can demonstrate library eligibility and continue to protect patron privacy by encouraging the use of free public library services for all immigrant populations.[4]

Public libraries in the United States have a long history of service to the foreign born. Federal outreach to immigrants through public libraries dates back before the World War I era (Burke, 2008; Jones, 1999). Materials in languages other than English, bilingual and bicultural staff members, literacy instruction, and English as a second language courses are some of the more common strategies.

This inclusiveness is further demonstrated in the *ALA Policy Manual* in Section 53, Intellectual Freedom, the Library Bill of Rights, followed by interpretations that specifically mention groups, including free access to minors (53.1.4), children and young adults to nonprint materials (53.1.13), and all persons regardless of sex, gender identity, or sexual orientation (53.1.15). Additionally, Section 54.3.2 provides for library services for people with disabilities. This policy is monitored by the association's Accessibility Assembly, which works to advance coordination and cooperation of efforts within ALA and the profession to meet the challenges of providing access to all. The Association of Specialized and Cooperative Library Agencies (2010) provides standards and guidelines for access to library services to the disabled and imprisoned.

Section 60, on diversity, is specifically directed to promoting library services to groups (rights relating to culture) and responsiveness to cultural imperatives (rights to a culture):

> The American Library Association (ALA) promotes equal access to information for all persons and recognizes the ongoing need to increase awareness of and responsiveness to the diversity of the communities we serve. ALA recognizes the critical need for access to library and information resources, services, and technologies by all people, especially those who may experience language or literacy-related barriers; economic distress;

cultural or social isolation; physical or attitudinal barriers; racism; discrimination on the basis of appearance, ethnicity, immigrant status, religious background, sexual orientation, gender identity, gender expression; or barriers to equal education, employment, and housing.

Libraries can and should play a crucial role in empowering diverse populations for full participation in a democratic society. In order to accomplish this, however, libraries must utilize multivariate resources and strategies. In the library workforce, concrete programs of recruitment, training, development, advancement and promotion are needed in order to increase and retain diverse library personnel who are reflective of the society we serve. Within the American Library Association and in the services and operations of libraries, efforts to include diversity in programs, activities, services, professional literature, products and continuing education must be ongoing and encouraged. (ALA, Governance Office, 2010)

In ALA's Core Values of Librarianship, diversity is mentioned along with access, confidentiality/privacy, and democracy. The diversity statement refers to "Libraries: An American Value" (Policy 53.8, adopted February 3, 1999), noting that "we value our nation's diversity and strive to reflect that diversity by providing a full spectrum of resources and services to the communities we serve." Diversity is also the first on the list of Key Action Areas, as approved by ALA Council in January 2006. Finally, in "ALA Ahead to 2010," cultural heritage is listed as a goal area to increase ALA's influence in promoting the preservation of our cultural heritage (ALA, 2008a).

Public librarians have been looking out for the cultural rights of their communities for many years. This is hard wired into the way we think about our service. This point is nicely and obliquely made by Thomas Clay Templeton (2008: 195) as he thinks about the library as place, either physically or virtually:

Place reminds us to tailor our professional work to the shifting concerns, and indeed the shifting criteria, of our shifting constituencies, rather than to a placeless professional vision of what librarianship, society, and literacy should be. The places of libraries in the lives of people are places we evolve together; otherwise the library is a site of domination or a hopeless utopian dream, literally "no place."

U.S. Public Library Service Responses as a Human Rights Typology Reflecting the IFLA Multicultural Library Manifesto

In this section we look at the PLA service response model (Nelson, 2008) and demonstrate where it parallels the IFLA Multicultural Library Manifesto. By comparing these two policy documents with the Universal Declaration of Human Rights, we begin to see a convergence of universal ideals. Public libraries in the United States have accepted the charge to provide services not just to individuals but to the demands of culturally or economically distinct groups of people, as shown in the terminology associated with planning and the future of twenty-firstcentury public libraries.

The practice of public librarianship in the twenty-first-century United States, as conceived by those involved in the development of the PLA New Planning for Results model, is about managing change (Nelson, 2008). *Strategic Planning for Results* identified 18 service responses that were selected by public librarians through several years of meetings and interactive discussion. These 18 service responses will guide the practice of public librarianship in the United States for the next decade. They provide a typology that we find is responsive to the Universal Declaration of Human Rights.

The IFLA Multicultural Library Manifesto states: "As libraries serve diverse interests and communities, they function as learning, cultural, and information centres. In addressing cultural and linguistic diversity, library services are driven by their commitment to the principles of fundamental freedoms and equity of access to information and knowledge for all, in the respect of cultural identity and values" (IFLA, 2008). Examining parallels between the IFLA Multicultural Library Manifesto and the PLA service response model provides the foundation for a human rights perspective.

In Figure 12.1 (pp. 352–353) we use the *Strategic Planning for Results* model (Nelson, 2008. 149–217) and include brief examples of public library liaisons, programs, and presentations aligned with the 18 service responses. We also include points from the IFLA Multicultural Library Manifesto (in bold), which identify key missions of information, literacy, education, and culture.

From the PLA service responses and the principles stated in the IFLA Multicultural Library Manifesto, we begin to see the way public librarianship faces the twenty-first century. Service responses such as promoting active civic participation, celebrating diversity, fostering community awareness, promoting informed decision making, and advancing service to immigrant populations have strong parallels with the Multicultural Library Manifesto.

Libraries of all types should reflect, support, and promote cultural and linguistic diversity at the international, national, and local levels, and thus work for cross-cultural dialogue and active citizenship. The ALA has an active commitment to these ideals, demonstrated by work on a statement, "Librarianship and Traditional Cultural Expression," which highlights the ways librarians can better manage cultural expression in their own collections and share expertise with cultures that choose to self-manage (ALA, Office for Information Technology Policy, 2010).

Figure 12.1. Comparison of PLA 18 Services Responses with IFLA Multicultural Library Manifesto, 2008

Service Response (Nelson, 2008)	Multicultural Guidelines (IFLA, 2008)
Be an Informed Citizen: Tax forms, e-government, civic engagement strategies; AARP tax advice; League of Women Voters.	Governments and other relevant decision-making bodies are encouraged to establish and adequately fund libraries and library systems to offer free library and information services to culturally diverse communities.
Build Successful Enterprises: Economic gardening, business reference services, supporting non-profits, public librarians embedded with local businesses.	
Celebrate Diversity: El día de los niños/El día de los libros; One Nation, Many Voices; Cultural competence; multicultural bibliographies; non-book collections of music, art. Black History Month; Coretta Scott King awards; resources at the Library of Congress and ALA.	Promote awareness of the positive value of cultural diversity and foster cultural dialogue; encourage linguistic diversity and respect for the mother tongue; safeguard linguistic and cultural heritage and give support to expression, creation, and dissemination in all relevant languages.
Connect to the Online World: Library computer centers; computer classes; job hunting online; library blogs, websites, social networking.	Encourage information literacy in the digital age, and the mastering of information and communication technologies; promote linguistic diversity in cyberspace; encourage universal access to cyberspace.
Create Young Readers: Storytime, literacy skills; puppet shows; book kits; services to daycare centers; Coretta Scott King Award.	
Discover Your Roots: Local history digitization; American Memory; genealogy classes; oral history; local exhibits; collaboration with DAR, historical societies; Ancestry.com databases.	Support the preservation of oral tradition and intangible cultural heritage.
Express Creativity: Poetry, art centers; teen video projects; dance; music at the library; concerts, plays; e-zines; shared book reviews; writer's workshops.	
Get Facts Fast: Virtual, chat reference; instant messaging; 211 services; website links; ready-reference collections.	
Know Your Community: Hurricane facts; social capital; civic engagement; participation in community task forces; development of a community information database.	Support inclusion and participation of persons and groups from all diverse cultural backgrounds.
Learn to Read and Write: Literacy and outreach; service to ex-offenders; family learning; recruiting, training, and hosting literacy tutors; after-school programs.	Provide referrals facilitating the harmonious coexistence of several languages, including learning of several languages from an early age.

(Continued)

Figure 12.1 *(Continued)*	
Make Career Choices: Job-hunting services; career advice; job fairs; résumé services; test preparation programs, materials; referrals.	
Make Informed Decisions: Health partnerships; investment workshops; parenting classes.	Support the exchange of knowledge and best practices with regard to cultural pluralism.
Satisfy Curiosity: Lifelong Learning: Elderhostel partnerships; active minds; senior center outreach; Let's Talk About It programs.	
Stimulate Imagination: Reading, Viewing, Listening for Pleasure: The Big Read; One Book, One Community; summer reading programs; readers' advisory, specifically multicultural readers' advisory; downloadable audio, video; author visits; book clubs; gaming tournaments.	
Succeed in School: After-school programs; school/library partnerships; community service opportunities; study rooms; library tours for classrooms; home schooling.	
Understand How to Find, Evaluate, and Use Information: National Forum on Information Literacy; research classes; consumer classes; reference services and interviews; classes on new technologies.	Encourage information literacy in the digital age, and the mastering of information and communication technologies.
Visit a Comfortable Place: Library as 3rd place; teen centers; fireplaces; drop-in centers; meeting rooms; seating groups; cafés; galleries; exhibit space; virtual social networking space.	
Welcome to the United States: Services to immigrants; citizenship and language classes; service to non-English speakers.	Special attention should be paid to groups that are often marginalized in culturally diverse societies: minorities, asylum seekers and refugees, residents with a temporary residence permit, migrant workers, and indigenous communities.

Libraries and Human Rights: The Future

In the 2010 Brookings Institution study *The State of Metropolitan America: On the Front Lines of Demographic Transformation,* the socioeconomic context for library service can be characterized in the face of five new realities: (1) growth and outward expansion of metropolitan America, (2) population diversification, (3) aging of the population, (4) uneven higher educational attainment, and (5) income polarization. These new realities are also reflected in the world at large.

The connection between human rights instruments and the configuration of current planning for U.S. public library service is becoming clearer every year. In the twenty-first century there will be a more universal way of thinking about public library service. For instance, the UNESCO/IFLA Public Library Manifesto proclaims "UNESCO's belief in the public library as a living force for education, culture and information, and as an essential agent for the fostering of peace and spiritual welfare through the minds of men and women" (UNESCO, 1994).

The ideals manifested in the knowledge and information sectors that include libraries are central to the World Summit on the Information Society (WSIS) initiative. The WSIS was established in response to the ever-widening gulf between knowledge and ignorance. Additionally, the WSIS responded to the development gap between the rich and the poor among and within countries. The WSIS has sought to bridge this digital divide and place the Millennium Development Goals on the communications technology-accelerated speedway to achievement (UNESCO, http://www.itu.int/wsis/basic/why.html).

The Tunis Commitment of the WSIS incorporated development and human rights to make the Millennium Development Goals a reality, and upheld the Universal Declaration of Human Rights (Berry, 2006; WSIS, 2005). Most pertinent to this discussion on the future of public libraries was affirmation of commitment to support, libraries, among other things:

> supporting educational, scientific, and cultural institutions, including libraries, archives and museums, in their role of developing, providing equitable, open and affordable access to, and preserving diverse and varied content, including in digital form, to support informal and formal education, research and innovation; and in particular supporting libraries in their public service role of providing free and equitable access to information and of improving ICT literacy and community connectivity, particularly in underserved communities. (WSIS, 2005)

In the monograph *Human Rights in the Global Information Society*, Adama Samassékou (2006: vii) has underscored that the development of the information society must be based on the framework of human rights. The barriers to doing this, even in the comparatively wealthy United States, are many. The Public Library Funding and Technology Access Study reports technological challenges in the United States including the need for equipment upgrades and broadband connectivity. The ability of public libraries to serve as community-based public Internet access points is an aspect of policy that the WSIS facilitates on a global scale (Mandel et al., 2010). WSIS stresses the human dimension of the information society; puts education, knowledge, information, and communication at the core of human progress, endeavor, and well-being; and seeks to create information-literate societies. The WSIS will facilitate a large participatory process toward inclusive, free, and open knowledge societies

(UNESCO, 2009). For placement of the human rights movement in a global perspective, Samuel Moyn's (2010) monograph *The Last Utopia* provides rich bibliographic documentation.

At this writing, the 2009 Millennium Development Goal report was released by the United Nations. Concern was expressed that global economic crises were slowing achievement of the goals (United Nations, 2009). However, we have shown that public librarians in the twenty-first century will be organizing their work from a viewpoint that holds a worldview with a human rights perspective. This has been explored in depth in Samek's (2007) book, *Librarianship and Human Rights*. Public librarians in the United States will work passionately on behalf of human capabilities in the twenty-first century (McCook & Phenix, 2008).

In *Public Libraries Services for the Poor* (Holt and Holt, 2010), the authors note that in the United States the library has great potential for helping the poor and disenfranchised. Librarians can do more for poor people. In a simple but lucid conclusion, they cite the St. Louis Public Library's mission of purposeful transformation and "organizing library services to improve individual, family and community life" (p. 149). A vision for expansive service to all is also true for all nations in the world. By keeping in mind the Millennium Development Goals in service of a human capabilities approach, the path will be clear to achieving universal human rights with the support and commitment of public librarians. This work, which is our heritage, is also the future of our work as public librarians.

Notes

1. The Office for Library Service to the Disadvantaged changed its name to the Office for Library Outreach Services in 1980, and then became the Office for Literacy and Outreach Services in 1995.

2. We recognize that the public library is an evolving institution. We recognize that the manifestation of public librarianship differs from nation to nation. We speak only about that which we know—the U.S. public library. See our essay "Public Librarianship" (McCook and Phenix, 2010).

3. On June 25, 1993, after the end of the cold war, representatives of 171 states adopted by consensus the Vienna Declaration and Programme of Action at the World Conference on Human Rights (United Nations, 1993). Ibrahim Fall, the secretary general of the conference, stated that the Vienna Declaration provided the international community with a new "framework of planning, dialogue and cooperation" that would enable a holistic approach to promoting human rights and involve actors at all levels—international, national, and local (UN-HCHR, 1995). The conference also included the examination of the link between development, democracy, and economic, social, cultural, civil, and political rights. It took historic new steps to promote and protect the rights of women, children, and indigenous peoples by creation of a new mechanism, a Special Rapporteur on Violence against Women, calling for the universal ratifi-

cation of the Convention on the Rights of the Child by 1995, and recommending the proclamation by the General Assembly of an international decade of the world's indigenous peoples. The Vienna Declaration (UN-HCHR, 1995) also made recommendations for strengthening the monitoring capacity of the United Nations system and called for the establishment of a High Commissioner for Human Rights by the General Assembly, which created the post on December 20, 1993. The Vienna + 5 Review (five years on) underscored the need to focus on development and democracy, noting that "respect for all human rights and fundamental freedoms, including the right to development, transparent and accountable governance and administration in all sectors of society, as well as effective participation by civil society, are essential parts of the necessary foundations for the realization of social- and people-centered sustainable development" (United Nations, Economic and Social Council, 1998). Of special interest is Section XI, which "affirmed that education on human rights and the dissemination of proper information, both theoretical and practical, play an important role in the promotion and respect of human rights with regard to all individuals without distinction of any kind, such as race, sex, language or religion, and this should be integrated in the education policies at the national as well as international levels." The Vienna + 5 Review includes among its conclusions: "In order to be fully respected and observed, human rights must be understood, promoted and implemented by the international community also from the perspectives of development, peace and security."

4. See the resolution passed by REFORMA's executive board, June 26, 2005, and then by the ALA Council: "Resolution in Support of Immigrants' Rights to Free Public Library Access," ALA Council Document #65, June 29, 2005.

> Resolution in Support of Immigrants' Rights to Free Public Library Access
> WHEREAS, The American Library Association is on record as opposing the REAL I. D. Act; and
> WHEREAS, this act will require all persons to present a standardized, state-issued ID, creating in effect a de facto national "identity card"; and
> WHEREAS, this card requires secure, machine readable identity information to be included on every state issued drivers' license or personal identification card, linking personal information such as social security numbers; and
> WHEREAS, the requirement of a state-issued driver's license or personal identification card denies many immigrants including children and young adult members of the family, free public access to books and reading materials necessary for their education and self-development; and
> WHEREAS, every state will be forced to comply with the uniform standards set by the Real ID Act by 2008 at the states' expense, forcing states to incur the costs, thus taking needed public dollars normally allocated for libraries and other public services; and
> WHEREAS, the use of this form of identification denies basic, fundamental, human rights to immigrants, in violation of the Universal Declaration of Human Rights, established under the vision and leadership of Eleanor Roosevelt; and
> WHEREAS, the use of the REAL ID violates the International Bill of Rights treaties including the International Covenant on Civil and Political Rights (ICCPR) as well as the

International Covenant on Economic, Social and Cultural Rights (ICESCR), two treaties commonly referred to as the "International Bill of Rights"; and therefore be it RESOLVED, that the American Library Association work with REFORMA and other affiliates to develop a public information strategy to inform and educate public libraries and member constituents about alternate forms of identification that will allow free public access to library services for ALL immigrant populations. (http://www.reforma .org/realIDres.htm)

References

American Library Association. 1996. *Intellectual Freedom Manual*. http://www.ala.org/ala/ aboutala/offices/oif/iftoolkits/ifmanual/intellectual.cfm.

————. 1997. "Resolution on IFLA, Human Rights, and Freedom of Expression." http://www .ftrf.org/ala/aboutala/offices/iro/awardsactivities/resolutionifla.cfm.

————. 2008a. *ALAhead to 2010: Strategic Plan*. http://www.ala.org/ala/aboutala/ missionhistory/plan/planningarchive/2010/index.cfm#Appendix.

————. 2008b. *How to Serve the World @ Your Library*. http://www.ala.org/ala/aboutala/ offices/olos/toolkits/nonenglishspeakers.cfm.

American Library Association, Governance Office. 2010. *ALA Policy Manual*. http://www.ala .org/ala/aboutala/governance/policymanual/index.cfm.

American Library Association, Office for Information Technology Policy. 2010. "Librarianship and Traditional Cultural Expressions: Nurturing Understanding and Respect." http://wo .ala.org/tce/.

Amnesty International. 2005. *Human Rights for Human Dignity: A Primer on Economic, Social and Cultural Rights*. London: Amnesty International Publications. http://www.amnesty .org/en/library/info/POL34/009/2005/en.

Association of Specialized and Cooperative Library Agencies. 2010. "Our Organization." http://www.ala.org/ala/mgrps/divs/ascla/asclaourassoc/ourassociation.cfm.

Berry, John W. 2006. "The World Summit on the Information Society (WSIS): A Global Challenge in the New Millennium." *Libri* 56: 1–15.

Brookings Institution. 2010. *State of Metropolitan America: On the Front Lines of Demographic Transformation*. Washington, DC: Brookings Institution.

Burke, Susan K. 2008. "Use of Public Libraries by Immigrants." *Reference and User Services Quarterly* 48 (Winter): 164–174.

Buschman, John E. 2009. "Just How Critical Should Librarianship Be of Technology?" In *Information Technology in Librarianship: New Critical Approaches*, edited by Gloria J. Leckie and John Buschman, 281–288. Westport, CT: Libraries Unlimited.

Byrne, Alex. 2007. *The Politics of Promoting Freedom of Information and Expression in International Librarianship: The IFLA/FAIFE Project*. Lanham, MD: Scarecrow Press.

Chaparro-Univazo, Sergio. 2007. "Where Social Justice Meets Librarianship." *Information for Social Change* 25 (Summer): 33–38. http://libr.org/isc/toc.html.

Cho, Eunice, Lisa A. Crooms, Heidi Dorow, Andy Huff, Ethel Long Scott, and Dorothy Q. Thomas. 2003. *Something Inside So Strong: A Resource Guide on Human Rights in the*

United States. Human Rights Network. http://www.ushrnetwork.org/files/ushrn/images/linkfiles/Something_Inside_So_Strong.pdf.

Comim, F., M. Qizilbash, and S. Alkire. 2008. *The Capability Approach: Concepts, Measures and Applications*. London: Cambridge University Press.

Davis, Karla Y. 2008. "African American Cultural Collections and Museums Archiving and Preserving Black History." *College and Research Libraries* 69 (December):695–698.

Edwards, Julie Biando, and Stephan P. Edwards. 2010. *Beyond Article 19: Libraries and Social and Cultural Rights*. Duluth, MN: Library Juice Press.

Falconer, Cobi. 2007. "You've Got to Have FAIFE." *Library Hi Tech News* 9/10: 22–25.

Forsythe, Ellen. 2005. "Public Libraries and the Millennium Development Goals." *IFLA Journal* 31: 315–323).

Hansen, Stephen A. 2006. "The Right to Take Part in Cultural Life." In *Human Rights in the World Community*, 3rd ed., edited by Richard Pierre Claude and Burns H. Weston, 223–232. Philadelphia: University of Pennsylvania Press.

Holt, Leslie Edmonds, and Glen E. Holt. 2010. *Public Library Services for the Poor: Doing All We Can*. Chicago: American Library Association.

International Federation of Library Associations and Institutions. 2008. "IFLA/UNESCO Multicultural Library Manifesto." http://www.ifla.org/en/publications/iflaunesco-multicultural-library-manifesto.

Jones, Plummer Alston. 1999. *Libraries, Immigrants, and the American Experience*. Westport, CT: Greenwood Press.

King, Martin Luther, Jr. 1967. *To Chart Our Course for the Future*. Atlanta: King Library and Archives, King Center.

Kunnemann, Rolf. 1995. "A Coherent Approach to Human Rights." *Human Rights Quarterly* 17, no. 2: 223–342.

Lindgren Alves, Jose A. 2000. "The Declaration of Human Rights in Postmodernity." *Human Rights Quarterly* 22: 478–500.

Mandel, Lauren H., Bradley Wade Bishop, Charles R. McClure, John Carlo Bertot, and Paul T. Jaeger. 2010. "Broadband for Public Libraries: Importance, Issues, and Research Needs." *Government Information Quarterly* 27: 280–291.

McCook, Kathleen de la Peña. 2002. *Rocks in the Whirlpool: Equity of Access and the American Library Association*. ERIC ED462981. Chicago: American Library Association. http://www.ala.org/ala/aboutala/missionhistory/keyactionareas/equityaction/rockswhirlpool.cfm.

McCook, Kathleen de la Peña, and Katharine J. Phenix. 2008. "Human Rights, Democracy and Librarians." In *The Portable MLIS*, edited by Ken Haycock and Brooke Sheldon, 22–34. Westport, CT: Libraries Unlimited.

———. 2010. "Public Librarianship." In *Encyclopedia of Library and Information Sciences*. 3rd ed. London: Taylor and Francis.

Moyn, Samuel. 2010. *The Last Utopia: Human Rights in History*. Cambridge, MA: Harvard University Press.

Nelson, Sandra. 2008. *Strategic Planning for Results*. Chicago: Public Library Association.

Nussbaum, Martha. 2007. "Human Rights and Human Capabilities." *Harvard Human Rights Journal* 20: 21–24.

Open Book Alliance. 2009. "Librarians' Concerns Linger." http://www.openbookalliance
.org/2009/12/librarians-concerns-linger/.

Samassékou, Adama. 2006. "The Promise of Information and Communication Societies." In
Human Rights in the Global Information Society, edited by Rikke Frank Jorgenesen, vii.
Cambridge, MA: MIT Press.

Samek, Toni. 2005. "Ethical Reflection on 21st Century Information Work: An Address for
Teachers and Librarians." *Progressive Librarian* 25: 43–61.

———. 2007. *Librarianship and Human Rights: A Twenty-first Century Guide*. Oxford:
Chandos.

Templeton, Thomas Clay. 2008. "Placing the Library: An Argument for the Phenomenological
and Constructivist Approach to the Human Geography of the Library." *Library Quarterly*
78, no. 2: 195–209.

UNESCO. 1976. "Recommendation on the Participation by the People at Large in Cultural Life
and Their Contribution to It." http://portal.unesco.org/en/ev.php-URL_ID=13097&URL_
DO=DO_TOPIC&URL_SECTION=201.html.

———. 1994. "Public Library Manifesto." http://www.ifla.org/en/publications/iflaunesco-
public-library-manifesto-1994.

———. 2001. *Universal Declaration on Cultural Diversity*. http://www2.ohchr.org/English/
law/diversity.htm.

———. 2005. *Convention on the Protection and Promotion of the Diversity of Cultural Expressions*. http://portal.unesco.org/en/cv.php-URL_ID=31038&URL_DO=DO_TOPIC&URL
_SECTION=201.html

———. 2009. "Fostering Information and Communication for Development: UNESCO's Follow-Up to the World Summit on the Information Society." http://unesdoc.unesco.org/
images/0018/001849/184921e.pdf.

United Nations. 1948. "Universal Declaration of Human Rights." http://www.un.org/en/
documents/udhr/.

———. 1993. "Vienna Declaration and Programme of Action." World Conference on Human
Rights.   http://www.unhchr.ch/huridocda/huridoca.nsf/(Symbol)/A.CONF.157.23.En?
OpenDocument.

———. 2009. *The Millennium Development Goals Report 2009*. New York: UN. http://www.un
.org/millenniumgoals/pdf/MDG_Report_2009_ENG.pdf.

———. 2010. "Millennium Development Goals." http://www.un.org/millenniumgoals/.

United Nations Development Programme. 2000. *Human Development Report 2000: Human
Rights and Human Development*. http://hdr.undp.org/en/reports/global/hdr2000/.

———. 2010. *What Will It Take to Achieve the Millennium Development Goals? An International Assessment*. New York: UNDP. http://content.undp.org/go/cms-service/stream/asset/
?asset_id=2620072.

United Nations, Economic and Social Council. 1998. "Follow-Up to the World Conference on
Human   Rights."   http://www.unhchr.ch/huridocda/huridoca.nsf/(Symbol)/E.CN.4.1998
.104*.En?OpenDocument.

United Nations, High Commissioner for Human Rights. 1951. "Convention on the Prevention and Punishment of the Crime of Genocide." http://www2.ohchr.org/english/law/genocide .htm.

———. 1965. "International Convention on the Elimination of All Forms of Racial Discrimination." http://www2.ohchr.org/english/law/cerd.htm.

———. 1966a. "International Covenant on Economic, Social, and Cultural Rights." http://www2.ohchr.org/english/law/pdf/cescr.pdf.

———. 1966b. "International Covenant on Civil and Political Rights." http://www2.ohchr .org/english/law/pdf/ccpr.pdf.

———. 1979. "Convention on the Elimination of All Forms of Discrimination against Women." http://www2.ohchr.org/english/law/cedaw.htm.

———. 1984. "Convention against Torture and Other Cruel, Inhuman, or Degrading Treatment or Punishment." http://www2.ohchr.org/english/law/cat.htm.

———. 1989. "Convention on the Rights of the Child." http://www2.ohchr.org/english/law/ crc.htm.

———. 1990. "International Convention on the Protection of the Rights of All Migrant Workers and Members of Their Families." http://www2.ohchr.org/english/law/cmw.htm.

———. 1995. *World Conference on Human Rights: 14–25 June 1993, Vienna, Austria.* http://www.ohchr.org/EN/AboutUs/Pages/ViennaWC.aspx.

———. 1996. International Bill of Human Rights. http://www.ohchr.org/Documents/Publications/ FactSheet2Rev.1en.pdf.

Weeramantry, C. G. 1997. *Justice without Frontiers: Furthering Human Rights.* The Hague: Kluwer.

World Summit on the Information Society. 2005. "Tunis Commitment." http://www.itu.int/ wsis/docs2/tunis/off/7.html.

Appendix A
Selected Readings

Links verified in autumn 2010.

1. The Landscape of Public Libraries in the Twenty-First Century

General

American Library Association. 2010. *Intellectual Freedom Manual*. 8th ed. Chicago: American Library Association.

American Library Association. "State of America's Libraries, 2010." http://www.ala.org/ala/newspresscenter/mediapresscenter/americaslibraries/index.cfm.

Amigos. http://www.amigos.org.

BCR (Bibliographical Center for Research). http://www.bcr.org.

Berry, John N. 2001. "A Model for the Public Sector." *Library Journal* 126 (March 1): 6.

Christensen, Karen, and David Levinson. 2007. *The Libraries We Love*. Great Barrington, MA: Berkshire.

Dawson, Alma, and Kathleen de la Peña McCook. 2006. "Rebuilding Community in Louisiana after the Hurricanes of 2005." *Reference and User Services Quarterly* 45 (Summer): 292–296.

Donelan, Molly, and Liz Miller. 2010. "Public Libraries Daring to Be Different." *Public Management Magazine* 92 (September).

Garceau, Oliver. 1949. *The Public Library in the Political Process: A Report of the Public Library Inquiry*. New York: Columbia University Press.

Henderson, E., K. Miller, T. Craig, S. Dorinski, M. Freeman, N. Isaac, J. Keng, L. McKenzie, P. O'Shea, C. Ramsey, and C. Sheckells. 2009. *Public Libraries Survey: Fiscal Year 2007*. Washington, DC: Institute of Museum and Library Services. http://harvester.census.gov/imls/pubs/pls/pub_detail.asp?id=122#.

Joeckel, Carleton Bruns. 1935. *The Government of the American Public Library*. Chicago: University of Chicago Press.

Lyrasis. http://www.lyrasis.org.

McClure, Charles, et al. 2009. "Hurricane Preparedness and Response for Florida Public Libraries." *Florida Libraries* 52 (Spring): 4–7.

Pacific Northwest Library Association (PNLA). http://www.pnla.org.

Public Agenda. 2006. *Long Overdue: A Fresh Look at Public and Leadership Attitudes about Libraries in the 21st Century*. ERIC. ED 493642. http://www.eric.ed.gov.

Public Library Association. http://www.ala.org/ala/mgrps/divs/pla/index.cfm.

Senville, Wayne. 2009. "Libraries at the Heart of Our Communities." *Planning Commissioners Journal* 75 (Summer): 12–18.

Shera, Jesse H. 1949. *Foundations of the Public Library: The Origins of the Public Library Movement in New England, 1629–1855*. Chicago: University of Chicago Press. Repr. Hamden, CT: Shoestring Press, 1965.

Southeastern Library Association (SELA). http://selaonline.org.

U.S. Department of the Interior, Bureau of Education. 1876. *Public Libraries in the United States of America: Their History, Condition, and Management. Special Report*. Washington, DC: U.S. Government Printing Office. Repr., as Monograph Series, no. 4, Champaign: University of Illinois, Graduate School of Library Science.

U.S. Institute of Museum and Library Services. 2008. *State Library Agency Survey: Fiscal Year, 2007*. Washington, DC: U.S. Institute of Museum and Library Services. http://harvester.census.gov/imls/pubs/Publications/StLA2007.pdf.

———. 2009. *Public Libraries Survey: Fiscal Year 2007*. Washington, DC: U.S. Institute of Museum and Library Services. http://harvester.census.gov/imls/pubs/pub_detail.asp?id= 122#.

Tribal Community Libraries

American Indian Library Association. http://www.ailanet.org.

American Indian Library Association. 1976. *American Indian Libraries Newsletter*.

American Library Association. Committee on Rural, Native and Tribal Libraries of All Kinds. http://www.ala.org/ala/mgrps/committees/ala/ala-ruralcom.cfm.

Grounds, Richard A., et al. 2003. *Native Voices: American Indian Identity and Resistance*. Lawrence: University Press of Kansas.

Hills, Gordon H. 1997. *Native Libraries: Cross-Cultural Conditions in the Circumpolar Countries*. Lanham, MD: Scarecrow Press.

Huhndorf, Shari M. 2009. *Mapping the Americas: The Transnational Politics of Contemporary Native Culture*. Ithaca: Cornell University Press.

International Indigenous Librarians Forum. http://www.trw.org.nz/iilf2009_about.php.

Patterson, Lotsee. 2000. "History and Status of Native Americans in Librarianship." *Library Trends* 49, no. 1 (Summer): 182–193.

———. 2001. "History and Development of Libraries on American Indian Reservations." In *International Indigenous Librarians' Forum Proceedings*, edited by Robert Sullivan, 38–44. Auckland, New Zealand: Te Ropu Whakahau.

Roy, Loriene. "If I Can Read, I Can Do Anything." School of Information, University of Texas at Austin. http://www.ischool.utexas.edu/~ifican.

———. 2000. "To Support and Model Native American Library Services." *Texas Library Journal* 76 (Spring): 32–35.

Roy, Loriene, and A. Arro Smith. 2002. "Supporting, Documenting and Preserving Tribal Cultural Lifeways: Library Services for Tribal Communities in the United States." *World Libraries* 12 (Spring): 28–31.

Roy, Loriene, et al. 2010. *Tribal Libraries, Archives and Museums: Preserving Our Language, Memory and Lifeways*. Lanham, MD: Scarecrow Press.

U.S. Institute of Museum and Library Services. Native American Library Services. http://www .imls.gov/applicants/grants/nativeservices.shtm.

U.S. National Commission on Libraries and Information Science. 1992. *Pathways to Excellence: A Report on Improving Library and Information Services for Native American Peoples*. Washington, DC: National Commission on Libraries and Information Science.

2. Brahmins, Bequests, and Determined Women: The Beginnings to 1918

Books and Chapters in Books

American Library Association. 1963. *Access to Public Libraries*. Chicago: American Library Association.

Amory, Hugh, and David D. Hall, eds. 2000. *A History of the Book in America*. Vol. 1 of *The Colonial Book in the Atlantic World*. New York: Cambridge University Press.

Anderson, Douglas. 2003. *William Bradford's Books: Of Plimmoth Plantation and the Printed Word*. Baltimore, MD: Johns Hopkins University Press.

Augst, Thomas, and Kenneth Carpenter. 2007. *Institutions of Reading: The Social Life of Libraries in the United States*. Amherst: University of Massachusetts Press.

Basbanes, Nicholas A. 1995. *A Fine Madness: Bibliophiles, Bibliomanes, and the Eternal Passion for Books*. New York: Henry Holt.

Battles, David M. 2009. *The History of Public Library Access for African Americans in the South or Leaving Behind the Plow*. Latham, MD: Scarecrow Press.

Bixby, A. F., and A. Howell. 1876. *Historical Sketches of the Ladies' Library Associations of the State of Michigan, 1876*. Adrian, MI: Times and Expositor Steam Print. Repr. in *The Status of Women in Librarianship, 1876–1976*, Kathleen Weibel, Kathleen Heim (de la Peña McCook), and Dianne J. Ellsworth, 3–4. Phoenix, AZ: Oryx Press, 1979.

Boston Public Library. 1852. *Report of the Trustees of the Public Library to the City of Boston*. Reproduced in Jesse H. Shera, *Foundations of the Public Library: The Origins of the Public Library Movement in New England, 1629–1855*. Chicago: University of Chicago Press, 1949. Repr., Hamden, CT: Shoestring Press, 1965, 267–290.

Boylan, Anne M. 1988. *Sunday School: The Formation of an American Institution, 1790–1880*. New Haven, CT: Yale University Press.

Brown, Richard D. 1989. *Knowledge Is Power: The Diffusion of Information in Early America, 1700–1865*. New York: Oxford University Press.

Casper, Scott E., Joanne D. Chaison, and Jeffrey D. Groves, eds. 2002. *Perspectives on American Book History: Artifacts and Commentary*. Amherst: University of Massachusetts Press.

Cazden, Robert E. 1978. "Libraries in the German-American Community and the Rise of the Public Library Movement." In *Milestones to the Present: Papers from Library History Seminar V*, 93–211. Syracuse, NY: Gaylord Professional Publications.

Cornelius, Janet Duitsman. 1991. *When I Can Read My Title Clear: Literacy, Slavery and Religion in the Antebellum South*. Columbia: University of South Carolina Press.

Dain, Phyllis P. 1972. *The New York Public Library: A History of Its Founding and Early Years*. New York: New York Public Library.

Davis, Donald G., Jr. 2002. *Winsor, Dewey, and Putnam: The Boston Experience*. Champaign: University of Illinois, Graduate School of Library and Information Science.

Davis, Donald G., Jr., and John Mark Tucker. 1989. *American Library History: A Comprehensive Guide to the Literature*. Santa Barbara, CA: ABC-CLIO.

Ditzion, Sidney H. 1947. *Arsenals of a Democratic Culture: A Social History of the American Public Library Movement in New England and the Middle States from 1850–1900*. Chicago: American Library Association.

Du Mont, Rosemary Ruhig. 1977. *Reform and Reaction: The Big City Public Library in American Life*. Westport, CT: Greenwood Press.

Edwards, Edward. 1859. *Memoirs of Libraries, Including a Handbook of Library Economy*. London: Trubner.

————. 1869. *Free Town Libraries, Their Function, Management, and History in Britain, France, Germany, and America*. London: Trubner.

Elliott, J. H. 2006. *Empires of the Atlantic World: Britain and Spain in America 1492–1830*. New Haven: Yale University Press.

Freeman, Robert S. 2003. "Harper & Brothers' Family and School District Libraries, 1830–1846." In *Libraries to the People: Histories of Outreach*, edited by Robert S. Freeman and David M. Hovde. Jefferson, NC: McFarland.

Freeman, Robert S., and David M. Hovde, eds. 2003. *Libraries to the People: Histories of Outreach*. Jefferson, NC: McFarland.

Garrison, Dee. 1979. *Apostles of Culture: The Public Librarian and American Society, 1876–1920*. New York: Free Press.

Gilmore, William J. 1989. *Reading Becomes a Necessity: Material and Cultural Life in Rural New England, 1780–1835*. Knoxville: University of Tennessee Press.

Gleason, Eliza Atkins. 1941. *The Southern Negro and the Public Library: A Study of Government and Administration of Public Library Service to Negroes in the South*. Chicago: University of Chicago Press.

Goetsch, Lori A., and Sarah B. Watstein. 1993. *On Account of Sex: An Annotated Bibliography on the History of Women in Librarianship, 1987–1992*. Metuchen, NJ: Scarecrow Press.

Graham, Patterson Toby. 2002. *A Right to Read: Segregation and Civil Rights in Alabama's Public Libraries, 1900–1965*. Tuscaloosa: University of Alabama Press.

Grotzinger, Laurel Ann, James Vinson Carmichael, and Mary Niles Maack. 1994. *Women's Work: Vision and Change in Librarianship*. Champaign: University of Illinois, Graduate School of Library and Information Science.

Hall, David D. 1989. *Worlds of Wonder, Days of Judgment: Popular Religious Belief in Early New England*. New York: Alfred A. Knopf.

Harris, Michael H. 1975. *Role of the Public Library in American Life: A Speculative Essay*. Occasional Paper No. 117. Champaign: University of Illinois, Graduate School of Library and Information Science.

————. 1995. *History of Libraries in the Western World*. 4th ed. Lanham, MD: Scarecrow Press.

Hayes, Kevin J. 1996. *A Colonial Woman's Bookshelf*. Knoxville: University of Tennessee Press.

Hildenbrand, Suzanne, ed. 1996. *Reclaiming the American Library Past: Writing the Women In*. Norwood, NJ: Ablex.

Hoyt, Dolores J. 1999. *A Strong Mind in a Strong Body: Libraries in the German-American Turner Movement*. New York: Peter Lang.

Jewett, Charles Coffin. 1851. "Report on the Public Libraries of the United States of America, January 1, 1850." In *Report of the Board of Regents of the Smithsonian Institution*. Washington, DC: Smithsonian Institution.

Joeckel, Carleton Bruns. 1935. *The Government of the American Public Library*. Chicago: University of Chicago Press.

Jones, Plummer Alston, Jr. 1999. *Libraries, Immigrants, and the American Experience*. Westport, CT: Greenwood Press.

Josey, E. J. 1970. *The Black Librarian in America*. Metuchen, NJ: Scarecrow Press.

Kaser, David. 1978. "Coffee House to Stock Exchange: A Natural History of the Reading Room." In *Milestones to the Present: Papers from Library History Seminar V*, edited by Harold Goldstein, 238–254. Syracuse, NY: Gaylord Professional Publications.

————. 1980. *A Book for a Six Pence: The Circulating Library in America*. Pittsburgh, PA: Beta Phi Mu.

Kelly, Thomas. 1957. *George Birbeck: Pioneer of Adult Education*. Liverpool, UK: Liverpool University Press.

Knight, Frances R. 2000. "A Palace for the People: The Relationships That Built the Boston Public Library." PhD diss., Oxford University.

Knowles, Malcolm S. 1977. *A History of the Adult Education Movement in the United States: Includes Adult Education Institutions through 1976*. Huntington, NY: Robert E. Krieger.

Kruger, Betsy, and Catherine A. Larson. 2000. *On Account of Sex: An Annotated Bibliography on the Status of Women in Librarianship, 1993–1997*. Lanham, MD: Scarecrow Press.

————. 2006. *On Account of Sex: An Annotated Bibliography on the Status of Women in Librarianship, 1998–2002*. Lanham, MD: Scarecrow Press.

Ladenson, Alex. 1982. *Library Law and Legislation in the United States*. Metuchen, NJ: Scarecrow Press.

Laugher, C. T. 1973. *Thomas Bray's Grand Design*. Chicago: American Library Association.

Lehmann-Haut, Hellmutt, Lawrence Wroth, and Rollo G. Silver. 1952. *The Book in America: A History of the Making and Selling of Books in the United States*. New York: Bowker.

Lehuu, Isabel. 2000. *Carnival on the Page: Popular Print Media in Antebellum America*. Chapel Hill: University of North Carolina Press.

Marshall, A. P. 1976. "Service to African-Americans." In *Century of Service: Librarianship in the United States and Canada*, edited by H. Jackson and E. J. Josey, 62–78. Chicago: American Library Association.

McCauley, Elfrieda B. 1971. "The New England Mill Girls: Feminine Influence in the Development of Public Libraries in New England, 1820–1860." PhD diss., Columbia University.

McCook, Kathleen de la Peña, and Katharine J. Phenix. 1984. *On Account of Sex: An Annotated Bibliography on the History of Women in Librarianship, 1977–1981*. Chicago: American Library Association.

———. 2010. "Public Librarianship." In *Encyclopedia of Library and Information Sciences*. Philadelphia: Taylor and Francis.

McHenry, Elizabeth. 2007. "An Association of Kindred Spirits: Black Readers and Their Reading Rooms." In *Institutions of Reading: The Social Life of Libraries in the United States*, edited by Thomas Augst and Kenneth Carpenter, 99–118. Amherst: University of Massachusetts Press.

McMullen, Haynes. 2000. *American Libraries before 1876*. Beta Phi Mu Monograph Series, no. 6. Westport, CT: Greenwood Press.

Miksa, Francis. 1982. "The Interpretation of American Public Library History." In *Public Librarianship: A Reader*, edited by Jane Robbins-Carter, 73–90. Littleton, CO: Libraries Unlimited.

Mitchell, Barbara A. 2007. "Boston Library Catalogues, 1850–1875: Female Labor and Technological Change." In *Institutions of Reading: The Social Life of Libraries in the United States*, edited by Thomas Augst and Kenneth Carpenter, 119–147. Amherst: University of Massachusetts Press.

Musmann, V. K. 1982. "Women and the Founding of Social Libraries in California, 1859–1910." PhD diss., University of Southern California.

Mussman, Klaus. 1998. "The Ugly Side of Librarianship: Segregation in Library Services from 1900–1950." In *Untold Stories: Civil Rights, Libraries and Black Librarianship*, 78–92. Champaign: University of Illinois, Graduate School of Library and Information Science.

Passet, Joanne. 1994. *Cultural Crusaders: Women Librarians in the American West, 1900–1917*. Albuquerque: University of New Mexico Press.

Pawley, Christine. 2003. "Reading *Apostles of Culture*: The Politics and Historiography of Library History." Foreword to reprint of Dee Garrison, *Apostles of Culture*. Madison: University of Wisconsin Press.

Phenix, Katharine J., and Kathleen de la Peña McCook. 1989. *On Account of Sex: An Annotated Bibliography on the History of Women in Librarianship, 1982–1986*. Chicago: American Library Association.

Raven, James. 2007. "Social Libraries and Library Societies in Eighteenth-Century North America." In *Institutions of Reading: The Social Life of Libraries in the United States*, edited by Thomas Augst and Kenneth Carpenter, 24–52. Amherst: University of Massachusetts Press.

Rice, S. P. 2004. *Minding the Machine: Languages of Class in Early Industrial America*. Berkeley: University of California Press.

Shera, Jesse H. 1949. *Foundations of the Public Library: The Origins of the Public Library Movement in New England, 1629–1855*. Chicago: University of Chicago Press. Repr., Hamden, CT: Shoestring Press, 1965.

Stielow, Frederick J., and James Corsaro. 1993. "The Carnegie Question and the Public Library Movement in Progressive Era New York." In *Carnegie Denied: Communities Rejecting*

Carnegie Library Construction Grants, 1898–1925, edited by Robert Sidney Martin, 35–51. Westport, CT: Greenwood Press.

Tucker, John M. 1998. *Untold Stories: Civil Rights, Libraries and Black Librarianship*. Champaign: University of Illinois, Graduate School of Library and Information Science.

Tyack, David B. 1967. *George Ticknor and the Boston Brahmins*. Cambridge, MA: Harvard University Press.

U.S. Department of the Interior, Bureau of Education. 1876. *Public Libraries in the United States of America: Their History, Condition, and Management. Special Report*. Washington, DC: U.S. Government Printing Office. Repr., as Monograph Series, no. 4, Champaign: University of Illinois, Graduate School of Library Science.

Wadlin, Horace Greeley. 1911. *The Public Library of the City of Boston: A History*. Boston: The Trustees.

Watson, Paula D. 2003. "Valleys without Sunsets: Women's Clubs and Traveling Libraries." In *Libraries to the People: Histories of Outreach*, edited by Robert S. Freeman and David M. Hovde, 73–95. Jefferson, NC: McFarland.

Weibel, Kathleen, Kathleen Heim (de la Peña McCook), and Dianne J. Ellsworth. 1979. *The Status of Women in Librarianship, 1876–1976*. Phoenix, AZ: Neal-Schuman.

Wellman, Hiller C., and Elizabeth Putnam Sohier. 1953. In *Pioneering Leaders in Librarianship*, edited by Emily Miller Danton. Boston: Greg Press.

Whitehill, Walter Muir. 1956. *Boston Public Library: A Centennial History*. Cambridge, MA: Harvard University Press.

Wiegand, Wayne A. 1986. "The Historical Development of State Library Agencies." In *State Library Services and Issues: Facing Future Challenges*, edited by Charles R. McClure, 1–16. Norwood, NJ: Ablex.

———. 1986. *The Politics of an Emerging Profession: The American Library Association, 1876–1917*. New York: Greenwood Press.

———. 1989. *An Active Instrument for Propaganda: The American Public Library during World War I*. Westport, CT: Greenwood Press.

Williams, Julie Hedgepeth. 1999. *The Significance of the Printed Word in Early America*. Westport, CT: Greenwood Press.

Wittmann, Reinhard. 1999. "Was There a Reading Revolution at the End of the Eighteenth Century?" In *A History of Reading in the West*, edited by Guglielmo Cavallo and Roger Chartier, 284–312. Amherst: University of Massachusetts Press.

Wolf, Edwin. 1988. *The Book Culture of a Colonial American City: Philadelphia Books, Bookmen, and Booksellers*. New York: Oxford University Press.

Wyss, Hilary E. 2000. *Writing Indians: Literacy, Christianity and Native Community in Early America*. Amherst: University of Massachusetts Press.

Young, Arthur P. 1981. *Books for Sammies: The American Library Association and World War I*. Pittsburgh, PA: Beta Phi Mu.

Zboray, Ronald J. 1993. *A Fictive People: Antebellum Economic Development and the Reading Public*. New York: Oxford University Press.

Zboray, Ronald, and Mary Saracino Zboray. 2000. *A Handbook for the Study of Book History in the United States*. Washington, DC: Center for the Book, Library of Congress.

Articles

Augst, Thomas. 2001. "American Libraries and Agencies of Culture." *American Studies* 42 (Fall): 12.

Blazek, R. 1979. "The Development of Library Service in the Nation's Oldest City: The St. Augustine Library Association, 1874–1880." *Journal of Library History* 14: 160–182.

Carmichael, J. V. J. 2005. "Southern Librarianship and the Culture of Resentment." *Libraries and Culture* 40 (Summer): 324–352.

Carnegie, Andrew. 1889. "The Best Fields for Philanthropy." *North American Review* 149, no. 397 (December)..

Cresswell, Stephen. 1996. "The Last Days of Jim Crow in Southern Libraries." *Libraries and Culture* 31 (Summer/Fall): 557–573.

Dawson, Alma. 2000. "Celebrating African-American Librarians and Librarianship." *Library Trends* 49 (Summer): 49–87.

Ditzion, Sidney H. 1940. "The District School Library, 1835–1855." *Library Quarterly* 10: 545–547.

Du Mont, Rosemary Ruhig. 1986. "Race in American Librarianship: Attitudes of the Library Profession." *Journal of Library History* 21 (Summer): 488–509.

Fain, Elaine. 1978. "The Library and American Education: Education through Secondary School." *Library Trends* (Winter): 327–352.

Glynn, T. 2005. "The New York Society Library: Books, Authority, and Publics in Colonial and Early Republican New York." *Libraries and Culture* 40 (Fall): 493–529.

Gunselman, C. 2004. "Cornelia Marvin and Mary Frances Isom: Leaders of Oregon's Library Movement." *Library Trends* 52 (Spring): 877–901.

Hall, David D. 1994. "Readers and Reading in America: Historical and Critical Perspectives." *Proceedings of the American Antiquarian Society* 104: 337–357.

Hansen, Debra G. 1999. "At the Pleasure of the Board: Women Librarians and the Los Angeles Public Library, 1880–1905." *Libraries and Culture* 34 (Fall): 311–346.

Harris, Michael H. 1973. "The Purpose of the American Public Library: A Revisionist Interpretation of History." *Library Journal* 98 (September 15): 2509–2514.

———. 1974. "Everett Ticknor and the Common Man: Fear of Societal Instability as the Motivation for the Founding of the Boston Public Library." *Libri* 24: 249–275.

———. 1976. "Public Libraries and the Decline of Democratic Dogma." *Library Journal* 101 (November 1): 2225–2230.

Harris, Steven R. 2003. "Civil Rights and the Louisiana Library Association." *Libraries and Culture* 38 (Fall): 322–350.

Held, Ray E. 1959. "The Early School District Library in California." *Library Quarterly* 29: 79.

Hill, Nanci Milone, et al. 2010. "LSTA Grants Help Promote Library and Extend Offerings." *Public Libraries* 49 (March/April): 9–13.

Houlette, W. D. 1934. "Parish Libraries and the Work of Rev. Thomas Bray." *Library Quarterly* 4: 588–609.

Malone, Cheryl Knott. 2000. "Books for Black Children: Public Library Collections in Louisville and Nashville, 1915–1925." *Library Quarterly* 70 (April): 179–200.

————. 2000. "Toward a Multicultural American Public Library History." *Libraries and Culture* 35 (Winter): 77–87.

Mattson, Kevin. 2000. "The Librarian as Secular Minister to Democracy: The Life and Ideas of John Cotton Dana." *Libraries and Culture* 35 (Fall): 514–534.

McCrossen, A. 2006. "'One Cathedral More' or 'Mere Lounging Place for Bummers'? The Cultural Politics of Leisure and the Public Library in Gilded America." *Libraries and Culture* 41 (Spring 2006): 169–188.

McMullen, Haynes. 1985. "The Very Slow Decline of the American Social Library." *Library Quarterly* 55: 207–225.

Nardini, Robert F. 2001. "A Search for Meaning: American Library Metaphors, 1876–1926." *Library Quarterly* 71 (April): 111–140.

Pollak, O. B. 2004. "The Library Spirit in Seward, Nebraska: 1888–1914." *Nebraska Library Association Quarterly* 35 (Spring): 15–20.

Richards, E. M. 1940. "Alexandre Vattemare and His System of International Exchanges." *Bulletin of the Medical Library Association* 32: 413–448.

Steiner, Bernard C. 1896. "Thomas Bray and His American Libraries." *American Historical Review* 2 (October): 59–75.

Story, R. 1975. "Class and Culture in Boston: The Athenaeum, 1807–1860." *American Quarterly* 27: 178–199.

Todd, Emily B. 2001. "Antebellum Libraries in Richmond and New Orleans and the Search for the Practices and Preferences of Real Readers." *American Studies* 42 (Fall): 195–209.

Tucker, Harold W. 1963. "The Access to Public Libraries Study." *ALA Bulletin* 57 (September): 742–745.

Watson, Paula D. 1994. "Founding Mothers: The Contribution of Women's Organizations to Public Library Development in the United States." *Library Quarterly* 64 (July): 237.

————. 1996. "Carnegie Ladies, Lady Carnegies: Women and the Building of Libraries." *Libraries and Culture* 31 (Winter): 159–196.

Wiegand, Wayne A. 2007. "The Rich Potential of American Public School Library History: Research Needs and Opportunities for Historians of Education and Librarianship." *Libraries and the Cultural Record* 42, no. 1: 57–74.

Young, Arthur P. 2002. "Books, Libraries and War." *Illinois Library Association Reporter* 20 (April): 10–11.

Law

Massachusetts, State of. Chapter 52. *1848 Acts and Resolves*. Boston: State of Massachusetts.

Websites

General Federation of Women's Clubs. http://www.gfwc.org.

Louisville Public Library. "A Separate Flame Western Branch: The First African-American Public Library." http://www.lfpl.org/western/htms/welcome.htm.

3. Public Library Growth and Values: 1918–Today

Books and Chapters in Books

American Library Association. 1936. *The Equal Chance: Books Help to Make It.* Chicago: American Library Association.

American Library Association, Commission on the Library and Adult Education. 1926. *Libraries and Adult Education.* Chicago: American Library Association.

American Library Association, Library Extension Board. 1926. *Library Extension: A Study of Public Library Conditions and Needs.* Chicago: American Library Association.

———. 1927. *Equalizing Library Opportunities.* Chicago: American Library Association.

———. 1927. *How to Organize a County Library Campaign.* Chicago: American Library Association.

American Library Association, Office for Intellectual Freedom. 2002. *Intellectual Freedom Manual.* 6th ed. Chicago: American Library Association.

Asheim, Lester. 1950. *A Forum on the Public Library Inquiry.* New York: Columbia University Press. Repr., Westport, CT: Greenwood Press, 1970.

Augst, Thomas, and Kenneth Carpenter. 2007. *Institutions of Reading: The Social Life of Libraries in the United States.* Amherst: University of Massachusetts Press.

Becker, Patti Clayton. 2005. *Books and Libraries in American Society during World War II: Weapons in the War of Ideas.* New York: Routledge.

Berelson, Bernard. 1949. *The Library's Public: A Report of the Public Library Inquiry.* New York: Columbia University Press.

Bowerman, George F. 1931. *Censorship and the Public Library.* New York: H. W. Wilson.

Brown v. Louisiana. 1966. 383 U.S. 131 (1966).

Bryan, Alice I. 1952. *The Public Librarian: A Report of the Public Library Inquiry.* New York: Columbia University Press.

Buschman, John E. 2003. *Dismantling the Public Sphere: Situating and Sustaining Librarianship in the Age of the New Public Philosophy.* Westport, CT: Libraries Unlimited.

Buschman, John, and Gloria J. Leckie, eds. 2007. *The Library as Place: History, Community, and Culture.* Westport, CT: Libraries Unlimited.

Carmichael, James V., Jr. 1988. *Tommie Dora Barker and Southern Librarianship.* Chapel Hill: University of North Carolina Press.

Carmichael, James Vinson. 1998. *Daring to Find Our Names: The Search for Lesbigay Library History.* Westport, CT: Greenwood Press.

Carnovsky, Leon, and Lowell A. Martin. 1944. *The Library and the Community.* Chicago: University of Chicago Press.

Carr, David. 2003. *The Promise of Cultural Institutions.* Walnut Creek, CA: AltaMira Press.

Casey, Genevieve M., ed. 1975. "Federal Aid to Libraries: Its History, Impact, Future." Special issue, *Library Trends* 24 (July).

Conable, Gordon. 2002. "Public Libraries and Intellectual Freedom." In *Intellectual Freedom Manual.* 6th ed. Chicago: American Library Association.

Cook, Karen. 2008 "Freedom Libraries in the 1964 Mississippi Freedom Summer Project: A History." Unpublished PhD diss., University of Alabama.

D'Angelo, Ed. 2006. *Barbarians at the Gate of the Public Library*. Duluth, MN: Library Juice Press.

Ditzion, Sidney H. 1947. *Arsenals of a Democratic Culture: A Social History of the American Public Library Movement in New England and the Middle States from 1850–1900*. Chicago: American Library Association.

Dix, William S., and Paul Bixler. 1954. *Freedom of Communications: Proceedings of the First Conference on Intellectual Freedom, New York City, June 28–29, 1952*. Chicago: American Library Association.

Garceau, Oliver. 1949. *The Public Library in the Political Process: A Report of the Public Library Inquiry*. New York: Columbia University Press.

Geller, Evelyn. 1984. *Forbidden Books in American Public Libraries, 1876–1939: A Study in Cultural Change*. Westport, CT: Greenwood Press.

Graham, Patterson Toby. 2002. *A Right to Read: Segregation and Civil Rights in Alabama's Public Libraries, 1900–1965*. Tuscaloosa: University of Alabama Press.

Healey, James Stewart. 1974. *John E. Fogarty: Political Leadership for Library Development*. Metuchen, NJ: Scarecrow Press.

Holley, Edward G., and Robert Schremser. 1983. *The Library Services and Construction Act: An Historical Overview from the Viewpoint of Major Participants*. Greenwich, CT: JAI Press.

Horrocks, Norman. 2005. *Perspectives, Insights and Priorities: 17 Leaders Speak Freely of Librarianship*. Lanham, MD: Scarecrow Press.

Joeckel, Carleton Bruns. 1935. *The Government of the American Public Library*. Chicago: University of Chicago Press.

———. 1943. *Post-War Standards for Public Libraries*. Chicago: American Library Association.

Joeckel, Carleton B., and Amy Winslow. 1948. *A National Plan for Public Library Service*. Chicago: American Library Association.

Johnson, Alvin. 1938. *The Public Library—A People's University*. New York: American Association for Adult Education.

Kister, Kenneth F. 2002. *Eric Moon: The Life and Library Times*. Jefferson, NC: McFarland.

Knight, Douglas M., and E. Shepley Nourse, eds. 1969. *Libraries at Large: Traditions, Innovations and the National Interest; The Resource Book Based on the Materials of the National Advisory Commission on Libraries*. New York: R. R. Bowker.

Knowles, Malcolm S. 1977. *A History of the Adult Education Movement in the United States: Includes Adult Education Institutions through 1976*. Huntington, NY: Robert E. Krieger.

Kramp, Robert Scott. 2010. *The Great Depression: Its Impact on Forty-Six Large American Public Libraries: An Analysis of Published Writings of Their Directors*. Duluth: Library Juice Press; University of Michigan, Library Science Dissertation, 1975.

Kranich, Nancy, ed. 2001. *Libraries and Democracy: The Cornerstones of Liberty*. Chicago: American Library Association.

Kunitz, Stanley. 2000. "The Layers." In *The Collected Poems*, 217–218. New York: W. W. Norton.

Lamont, Bridget L. 1998. "The Legacy of the Library Services and Construction Act in Illinois." *Illinois Libraries* 80 (Summer): 93–184.

LaRue, James. 2007. *The New Inquisition: Understanding and Managing Intellectual Freedom Challenges.* Westport, CT: Libraries Unlimited.

Latham, Joyce M. 2007. "White Collar Read: The American Public Library and the Left-Led CIO: A Case Study of the Chicago Public Library, 1929–1952." Unpublished PhD diss., University of Illinois at Urbana-Champaign.

Learned, William S. 1924. *The American Public Library and the Diffusion of Knowledge.* New York: Harcourt.

Leigh, Robert D. 1950. *The Public Library in the United States: The General Report of the Public Library Inquiry.* New York: Columbia University Press.

Marshall, A. P. 1976. "Service to African-Americans." In *Century of Service: Librarianship in the United States and Canada,* edited by H. Jackson and E. J. Josey, 62–78. Chicago: American Library Association.

Martin, Lowell A. 1962. "LSA and Library Standards." In *The Impact of the Library Services Act,* edited by Donald E. Strout, 1–16. Champaign: University of Illinois.

———. 1967. *Baltimore Reaches Out: Library Services to the Disadvantaged.* Baltimore, MD: Enoch Pratt Free Library.

———. 1969. *Library Response to Urban Change: A Study of the Chicago Public Library.* Chicago: American Library Association.

Mason, Marilyn Gell. 1983. *The Federal Role in Library and Information Services.* White Plains, NY: Knowledge Industry Publications.

McCook, Kathleen de la Peña. 1994. *Toward a Just and Productive Society: An Analysis of the Recommendations of the White House Conference on Library and Information Services.* Washington, DC: National Commission on Libraries and Information Science.

McCook, Kathleen de la Peña, and Katharine J. Phenix. 2008. "Human Rights, Democracy and Librarians." In *The Portable MLIS,* edited by Ken Haycock and Brooke E. Sheldon, 23–34. Westport, CT: Greenwood Press.

Milam, Carl H. 1922. *What Libraries Learned from the War.* Washington, DC: U.S. Office of Education.

Molz, Redmond Kathleen. 1984. *National Planning for Library Service: 1935–1975.* Chicago: American Library Association.

Monroe, Margaret E. 1963. *Library Adult Education: The Biography of an Idea.* New York: Scarecrow Press.

———. 2006. *Memoirs of a Public Librarian.* Madison, WI: School of Library and Information Studies.

Monypenny, Phillip. 1966. *The Library Functions of the States.* Chicago: American Library Association.

Most, Linda R. 2009. "The Rural Public Library as Place in North Florida." PhD diss., Florida State University.

Nasaw, David. 2006. *Andrew Carnegie.* New York: Penguin Press.

Pawley, Christine. 2007. "Blood and Thunder on the Bookmobile: American Public Libraries and the Construction of the Reader, 1950–1995." In *Institutions of Reading: The Social Life of Libraries in the United States*, edited by Thomas Augst and Kenneth Carpenter, 264–282. Amherst: University of Massachusetts Press.

Public Library Association, Goals, Guidelines and Standards Committee. 1979. *The Public Library Mission Statement and Its Imperatives for Service*. Chicago: American Library Association.

Pungitore, Verna L. 1995. *Innovation and the Library: The Adoption of New Ideas in Public Libraries*. Westport, CT: Greenwood Press.

Raber, Douglas. 1997. *Librarianship and Legitimacy: The Ideology of the Public Library Inquiry*. Westport, CT: Greenwood Press.

Reagan, Patrick D. 2000. *Designing a New America: The Origins of New Deal Planning, 1890–1943*. Amherst: University of Massachusetts Press.

Robbins, Louise S. 1996. *Censorship and the American Library: The American Library Association's Response to Threats to Intellectual Freedom: 1939–1969*. Westport, CT: Greenwood Press.

Shera, Jesse H. 1949. *Foundations of the Public Library: The Origins of the Public Library Movement in New England, 1629–1855*. Chicago: University of Chicago Press. Repr., Hamden, CT: Shoestring Press, 1965.

Sherrill, Laurence L. 1970. *Library Service to the Unserved: Papers Presented at the University of Wisconsin–Milwaukee, School of Library and Information Science, November 16–18, 1967*. New York: Bowker.

Sullivan, Peggy. 1976. *Carl H. Milam and the American Library Association*. New York: H. W. Wilson.

Thomison, Dennis. 1978. *A History of the American Library Association, 1876–1972*. Chicago: American Library Association.

U.S. National Commission on Libraries and Information Science. 1975. *Toward a National Program for Library and Information Services: Goals for Action*. Washington, DC: U.S. Government Printing Office.

———. 1992. *Pathways to Excellence: A Report on Improving Library and Information Services for Native American Peoples*. Washington, DC: Government Printing Office.

———. 1995. "NCLIS at 25." Washington, DC: U.S. National Commission on Libraries and Information Science. ERIC.

———. 1999. "NCLIS Adopts 'Principles for Public Service.'" Washington, DC: U.S. National Commission on Libraries and Information Science. ERIC.

———. 2008. *Meeting the Information Needs of the American People, Past Actions and Future Initiatives*. Washington, DC: U.S. National Commission on Libraries and Information Science. ERIC 500878.

Van Fleet, Connie. 1990. "Lifelong Learning Theory and the Provision of Adult Services." In *Adult Services: An Enduring Focus for Public Libraries*, edited by Kathleen M. Heim (de la Peña McCook) and Danny P. Wallace, 166–211. Chicago: American Library Association.

Wertheimer, Andrew B. 2004. "Japanese American Community Libraries in America's Concentration Camps, 1942–1946." Unpublished PhD diss., University of Wisconsin–Madison.

White House Conference on Library and Information Services. 1980. *Information for the 1980s: Final Report of the White House Conference on Library and Information Services, 1979.* Washington, DC: National Commission on Libraries and Information Science.

——. 1991. *Information 2000: Library and Information Services for the 21st Century.* Washington, DC: The Conference.

White House Conference on Library and Information Services Task Force. 1997. *Summary of Actions to Implement the 96 Recommendations and Petitions of the 1991 White House Conference on Library and Information Services: March 1994 through December 1996.* Washington, DC: National Commission on Libraries and Information Science. purl.access.gpo .gov/GPO/LPS4122.

Wiegand, Wayne A. 1989. *An Active Instrument for Propaganda: The American Public Library during World War I.* Westport, CT: Greenwood Press.

Wiegand, Shirley A., and Wayne A. Wiegand. 2007. *Books on Trial: Red Scare in the Heartland.* Norman: University of Oklahoma Press.

Wilson, Louis R., and Edward A. Wight. 1935. *County Library Service in the South: A Study of the Rosenwald County Library Demonstration.* Chicago: University of Chicago Press.

Zinn, Howard. 1997. "A Quiet Case of Social Change." In *The Zinn Reader: Writings on Disobedience and Democracy*, 31–39. New York: Seven Stories Press.

Articles

"ALA Responds to CIPA Decision." 2003. *Newsletter on Intellectual Freedom* (September): 175.

Berelson, Bernard. 1938. "The Myth of Library Impartiality." *Wilson Library Bulletin* 13 (October): 87–90.

Berninghausen, David K. 1948. "Library Bill of Rights." *ALA Bulletin* 42 (July/August): 285.

Berry, John N.. 2005. "Election 2004: The Library Fails Again." *Perspectives, Insights and Priorities: 17 Leaders Speak Freely of Librarianship*, edited by Norman Horrocks, 13–17. Lanham, MD: Scarecrow Press.

——. 2007. "The Politics of NCLIS." *Library Journal* 132 (March): 10.

Budd, John M., and Cynthia Wyatt. 2002. "'Do You Have Any Books On—': An Examination of Public Library Holdings." *Public Libraries* 41 (March/April): 107–112.

Burke, Susan K. 2007. "The Use of Public Libraries by Native Americans." *Library Quarterly* 77 (October): 429–461.

Buschman, John. 2007. "Democratic Theory in Library Information Science: Toward an Emendation." *Journal of the American Society for Information Science and Technology* 58, no. 10 (August): 1483–1496.

Carmichael, James V., Jr. 1992. "Women in Southern Library Education, 1905–1945." *Library Quarterly* 62 (April): 169–216.

Estes, Rice. 1960. "Segregated Libraries." *Library Journal* (December 15): 4418–4421.

Fenwick, Sara Innis. 1976. "Library Services to Children and Young People." *Library Trends* 25 (Summer): 329–360.

Fichter, Darlene, and Jeff Wisniewski. 2009. "Social Media Metrics: Tracking Your Impact." *Online* 33 (January/February): 54–57.

Fiels, Keith Michael. 2009. "In Tough Economic Times." *American Libraries* (March): 8.

Fitzpatrick, S. 2009. "Budget Cuts Continue to Loom Over U.S. Libraries." *American Libraries* (May): 17–18.

Fry, James W. 1975. "LSA and LSCA, 1956–1973: A Legislative History." *Library Trends* 24 (July): 7–28.

Fuller, Peter. 1994. "The Politics of LSCA during the Reagan and Bush Administrations." *Library Quarterly* 64 (July): 294–318.

Graham, Frank P. 1932. "Citizens' Library Movements." *Library Extension News* 14 (May): 2.

Guss, Emily. 2010. "Cultural Record Keepers: Vivian G. Harsh Collection of Afro-American History and Literature, Carter G. Woodson Regional Library, Chicago Public Library." *Libraries and the Cultural Record* 45, no. 3: 359–363.

Haines, Helen E. 1924. "Modern Fiction and the Public Library." *Library Journal* 49 (May 15): 458–460.

Hildenbrand, Suzanne. 2000. "Library Feminism and Library Women's History: Activism and Scholarship, Equity and Culture." *Libraries and Culture* 35 (Winter): 51–65.

Hill, Nanci Milone. 2010. "LSTA Grants Help Promote Library and Extend Offerings." *Public Libraries* 49 (March/April): 9–13.

Intellectual Freedom Manual. 2009. IFC Report to Council. January 28.

Jaeger, Paul T., and John Carlo Bertot. 2009. "E-government Education in Public Libraries." *Journal of Education for Library and Information Science* 50 (Winter): 39–49.

Jaeger, Paul T., and Zheng Yan. 2009. "One Law with Two Outcomes: Comparing the Implementation of CIPA in Public Libraries and Schools." *Information Technology and Libraries* 28 (March): 6–14.

Jenkins, Christine A. 2000. "The History of Youth Services Librarianship. A Review of the Research Literature." *Libraries and Culture* 35 (Winter): 103–140.

Jones, Barbara M. 2009. "'Librarians Shushed No More': the USA Patriot Act, the 'Connecticut Four,' and Professional Ethics." *Newsletter on Intellectual Freedom* 58, no. 6: 195, 221–223.

Kelly, Melody S. 2003. "Revisiting C. H. Milam's 'What Libraries Learned from the War' and Rediscovering the Library Faith." *Libraries and Culture* 38 (Fall): 378–388.

Kunitz, Stanley. 1936. "The Spectre at Richmond." *Wilson Library Bulletin* (June): 592–593.

———. 1939. "That Library Serves Best." *Wilson Library Bulletin* (December): 314.

Kurutz, Gary F. 2009. "'It's a Long Trip from Headquarters': An Exhibit Celebrating Early County Library Service in California." *California State Library Foundation Bulletin*, 13–19.

Latham, Joyce M. 2010. "Clergy of the Mind: Alvin S. Johnson, William S. Learned, the Carnegie Corporations, and the American Library Association." *Library Quarterly* 80, no. 3: 249–265.

Lee, Dan R. 1991. "Faith Cabin Libraries: A Study of an Alternative Library Service in the Segregated South, 1932–1960." *Libraries and Culture* 26 (Winter): 169–182.

"Library Projects under Public Works, Civil Works and Relief Administrations." 1933. *ALA Bulletin* 27 (December): 539.

Lincove, David A. 1994. "Propaganda and the American Public Library from the 1930s to the Eve of World War II." *RQ* 33 (Summer): 510–523.

Lingo, Marci. 2003. "Forbidden Fruit: The Banning of *The Grapes of Wrath* in the Kern County Free Library." *Libraries and Culture* 38 (Fall): 351–377.

"Looking Toward National Planning." 1934. *ALA Bulletin* 28 (August): 453–460.

Maack, Mary Niles. 1994. "Public Libraries in Transition: Ideals, Strategies and Research." *Libraries and Culture* 29 (Winter): 79.

Mallory, Mary. 1995. The Rare Vision of Mary Utopia Rothrock: Organizing Regional Library Services in the Tennessee Valley." *Library Quarterly* 65 (January): 62–88.

Martin, Robert S. 2003. "Cultural Policies in Knowledge Societies: The United States of America." UNESCO Ministerial Roundtable: Toward Knowledge Societies. UNESCO Headquarters, Paris, France, October 10.

Martin, Robert S., and Orvin Lee Shiflett. 1996. "Hampton, Fisk and Atlanta: The Foundations, the American Library Association and Library Education for Blacks, 1925–1941." *Libraries and Culture* 31 (Spring): 300–325.

McCook, Kathleen de la Peña. 2001. "Authentic Discourse as a Means of Connection between Public Library Service Responses and Community Building Initiatives." *Reference and User Services Quarterly* 40 (Winter): 127–133.

McCook, Kathleen de la Peña, and Peggy Barber. 2002. "Public Policy as a Factor Influencing Adult Lifelong Learning, Adult Literacy and Public Libraries." *Reference and User Services Quarterly* 42, no. 1 (Fall): 66–75.

McCook, Kathleen de la Peña, and Maria A. Jones. 2002. "Cultural Heritage Institutions and Community Building." *Reference and User Services Quarterly* 41 (Summer): 326–329.

McReynolds, Rosalee. 1990/1991. "The Progressive Librarians Council and Its Founders." *Progressive Librarian* 2 (Winter): 23–29.

Milam, Carl H. 1934. "National Planning for Libraries." *ALA Bulletin* 28 (February): 60–62.

Miller, Rebecca. 2010. "Losing Libraries/Saving Libraries." *Library Journal* 135 (August): 20–21.

"A National Plan for Libraries." 1935. *ALA Bulletin* 29 (February): 91–98.

"A National Plan for Libraries." 1939. *ALA Bulletin* 33 (February): 136–150.

Preer, Jean. 2010. "'Wake Up and Read!' Book Promotion and National Library Week, 1958." *Libraries and the Cultural Record* 45: 92–106.

Price, Lee. 2008. "Libraries Take the Big Read Challenge." *Public Libraries* 47 (January/February): 42–45.

Public Library Association, Public Library Principles Task Force. 1982. "The Public Library: Democracy's Resource, a Statement of Principles." *Public Libraries* 21: 92.

Raber, Douglas. 1995. "Ideological Opposition to Federal Library Legislation: The Case of the Library Services Act of 1956." *Public Libraries* 34 (May/June): 162–169.

"Resolution on the USA PATRIOT Act and Related Measures That Infringe on the Rights of Library Users." 2003. *Newsletter on Intellectual Freedom* (May): 93.

Rioux, Kevin. 2010. "Metatheory in Library and Information Science: A Nascent Social Justice Approach." *Journal of Education for Library and Information Science* 51 (Winter): 9–17.

Robbins, Louise S. 1995. "After Brave Words, Silence: American Librarianship Responds to Cold War Loyalty Programs, 1947–1957." *Libraries and Culture* 30 (Fall): 345–365.

————. 1996. "Champions of a Cause: American Librarians and the Library Bill of Rights in the 1950s." *Library Trends* 45 (Summer): 291–311.

————. 2001. "The Overseas Library Controversy and the Freedom to Read: U.S. Librarians and Publishers Confront Joseph McCarthy." *Libraries and Culture* 36 (Winter): 27–39.

————. 2005. "Changing the Geography of Reading in a Southern Border State: The Rosenwald Fund and the WPA in Oklahoma." *Libraries and Culture* 40 (Summer): 353–367.

————. 2007. "Responses to the Resurrection of Miss Ruth Brown: An Essay on the Reception of a Historical Case Study." *Libraries and the Cultural Record* 42: 422–437.

Shaw, Tamara. 2007. "Doing Their Part: The Services of the San Diego Public Library during World War II." *Library Trends* 55 (Winter): 570–582.

Stephens, Annabel K. 2004. "The Founding and Early Development of Alabama Public Libraries: A Content Analysis of 116 of the Libraries' Written Histories." *Alabama Librarian* 54 (2004): 32–38.

Sticlow, Frederick J. 1983. "Censorship in the Early Professionalization of American Libraries." *Journal of Library History* 18 (Winter): 42–47.

. 1990. "Librarian Warriors and Rapprochement: Carl Milam, Archibald MacLeish and World War II." *Libraries and Culture* 25 (Fall): 516.

Swain, Martha H. 1995. "A New Deal in Libraries: Federal Relief Work and Library Service, 1933–1943." *Libraries and Culture* 30: 265–283.

"12 Ways Libraries Are Good for the Country." 1995. *American Libraries* 26 (December): 1113–1119.

Willingham, Taylor L. 2008. "Libraries as Civic Agents." *Public Library Quarterly* 27: 97–110.

Websites

American Library Association, Office for Intellectual Freedom. "Interpretations of the Library Bill of Rights." http://www.ala.org/ala/issuesadvocacy/intfreedom/librarybill/interpretations/default.cfm.

American Library Association, Office for Library Advocacy. http://www.ala.org/ala/aboutala/offices/ola/index.cfm.

American Library Association, Washington Office. http://www.ala.org/ala/aboutala/offices/wo/index.cfm.

Rettig, Jim. 2008. "Libraries Stand Ready to Help in Tough Economic Times." *Huffington Post* (December 11). http://www.huffingtonpost.com/jim-rettig/libraries-stand-ready-to_b_150268.html.

San Diego Public Library. 2010. "Read/San Diego." http://www.sandiego.gov/public-library/services/read.shtml.

U.S. Institute of Museum and Library Services. 1996. "Museum and Library Services Act of 1996." http://www.imls.gov/about/services1996.shtm.

————. 2010. "Mission." http://www.imls.gov/about/about.shtm.

4. Statistics, Standards, Planning, Results, and Quality of Life

Books and Chapters in Books

American Library Association, Committee on Economic Opportunity Programs. 1969. *Library Service to the Disadvantaged: A Study Based on Responses to Questionnaires from Public Libraries Serving Populations Over 15,000.* Chicago: American Library Association.

American Library Association, Coordinating Committee on Revision of Public Library Standards. 1956. *Public Library Service: A Guide to Evaluation with Minimum Standards.* Chicago: American Library Association.

————. 1956. *Public Library Services; Supplement: Costs of Public Library Services in 1956.* Chicago: American Library Association.

American Library Association, Public Library Association, Standards Committee. 1967. *Minimum Standards for Public Library Systems, 1966.* Chicago: American Library Association.

Bassman, Keri, et al. 1998. *How Does Your Public Library Compare? Service Performance of Peer Groups.* Washington, DC: National Center for Education Statistics. October 27. http://nces.ed.gov/pubs98/98310.pdf.

Bertot, John Carlo, Charles R. McClure, and Joe Ryan. 2001. *Statistics and Performance Measures for Public Library Networked Services.* Chicago: American Library Association.

Chief Officers of State Library Agencies. 2009. "Member Profiles." http://www.cosla.org/profiles/.

Chute, Adrienne. 2003. "National Center for Education Statistics Library Statistics Program." In *The Bowker Annual Library and Book Trade Almanac,* 95–102. New York: R. R. Bowker.

Curran, Charles C., and F. William Summers. 1990. *Library Performance, Accountability and Responsiveness: Essays in Honor of Ernest De Prospo.* Norwood, NJ: Ablex.

De Prospo, Ernest R., Ellen Altman, and Kenneth Beasley. 1973. *Performance Measures for Public Libraries.* Chicago: American Library Association.

Durrance, Joan C., and Karen E. Fisher. 2005. *How Libraries and Librarians Help: Assessing Outcomes in Your Library.* Chicago: American Library Association.

Fair, E. M. 1934. *Countywide Library Service.* Chicago: American Library Association.

Garceau, Oliver. 1949. *The Public Library in the Political Process: A Report of the Public Library Inquiry.* New York: Columbia University Press.

Goldhor, Herbert. 1983. "U.S. Public Library Statistics in Series: A Bibliography and Subject Index." In *Bowker Annual of Library and Book Trade Information.* 28th ed, 327–335. New York: R. R. Bowker.

Hamilton-Pennell, Christine. 2010. "Public Library Standards: A Review of Standards and Guidelines from the Fifty States of the U.S. for the Colorado, Mississippi, and Hawaii State Libraries." Mosaic Knowledge Works. Chief Officers of State Library Agencies. http://www.cosla.org.

Harrington, Michael. 1962. *The Other America: Poverty in the United States.* New York: Macmillan.

Hennen, Thomas J., Jr. 2004. *Hennen's Public Library Planner: A Manual and Interactive CD-ROM.* New York: Neal-Schuman.

Hill, Chrystie. 2009. *Inside, Outside and Online: Building Your Library Community*. Chicago: American Library Association.

Himmel, Ethel, and William James Wilson, with the ReVision Committee of the Public Library Association. 1998. *Planning for Results: A Public Library Transformation Process*. Chicago: American Library Association.

Joeckel, Carleton Bruns. 1935. *The Government of the American Public Library*. Chicago: University of Chicago Press.

———. 1943. *Post-War Standards for Public Libraries*. Chicago: American Library Association.

Joeckel, Carleton B., and Amy Winslow. 1948. *A National Plan for Public Library Service*. Chicago: American Library Association.

Johnson, Debra Wilcox. 1995. *An Evaluation of the Public Library Development Program*. Chicago: Public Library Association.

Lance, Keith Curry, et al. 2002. *Counting on Results: New Tools for Outcome-Based Evaluation for Public Libraries*. Aurora, CO: Bibliographical Center for Research. http://www.lrs.org/documents/cor/CoRFin.

Leigh, Robert D. 1950. *The Public Library in the United States: The General Report of the Public Library Inquiry*. New York: Columbia University Press.

Lynch, Mary Jo. 1987. *Libraries in an Information Society: A Statistical Summary*. Chicago: American Library Association.

———. 1983. *Sources of Library Statistics: 1972–1982*. Chicago: American Library Association.

Martin, Allie Beth. 1972. *A Strategy for Public Library Change: Proposed Public Library Goals—Feasibility Study*. Chicago: American Library Association.

Matthews, Joseph R. 2007. *The Evaluation and Measurement of Library Services*. Westport, CT: Libraries Unlimited.

McClure, Charles R. 1987. *Planning and Role Setting for Public Libraries: A Manual of Options and Procedures*. Chicago: American Library Association.

McClure, Charles R., and Paul T. Jaeger. 2009. *Public Libraries and Internet Service Roles: Measuring and Maximizing Internet Services*. Chicago: American Library Association.

McCook, Kathleen de la Peña. 1982. "Stimulation." In *The Service Imperative for Libraries: Essays in Honor of Margaret E. Monroe*, 120–154. Littleton, CO: Libraries Unlimited.

Møller, Valerie, and Dennis Huschka. 2009. *Quality of Life and the Millennium Challenge*. New York: Springer.

Nelson, Sandra. 2001. *The New Planning for Results: A Streamlined Approach*. Chicago: American Library Association.

———. 2008. *Strategic Planning for Results*. Chicago: American Library Association.

———. 2009. *Implementing for Results: Your Strategic Plan in Action*. Chicago: American Library Association.

Nelson, Sandra, Ellen Altman, and Diane Mayo. 2000. "Managing Your Library's Staff." In *Managing for Results: Effective Resource Allocation for Public Libraries*, 29–110. Chicago: American Library Association.

O'Donnell, Peggy. 1988. *Public Library Development Program: Manual for Trainers*. Chicago: American Library Association.

Palmour, Vernon E., et al. 1980. *A Planning Process for Public Libraries*. Chicago: American Library Association.

Public Library Association, Goals, Guidelines and Standards Committee. 1979. *The Public Library Mission Statement and Its Imperatives for Service*. Chicago: American Library Association.

Public Library Association, Public Library Data Service. 1992–present. *Statistical Report* (annual). Chicago: Public Library Association. Continues *Public Library Data Service Statistical Report*. Chicago: Public Library Association, 1988–1991. Also as a database, see PLA website: http://www.ala.org/ala/mgrps/divs/pla/plapublications/pldsstatreport/index.cfm.

Public Library Association, Standards Committee. 1967. *Minimum Standards for Public Library Systems, 1966*. Chicago: American Library Association.

Pungitore, Verna L. 1995. *Innovation and the Library: The Adoption of New Ideas in Public Libraries*. Westport, CT: Greenwood Press.

Samek, Toni. 2001. *Intellectual Freedom and Social Responsibility in American Librarianship, 1967–1974*. Chicago: American Library Association.

Stephens, Annabel K. 1996. *Assessing the Public Library Planning Process*. Norwood, NJ: Ablex.

U.S. National Commission on Libraries and Information Science. 1989. *An Action Plan for a Federal State Cooperative System for Public Library Data*. ERIC: ED311919.

Van House, Nancy, et al. 1987. *Output Measures for Public Libraries: A Manual of Standardized Procedures*. Chicago: American Library Association.

Wallace, Danny P., and Connie Jean Van Fleet. 2001. *Library Evaluation: A Casebook and Can-Do Guide*. Englewood, CO: Libraries Unlimited.

Walter, Virginia A. 1992. *Output Measures for Public Library Service to Children: A Manual of Standardized Procedures*. Chicago: American Library Association.

———. 1995. *Output Measures and More: Planning and Evaluating Public Library Services for Young Adults*. Chicago: American Library Association.

Zweizig, Douglas L. 1996. *The Tell It! Manual: The Complete Program for Evaluating Library Performance*. Chicago: American Library Association.

Zweizig, Douglas L., and Eleanor Jo Rodger. 1982. *Output Measures for Public Libraries*. Chicago: American Library Association.

Articles

Balcom, Kathleen Mehaffey. 1986. "To Concentrate and Strengthen: The Promise of the Public Library Development Program." *Library Journal* 111 (June 15): 36–40.

Blasingame, Ralph, Jr., and Mary Jo Lynch. 1974. "Design for Diversity: Alternatives to Standards for Public Libraries." *PLA Newsletter* 13: 4–22.

Bloss, Meredith. 1976. "Standards for Public Library Service—Quo Vadis?" *Library Journal* 101 (June): 1259–1262.

Brown, Jeffrey L. 2001. "Making a Huge Difference in So Many Little Ways." *Public Libraries* 40 (January/February): 24.

Childers, Thomas. 1975. "Statistics That Describe Libraries and Library Service." *Advances in Librarianship* 5: 107–120.

Davis, Denis M. 2004. "NISO Standard Z39.7—the Evolution to a Data Dictionary for Library Metrics and Assessment Methods." *Serials Review* 30, no. 1: 15–24.

———. 2008. "A Comparison of Public Library Data PLDS in Context." *Public Libraries* 47 (September/October): 20–25.

Durrance, Joan C., and Karen E. Fisher-Pettigrew. 2003. "Determining How Libraries and Librarians Help." *Library Trends* 51 (Spring): 541–570.

Flagg, Gordon. 2009. "HALPR Library Rankings Mark 10th Anniversary with Ohio on Top." *American Libraries* 40 (August/September): 26.

"Goals and Guidelines for Community Service." 1975. *PLA Newsletter* 14: 9–13.

Goldhor, Herbert. 1976. "Indices of American Public Library Statistics." *Illinois Libraries* 58 (February): 152–158.

Heckman, James. 2000. "Causal Parameters and Policy Analysis in Economics: A Twentieth Century Retrospective." *Quarterly Journal of Economics* 115 (February): 45–97.

Henderson, E., K. Miller, T. Craig, S. Dorinski, M. Freeman, N. Isaac, J. Keng, P. O'Shea, and P. Schilling. 2010. *Public Libraries Survey: Fiscal Year 2008* (IMLS-2010–PLS-02). Washington, DC: Institute of Museum and Library Services. http://harvester.census.gov/imls/pubs/Publications/pls2008.pdf.

Hennen, Thomas J., Jr. 1999. "Go Ahead, Name Them: America's Best Public Libraries." *American Libraries* 30 (January): 72–76.

———. 1999. "Great American Public Libraries: HAPLR Ratings: Round Two." *American Libraries* 30 (September): 64–68.

———. 2000. "Great American Public Libraries: HAPLR Ratings: 2000." *American Libraries* 31 (November): 50–54.

———. 2000. "Why We Should Establish a National System of Standards." *American Libraries* 31 (March): 43–45.

———. 2002. "Are Wider Library Units Wiser?" *American Libraries* 33, no. 6 (June/July): 65–70. (Also titled, "Wider and Wiser Units.") http://www.haplr-index.com/wider_and_wiser_units.htm.

———. 2002. "Great American Public Libraries: HAPLR Ratings: 2002." *American Libraries* 33 (October): 64–68.

———. 2003. "Great American Public Libraries: HAPLR Ratings: 2003." *American Libraries* 34 (October): 44–49.

———. 2004. "Great American Public Libraries: HAPLR Ratings: 2004." *American Libraries* 35 (October): 54–59.

———. 2005. "Great American Public Libraries: HAPLR Ratings: 2005." *American Libraries* 36 (October): 42–48.

———. 2006. "Hennen's American Public Library Ratings 2006." *American Libraries* 37 (November): 40–42.

————. 2008. "Hennen's American Public Library Ratings 2008." *American Libraries* 39 (October): 56–61.

————. 2009. "HALPR 2009: 10th Anniversary Edition." http://www.haplr-index.com/ haplr_ 2009_10thAnniv_AmerLibrArticle.htm.

————. 2010. "HALPR 2010." http://www.haplr-index.com/2010_haplr_edition.htm.

Hildreth, Susan. 2007. "Engaging Your Community: A Strategy for Relevance in the Twenty-First Century." *Public Libraries* 46 (May/June): 7–9.

Johnson, Catherine A. 2010. "Do Public Libraries Contribute to Social Capital? A Preliminary Investigation into the Relationship." *Library and Information Science Research* 32: 147–155.

Johnson, Debra Wilcox. 1993. "Reflecting on the Public Library Data Service Project: Public Libraries over Five Years, 1987–1991." *Public Libraries* 32 (September/October): 259–261.

Kniffel, Leonard. 2008. "Public Library Ratings Corrected." *American Libraries* 39 (November): 54–55.

————. 2009. "LJ Index: Too Much Too Late." American Libraries Online. http:// americanlibrariesmagazine.org/2009/03/03/lj-index-too-much-too-late.

Kunitz, Stanley. 1936. "The Spectre at Richmond." *Wilson Library Bulletin* (June): 592–593.

Lance, Keith Curry. 2008. "The New 'LJ' Index." *Library Journal* 133 (June): 38–41.

Lance, Keith Curry, and Marti A. Cox. 2000. "Lies, Damn Lies and Indexes." *American Libraries* 31 (June/July): 82–87.

Lance, Keith Curry, and Ray Lyons. 2009. "America's Star Libraries: The 'LJ' Index of Public Library Service 2009, Round 2." *Library Journal* 134 (November): 18–26.

————. 2010. "America's Star Libraries: The 'LJ' Index of Public Library Service, 2010." *Library Journal* 135 (October).

"LPN Talks with Retiring ORS Director Mary Jo Lynch." 2004. *Library Personnel News* 16 (Winter): 2–3.

Lynch, Mary Jo. 1981. "The Public Library Association and Public Library Planning." *Journal of Library Administration* 2 (Summer/Fall/Winter): 29–41.

————. 1985. "Analysis of Library Data Collection and Development of Plans for the Future: A Project Summary." *The Bowker Annual of Library and Book Trade Information*. New York: Bowker.

————. 1985. "Public Library Statistics, the National Center for Education Statistics, and the Public Library Community." *Public Libraries* 24 (Summer): 62–64.

————. 1988. "An Impossible Dream Come True?" *Public Libraries* 27 (Winter): 170–171.

————. 1991. "New, National and Ready to Fly: The Federal State Cooperative System (FSCS) for Public Library Data." *Public Libraries* 30 (November/December): 358–361.

Lyons, Ray, and Keith Curry Lance. 2009. "America's Star Libraries: The LJ Index of Public Library Service." *Library Journal* 134 (February 15): 26–27.

Martin, Lowell. 1972. "Standards for Public Libraries." *Library Trends* 21 (October): 164–177.

McClure, Charles R., et al. 2006. "Politics and Advocacy: The Role of Networking in Selling the Library to Your Community." *Public Library Quarterly* 25, no. 1/2: 137–154.

McCook, Kathleen de la Peña, and Kristin Brand. 2001. "Community Indicators, Genuine Progress and the Golden Billion." *Reference and User Services Quarterly* 40 (Summer): 337–340.

Milam, D. P. 2008. "Public Library Strategies for Building Stronger Economies and Communities." *National Civic Review* 97 (Fall): 11–16.

Molyneux, B. 2005. "U.S. Public Library Data: A Unified Field Theory." *Public Library Quarterly* 24, no. 3: 3–19.

Molyneux, Robert E. 2008. "Squeeze Play: Public Library Circulation and Budget Trends, FY1992–FY2004." *Public Library Quarterly* 26: 101–107.

Moorman, John A. 1997. "Standards for Public Libraries: A Study in Quantitative Measures of Library Performance as Found in State Public Library Documents." *Public Libraries* 36 (January/February): 32–39.

Pecoraro, John. 2009. "What's It Worth? The Value of Library Services as an Advocacy Tool." *Texas Library Journal* 85 (Spring): 8–9.

Public Library Association, Goals, Guidelines and Standards Committee. 1973. "Community Library Services: Working Papers on Goals and Guidelines." *Library Journal* 96: 2603–2609.

Public Library Association, Public Library Principles Task Force. 1982. "The Public Library: Democracy's Resource, a Statement of Principles." *Public Libraries* 21 (fall): 92.

Pungitore, Verna L. 1992. "Dissemination of the Public Library Planning Process among Smaller Libraries." *Library Quarterly* 62 (October): 375–407.

———. 1993. "Planning in Smaller Libraries: A Field Study." *Public Libraries* 32 (November/December): 331–336.

Raber, Douglas. 1995. "A Conflict of Cultures: Planning vs. Tradition in Public Libraries." *RQ* 35 (Fall): 50–63.

Robinson, Charles W. 1983. "Libraries and the Community." *Public Libraries* 22 (Spring): 7–13.

Schick, Frank L. 1971. "Library Statistics: A Century Plus." *American Libraries* 2: 727–741.

Senville, Wayne. 2009. "Libraries at the Heart of Our Communities." *Planning Commissioners Journal* 75 (Summer): 12–18.

Smith, Nancy Milner. 1994. "State Library Agency Use of Planning and Role Setting for Public Libraries and Output Measures for Public Libraries." *Public Libraries* 33 (July/August): 211–212.

"Standards for Public Libraries." 1933. *ALA Bulletin* 27 (November): 513–514.

Steffen, Nicolle O., and Keith Curry Lance. 2002. "Who's Doing What: Outcome-Based Evaluation and Demographics in the 'Counting on Results Project.'" *Public Libraries* 43 (September/October): 271–279.

Steffen, Nicolle O., Keith Curry Lance, and Rochelle Logan. 2002. "Time to Tell the Whole Story: Outcome-Based Evaluation and the 'Counting on Results Project.'" *Public Libraries* 43 (July/August): 222–228.

Tucker, Harold W. 1963. "The Access to Public Libraries Study." *ALA Bulletin* 57 (September): 742–745.

Varvel, V. E., Jr., and X. Lei. 2009. "Characteristics and Trends: In the *Public Library Data Service* 2008 Report." *Public Libraries* 48, no. 2 (March/April): 6–12.

Varvel, Virgil E. 2010. "Characteristics and Trends in the *Public Library Data Service* 2010 Statistical Report." *Public Libraries* 49, no. 6 (November/December): 34–42.

Varvel, Virgil E., Jr. 2010. "Characteristics and Trends: In the *Public Library Data Service* Report." *Public Libraries* 49, no. 3 (May/June): 36–44.

Weech, Terry L. 1988. "Small Public Libraries and Public Library Standards." *Public Libraries* (Summer): 72–74.

Williams, Robert V. 1991. "The Making of Statistics of National Scope on American Libraries, 1836–1986: Purposes, Problems, and Issues." *Libraries and Culture* 26 (Spring): 464–485.

Yan, Quan Liu, and Douglas L. Zweizig. 2000. "Public Library Use of Statistics: A Survey Report." *Public Libraries* 39 (March/April): 98–105.

———. 2001. "The Use of National Public Library Statistics by Public Library Directors." *Library Quarterly* 71 (October): 467–497.

Zweizig, Douglas L. 1985. "Any Number Can Play: The First National Report of Output Measures Data." *Public Libraries* 24 (Summer): 50–53.

Websites

American Library Association. 1948. "Post-War Planning Committee File, 1941–1948 / The American Library Association Archives." The University of Illinois at Urbana-Champaign. http://www.library.illinois.edu/archives/ala/holdings/?p=collections/controlcard&id=785.

———. 2009. "Advocating in a Tough Economy Toolkit." http://www.ala.org/ala/issuesadvocacy/advocacy/advocacyuniversity/toolkit/index.cfm.

American National Standards Institute. http://www.ansi.org.

"America's Star Libraries." 2009. *Library Journal.* http://www.libraryjournal.com/article/CA6629180.html.

"America's Star Libraries." 2010. http://www.libraryjournal.com/lj/home/887076-264/announcing_americas_star_libraries_.html.csp.

Bibliostat Connect. http://www.btol.com/ps_details.cfm?id=222.

Chief Officers of State Library Agencies. http://www.cosla.org.

Community Indicators Consortium. http://www.communityindicators.net/.

Connecticut. "Social Indicator Statistics." http://www.cslib.org/pathfinders/SocialStats.htm.

Hennen's American Public Library Ratings. http://www.haplr-index.com/index.html.

Hennepin County Community Indicators. http://www.co.hennepin.mn.us.

Information Use Management and Policy Institute. Florida State University. http://www.ii.fsu.edu/index.cfm.

International Institute for Sustainable Development. Compendium of Sustainable Development Indicator Initiatives. http://www.iisd.org/measure/compendium.

Library Research Service. 2009. "National Public Library Statistics." http://www.lrs.org/public/national.php.

McClure, Charles R. 2005–2009. "Increasing the Effectiveness of Evaluation for Improved Public Library Decision Making." Information Use Management and Policy Institute, Florida State University. http://www.ii.fsu.edu/projects/effective-eval/.

National Information Standards Association. http://www.niso.org/index.html.

National Information Standards Organization. 2004. *Information Services and Use: Metrics and Statistics for Libraries and Information Providers-Data Dictionary*, NISO Z39.7-2004. http://www.niso.org/dictionary/toc.

New York State Library. "Bibliostat Connect: Easy Online Access to Public Library Statistics from Your State Library." http://www.nysl.nysed.gov/libdev/libs/biblcnct.htm.

Oregon State Library. "Reporting Public Library Statistics." http://www.osl.state.or.us/home/libdev/reportpublibstats.html.

PLAblog. http://plablog.org/.

Redefining Progress. 2006. *Community Indicators Handbook*. Community Indicators Consortium. http://www.communityindicators.net/.

Texas State Library and Archives Commission. "Public Library Standards." http://www.tsl.state.tx.us/plstandards/.

U.S. Institute of Museum and Library Services. "Compare Public Libraries." harvester.census.gov/imls/compare/index.asp.

———. "Outcomes Based Assessment." http://www.imls.gov/applicants/basics.shtm.

———. 2009. *Public Libraries in the United States, 2007*. http://harvester.census.gov/imls/pubs/pls/index.asp.

———. 2010. *Public Libraries Survey: Fiscal Year 2008* (IMLS-2010–PLS-02). Washington, DC: Institute of Museum and Library Services. http://harvester.census.gov/imls/pubs/Publications/pls2008.pdf.

U.S. National Center for Education Statistics. "Public Libraries Data." http://nces.ed.gov/pubsearch/.

———. "Public Library Peer Comparison Tool." Moved to IMLS: "Compare Public Libraries" at http://harvester.census.gov/imls/compare/index.asp.

U.S. National Commission on Libraries and Information Science. "Library Statistics Cooperative Program." Now at IMLS, Library Statistics: http://harvester.census.gov/imls/search/index.asp.

———. "The Federal-State Cooperative System (FSCS) for Public Library Data." See IMLS, Library Statistics: http://harvester.census.gov/imls/pub_survdesign.asp.

Valentine, Patrick M. 1998. "Mollie Huston Lee: Founder of Raleigh's Public Black Library." *North Carolina Libraries* 56 (Spring): 23–26.

WebJunction. Public Library Standards. Connecticut. http://ct.webjunction.org/tech-security/articles/content/436213.

WebJunction. Public Library Standards. Indiana. http://in.webjunction.org/in/plstandards/-/resources/overview.

Williams, Robert V., and Mittie Kristina McLean. 2008. *A Bibliographical Guide to a Chronological Record of Statistics of National Scope on Libraries in the United States*. University of South Carolina, School of Library and Information Science. http://www.libsci.sc.edu/bob/LibraryStatistics/LibraryStatisticsGuide.html.

5. Organization, Law, Advocacy, Funding, and Politics

Books and Chapters in Books

American Library Association. 1930. *American Library Laws*. Volumes and supplements published 1930, 1943, 1962 (supplements 1965–1970), 1972 (supplements 1972–1978), 1983. Chicago: American Library Association.

Buschman, John E. 2003. *Dismantling the Public Sphere: Situating and Sustaining Librarianship in the Age of the New Public Philosophy*. Westport, CT: Libraries Unlimited.

Christensen, Karen. 2007. *Heart of the Community: The Libraries We Love*. Great Barrington, MA: Berkshire.

Dowlin, Ken. 2008. *Getting the Money: How to Succeed in Fundraising for Public and Nonprofit Libraries*. Westport, CT: Libraries Unlimited.

Fiels, Keith Michael, Joan Neumann, and Eva R. Brown. 1991. *Multitype Library Cooperation State Laws, Regulations and Pending Legislation*. Chicago: Association of Specialized and Cooperative Library Agencies.

Garceau, Oliver. 1949. *The Public Library in the Political Process: A Report of the Public Library Inquiry*. New York: Columbia University Press.

Halsey, Richard Sweeney. 2003. *Lobbying for Public and School Libraries: A History and Political Playbook*. Lanham, MD: Scarecrow Press.

Healey, James S. 1974. *John E. Fogarty: Political Leadership for Library Development*. Metuchen, NJ: Scarecrow Press.

Held, Ray E. 1973. *The Rise of the Public Library in California*. Chicago: American Library Association.

Himmel, Ethel E., William J. Wilson, and GraceAnne DeCandido. 2000. *The Functions and Roles of State Library Agencies*. Chicago: American Library Association.

Holley, Edward G., and Robert Schremser. 1983. *The Library Services and Construction Act: An Historical Overview from the Viewpoint of Major Participants*. Greenwich, CT: JAI Press.

Hughes, Kathleen M. 2009. *The PLA Reader for Public Library Directors and Managers*. New York: Neal-Schuman.

Imholz, Susan, and Jennifer Weil Arns. 2007. *Worth Their Weight: An Assessment of the Evolving Field of Library Valuation*. New York: Americans for Libraries Council.

Joeckel, Carleton Bruns. 1935. *The Government of the American Public Library*. Chicago: University of Chicago Press.

Josey, E. J. 1980. *Libraries and the Political Process*. New York: Neal-Schuman.

———. 1987. *Libraries, Coalitions and the Public Good*. New York: Neal-Schuman.

Josey, E. J., and Kenneth D. Shearer. 1990. *Politics and the Support of Libraries*. New York: Neal-Schuman.

Krane, Dale, Platon N. Rigos, and Melvin Hill Jr. 2001. *Home Rule in America: A Fifty-State Handbook*. Washington, DC: CQ Press.

Kranich, Nancy C. 2001. "Libraries, the New Media, and the Political Process." In *Libraries and Democracy*, edited by Nancy Kranich, 108–112. Chicago: American Library Association.

Ladenson, Alex. 1982. *Library Law and Legislation in the United States*. Metuchen, NJ: Scarecrow Press.

Lipinski, Tomas A. 2002. *Libraries, Museums and Archives: Legal Issues and Ethical Challenges in the New Information Era*. Lanham, MD: Scarecrow Press.

Manjarrez, C., L. Langa, and K. Miller. 2009. *A Catalyst for Change: LSTA Grants to States Program Activities and the Transformation of Library Services to the Public* (IMLS-2009-RES-01). Washington, DC: Institute of Museum and Library Services. http://www.imls.gov/pdf/CatalystForChange.pdf.

Merola, Marci. 2008. *Library Advocate's Handbook*. Chicago: American Library Association, Office for Library Advocacy.

Merrill, Julia Wright. 1942. *Regional and District Library Laws*. Chicago: American Library Association.

Mersel, Jules. 1969. *An Overview of the Library Services and Construction Act, Title 1*. New York: R. R. Bowker.

Minow, Mary, and Tomas A. Lipinski. 2003. *The Library's Legal Answer Book*. Chicago: American Library Association.

Tolman, Frank Leland. 1937. *Digest of County Library Laws of the United States*. Chicago: American Library Association.

Turner, Anne M. 2000. *Vote Yes for Libraries: A Guide to Winning Ballot Measure Campaigns for Library Funding*. Jefferson, NC: McFarland.

Wallace, Linda K. 2000. *Library Advocates Handbook*. Chicago: American Library Association.

Yust, William F. 1911. *Library Legislation*. Chicago: American Library Association.

Articles

"Advocacy Grows at Your Library." 2004. *American Libraries* 35 (February): 32–36.

Berry, John N. 2009. "No Villains: Threatened Cuts and Partial Restorations Point Out the Ambiguous Politics of Library Funding." *Library Journal* (September 15): 24–25.

Bertot, John Carlo, Charles R. McClure, and Joe Ryan. 2002. "Impact of External Technology Funding Programs for Public Libraries: A Study of LSTA, E-Rate, Gates and Others." *Public Libraries* 41 (May/June): 166–171.

Brawner, Lee. 1993. "The People's Choice." *Library Journal* (January): 59–62.

Brey-Casiano, Carol. 2005. "Grassroots Advocacy Works." *American Libraries* 36 (June/July): 5.

Budd, John. 2008. "Public Library Leaders." *Public Library Quarterly* 26, no. 3: 1–14.

Burger, Leslie. 2007. "I Love Libraries." *American Libraries* 38 (January): 6.

Byrnes, Shirley M. 2005. "Advocacy and Illinois Regional Library Systems." *Illinois Libraries* 86 (December): 80–81.

Coffman, Steve. 2004. "Saving Ourselves: Plural Funding for Public Libraries." *American Libraries* 35 (February): 37–39.

Dain, Phyllis. 1996. "American Public Libraries and the Third Sector: Historical Reflections and Implications." *Libraries and Culture* 31 (Winter): 56–84.

Fry, James W. 1975. "LSA and LSCA, 1956–1973: A Legislative History." *Library Trends* 24 (July): 7–28.

Goldberg, B. 2008. "Voters Buck Gloomy Economic Outlook to Fund Libraries." *American Libraries* 39 (December): 23.

Goldhor, Herbert. 1943. "Civil Service in Public Libraries." *Library Quarterly* 13 (July): 187–211.

Gordon, Andrew C., et al. 2003. "The Gates Legacy." *Library Journal* (March 1): 44–48.

Hennen, Thomas J., Jr. 2002. "Are Wider Library Units Wiser?" *American Libraries* 33, no. 6 (June/July): 65–70. (Also titled, "Wider and Wiser Units.") http://www.haplr-index.com/wider_and_wiser_units.htm.

————. 2005. "Is There a Library Consolidation in Your Future?" *American Libraries* 36 (October): 49–51.

Herrera, L. 2003. "It's Our Turn." *Public Libraries* 42 (November/December): 343.

Hilyard, Nann Blaine. 2009. "Cultivating Support for Library Advocacy." *Public Libraries* 48 (May/June): 16–19.

Holland, Suzann, and Amanda Verploeg. 2009. "No Easy Targets: Six Libraries in the Economy's Dark Days." *Public Libraries* 48 (July/August): 27–38.

Jaeger, Paul T., and Zheng Yan. 2009. "One Law with Two Outcomes: Comparing Implementation of CIPA in Public Libraries and Schools." *Information Technology and Libraries* 28 (March): 6–14.

Kniffel, Leonard. 2008. "8 Years Later: Laura Bush, Librarian in the White House." *American Libraries* 39 (December): 42–47.

Krois, Jerome W. 2002. "An Introduction to Public Library Foundations: A Members' Guide." *Unabashed Librarian* 122: 22–26.

Ladenson, Alex. 1970. "Library Legislation: Some General Considerations." *Library Trends* 19 (October): 175–181.

Landgraf, G. 2008. "Minneapolis Public Library Merges with Hennepin County Library." *American Libraries* 39 (March): 19.

"A National Plan for Libraries." 1935. *ALA Bulletin* 29 (February): 91–98.

"A National Plan for Libraries." 1939. *ALA Bulletin* 33 (February): 136–150.

Reed, Sally Gardner. 2004. "FOLUSA Turns 25." *American Libraries* 35 (February): 40–41.

————. 2009. "Amalgamating for Advocacy." *American Libraries* 40 (March): 34–36.

Richards, Susan L. 1996. "Library Philanthropy with a Personal Touch: Phoebe Apperson Hearst and the Libraries of Lead and Anaconda." *Libraries and Culture* 31 (Winter): 197–208.

Schaefer, Steve W. 2001. "Going for the Green: How Public Libraries get State Money." *Public Libraries* 40 (September/October): 298–304.

Schuman, Patricia. 1999. "Speaking Up and Speaking Out: Ensuring Equity through Advocacy." *American Libraries* 30 (October): 50–53.

"State Library Agencies Get Requested Fed Funding." 2009. *Library Journal* 134 (April 1): 13.

Stevenson, Siobhan. 2006–2007. "Philanthropy's Unintended Consequences: Public Libraries and the Struggle Over Free Versus Proprietary Software." *Progressive Librarian* 28 (Winter): 64–77.

"Straight Answers from George Christian and Peter Chase." 2006. *American Libraries* 37 (August): 22.

Websites

Alliance for Regional Stewardship. http://www.acce.org/ars/about-the-alliance-for-regional-stewardship/.

American Library Association, Federal Library Legislative and Advocacy Network. http://www.ala.org/ala/issuesadvocacy/advocacy/federallegislation/getinvolved/fllan/index.cfm.

American Library Association, Office for Library Advocacy. http://www.ala.org/ala/aboutala/offices/ola/index.cfm.

American Library Association, Washington Office. http://www.ala.org/ala/aboutala/offices/wo/index.cfm.

Association of Library Trustees, Advocates, Friends and Foundations. http://www.ala.org/ala/mgrps/divs/altaff/index.cfm.

Bill and Melinda Gates Foundation. "Libraries." http://www.gatesfoundation.org/topics/Pages/libraries.aspx.

Brevard Library Foundation. http://www.brevardlibraryfoundation.org/index.html.

California State Library. 2008. *LSTA Five-Year Plan 2008-2012*. http://www.library.ca.gov/grants/lsta/docs/STATE_PLAN_08_12.pdf.

Chicago Public Library Foundation. http://www.chicagopubliclibraryfoundation.org.

Chief Officers of State Library Agencies. http://www.cosla.org.

Council on Foundations. Community Foundations. http://www.cof.org.

Foundation Center. http://www.foundationcenter.org.

GEOLIB. http://www.geolib.org.

Georgia Public Library Service. 2007. *Library Services and Technology Act Five Year Plan for Georgia's Libraries 2008–2012*. http://www.georgialibraries.org/lib/lsta/5yr_plan2008_12.pdf.

LSTA Five-Year Plans. http://www.cosla.org/content.cfm/id/lsta_five_year_plans.

National Association of Counties. http://www.naco.org.

National Governors Association. http://www.nga.org.

Netter Center for Community Partnerships. 2008. "Anchor Institution Toolkit: A Guide for Neighborhood Revitalization." University of Pennsylvania. http://www.upenn.edu/ccp/resources/publications/anchor-toolkit-200803.pdf.

The Public Access to Computing Project: Legacy of Gates U.S. Library Project. http://www.webjunction.org/pacomputing.

U.S. Census Bureau. 2010. "State and County Quick Facts." http://quickfacts.census.gov/qfd/states/00000.html.

U.S. Conference of Mayors. http://www.usmayors.org.

U.S. Institute of Museum and Library Services. http://www.imls.gov/index.shtm.

———. "Grants to State Library Agencies." http://www.imls.gov/programs/programs.shtm.

———. 2009. *Public Libraries Survey: Fiscal Year 2007*. Washington, DC: Institute of Museum and Library Services. http://harvester.census.gov/imls/pubs/pls/pub_detail.asp?id=122#.

———. 2010. *Public Libraries Survey: Fiscal Year 2008*, pp. 43–44. Washington, DC: Institute of Museum and Library Services. http://harvester.census.gov/imls/pubs/Publications/pls2008.pdf.

6. Administration and Staffing

Books and Chapters in Books

Altman, Ellen, and Roberta Bowler. 1980. *Local Public Library Administration.* Chicago: American Library Association.

Association for Library and Information Science Education. Annual. *Library and Information Science Education Statistical Report.* http://www.alise.org.

Avery, Elizabeth Fuseler, et al. 2001. *Staff Development: A Practical Guide.* 3rd ed. Chicago: American Library Association.

Baugham, James C. 1993. *Policymaking for Public Library Trustees.* Englewood, CO: Libraries Unlimited.

Bostwich, Arthur. 1927. *The Trustee and His Library.* Chicago: American Library Association.

Brumley, Rebecca. 2005. *The Neal-Schuman Directory of Public Library Job Descriptions.* New York: Neal-Schuman.

Childers, Thomas, and Nancy Van House. 1993. *What's Good? Describing Your Public Library's Effectiveness.* Chicago: American Library Association.

Dixon, Sandy. 2001. *Iowa Public Library Director's Handbook, 2001.* Des Moines, IA: State Library of Iowa.

Donovan, Georgie L., and Miguel A. Figueroa. 2009. *Staff Development Strategies That Work.* New York: Neal-Schuman.

Driggers, Preston F., and Eileen Dumas. 2002. *Managing Library Volunteers: A Practical Toolkit.* Chicago: American Library Association.

Garceau, Oliver. 1949. "The Governing Authority of the Public Library." In *The Public Library in the Political Process: A Report of the Public Library Inquiry*, 53–110. New York: Columbia University Press.

Getz, Malcolm. 1980. *Public Libraries: An Economic View.* Baltimore, MD: Johns Hopkins University Press.

Gillespie, Kellie M. 2004. *Teen Volunteer Services in Libraries.* Lanham, MD: VOYA Books.

Healey, Paul D. 2008. *Professional Liability Issues for Librarians and Information Professionals.* New York: Neal-Schuman.

Hernon, Peter. 2010. *Shaping the Future: Advancing the Understanding of Leadership.* Santa Barbara, CA: Libraries Unlimited.

Hernon, Peter, Ronald R. Powell, and Arthur P. Young. 2003. *The Next Library Leadership: Attributes of Academic and Public Library Directors.* Westport, CT: Greenwood Press.

Hopper, Lyn. 2008. *Georgia Public Library Trustee Manual.* Georgia Public Library Service. http://www.georgialibraries.org/lib/publications/trusteemanual.

Hughes, Kathleen. 2009. *The PLA Reader for Public Library Directors and Managers.* New York: Neal-Schuman.

Illinois Library Association. 2009. *Serving Our Public 2.0: Standards for Public Libraries 2009.*

Joeckel, Carleton Bruns. 1935. "Municipal Libraries Managed by Boards: Organization of the Library Board; Municipal Libraries: Power and Functions of the Library Board; and an Appraisal of the Library Board as a Governmental Agency." In *The Government of the American Public Library*, 170–262. Chicago: University of Chicago Press.

Kay, Linda. 2002. *New Jersey Public Libraries: A Manual for Trustees.* Trenton, NJ: New Jersey State Library.

Landau, Herbert B. 2008. *The Small Public Library Survival Guide: Thriving on Less.* Chicago: American Library Association.

Larson, Jeanette, and Herman Totten. 1998. *Model Policies for Small and Medium Public Libraries.* New York: Neal-Schuman.

Lubans, John. 2010. *Leading from the Middle.* Santa Barbara, CA: Libraries Unlimited/ABC-CLIO.

Massis, Bruce E. 2003. *The Practical Library Manager.* Binghamton, NY: Haworth Information Press.

Mayo, Diane, and Jeanne Goodrich. 2002. *Staffing for Results.* Chicago: American Library Association.

McCook, Kathleen de la Peña. 2010. "Unions in Public and Academic Libraries." In *Encyclopedia of Library and Information Science*. London: Taylor and Francis.

Miller, Ellen G., and Patricia H. Fisher. 2007. *Library Board: Strategic Guide.* Lanham, MD: Scarecrow Press.

Moore, Mary Y. 2010. *The Successful Library Trustee Handbook.* 2nd ed. Chicago: American Library Association.

Nelson, Sandra S., and June Garcia. 2003. *Creating Policies for Results: From Chaos to Clarity.* Chicago: American Library Association.

Nelson, Sandra, Ellen Altman, and Diane Mayo. 2000. *Managing for Results: Effective Resource Allocation for Public Libraries.* Chicago: American Library Association.

Owens, Stephen. 1996. *Public Library Structure and Organization in the United States.* Washington, DC: National Center for Education Statistics.

Pearlmutter, Jane, and Nelson, Paul. 2011. *Small Public Library Management.* Chicago: American Library Association.

Prentice, Anne E. 1973. *The Public Library Trustee.* Metuchen, NJ: Scarecrow.

Pungitore, Verna L. 1989. "Governance of Public Libraries." In *Public Librarianship: An Issues Oriented Approach*, 47–58. New York: Greenwood Press.

Reed, Sally Gardner, and Beth Nawalinski. 2008. *Even More Great Ideas for Libraries and Friends.* New York: Neal-Schuman.

Robbins, Jane B. 1975. *Citizen Participation and the Public Library.* Metuchen, NJ: Scarecrow Press.

Robinson, Maureen K. 2001. *Non-profit Boards That Work: Ending One-Size-Fits-All Governance.* New York: John Wiley and Sons.

Roy, Loriene. 2006. *Bridging Boundaries to Create a New Workforce: A Survey of SPECTRUM Scholarship Recipients, 1998–2003.* Chicago: American Library Association.

Sager, Donald J. 1989. *Managing the Public Library*. Boston: G. K. Hall.

———. 2000. *Small Libraries: Organization and Operation*. Ft. Atkinson, WI: Highsmith Press.

Saulmon, Sharon A. 1997. *Sample Evaluations of Library Directors*. Chicago: American Library Trustee Association/American Library Association.

Singer, Paula M. 2002. *Developing a Compensation Plan for Your Library*. Chicago: American Library Association.

Stanley, Mary J. 2008. *Managing Library Employees*. New York: Neal-Schuman.

Sullivan, Peggy, and William Ptacek. 1982. *Public Libraries: Smart Practices in Personnel*. Littleton, CO: Libraries Unlimited.

Thompson, Susan M. 2009. *Core Technology Competencies for Librarians and Library Staff*. New York: Neal-Schuman.

Todaro, Julie, and Marl L. Smith. 2006. *Training Library Staff and Volunteers to Provide Extraordinary Customer Service*. New York: Neal-Schuman.

Urban Libraries Council. 1997. *Governing and Funding Metropolitan Public Libraries*. Evanston, IL: Urban Libraries Council.

Urban Libraries Council. 2010. *Partners for the Future: Public Libraries and Local Governments Creating Sustainable Communities*. [Chicago, IL]: Urban Libraries Council.

U.S. Institute of Museum and Library Services. 2010. *Public Libraries Survey: Fiscal Year 2008* (IMLS-2010–PLS-02). Washington, DC: Institute of Museum and Library Services. http://harvester.census.gov/imls/pubs/Publications/pls2008.pdf.

Wade, Gordon S. 1991. *Working with Library Boards of Trustees: A How-to-Do-It Manual*. New York: Neal-Schuman.

Weingand, Darlene E. 2001. *The Administration of the Small Public Library*. Chicago: American Library Association.

Wheeler, Joseph Lewis, Herbert Goldhor, and Carlton C. Rochell. 1981. *Wheeler and Goldhor's Practical Administration of Public Libraries*. New York: Harper and Row.

Winston, Mark. 1999. *Managing Multiculturalism and Diversity in the Library: Principles and Issues for Administrators*. Binghamton, NY: Haworth Press.

Wisconsin Department of Public Instruction, Division of Libraries, Technology and Community Learning. 2000. *Certification Manual for Wisconsin Public Library Directors*. Madison, WI: Wisconsin Department of Public Instruction.

Young, Virginia. 1995. *The Library Trustee: A Practical Handbook*. 5th ed. Chicago: American Library Association.

Articles

Ames, Kathyrn S., and Greg Heid. 2009. "The Role of the Library Board of Trustees in the Construction of a Public Library." *Georgia Library Quarterly* 46 (Winter): 9–14.

Arns, Jennifer. 2007. "Challenges in Governance: The Leadership Characteristics and Behaviors Valued by Public Library Trustees in Times of Conflict and Contention." *The Library Quarterly* 77: 287–310.

Auld, Hampton. 2002. "The Benefits and Deficiencies of Unions in Public Libraries." *Public Libraries* 41 (May/June): 135–142.

Batson, C. Daniel, and Nadia Ahmad. 2002. "Four Motives for Community Involvement." *Journal of Social Issues* 58 (Fall): 429–445.

Bernier, Anthony. 2009. "Young Adult Volunteering in Public Libraries: Managerial Implications." *Library Leadership and Management* 23 (Summer): 133–139.

Berry, John N. 2009. "Team Cedar Rapids." *Library Journal* 134 (January 1): 28–30.

Brown, Jeanne M. 2010. "Informal Assessment for Library Middle Managers." *Library Leadership and Management* 24 (Winter): 18–22.

Callen, J. L., A. Klein, and D. Tinkelman. 2003. "Board Composition, Committees and Organizational Efficiency." *Nonprofit and Voluntary Sector Quarterly* 32 (December): 493–520.

Casey, James B. 2002. "The 1.6% Solution." *American Libraries* 33 (April): 85–86.

Christenson, John. 1995. "The Role of the Public Library Trustee." *Library Trends* 44: 63–76.

Clay, Edwin S., III, and Patricia C. Bangs. 2000. "Entrepreneurs in the Public Library: Reinventing an Institution." *Library Trends* 48 (Winter): 606–618.

Farmer, Leslie. 2003. "Teen Library Volunteers." *Public Libraries* 42 (May/June): 141–142.

Fay, Diane. 2008. "Joining a Union." *Library Worklife* 5 (July).

Fisher, William, and Lisa Rosenblum. 2008. "Now What Do I Do? Some Reflections on Becoming a First-Time Public Library Director." *Library Administration and Management* 22 (Winter): 15–23.

Florida Library Association, Friends and Trustees Section. 2000. "Floridians Value Their Libraries." *Florida Libraries* 43 (Fall): 18.

Frank, Donald G. 1997. "Activity in Professional Associations: The Positive Difference in a Librarian's Career." *Library Trends* 46 (Fall): 307–317.

Freedman, Maurice J. 2002. "The Campaign for America's Librarians." *American Libraries* 33 (August): 7.

Freedman, Maurice (Mitch) J. 2003. "For the People Who Work in Libraries." *Library Journal* 128 (April 2): 46.

Gardyn, R. 2003. "Building Board Diversity." *Chronicle of Philanthropy*. December 11. http://philanthropy.com/free/articles/v16/i05/05002501.htm.

Gibbs, P., et al. 2007. "Public Library Trustees: Characteristics and Educational Preferences." *Public Library Quarterly* 26 (October): 21–43.

Glennon, Michael. 1997. "Developing and Passing a Bond Issue: A Trustee's View." *Public Libraries* 36 (January/February): 24–28.

Goodrich, Jeanne. 2005. "Staffing Public Libraries: Are There Models or Best Practices?" *Public Libraries* 44 (September/October): 277–281.

Hague, Rodger. 1999. "A Short History of the Stevens County Rural Library District." *Alki* 15 (July): 22–23.

Hider, Philip. 2008. "Using the Contingent Valuation Method for Dollar Valuations of Library Services." *Library Quarterly* 78 (October): 437–458.

Hill, Nanci Milone. 2009. "Across the Spectrum." *Public Libraries* 48 (March/April): 15.

Hilyard, Nann Blaine. 2003. "Our Trusty Trustees." *Public Libraries* 42 (July/August): 220–223.

Holley, Carroll, and Linda Klancher. 2002. "Labor Unions in Public Libraries: A Perspective from Both Sides of the Issue." *Public Libraries* 41 (May/June): 138.

Jatkevicius, Jim. 2010. "Libraries and the Lessons of Abilene: Managing Agreement for the Sake of Transparency and Organizational Communication." *Library Leadership and Management* 24, no. 3 (Summer): 77–82.

Johnson, Cameron. 2002. "Professionalism, Not Paternalism." *Public Libraries* 41 (May/June): 139–140.

Jordan, Amy. 2002. "Can Unions Solve the Low-Pay Dilemma?" *American Libraries* 33 (January): 65–69.

Kelley, H. Neil. 1999. "Portrait of the Illinois Trustee Community." *Illinois Libraries* 81 (Fall): 222–225.

Kinnaly, Gene. 2002. "Pay Equity, Support Staff, and ALA." *Library Mosaics* 13 (March/April): 8–10.

Kraemer, Jean T. 1990. "The Library Trustee as a Library Activist." *Public Libraries* 29 (July/August): 220–223.

Lang, Shirley. 2009. "From the Other Side." *Public Libraries* 47 (September/October): 28–29.

Lynch, Mary Jo. 2003. "Public Library Staff: How Many Is Enough?" *American Libraries* 32 (May): 58–59.

Maatta, Stephanie. 2009. "Placements and Salaries." *Library Journal* (October 15).

Marshall, Joanne Gard, Paul Solomon, and Susan Rathbun-Grubb. 2009. "Workforce Issues in Library and Information Science." *Library Trends* 58 (Fall): 121–126.

Martinez, Elizabeth. 2009. "We're Back!" *American Libraries* 40 (March): 42–44.

McCook, Kathleen de la Peña, ed. 2000. "Ethnic Diversity in Library and Information Science." Special issue, *Library Trends* 49 (Summer): 1–214.

———. 2009. "There Is Power in a Union." *Progressive Librarian* 32 (Winter/Spring): 55–67.

Milden, James T. 1977. "Women, Public Libraries and Library Unions." *Journal of Library History* 12 (Spring): 150–158.

Miller, Ellen G. 2001. "Getting the Most from Your Boards and Advisory Councils." *Library Administration and Management* 15 (Fall): 204–212.

Musick, Marc A., John Wilson, and William B. Bynum Jr. 2000. "Race and Formal Volunteering: The Differential Effects of Class and Religion." *Social Forces* 78 (June): 1539–1570.

Naylor, Richard J. 2000. "Core Competencies: What They Are and How to Use Them." *Public Libraries* 39 (March/April): 108–114.

Nicol, Erica A., and Corey M. Johnson. 2008. "Volunteers in Libraries: Program Structure, Evaluation, and Theoretical Analysis." *Reference and User Services Quarterly* 48 (Winter): 154–163.

Oder, Norman. 2008. "IMLS: $20.3M for Recruitment." *Library Journal* 133 (August): 16.

Omoto, Alan M., and Mark Snyder. 2002. "Considerations of Community: The Context and Process of Volunteerism." *American Behavioral Scientist* 45 (January): 848–867.

Price, Lee. 2007. "With a Little Help from My Friends." *Public Libraries* 46 (September/October): 43–46.

Rathbun-Grubb, Susan, and Joanne Gard Marshall. 2009. "Public Librarianship as a Career: Challenges and Prospects." *Library Trends* 58 (Fall): 263–275.

"Recruitment of Public Librarians." 2000. *Public Libraries* 39 (May/June): 168–172.

Reed, Sally Gardner. 2009. "Amalgamating for Advocacy." *American Libraries* 40 (March): 34–36.

Robbin, Alice. 2000. "We the People: One Nation, a Multicultural Society." *Library Trends* 49 (Summer): 6–48.

Roberts, John J. 2010. "Volunteering with Friends Groups Is Rewarding Experience." *Georgia Library Quarterly* 47 (Winter): 6.

Sager, Donald J. 2001. "Evolving Virtues: Public Library Administrative Skills." *Public Libraries* 40 (September/October): 268–272.

Scheppke, Jim. 1991. "The Governance of Public Libraries: Findings of the PLA Governance of Public Libraries Committee." *Public Libraries* 30 (September/October): 288–294.

Sheketoff, Emily. 2009. "Employee Free Choice Act." *Progressive Librarian* 32 (Winter/ Spring): 76.

Shoaf, Eric C. 2009. "Library Leadership in Action." *Library Leadership and Management* 23 (Spring): 75–79.

Sparanese, Ann, C. 2002. "Unions in Libraries: A Positive View." *Public Libraries* 41 (May/June): 140–141.

Strudwick, Jane. 2006. "A Selected Bibliography of Library Disaster Stories: Before, During, and After." *Public Library Quarterly* 25, no. 3/4: 7–16.

Thomas, Mary Augusta. 2009. "Interview with Ginnie Cooper." *Library Leadership and Management* 23 (Fall): 177–178.

Valentine, Patrick M. 1996. "Steel, Cotton and Tobacco: Philanthropy and Public Libraries in North Carolina, 1900–1940." *Libraries and Culture* 31 (Spring): 272–298.

Young, Virginia. 1977. "Library Governance by Citizen Boards." *Library Trends* 25 (Fall): 287–297.

Websites

Akron-Summit County Public Library. "Organization Chart." http://www.akronlibrary.org/ad-org.html.

American Indian Library Association. http://www.ailanet.org.

American Library Association. "Key Action Area. Education and Continuous Learning." http://www.ala.org/ala/aboutala/missionhistory/keyactionareas/index.cfm.

———. "Learning Round Table." http://www.ala.org/ala/mgrps/rts/clenert/index.cfm.

———. "Library and Information Studies and Human Resource Utilization: Policy Statement. Policy 54.1." http://www.ala.org/ala/aboutala/governance/policymanual/index.cfm.

———. "Library Careers." http://www.ala.org/ala/educationcareers/careers.

———. "Library Support Staff Interests Round Table." http://www.ala.org/ala/mgrps/rts/lssirt/index.cfm.

———. 2008. *Standards for Accreditation of Master's Programs in Library and Information Studies.* Chicago: American Library Association. http://www.ala.org/ala/educationcareers/education/accreditedprograms/standards/index.cfm.

American Library Association-Allied Professional Association. 2007. *Advocating for Better Salaries and Pay Equity Toolkit.* http://www.ala-apa.org/files/2010/07/toolkit.pdf.

————. 2010. "Certification News." http://www.ala-apa.org/certification/certification.html.

American Library Association, Association of Library Trustees, Advocates, Friends and Foundations. "Organizational Tools for Trustees. Ethics Policy." http://www.ala.org/ala/mgrps/divs/altaff/trustees/orgtools/index.cfm.

American Library Association, Human Resource Development and Recruitment Office. http://www.ala.org/ala/aboutala/offices/hrdr/index.cfm.

Asian/Pacific American Library Association. http://www.apalaweb.org.

Association for Library and Information Science Education. http://www.alise.org.

Association for Research on Nonprofit Organizations and Voluntary Action. http://www.arnova.org.

Association of Library Trustees, Advocates, Friends and Foundations. Organizational Tools for Trustees. http://www.ala.org/ala/mgrps/divs/altaff/trustees/orgtools/index.cfm.

Bedford Free Library. http://www.bedfordlibrary.net.

Bedford, Town of. http://www.town.bedford.ma.us.

Black Caucus of the American Library Association. http://www.bcala.org.

BoardSource (Building Effective Nonprofit Boards). http://www.boardsource.org.

Center on Budget and Policy Priorities. 2010. "New Fiscal Year Brings Continued Trouble for States Due to Economic Downturn." http://www.cbpp.org/cms/index.cfm?fa=view&id=1283.

Chinese-American Librarians Association. http://www.cala-web.org.

Denver Public Library. "Organization Chart." http://denverlibrary.org/files/org_chart.pdf.

Georgia Board of Librarians. http://sos.georgia.gov/plb/librarians/.

Kentucky State Board for the Certification of Librarians. http://www.kdla.ky.gov/libsupport/certification.htm.

Los Angeles Public Library. "Volunteer Opportunities at the Los Angeles Public Library." http://www.lapl.org/about/volunteer.html.

Lynch, Mary Jo. "Spending on Staff Development—2001." American Library Association, Office for Research and Statistics. http://www.ala.org (enter "staff development" in search box).

"Missouri Public Library Standards: An Implementation Plan." 2005. http://www.sos.mo.gov/library/libstan.pdf.

New York State Library. "Public Library Certification Process." http://www.nysl.nysed.gov/libdev/cert.

————. 2010. "Continuing Education for Public Librarian Certification." http://www.nysl.nysed.gov/libdev/cert/conted.htm.

Public Library Association. "Public Librarian Recruitment." http://www.pla.org.

REFORMA—National Association to Promote Library and Information Services to Latinos and the Spanish-Speaking. http://www.reforma.org.

Seattle Public Library. "Volunteer Opportunities." http://www.spl.org/default.asp?pageID=about_support_volunteering_opportunities.

U.S. Corporation for National and Community Service. http://www.nationalservice.gov.

U.S. Department of Labor, Bureau of Labor Statistics. *Occupational Outlook Handbook; Occupational Outlook Quarterly; Occupational Employment Statistics.* http://www.bls.gov.

U.S. Institute of Museum and Library Services. 2009. "Laura Bush 21st Century Librarian Program." http://www.imls.gov/news/2009/061709b_list.shtm.

———. 2010. *Public Libraries Survey: Fiscal Year 2008* (IMLS-2010–PLS-02). Washington, DC: Institute of Museum and Library Services. http://harvester.census.gov/imls/pubs/Publications/pls2008.pdf.

Washington State Library. "Certification of Librarians." http://www.secstate.wa.gov/library/libraries/training/certification.aspx.

Webjunction. 2009. "Libraries as Learning Organizations." http://www.webjunction.org/learning-organization/-/articles/content/61714988.

"Wisconsin Public Library Standards." 2005. http://dpi.wi.gov/pld/standard.html.

Examples of Trustee and Board Materials Developed by States

Hopper, Lyn. 2008. *Georgia Public Library Trustee Manual*. Georgia Public Library Service. http://www.georgialibraries.org/lib/publications/trusteemanual.

Michigan Library Association, Trustee and Advocates Division. 2006. "Basic Training for Trustees." http://www.mla.lib.mi.us/tad.

Michigan Library Quality Services Audit Checklist. History, Getting Started, and FAQ. http://www.michigan.gov/mde/0,1607,7-140-54504_18668_45510—-,00.html.

Mississippi Library Commission. "Library Boards of Trustees." http://www.mlc.lib.ms.us/ServicesToLibraries/ladv_board.html.

New York State Association of Library Boards. 2005. *Handbook for Library Trustees of New York State*. http://www.nysalb.org/reference/2005Handbook.pdf.

Office of Library and Information Services. *Rhode Island Public Library Trustees Handbook*. http://www.olis.state.ri.us/pubs/trustees/section1.pdf.

Wisconsin Department of Public Instruction. 2009. *Trustee Essentials: A Handbook for Wisconsin Public Library Trustees*. http://dpi.state.wi.us/pld/handbook.html.

7. Structure and Infrastructure

Books and Chapters in Books

Alire, Camila A. 2000. *Library Disaster Planning and Recovery Handbook*. New York: Neal-Schuman.

American Library Association. Annually revised. "Library Services for People with Disabilities." In *ALA Policy Manual*, 54.3.2. Chicago: American Library Association. http://www.ala.org/ala/aboutala/governance/policymanual.

American Library Association, Coordinating Committee on Revision of Public Library Standards. 1956. *Public Library Service: A Guide to Evaluation with Minimum Standards*. Chicago: American Library Association.

American Library Association, Public Library Association, Standards Committee. 1967. *Minimum Standards for Public Library Systems, 1966*. Chicago: American Library Association.

Bertot, J. C., Lesley A. Langa, Juston M. Grimes, Kathryn Sigler, and Shannon N. Simmons. 2010. *2009–2010 Public Library Funding and Access Survey.* American Library Association. http://www.plinternetsurvey.org/?q=node/13.

Bertot, J. C., C. R. McClure, C. B. Wright, E. Jensen, and S. Thomas. 2009. *Public Libraries and the Internet 2009: Survey Results and Findings.* College Park, MD: Center for Library and Information Innovation. http://www.plinternetsurvey.org/?q=node/13.

Bobinski, George S. 1969. "Carnegie Library Architecture." In *Carnegie Libraries: Their History and Impact on American Library Development*, 57–75. Chicago: American Library Association.

Brawner, Lee, and Donald K. Beck Jr. 1996. *Determining Your Public Library's Future Size: A Needs Assessment and Planning Model.* Chicago: American Library Association.

Breisch, Kenneth A. 2003. *Henry Hobson Richardson and the Small Public Library in America: A Study in Typology.* Cambridge, MA: MIT Press.

Bryan, Cheryl. 2007. *Managing Facilities for Results.* Chicago: American Library Association.

Building Blocks for Planning Functional Library Space. 2001. Edited by LAMA BES Facilities Committee. Lanham, MD: Scarecrow Press.

Bundy, Alan. 2003. "Joint-Use Libraries: The Ultimate Form of Cooperation." In *Planning the Modern Public Library Building*, edited by Gerard McCabe and James Kennedy. Westport, CT: Libraries Unlimited.

Buschman, John, and Gloria J. Leckie, eds. 2007. *Library as Place: History, Community and Culture.* Westport, CT: Libraries Unlimited.

Christensen, Karen, and David Levinsen. 2007. *A Heart of the Community: The Libraries We Love.* Great Barrington, MA: Berkshire.

Dahlgren, Anders C. 1996. *Planning the Small Library Facility.* 2nd ed. Chicago: American Library Association.

Davis, Denise M., John Carlo Bertot, and Charles R. McClure. 2008. *Libraries Connect Communities: Public Library Funding and Technology Access Study 2007–2008.* Chicago: American Library Association. http://www.ala.org/ala/research/initiatives/plftas/previousstudies.

———. 2009. *Libraries Connect Communities 3: Public Library Funding and Technology Access Study 2008–2009.* Chicago: American Library Association. http://www.ala.org/ala/research/initiatives/plftas/previousstudies.

Dudley, Michael. Forthcoming (2012). *Public Libraries and Resilient Cities: Creating Sustainable and Equitable Places.* Chicago: ALA Editions.

Feinberg, Sandra, and James R. Keller. 2010. *Designing Space for Children and Teens in Libraries and Public Spaces.* Chicago: American Library Association.

Feinberg, Sandra, Joan F. Kuchner, and Sari Feldman. 1998. *Learning Environments for Young Children: Rethinking Library Spaces and Services.* Chicago: American Library Association.

Fisher, Karen, et al. 2007. "Seattle Public Library as Place: Reconceptualizing Space, Community, and Information at the Central Library." In *Library as Place: History, Community and Culture*, 135–160. Westport, CT: Libraries Unlimited.

Henderson, Everett. 2009. *Service Trends in U.S. Public Libraries, 1997–2007.* Washington, DC: Institute of Museum and Library Services. http://www.imls.gov/pdf/Brief2010_01.pdf.

Institute of Museum and Library Services. "Status of Technology and Digitization in the Nation's Museums and Libraries, 2006 Report." ED495804.

Joeckel, Carleton B., and Amy Winslow. 1948. *A National Plan for Public Library Service*. Chicago: American Library Association.

Jones, Theodore. 1997. *Carnegie Libraries Across America: A Public Legacy*. New York: John Wiley.

Kahn, Miriam. 2003. *Disaster Response and Planning for Libraries*. Chicago: American Library Association.

Kahn, Miriam B. 2008. *The Library Security and Safety Guide to Prevention, Planning, and Response*. Chicago: American Library Association.

Kroski, Ellyssa. 2008. *Web 2.0 for Librarians and Information Professionals*. New York: Neal-Schuman.

———. 2010. *Tech Set Series*. New York: Neal-Schuman.

Latimer, Karen, and Hellen Niegaard, eds. 2007. *IFLA Library Building Guidelines: Developments and Reflections*. Munich: K. G. Saur.

Library of Congress, National Library Service for the Blind and Physically Handicapped. 2009. *Guide to State Laws Relating to Library Services for Blind and Physically Handicapped Individuals*. Washington, DC: Library of Congress.

Lushington, Nolan. 2002. *Libraries Designed for Users: A 21st Century Guide*. New York: Neal-Schuman.

Manjarrez, C., L. Langa, and K. Miller. 2009. *A Catalyst for Change: LSTA Grants to States Program Activities and the Transformation of Library Services to the Public* (IMLS-2009-RES-01). Washington, DC: Institute of Museum and Library Services. http://www.imls.gov/pdf/CatalystForChange.pdf.

Mattern, Shannon. 2005. *Public Places, Info Spaces: Creating the Modern Urban Library*. Washington, DC: Smithsonian.

———. 2007. *The New Downtown Library*. Minneapolis: University of Minnesota Press.

Mayo, Diane. 2005. *Technology for Results: Developing Service-Based Plans*. Chicago: American Library Association.

Mayo, Diane, and Sandra Nelson. 1999. *Wired for the Future: Developing Your Library Technology Plan*. Chicago: American Library Association.

McBane, Sam Mulford, and Ned A. Himmel. 2009. *How Green Is My Library?* Westport, CT: Libraries Unlimited.

McCabe, Gerald B. 2000. *Planning for a New Generation of Public Library Buildings*. Westport, CT: Greenwood Press.

———. 2003. *Planning the Modern Public Library Building*. Westport, CT: Libraries Unlimited.

McCarthy, Rick. 2007. *Managing Your Library Construction Project*. Chicago: American Library Association.

McClure, Charles R., and Paul T. Jaeger. 2009. *Public Libraries and Internet Service Roles: Measuring and Maximizing Internet Services*. American Library Association.

McNeil, Beth, and Denise J. Johnson. 1966. *Patron Behavior in Libraries: A Handbook of Positive Approaches to Negative Situations*. Chicago: American Library Association.

McCook, Kathleen de la Peña. 2000. *A Place at the Table: Participating in Community Building*. Chicago: American Library Association.

———. 2002. *Rocks in the Whirlpool: The American Library Association and Equity of Access*. ERIC. ED462981. Chicago: American Library Association.

Miller, Kathryn. 2010. *Public Libraries Going Green*. Chicago: American Library Association.

Mosely, Pixley Ann, and Wendi Arant-Kaspar. 2009. "LLAMA News Section." *Library Leadership and Management* 23 (Summer): 52–55.

Murphy, Tish. 2007. *Library Furnishings: A Planning Guide*. Jefferson, NC: McFarland.

Polanka, Sue. 2011. *No Shelf Required: E-Books in Libraries*. Chicago: American Library Association.

Public Library Association, Standards Committee. 1967. *Minimum Standards for Public Library Systems, 1966*. Chicago: American Library Association.

Public Library Funding & Technology Access Study, 2009-2010. 2010. Chicago: American Library Association.

Putnam, Robert D., and Lewis M. Feldstein. 2003. "Branch Libraries: The Heartbeat of the Community." In *Better Together: Restoring the American Community*, 34–54. New York: Simon and Schuster.

Rabun, J. Stanley. 2000. *Structural Analysis of Historic Buildings: Restoration, Preservation and Adaptive Reuse Applications for Architects and Engineers*. New York: Wiley.

Rivers, Vicki. 2004. *The Branch Manager's Handbook*. Jefferson, NC: McFarland.

Rubin, Rhea J. 2001. *Planning for Library Services for People with Disabilities*. Chicago: American Library Association.

Sannwald, William W. 2009. *Checklist of Building Design Considerations*. 5th ed. Chicago: American Library Association.

Shuman, Bruce A. 1999. *Library Security and Safety Handbook: Prevention, Policies, and Procedures*. Chicago: American Library Association.

Switzer, Teri R. 1999. *Safe at Work? Library Security and Safety Issues*. Lanham, MD: Scarecrow Press.

Thenell, Jan. 2004. *The Library's Crisis Communications Planner: A PR Guide for Handling Every Emergency*. Chicago: American Library Association.

Todaro, Julie Beth. 2009. *Emergency Preparedness for Libraries*. Lanham, MD: Government Institutes.

2009–2010 Public Library Funding and Technology Access Survey: Survey Findings and Results. Chicago: American Library Association. http://www.ala.org/ala/research/initiatives/plftas/2009_2010/summary0910.pdf.

Universal Service Administrative Company. 2010. http://www.universalservice.org.

U.S. Institute of Museum and Library Services. 2009. *Public Libraries Survey: Fiscal Year 2007*. Washington, DC: Institute of Museum and Library Services. http://harvester.census.gov/imls/pubs/pls/pub_detail.asp?id=122#.

———. 2010. *Public Libraries Survey: Fiscal Year 2008* (IMLS-2010–PLS-02). Washington, DC: Institute of Museum and Library Services.http://harvester.census.gov/imls/pubs/Publications/pls2008.pdf.

U.S. Institute of Museum and Library Services, State Programs. "5 Year Plans." http://www
.imls.gov/programs/5yearplans.shtm.
———. "5-Year Evaluations: 2003–2007." http://www.imls.gov/programs/5yearevals.shtm.
U.S. National Commission on Libraries and Information Science. 1992. *Pathways to Excellence: A Report on Improving Library and Information Services for Native American Peoples.*
Washington, DC: National Commission on Libraries and Information Science.
Van Slyck, Abigail Ayres. 1995. *Free to All: Carnegie Libraries and American Culture,
1890–1920.* Chicago: University of Chicago Press.
Vollmer, Timothy. 2010. "There's an App for That! Libraries and Mobile Technology: An Intro-
duction to Public Policy Considerations." Washington, DC: ALA Office for Information
Technology Policy. http://www.ala.org/ala/aboutala/offices/oitp/publications/policybriefs/
mobiledevices.pdf.
Wilkinson, Frances C., Linda K. Lewis, and Nancy K. Dennis. 2010. *Comprehensive Guide to
Emergency Preparedness and Disaster Recovery.* Chicago: Association of College and Re-
search Libraries.
Willis, Mark R. 1999. *Dealing with Difficult People in the Library.* Chicago: American Library
Association.
Windhausen, John, Jr., and Marijke Visser. 2009. *Fiber to the Library: How Public Libraries
Can Benefit from Using Fiber Optics for their Broadband Internet Connection.* Washington,
DC: ALA Office for Information Technology Policy. http://www.ala.org/ala/issuesadvocacy/
telecom/index.cfm.
Woodward, Jeannette. 2010. *Countdown to a New Library*, 2nd ed. Chicago: American Library
Association.

Articles

Antonelli, Monika. 2008. "The Green Library Movement: An Overview of Green Library Literature from 1979 to the Future of Green Libraries." *Electronic Green Journal* 27 (Fall).
http://escholarship.org/uc/item/39d3v236.
Balas, Janet L. 2009. "The Library for the Mobile Patron." *Computers in Libraries* 29 (May):
33.
———. 2009. "Excellence in Service in the Virtual Library." *Computers in Libraries* 29 (January): 33.
Ball, Mary Alice. 2009. "Aggregating Broadband Demand: Surveying the Benefits and Challenges for Public Libraries." *Government Information Quarterly* 26 (October): 551–558.
Becker, Samantha, et al. 2010. *Opportunity for All: How the American Public Benefits from
Internet Access at U.S. Libraries* (IMLS-2010-RES-01). Washington, DC: Institute of Mu-
seum and Library Services.
Berry, John N., III. 2004. "The San Jose Model: Gale/*Library Journal* Library of the Year.
2004: San Jose Public Library and San Jose State University Library." *Library Journal* 129
(June 15): 34.
Berry, Louise Parker, and Alan Kirk Gray. 2009. "State of the Art in Darien." *Library Journal*
(Spring): 6–9.

Bertot, John Carlo. 2001. "Measuring Service Quality in the Networked Environment: Approaches and Considerations." *Library Trends* 49 (Spring): 758–775.

Bertot, John Carlo, Charles R. McClure, and Joe Ryan. 2002. "Impact of External Technology Funding Programs for Public Libraries: A Study of LSTA, E-Rate, Gates and Others." *Public Libraries* 41 (May/June): 166–171.

Blumenstein, Lynn. 2009. "San Jose's Green Art." *Library Journal, Library by Design* (Spring): 24–25.

———. 2010. "Small Footprint with Big Impact." *Library Journal, Library by Design* 30 (Spring): 30.

Bracquet, Donna. 2009. "Information Needs in a Hurricane Gustav Evacuation Shelter: Reflections on a Librarian's Volunteer Experience." *Southeastern Librarian* 57 (Fall): 16–28.

Brehm-Heeger, Paula, and Greg Edwards. 2010. "Remaking One of the Nation's Busiest Main Libraries." *Public Libraries* 49, no. 5 (September/October): 40–44.

Brevik, Patricia Senn, et al. 2005. "We're Married! The Rewards and Challenges of Joint Libraries." *Journal of Academic Librarianship* 31 (September): 401–408.

Broome, Beth. 2009. "Marlon Blackwell Renews the Dignity of the Aging Fulbright Building." *Architectural Record* 197 (June): 86–90.

Bryan, Cheryl. 2009. "Beginning Your Green Building." *Library Journal* (Fall): 31.

"Building for the Future." 2003. *American Libraries* 34 (April): 41–62.

Burke, Susan K. 2009. "Perceptions of Public Library Accessibility for People with Disabilities." *Reference Librarian* 50 (January/March): 43–54.

Campbell, Anne L. 2003. "Magical Models." *Library Journal* (February 15): 38–40.

Dawson, Alma, and Kathleen de la Peña McCook. 2006. "Rebuilding Community in Louisiana after the Hurricanes of 2005." *Reference and User Services Quarterly* 45 (Summer): 292–296.

D'Elia, George, et al. 2002. "The Impact of the Internet on Public Library Use: An Analysis of the Current Consumer Market for Library and Internet Services." *Journal of the American Society for Information Science and Technology* 53: 802–820.

Dorr, Jessica, and Richard Akeroyd. 2001. "New Mexico Tribal Libraries: Bridging the Digital Divide." *Computers in Libraries* 21, no. 8 (October): 36–43. http://www.infotoday.com/cilmag/oct01/dorr&akeroyd.htm.

Duggar, David. 2009. "Atkins Branch: Shreveport's Seaport." *Louisiana Libraries* 71 (Winter): 21–24.

Ellis, Jamie Bounds, and Jane Shambra. 2008. "Reshaping Public Services after a Disaster." *Mississippi Libraries* 72 (Fall): 51–53.

Fackerell, Reita. 2008. "So You Think You Are Ready for a Disaster? Don't Be So Sure . . . Learning from the Seaside Public Library Experience." *OLA Quarterly* 14 (Winter): 15–16.

Fichter, Darlene, and Jeff Wisniewski. 2009. "Social Media Metrics: Tracking Your Impact." *Online* 33 (January/February): 54–57.

Flagg, Gordon. 2009. "Libraries Get Broadband Stimulus Grants." *American Libraries Online* (December 21): 23–28.

Fleischer, S. Victor, and Mark J. Heppner. 2009. "Disaster Planning for Libraries and Archives: What You Need to Know and How to Do It." *Library and Archival Security* 22, no. 2: 125–140.

"Florida Library Merges Branch, Social Services." 2009. *Library Journal* 134 (August):10.

Forrest, Charles. 2002. "Building Libraries and Library Building Awards—Twenty Years of Change: An Interview with Anders C. Dahlgren." *Library Administration and Management Journal* 16 (Summer): 120–125.

Fox, Bette-Lee. 2009. "Library Buildings 2009: The Constant Library." *Library Journal* (December 15).

Gisolfi, Peter. 2009. "A Green Library Inside and Out." *Library Journal: Library by Design* (Spring): 8.

Gordon, Andrew C., et al. 2003. "The Gates Legacy." *Library Journal* (March 1): 44–48.

Greenwood, Bill. 2009. "Bill and Melinda Gates Foundation Targets Library Internet Speeds." *Computers in Libraries* 29 (March): 32.

Gregory, Gwen. 1999. "The Library Services and Technology Act: How Changes from LSCA Are Affecting Libraries." *Public Libraries* 38 (November/December): 378–382.

Hadro, Josh. 2009. "Interfaces Galore for Mobile Devices." *Library Journal* 134 (March 1): 19–20.

Halverson, Kathleen, and Jean Plotas. 2006. "Creating and Capitalizing on the Town/Gown Relationship: An Academic Library and a Public Library Form a Community Partnership. *Journal of Academic Librarianship* 32 (November): 624–629.

Hatfield, Jean. 2008. "Doing What We Do Best." *Public Libraries* 47 (July/August): 19–20.

Haycock, Ken. 2006. "Dual Use Libraries: Guidelines for Success." *Library Trends* 54 (Spring): 488–500.

Henderson, Jill. 2007. "Exploring the Combined Public/School Library." *Knowledge Quest* 35 (January/February): 34–37.

Hilyard, Nann Blaine. 2008. "The Heart of the Neighborhood: Branch Librarian Today." *Public Libraries* 47 (July/August): 15.

Houser, John. 2009. "Open Source Public Workstations in Libraries." *Library Technology Reports* 45 (April).

Jaeger, Paul T., and Charles R. McClure. 2004. "Potential Legal Challenges to the Application of the Children's Internet Protection Act (CIPA) in Public Libraries: Strategies and Issues." *First Monday* 9 (February). http://firstmonday.org/issues/issue9_2/jaeger/index.html.

Jeffers, Eugene J. 2009. "Electronic Outreach and Our Internet Patrons." *Public Libraries* 48 (January/February): 21–22.

Kenney, Brian. 2001. "Minneapolis PL to Revitalize Its Downtown." *Library Journal* 126 (June 15): 12.

Kent, Fred, and Phil Myrick. 2003. "How to Become a Great Public Space." *American Libraries* 34 (April): 72–76.

King, David Lee. 2009. "Building a Digital Branch." *American Libraries* (October): 43.

———. 2009. "Building the Digital Branch: Guidelines for Transforming Your Library Website." *Library Technology Reports* 45 (August/September).

Kirsten, Marie L. 2007. "One Plus One Equals Three: Joint-Use Libraries in Urban Areas—The Ultimate Form of Library Cooperation." *Library Administration and Management* 21 (Winter): 23–28.

Kline, Kerry A. 2002. "Libraries, Schools and Wired Communities in Rural Areas and the Changing Communications Landscape." *Rural Libraries* 22, no. 2: 13–41.

Kniffel, Leonard. 2003. "Bill Gates: Why He Did It." *American Libraries* 34 (December): 48–53.

Kolleeny, Jane F. 2008. "Gentry Public Library." *Architectural Record* 196 (October): 138+.

Lane, Christian K. 1989. "Chicago Public Library Competition." *Chicago Architectural Journal* 7: 6–27.

MacDougall, Harriet D., and Nora J. Quinlan. 2001. "Staffing Challenges for a Joint-Use Library: The Nova Southeastern University and Broward County Experience." *Resource Sharing and Information Networks* 15: 131–150.

Mandel, Lauren H., Bradley Wade Bishop, Charles R. McClure, John Carlo Bertot, and Paul T. Jaeger. 2010. "Broadband for Public Libraries: Importance, Issues, and Research Needs." *Government Information Quarterly* 27 (July): 280–291.

McClure, Charles R., et al. 2009. "Hurricane Preparedness and Response for Florida Public Libraries: Best Practices and Strategies." *Florida Libraries* 52 (Spring): 4–7.

Miller, William. 2001. "Joint-Use Libraries: Introduction." *Resource Sharing and Information Networks* 15: 131–150.

Murdock, James. 2008. "Mulberry Street Branch, New York City." *Architectural Record* 196 (February): 148–151.

"Narratives from the Storm." 2008. *Texas Library Journal* 84, no. 4 (Winter): 162, 164–166.

Németh, Jeremy, and Stephan Schmidt. 2007. "Toward a Methodology for Measuring the Security of Publicly Accessible Spaces." *Journal of the American Planning Association* 73 (Summer): 283–297.

Oder, Norman. 2007. "Gates Offers New Grant Program." *Library Journal* 132 (February 15): 16–17.

———. 2008. "Hurricanes Hurt Gulf Coast PLs." *Library Journal* 133 (October): 15.

Olliver, James, and Susan Anderson. 2001. "Seminole Community Library: Joint-Use Library Services for Community and the College." *Resource Sharing and Information Networks* 15: 89–102.

Peltier-Davis, Cheryl. 2009. "Web 2.0, Library 2.0, Library User 2.0, Librarian 2.0: Innovative Services for Sustainable Libraries." *Computers in Libraries* 29 (November/December): 16–21.

Persichini, G., et al. 2008. "E-branch in a Box: How Idaho Libraries Created an Easy and Sustainable Web Presence." *PNLA Quarterly* 72 (winter): 18–19.

Porter, Michael, and David Lee King. 2010. "Premium Web Tools for Public Libraries." *Public Libraries* 49 (September/October): 22–23.

Sampson, Joann. 2009. "Outreach as Virtual Branch." *Public Libraries* 48 (January/February): 23–24.

Senville, Wayne. 2009. "Libraries: The Hubs of Our Communities." *Planning Commissioners Journal* 75 (Summer): 12–18.

"Six Chicago Architects: Impressions of the Chicago Public Library Competition." 1989. *Chicago Architectural Journal* 7: 28–37.

Slavick, Steven. 2009. "Problem Situations, Not Problem Patrons." *Public Libraries* 48, no. 6 (November/December): 38–42.

Stone, Amy. 2005. "Gates Foundation Gives Away $10 Million." *American Libraries* 36 (February): 112, 14.

"Supreme Court Upholds CIPA." 2003. *Newsletter on Intellectual Freedom* 52 (September): 173, 187–191.

Trapskin, Ben. 2008. "A Changing of the Guard: Emerging Trends in Public Library Security." *Library and Archival Security* 21 (September): 69–76.

"2009 Library Design Showcase." 2009. *American Libraries* 40 (April): 30–42.

"2010 Library Design Showcase." 2010. *American Libraries* 41 (April): 38–45.

Urbanska, Wanda. 2009. "A Greener Library, A Greener You." *American Libraries* 40 (April): 52–55.

Waller, Elizabeth, and Patricia Bangs. 2007. "Embracing the Problem Customer." *Public Libraries* 46 (September/October): 27–28.

Zach, Lisl, and Michelynn McKnight. 2010. "Innovative Services Improvised during Disasters: Evidence-Based Education Modules to Prepare Students and Practitioners for Shifts in Community Information Needs." *Journal of Education for Library and Information Science* 51 (Spring): 76–85.

———. 2010. "Special Services in Special Times: Responding to Changed Information Needs during and after Community-Based Disasters." *Public Libraries* 49 (March/April): 37–43.

Websites

ADA Accessibility Guidelines for Buildings and Facilities. 2010. http://www.access-board.gov/adaag/html/adaag.htm.

ALA TechSource. http://www.alatechsource.org.

American Institute of Architects. "2009 AIA/ALA Building Awards." http://www.aia.org/press/AIAB061549.

American Library Association. "Disaster Preparedness and Recovery." http://www.ala.org/ala/issuesadvocacy/advocacy/federallegislation/govinfo/disasterpreparedness/index.cfm.

American Library Association, Office for Information Technology Policy. http://www.ala.org/ala/aboutala/offices/oitp/index.cfm#.

American Library Association, Office for Literacy and Outreach Services. 2008. *Handbook for Mobile Library Staff.* http://www.ala.org/ala/aboutala/offices/olos/bookmobiles/mobileservices.cfm.

———. 2010. "Services to Bookmobile Communities." http://www.ala.org/ala/aboutala/offices/olos/bookmobiles.cfm.

American Library Association, Social Responsibilities Round Table. Task Force on the Environment. http://www.ala.org/ala/mgrps/rts/srrt/tfoe/taskforceenvironment.cfm.

Association of Bookmobile and Outreach Services. http://www.abos-outreach.org.

———. 2008. *National Bookmobile Guidelines.* http://www.abos-outreach.org/2008BookmobileGuidelines.pdf.

Bill and Melinda Gates Foundation. "Libraries." http://www.gatesfoundation.org.

———. 2010. "Funding for United States Libraries." http://www.gatesfoundation.org/grantseeker/Pages/funding-united-states-libraries.aspx.

BroadbandUSA. http://broadbandusa.gov/index.htm.

Buffalo and Erie County Public Library. "Downloads to Go." http://buffalo.lib.overdrive.com/8FA99691-6BC2-42D6-B5DB-C53F1325CEC9/10/400/en/Help-QuickStartGuide.htm.

Center for Library and Information Innovation. http://clii.umd.edu.

Chicago Public Library. "The Development of a Central Library, 1990–2004." http://www.chipublib.org/aboutcpl/history/hist1990.php.

Chiefs Officers of State Library Agencies. http://www.cosla.org.

Dahlgren, Anders C. 2009. *Public Library Space Needs: A Planning Outline/2009.* Wisconsin Department of Public Instruction, Public Library Development. http://dpi.wi.gov/pld/pdf/plspace.pdf.

Dempsey, Lorcan. 2009. "Always On: Libraries in a World of Permanent Connectivity." *First Monday* 14 (January). http://firstmonday.org/htbin/cgiwrap/bin/ojs/index.php/fm/article/viewArticle/2291/2070.

Distant Librarian. 2009. "DC Public Library Announces iPhone App for Their Catalog." http://distlib.blogs.com/distlib/2009/01/dc-public-libra.html.

Dorr, Jessica, and Richard Akeroyd. 2001. "New Mexico Tribal Libraries: Bridging the Digital Divide." *Computers in Libraries* 21, no. 8 (October): 36–43. http://www.infotoday.com/cilmag/oct01/dorr&akeroyd.htm.

Green Libraries. http://www.greenlibraries.org.

Hennepin County Public Library. http://www.hclib.org/pub/.

Horrigan, John. 2009. *Wireless Internet Use.* Pew Internet and American Life Project. http://pewinternet.org/Reports/2009/12-Wireless-Internet-Use.aspx.

Johnson, L., A. Levine, and R. Smith. 2009. The 2009 Horizon Report. Austin, TX: New Media Consortium. http://wp.nmc.org/horizon2009/.

Jones, Sydney, and Susannah Fox. 2009. *Generations Online.* Pew Internet and American Life Project. http://pewinternet.org/Reports/2009/Generations-Online-in-2009.aspx.

Kansas City Public Library. http://www.kclibrary.org/library-history.

LAMA Building Consultants List. http://scs.ala.org/lbcl/search/.

Library of Congress, National Library Service for the Blind and Physically Handicapped. http://www.loc.gov/nls.

Library Technology Guides. "Key Resources and Content Related to Library Automation." http://www.librarytechnology.org.

Libris Design. 2008. http://www.librisdesign.org.

LITAblog. Library and Information Technology Association. http://litablog.org/.

LYRASIS. http://www.lyrasis.org.

NYPL Labs. http://labs.nypl.org.

OCLC. 2010. "Support and Training." http://www.oclc.org/us/en/supportandtraining/default.htm.

Oklahoma Territorial Museum and Carnegie Library. http://www.okhistory.org/outreach/museums/territorialmuseum.html.

Public Access Computing Project. Webjunction. http://www.webjunction.org/public-access/-/resources/overview.

Project for Public Spaces. http://www.pps.org.

Seattle Public Library. 2008. *Libraries for All: A Report to the Community.* http://www
.spl.org/pdfs/libraries_for_all_report.pdf.

Tompkins County Public Library. http://tcpl.org/.

Universal Service Administrative Company. http://www.universalservice.org/sl/.

Urban Libraries Council. 2005. *The Engaged Library: Chicago Stories of Community Building.*
Evanston, IL: ULC. http://urbanlibraries.org/associations/9851/files/ULC_PFSC_Engaged
_0206.pdf.

U.S. Access Board. "Accessibility Guidelines and Standards." http://www.access-board.gov/
gs.htm.

U.S. Department of Education, Office of Educational Research and Improvement. *Biennial
Evaluation Report, 1995–1996. Public Library Construction and Technology Enhancement
Grants to State Library Agencies* (CFDA No. 84-154). http://www.ed.gov/pubs/Biennial/95-
96/eval/603-97.pdf.

U.S. Federal Communications Commission. 2010. "Universal Service." http://www.fcc.gov/
wcb/tapd/universal_service.

U.S. Green Building Council. http://www.usgbc.org.

U.S. Institute of Museum and Library Services. 2009. *Public Libraries Survey. Fiscal Year
2007.* Washington, DC: Institute of Museum and Library Services. http://harvester.
census.gov/imls/pubs/pls/pub_detail.asp?id=122#.

U.S. Institute of Museum and Library Services, State Programs. "5-Year Evaluations: 2003–
2007." http://www.imls.gov/programs/5yearevals.shtm.

U.S. National Telecommunications and Information Administration, Broadband Technology
Opportunities Program. 2010. http://www.ntia.doc.gov/broadbandgrants.

U.S. National Telecommunications and Information Administration, Technology Opportunities
Program. http://www.ntia.doc.gov/otiahome/top/index.html.

Webjunction. http://www.webjunction.org.

Wisconsin Department of Public Instruction, Public Library Development. 2009. *Public
Library Space Needs: A Planning Outline/2009.* http://dpi.wi.gov/pld/plspace.html.

Wisconsin Public Library Standards. 4th ed. 2005. http://dpi.wi.gov/pld/standard.html.

WorldCat Mobile. http://www.worldcat.org/wcpa/content/mobile.

Video

MARZ Associates, in association with WGBH, Boston. 1989. "Design Wars." *Nova.* VHS.
Boston: WGBH Educational Foundation.

8. Adult Services

Books and Chapters in Books

American Library Association. 1926. *Libraries and Adult Education: Report of a Study Made
by the American Library Association.* Chicago: American Library Association.

———. 2010. *Intellectual Freedom Manual.* 8th ed. Chicago: American Library Association.

———. Annual. "Library Services for People with Disabilities" (54.3.1); "Minority Concerns" (60); "Goals for Indian Library and Information Services" (60.3); "Library Services for the Poor" (61). In *ALA Policy Manual*. Chicago: American Library Association.

Berelson, Bernard. 1949. *The Library's Public*. New York: Columbia University Press.

Birge, Lynn E. 1981. *Serving Adult Learners: A Public Library Tradition*. Chicago: American Library Association.

Buschman, John E. 2003. *Dismantling the Public Sphere: Situating and Sustaining Librarianship in the Age of the New Public Philosophy*. Westport, CT: Libraries Unlimited.

Carr, David. 2003. *The Promise of Cultural Institutions: American Association for State and Local History*. Walnut Creek, CA: Altamira Press.

———. 2006. *A Place Not a Place: Reflection and Possibility in Museums and Libraries*. Lanham, MD: Altamira Press.

Christensen, Karen, and David Levinson, eds. 2003. *Encyclopedia of Community*. Thousand Oaks, CA: Sage. See especially the articles, "Information Communities," 657–660; "Public Libraries," 1114–1117; and "Libraries Build Community," Appendix 2, 1533–1551.

Davies, D. W. 1974. *Public Libraries as Culture and Social Centers: The Origins of the Concept*. Metuchen, NJ: Scarecrow Press.

Estabrook, Leigh S., et al. 2007. *Information Searches That Solve Problems How People Use the Internet, Libraries, and Government Agencies When They Need Help*. Washington, DC: Pew Internet and American Life Project. http://www.pewinternet.org/Reports/2007/Information-Searches-That-Solve-Problems.aspx.

Freeman, Robert S., and David M. Hovde, eds. 2003. *Libraries to the People: Histories of Outreach*. Jefferson, NC: McFarland.

Heim, Kathleen M., and Harry D. Nuttall. 1990. *Adult Services: A Bibliography and Index. A Component of the Adult Services in the Eighties Project*. ERIC ED320609. Baton Rouge: Louisiana State University.

Heim, Kathleen M., and Danny P. Wallace. 1990. *Adult Services: An Enduring Focus for Public Libraries*. Chicago: American Library Association.

Herald, Diana Tixier. 2000. *Genreflecting: A Guide to Reading Interests in Genre Fiction*. 5th ed. Englewood, CO: Libraries Unlimited.

Jaeger, Paul T., and Gary Burnett. 2010. *Information Worlds: Behavior, Technology and Social Context in the World of the Internet*. London: Routledge.

Johnson, Alvin. 1938. *The Public Library—A People's University*. New York: American Association for Adult Education.

Josey, E. J. 1994. "Race Issues in Library History." In *Encyclopedia of Library History*, edited by W. A. Wiegand and D. G. Davis, 533–537. New York: Garland.

Kaestle, Carl F., and Janice A. Radway. 2009. *Print in Motion: The Expansion of Reading in the United States, 1880–1940*. Chapel Hill: University of North Carolina Press.

Learned, William S. 1924. *The American Public Library and the Diffusion of Knowledge*. New York: Harcourt.

Lee, Robert Ellis. 1966. *Continuing Education for Adults through the American Public Library 1833–1966*. Chicago: American Library Association.

Lyman, Helen. 1954. *Adult Education Activities in Public Libraries*. Chicago: American Library Association.

Maatta, Stephanie L. 2010. *A Few Good Books: Using Contemporary Readers' Advisory Strategies to Connect Readers with Books*. New York: Neal-Schuman.

Martin, Robert. 2001. "Welcoming Remarks." 21st Century Learner Conference. Institute of Museum and Library Services. November 7.

Mathews, Virginia H. 2004. "Libraries." *Citizens and Advocacy: The Lasting Effects of Two White House Conferences on Library and Information Services*. Washington, DC: White House Conference on Libraries and Information Services Taskforce.

McClure, Charles R. 1987. *Planning and Role Setting for Public Libraries: A Manual of Options and Procedures*. Chicago: American Library Association.

McClure, Charles R., and Paul T. Jaeger. 2009. *Public Libraries and Internet Service Roles: Measuring and Maximizing Internet Services*. Chicago: American Library Association.

McCook, Kathleen de la Peña. 1990. "Adult Services: An Enduring Focus." In *Adult Services: An Enduring Focus for Public Libraries*, edited by Kathleen M. Heim (de la Peña McCook) and Danny P. Wallace, 11–26. Chicago: American Library Association.

———. 1991. "The Developing Role of Public Libraries in Adult Education: 1966 to 1991." In *Partners for Lifelong Learning: Public Libraries and Adult Education*, 21–53. Washington, DC: U.S. Department of Education.

———. 2002. *Rocks in the Whirlpool: The American Library Association and Equity of Access*. ERIC ED462981. Chicago: American Library Association.

Monroe, Margaret E. 1963. *Library Adult Education: The Biography of an Idea*. New York: Scarecrow Press.

Nelson, Sandra. 2001. *The New Planning for Results: A Streamlined Approach*. Chicago: American Library Association.

———. 2008. *Strategic Planning for Results*. Chicago: American Library Association.

———. 2009. *Implementing for Results: Your Strategic Plan in Action*. Chicago: American Library Association.

Schlachter, Gail A. 1982. *The Service Imperative for Libraries: Essays in Honor of Margaret E. Monroe*. Littleton, CO: Libraries Unlimited.

Smallwood, Carol. 2010. *Librarians as Community Partners: An Outreach Handbook*. Chicago: American Library Association.

Smith, Helen Lyman. 1954. *Adult Education Activities in Public Libraries*. Chicago: American Library Association.

Tucker, John Mark. 1998. *Untold Stories: Civil Rights, Libraries, and Black Librarianship*. Champaign, IL: Publications Office, Graduate School of Library and Information Science.

Venturella, Karen M. 1998. *Poor People and Library Services*. Jefferson, NC: McFarland.

Wallace, Danny P. 1990. "The Character of Adult Services in the Eighties." In *Adult Services: An Enduring Focus for Public Libraries*, edited by Kathleen M. Heim and Danny P. Wallace, 27–165. Chicago: American Library Association.

Weibel, Kathleen. 1982. *The Evolution of Library Outreach 1960–75 and Its Effect on Reader Services: Some Considerations*. Occasional Paper No. 16. Urbana, IL: Graduate School of Library and Information Science. ERIC ED231376.

Articles

American Library Association, Board on Library and Adult Education. 1935. "The Library and Adult Education: 1924–1934." *ALA Bulletin* 29 (June): 316–323.

Blayney, M. S. 1977. "Libraries for the Millions: Adult Public Libraries and the New Deal." *Journal of Library History* 12: 235–249.

Birch, Eugenie. 2007. "Special Report: Anchor Institutions." *Next American City* (Summer). http://americancity.org/magazine/article/special-report-anchor-institutions-birch.

Brown, Walter L. 1917. "The Changing Public." *ALA Bulletin* 11 (July): 91–95.

Buschman, John. 2005. "Libraries and the Decline of Public Purpose." *Public Library Quarterly* 24: 1–12.

Camaratta, Maria A. 2009. "Library Service to People with Mental Challenges." *Public Libraries* 48 (May/June): 4–12.

Chatman, Elfreda A., and Pendleton, V. E. M. 1995. "Knowledge Gap, Information Seeking and the Poor." *Reference Librarian* 40: 135–145.

Dane, William J. 1990. "John Cotton Dana: A Contemporary Appraisal of His Contributions and Lasting Influence on the Library and Museum Worlds 60 Years after His Death." *Art Libraries Journal* 15: 5–9.

"A Decade of Words and Wonder." 2010. *Library of Congress Information Bulletin* 69, no. 6 (June): 116–117.

Gieskes, Lisa. 2009. "ALA Task Force Member Survey on Policy 61. Library Services for the Poor." *Progressive Librarian* 32 (Winter/Spring): 82–87.

Graham, Elizabeth, and Roberta Sparks. 2010. "Libraries as a Catalyst for Economic Growth and Community Development: A Mayor's Summit on Public Libraries." *Texas Library Journal* 86 (Spring): 30–31.

Hansen, Andrew M. 1995. "RASD: Serving Those Who Serve the Public." *RQ* 34 (Spring): 314–338.

Heim, Kathleen M. 1986. "Adult Services as Reflective of the Changing Role of the Public Library." *RQ* 26 (Winter): 180–187.

Hicks, Jack Alan. 1998. "Planning Successful Author Programming." *Public Libraries* 37 (July/August): 237–238.

Jensen, Leif, and Tim Slack. 2003. "Underemployment in America: Measurement and Evidence." *American Journal of Community Psychology* 12 (September): 21–31.

Lamolinara, Guy. 2010. "The National and International Roles of the Center for the Book." *Libraries and the Cultural Record* 45, no. 1: 37–55.

Latham, Joyce M. 2010. "Clergy of the Mind: Alvin S. Johnson, William S. Learned, the Carnegie Corporations and the American Library Association." *Library Quarterly* 80, no. 3: 249–265.

Leckie, Gloria J., and Lisa M. Given. 2005. "Understanding Information-Seeking: The Public Library Context." *Advances in Librarianship* 29: 1–72.

"Library Rights of Adults." 1970. *ASD Newsletter* 8 (Winter): 2–3.

Maack, Mary Niles. 2010. "John Y. Cole: Librarian, Bookman, and Scholar." *Libraries and the Cultural Record* 45, no. 1: 1–4.

MacCreaigh, Erica. 2010. "Tough Times after Hard Times: How Public Libraries Can Ease the Reentry Process for Ex-offenders." *Interface* (Winter). http://ascla.ala.org/interface/.

Martin, Robert K. 2001. 21st Century Learners Conference. Institute of Museum and Library Services. November 7.

McCook, Kathleen de la Peña. 1992. "Where Would We Be Without Them? Libraries and Adult Education Activities: 1966–1991." *RQ* 32 (Winter): 245–253.

Milam, D. P. 2008. "Public Library Strategies for Building Stronger Economies and Communities." *National Civic Review* 97 (Fall): 11–16.

Monroe, Margaret E., and Kathleen M. Heim. 1979. "Emerging Patterns of Community Service." *Library Trends* 28 (Fall): 129–138.

"New Family Literacy Focus Initiative Begins." 2010. *American Libraries* 41, no. 3 (March): 13.

Stephens, Annabel K. 2006. "Twenty-first Century Public Library Adult Services." *Reference and User Services Quarterly* 45 (Spring): 223–235.

Stevenson, Grace T. 1954. "The ALA Adult Education Board." *ALA Bulletin* 48 (April): 226–231.

Stone, C. Walter. 1953. "Adult Education and the Public Library." *Library Trends* 1 (April): 437–453.

Swain, Martha H. 1995. "A New Deal in Libraries: Federal Relief Work and Library Service, 1933–1943." *Libraries and Culture* 30 (Summer): 265–283.

Taylor, Edward W. 2010. "Cultural Institutions and Adult Education." *New Directions for Adult and Continuing Education* 127 (Fall): 5–14.

Trott, Barry. 2008. "Building on a Firm Foundation: Readers' Advisory over the Next Twenty-Five Years." *Reference and User Services Quarterly* 48 (Winter): 132–135.

Van Fleet, Connie. 1987. "ASE: Adult Services in the Eighties." *RQ* 26 (Spring): 302–303.

Wellman, Hiller C. 1915. "The Library's Primary Duty." *ALA Bulletin* 9 (July): 89–93.

Websites

American Library Association, Office for Diversity. http://www.ala.org/diversity.

American Library Association, Office for Literacy and Outreach Services. http://www.ala.org/ala/aboutala/offices/olos/index.cfm.

American Library Association, Office for Public Programs. http://www.ala.org/ala/aboutala/offices/ppo/index.cfm.

Association of Specialized and Cooperative Library Agencies. Libraries Serving Special Populations Section of the American Library Association. http://www.ala.org/ala/mgrps/divs/ascla/asclaourassoc/asclasections/lssps/lssps.cfm.

Library of Congress, Center for the Book. http://www.read.gov/cfb/.

———. "State Center Affiliates." http://www.read.gov/cfb/affiliates.html.

Public Library Association. "Communities of Practice." http://www.ala.org/ala/mgrps/divs/pla/plagroups/placops/index.cfm.

Reference and User Services Association. http://www.ala.org/ala/mgrps/divs/rusa/index.cfm.

————. "Notable Books. For Adults." http://www.ala.org/ala/mgrps/divs/rusa/awards/notablebooks/index.cfm.

U.S. Institute of Museum and Library Services. http://www.imls.gov/index.shtm.

Specific Service Responses

(Organized in order of Nelson, 2008. *Strategic Planning for Results*, 143–217.)

Be an Informed Citizen: Local, National and World Affairs (Public Sphere; Nelson, 2008: 149–152)

American Library Association, Government Documents Round Table. http://www.ala.org/ala/mgrps/rts/godort/index.cfm.

American Library Association, Public Programs Office. http://www.ala.org/ala/aboutala/offices/ppo/index.cfm.

Clark, Wayne. 2000. *Activism in the Public Sphere: Exploring the Discourse of Political Participation*. Burlington, VT: Aldershot.

Community Information Needs. http://www.informationneeds.org.

Hill, Chrystie. 2009. *Inside, Outside, and Online*. Chicago: American Library Association.

Knight Commission on the Information Needs of Communities in a Democracy. 2009. *Informing Communities: Sustaining Democracy in the Digital Age*. Washington, DC: Aspen Institute.

Kranich, Nancy. 2010. "Promoting Adult Learning through Civil Discourse in the Public Library." *New Directions for Adult and Continuing Education* no. 127 (Fall): 15–24.

————, ed. 2001. *Libraries and Democracy: The Cornerstones of Liberty*. Chicago: American Library Association.

McCabe, Ronald B. 2001. *Civic Librarianship: Renewing the Social Mission of the Public Library*. Lanham, MD: Scarecrow Press.

McCook, Kathleen de la Peña. 2000. *A Place at the Table: Participating in Community Building*. Chicago: American Library Association.

————. 2001. "Authentic Discourse as a Means of Connection between Public Library Service Responses and Community Building Initiatives." *Reference and User Services Quarterly* 40 (Winter): 127–133.

————. 2003. "Public Libraries and Community." In *Encyclopedia of Community*, edited by Karen Christensen and David Levinson, 1114–1111. Thousand Oaks, CA: Sage.

Molz, Redmond Kathleen, and Phyllis Dain. 1999. *Civic Space/Cyberspace: The American Public Library in the Information Age*. Cambridge, MA: MIT Press.

Morrison, Andrea M. 2008. *Managing Electronic Government Information in Libraries*. Chicago: American Library Association.

Preer, Jean L. 1993. "The American Heritage Project: Librarians and the Democratic Tradition in the Early Cold War." *Libraries and Culture* 28 (Spring): 165–188.

————. 2008. "Promoting Citizenship: How Librarians Helped Get Out the Vote in the 1952 Presidential Election." *Libraries and the Cultural Record* 43, no. 1: 1–28.

Programming Librarian. http://programminglibrarian.org.

Ristau, Stephen. 2010. "Get Involved: Promoting Civic Engagement through California Public Libraries." *California State Library Foundation Bulletin*: 12–14.

Swain, Martha H. 1995. "A New Deal in Libraries: Federal Relief Work and Library Service, 1933–1943." *Libraries and Culture* 30: 265–283.

Willingham, Taylor L. 2008. "Libraries as Civic Agents." *Public Library Quarterly* 27: 97–110.

Build Successful Enterprises: Business and Nonprofit Support (Information; Nelson, 2008: 153–157)

Bleiweiss, Maxine. 1997. *Helping Business: The Library's Role in Community Economic Development*. New York: Neal-Schuman.

Boston Public Library. http://www.bpl.org/research/kbb/kbbhome.htm.

BRASS Business Reference in Public Libraries Committee. "Public Libraries Briefcase." http://www.ala.org/ala/mgrps/divs/rusa/sections/brass/brasspubs/publibbrief/publiclibraries .cfm.

Brooklyn Public Library. "Business Library." http://www.brooklynpubliclibrary.org/business.

Durrance, Joan C. 1993. *Serving Job Seekers and Career Changers*. Chicago: Public Library Association.

Graham, Elizabeth, and Roberta Sparks. 2010. "Libraries as a Catalyst for Economic Growth and Community Development: A Mayor's Summit on Public Libraries." *Texas Library Journal* 86 (Spring): 30–31.

Hatton, Jason, et al. 2008. "Making the Library Visible to the Business and Nonprofit Communities." *Indiana Libraries* 27: 33–34.

Los Angeles Public Library. http://www.lapl.org/central/business.html.

Meyers, Arthur S. 2002. "A Fifty-Five Year Partnership: ALA and the AFL-CIO." *Library Trends* 51 (Summer): 36–49.

New York Public Library. http://www.nypl.org/locations/sibl.

Reference and User Services Association. BRASS. Business Reference and Services Section. http://www.ala.org/ala/mgrps/divs/rusa/sections/brass/index.cfm.

Weiss, Luise. 2010. *Small Business and the Public Library*. Chicago: American Library Association.

Welch, Jeanie M. 2005. "Silent Partners: Public Libraries and Their Services to Small Businesses and Entrepreneurs." *Public Libraries* 44 (September/October): 282–286.

Celebrate Diversity: Cultural Awareness (Cultural Heritage; Nelson, 2008: 158–161)

American Library Association, Ethnic and Multicultural Information Exchange Round Table. http://www.ala.org/ala/mgrps/rts/emiert/index.cfm.

American Library Association, Gay, Lesbian, Bisexual, and Transgendered Round Table. http://www.ala.org/ala/mgrps/rts/glbtrt/index.cfm.

American Library Association, Office for Diversity. http://www.ala.org/ala/aboutala/offices/ diversity/index.cfm.

Balderrama, Sandra Ríos. 2000. "This Trend Called Diversity." *Library Trends* 49 (Summer): 194–214.

Bell, Gladys Smiley. 2009. *Gathering at the Waters, Embracing Our Spirits, Telling Our Stories: Proceedings of the First Joint Conference of Librarians of Color, Dallas, Texas, October 11–15, 2006.* http://www.nxtbook.com/nxtbooks/hall-erickson/jclc_2006conf/.

Carmichael, James V., Jr. 1998. *Daring to Find Our Names: The Search for Lesbigay Library History.* Westport, CT: Greenwood Press.

Dawson, Alma. 2000. "Celebrating African-American Librarians and Librarianship." *Library Trends* 49 (Summer): 49–87.

Güereña, Salvador, and Edward Erazo. 2000. "Latinos and Librarianship." *Library Trends* 49 (Summer): 139–181.

Jones, Alston Plummer, Jr. 2004. *Still Struggling for Equality: American Public Library Services with Minorities.* Westport, CT: Libraries Unlimited.

Joyce, Steven. 2000. "Lesbian, Gay and Bisexual Library Service: A Review of the Literature." *Public Libraries* 39 (September/October): 270–279.

Kniffel, Leonard. 2009. "New Survey Finds Cultural Consumers Love Public Libraries, Support Public Funding." *American Libraries* 40 (December): 21.

Liu, Mengxiong. 2000. "The History and Status of Chinese Americans in Librarianship." *Library Trends* 49 (Summer): 109–137.

McCook, Kathleen de la Peña, ed. 2000. "Ethnic Diversity in Library and Information Science." Special issue, *Library Trends* 49 (Summer): 1–214.

Overall, Patricia Montile. 2009. "Cultural Competence: A Conceptual Framework for Library and Information Science Professionals." *Library Quarterly* 79 (April): 175–204.

Patterson, Lotsee. 2000. "History and Status of Native Americans in Librarianship." *Library Trends* 49, no. 1 (Summer): 182–193.

Rothbauer, Paulette. 2006. "Locating the Library as Place among Lesbian, Gay, Bisexual, and Queer Patrons." In *Library as Place: History, Community and Culture*, edited by John Buschman and Gloria J. Leckie, 101–115. Westport, CT: Libraries Unlimited.

Roy, Loriene. 2000. "To Support and Model Native American Library Services." *Texas Library Journal* 76 (Spring): 32–35.

Yamashita, Kenneth A. 2000. "Asian/Pacific American Librarians Association: A History of APALA and Its Founders." *Library Trends* 49 (Summer): 88–108.

Connect to the Online World: Public Internet Access (Information; Nelson, 2008: 162–164)

American Library Association. "Public Library Funding and Technology Access Study." http://www.ala.org/ala/research/initiatives/plftas/index.cfm.

American Library Association, Office for Research and Statistics. 2009. "Internet Connectivity in U.S. Public Libraries." http://www.ala.org/ala/research/initiatives/plftas/issuesbriefs/connectivitybrief_2009_10_final.pdf.

American Library Association and Florida State University. 2007. *Libraries Connect Communities: Public Library Funding and Technology Access Study, 2006–2007.* ALA Research Series. Chicago: American Library Association.

Ball, Mary Alice. 2008. "Connecting with Connectivity: Why Librarians Need to Care." *Public Libraries* 47, no. 3 (May/June): 52–56.

———. 2009. "Aggregating Broadband Demand: Surveying the Benefits and Challenges for Public Libraries." *Government Information Quarterly* 26 (October): 551–558.

Ball, Mary Alice, and Wendy Knapp. 2009. "Leveraging Funding to Enhance Broadband Access." *Public Libraries* 48 (September/October): 48–55.

Becker, Samantha, et al. 2009. "Communicating the Impact of Free Access to Computers and the Internet in Public Libraries: A Mixed Methods Approach to Developing Outcome Indicators." *Public Library Quarterly* 28 (April/June): 109–119.

Bertot, John Carlo. 2009. "Public Access Technologies in Public Libraries: Effects and Implications." *Information Technology and Libraries* 28 (June): 81–92.

Bertot, John Carlo, and Denise M. Davis. 2006. "Public Library Public Access Computing and Internet Access: Factors Which Contribute to Quality Services and Resources." *Public Library Quarterly* 25, no. 1/2: 27–42.

Bertot, John Carlo, and Charles R. McClure. 2007. "Assessing Sufficiency and Quality of Bandwidth for Public Libraries." *Information Technology and Libraries* 26 (March): 14–22.

Bertot, John Carlo, et al. 2008. "The Impacts of Free Public Internet Access on Public Library Patrons and Communities." *Library Quarterly* 78 (July): 285–301.

Henderson, Everett. 2009. *Service Trends in U.S. Public Libraries, 1997–2007*. Washington, DC: Institute of Museum and Library Services.

Jaeger, Paul T., et al. 2005. "The E-Rate Program and Libraries and Library Consortia, 2000–2004: Trends and Issues." *Information Technology and Libraries* 24, no. 2: 57–67.

———. 2006. "The Policy Implications of Internet Connectivity in Public Libraries." *Government Information Quarterly* 23: 123–141.

Lehman, Tom, and Terry Nikkel. 2008. *Making Library Web Sites Usable: A LITA Guide*. New York: Neal-Schuman.

Lietzau, Zeth. 2009. "U.S. Public Libraries and Web 2.0: What's Really Happening?" *Computers in Libraries* 29 (October): 6–10.

McClure, Charles R., et al. 2006. "Politics and Advocacy: The Role of Networking in Selling the Library to Your Community." *Public Library Quarterly* 25: 137–154.

———. 2007. "The Looming Infrastructure Plateau? Space, Funding, Connection Speed, and the Ability of Public Libraries to Meet the Demand for Free Internet Access." *First Monday* (Online) 12, no. 12 (December).

McClure, Charles R., and Paul T. Jaeger. 2009. *Public Libraries and Internet Service Roles: Measuring and Maximizing Internet Services*. Chicago: American Library Association.

Sheketoff, Emily. 2009. "Public Libraries and the American Recovery and Reinvestment Act." *Public Libraries* 48 (July/August): 44–51.

Vollmer, Timothy. 2010. "There's an App for That! Libraries and Mobile Technology: An Introduction to Public Policy Considerations." Washington, DC: ALA Office for Information Technology Policy. http://www.ala.org/ala/aboutala/offices/oitp/publications/policybriefs/mobiledevices.pdf.

Weingarten, Rick, et al. 2007. *Public Library Connectivity Project: Findings and Recommendations*. Washington, DC: ALA Office for Information Technology Policy.

Create Young Readers: Early Literacy (Education; Nelson, 2008: 165–168)

Albright, Meagan, et al. 2009. "The Evolution of Early Literacy: A History of Best Practices in Storytimes." *Children and Libraries* 7 (Spring): 13–18.

Ash, Viki, and Elaine Meyers. 2009. "Every Child Ready to Read @ Your Library." *Children and Libraries* 7 (Spring): 3–7.

Every Child Ready to Read @ Your Library. http://www.ala.org/ala/mgrps/divs/alsc/ecrr/index.cfm.

Feinberg, Sandra, et al. 2007. *The Family-Centered Library Handbook*. New York: Neal-Schuman.

Ghoting, Saroj Nadkarni, and Pamela Martin-Díaz. 2010. *Early Literacy Reading Programs @ Your Fingertips*. Chicago: American Library Association.

Hughes-Hassell, Sandra, et al. 2007. "Making Storytime to Children of Working Parents: Public Libraries and the Scheduling of Children's Literacy Programs." *Children and Libraries* 5 (Summer/Fall): 43–48.

Marino, Jane. 2007. *Babies in the Library*. Lanham, MD: Scarecrow Press.

Nichols, Judy. 2007. *Storytimes for Two-Year-Olds*. Chicago: ALA Editions.

Queen, Priscilla. 2008. "Libraries Wanted: Boosting Our Role in Early Childhood Communities." *Colorado Libraries* 34, no. 4: 12–16.

Discover Your Roots: Genealogy and Local History (Cultural Heritage; Nelson, 2008: 169–172)

American Association for State and Local History. http://www.aaslh.org.

Archibald, Robert R. 1999. *A Place to Remember: Using History to Build Community*. Walnut Creek, CA: Rowman and Littlefield.

Bachowski, Donna. 2009. "Orlando Memory: Capturing Community Memories." *Florida Libraries* 52 (Fall): 8–9.

Carr, David. 2003. *The Promise of Cultural Institutions: American Association for State and Local History*. Walnut Creek, CA: Altamira Press.

Given, Lisa M., and LiAnne McTavish. 2010. "What's Old Is New Again: The Reconvergence of Libraries, Archives and Museums in the Digital Age." *Library Quarterly* 80 (January): 7–32.

Huwe, Terence K. 2010. "Online History-Keeping for Outreach and Community Development." *Computers in Libraries* 30 (January/February): 35–37.

Jones, Christopher. 2010. "Preserving History in Charlotte County." *Florida Libraries* 53 (Spring): 4–5.

Kaplan, Paul. 2007. "How Public Libraries Can Provide Basic Genealogy Instruction." *Illinois Libraries* 86 (Spring): 16–20.

Linderman, Eric. 2009. "Archives in Public Libraries." *Public Libraries* 48 (January/February): 46–51.

Reference and User Services Association. 1999. "Guidelines for Developing Beginning Genealogical Collections and Services." http://www.ala.org/ala/mgrps/divs/rusa/resources/guidelines/guidelinesdeveloping.cfm.

Reference and User Services Association, History Section, Local History Committee. 2006. "Guidelines for Establishing Local History Collections." http://www.ala.org/ala/mgrps/ divs/rusa/resources/guidelines/guidelinesestablishing.cfm.

Rendfeld, Connie. 2008. "Indiana Memory: The Making of a Statewide Digital Library." *Indiana Libraries* 27, no. 2: 23–25.

Simpson, Jack. 2009. *Basics of Genealogy Reference.* Westport, CT: Libraries Unlimited.

Express Creativity: Create and Share Content (Cultural Heritage; Nelson, 2008: 173–176)

Cohen, Alex. 2009. "Learning Spaces in Public Libraries." *Public Library Quarterly* 28 (July/September): 227–233.

Favreau, Karen. 2007. "A Library and an Art Center." *American Libraries* 38 (February): 38–40.

Hustedde, Hedy N. R. 2005. "Emily Dickinson Lives! @ the Bettendorf Public Library." *Public Libraries* 44 (September/October): 287–291.

Nelson, Sarah. 2007. "Multnomah County Library Champions Portland Zine Scene." *OLA Quarterly* 17 (Summer): 17–19.

Rangeview Libraries, Adams County, CO. http://www.anythinklibraries.org.

Robertson, Deborah A. 2005. *Cultural Programming for Libraries: Linking Libraries, Communities, and Culture.* Chicago: American Library Association.

Get Facts Fast: Ready Reference (Information; Nelson, 2008: 177–179)

ASKaLibrarian. http://info.askalibrarian.org/index.php.

Curry, Ann, and Gayle J. E. Harris. 2000. "Reference Librarians' Attitudes Toward the World Wide Web." *Public Library Quarterly* 18: 25–38.

Janes, Joseph, and Chrystie Hill. 2002. "Finger on the Pulse: Librarians Describe Evolving Reference Practice in an Increasingly Digital World." *Reference and User Services Quarterly* 42 (Fall): 54–65.

Kern, M. Kathleen. 2009. *Virtual Reference Best Practices.* Chicago: American Library Association.

Leckie, Gloria J., and Lisa M. Given. 2005. "Understanding Information-Seeking: The Public Library Context." *Advances in Librarianship* 29: 1–72.

Reference and User Services Association. 2000. "Guidelines for Information Services." http://www.ala.org/ala/mgrps/divs/rusa/resources/guidelines/guidelinesinformation.cfm.

———. 2003. "Professional Competencies for Reference and User Services Librarians." http://www.ala.org/ala/mgrps/divs/rusa/resources/guidelines/professional.cfm.

———. 2006. "Guidelines for Behavioral Performance of Reference and Information Service Providers." http://www.ala.org/ala/mgrps/divs/rusa/resources/guidelines/guidelinesbehavioral.cfm.

———. 2006. "Guidelines for Cooperative Reference Services." http://www.ala.org/ala/ mgrps/divs/rusa/resources/guidelines/guidelinescooperative.cfm.

————. 2008. "Definitions of Reference." http://www.ala.org/ala/mgrps/divs/rusa/resources/guidelines/definitionsreference.cfm.

————. 2010. "Guidelines for Implementing and Maintaining Virtual Reference Services." *Reference and User Services Quarterly* 50 (Fall): 92–96.

Know Your Community: Community Resources and Services (Public Sphere; Nelson, 2008: 180–183)

Bajjaly, Stephen T. 1999. *The Community Networking Handbook*. Chicago: ALA Editions.

Barker, Anne, et al. 2008. "Committed to the Community: A Community Services Website." *Texas Library Journal* 84 (Summer): 56, 58–59.

Chepesiuk, Ron. 2001. "Dial 211: Libraries Get Involved with a New Social Service Initiative. *American Libraries* 32 (December): 44–46.

Childers, Thomas. 1984. *Information and Referral: Public Libraries*. Norwood, NJ: Ablex.

Croneberger, Robert. 1975. *The Library as a Community Information and Referral Center*. ERIC ED108653. Morehead State University, KY: Appalachian Adult Education Center.

Croneberger, Robert, and Carolyn Luck. 1975. "Defining Information and Referral Service." *Library Journal* 100 (November 1): 1984–1987.

Curley, Arthur. 1979. "Information from the People to the People." *American Libraries* 10 (July): 316–320.

Drueke, Jeanetta. 2006. "Researching Local Organizations: Simple Strategies for Building Social Capital." *Reference and User Services Quarterly* 45 (Summer): 327–333.

Durrance, Joan C., and Karen E. Fisher. 2005. *How Libraries and Librarians Help: A Guide to Identifying User-Centered Outcomes*. Chicago: American Library Association.

Durrance, Joan C., and Karen E. Fisher-Pettigrew. 2003. "Determining How Libraries and Librarians Help." *Library Trends* 51 (Spring): 541–570.

Durrance, Joan C., and Karen E. Pettigrew. 2002. *Online Community Information: Creating a Nexus at Your Library*. Chicago: American Library Association.

Fredericks, Nancy. 2009. "Electronic Tools and E-government Services." *Florida Libraries* 52 (Fall): 4–6.

Jaeger, Paul T., and John Carlo Bertot. 2009. "E-government Education in Public Libraries: New Service Roles and Expanding Social Responsibilities." *Journal of Education for Library and Information Science* 50 (Winter): 39–49.

Jaeger, Paul T., and K. R. Fleischmann. 2007. "Public Libraries, Values, Trust, and E-government." *Information Technology and Libraries* 26 (4): 35–43.

Jones, Clara S. 1978. *Public Library Information and Referral Service*. Syracuse, NY: Gaylord Professional Publications.

LINC at the Memphis Public Library. http://www.memphislibrary.org/linc/211.htm.

Maas, Norman L., and Dick Manikowski. 1997. *Guidelines for Establishing Community Information and Referral Services in Public Libraries*. 4th ed. Chicago: American Library Association.

McClure, Charles R., and Paul T. Jaeger. 2009. *Public Libraries and Internet Service Roles: Measuring and Maximizing Internet Services*. Chicago: American Library Association.

McCook, Kathleen de la Peña. 2000. "Service Integration and Libraries." *Reference and User Services Quarterly* 40 (Winter): 22–25.

Owens, Major R., and Miriam Braverman. 1974. *The Public Library and Advocacy: Information for Survival.* New York: Teachers College Press.

Pettigrew, Karen E., Joan C. Durrance, and Kenton T. Unruh. 2002. "Facilitating Community Information Seeking." *Journal of the American Society for Information Science and Technology* 53, no. 11 (September 6).

Saxton, Matthew, et al. 2007. "2-1-1 Information Services: Outcomes Assessment, Benefit-Cost Analysis and Policy Issues." *Government Information Quarterly* 24 (January): 186–215.

Smallwood, Carol. 2010. *Librarians as Community Partners: An Outreach Handbook.* Chicago: American Library Association.

United Way, Alliance for Information and Referral Services. "2–1–1. Get Connected. Get Answers." http://211us.org/.

"Using the Internet: Findings from Three Public Library-Community Network Systems." *Journal of the American Society for Information Science and Technology* 53 (September): 894–903.

U.S. National Commission on Libraries and Information Science. 1983. *Final Report to the National Commission on Libraries and Information Science from the Community Information and Referral Task Force.* ERIC ED241014. Washington, DC: National Commission on Libraries and Information Science.

Learn to Read and Write: Adults, Teens and Family Literacy (Education; Nelson, 2008: 184–187)

"The American Dream Begins @ Your Library." 2010. http://www.americandreamtoolkit.org.

American Library Association. "BuildLiteracy." http://www.buildliteracy.org.

———. "Literacy Assembly." http://connect.ala.org/node/71957.

American Library Association, Office for Literacy and Outreach Services. http://www.ala.org/ala/aboutala/offices/olos/index.cfm.

Baer, J., M. Kutner, and J. Sabatini. 2009. *Basic Reading Skills and the Literacy of America's Least Literate Adults: Results from the 2003 National Assessment of Adult Literacy (NAAL) Supplemental Studies* (NCES 2009-481). Washington, DC: National Center for Education Statistics, Institute of Education Sciences, U.S. Department of Education. http://nces.ed.gov/pubs2009/2009481.pdf.

Belzer, Alisa. 2007. "Implementing the Workforce Investment Act from in Between: State Agency Responses to Federal Accountability Policy in Adult Basic Education." *Educational Policy* 21 (September): 555–588.

Chisman, Forrest P. 2010. *Local Perspectives on WIA Reauthorization from a CAAL Roundtable.* Council for the Advancement of Adult Literacy. http://www.caalusa.org/LPP.pdf.

Coleman, Jean Ellen. 1996. "Literacy Education Programs in Public Libraries as a response to a Socio-educational Need: Four Case Studies. PhD diss., Rutgers, the State University of New Jersey.

DeCandido, GraceAnne, ed. 2001. *Literacy and Libraries: Learning from Case Studies*. Chicago: American Library Association.

Demetrion, George. 2005. *Conflicting Paradigms in Adult Literacy Education: In Quest of a U.S. Democratic Politics of Literacy*. Mahwah: NJ: Erlbaum.

Feinberg, Sandra. 2007. *The Family-Centered Library Handbook*. New York: Neal-Schuman.

Hopkins, John L., et al. 2009. "Conflict and Collaboration: Providers and Planners Implementing the Workforce Investment Act (WIA)." *Adult Education Quarterly* 59 (May): 208–226.

"Libraries, Literacy and Learning in the 21st Century." 2005. *American Libraries* 36 (August): supplement. Los Angeles Public Library. http://www.lapl.org/literacy/main.html.

Lyman, Helen H. 1973. *Library Materials in Service to the Adult New Reader*. Chicago: American Library Association.

———. 1976. *Reading and the Adult New Reader*. Chicago: American Library Association.

———. 1977. *Literacy and the Nation's Libraries*. Chicago: American Library Association.

McCook, Kathleen de la Peña. 2005–2006. "Adult Literacy Practice and Theories: The Writings of George Demetrion." *Progressive Librarian* 26 (Winter): 76–78.

McCook, Kathleen de la Peña, and Peggy Barber. 2002. *Chronology of Milestones for Libraries and Adult Lifelong Learning and Literacy*. ERIC ED458888. Washington, DC.

———. 2002. "Public Policy as a Factor Influencing Adult Lifelong Learning, Adult Literacy and Public Libraries." *Reference and User Services Quarterly* 42, no. 1 (Fall): 66–75.

Miami-Dade Public Library System. Project L.E.A.D. (Literacy for Every Adult in Dade). http://www.mdpls.org/services/outreach/lead.asp.

National Assessments of Adult Literacy. http://nces.ed.gov/naal.

National Coalition for Literacy. http://www.national-coalition-literacy.org/.

National Commission on Adult Literacy and Council for Advancement of Adult Literacy. 2008. *Reach Higher, America: Overcoming Crisis in the U.S. Workforce: Report of the National Commission on Adult Literacy*. New York: Council for Advancement of Adult Literacy.

New York State. "Adult Literacy Library Services." http://www.nysl.nysed.gov/libdev/literacy/.

Penny, Victoria. 2005. "Motheread/Fatheread: A True Partnership in Tunica County." *Mississippi Libraries* 69 (Fall): 70–71.

Petruzzi, Tony, and Mary Frances Burns. 2006. "A Literacy Center Where? A Public Library Finds Space to Promote and Provide Family Learning Activities." *Public Library Quarterly* 25: 191–197.

Proliteracy. http://www.proliteracy.org.

Rolstad, Gary O. 1990. "Literacy Services in Public Libraries." In *Adult Services: An Enduring Focus for Public Libraries*, edited by Kathleen M. Heim and Danny P. Wallace, 245–265. Chicago: American Library Association.

Sanders, J. 2008. "Bylaws Changes Will Create a More Inclusive PLA." *Public Libraries* 47 (January/February): 7–8.

Tulsa City County Library. http://www.tulsalibrary.org/literacy/.

U.S. National Center for Education Statistics. 2002. *Programs for Adults in Public Library Outlets*. Washington, DC: National Center for Education Statistics.

Make Career Choices: Job and Career Development (Education; Nelson, 2008: 188–190)

American Library Association, Office for Research and Statistics. 2009. "Job-Seeking in U.S. Public Libraries." http://www.ala.org/ala/research/initiatives/plftas/issuesbriefs/JobBrief 2009_2F.pdf.

Baumann, Michael. 2009. "Public Libraries Step into Job-Search Niche." *Information Today* 26, no. 10: 1, 43.

Durrance, Joan C. 1993. *Serving Job Seekers and Career Changers.* Chicago: Public Library Association.

Jerrard, Jane. 2009. *Crisis in Employment: A Librarian's Guide to Helping Job Seekers.* Chicago: American Library Association.

New York Public Library. "Job Search Central." http://www.nypl.org/locations/tid/65/node/40820.

North Carolina State Library. "Job Search Toolkit." http://statelibrary.ncdcr.gov/ld/jobsearchtoolkit.html.

Reference and User Services Association, Business Reference and Services Section. http://www.ala.org/ala/mgrps/divs/rusa/sections/brass/index.cfm.

Tacoma Public Library. "Education and Job Center." http://www.tpl.lib.wa.us/Page.aspx?nid=216.

Make Informed Decisions: Health, Wealth and Other Life Choices (Information; Nelson, 2008: 191–194)

Bell, Lori, Tom Peters, Margaret Monsour, and Kitty Pope. 2009. "Financial Information Literacy Services at Your Library." *Searcher* 17 (June): 18–21, 53.

OCLC. 2010. *How Libraries Stack Up: 2010.* http://www.oclc.org/reports/pdfs/214109usf_how_libraries_stack_up_gray.pdf.

Reference and User Services Association. 2001. "Guidelines for Medical, Legal and Business Responses." http://www.ala.org/ala/mgrps/divs/rusa/resources/guidelines/guidelinesmedical.cfm.

Rena, Ren, et al. 2009. "Partnerships for a Healthy Community: Laredo Public Library's Children's Health Fair and Outreach Program." *Texas Library Journal* 85 (Summer): 63–64.

Tashbrook, Linda. 2009. "Aiming High, Reaching Out and Doing Good: Helping Homeless Library Patrons with Legal Information." *Public Libraries* 48 (January/February): 38–45.

Satisfy Curiosity: Lifelong Learning (Cultural Heritage; Nelson, 2008: 195–198)

American Library Association, Office for Public Programs. http://www.ala.org/ala/aboutala/offices/ppo/index.cfm.

Brack, Lori, and Joe McKenzie. 2007. "CLASS: The Future of Adult Programming in the Public Library." *Public Libraries* 46 (May/June): 40–44.

Burge, Elizabeth J. 1983. "Adult Learners, Learning and Public Libraries." Special issue, *Library Trends* 31 (Spring).

Carr, David. 2003. *The Promise of Cultural Institutions.* Walnut Creek, CA: AltaMira Press.

Dilevko, Juris, and Lisa Gottlieb. 2003. "Resurrecting a Neglected Idea: The Re-introduction of Library-Museum Hybrids." *Library Quarterly* 73 (April): 160–198.

Elmborg, Jim. 2010. "Literacies, Narratives, and Adult Learning in Libraries." *New Directions for Adult and Continuing Education* no. 127 (Fall): 67–76.

Falk, John H., and Lynn D. Dierking. 2000. *Learning from Museums: Visitor Experiences and the Making of Meaning*. Walnut Creek, CA: Rowman and Littlefield.

Hinchcliffe, Geoffrey, and Lorella Terzi. 2009. "Capabilities and Education." *Studies in Philosophy and Education* 28 (September): 387–390.

Houle, Cyril O. 1979. "Seven Adult Educational Roles of the Public Library." In *As Much to Learn as to Teach: Essays in Honor of Lester Asheim*, edited by Joel M. Lee and Beth A. Hamilton, 94–116. Hamden, CT: Linnet.

Jarvis, Peter. 2010. *Adult Education and Lifelong Learning*. London: Routledge.

Lear, Brett W. 2002. *Adult Programs in the Library*. Chicago: American Library Association.

Library of Congress. "National Book Festival." http://www.loc.gov/bookfest/.

Library of Congress, Center for the Book. http://www.read.gov/cfb/.

———. "State Center Affiliates." http://www.read.gov/cfb/state-affiliates.php.

McCook, Kathleen de la Peña, and Maria A. Jones. 2002. "Cultural Heritage Institutions and Community Building." *Reference and User Services Quarterly* 41 (Summer): 326–329.

Monroe, Margaret E. 1981. "The Cultural Role of the Public Library." *Advances in Librarianship* 11: 1–49.

National Endowment for the Humanities. http://www.neh.gov.

———. "State Humanities Councils." http://www.neh.gov/whoweare/statecouncils.html.

Rubin, Rhea Joyce. 1997. *Humanities Programming: A How-to-Do-It Manual*. New York: Neal-Schuman.

U.S. Department of Education. 2000. *Lifelong Learning NCES Task Force: Final Report, Volume II, Working Paper No. 2000-16b*. Washington, DC: U.S. Department of Education.

Van Fleet, Connie. 1990. "Lifelong Learning Theory and the Provision of Adult Services." In *Adult Services: An Enduring Focus for Public Libraries*, edited by Kathleen M. Heim and Danny P. Wallace, 166–211. Chicago: American Library Association.

Van Fleet, Connie, and Douglas Raber. 1990. "The Public Library as a Social/Cultural Institution: Alternative Perspectives and Changing Contexts." In *Adult Services: An Enduring Focus for Public Libraries*, edited by Kathleen M. Heim and Danny P. Wallace, 456–500. Chicago: American Library Association.

Watkins, Christine. 2000. "Live at the Library 2000: Building Cultural Communities." *American Libraries* 31 (June/July): 69.

Stimulate Imagination: Reading, Viewing and Listening for Pleasure (Cultural Heritage; Nelson, 2008: 199–202)

Adult Reading Round Table. http://www.arrtreads.org.

American Library Association. "Notable Books." http://www.ala.org/ala/mgrps/divs/rusa/awards/notablebooks/index.cfm.

American Library Association, Office for Public Programs. http://www.ala.org/ala/aboutala/offices/ppo/index.cfm.

American Library Association, Video Round Table. http://www.ala.org/ala/mgrps/rts/vrt/index
.cfm.

Appleyard, J. A. 1990. *Becoming a Reader: The Experience of Fiction from Childhood to Adult-
hood.* New York: Cambridge University Press.

Balcom, Ted. 1992. *Book Discussion for Adults: A Leader's Guide.* Chicago: American Library
Association.

———. 2002. "The Adult Reading Round Table." *Reference and User Services Quarterly* 41
(Spring): 238–243.

Beam, Alex. 2009. *A Great Idea at the Time: The Rise, Fall and Curious Afterlife of the Great
Books.* New York: Public Affairs.

Brandehoff, Susan E. 1996. "ALA's Touring Shows Spur Programs: Traveling Exhibits ALA
Has Developed since 1983." *American Libraries* 27 (January): 85–86.

Burgin, Robert. 2004. *Nonfiction Readers' Advisory.* Westport, CT: Libraries Unlimited.

Carpenter, Kenneth E. 1996. *Toward a History of Libraries and Culture in America.* Washington, DC: Library of Congress.

Carr, David. 2006. *A Place Not a Place: Reflection and Possibility in Museums and Libraries.*
Lanham, MD: Altamira Press.

Carrier, Esther Jane. 1965. *Fiction in Public Libraries, 1876–1900.* New York: Scarecrow
Press.

———. 1985. *Fiction in Public Libraries, 1900–1950.* Littleton, CO: Libraries Unlimited.

Crawford, Walt. 2003. "Thinking about Complex Media." *American Libraries* 34 (December):
59.

Farr, Cecilia Konchar. 2004. *Reading Oprah: How Oprah's Book Club Changed the Way America Reads.* Albany: State University of New York Press.

Goodes, Pamela A. 1998. "Writers Live at the Library." *Public Libraries* 37 (July/August):
240–241.

Gray, William S., and Ruth Munroe. 1929. *The Reading Interests and Habits of Adults.* New
York: Macmillan.

Haines, Helen E. 1924. Modern Fiction and the Public Library. *Library Journal* 49 (May 15):
458–460.

———. 1935. *Living with Books: The Art of Book Selection.* New York: Columbia University
Press.

Hawthorne, Karen, and Jane E. Gibson. 2002. *Bulletin Board Power: Bridges to Lifelong
Learning.* Greenwood Village, CO: Libraries Unlimited.

Herald, Diana Tixier. 2005. *Genreflecting: A Guide to Reading Interests in Genre Fiction.* 5th
ed. Englewood, CO: Libraries Unlimited.

Holt, Leslie Edmonds, and Glen E. Holt. 2010. *Public Library Services for the Poor.* Chicago:
American Library Association.

Hooper, Brad. 2010. "Selling the Classics." *Public Libraries* 49 (January/February): 26–33.

Howell, R. Patton. 1989. *Beyond Literacy: The Second Gutenberg Revolution.* San Francisco:
Saybrook.

Kaestle, Carl F., and Janice A. Radway. 2009. *Print in Motion: The Expansion of Publishing and Reading in the United States, 1880–1940*. Chapel Hill: University of North Carolina Press.

Kaplan, Paul. 1998. "The Benefits of Local Author Programs." *Public Libraries* 37 (July/August): 238.

Karetzky, Stephen. 1982. *Reading Research and Librarianship: A History and Analysis*. Westport, CT: Greenwood Press.

Kniffel, Leonard. 2001. "Authors Take Center Stage at First National Book Festival." *American Libraries* 32 (October): 16–17.

Korda, Michael. 2001. *Making the List: A Cultural History of the American Best Seller, 1900–1999*. New York: Barnes and Noble.

Langemack, Chapple. 2007. *The Author Event Primer*. Westport, CT: Libraries Unlimited.

Lesesne, Teri S. 2009. "Reading with Your Ears or with Your Eyes: Does It Matter?" *Voice of Youth Advocates* 32 (April): 44–46.

Library of Congress. "National Book Festival." http://www.loc.gov/bookfest/.

Library of Congress, Center for the Book. http://www.read.gov/cfb/.

———. "State Center Affiliates." http://www.read.gov/cfb/state-affiliates.php.

Library of Congress, National Library Service for the Blind and Physically Handicapped. http://www.loc.gov/nls/.

Long, Sarah Ann. 2001. "Foreword." In *Civic Librarianship: Renewing the Social Mission of the Public Library*, edited by Ronald B. McCabe, vii–ix. Lanham, MD: Scarecrow Press.

Manguel, Alberto. 1996. *A History of Reading*. New York: Penguin.

———. 2010. *A Reader on Reading*. New Haven, CT: Yale University Press.

McCook, Kathleen de la Peña. 1993. "Considerations of Theoretical Bases for Readers' Advisory Services." In *Developing Readers' Advisory Services: Concepts and Commitments*, edited by Kathleen de la Peña McCook and Gary O. Rolstad, 7–12. New York: Neal-Schuman.

———. 1993. "The First Virtual Reality." *American Libraries* 24 (July/August): 626–628.

McCook, Kathleen de la Peña, and Gary O. Rolstad, eds. 1993. *Developing Readers' Advisory Services: Concepts and Commitments*. New York: Neal-Schuman.

Merola, Marci. 2009. "Book Festival Draws Record Crowd." *American Libraries* 40 (November): 19.

Moyer, Jessica E. 2005. "Adult Fiction Reading: A Literature Review of Readers' Advisory Services, Adult Fiction Librarianship and Fiction Readers." *Reference and User Services Quarterly* 44 (Spring): 220–226, 229–231.

———. 2007. "Learning from Leisure Reading: A Study of Adult Public Library Patrons." *Reference and User Services Quarterly* 46 (Summer): 66–79.

Moyer, Jessica E., and Kaite Mediatore Stover. 2010. *The Readers' Advisor Handbook*. Chicago: American Library Association.

National Endowment for the Arts. 2004. *Reading at Risk: A Survey of Literary Reading in America*. Washington, DC: National Endowment for the Arts.

Nell, Victor. 1988. *Lost in a Book: The Psychology of Reading for Pleasure*. New Haven, CT: Yale University Press.

Nordmeyer, Ricki. 2001. "Readers' Advisory Websites." *Reference and User Services Quarterly* 41 (Winter): 139–143.

Pawley, Christine. 2010. *Reading Places: Literacy, Democracy, and the Public Library in Cold War America*. Amherst: University of Massachusetts Press.

Pearl, Nancy. 2002. *Now Read This II: A Guide to Mainstream Fiction, 1990–2001*. Greenwood Village, CO: Libraries Unlimited.

———. 2003. *Book Lust: Recommended Reading for Every Mood, Moment and Reason*. Seattle, WA: Sasquatch Books.

Peters, Thomas A. 2009. *Library Programs Online*. Westport, CT: Libraries Unlimited.

Polanka, Sue. 2010. *No Shelf Required: E-books in Libraries*. Chicago: American Library Association.

Price, Lee. 2009. "Celebrating the Humanities." *Public Libraries* 483 (May/June): 23–25.

Radway, Janice A. 1997. *A Feeling for Books: The Book-of-the-Month Club, Literary Taste, and Middle Class Desire*. Chapel Hill: University of North Carolina Press.

Reference and User Services Association. "Notable Books for Adults." http://www.ala.org/ala/mgrps/divs/rusa/awards/notablebooks/index.cfm.

Ross, Catherine Sheldrick. 2006. *Reading Matters: What the Research Reveals about Reading, Libraries and Community*. Westport, CT: Libraries Unlimited.

———. 2009. "Public Libraries, Pleasure Reading and Models of Reading." *Library Trends* 57 (Spring): 632–656.

Sager, Donald J., ed. 1998. "Authors in Public Libraries." *Public Libraries* 37 (July/August): 237–241.

Sulwak, Dale. 1999. *A Passion for Books*. New York: St. Martin's Press.

Saricks, Joyce G. 2005. *Readers' Advisory Services in the Public Library*. 3rd ed. Chicago: American Library Association.

———. 2009. "Celebrate ARRT." *Booklist* 105: 24.

———. 2009. *The Readers' Advisory Guide to Genre Fiction*. Rev. ed. Chicago: American Library Association.

Shearer, Kenneth D. 1996. *Guiding the Reader to the Next Book*. New York: Neal-Schuman.

Shearer, Kenneth D., and Robert Burgin. 2002. *Readers' Advisor's Companion*. Littleton, CO: Libraries Unlimited.

Shorris, Earl. 2000. "Promoting the Humanities, or How to Make the Poor Dangerous." *American Libraries* 31 (May): 46–48.

———. 2000. *Riches for the Poor*. New York: W. W. Norton.

Smith, Duncan. 2000. "Talking with Readers: A Competency Based Approach to Readers' Advisory Services." *Reference and User Services Quarterly* 40 (Winter): 135–142.

Stover, Kaite Mediatore. 2009. "Stalking the Wild Appeal Factor: Readers' Advisory and Social Networking Sites." *Reference and User Services Quarterly* 48 (Spring): 243–246, 269.

Trott, Barry. 2010. "Helen E. Haines: A Life with Books." *Reference and User Services Quarterly* 50 (Fall): 14–17.

Trott, Barry, and Duncan Smith. 2009. "Your Brain on Fiction." *Reference and User Services Quarterly* 49 (Fall): 38–42.

Waples, Douglas, and Ralph W. Tyler. 1931. *What People Want to Read About: A Study of Group Interests and a Survey of Problems in Adult Reading*. Chicago: University of Chicago Press.

Weiner, Stephen. 1998. "Authors Are a Community's Celebrities." *Public Libraries* 37 (July/August): 240.

Wilson, Louis R. 1938. *The Geography of Reading: A Study of the Distribution and Status of Libraries in the United States*. Chicago: University of Chicago Press.

Wyatt, Neal. 2002. "A Year Inside Notable Books." *Reference and User Services Quarterly* 41 (Summer): 340–343.

———. 2008. "RA ToolKit." *Library Journal* 133 (June 15): 42–45.

Succeed in School: Homework Help (Education; Nelson, 2008: 203–206)

Association of College and Research Libraries. 2008. "Guidelines for Distance Learning Library Services." http://www.ala.org/ala/mgrps/divs/acrl/standards/guidelinesdistancelearning.cfm.

Davis, Elizabeth. 2008. "Homeschooling @ Your Library." *Public Libraries* 47 (May/June): 20–21.

Feinberg, Sandra. 2007. *The Family-Centered Library Handbook*. New York: Neal-Schuman.

Intner, Carol F. 2010. *Homework Help from the Library*. Chicago: American Library Association.

Michaelson, Judy. 2009. "Online Homework Help: Evaluating the Options." *Young Adult Library Services* 7 (Winter): 25–28.

Understand How to Find, Evaluate, and Use Information: Information Fluency (Education; Nelson, 2008: 207–209)

American Library Association. 1989. "Presidential Commission on Information Literacy: Final Report." January 10. http://www.ala.org/ala/mgrps/divs/acrl/publications/whitepapers/presidential.cfm.

Andersen, Jack. 2006. "The Public Sphere and Discursive Activities: Information Literacy as Sociopolitical Skills." *Journal of Documentation* 62: 213–228.

Association for College and Research Libraries. "Information Literacy Toolkit." http://www.ala.org/ala/mgrps/divs/acrl/issues/infolit/standards/standardstoolkit.cfm.

Buschman, John. 2009. "Information Literacy, and 'New' Literacies, and Literacy." *Library Quarterly* 79 (January): 95–118.

Curzon, Susan Carol, and Lynn D. Lampert. 2007. *Proven Strategies for Building an Information Literacy Program*. New York: Neal-Schuman.

Julien, Heidi, and Cameron Hoffman. 2008. "Information Literacy Training in Canada's Public Libraries." *Library Quarterly* 78 (January): 19–41.

National Forum on Information Literacy. http://www.infolit.org/welcome.

Obama, Barack. 2009. "Presidential Proclamation: National Literacy Awareness Month." http://www.whitehouse.gov/the_press_office/Presidential-Proclamation-National-Information-Literacy-Awareness-Month.

Reference and User Services Association. 2006. "Guidelines for the Introduction of Electronic Information Resources to Users." http://www.ala.org/ala/mgrps/divs/rusa/resources/guidelines/guidelinesintroduction.cfm.

WebJunction. 2010. "National Leadership Grant to Look at Online Patron Instruction in Public Libraries. http://www.webjunction.org/patron-training-research.

Visit a Comfortable Place: Physical and Virtual Spaces (Public Sphere; Nelson, 2008: 210–213)

Balas, Janet L. 2009. "Excellence in Service in the Virtual Library." *Computers in Libraries* 29 (January): 33.

Ball, Mary Alice. 2009. "Aggregating Broadband Demand: Surveying the Benefits and Challenges for Public Libraries." *Government Information Quarterly* 26 (October): 531–558.

Burke, Susan K. 2009. "Perceptions of Public Library Accessibility for People with Disabilities." *Reference Librarian* 50 (January/March): 43–54.

Buschman, John, and Gloria J. Leckie, eds. 2007. *Library as Place: History, Community and Culture.* Westport, CT: Libraries Unlimited.

Christensen, Karen, and David Levinson. 2007. *A Heart of the Community: The Libraries We Love.* Great Barrington, MA: Berkshire.

Davis, Denise M., John Carlo Bertot, and Charles R. McClure. 2008. *Libraries Connect Communities: Public Library Funding and Technology Access Study 2007–2008.* Chicago: American Library Association. http://www.ala.org/ala/research/initiatives/plftas/previous studies/0708/LibrariesConnectCommunities.pdf.

Greenwood, Bill. 2009. "Bill and Melinda Gates Foundation Targets Library Internet Speeds." *Computers in Libraries* 29 (March): 32.

Hill, Nanci Milone. 2008. "Meeting Rooms." *Public Libraries* 47 (November/December): 17.

Hilyard, Nann Blaine. 2008. "The Heart of the Neighborhood: Branch Libraries Today." *Public Libraries* 47 (July/August): 15.

Houser, John. 2009. "Open Source Public Workstations in Libraries." *Library Technology Reports* 45 (April).

Kelman, Ari. 2001. "The Sound of the Civic: Reading Noise at the New York Public Library." *American Studies* 42 (Fall): 23–41.

King, David Lee. 2009. "Building the Digital Branch: Guidelines for Transforming Your Library Website." *Library Technology Reports* 45 (August/September).

Kniffel, Leonard. 2007. "Supreme Court Won't Hear Meeting Room Appeal." *American Libraries* 38 (November): 18.

Lehman, Tom, and Terry Nikkel. 2008. *Making Library Web Sites Usable: A LITA Guide.* New York: Neal-Schuman.

Lehrman, Leonard. 1995. "Hear the Music: Concerts in Libraries." *Wilson Library Bulletin* 69 (February): 30–32.

Mattern, Shannon. 2007. *The New Downtown Library.* Minneapolis: University of Minnesota Press.

McCabe, Ron. 2009. "The Library Commons." *Voice of Youth Advocate* 32 (October): 296–297.

McClure, Charles R., and Paul T. Jaeger. 2009. *Public Libraries and Internet Service Roles: Measuring and Maximizing Internet Services.* Chicago: American Library Association.

Peltier-Davis, Cheryl. 2009. "Web 2.0, Library 2.0, Library User 2.0, Librarian 2.0: Innovative Services for Sustainable Libraries." *Computers in Libraries* 29 (November/December): 16–21.

Price, Lee. 2009. "Celebrating the Humanities." *Public Libraries* 48 (Mary/June): 23–25.

———. 2009. "The Story of the H.O.M.E. Page Café." *Public Libraries* 48 (January/February): 32–34.

Putnam, Robert D., and Lewis M. Feldstein. 2003. "Branch Libraries: The Heartbeat of the Community." In *Better Together: Restoring the American Community*, 34–54. New York: Simon and Schuster.

Romano, T. Wayne. 2007. "Piano Concerts at Danville Public Library." *Virginia Libraries* 53 (October/November/December): 21–22.

Russo, Stacy Shotsberger. 2008. *The Library as Place in California*. Jefferson, NC: McFarland.

Senville, Wayne. 2009. "Libraries: The Hubs of Our Communities." *Planning Commissioners Journal* 75 (Summer): 12–18.

Simon, Scott J. 2008. "Jamming in the Stacks: Music as a Progressive Librarian Ideal." *Progressive Librarian* 31 (Summer): 37–45.

Swisher, Susan Herrick. 2007. "'A' Is for Art, Not Age: The Hammond Public Library's Annual Senior Art Exhibit." *Indiana Libraries* 26, no. 2: 38–39.

Urbanska, Wanda. 2009. "A Greener Library, A Greener You." *American Libraries* 40 (April): 52–55.

Wise, Mary. 2005. "Books, Hot Coffee and a Comfortable Chair." *Alki* 21 (March): 11–12.

Welcome to the United States: Services for New Immigrants (Information; Nelson, 2008: 214–217)

Adkins, Denise, et al. 2009. "Describing Vernacular Literacy Practices to Enhance Understanding of Community Information Needs: A Case Study with Practical Implications." *Reference and User Services Quarterly* 49 (Fall): 64–71.

Avila, Salvador. 2008. *Crash Course in Serving Spanish-Speakers*. Westport, CT: Libraries Unlimited.

Burke, Susan K. 2008. "Use of Public Libraries by Immigrants." *Reference and User Services Quarterly* 48 (Winter): 164–174.

Cuban, Sondra. 2007. *Serving New Immigrant Communities in the Library*. Westport, CT: Libraries Unlimited.

Davis, Denise M. 2009. "Outreach to Non-English Speakers in U.S. Public Libraries." *Public Libraries* 48 (January/February): 13–19.

Dezarn, L. M. 2008. "The Challenge of Latino Immigration for the Rural Library." *Bookmobile and Outreach Services* 11: 25–45.

Eitner, Mike. 2006. "The Vietnamese Collection at the Denver Public Library: Evolving Needs and Preferences." *Colorado Libraries* 32 (Fall): 19–20.

Güereña, Salvador. 2000. *Library Services to Latinos*. Jefferson, NC: McFarland.

Jeffers, Eugene J. 2009. "Electronic Outreach and Our Internet Patrons." *Public Libraries* 48 (January/February): 21–23.

Klopstein, Emily, et al. 2009. "Welcoming Newcomers with Practical Library Programs." *Public Libraries* 48 (November/December): 43–47.

Koontz, Christine M., and Dean K. Jue. 2008. *Serving Non-English Speakers in U.S. Public Libraries: 2007 Analysis of Library Demographics, Services and Programs*. Chicago: American Library Association.

"Library Services for Immigrants, An Abridged Version." 2009. *Public Library Quarterly* 28 (April/June): 120–126.

McCook, Kathleen de la Peña. 2007. "Librarians as Advocates for the Human Rights of Immigrants." *Progressive Librarian* 29 (Summer): 51–54.

McMullen, C. 2008. "'Official English' Legislation and Its Effect on Limited English Proficient People." *DttP* 36 (Winter): 15–19, 35.

Naficy, Homa. 2009. "Centering Essential Immigrants Help on the Library Web Site: The American Place (TAP) at Hartford Public Library." *Public Library Quarterly* 28, no. 2 (April/June): 162–175.

Reference and User Services Association. 2007. "Guidelines for the Development and Promotion of Multilingual Collections and Services." http://www.ala.org/ala/mgrps/divs/rusa/resources/guidelines/guidemultilingual.cfm.

REFORMA. 2006. "Librarian's Toolkit for Responding Effectively to Anti-immigrant Sentiment." http://www.reforma.org/ToolkitPartI.htm.

Roy, Loriene. 2007. "Circle of Community." *American Libraries* 38: 6.

Salem, Bryan. 2010. "Cultivating the Enjoyment of Reading: The Prospects of Using a Leveled Library to Support English Language Learners." *PNLA Quarterly* 74, no. 2: 27–37.

Voss, Joyce. 2005. "Outreach Services to the Backstretch of Arlington Park Race Track." *Public Libraries* 44 (November/December): 325–326.

9. Youth Services

Books and Parts of Books

Alire, Camila, and Jacqueline Ayala. 2007. *Serving Latino Communities*. New York: Neal-Schuman.

American Association of School Librarians. 2007. *Standards for the 21st Century Learner*. Chicago: American Association of School Librarians.

———. 2009. *Standards for the Twenty-first Century Learner in Action*. Chicago: American Association of School Librarians.

American Association of School Librarians and Association for Educational Communications and Technology. 1998. *Information Power: Building Partnerships for Learning*. Chicago: American Library Association.

American Library Association. 1984. *Realities: Educational Reform in a Learning Society*. Chicago: American Library Association.

———. 2010. *Intellectual Freedom Manual*. 8th ed. Chicago: American Library Association.

Aries, Philipe. 1962. *Centuries of Childhood*. New York: Random House.

Association for Library Service to Children. 2000. *Intellectual Freedom for Children: The Censor Is Coming*. Chicago: American Library Association.

————. 2009. *Competencies for Librarians Serving Children in Public Libraries*. http://www .ala.org/ala/mgrps/divs/alsc/edcareeers/alsccorecomps/index.cfm.

Association for Library Services to Children, Intellectual Freedom Committee. 2007. *Kids, Know Your Rights: A Young Person's Guide to Intellectual Freedom*. http://www.ala.org/ ala/mgrps/divs/alsc/issuesadv/intellectualfreedom/kidsknowyourrights.pdf.

Baker, Augusta, and Ellin Greene. 1987. *Storytelling Art and Technique*. New York: Bowker.

Benton Foundation. 1996. *Buildings, Books, and Bytes: Libraries and Communities in the Digital Age*. Washington, DC: Benton Foundation.

Blowers, Helene, and Robin Bryan. 2004. *Weaving a Library Web: A Guide to Developing Children's Websites*. Chicago: American Library Association.

Boyer, Ernest L. 1991. *Ready to Learn: A Mandate for the Nation*. Princeton, NJ: Princeton University Press.

Bransford, John D., Ann L. Brown, and Rodney R. Cocking, eds. 1999. *How People Learn: Brain, Mind, Experience, and School*. Washington, DC: National Academy Press.

Braun, Linda. 2010. *Children and the Internet: Policies That work*. Chicago: PLA/ALSC. http:// www.ala.org/ala/mgrps/divs/alsc/issuesadv/internettech/childrentheinternetpoliciesthatwork/ index.cfm.

Braverman, Miriam. 1979. *Youth, Society and the Public Library*. Chicago: American Library Association.

Bredekamp, Sue, ed. 1987. *Developmentally Appropriate Practice in Early Childhood Programs Serving Children from Birth through Age 8*. Exp. ed. Washington, DC: National Association for the Education of Young Children.

Broderick, Dorothy. 1965. *An Introduction to Children's Work in Public Libraries*. New York: H. W. Wilson.

Brophy, Peter. 2007. *The Library in the Twenty-first Century*. London: Facet.

Brown, Carol R. 2002. *Interior Design for Libraries: Drawing on Function and Appeal*. Chicago: American Library Association.

Cerny, Rosanne, Penny Markey, Amanda Williams, and the Association for Library Service to Children. 2006. *Outstanding Library Service to Children: Putting the Core Competencies to Work*. Chicago: American Library Association.

Chelton, Mary K. 2000. *Excellence in Library Services to Young Adults: The Nation's Top Programs*. Chicago: American Library Association.

Connor, Jane Gardner. 1990. *Children's Library Services Handbook*. Phoenix, AZ: Oryx.

Council on Interracial Books for Children. 1980. *Guidelines for Selecting Bias-Free Textbooks and Storybooks*. New York: Council on Interracial Books for Children.

Cross, Gary. 1997. *Kids' Stuff: Toys and the Changing World of American Childhood*. Cambridge, MA: Harvard University Press.

Day, Frances Ann. 1999. *Multicultural Voices in Contemporary Literature: A Resource for Teachers*. Rev. ed. Portsmouth, NH: Heinemann.

DeBell, Matthew, and Chris Chapman. 2003. *Computer and Internet Use by Children and Adolescents in 2001*. Washington, DC: U.S. Department of Education. http://nces.ed.gov/ pubsearch/pubsinfo.asp?pubid=2004014.

DeWitt Wallace-Reader's Digest Fund. 1999. *Public Libraries as Partners in Youth Development*. New York: DeWitt Wallace-Reader's Digest Fund.

Diamant-Cohen, Betsy. 2010. *Children's Services: Partnerships for Success*. Chicago: American Library Association.

Doyle, Christina S. 1994. *Information Literacy in an Information Society: A Concept for the Information Age*. ED372763. Syracuse, NY: ERIC Clearing House on Information and Technology, Syracuse University.

Dresang, Eliza T. 1999. *Radical Change: Books for Youth in a Digital Age*. New York: H. W. Wilson.

———. 2000. "Outstanding Literature: Pura Belpré and Américas Selections with Special Appeal in the Digital Age." In *Library Services to Youth of Hispanic Heritage*, edited by Barbara Immroth and Kathleen de la Peña McCook, 69–87. Jefferson, NC: McFarland.

Dresang, Eliza T., Melissa Gross, and Leslie Edmonds Holt. 2006. *Dynamic Youth Services through Outcome-Based Planning and Evaluation*. Chicago: American Library Association.

East, Kathy, and Rebecca L. Thomas. 2007. *Across Cultures: A Guide to Multicultural Literature for Children*. Westport, CT: Libraries Unlimited.

Evans, Sara M., and Harry C. Boyte. 1986. *Free Spaces: The Sources of Democratic Change in America*. New York: Harper and Row.

Fasick, Adele M., and Leslie E. Holt. 2008. *Managing Children's Services in the Public Library*. 3rd ed. Westport, CT: Libraries Unlimited.

Federal Interagency Forum on Child and Family Statistics. 1999. *America's Children: Key National Indicators of Well-Being*. Washington, DC: U.S. Government Printing Office.

Feinberg, Sandra, Joan F. Kuchner, and Sari Feldman. 1998. *Learning Environments for Young Children: Rethinking Library Spaces and Services*. Chicago: American Library Association.

Fletcher, William I. 1876. "Public Libraries and the Young." In *Public Libraries in the United States: Their History, Condition and Management*, 412–418. Washington, DC: Department of the Interior, Bureau of Education.

Furness, A. 2008. *Helping Homeschoolers in the Library*. Chicago: American Library Association.

Garbarino, James, et al. 1992. *Children in Danger: Coping with the Consequences of Community Violence*. San Francisco: Jossey-Bass.

Gleason, Eliza Atkins. 1941. *The Southern Negro and the Public Library: A Study of Government and Administration of Public Library Service to Negroes in the South*. Chicago: University of Chicago Press.

Gnehm, Kurstin Finch. 2002. *Youth Development and Public Libraries: Tools for Success*. Evanston, IL: Urban Libraries Council.

Gonzalez, Lucia M. 2000. "Developing Culturally Integrated Children's Programs." In *Library Services to Youth of Hispanic Heritage*, edited by Barbara Immroth and Kathleen de la Peña McCook, 19–21. Jefferson, NC: McFarland.

Gregory, Vicki L., Marilyn Stauffer, and Thomas Keene Jr. 1999. *Multicultural Resources on the Internet: The United States and Canada*. New York: Neal-Schuman.

Gross, Elizabeth Henry. 1963. *Children's Services in Public Libraries*. Chicago: American Library Association.

Halperin, Wendy Anderson. 1998. *Once upon a Company: A True Story*. New York: Orchard.

Hawes, Joseph M. 1991. *The Children's Rights Movement: A History of Advocacy and Protection*. Boston: Twayne.

Healy, Jane M. 1998. *Failure to Connect: How Computers Affect our Children's Minds—for Better and Worse*. New York: Simon and Schuster.

Heyns, Barbara. 1978. *Summer Learning and the Effects of Schooling*. New York: Academic Press.

Hildebrand, Janet. 1997. "Is Privacy Reserved for Adults? Children's Rights at the Public Library." In *School Library Journal's Best: A Reader for Children's, Young Adult, and School Librarians*, edited by Lillian N. Gerhardt, 419–422. New York: Neal-Schuman.

Himmel, Ethel, and William James Wilson. 1998. *Planning for Results: A Public Library Transformation Process*. Chicago: American Library Association.

Immroth, Barbara, and Kathleen de la Peña McCook. 2000. *Library Services to Youth of Hispanic Heritage*. Jefferson, NC: McFarland.

Intner, Carol F. 2010. *Homework Help from the Library*. Chicago: American Library Association.

Jeffery, Debby Ann. 1995. *Literate Beginnings: Programs for Babies and Toddlers*. Chicago: American Library Association.

Jones, Dolores Blythe, and Anne H. Lundin. 1998. *Building a Special Collection of Children's Literature in Your Library*. Chicago: American Library Association.

Jones, Patrick. 1998. *Connecting Young Adults and Libraries: A How-to-Do-It Manual*. 2nd ed. New York: Neal-Schuman.

Jones, Patrick, and Linda L. Waddle. 2002. *New Directions for Library Service to Young Adults*. Chicago: American Library Association.

Kafai, Yasmin. 1993. *Minds in Play: Computer Game Design as a Context for Children's Learning*. Hillsdale, NJ: Erlbaum.

Kleiner, Anne, and Laurie Lewis. 2003. *Internet Access in U.S. Public Schools and Classrooms: 1994–2002*. Washington, DC: U.S. Department of Education. http://nces.ed.gov/pubsearch/pubsinfo.asp?pubid=2004011.

Kohn, Alfie. 1992. *No Contest: The Case against Competition*. Boston: Houghton Mifflin.

———. 1993. *Punished by Rewards: The Trouble with Gold Stars, Incentive Plans, A's, Praise, and Other Bribes*. Boston: Houghton Mifflin.

Kruse, Ginny Moore, and Kathleen Horning. 1991. *Multicultural Literature for Children and Young Adults*. Madison, WI: Wisconsin Department of Public Instruction.

Kuharets, Olga R., ed. 2001. *Venture into Cultures*. 2nd ed. Chicago: American Library Association.

Kuipers, Barbara. 1995. *American Indian Reference and Resource Books for Children and Young Adults*. 2nd ed. Englewood, CO: Libraries Unlimited.

Kuklin, Susan. 1998. *Iqbal Masih and the Crusaders against Child Slavery*. New York: Holt.

Large, Andrew. 2009. "Children and Information Technology." In *Information Technology in Librarianship: New Critical Approaches*, edited by Gloria J. Leckie and John Buschman, 181–203. Westport, CT: Libraries Unlimited.

Leckie, Gloria J., and John Buschman, eds. 2009. *Information Technology in Librarianship: New Critical Approaches*. Westport, CT: Libraries Unlimited.

Leslie, R., et al. 2001. *Igniting the Spark: Library Programs That Inspire High School Patrons*. Westport, CT: Libraries Unlimited.

Long, Harriet G. 1969. *Public Library Service to Children: Foundation and Development*. Metuchen, NJ: Scarecrow Press.

Lundin, Anne H., and Carol W. Cubberley. 1995. *Teaching Children's Literature: A Resource Guide with a Directory of Courses*. Jefferson, NC: McFarland.

Mathews, Joe. 2010. "Evaluating Summer Reading Programs: Suggested Improvements." *Public Libraries* 49 (July/August): 34–40.

McClure, Charles R. 1987. *Planning and Role Setting for Public Libraries: A Manual of Options and Procedures*. Chicago: American Library Association.

McClure, Charles R., and Paul T. Jaeger. 2009. *Public Libraries and Internet Service Roles: Measuring and Maximizing Internet Services*. Chicago: American Library Association.

McCook, Kathleen de la Peña, ed. 2000. "Ethnic Diversity in Library and Information Science." Special issue, *Library Trends* 49 (Summer): 1–214.

McDowell, Kathleen. 2007. "The Cultural Origins of Youth Services Librarianship, 1876–1900." PhD diss., University of Illinois at Urbana-Champaign.

Mediavilla, Cindy. 1998. "Homework Assistance Programs in Public Libraries: Helping Johnny Read." In *Young Adults and Public Libraries: A Handbook of Materials and Services*, edited by Mary Anne Nichols and C. Allen Nichols, 181–189. Westport, CT: Greenwood Press.

Metoyer-Duran, Cheryl. 1993. *Gatekeepers in Ethnolinguistic Communities*. Norwood, NJ: Ablex.

Miller, Marilyn L. 2003. "Public Library Service to Children." In *Encyclopedia of Library and Information Science*, 2nd ed.: 2397–2407. http://www.informaworld.com/10.1081/E-ELIS -120008737.

Minkel, Walter, and Roxanne Hsu Feldman. 1999. *Delivering Web Reference Services to Young People*. Chicago: American Library Association.

Molz, Redmond Kathleen, and Phyllis Dain. 1999. *Civic Space/Cyberspace: The American Public Library in the Information Age*. Cambridge, MA: MIT Press.

Moore, Anne Carroll. 1969. *My Roads to Childhood: Views and Reviews of Children's Books*. Boston: Horn Book.

Murnane, Richard J., and Frank Levy. 1996. *Teaching the New Basic Skills: Principles for Educating Children to Thrive in a Changing Economy*. New York: Free Press.

Muse, Daphne, ed. 1997. *The New Press Guide to Multicultural Resources for Young Readers*. New York: New Press.

National Education Association. 1899. *Report of the Committee on the Relations of Public Libraries to Public Schools*. Washington, DC: National Education Association.

National Reading Panel. 2000. *Report of the National Reading Panel: Teaching Children to Read: An Evidence-Based Assessment of the Scientific Research Literature on Reading and Its Implications for Reading Instruction*. Washington, DC: National Institute of Child Health and Human Development, National Institutes of Health.

National Research Council. 1998. *Starting Out Right: A Guide to Promoting Children's Reading Success*, edited by Susan M. Burns, Peg Griffin, and Catherine E. Snow. Washington, DC: National Academy Press.

Negroponte, Nicholas. 1995. *Being Digital*. New York: Knopf.

Nelson, Sandra. 2008. *Strategic Planning for Results*. Chicago: American Library Association.

Nespecca, Sue McCleaf. 1994. *Library Programming for Families with Young Children*. New York: Neal-Schuman.

New York Library Association, Task Force on Standards for Youth Services. 1984. *Standards for Youth Services in Public Libraries of New York State*. New York: Youth Services Section of NYLA.

Nichols, May Anne, and C. Allen Nichols. 1998. *Young Adults and Public Libraries*. Westport, CT: Greenwood Press.

Nilsen, Alleen, and Kenneth L. Donelson. 2001. *Literature for Today's Young Adults*. 6th ed. New York: Longman.

Odean, Kathleen. 2003. *Great Books for Babies and Toddlers: More Than 500 Recommended Books for Your Child's First Three Years*. New York: Ballantine.

O'Dell, K. 2002. *Library Materials and Services for Teen Girls*. Greenwood Village, CO: Libraries Unlimited.

Olcott, Frances Jenkins. 1905. "Rational Library Work with Children and the Preparation for It." In *Proceedings of the American Library Association Conference*, 71–75. Chicago: American Library Association.

Palfrey, John, and Urs Gasser. 2008. *Born Digital: Understanding the First Generation of Digital Natives*. New York: Basic Books.

Papert, Seymour. 1993. *The Children's Machine: Rethinking School in the Age of the Computer*. New York: Basic Books.

Pierce, Jennifer Burek. 2008. *Sex, Brains, and Video Games: A Librarian's Guide to Teens in the Twenty-first Century*. Chicago: American Library Association.

Power, Effie. 1930. *Library Service for Children: Library Curriculum Studies*. Chicago: American Library Association.

Reed, Sally Gardiner, and Beth Nawalinsky. 2008. *Even More Great Ideas for Libraries and Friends*. New York: Neal-Schuman.

Reid, R. 2002. *Something Funny Happened at the Library: How to Create Humorous Programs for Children and Young Adults*. Chicago: American Library Association.

Rheingold, Howard. 1993. *The Virtual Community: Homesteading on the Electronic Frontier*. Reading, MA: Addison-Wesley.

Riechel, Rosemarie. 1991. *Reference Services for Children and Young Adults*. Hamden, CT: Library Professional Publications.

Rollock, Barbara T. 1988. *Public Library Services for Children*. Hamden, CT: Shoestring Press.

Roman, Susan. 2010. *Dominican Study: Public Library Summer Reading Programs Close the Reading Gap*. River Forest, IL: Dominican University.

Roman, Susan, Deborah T. Carran, and Carole D. Fiore. 2010. "Public Library Summer Reading Programs Close the Reading Gap." *Illinois Library Association Reporter* 28 (August): 20–22.

Rong, Xue Lan, and Judith Preissle. 1998. *Educating Immigrant Students: What We Need to Know to Meet the Challenges*. Thousand Oaks, CA: Corwin/Sage.

Rovenger, Judith, and Ristiina Wigg. 1986. *Libraries Serving Youth: Directions for Service in the 1990s*. New Paltz: New York Library Association.

Rushkoff, Douglas. 1998. *Playing the Future: How Kids' Culture Can Teach Us to Thrive in an Age of Chaos*. New York: HarperCollins.

Sanders, Rickie, and Mark T. Mattson. 1998. *Growing Up in America: An Atlas of Youth in the USA*. New York: Simon and Schuster/Macmillan.

Sayers, Frances Clarke. 1972. *Anne Carroll Moore*. New York: Atheneum.

Scales, Pat. 2009. *Protecting Intellectual Freedom in Your School Library: Scenarios from the Front Lines*. Chicago: American Library Association.

Schall, Lucy. 2001. *Booktalks Plus: Motivating Teens to Read*. Englewood, CO: Libraries Unlimited.

———. 2003. *Booktalks and More: Motivating Teens to Read*. Westport, CT: Libraries Unlimited.

Sims, Rudine. 1982. *Shadow and Substance: Afro-American Experience in Contemporary Children's Fiction*. Urbana, IL: National Council of Teachers of English.

Slapin, Beverly, and Doris Seala, eds. 1992. *Through Indian Eyes: The Native Experience in Books for Children*. 3rd ed. Philadelphia, PA: New Society.

Smith, Henrietta M. 1994. *The Coretta Scott King Awards Book: From Visions to Reality*. Chicago: American Library Association.

———. 1999. *The Coretta Scott King Awards Book, 1970–1999*. Chicago: American Library Association.

———. 2004. *The Coretta Scott King Awards Book, 1970–2004*. Chicago: American Library Association.

———. 2009. *The Coretta Scott King Awards, 1970-2009*. Chicago: American Library Association.

Smith, Laura. 1992. *Children's Book Awards International, 1990 through 2000*. Jefferson, NC: McFarland.

Sommerville, John. 1982. *The Rise and Fall of Childhood*. Beverly Hills, CA: Sage.

Staerkel, Kathleen, Mary Fellows, and Sue McCleaf Nespecca. 1995. *Youth Services Librarians as Managers: A How-to Guide from Budgeting to Personnel*. Chicago: American Library Association/Association for Library Service to Children.

Steiner, Stanley F. 2001. *Promoting a Global Community through Multicultural Children's Literature*. Englewood, CO: Libraries Unlimited.

Sullivan, Michael. 2005. *Fundamentals of Children's Services*. Chicago: American Library Association.

Tapscott, Don. 1998. *Growing Up Digital: The Rise of the Net Generation*. New York: McGraw-Hill.

Teale, William H. 1995. "Public Libraries and Emergent Literacy: Helping Set the Foundation for School Success." In *Achieving School Readiness: Public Libraries and National Education Goal No. 1*, edited by Barbara Froling Immroth and Viki Ash-Geisler. Chicago: American Library Association.

Thomas, Fannette H. 1982. "The Genesis of Children's Library Services in the American Public Library, 1876–1906." PhD diss., University of Wisconsin-Madison.

Turkle, Sherry. 1995. *Life on the Screen: Identity in the Age of the Internet*. New York: Simon and Schuster.

U.S. Census Bureau. 1993. *We the American Children*. Washington, DC: U.S. Department of Commerce, Census Bureau.

U.S. Department of Employment and Training. 1998. *Dictionary of Occupational Titles*. CD-ROM. U.S. Employment Service.

U.S. Institute of Museum and Library Services. 2009. *Public Libraries Survey: Fiscal Year 2007*. Washington, DC: U.S. Institute of Museum and Library Services. http://harvester .census.gov/imls/pubs/pls/pub_detail.asp?id=122#.

U.S. National Center for Education Statistics. 1988. *Services and Resources for Young Adults in Public Libraries*. Washington, DC: Government Printing Office.

———. 1995. *Services and Resources for Children and Young Adults in Public Libraries*. Washington, DC: U.S. Department of Education.

Walter, Virginia A. 1992. *Output Measures for Public Library Service to Children: A Manual of Standardized Procedures*. Chicago: American Library Association.

———. 1995. *Output Measures and More: Planning and Evaluating Public Library Services for Young Adults*. Chicago: American Library Association.

———. 2001. *Children and Libraries: Getting It Right*. Chicago: American Library Association.

———. 2010. *Twenty-first Century Kids, Twenty-first Century Librarians*. Chicago: American Library Association.

Walter, Virginia A., and Elaine Meyers. 2003. *Teens and Libraries: Getting It Right*. Chicago: American Library Association.

Willett, Holly G. 1995. *Public Library Youth Services: A Public Policy Approach*. Norwood, NJ: Ablex.

Wishy, Bernard. 1968. *The Child and the Republic: The Dawn of Modern American Child Nurture*. Philadelphia, PA: University of Pennsylvania Press.

Yaakov, Juliette, and Anne Price. 2003. *Children's Catalog*. New York: H. W. Wilson.

Young Adult Library Services Association. 2010. *YALSA's Competencies for Librarians Serving Youth: Young Adults Deserve the Best*. http://www.ala.org/ala/mgrps/divs/yalsa/profdev/ yadeservethebest_201.pdf.

Ziarnik, N. 2003. *Schools and Public Libraries*. Chicago: American Library Association.

Articles

Agosto, Denise. 2007. "Why Do Teens Use Libraries?" *Public Libraries* 46 (May): 55–61.

Aldrich, Stacey. 1999. "Sound Bytes of Possibilities." *Journal of Youth Services in Libraries* 12 (Winter): 5–9.

Anderson, Sheila B. 2000. "I Stink and My Feet Are Too Big! Training Librarians to Work with Teens." *Voice of Youth Advocates* 22 (February): 388–390.

Anderson, Sheila B., and John P. Bradford. 2001. "State-Level Commitment to Public Library Services to Young Adults." *Journal of Youth Services in Libraries* 14 (Spring): 23–27.

Ash, Viki, and Elaine Meyers. 2009. "Every Child Ready to Read @ Your Library: How It All Began." *Children and Libraries* 7: 3–7.

Barban, L. 2003. "More Than 'May I Help You': The Assertive Children's Librarian." *Public Libraries* 42 (March/April): 73–74.

Bernier, Anthony, Mary K. Chelton, Christine A. Jenkins, and Jennifer Burek Pierce. 2005. "Two Hundred Years of Young Adult Library Services History: A Chronology." *Voice of Youth Advocates* 28, no. 2: 106–111.

Bingham, Anne. 2002. "Goin' Someplace Special: Trends in Children's Literature." *Alki* 18 (July): 14–15.

Bird, B. 2002. "Solving the Mystery: Children's Librarianship and How to Nurture It." *Australasian Public Libraries and Information Services* 15 (March): 14–23.

Bishop, Kay, and Pat Bauer. 2002. "Attracting Young Adults to Public Libraries: Frances Henne/YALSA/VOYA Research Grant Results." *Journal of Youth Services in Libraries* 15 (Winter): 36–44.

Bitterman, Lisa. 2002. "Across Towns and Across Times: Library Service to Young People in Rural Libraries." *Rural Libraries* 22: 43–62.

Borawski, Christopher. 2009. "Beyond the Book: Literacy in the Digital Age." *Children and Libraries* 7: 53–54.

Campbell, Patty. 1994. "The Sand in the Oyster: White Children's Book Authors' Books on Multicultural Topics." *Horn Book Magazine* 70 (July/August): 491.

Carter, Betty, and Pam Spencer Holley. 2007. "John, Paul, George, and YALSA." *School Library Journal* 53, no. 2: 34–37.

Carty, Natasha S. 2003. "Teen Zone: C. Burr Artz Library, Frederick County Public Libraries, Frederick, Maryland." *Voice of Youth Advocates* 26 (August): 204–205.

Chelton, Mary K. 1997. "Three in Five Public Library Users Are Youth." *Public Libraries* (March/April): 104–108.

———. 2007. "Remembering YALSA: The View of the 'Oldest Living YA Librarian'." *Young Adult Library Services* 6, no. 1: 32–34.

Cox, R. O. 2002. "Lost Boys." *Voice of Youth Advocates* 25 (June): 172–173.

Cresswell, Stephen. 1996. "The Last Days of Jim Crow in Southern Libraries." *Libraries and Culture* 31 (Summer/Fall): 557–573.

Crew, Hilary S. 2002. "Five Foot Bookshelf: Essential Books for Professionals Who Serve Teens." *Voice of Youth Advocates* 25 (October): 260.

Curran, Charles. 1990. "Information Literacy and the Public Librarian." *Public Libraries* 29 (November/December): 349–353.

Danley, Elizabeth. 2003. "The Public Children's Librarian as Educator." *Public Libraries* 42 (March/April): 98–101.

De Groot, Joanne, and Jennifer Branch. 2009. "Solid Foundations: A Primer on the Crucial, Critical, and Key Roles of School and Public Libraries in Children's Development." *Library Trends* 58 (Summer): 51–62.

DeMarco, P. 2003. "Teens Are a Work in Progress: Finding Our Way in a Construction Zone." *Voice of Youth Advocates* 25 (February): 440–442.

Dresang, Eliza T. 2006. "Intellectual Freedom and Libraries: Complexity and Change in the Twenty-first-Century Digital Environment." *Library Quarterly* 76 (April): 169–192.

Dresang, Eliza T., et al. 2003. "Project CATE: Using Outcome Measures to Assess School-Age Children's Use of Technology in Urban Public Libraries: A Collaborative Research Process." *Library and Information Science Research* 25, no. 1: 19–42.

Fenwick, Sara Innis. 1976. "Library Services to Children and Young People." *Library Trends* 25 (Summer): 329–360.

Fine, J. R. 2001. "From the Field: Reaping the Benefits of Partnerships." *Journal of Youth Services in Libraries* 15 (Fall): 16–22.

Fisher, H. 2000. "Children's and Young Adult Service: Like a Box of Chocolates." *Australasian Public Libraries and Information Services* 13 (May): 113–118.

Fitzgibbons, Shirley. 2001. "Libraries and Literacy: A Preliminary Survey of the Literature." *IFLA Journal* 27: 91–106.

Goldsmith, F. 2001. "Literacy Daycamp at the Library: Collaborating with Coworkers and Teens." *Voice of Youth Advocates* 23 (February): 408–409.

Gorman, M. 2002. "Wiring Teens to the Library." *Library Journal Part Net Connect* (Summer): 18–20.

Hake, K. 2000. "Programming and Children's Services." *Bookmobiles and Outreach Services* 3, no. 2: 7–10.

Hamilton, Virginia. 1999. "Sentinels in Long Still Rows." *American Libraries* 30 (June/July): 68–71.

Henricks, S. 2001. "Reconnecting with Teens." *Unabashed Librarian* 121: 24–28.

Hernandez-Delgado, Julio. 1992. "Pura Teresa Belpre: Story Teller and Pioneer Puerto Rican Librarian." *Library Quarterly* 62 (October): 425–440.

Hewins, Caroline. 1892. "Yearly Report on Boys' and Girls' Reading." *Library Journal* 7 (July/August): 182–190.

Hill, Nanci Milone. 2008. "Teens—Perpetual Problem, or Golden Opportunity?" *Public Libraries* 47 (January/February): 24–32.

Hilyard, N. B. 2002. "Assets and Outcomes: New Directions in Young Adult Services in Public Libraries." *Public Libraries* 41 (August/September): 195–199.

Hughes-Hassell, Sandra, and Kay Bishop. 2004. "Using Focus Group Interviews to Improve Library Services for Youth." *Teacher Librarian* 32, no. 1: 8–12.

Hunenberg, D. 2002. "Duh!!! Seven Tips for Improving Customer Service to Teens." *Unabashed Librarian* 125: 10–12.

Ishizuka, K. 2003. "Girl Scouts Build Big Ugly Library." *School Library Journal* 49 (March): 26.

Jaeger, Paul T., and Yan Zheng. 2009. "One Law with Two Outcomes: Comparing the Implementation of CIPA in Public Libraries and Schools." *Information Technology and Libraries* 28 (March): 6–14.

Janes, J. 2003. "Digital Reference for Teens." *Voice of Youth Advocates* 25 (February): 451.

Jenkins, Christine A. 1996. "Women of ALA Youth Services and Professional Jurisdiction: Of Nightingales, Newberies, Realism, and the Right Books, 1937–1945." *Library Trends* 44 (Spring): 813–839.

————. 2000. "The History of Youth Services Librarianship: A Review of the Research Literature." *Libraries and Culture* 35 (Winter): 103–139.

Jones, Patrick. 2001. "Showing You the Money: LSTA Funds and Fifty-two Resources to Find Funding for Youth Services in Libraries." *Journal of Youth Services in Libraries* 15 (Fall): 33–38.

————. 2001. "Why We Are Kids' Best Assets." *School Library Journal* 47 (November): 44–47.

Jones, Plummer Alston. 2004. *Still Struggling for Equality: American Public Library Services with Minorities*. Westport, CT: Libraries Unlimited.

Kimball, Melanie A. 2007. "From Refuge to Risk: Public Libraries and Children in World War I." *Library Trends* 55 (Winter): 454–463.

Kimball, Melanie A., et al. 2004. "Effie Louise Power: Librarian, Educator, Author." *Library Trends* 52 (Spring): 924–951.

Kinney, M. S. 2001. "A Bird's (or State's) Eye View of Cooperation." *Journal of Youth Services in Libraries* 15 (Fall): 25.

Lee, R. 2000. "Remember All the Nifty Children's Programs You Had? Programs Like . . ." *American Libraries* 31 (February): 46–47.

Lepore, Jill. 2008. "The Lion and the Mouse: The Battle That Reshaped Children's Literature." *The New Yorker*. http://www.newyorker.com/reporting/2008/07/21/080721fa_fact_lepore.

Lundin, Anne. 1996. "The Pedagogical Context of Women in Children's Services and Literature Scholarship." *Library Trends* 44 (Winter): 840–850.

Machado, Julie, et al. 2000. "A Survey of Best Practices in Youth Services around the Country." *Journal of Youth Services in Libraries* 13 (Winter): 30–35.

MacRae, Cathi Dunn. 2007. "The Power of Radically Trusting Teens." *Voice of Youth Advocates* 30, no. 2: 101.

McCook, Kathleen de la Peña. 2001. "Authentic Discourse as a Means of Connection between Public Library Service Responses and Community-Building Initiatives." *Reference and User Services Quarterly* 41 (Winter): 127–133.

McCook, Kathleen de la Peña, and Rachel Meyer. 2001. "Public Libraries and Comprehensive Community Initiatives for Youth Development." *Public Libraries* 40 (September/October): 282–288.

McDowell, Kate. 2009. "Surveying the Field: The Research Model of Women in Librarianship, 1882–1898." *Library Quarterly* 79, no. 3: 279–300.

McKechnie, L. E. F. 2001. "Children's Access to Services in Canadian Public Libraries." *Canadian Journal of Information and Library Science* 26 (December): 37–55.

McNeil-Nix, H. 2001. "Family Friendly Libraries Are Us." *Journal of Youth Services in Libraries* 14 (Winter): 17–19.

Meyers, Elaine. 2001. "The Road to Coolness: Youth Rock the Public Library." *American Libraries* 32 (February): 46–48.

————. 2002. "Youth Development and Libraries: A Conversation with Karen Pittman." *Public Libraries* 41 (September/October): 256–260.

Minkel, Walter. 2002. "When Homework Is Good Politics." *School Library Journal* 48 (April): 39.

———. 2003. "We're Not Just a Building." *Library Journal Part Net Connect* (Spring): 26–27.

Moore, Anne Carroll. 1898. "Special Training for Children's Librarians." *Library Journal* 12 (August): 81.

Nesbitt, Elizabeth. 1954. "Library Service to Children." *Library Trends* 3 (October): 118–128.

O'Driscoll, J. A. 2000. "Recipe for Young Adult Spaces and Services." *Voice of Youth Advocates* 23 (April): 27.

Overall, Patricia Montile. 2009. "Cultural Competence: A Conceptual Framework for Library and Information Science Professionals." *Library Quarterly* 79 (April): 175–204.

Petrilli, Ken. 2009. "Banned Books Week: Celebrating Your (and Your Teens!) Freedom to Read." *Young Adult Library Services* 7 (Summer): 4–5.

Phares, C. 2001. "Super Duper Program Planning." *Mississippi Libraries* 65 (Fall): 74–77.

"Programs for School-Aged Youth in Public Libraries: Report of a Survey Conducted for the DeWitt Wallace-Reader's Digest Fund." 1999. *Teacher Librarian* 27 (October): 71–72.

Rackes, Judiann M. 2010. "The Power of Partnerships: Opening Children's Minds through Collaborative Early Learning Programs." *Florida Libraries* 55 (Fall): 8–10.

Rock, F., et al. 2002. "Children Are Service Users Too." *Public Library Journal* 17 (Spring): 8–10.

Rollock, Barbara T. 1988. *Public Library Services for Children*. Hamden, CT: Shoe String Press.

Ryan, S. 2000. "It's Hip to Be Square." *School Library Journal* 46 (March): 138–141.

Sasse, Margo. 1973. "Invisible Women: The Children's Librarian in America." *School Library Journal* 19 (January 15): 213–217.

Saunders, M. 2003. "The Young Adult Outpost: A Library Just for Teens." *Public Libraries* 42 (March/April): 113–116.

Sayers, Frances Clarke. 1963. "The Origins of Public Library Work with Children." *Library Trends* 12 (July): 6–13.

Schmitzer, Jeanne C. 2003. "VOYA's Most Valuable Program for 2003: Making Personal Connections with History." *Voice of Youth Advocates* 26 (October): 276–228.

Schulte-Cooper, L. 2003. "ALSC Builds a Future for Children." *American Libraries* 34 (April): 10.

Sexton, J. 2002. "From Hanging Out to Homework: Teens in the Library." *OLA Quarterly* 8 (Fall): 10–12, 19.

Sloan, C., et al. 2000. "The Extra Mile." *School Librarian* 48 (Winter): 183.

St. Lifer, E. 2002. "The Future of Youth Services." *School Library Journal* 48 (July): 9.

Sullivan, E. T. 2001. "Teenagers Are Not Luggage; They Don't Need Handling." *Public Libraries* 40 (March/April): 75–77.

Thomas, Fannette H. 1990. "Early Appearances of Children's Reading Rooms in Public Libraries." *Journal of Youth Services* (Summer): 81–85.

Thompson, J. 2003. "After School and Online." *Library Journal Part Net Connect* (Winter): 35–37.

Valenza, Joyce Kasman, and Doug Johnson. 2009. "Things That Keep Us Up at Night." *School Library Journal* 55: 29–32.

Vandergrift, Kay. 1996. "Female Advocacy and Harmonious Voices: A History of Public Library Services and Publishing for Children in the United States." *Library Trends* 44 (Spring): 683–718.

Viti, Thomas. 1997. "The Role of the Public Library in Homework Assistance." *Public Libraries* 36 (January/February): 21–22.

"Volume of Children's Work in the United States." 1913. *ALA Bulletin* 7: 287–290.

Walter, Fran K. 1941. "A Poor but Respectable Relation—the Sunday School Library." *Library Quarterly* 12 (July): 734.

Walter, Virginia A. 2001. "The Once and Future Library." *School Library Journal* 47 (January): 48–53.

———. 2002. "Library Services to Children: Future Tense." *Journal of Youth Services in Libraries* 15 (Spring): 18–20.

———. 2003. "Public Library Services to Children and Teens: A Research Agenda." *Library Trends* 51 (Spring): 571–589.

———. 2009. "The Children We Serve: Five Notions of Childhood Suggest Ways to Think about the Services We Provide." *American Libraries* 40 (October): 52–55.

Weinberg, Kathie. 2009. "House Calls: Teen Space Makeover; Teens and Local Newspaper Collaborate for Affordable Changes." *Voice of Youth Advocates* 32 (December): 386–387.

White, Dan R. 2002. "Working Together to Build a Better World: The Importance of Youth Services in the Development and Education of Children and Their Parents." *OLA Quarterly* 8 (Fall): 13–19.

Winston, M. D., et al. 2001. "Reference and Information Services for Young Adults: A Research Study of Public Libraries in New Jersey." *Reference and User Services Quarterly* 41 (Fall): 45–50.

Wright, Lisa A. 1996. "Public Library Circulation Rises along with Spending." *American Libraries* 27 (October): 57–58.

YALSA Research Committee. 2001. "Current Research Related to Young Adult Services." *Journal of Youth Services in Libraries* 14 (Winter): 20, 25–30.

Young Adult Library Services Association. 2010. "YALSA's Competencies for Librarians Serving Youth: Young Adults Deserve the Best." http://www.ala.org/ala/mgrps/divs/yalsa/profdev/yacompetencies2010.cfm.

"Youth and Library Use Studies Show Gains in Serving Young Adults." 2007. *Young Adult Library Services* 6 (Fall): 45.

Websites of Youth-Related Associations

American Association of School Librarians (AASL). http://www.ala.org/ala/mgrps/divs/aasl/index.cfm.

This is the website for AASL, a division of the ALA for school librarians and school library media specialists. Included are conference and event information, the new national guidelines and standards, professional materials for handling book and material challenges, resources on Internet filtering, and AASL mission and position statements.

American Library Association. Ethnic and Multicultural Information Exchange Round Table. http://www.ala.org/ala/mgrps/rts/emiert/index.cfm.

The Ethnic and Multicultural Information Exchange Round Table from the American Library Association promotes and provides information on recommended ethnic collections, services, and programs. The website provides information regarding ethnic and multicultural programs, the organization's most recent publications, including the *EMIE Bulletin*, and the nominations and selections for the Coretta Scott King Award and the Multicultural Awards for children's literature.

Association for Library Service to Children (ALSC). http://www.ala.org/ala/mgrps/divs/alsc/index.cfm.

Supporting children's librarianship is the stated goal of the ALSC, a division of the ALA. Through the ALSC website, members and nonmembers can discover association news, conference information, and links to various related websites. School and public librarians who work with children will find this site useful and members will find a direct route to involvement in the association.

Children's Book Committee at Bank Street College. http://www.bankstreet.edu/bookcom.

The Children's Book Committee at Bank Street College was formed 75 years ago with the purpose of selecting the best children's books published each year. The site provides information on the committee, its book awards and publications, and its annual list of the 600 best children's books.

The Children's Book Council (CBC). http://www.cbcbooks.org.

The CBC has been in existence since 1945 and provides various opportunities for encouraging reading in children. The CBC Online has links of interest to publishers, authors, teachers, librarians, booksellers, and parents. In addition, special events are highlighted and presented. The Teachers and Librarians Page features information about new books, noteworthy authors and illustrators, bibliographies, reading activities, featured topic forums, and authors. Members of the CBC will find this site useful for council news, while librarians and teachers will discover useful ideas for use in the classroom.

Children's Literature Assembly (CLA). http://www.childrensliteratureassembly.org.

Affiliated with the National Council of Teachers of English, the CLA promotes children's literature and its teaching. The site includes the CLA's annual list of notable children's trade books in the language arts, its annual report, and a list of the Orbis Pictus Award for Outstanding Nonfiction for Children.

Children's Literature Association. http://www.childlitassn.org.

Promoting scholarship and research in children's literature, the Children's Literature Association webpage presents membership information, an overview of the association, conference information, and links to its publications, including a topical index to *ChLA Quarterly*. While designed to promote and support the association, this website will provide the general learner with information.

International Board on Books for Young People (IBBY). http://www.ibby.org.

IBBY is a nonprofit organization that represents an international network of people from all over the world who are committed to bringing books and children together. The website also contains information on the Hans Christian Andersen Award.

Society of Children's Book Writers and Illustrators (SCBWI). http://www.scbwi.org.

Representing the writer's side of children's literature, SCBWI is the only professional organization dedicated to the writers and illustrators of children's books. The site provides information about the children's publishing industry as well as the Golden Kite Award lists and selected SCBWI publications.

Young Adult Library Services Association (YALSA). http://www.ala.org/ala/mgrps/divs/yalsa/aboutyalsab/aboutyalsa.cfm.

The website for the YALSA division of the American Library Association contains information on the association's guidelines, publications, campaigns, and recommendations in the form of booklists and book awards. It also includes a professional development center with information for those who work with young adults.

Websites for Resources to Serve Youth

ALAN Review. http://scholar.lib.vt.edu/ejournals/ALAN.

ALFY. http://www.ALFY.com.

American Library Association. "Associations for Ethnic Librarians." http://www.ala.org/ala/aboutala/offices/diversity/ethniclibrariansassociations.cfm.

————. "Banned Books." http://www.ala.org/ala/issuesadvocacy/banned/index.cfm.

————, "Best Books for Young Adults." *Booklist*. http://www.ala.org/ala/mgrps/divs/yalsa/booklistsawards/bestbooksya/bbyahome.cfm.

————. "Children's Notable Lists." http://www.ala.org/ala/mgrps/divs/alsc/awardsgrants/notalists/index.cfm.

————. "Great Web Sites for Kids." http://www.ala.org/gwstemplate.cfm?section=greatwebsites&template=/cfapps/gws/default.cfm.

————. "Pura Belpré Award." http://www.ala.org/ala/mgrps/divs/alsc/awardsgrants/bookmedia/belpremedal/belpreabout/index.cfm.

Anne Frank Online. http://www.annefrank.com.

Barahona Center for the Study of Books in Spanish for Children and Adolescents. http://www2.csusm.edu/csb.

Ben's Guide to U.S. Government for Kids. http://bensguide.gpo.gov.

BookList Magazine. http://www.ala.org/ala/aboutala/offices/publishing/booklist_publications/booklist/booklist.cfm.

"Booktalking: Quick and Simple." http://nancykeane.com/booktalks.

Brown v. Board of Education. http://www.nps.gov/brvb/index.htm.

Caldecott Medal Home Page. http://www.ala.org/ala/mgrps/divs/alsc/awardsgrants/bookmedia/caldecottmedal/caldecottmedal.cfm.

Children's Literature Web Guide. http://www.acs.ucalgary.ca/~dkbrown.

Child Trends. http://www.childtrends.org.

Chiles: Children and Libraries en Espanola. http://www.chil-es.org/home/.

Coretta Scott King Award. http://www.ala.org/ala/mgrps/rts/emiert/cskbookawards/index.cfm.

Dia de los Niños, Dia de los Libros. http://www.reforma.org/Dia.htm.

Discovery Channel. http://dsc.discovery.com.

Filamentality. http://www.kn.pacbell.com/wired/fil.

Gay and Lesbian Characters and Themes in Children's Literature. http://www.armory.com/~web/gaybooks.html.

Horn Book. http://www.hbook.com.

International Children's Digital Library. http://en.childrenslibrary.org/.

International Reading Association. http://www.reading.org.

Internet Public Library. http://www.ipl.org.

Kay E. Vandergrift's Special Interest Page. http://www.scils.rutgers.edu/~kvander.

Kids Count. http://www.aecf.org/MajorInitiatives/KIDSCOUNT.aspx.

Kids.Gov: The Official Kids Portal to the U.S. Government. http://www.kids.gov/.

Library of Congress. "National Book Festival." http://www.loc.gov/bookfest.

Library of Congress, National Library Service for the Blind and Physically Handicapped. http://www.loc.gov/nls.

Media Awareness Network. http://www.media-awareness.ca/english.

National Center for Family Literacy. http://www.famlit.org.

National Latino Children's Institute. http://www.nlci.org/common/index2.htm.

Newbery Medal Home Page. http://www.ala.org/ala/mgrps/divs/alsc/awardsgrants/bookmedia/newberymedal/newberymedal.cfm.

Reading Is Fundamental for Literacy. http://www.rif.org.

U.S. Census Bureau. "Kids' Corner." http://factfinder.census.gov/home/en/kids/kids.html.

U.S. General Services Administration. 2010. Kids.gov: The Official Kids' Portal for the U.S. Government. http://www.kids.gov/.

Virginia Hamilton Literary Award. http://virginia-hamilton.slis.kent.edu/awards.html.

Voices from the Gaps. http://voices.cla.umn.edu.

YALSA Booklists and Book Awards. http://www.ala.org/ala/mgrps/divs/yalsa/booklistsawards/booklistsbook.cfm.

Specific Service Responses

(Organized in order of Nelson, 2008: 143–217.)

Be an Informed Citizen: Local, National and World Affairs (Public Sphere; Nelson, 2008: 149–152)

Ben's Guide to U.S. Government for Kids. http://bensguide.gpo.gov.

Kids.Gov: The Official Kids Portal to the U.S. Government. http://www.kids.gov/.

U.S. Census Bureau. "Kids' Corner." http://factfinder.census.gov/home/en/kids/kids.html.

U.S. Department of Homeland Security, U.S. Citizenship and Immigration Services, Office of Citizenship. 2009. *Expanding ESL, Civics, and Citizenship Education in Your Community: A Start-Up Guide*. http://www.uscis.gov/files/nativedocuments/M-677.pdf.

Veccia, Susan H. 2003. *Uncovering Our History: Teaching with Primary Sources*. Chicago: American Library Association.

Ziegenbein, Sarah. 2008. "Government Documents and Children." *Arkansas Libraries* 65 (Summer): 6–8.

Build Successful Enterprises: Business and Nonprofit Support (Information; Nelson, 2008: 153–157)

Diamant-Cohen, Betsy. 2010. *Children's Services: Partnerships for Success*. Chicago: American Library Association.

Jerrard, Jane. 2009. *Crisis in Employment: A Librarian's Guide to Helping Job Seekers*. Chicago: American Library Association.

Smallwood, Carol. 2010. *Librarians as Community Partners: An Outreach Handbook*. Chicago: American Library Association.

Weiss, Luise, Sophia Serlis-McPhillips, and Elizabeth Malafi. 2010. *Small Business and the Public Library: Strategies for a Successful Partnership*. Chicago: American Library Association.

Celebrate Diversity: Cultural Awareness (Cultural Heritage; Nelson, 2008:158–161)

Agosto, Denise E. 2001. "Bridging the Cultural Gap: Ten Steps Toward a More Multicultural Youth Library." *Journal of Library Services in Libraries* 4 (Spring): 38–41.

Alexander, Linda B., and Nahyun Kwon, eds. 2010. *Multicultural Programs for Tweens and Teens*. Chicago: American Library Association.

American Library Association. "Associations for Ethnic Librarians." http://www.ala.org/ala/aboutala/offices/diversity/ethniclibrariansassociations.cfm.

Curry, Ann. 2005. "If I Ask, Will They Answer? Evaluating Public Library Reference Service to Gay and Lesbian Youth." *Reference User Services Quarterly* 45, no. 1: 65–75.

Dunkley, Cora Phelps. 2010. "The Religious Aspects in Virginia Hamilton's *The People Could Fly* and Other Sources." In *Adventures, Fantasy, and Dreams in Children's Literature*, edited by Judith Lynne McConnell-Farmer. Cambridge, UK: Linton Atlantic Books.

East, Kathy, and Rebecca L. Thomas. 2007. *Across Cultures: A Guide to Multicultural Literature for Children*. Westport, CT: Libraries Unlimited.

Ethnic and Multicultural Information Exchange Round Table. 2005. "Humor in Multicultural Literature." http://www.ala.org/ala/mgrps/rts/emiert/usefullinks/humorlit.pdf.

———. 2005. "Those Who Forget the Past." http://www.ala.org/ala/mgrps/rts/emiert/usefullinks/armeniagen.pdf.

———. 2006. "Contemporary Immigrant Experiences in Children's Books." http://www.ala.org/ala/mgrps/rts/emiert/usefullinks/contempimmigrant.pdf.

Farrelly, Michael Garrett. 2007. "More on Serving Gay Youth." *Public Libraries* 46 (May/June): 38–39.

Feinberg, Sandra, and Caryn Rogoff. 1998. "Diversity Takes Children to a Friendly Family Place." *American Libraries* 29 (August): 50–52.

Howrey, Sara P. 2003. "De Colores: The Universal Language of Bilingual Storytime." *American Libraries* 34 (October): 38–40, 42–43.

Hoyle, Karen Nelson. 2008. "Forty Years and Still Vibrant: ALSC's Batchelder Award." *Children and Libraries* 6 (Summer/Fall): 14–18.

Kuharets, Olga R., ed. 2001. *Venture into Cultures*. 2nd ed. Chicago: American Library Association.

Pavon, Ana Elba, and Diana Borrego. 2002. *25 Latino Craft Projects*. Chicago: American Library Association.

Rockefeller, Elsworth. 2008. "Striving to Serve Diverse Youth." *Public Libraries* 47 (January/February): 50–55.

Schon, I. 1978. *A Bicultural Heritage: Themes for the Exploration of Mexican and Mexican-American Culture through Books for Children and Adolescents*. Lanham, MD: Scarecrow Press.

Schon, Isabel. 2006. "Opening New Worlds for Latino Children—Librarians Can Play a Special Role in Serving the Literature Needs of a Growing Minority Group." *American Libraries* 37: 48.

Treviño, Rose Zertuche. 2009. *Read Me a Rhyme in Spanish and English/Léame una rima en español e inglés*. Chicago: American Library Association.

Wertsman, Vladimir F. 2003. *Directory of Ethnic and Multicultural Publishers, Distributors and Resource Organizations*. 5th ed. Niles, IL: Ethnic and Multicultural Information Exchange Round Table.

Yokota, Junko. 2009. "Asian-Americans in Literature for Children and Young Adults." *Teacher Librarian* 36, no. 3: 15–19.

Connect to the Online World: Public Internet Access (Information; Nelson, 2008: 162–164)

Aiken, Julian. 2006. "Hands Off MySpace." *American Libraries* 37 (August): 33.

Braun, Linda W. 2009. "Using Technology to Market Teen Library Programs and Services: Is a Web Site the Answer?" *Voice of Youth Advocates* 31, no. 6: 510–511.

Farmer, L. S. J. 2005. *Digital Inclusion, Teens, and Your Library: Exploring the Issues and Acting on Them*. Westport, CT: Libraries Unlimited.

Farrelly, Michael Garrett. 2009. "Tweet, Tweet." *Public Libraries* 48 (January/February): 35–36.

McLean, C. D. 2007. "Building Teen Communities Online: Listen, Listen, and Listen." *Young Adult Library Services* 5 (Summer): 21–26.

Porter, Michael, and David Lee King. 2008. "What's the Internet Spotlight for Your YA Services?" *Public Libraries* 47 (January/February): 38–41.

Saxton, B. 2008. "Information Tools: Using Blogs, RSS, and Wikis as Professional Resources." *Young Adult Library Services* 6 (Winter): 27–29.

Create Young Readers: Early Literacy (Education; Nelson, 2008: 165–168)

Albright, Meagan, Kevin Delecki, and Sarah Hinkle. 2009. "The Evolution of Early Literacy: A History of Best Practices in Storytime." *Children and Libraries* 7 (Spring): 13–18.

Arnold, Renae. 2002. "Coming Together for Children: A Guide to Early Learning Childhood Programming." *Journal of Youth Services in Libraries* 15 (Winter): 24–30.

Ash, Viki, and Elaine Meyers. 2009. "Every Child Ready to Read @ Your Library." *Children and Libraries* 7 (Spring): 3–7.

Association for Library Service to Children and Public Library Association. 2010. "Every Child Ready to Read @ Your Library Website." http://www.ala.org/ala/mgrps/divs/alsc/ecrr/index.cfm.

Bailey, Alan R. 2009. "Early Essentials: Developing and Sustaining Birth–Kindergarten Library Collections." *Children and Libraries* 7 (Winter): 17–24.

Balkin, Al. 2009. *Tune Up to Literacy: Original Songs and Activities for Kids*. Chicago: American Library Association.

De Groot, Joanne, and Jennifer Branch. 2009. "Solid Foundations: A Primer on the Crucial, Critical, and Key Roles of School and Public Libraries in Children's Development." *Library Trends* 58 (Summer): 51–62.

Diamant-Cohen, Betsy, and Saroj Nadkami Ghoting. 2010. *The Early Literacy Kit: A Handbook of Tip Cards*. Chicago: American Library Association.

Epstein, Connie C. 2001. "Create a World for Young Readers." *The Writer* 114 (June): 34.

Feinberg, Sandra, et al. 2007. *The Family-Centered Library Handbook*. New York: Neal-Schuman.

Howrey, Sara P. 2003. "De Colores: The Universal Language of Bilingual Storytime." *American Libraries* 34 (October): 38–40, 42–43.

Marino, Jane. 2007. *Babies in the Library*. Lanham, MD: Scarecrow Press.

McKechnie, Lynne. 2006. "Observations of Babies and Toddlers in Library Settings." *Library Trends* 55 (Summer): 190–201.

Smith, Sandra. 2008. "The Library Has Legs: An Early Childhood Literacy Outreach Program in Victoria." *Australas Public Libraries Information Services* 21, no. 4: 154–156.

Trabucco, D., et al. 2003. "Early Literacy and a Little Read Wagon." *Texas Library Journal* 79 (Spring): 8–11.

Discover Your Roots: Genealogy and Local History (Cultural Heritage; Nelson, 2008: 169–172)

U.S. Census Bureau. "Kids' Corner." http://factfinder.census.gov/home/en/kids/kids.html.

U.S. Gen Web Kidz. http://www.rootsweb.ancestry.com/~usgwkidz/.

Veccia, Susan H. 2003. *Uncovering Our History: Teaching with Primary Sources*. Chicago: American Library Association.

Wolfman, Ira. 2002. *Climbing Your Family Tree: Online and Offline Genealogy for Kids: The Official Ellis Island Handbook*. New York: Workman.

Express Creativity: Create and Share Content (Cultural Heritage; Nelson, 2008: 173–176)

Bane, Rebecca. 2008. "Let's Pretend: Exploring the Value of Play at the Library." *Children and Libraries* 6 (Summer/Fall): 21–23.

Brown, Amy. 2009. "Don't Stop the Music!: Creating Tuneful Times at Your Library." *Children and Libraries* 7 (Summer/Fall): 36–42.

Farrelly, Michael Garrett. 2006. "The Possibilities of YouTube." *Public Libraries* 45 (September/October): 34–35.

Prichard, Heather. 2008. "Write Here, Write Now." *Young Adult Library Services* 6 (Summer): 19–23.

Vardell, Sylvia M. 2006. "A Place for Poetry: Celebrating the Library in Poetry." *Children and Libraries* 4 (Summer/Fall): 35–41.

———. 2006. *Poetry Aloud Here!: Sharing Poetry with Children in the Library*. Chicago: American Library Association.

Get Facts Fast: Ready Reference (Information; Nelson, 2008: 177–179)

Bishop, Kay, et al. 2001. "Responding to Developmental Stages in Reference Service to Children." *Public Libraries* 40 (November/December): 354–358.

Curry, Ann. 2005. "If I Ask, Will They Answer?: Evaluating Public Library Reference Service to Gay and Lesbian Youth." *Reference User Services Quarterly* 45, no. 1: 65–75.

Czarnecki, Kelly. 2008. "Building Community as a Library in a 3D Environment." *Australasian Public Libraries Information Services* 21 (March): 25–27.

Farrelly, Michael Garrett. 2009. "Tweet, Tweet." *Public Libraries* 48 (January/February): 35–36.

Flowers, Sarah. 2008. "Guidelines for Library Services to Teens." *Young Adult Library Services* 6 (Spring): 4–7.

Gross, M. 2000. "The Imposed Query and Information Services for Children." *Journal of Youth Services in Libraries* 13 (Winter): 10–17.

Hedreen, Rebecca C., Jennifer L. Johnson, Mack A. Lundy, Peg Burnette, Carol Perryman, Guus Van Den Brekel, J. J. Jacobson, Matt Gullett, and Kelly Czarnecki. 2008. "Exploring Virtual Librarianship: Second Life Library 2.0." *Internet Reference Services Quarterly* 13, no. 2–3: 167–195.

King, David L., and Stephanie W. Brown. 2009. "Emerging Trends, 2.0, and Libraries." *Serials Librarian* 56, no. 1: 32–43.

Know Your Community: Community Resources and Services (Public Sphere; Nelson, 2008: 180–183.

Cheumwattana, A., et al. 2002. "Small Is Beautiful: The Library Train for Homeless Children." *Library Management* 23, no. 1/2: 88–92.

Costello, J., et al. 2001. "Promoting Public Library Partnerships with Youth Agencies." *Journal of Youth Services in Libraries* 15 (Winter): 8–15.

Geloff, K., et al. 2002. "Library Services to Homeless Youth." *Alki* 18 (July): 16.

Lukenbill, W. Bernard. 2006. "Helping Youth at Risk: An Overview of Reformist Movements in American Public Libraries to Youth." *New Review of Children's Literature and Librarianship* 12, no. 2: 197–213.

Reed, Sally Gardiner, and Beth Nawalinsky. 2008. *Even More Great Ideas for Libraries and Friends*. New York: Neal-Schuman.

Woelfer, Jill Palzkill, and David G. Hendry. 2010. "Stabilizing Homeless Young People with Information and Place." *Journal of the American Society for Information Science and Technology* 60 (November): 2300–2312.

Learn to Read and Write: Adults, Teens and Family Literature (Education; Nelson,2008: 184–187)

Fiore, Carole. 2007. "Summer Library Reading Programs." *New Directions for Youth Development* 114: 85–98.

Krashen, S., and F. Shin. 2005. "Summer Reading and the Potential Contribution of the Public Library in Improving Reading for Children of Poverty." *Public Library Quarterly* 23, no. 3: 99–109.

Petruzzi, Tony, and Mary Frances Burns. 2006. "A Literacy Where? A Public Library Finds Space to Promote and Provide Family Learning Activities." *Public Library Quarterly* 191, no. 7: 25.

Saldaña, René. 2009. "The Bilingual Book Club: A Family Affair." *Teacher Librarian* 36 (Fall): 27–32.

Thiang, Alicia. 2008. "Alter Ego: An Interactive Public Library Literacy Program for Disadvantaged Children." *Australas Public Libraries Information Services* 21, no. 3: 106–108.

Treviño, Rose Zertuche. 2009. *Read me a Rhyme in Spanish and English/Léame una rima en español e inglés*. Chicago: American Library Association.

Make Career Choices: Job and Career Development (Education; Nelson,2008)

Cheney, Amy. 2006. "Today's Techie, Training Teens." *Library Journal* 131, no. 5: 18.

Fourie, J. A. 2007. "Educational and Vocational Guidance and Information Services for the Youth in Public Libraries." *South African Journal of Library and Information Science* 73, no. 1: 51–63.

———. 2009. "A Theoretical Model for the Provision of Educational and Career Guidance and Information Services for High School Learners in Public Libraries." *Mousaion* 27, no. 1: 1–23.

Williams, Cynthia. 2004. "Helping Teens Enter the World of Work." *Voice Youth Advocates* 27, no. 4: 281.

Make Informed Decisions: Health, Wealth and Other Life Choices (Information; Nelson,2008: 188–190)

Bussmann, I., et al. 2000. "New Services to Develop Children's and Young People's Information Skills–the European Projects CHILIAS and VERITY." *New Review of Children's Literature and Librarianship* 6: 137–146.

Hughes-Hassell, Sandra, Dana Hanson-Baldauf, and Jennifer E. Burke. 2008. "Urban Teenagers, Health Information, and Public Library Web Sites." *Young Adult Library Services* 6 (Summer): 35–42.

Levine, A. 2002. "Providing Information on Sexuality: Librarians Can Help Youth Become Sexually Healthy Adults." *Journal of Youth Services in Libraries* 15 (Winter): 45–48.

Ren, Rena, Keith Cogdill, and Alex Potemkin. 2009. "Partnerships for a Healthy Community." *Public Libraries* 48 (January/February): 59–61.

Satisfy Curiosity: Lifelong Learning (Cultural Heritage; Nelson, 2008: 195–198)

Blumson, L. 2003. "Libraries for Lifelong Learning in Queensland: Towards the Smart State." *Australasian Public Libraries and Information Services* 16 (March): 17–20.

Honnold, RoseMary. 2004. "Connecting Teens with Generations A–Z." *Public Libraries* 43 (September/October): 281–284.

Long, Sarah. 2005. "Program Puts Kids, Mentors on Same Page." *Library Mosaics* 16 (July/August): 18.

Stimulate Imagination: Reading, Viewing and Listening for Pleasure (Cultural Heritage; Nelson, 2008: 199–202)

American Library Association. 2010. "Coretta Scott King/Virginia Hamilton Award for Lifetime Achievement." http://www.ala.org/ala/mgrps/rts/emiert/index.cfm.

Booth, Heather. 2005. "RA for YA: Tailoring the Readers Advisory Interview to the Needs of Young Adult Patrons." *Public Libraries* 44 (January/February): 33–36.

Cart, Michael. 2007. "Teens and the Future of Reading." *American Libraries* 38 (October): 53–54.

———. 2010. *Young Adult Literature: From Romance to Realism*. Chicago: American Library Association.

Farrelly, Michael Garrett. 2007. "YA Services in a Post–Harry Potter World." *Public Libraries* 46 (September/October): 48–49.

Goldsmith, Francisca. 2010. *The Reader's Advisory Guide to Graphic Novels*. Chicago: American Library Association.

Hoyle, Karen Nelson. 2008. "Forty Years and Still Vibrant: ALSC's Batchelder Award." *Children and Libraries* 6 (Summer/Fall): 14–18.

Locke, Jill. 1992. "Summer Reading Activities—Way Back When." *Journal of Youth Services in Libraries* 6 (Fall): 72–77.

Lundin, Anne H. 1993. "The Company We Keep: Advisory Services for Youth." *Collection Building* 12: 45–56.

Mori, Maryann. 2007. "Graphic Novels: Leading the Way to Teen Literacy and Leadership." *Indiana Libraries* 26, no. 3: 29–32.

Price, Lee. 2008. "Libraries Take the Big Read Challenge." *Public Libraries* 47 (January/February): 42–45.

Roman, Susan. 2010. *Dominican Study: Public Library Summer Reading Programs Close the Reading Gap*. River Forest, IL: Dominican University.

Smith, Henrietta M. 1994. *The Coretta Scott King Awards Book: From Visions to Reality*. Chicago: American Library Association.

————. 1999. *The Coretta Scott King Awards Book, 1970–1999*. Chicago: American Library Association.

————. 2004. *The Coretta Scott King Awards Book, 1970–2004*. Chicago: American Library Association.

————. 2009. *The Coretta Scott King Awards, 1970–2009*. Chicago: American Library Association.

Smith, Laura. 2003. *Children's Book Awards International, 1990 through 2000*. Jefferson, NC: McFarland.

Snowball, Clare. 2008. "Teenagers Talking About Reading and Libraries." *Australian Academic and Research Libraries* 39, no. 2: 106–118.

Succeed in School: Homework Help (Education; Nelson,2008: 203–206)

Chernek, V. 2002. "Baltimore County Students and Parents Say Yes! to Library Summer School Program Involving Online Instruction and Tutoring." *Book Report* 20 (January/February): 49.

Clark, Marilyn L. 1997. "The Public Library and Homework Help." *Public Libraries* 36 (January/February): 19–20.

Danley, Elizabeth. 2003. "The Public Children's Librarian as Educator." *Public Libraries* 42 (March/April): 98–101.

Fiore, Carole. 2007. "Summer Library Reading Programs." *New Directions for Youth Development* 114: 85–98.

Fitzgibbons, Shirley. 2001. "School and Public Library Relationships." *Journal of Youth Services in Libraries* 13 (Spring): 3–7.

Furness, Adrienne. 2008. *Helping Homeschoolers in the Library*. Chicago: American Library Association.

Hilyard, Nann B. 2008. "Welcoming Homeschoolers to the Library." *Public Libraries* 47 (May/June): 17–18.

Intner, Carol F. 2010. *Homework Help from the Library*. Chicago: American Library Association.

Katz, Jeff. 2009. "A Common Purpose: Public/School Library Cooperation and Collaboration." *Public Libraries* 48 (May/June): 28–31.

Krashen, S., and F. Shin. 2005. "Summer Reading and the Potential Contribution of the Public Library in Improving Reading for Children of Poverty." *Public Library Quarterly* 23, no. 3: 99–109.

Lu, Ya-Ling. 2009. "Engaging Students with Summer Reading: An Assessment of a Collaborative High School Summer Reading Program." *Journal of Education for Library and Information Science* 50 (Spring): 90–106.

Martinez, Gilda. 2008. "Public Libraries—Community Organizations Making Outreach Efforts to Help Young Children Succeed in School." *School Community Journal* 18, no. 1: 93–104.

Mediavilla, Cindy. 1998. "Homework Assistance Programs in Public Libraries: Helping Johnny Read." In *Young Adults and Public Libraries: A Handbook of Materials and Services*, edited by Mary Anne Nichols and C. Allen Nichols, 181–189. Westport, CT: Greenwood Press.

Rua, Robert J. 2008. "After-School Success Stories." *American Libraries* 39 (November): 46–48.

Scheps, Susan G. 1999. "Homeschoolers in the Library." *School Library Journal* 45 (February): 38–39.

Woolls, Blanche. 2001. "Public Libraries–School Library Cooperation: A View from the Past with a Predictor for the Future." *Journal of Youth Services in Libraries* 14 (Spring): 8–10.

Ziarnik, Natalie Reif. 2002. *School and Public Libraries: Developing the Natural Alliance*. Chicago: American Library Association.

Understand How to Find, Evaluate, and Use Information: Information Fluency (Education; Nelson,2008: 207–209)

American Association of School Librarians. 2009. *Standards for the Twenty-first Century Learner in Action*. Chicago: American Association of School Librarians.

American Association of School Librarians and Association for Educational Communications and Technology. 1998. *Information Power: Building Partnerships for Learning*. Chicago: American Library Association.

Cuban, Sondra, and Larry Cuban. 2007. *Partners in Literacy: Schools and Libraries Building Communities through Technology*. Chicago: American Library Association.

Gilton, Donna L. 2008. "Information Literacy as a Department Store." *Young Adult Library Services* 6 (Winter): 39–44.

McCarter, Monica. 2003. "At-Risk Students and Cooperative Learning: Best Practices for Library Instruction Based on Students' Psychological, Cognitive, and Emotional Levels." *Current Studies in Librarianship* 27 (Spring/Fall): 51–59.

Visit a Comfortable Place: Physical and Virtual Spaces (Public Sphere; Nelson, 2008: 210–213)

Aiken, Julian. 2006. "Hands Off MySpace." *American Libraries* 37 (August): 33.

Bernier, Anthony. 2009. "A Space for Myself to Go: Early Patterns in Small YA Spaces." *Public Libraries* 48 (September/October): 33–47.

Blowers, Helene, and Robin Bryan. 2004. *Weaving a Library Web: A Guide to Developing Children's Websites*. Chicago: American Library Association.

Bolan, Kimberly. 2006. "Looks Like Teen Spirit." *School Library Journal* 52 (November): 44–48.

———. 2009. *Teen Spaces: The Step-by-Step Library Makeover*. 2nd ed. Chicago: American Library Association.

Brown, Carol R. 2002. *Interior Design for Libraries: Drawing on Function and Appeal*. Chicago: American Library Association.

Cranz, Galen, and Eunah Cha. 2006. "Body-Conscious Design in a Teen Space." *Public Libraries* 45 (November/December): 48–56.

Czarnecki, Kelly. 2008. "Top Fifty Gaming Core Collection Titles." *Young Adult Library Services* 6, no. 2: 36–38.

Danforth, Liz. 2010. "Rethinking Your Strategy." *Library Journal* 135 (February 15): 73.

Farrelly, Michael Garrett. 2006. "Does Your Space Appeal to Teens?" *Public Libraries* 45 (May/June): 40–41.

———. 2006. "The Possibilities of YouTube." *Public Libraries* 45 (September/October): 34–35.

———. 2008. "Guitar Hero and Rock Band: Games That Are Fun and Educational." *Public Libraries* 47 (March/April): 40–41.

———. 2009. "Tweet, Tweet." *Public Libraries* 48 (January/February): 35–36.

———. 2010. *Make Room for Teens! A Guide for Developing Teen Spaces in the Library*. Santa Barbara, CA: Libraries Unlimited.

Feinberg, Sandra, and James R. Keller. 2010. *Designing Space for Children and Teens in Libraries and Public Places*. Chicago: American Library Association.

Gorman, Michele, and Tricia Suellentrop. 2009. *Connecting Young Adults and Libraries*, 4th ed. New York: Neal-Schuman.

Hedreen, Rebecca C., Jennifer L. Johnson, Mack A. Lundy, Peg Burnette, Carol Perryman, Guus Van Den Brekel, J. J. Jacobson, Matt Gullett, and Kelly Czarnecki. 2008. "Exploring Virtual Librarianship: Second Life Library 2.0." *Internet Reference Services Quarterly* 13, no. 2–3: 167–195.

Herald, Diana Tixier, and Diane P. Monnier. 2007. "The Beasts Have Arrived." *Voice of Youth Advocates* 30 (June): 116–119.

Holt, Glen E. 2008. "ImaginOn, the First Twenty-first-Century Public Library Building in the U.S." *Public Library Quarterly* 27, no. 2: 174–191.

Iser, Stephanie, and Joseph Wilk. 2008. "Get Ready for Teen Tech Week 2008." *Public Libraries* 47 (January/February): 16–19.

Kenney, Brian. 2006. "Welcome to the Fun House." *Library Journal* (Spring): 8–13.

King, David L., and Stephanie W. Brown. 2009. "Emerging Trends, 2.0, and Libraries." *Serials Librarian* 56, no. 1: 32–43.

Scordato, Julie. 2008. "Gaming as a Library Service." *Public Libraries* 47 (January/February): 67–73.

Suellentrop, Tricia. 2008. "It's Not About You." *School Library Journal* 54 (April): 27.

Wernett, Lisa C. 2008. "Teen Space and the Community's Living Room: Incorporating Teen Areas into Rural Libraries." *PNLA Quarterly* 72, no. 4: 7–18.

Young Adult Library Association. 2009. *Teens and Social Networking in School and Public Libraries: A Toolkit for Librarians and Library Workers*. http://www.ala.org/ala/mgrps/divs/yalsa/profdev/socialnetworkingtool.pdf.

Welcome to the United States: Services for New Immigrants (Information; Nelson, 2008: 214–217)

Diamant-Cohen, Betsy, and Anne Calderon. 2009. "Buena Casa Buena Brasa." *American Libraries* 40 (December): 41–43.

Fredericks, Nancy. 2005. "Another Day in the Life." *Young Adult Library Services* 3 (Spring): 15–16.

Lukenbill, W. Bernard. 2006. "Helping Youth at Risk: An Overview of Reformist Movements in American Public Libraries to Youth." *New Review of Children's Literature and Librarianship* 12, no. 2: 197–213.

U.S. Department of Homeland Security, U.S. Citizenship and Immigration Services, Office of Citizenship. 2009. *Expanding ESL, Civics, and Citizenship Education in Your Community: A Start-Up Guide.* http://www.uscis.gov/files/nativedocuments/M-677.pdf.

———. 2009. *Welcome to the United States: A Guide for New Immigrants.* http://www.uscis.gov/portal/ site/uscis.

10. The Interconnective Nature of the Public Library

Books and Chapters in Books

Alliance for Regional Stewardship. 2003. *Inclusive Stewardship: Emerging Collaborations between Neighborhoods and Regions.* Denver, CO: The Alliance.

American Association of State Libraries. 1963. *Standards for Library Functions at the State Level.* Chicago: American Library Association.

———. 1970. *Standards for Library Functions at the State Level.* 2nd ed. Chicago: American Library Association.

Association of Specialized and Cooperative Library Agencies. 1985. *Standards for Library Functions at the State Level.* 3rd ed. Chicago: American Library Association.

———. 1990. *Standards for Cooperative Multitype Library Organizations.* Chicago: American Library Association.

Becker, Joseph. 1979. "Network Functions." In *The Structure and Governance of Library Networks*, edited by Alan Kent and Thomas J. Galvin, 89. New York: Marcel Dekker.

Borrett, Rochelle M., and Danielle Patrick Milam. 2008. *Welcome, Stranger: Public Libraries Build the Global Village: Toolkit.* Chicago, IL: Urban Libraries Council.

Bundy, Alan. 2003. "Joint-Use Libraries: The Ultimate Form of Cooperation." In *Planning the Modern Library Building*, edited by Gerald B. McCabe and James R. Kennedy, 129–148. Westport, CT: Libraries Unlimited.

Dawson, Alma, and Florence M. Jumonville. 2003. *A History of the Louisiana Library Association, 1925–2000.* Baton Rouge: Louisiana Library Association.

Fiels, Keith Michael, Joan Neumann, and Eva R. Brown. 1991. *Multitype Library Cooperation State Laws, Regulations and Pending Legislation.* Chicago: Association of Specialized and Cooperative Library Agencies.

Frug, Gerald E. 1999. *City Making: Building Communities without Building Walls.* Princeton, NJ: Princeton University Press.

Healey, James S. 1974. *John E. Fogarty: Political Leadership for Library Development.* Metuchen, NJ: Scarecrow Press.

Henderson, E., et al. 2009. *State Library Agencies Survey: Fiscal Year 2008* (IMLS-2010–StLA-01). Washington, DC: Institute of Museum and Library Services.

Himmel, Ethel, and Bill Wilson. 2008. *Library Services and Technology Act: Grants to States Program Trends Analysis, Report to IMLS.* Washington, DC; Institute of Museum and Library Services.

Himmel, Ethel E., William J. Wilson, and GraceAnne DeCandido. 2000. *The Functions and Roles of State Library Agencies*. Chicago: American Library Association.

Information Today. 2010. *American Library Directory: 2010–2011*. Medford, NJ: Information Today.

Jank, David. 2010. "Collaborative Systems and Groupware." In *Encyclopedia of Library and Information Sciences*, 3rd ed., 1:1, 1088–1096.

Jordan, Jay. 2010. "OCLC: A Worldwide Library Cooperative." *Encyclopedia of Library and Information Sciences*, 3rd ed., 1:1, 3924–3937.

Keller, Shelly G., ed. 1997. *Proceedings of the Convocation on Providing Public Library Service to California's 21st Century Population*. ERIC ED422000. Sacramento, California, May 22–23.

Kifer, Ruth E., and Jane E. Light. 2010. "Shared Libraries." In *Encyclopedia of Library and Information Sciences*, 3rd ed., 1:1, 4741–4746.

Knight, Douglas M., and E. Shepley Nourse, eds. 1969. *Libraries at Large: Traditions, Innovations and the National Interest; The Resource Book Based on the Materials of the National Advisory Commission on Libraries*. New York: R. R. Bowker.

Kretzmann, Jody, and Susan Rans. 2005. *The Engaged Library: Chicago Stories of Community Building*. Chicago, IL: Urban Libraries Council.

Laughlin, Sara. 2000. *Library Networks in the New Millennium: Top Ten Trends*. Chicago: American Library Association.

Long, Sarah Ann. 1995. "Systems, Quo Vadis? An Examination of the History, Current Status and Future Role of Regional Library Systems." *Advances in Librarianship* 19: 118.

———. 2000. "Foreword." In *A Place at the Table: Participating in Community Building*, by Kathleen de la Peña McCook, vii. Chicago: American Library Association.

McCook, Kathleen de la Peña. 2000. *A Place at the Table: Participating in Community Building*. Chicago: American Library Association.

Molz, Redmond Kathleen. 1975. *Federal Policy and Library Support*. Cambridge, MA: MIT Press.

Monypenny, Phillip. 1966. *The Library Functions of the States*. Chicago: American Library Association.

Nelson Associates. 1969. *Public Library Systems in the United States: A Survey of Multi-jurisdictional Systems*. Chicago: American Library Association.

Nelson Associates, in association with National Advisory Commission on Libraries. 1967. *American State Libraries and State Library Agencies: An Overview with Recommendations*. ERIC ED022486. New York: National Advisory Commission on Libraries. Repr., in *Libraries at Large: Traditions, Innovations and the National Interest*, edited by Douglas M. Knight and E. Shepley Nourse, 400–411. New York: R. R. Bowker, 1969.

Nicely, Donna, and Beth Dempsey. 2005. "Building a Culture of Leadership: ULC's Executive Leadership Institute Fills Libraries' Biggest Training Void." *Public Libraries* 44 (September/October): 297–300.

North Dakota Library Association. 2006. *Dakota Gold: NDLA Celebrates 100 Years; Centennial Cookbook and History*. Bismarck: North Dakota Library Association.

Public Library Association. 1967. *Minimum Standards for Public Library Systems, 1966*. Chicago: American Library Association.

Shavit, David. 1985. *Federal Aid and State Library Agencies: Federal Policy Implementation*. Westport, CT: Greenwood Press.

St. Angelo, Douglas. 1971. *State Library Policy, Its Legislative and Environmental Contexts*. Chicago: American Library Association.

U.S. Bureau of Education. 1876. *Public Libraries in the United States of America: Their History, Condition, and Management. Special Report*. Washington, DC: U.S. Government Printing Office. Repr. as Monograph Series, no. 4, Champaign: University of Illinois, Graduate School of Library Science.

U.S. Institute of Museum and Library Services. 2009. *A Catalyst for Change: LSTA Grants to States Program Activities and the Transformation of Library Services to the Public*. Washington, DC: Institute of Museum and Library Services.

U.S. National Advisory Commission on Libraries. 1969. *Libraries at Large: Traditions, Innovations, and the National Interest*, edited by Douglas M. Knight and E. Shepley Nourse. New York: R. R. Bowker.

U.S. National Center for Education Statistics. 2004. *State Library Agencies, Fiscal Year 2002*. Washington, DC: U.S. Department of Education. http://nces.ed.gov/pubs2004/2004304.pdf.

Wilt, Catherine C. 2010. "Regional Library Networks: United States." In *Encyclopedia of Library and Information Sciences*, 3rd ed., 1:1, 4492–4497.

Articles

Altshuler, Alyssa. 2005. "The Virginia Library Association: A Retrospective." *Virginia Libraries* 51 (July/August/September): 5–10.

Anderson, Kathy. 2010. "LYRASIS: A Collaborative Success Story." *Collaborative Librarianship* 2, no. 2: 105–108. http://collaborativelibrarianship.org/index.html

Bailey-Hainer, Brenda. 2010. "Reinventing Cooperation Is Our Future." *Interface* (Winter). http://ascla.ala.org/interface.

Banush, David. 2010. "Cooperative Cataloging at the Intersection of Tradition and Transformation: Possible Futures for the Program for Cooperative Cataloging." *Cataloging and Classification Quarterly* 48, no. 2/3: 247–257.

Basolo, Victoria. 2003. "U.S. Regionalism and Rationality." *Urban Studies* 40 (March): 447–462.

Clyke, Frank, Kurt, Michael M. Moodie, and Robert E. Fistick. 2007. "Serving the Blind and Physically Handicapped in the United States of America." *Library Trends* 55, no. 4: 796–808.

Davis, Denise M. 2010. "E-books: Collection Vortex or Black Hole?" *Public Libraries* 49 (July/August): 10–14.

Dornseif, Karen, and Ken Draves. 2003. "The Joint-Use Library: The Ultimate Collaboration." *Colorado Libraries* 29 (Spring): 5–7.

Fichter, D. 2005. "The Many Forms of E-collaboration: Blogs, Wikis, Portals, Groupware, Discussion Boards, and Instant Messaging." *Online* 29 (July/August): 48–50.

Frank, Donald G. 1997. "Activity in Professional Associations: The Positive Difference in a Librarian's Career." *Library Trends* 46, no. 2: 307–319.

Frederiksen, Linda. 2009. "A Century of Cooperation: The Pacific Northwest Library Association, 1909–2009." *PNLA Quarterly* 73 (Summer): 5–35.

Frug, Gerald. E. 2002. "Beyond Regional Government." *Harvard Law Review* 115 (May): 1763–1836.

Fry, James W. 1975. "LSCA and LSCA, 1956–1973: A Legislative History." *Library Trends* 24 (July): 7–26.

Helfer, Doris Small. 2002. "OCLC's March into the 21st Century." *Searcher* 10 (February): 66–69.

Hill, Nanci Milone. 2010. "Dewey or Don't We?" *Public Libraries* 49 (July/August): 14–20.

Hill, Nanci Milone, Jan Dempsey, Kate Skarbek, Gerri Guyote, and Kathy Moran-Wallace. 2010. "LSTA Grants Help Promote Library and Extend Offerings." *Public Libraries* 49 (March/April): 9–13.

Interface. Newsletter of the Association of Specialized and Cooperative Library Agencies. http://ascla.ala.org/interface/.

Ison, Jan. 2005. "Multitype Cooperation—the Competitive Advantage." *Illinois Libraries* 86 (December) 57–59.

Kniffel, Leonard. 2010. "With No Check in the Mail, Illinois Cooperatives Lay Off Dozens." *American Libraries* (May 10). http://americanlibrariesmagazine.org/news/05102010/no check-mail-illinois-cooperatives-lay-dozens.

Lipscomb, C. E. 2002. "Lister Hill and His Influence." *Journal of the Medical Library Association* 90, no. 1 (January): 109–110.

Long, Sarah. 2004. "The Story of the Light Bulb Group." *Interface* 26 (Summer).

———. 2005. "Top 10 Reasons Why Regional Library Systems Are Vital in 2005—and Beyond." *Illinois Libraries* 86: 68–69.

Marie, Kirsten L. 2007. "One Plus One Equals Three: Joint-Use Libraries in Urban Areas—the Ultimate Form of Library Cooperation." *Library Administration and Management* 21, no. 1: 23–28.

Mason, Marilyn Gell. 2009. "WebJunction: A Community for Library Staff." *Journal of Library Administration* 49 (October): 701–705.

Nicely, Donna, and Beth Dempsey. 2005. "Building a Culture of Leadership: ULC's Executive Leadership Institute Fills Libraries' Biggest Training Void." *Public Libraries* 44 (September/October): 297–300.

Raber, Douglas. 1995. "Ideological Opposition to Federal Library Legislation: The Case of the Library Services Act of 1956." *Public Libraries* (May/June): 162–169.

Sager, Donald J. 2000. "Before the Memory Fades: Public Libraries in the Twentieth Century." *Public Libraries* 39 (March/April): 73–77.

"SOLINET + PALINET = LYRASIS." 2010. *Library Journal* 134 (March): 16.

Tennant, Roy. 2010. "The Decade of Massive Cooperation." Tennant Digital Libraries Blog. *Library Journal Online*. January 10. http://blog.libraryjournal.com/tennantdigitallibraries/2010/01/03/the-decade-of-massive-cooperation/.

Wheeler, Stephen M. 2002. "The New Regionalism: Key Characteristics of an Emerging Movement." *Journal of the American Planning Association* 68 (Summer): 267–278.

Woodsworth, Anne. 1991. "Governance of Library Networks: Structures and Issues." *Advances in Librarianship* 15: 155–174.

Young, Jeffrey R. 2010. "Library-Services Companies Sue OCLC, Alleging Anticompetitive Practices." *Chronicle of Higher Education*. July 29. http://chronicle.com/article/Library-Services-Companies-Sue/123718/.

Websites

ALA Connect. http://connect.ala.org/about.

American Library Association, Chapter Relations Office. http://www.ala.org/ala/mgrps/affiliates/chapters/state/stateregional.cfm.

American Planning Association. http://www.planning.org.

AMIGOS. http://www.amigos.org.

Association for Rural and Small Libraries. http://www.arsl.info/about/.

Association of Bookmobile and Outreach Services. http://www.abos-outreach.org/.

———. 2008. "Guidelines." http://www.abos-outreach.org/2008BookmobileGuidelines.pdf.

Association of Specialized and Cooperative Library Agencies, InterLibrary Cooperation and Networking Section. http://www.ala.org/ala/mgrps/divs/ascla/asclaourassoc/asclasections/ican/ican.cfm.

Association of Specialized and Cooperative Library Agencies, State Library Agency Section. http://www.ala.org/ala/mgrps/divs/ascla/ascla.cfm.

BayNet. Bay Area Library and Information Network. http://www.baynetlibs.org.

Chief Officers of State Library Agencies. http://www.cosla.org.

Citizens Network for Sustainable Development. http://www.citnet.org.

Connecticut Library Consortium. http://www.ctlibrarians.org.

Florida Library Association. http://www.flalib.org.

Himmel, Ethel E., and William J. Wilson. 2004. "Library Systems and Cooperatives." Himmel and Wilson Library Consultants. http://www.libraryconsultant.com.

ILLINET. http://www.cyberdriveillinois.com/departments/library/who_we_are/.

INCOLSA. Indiana Cooperative Library Services Authority. http://www.incolsa.net.

Library of Congress, National Library Service for the Blind and Physically Handicapped. http://www.loc.gov/nls.

LYRASIS. http://www.lyrasis.org.

Midwest Collaborative for Library Services. http://www.mcls.org/cms/sitem.cfm.

MINITEX. http://www.minitex.umn.edu.

Missouri Library Network Corporation. http://www.mlnc.org.

National Association of Regional Councils. http://www.narc.org.

NEBASE, Nebraska's OCLC Connection. http://www.nlc.state.ne.us/netserv/nebase/nebserv.html.

NYLINK. http://nylink.suny.edu (phasing down operations by 2011).

OCLC. United States. http://www.oclc.org/us/en/default.htm.

OCLC Eastern Service Center. http://www.oclc.org/eastern/default.htm.

OCLC Regional Service Providers. http://oclc.org/contacts/regional/default.htm.

OCLC Western Service Center. http://www.oclc.org/western/.

OHIONET. http://www.ohionet.org.

Public Library Association. 2010. Strategic Plan. http://www.ala.org/ala/mgrps/divs/pla/plaabout/plagovernance/plastrategicplan/index.cfm.

PUBLIB Electronic Discussion List. http://lists.webjunction.org/publib/.

South Dakota Library Association. http://sdlibraryassociation.org.

Tampa Bay Library Consortium. http://www.tblc.org.

Urban Libraries Council. http://urbanlibraries.org/index.cfm.

Webjunction. Project Compass. http://www.webjunction.org/project-compass.

Wisconsin Library Services. http://www.wils.wisc.edu.

11. Global Perspectives on Public Libraries

Books and Chapters in Books

Abdullahi, Ismael, ed. 2009. *Global Library and Information Science*. Munich: K. G. Saur.

Alyaqou, Hayat. 2009. "Middle East." In *Global Library and Information Science*, edited by Ismael Abdullahi, 421–439. Munich: K. G. Saur.

Black, Alistair. 1996. *A New History of the English Public Library: Social and Intellectual Contexts, 1850–1940*. London: University of Leicester Press.

———. 2000. *The Public Library in Britain, 1914–2000*. London: British Library.

Bukenya, Isaac Kigongo. 2009. "Africa." In *Global Library and Information Science*, edited by Ismael Abdullahi, 21–44. Munich: K. G. Saur.

Caballero, Maria Cristina. 2003. *Bibliored: Colombia's Innovative Library Network*. Washington, DC: Council on Library and Information Resources.

Carnegie Corporation of New York. 2000. *Revitalizing African Libraries*. Carnegie Corporation of New York.

Carroll, Frances, and John Frederick Harvey. 2001. *International Librarianship: Cooperation and Collaboration*. Lanham, MD: Scarecrow Press.

Coombs, Douglas. 1988. *Spreading the Word: The Library Work of the British Council*. London: Mansell.

Ford, Barbara J. 2008. "LIS Professionals in a Global Society." In *The Portable MLIS*. Westport, CT: Libraries Unlimited.

Greenhalgh, Liz, Ken Worpole, and Charles Landry. 1995. *Libraries in a World of Cultural Change*. London: UCL Press.

Häggström, Britt Marie. 2004. *The Role of Libraries in Lifelong Learning: Final Report of the IFLA Project under the Section for Public Libraries*. International Federation of Library Associations. http://archive.ifla.org/VII/s8/proj/Lifelong-LearningReport.pdf.

Hanratty, Catherine, and John Sumsion. 1996. *International Comparison of Public Library Statistics*. Loughborough, UK: Loughborough University, Library and Information Statistics Unit.

Heaney, Michael. 2009. *Library Statistics for the Twenty-first Century World: Proceedings of the Conference Held in Montréal on 18–19 August 2008 Reporting on the Global Library Statistics Project*. Munich: K. G. Saur.

Henry, Carol K., and Donald G. Davis Jr. 2002. *IFLA 75th Anniversary*. The Hague, Netherlands: IFLA.

International Federation of Library Associations and Institutions. 2001. *The Public Library Service: IFLA/UNESCO Guidelines for Development*. Munich: K. G. Saur.

International Federation of Library Associations and Institutions and Freedom of Access to Information and Freedom of Expression. 2001. *Libraries and Intellectual Freedom: IFLA/FAIFE World Report: Denmark*. Denmark: IFLA/FAIFE Office.

Issak, Aissa. 2000. *Public Libraries in Africa: A Report and Annotated Bibliography*. Oxford: International Network for the Availability of Scientific Publications.

Jones, Chris, et al. 2009. "Australia." In *Global Library and Information Science*, edited by Ismael Abdullahi, 223–242. Munich: K. G. Saur.

Koontz, Christie, and Barbara Gubbin. 2010. *IFLA Public Library Service Guidelines*. Berlin: De Gruyter/Saur.

Koops, Willem R. H., and Joachim Wieder. 1977. *IFLA's First Fifty Years: Achievement and Challenge in International Librarianship*. Munich: Verlag Dokumentation.

Koren, Marian. 2009. "Europe." In *Global Library and Information Science*, edited by Ismael Abdullahi, 311–328. Munich: K. G. Saur.

Laubier, Guillaume de, and Jacques Bosser. 2003. *The Most Beautiful Libraries in the World*. New York: Harry N. Abrams.

Leyva, Elsa M. Ramirez. 2009. "Latin America." In *Global Library and Information Science*, edited by Ismael Abdullahi, 367–381. Munich: K. G. Saur.

McCook, Kathleen de la Peña, Barbara J. Ford, and Kate Lippincott. 1998. *Libraries: Global Reach—Local Touch*. Chicago: American Library Association.

Poll, Roswitha. 2009. "Standardisation of Library Statistics." In *Library Statistics for the Twenty-First Century World: Proceedings of the Conference Held in Montreal on 18–19 August 2008 Reporting on the Global Library Statistics Project*, edited by Michael Heaney, 27–30. Munich: K. G. Saur.

Stam, David H., ed. 2001. *International Dictionary of Library Histories*. Chicago: Fitzroy Dearborn.

Stringer, Roger. 2002. *The Book Chain in Anglophone Africa: A Survey and Directory*. Oxford: International Network for the Availability of Scientific Publications.

Sturges, Paul, and Richard Neill. 1998. *The Quiet Struggle: Information and Libraries for the People of Africa*. 2nd ed. London: Mansell.

Swedish Library Association. 1999. *Library at the Centre of the World: Multicultural Library Services*. Lund, Sweden: Committee on Multicultural Library Services of the Swedish Library Association.

Thorhauge, J., G. Larsen, et al. 1997. *Public Libraries and the Information Society*. Luxembourg: European Commission.

UNESCO. 1998. *World Culture Report 1998: Culture, Creativity and Markets*. France: UNESCO.

———. 2010. *Education for All Global Monitoring Report—2010. Reaching the Marginalized*. London: Oxford University Press.

United Nations Development Programme. 2010. *Beyond the Midpoint: Achieving the Millennium Development Goals*. New York: United Nations. http://content.undp.org/go/cms-service/stream/asset/?asset_id=2223855.

Vashishth, C. P., ed. 1995. *Libraries as Rural Community Resource Centres: Papers and Proceedings of the Workshop on Rural Community Resource Centres*. Delhi: B. R. Publishing.

Wedgeworth, Robert. 1998. "Global Perspective." In *Libraries: Global Reach-Local Touch*, edited by Kathleen de la Peña McCook, Barbara J. Ford, and Kate Lippincott, 6–11. Chicago: American Library Association.

Wendell, Laura. 1998. *Libraries for All: How to Start and Run a Basic Library*. Paris: UNESCO.

Wedgeworth, Robert. 1998. "Global Perspective." In *Libraries: Global Reach Local Touch*, edited by Kathleen de la Peña McCook, Barbara J. Ford, and Kate Lippincott, 6–11. Chicago: American Library Association.

Windau, Bettina, ed. 1999. *International Network of Public Libraries*. 6 vols. Lanham, MD: Scarecrow Press.

Yang, Mei-Hwa. 2009. "Asia." In *Global Library and Information Science*, edited by Ismael Abdullahi, 137–157. Munich: K. G. Saur.

Yitai, Cong, and C. E. Gorman. 2000. *Libraries and Information Services in China*. Lanham, MD: Scarecrow Press.

Articles

Atuti, Richard M. 1999. "Camel Library Service to Nomadic Pastoralists: The Kenyan Scenario." *IFLA Journal* 25: 152–158.

Auld, Hampton. 2002. "Public Libraries in the Developing World." *Public Libraries* 41 (January/February): 25–33.

Birdi, Briony, and Kerry Wilson. 2008. "The Public Library, Exclusion and Empathy: A Literature Review." *Library Review* 57, no. 8: 576–592.

Campbell, Harry C. 2002. "Library Universality in a Divided World." *IFLA Journal* 28: 118–135.

Clifford, Nerida. 2003. "International Public Library Trends." *Australasian Public Libraries and Information Services* 16 (September): 115–122.

Davis, Donald G., Jr., Olga Diakonova, and Ludmila Kozlova. 2003. "Strengthening Links between Library Associations and Their Members: The 25th Anniversary of the IFLA Section of Library and Information Science Journals." *IFLA Journal* 29, no. 3: 235–244.

Ellis, Simon, Michael Heaney, Pierre Meunier, and Roswitha Poll. 2009. "Global Library Statistics." *IFLA Journal* 35, no. 2: 123–130.

Erickson, Carol A., and Abbagliati Boils. 2003. "Chile's Information Transformation." *American Libraries* 34 (January): 52–54.

Ford, Barbara. 2002. "International Public Librarianship." *Public Libraries* 41 (January/February): 12.

Forsyth, Ellen. 2005. "Public Libraries and the Millennium Development Goals." *IFLA Journal* 31, no. 4: 315–323.

Gould, Elizabeth, and Ricardo Gomez. 2010. "New Challenges for Libraries in the Information Age: A Comparative Study of ICT in Public Libraries in 25 Countries." *Information Development* 26 (May): 166–176.

Haratsis, Brian. 1995. "Justifying the Economic Value of Public Libraries in a Turbulent Local Government Environment." *Australasian Public Libraries and Information Services* 8: 164–172.

Hassner, Karen. 2004. "Promoting the Public Library Guidelines." *IFLA Section of Public Libraries Newsletter* 29 (February): 22.

International Federation of Library Associations and Institutions, Public Libraries Section. 2009. "10 Ways to Make a Public Library Work." http://www.ifla.org/files/public-libraries/publications/10-ways-to-make-a-public-library-work.pdf.

Kalantry, Sital, et al. 2010. "Enhancing Enforcement of Economic, Social, and Cultural Rights Using Indicators: A Focus on the Right to Education in the ICESCR." *Human Rights Quarterly* 32 (May): 253–310.

Muhamad-Brandner, Catharina. 2008. "Indigenous Cyberspace: The Maori Renaissance and Its Influence on the Web Space of Aotearoa/New Zealand." *Information Studies* 14 (April): 85–98.

Onwubiko, Chidi P. C. 1996. "The Practice of Amadi's Barefoot Librarianship in African Public Libraries." *Library Review* 45: 39–47.

Panella, Nancy. 2009. "The Library Services to People with Special Needs Section of IFLA: An Historical Overview." *IFLA Journal* 35, no. 3: 258–271.

Paola Picco, M. 2008. "Quebec's Public Libraries: An Overview of Their History and Current Situation." *Public Library Quarterly* 27, no. 2: 139–150.

Payne, Beth A. 2002. "Creating a Nation's First Public Library." *Public Libraries* 41 (January/February): 49–51.

Poustie, Kay. 1999. "The Bertelsmann International Network of Public Libraries: A Model of Public Library Cooperation on an International Scale." *Asian Libraries* 8, no. 11: 422–430.

Rahman, Faizur. 2000. "Status of Rural and Small Libraries in Bangladesh: Directions for the Future." *Rural Libraries* 20: 52–64.

Roy, Loriene. 2000. "The International Indigenous Librarians' Forum: A Professional Life-Affirming Event." *World Libraries* 10 (Spring/Fall): 19–30.

Rudolf, Málek. 1970. "On the Origin of the International Organization of Librarians (IFLA): The Congress of Librarians in Prague, 1926." *Libri* 20: 222–224.

Sager, Donald. J. 2000. "The Sister Libraries Program." *Public Libraries* 39 (July/August): 195–199.

Sears, Rebecca, and Michael Crandall. 2010. "Bridging between Libraries and Information and Communication Technologies for Development." *IFLA Journal* 36 (March): 70–73.

Strong, Gary E. 2002. "International Experiences at the Queens Borough Public Library." *Public Libraries* 41 (January/February): 41–43.

Sturges, R. P. 2001. "The Poverty of Librarianship: An Historical Critique of Public Librarianship in Anglophone Africa." *Libri* 51 (March): 38–48.

Sukkar, Deanna. 2008. "The Road to Global Connections and Better Lives." *Alki* 24, no. 3: 5–6, 11.

"The 25th Anniversary of the IFLA Section of Library and Information Science Journals." *IFLA Journal* 29: 235–244.

Wieder, Joachim, and Harry Campbell. 2002. "IFLA's First Fifty Years." *IFLA Journal* 28: 107–117.

Websites

African Books Collective. http://www.africanbookscollective.com.

American Library Association, International Relations Round Table. 2009. http://www.ala.org/ala/mgrps/rts/irrt/index.cfm.

———. "Official Manual." http://www.ala.org/ala/mgrps/rts/irrt/irrtcommittees/offmanual 011609rev.pdf.

Bill and Melinda Gates Foundation. "International Library Initiatives." http://www .gatesfoundation.org.

———. 2008. "Mobile Classrooms Reach Rural Mexico." http://www.gatesfoundation.org/atla/Pages/2008-vasconcelos-program.aspx.

Book Aid International. http://www.bookaid.org/cms.cgi/site/index.htm.

Canadian Organization for Development through Education. http://www.codecan.org/en/code.

Carnegie Corporation. "Higher Education and Libraries in Africa." http://carnegie.org/programs/higher-education-and-libraries-in-africa/.

Carnegie United Kingdom Trust. http://www.carnegieuktrust.org.uk.

Council on Library and Information Resources. "Access to Learning Award." http://www .clir.org/fellowships/gates/gates.html.

Europeana. http://europeana.eu/portal/.

European Commission. http://ec.europa.eu/.

International Federation of Library Associations and Institutions. "Core Values." http:// www.ifla.org.

———. "Glasgow Declaration." http://www.ifla.org/faife/policy/iflastat/gldeclar-e.html.

———. 2005. "Meeting User Needs: A Checklist for Best Practices." http://archive.ifla .org/VII/s8/proj/Mtg_UN-Checklist.pdf.

———. 2010. *World Report 2010*. http://www.ifla-world-report.org/.

International Federation of Library Associations and Institutions, Action for Development through Libraries Programme. http://www.ifla.org/en/alp.

International Network for the Availability of Scientific Publications. http://www.inasp.info.

International Network of Public Libraries. http://www.public-libraries.net.

Norwegian Agency for Development Cooperation. http://www.norad.no/en/.

Open Society Institute, Soros Foundation. http://www.soros.org.

UNESCO. http://www.unesco.org.

————. "The IFLA/UNESCO Public Library Manifesto." http://www.ifla.org/en/publications/iflaunesco-public-library-manifesto-1994.

————. "Libraries Portal." http://www.unesco-ci.org/cgi-bin/portals/libraries/page.cgi?d=1.

————. 2009. *The 2009 UNESCO Framework for Cultural Statistics*. Montreal, Canada. http://www.uis.unesco.org/template/pdf/cscl/framework/FCS_2009_EN.pdf.

United Nations. "Millennium Development Goals." http://www.un.org/millenniumgoals/bkgd.shtml.

University of Illinois Library at Urbana-Champaign, Mortenson Center for International Library Programs. http://www.library.uiuc.edu/mortenson.

World Summit on the Information Society. 2010. "WSIS Forum 2010." http://www.itu.int/wsis/implementation/2010/forum/geneva/.

12. The Future of Public Libraries in the Twenty-First Century: Human Rights and Human Capabilities

"ALA Joins Anti-National ID Campaign." 2007. *American Libraries* 38 (June/July): 22.

American Library Association. 2010. *Equity of Access*. http://www.ala.org/ala/issuesadvocacy/access/equityofaccess/index.cfm.

————. 2010. *Intellectual Freedom Manual*. 8th ed. Chicago: American Library Association.

American Library Association, Social Responsibilities Round Table. 1969. *SRRT Newsletter*. http://www.libr.org/srrt/newsletter.html.

American Library Association, Task Force on Cultural Expression. 2011. "Presidential Task Force on Traditional Cultural Expressions Report. http://connect.ala.org/node/123944.

Bacon, David. 2010. "Equality and Rights for Immigrants—the Key to Organizing Unions." *Monthly Review* 62 (October): 34–48.

Berry, John W. 2006. "The World Summit on the Information Society (WSIS): A Global Challenge in the New Millennium." *Libri* 56: 1–15.

Bertot, John C., Paul T. Jaeger, and Justin M. Grimes. 2010. "Using ICTs to Create a Culture of Transparency: E-government and Social Media as Openness and Anti-corruption Tools for Societies." *Government Information Quarterly* 27 (July): 264–271.

Britz, Johannes J. 2008. "Making the Global Information Society Good: A Social Justice Perspective on the Ethical Dimensions of the Global Information Society." *Journal of the American Society for Information Science and Technology* 59 (May): 1171–1183.

Budd, John. 2008. *Self-Examination: The Present and Future of Librarianship*. Westport, CT: Libraries Unlimited.

Burke, Susan K. 2008. "Use of Public Libraries by Immigrants." *Reference and User Services Quarterly* 48 (Winter): 164–174.

Buschman, John E. 2007. "Democratic Theory in Library Information Science: Toward an Emendation." *Journal of the American Society for Information Science and Technology* 58, no. 10 (August): 1483–1496.

————. 2009. *Information Technology in Librarianship: New Critical Approaches*. Westport, CT: Libraries Unlimited, 281–288.

Byrne, Alex. 2007. *The Politics of Promoting Freedom of Information and Expression in International Librarianship: The IFLA/FAIFE Project*. Lanham, MD: Scarecrow Press.

Comim, F., M. Qizilbash, and S. Alkire. 2008. *The Capability Approach: Concepts, Measures and Applications*. New York: Cambridge University Press.

Dembour, Marie-Bénédicte. 2010. "What Are Human Rights? Four Schools of Thought." *Human Rights Quarterly* 32: 1–20.

Donelan, Molly, and Liz Miller. 2010. "Public Libraries Daring to Be Different." *Public Management Magazine* 92 (September).

Edwards, Julie Biando, and Stephan P. Edwards. 2010. *Beyond Article 19: Libraries and Social and Cultural Rights*. Duluth, MN: Library Juice Press.

Gehner, John. 2010. "Libraries, Low-Income People, and Social Exclusion." *Public Library Quarterly* 29, no. 1: 39–47.

Glendon, Mary Ann. 2001. *A World Made New: Eleanor Roosevelt and the Universal Declaration of Human Rights*. New York: Random House.

Hall, Peter Dobkin. 1996. "'To Make Us Bold and Learn to Read—to Be Friends to Each Other, and Friends to the World': Libraries and the Origins of Civil Society in the United States." *Libraries and Culture* 31 (Winter): 14–35.

Information for Social Change. 1994. http://www.libr.org/isc/.

International Federation of Library Associations and Institutions. 2002. "IFLA Internet Manifesto." http://www.ifla.org/publications/the-ifla-internet-manifesto.

————. 2009. *Multicultural Communities: Guidelines for Library Services*. 3rd ed. http://www.ifla.org/files/library-services-to-multicultural-populations/publications/multicultural-communities-en.pdf.

Jaeger, Paul T., and John Bertot. 2009. "E-government Education in Public Libraries: New Service Roles and Expanding Social Responsibilities." *Journal of Education for Library and Information Science* 50 (Winter): 39–49.

Jones, Plummer Alston. 2004. *Still Struggling for Equality: American Public Library Services with Minorities*. Westport, CT: Libraries Unlimited.

Journal of Information Ethics. 1992. Jefferson, NC: McFarland. http://www.mcfarlandpub.com.

Kagan, Al. 2008. "An Alternative View on IFLA, Human Rights, and the Social Responsibility of International Librarianship." *IFLA Journal* 34 no. 3: 230–237.

Koontz, Christie, and Barbara Gubbin. 2010. *IFLA Public Library Service Guidelines*. Berlin: De Gruyter Saur.

Kranich, Nancy. 2005. "Civic Partnerships: The Role of Libraries in Promoting Civic Engagement." *Resource Sharing and Information Networks* 18, no. 1–2: 89–103.

Leckie, Gloria J., and John Buschman. 2009. *Information Technology in Librarianship: New Critical Approaches*. Westport, CT: Libraries Unlimited.

Lewis, Alison M. 2008. *Questioning Library Neutrality: Essays from Progressive Librarians*. Duluth, MN: Library Juice Press.

McCook, Kathleen de la Peña. 2009. "Human Rights as a Framework for Reflection in Service Learning: 'Para que Otro Mundo es posible.'" In *Service Learning*, 5–15. Chicago: American Library Association.

———. 2010. "Jean E. Coleman Library Outreach Lecture: 'Librarians and Human Rights.'" Washington, DC: American Library Association Annual Conference.

McCook, Kathleen de la Peña, and Katharine J. Phenix. 2008. "Human Rights, Democracy, and Librarians." In *The Portable MLIS*, edited by Ken Haycock and Brooke E. Sheldon. Westport, CT: Libraries Unlimited.

———. 2007. "Librarians as Advocates for the Human Rights of Immigrants." *Progressive Librarian* 29 (Summer): 51–54.

———. 2010. "Public Librarianship." In *Encyclopedia of Library and Information Sciences*, 3rd ed. London: Taylor and Francis.

Moyn, Samuel. 2010. *The Last Utopia: Human Rights in History*. Cambridge, MA: Harvard University Press.

Phenix, Katharine J., and Kathleen de la Peña McCook. 2005. "Human Rights and Librarians." *Reference and User Services Quarterly* 45 (Fall): 23–26.

———. 2009. "Librarians and Human Rights: Writings in the First Decade of the 21st Century." *SRRT Newsletter* (September): 7–9.

Preer, Jean L. 2008. *Library Ethics*. Westport, CT: Libraries Unlimited.

Progressive Librarian. 1990. New York: Progressive Librarians Guild. http://www.libr.org/PL/contents.html.

Raab, Ralph. 2010. "Books and Literacy in the Digital Age." *American Libraries* 41: 34–37.

REFORMA. 2010. "El Día de los Niños/El Día de los Libros." http://www.reforma.org/Dia.htm.

Ren, Rena, Keith Cogdill, and Alex Potemkin. 2009. "Partnerships for a Healthy Community: Laredo Public Library's Children's Health Fair and Outreach Program." *Public Libraries* 48 (January/February): 59–61.

Reznowski, Gabriella. 2009. "American Libraries and Linguistic Diversity: Policies, Controversies and Ideological Fences." *Libri* 59 no. 3: 155–165.

Rioux, Kevin. 2010. "Metatheory in Library and Information Science: A Nascent Social Justice Approach." *Journal of Education for Library and Information Science* 51 (Winter): 9–17.

Roosevelt, Eleanor. 1953. Remarks at the United Nations, March 27.

Samek, Toni. 2007. *Librarianship and Human Rights: A Twenty-first Century Guide*. Oxford: Chandos.

———. 2008. "An Introduction to Librarianship for Human Rights." In *Educating for Human Rights and Global Citizenship*, edited by Ali A. Abdi and Lynette Shultz. Albany: State University of New York Press.

United Nations. 2010. "Millennium Development Goals." http://www.un.org/millenniumgoals/.

United Nations, High Commissioner for Human Rights. 2004. *World Programme for Human Rights Education*. http://www2.ohchr.org/english/issues/education/training/programme.htm.

United Nations Development Programme. *Human Development Reports*. http://hdr.undp.org/en/reports/global/hdr2010/.

————. *Origins of the Human Development Approach*. http://hdr.undp.org/en/humandev/origins/.

Wallace, David A. 2010. "Locating Agency: Interdisciplinary Perspectives on Professional Ethics and Archival Morality." *Journal of Information Ethics* 19: 172–189.

Appendix B
21st Century Learner Conference, U.S. Institute of Museum and Library Services: Welcoming Remarks

Robert S. Martin, Director

November 7, 2001

Good afternoon, and welcome. I am Robert Martin, director of the Institute of Museum and Library Services, and it is my pleasure to welcome you on behalf of the staff of IMLS to this conference on the twenty-first-century learner. Thank you for coming to what we expect to be an extremely interesting and stimulating conversation on the role that libraries and museums play in support of informal education.

The Institute of Museum and Library Services was created in 1996 by the Museum and Library Services Act, which essentially merged the federal programs for supporting the nation's museums and libraries, transferring the library programs out of the Department of Education and grafting them onto what had been the Institute of Museum Services. The rationale that drove this merger was the simple recognition that museums and libraries are both social agencies for public education. This conference today is designed to focus our attention on this common mission of museums and libraries, to reaffirm its central importance, and to explore some new and innovative approaches to addressing our educational responsibilities.

I am pleased to be leading this fine agency. IMLS is the primary source of federal grants for the nation's libraries and museums. It is an independent federal agency that fosters leadership, innovation, and a lifetime of learning. Our major goal is to provide grants and leadership activities that help build the educational capacity of our constituency. Our grants build institutional capacity, support core library and museum services, and encourage excellence. IMLS is a catalyst for leadership. We take an active part in championing the role libraries and museums play in our society. As a federal agency we have a responsibility to place a national spotlight on the outstanding work that you do and on the enormous contributions you make. We do this in a number of ways through conferences, such as this one, through encouraging best practices through our website and National Awards Program, by offering training on outcome-based evaluation and through our publications. All of our leadership activities endeavor to establish that libraries and museums are essentially educational institutions.

Libraries and museums provide a plethora of resources and services for their communities. They preserve our rich and diverse culture and history and transmit it from one generation to the next. They provide social settings for numerous community activities. They support economic development. They provide extraordinary opportunities for recreation and enjoyment. And perhaps most important, they serve as a primary social agency in support of education, providing resources and services that complement the structures of formal education and extend education into an enterprise that lasts the length of the lifetime. In my view, all of the numerous and varied roles and functions that libraries and museums play in their communities fall into one of three overlapping categories: education, information, and recreation. Of these the most important is education.

I am a historian by both training and inclination, and so I want to review for a minute the history of our educational mission. What we know today as the American public library first came into existence in Boston about 150 years ago. There was no doubt in the minds of the founders of the Boston Public Library that its mission was to be primarily educational. In their report to the Boston City Council, the trustees of the library proposed that the public library in Boston would be "the crowning glory of our system of City schools" and have "the utmost importance as the means of completing our system of public education." George Ticknor, the leader of the civic library movement in Boston, often spoke of the role of the library in terms of its educational mission. Communities that followed the Boston model and founded libraries in the 1850s and 1860s were explicit in citing the library's purpose to support and extend the agencies of formal education in the community.

The education theme has remained a constant in the discourse of the American library profession. In 1946 ALA promulgated a new National Plan for Public Library Service, which again asserted that "the public library is an essential unit in the American educational system. . . . It comes closer than any other institution to being the capstone of our educational system."

In 1955, testimony in support of the first federal legislation to support library development, the Library Services Act, consistently argued the educational importance of the public library, asserting that libraries were second only to schools in the capacity to educate citizens. Librarian of Congress L. Q. Mumford testified that "for most people the public library is the chief—and sometimes the only—means of carrying on their education after they leave school."

Similarly, museums in America began with an essentially educational purpose. In Europe the first museums were established to preserve royal collections; in America they were often founded with the notion of public education clearly in mind. Long before the Tax Reform Act of 1969 officially designated museums as educational institutions, American museums embraced the notion that they should communicate the essence of ideas, impart knowledge, encourage curiosity, and promote esthetic sensibility. If collections are the heart of museums, what we have come to call education is the spirit.

One of the earliest museums in America was the Peale Museum in Philadelphia, established by Charles Willson Peale in 1786. Peale saw his museums as a commercial as well as an educational undertaking; he understood the need to connect his content to his audience's interests in a lively manner if he expected them to pay the admission fees that his museum required for its operation. Peale's museum was characteristic of a genre that saw its collections as representing the entire world. Its collections grew to over 100,000 specimens, collected and exhibited with two purposes in mind—to educate and to entertain. It is important to remember that early museums such as Peale's developed long before universal public schooling became common; they, along with the church and the library, were important institutions concerned with public education.

Over the years this essential educational focus has ebbed and flowed. At some times our institutions are more true to their historical beginnings than at other times. Museums have struggled over the primacy of their educational mission as opposed to the primacy of their collecting and scholarship mission. Libraries have clashed over whether their primary mission is to provide information or knowledge. I am especially concerned that in recent years the importance of education has almost disappeared from the rhetoric of librarians, replaced by a focus on information. Providing information and supporting education are not the same things. There is a difference between information and knowledge, and the most important role of the library is not providing access to information; it is supporting, enhancing, and facilitating the transfer of knowledge—in other words, education.

This conference is delivered in the spirit of John Cotton Dana, a person who is very important to both libraries and museums. He was director of the Free Public Library of Newark from 1901 until his death in 1929 and simultaneously the director of the Newark Museum Association from 1909 until his death. He was one of the most passionate promulgators of museum and libraries as institutions of learning. He believed education was a social responsibility and should be their primary missions.

I would be remiss if I failed to mention in my remarks the terrible events that took place on September 11. All of us were transformed by those events. Perhaps we all now share a sense of having entered a dreadful new age in which cherished features of our existence that we once took for granted seem remote and distant. But in the past weeks we have also witnessed marvelous examples of museums and libraries reaffirming their central role in the life of their communities. We must take inspiration from these examples. We must actively assert the fundamental role that museums and libraries play in our democratic society.

Our country's libraries and museums are uniquely American institutions. As the National Foundation for the Art and Humanities Act says, "Democracy demands wisdom and vision in its citizens." We know that for democracy to survive and thrive, for people to be able to participate freely and effectively in governing themselves, citizens must be both educated and informed. Our founding fathers knew this, and often spoke of the importance of education. Many might quote Jefferson or Madison at a time like this, but you know, I am a Texan, and so I would like to quote a famous Texan in support of my point. The second president of the Republic of Texas, Mirabeau Buonapart Lamar, put it as well as anyone when he said, "the cultivated mind is the guardian genius of Democracy." Libraries and museums cultivate minds. They are central to educating and informing the citizens of our country. They preserve our rich and diverse culture and history and transmit it from one generation to the next. They are cornerstones of community engagement and help us find connections to each other and the world in which we live. And they provide rich and stimulating opportunities for recreation and enjoyment.

This work is so important. In these troubled times, let us not forget that the work we do in museums and libraries is important. It is fundamental to what we believe and who we are as a people. And we must carry that message forward to the public and elected officials to ensure that museums and libraries have the resources they need to provide essential programs and services to the communities that they serve.

We hope this conference on the twenty-first-century learner will develop some new insights into how we might accomplish this. This conference was the inspiration of a very special person at the IMLS, Beverly Sheppard. Beverly came to the IMLS to serve as the deputy director for museum services. When Diane Frankel left in 1999, Beverly was made acting director. Shortly thereafter the deputy for library services left, and for more than two years Beverly Sheppard really did three jobs. The fact that most people in the museum and library world never noticed is a tribute to Beverly's energy, skill, and vision. I want to recognize her leadership today. She had the initial idea for this conference, and she is largely responsible for the shape and content of the program. And I will now turn the podium over to Beverly to provide an overview of what is to come.

Note

After the events of September 11, 2001, the nation was in mourning. I felt that this conference was a beacon of hope and my husband, Bill McCook, and my dear friend the Louisiana state librarian for computing services, Sara M. Taffae, drove with me from Tampa, Florida, to this conference. Dr. Robert Martin's remarks were initially posted at the IMLS website, but they were taken down after 2008. I am reproducing these remarks here because I believe that this historic conference which took place at such a turning point in the history of the United States was also a turning point in public library development.—K.dlPMc.

Appendix C

Community Foundations and the Public Library: Libraries for the Future

Diantha Dow Schull and William Zeisel

Libraries for the Future (LFF) was a national nonprofit organization that championed the role of libraries in American life and helped individual libraries become more effective community institutions of the future. Founded in 1992, LFF mobilized private and public support for libraries, schools, and community partners to achieve equal access to the information and knowledge essential for a democratic society. LFF ceased operations in March 2009. The classic report "Community Foundations and the Public Library," based on data gathered in 1990–1991, is a foundational document for understanding the development of community foundations. This brief report is reproduced below because I have been unable to find it in any library and I feel that it should be available to those wishing to understand the scope of funding options for public libraries.

Introduction

Community foundations and public libraries are local institutions that receive little attention in the media yet perform vital services for most communities in the United States. If these two institutions receive little public attention, the relationship between them is even more poorly known to the general populace and, indeed, to officials, policymakers, and other local leaders. Traditionally, public libraries have received most of their capital and operating income from taxes, with occasional small additions from the federal government and private foundations. Little noticed has been the growing importance, during the past two decades, of the community foundation as an often crucial source of support for many libraries. Mutual interest is one reason for the closer relations between libraries and community foundations, both of which are local

475

institutions seeking to promote local interests. Cost effectiveness is another, as local institutions seek to achieve economies of scale by combining resources and cooperating on large projects. Efficiency is a third factor, because the key people in libraries and community foundations often know one another through local affairs and interaction, which means that there is less need to provide the potential funder with basic information, and also less need to explain the need for support.

In an effort to analyze this little-known nexus, LFF examined 150 community foundations, a sample diverse enough in geographical region and size of foundations to assess national trends. In addition, LFF sent survey questionnaires to the 150 foundations and received responses from more than half. The discussion that follows, based almost entirely on this research, suggests that the community foundation is far more important to public libraries than might be thought, and that through public libraries community foundations might be able to enhance their mission of serving the local community.

Basics about Community Foundations

A community foundation is a charitable, nonprofit corporation that holds and administers investments, as trusts and endowments, with the goal of advancing the public good by providing grants for local organizations and individuals. The first community foundation was established in Cleveland in 1914, and by the early 1960s more than 170 cities and towns had followed that example. Today an estimated 400 community foundations exist nationwide. They range in asset base from the largest, the New York Community Trust, and the second largest, the pioneering Cleveland Foundation ($693.6 million in 1991), to scores of small entities that hold no more than a few million dollars in investments.

Foundations typically begin with an initial donation or bundle of donations, which form the core endowment. Impetus for creating New Jersey's Westfield Foundation came from a group of local citizens, led by the town's mayor, who wanted "to give local philanthropy the flexibility and permanence of management needed for efficient and relevant responses to changing circumstances in the Westfield community." Over time local donors, including individuals, estates, businesses, and corporations, contributed additional funds. The Westfield Foundation began in 1975 with $2,000 of assets, and made its first grants in 1980 when its asset base reached $100,000. In 1981 the fund was augmented greatly by a transfer of more than $600,000 in assets from a local private foundation that supported scholarships and grants to schools, day care centers, and other entities. The transfer, made to achieve administrative efficiency, led to others in later years, including one of nearly $96,000 by the Friends of the Westfield Memorial Library. At the end of 1991, the Westfield Foundation held $2.5 million in assets, including 31 endowments and special-purpose funds managed for community groups, such as the United Way and the Westfield Rotary Club Foundation.

The community foundation typically defines its service area as a city, metropolitan area, county, or region. California's Humboldt Area Foundation covers a large county on the North Coast; several thousand miles to the east the Community Foundation of Southeastern Connecticut has 11 counties in its service area. The Community Foundation for Greater New Haven, which serves Connecticut's largest metropolitan area, describes itself as "a tool for the many, many levels of community life that exist here—on the streets of a neighborhood, within the boundaries of a town or city, across the region, or within some otherwise defined community linked by a common purpose."

Community foundations commonly divide their funds into several categories. So-called designated funds are established to benefit a specific organization. Among the funds of the Community Foundation of Greater New Haven are the Howard H. Bradley Trust, established in 1982 to benefit the Mt. Carmel Library, and the Mary W. and Robert Pryde Library fund, created in 1976 for the Town of Orange Library. Another fiscal category is donor-advised funds, which as the name suggests are administered in consultation with the donor. A third kind of fund, the discretionary fund, has the fewest strings attached.

Support to Public Libraries

The recipients of foundation grants vary widely. The Community Foundation of Southeastern Connecticut lists possible recipients as "charitable organizations" and the goal of the grants "to meet medical, educational, social welfare, cultural, environmental and civic needs" within the 11-county region. Public libraries receive grants under a variety of rubrics and funds, including education, culture, humanities, arts, community services, and services for the handicapped, especially the blind and visually impaired. In addition, foundations award grants for general community benefit, as when a library seeks help in paying for the computerization of its catalog or integration of its catalog with a county, state, or regional catalog. In the LFF survey most grants were used for unrestricted or capital expenses, including construction, books, equipment, computerization, staff, a bookmobile, and capital campaigns. Other, generally more modest grants were for special programs, reading groups, literacy programs, cataloging, planning, research and job centers, and video and other media. Several grants were for children's libraries, and some respondents indicated that their grants enabled library services to rural communities.

Of the 150 community foundations surveyed by LFF, three-fourths had provided support to public libraries. In a mail survey LFF asked 150 community foundations about their interest in and support for public libraries. Eighty-eight responded, including 26 of the nation's top 50 in market value. Of the respondents, 84 percent reported that they had funded public libraries, mostly through their discretionary funds. In general, respondents reported that their support for public libraries had remained relatively constant or increased over the years.

A foundation's interest in libraries may vary considerably over the span of years. For example, since 1956 the Scranton Area Foundation has provided grants, mostly under $5,000, to local public libraries. However, in 1987 it gave a $100,000 grant to the Scranton Public Library for a children's library, with the hope that by demonstrating support "others in the community would follow suit and this important community need would be met." Nebraska's Fremont Area Foundation, one of the nation's largest community foundations with assets of about $62 million (market value), provided the city of Fremont with $94,000 in 1991, toward the library's operating budget, plus smaller amounts for specific needs such as a CD-ROM station. It also provided grants as small as $100 and $700 to other public libraries.

Relatively few grants to libraries were greater than $10,000. Table 1 shows that of 176 grants made in 1990–1991, approximately one-quarter were in the more-than-$10,000 category.

The average (mean) grant was about $26,000, which is a substantial amount for most library budgets, but the median was only about $2,000. Most grants are very small indeed, typically around $1,000 or $2,000, and seldom over $5,000, and would significantly affect the overall level of private support only for the smallest libraries. The reason for the great difference between average and median sizes of grants is that a few large grants accounted for most of the dollars awarded. In fact, grants less than $10,000 were less than 7 percent of all grant dollars awarded, as shown in Table 2.

The low median size of grants should not be interpreted to mean that the smaller grants were of little consequence. One of the special attributes of the community foundation is its knowledge of local conditions, which permits it to make efficient use of dollars, particularly in situations where a small amount of money can make a big dif-

Table 1. Number of Grants to Public Libraries, from 150 Community Foundations, 1990–1991

Grant Size	No. of Foundations	No. of Grants
$10,000	23	45
Under $10,000	65	131
Total	88	176

Table 2. Amount of Support to Public Libraries, from 150 Sampled Community Foundations, by Size of Grant, 1990–1991	
Grant Size	Award
$10,000+	$4,207,647
Under $10,000	$276,646
Total	$4,484,293

ference. The librarian of Nebraska's North Bend Public Library, writing about a campaign to automate the checkout system, gratefully acknowledged a $350.00 grant from the Fremont Area Community Foundation, which "helped us reach our goal of $4,000.00, which seemed impossible for our little town." The Idaho Community Foundation in 1991 provided two small grants ($2,000 and $1,000) that paid for a new computer at the Pocatello Public Library and a theater performance sponsored by Community Library of Cottonwood. Fine-tuned giving of this nature is possible only when the funder and the recipient know each other well.

Comparison with Private Foundations

Community foundations, when compared with their more visible cousins, private foundations, are generous in supporting public libraries. The sampled foundations awarded a total of nearly $5 million in a recent year. Should the approximately 250 community foundations not sampled follow the same pattern, they would award another $7 million annually, for a total of $12 million from all community foundations.

These are small amounts when compared to the total operating budgets of the nation's public libraries—nearly $5 billion annually—but they are large when compared to grant support from the nation's private foundations (Ford, Mellon, Carnegie, etc.). A recent study by LFF concluded that foundations, including both private and community foundations, provide only $20 to $30 million annually to public libraries. If community foundations provide approximately $12 million of that amount, private foundations are supplying the rest, which means roughly $8–18 million each year. It is thus possible that in some years libraries receive more support from community foundations than from private foundations. However, unlike the Fords, Mellons, and Carnegies, community foundations do not have the potential for conceiving and implementing a broad national strategy, although many such foundations, acting along similar lines (whether by design or accident), might have a considerable impact on certain aspects of library operations and infrastructure.

Other Contributions to Public Libraries

Aside from direct grants, community foundations can also provide services of benefit to other organizations, including libraries. Many public libraries have discovered that they can reduce bookkeeping, accounting, and investment costs by transferring management of their endowment to a community foundation. The Community Foundation of Greater New Haven administers the Hamden Library Gift Fund and the funds of the Friends of the New Haven Free Public Library. California's Humboldt Area Foundation administers the Humboldt County Library Building Fund, which in 1993 donated $10,000 to the library's Construction Advisory Committee. The San Francisco Foundation provides bookkeeping for the Library Foundation of San Francisco's Campaign for the New Main Library. The Arkansas Community Foundation, which manages several funds for libraries, has been receiving inquiries about setting up funds for other libraries. In Ohio, to cite another example, the Columbus Foundation administers the $70,480 Columbus Metropolitan Library Endowment Fund, established in 1990 from the estate of an "avid library user."

Yet another service of the community foundation is to provide advice and seed money. California's Glendale Community Foundation helped the library establish an endowment fund by awarding local Friends a $3,000 grant to seed a "funding tree," placed on the wall of the main library. In return for a gift, library supporters could have their names engraved on the leaves. North Carolina's Cumberland Community Foundation helped the local library establish its own endowment and manage it, because "a local endowment makes a good library great and helps limit vagaries of public budgets."

Mutual Benefits

Public libraries and community foundations, as important local institutions, have a mutual self-interest in cooperating through grant support and shared or delegated services. The benefits to the public library are, first, additional funding; second, greater visibility in the community (since grants often come with some fanfare); and third, enhanced potential for grants in the future. The process of obtaining a grant from a community foundation is usually quicker and simpler than applying for one from a major private foundation, in part because the staff at the community foundation are already familiar with local needs and people. Since librarians and community foundation staff share a community, they are likely to be part of the same social and professional networks and may therefore more efficiently work for their common goals.

From the perspective of the community foundation the benefits are obvious but perhaps not as great as they might be if foundations were better able to look beyond the stereotype of the public library as mainly a collection of books and periodicals. The giving of grants satisfies the community foundation's major reason for being, which is to advance the public good locally. However, the good that is advanced through grants to public libraries may reflect an outdated view of the library's importance as a community institution.

Beyond books, beyond the dispensing of information, beyond providing a place to read and think, the public library exists as a civic institution. Funded largely by the community it serves, governed locally, patronized mainly by the people who live around it, the library is a central physical and social place without parallel elsewhere in the community. Through Friends groups, the governing board, volunteers, and individual contributions of time and effort, the library provides a way for people to participate in the community. It is also a way for the community to reach out to all its members, even those long ignored or isolated, through new, more action-oriented library-based projects and services.

Libraries around the nation have introduced innovative programs aimed at disadvantaged children and parents, as a way of helping people help themselves out of poverty. Activities for infants and preschoolers inculcate the habits of reading and thinking, which are then instilled into students through after-school study programs, homework workshops, activities for latchkey children, and other efforts offered by many libraries. Programs for senior citizens, including even outreach to nursing homes and community centers, help people stay mentally engaged throughout life. Centers for job and career information and health information empower individuals with data and referrals, while new centers for environmental information and programs on civic issues support local activism and problem solving and stimulate citizen participation. Every interaction between residents, as mediated through the library, strengthens the sense of shared identity and interests and increases the community's social capital.

Viewed in this light, libraries appear as far more central to the community and more likely to merit foundation support. A foundation, for its part, could find many opportunities in the library, including a new venue for public programs and a largely unexploited access route to reaching local residents. Exactly what this would mean in terms of dollars and programs would depend on the local situation, but the important step is to acknowledge that the public library has changed enough in recent years to warrant a major reassessment by community foundation leaders.

Conclusion

Community foundations and public libraries share many common interests, which have often led them to establish close working relationships in recent years. Community foundations annually provide a major share of philanthropic support to public libraries, and the share could increase with better understanding of the new library and its centrality to the community. Though both community foundations and public libraries are local institutions, in their totality they represent a vital part of the national infrastructure and should be analyzed in that light. As a national issue their mutually rewarding interaction deserves far more attention and discussion among experts, policymakers, legislators, library professionals, philanthropic leaders, and representatives of the general public.

Appendix D
Bibliography of National Statistics on Public Libraries

Arranged chronologically rather than alphabetically by author name.

1850 to 1900

Government Publications

Jewett, Charles Coffin. 1851. "Report on the Public Libraries of the United States of America, January 1, 1850." In *Report of the Board of Regents of the Smithsonian Institution*. Washington, DC: Smithsonian Institution.

Rhees, William Jones. 1859. *List of Public Libraries, Institutions and Societies in the United States and British Provinces of North America*. Washington, DC: Smithsonian Institution.

U.S. Bureau of Education. 1870. *Report of the Commissioner of Education Made to the Secretary of the Interior for the Year 1870, with Accompanying Papers*. Includes table, "Principal Libraries of the United States, Exclusive of Those Connected with Colleges, etc." Washington, DC: U.S. Government Printing Office.

U.S. Office of Education. 1876. *Public Libraries in the United States of America; Their History, Condition, and Management. Special Report*. Washington, DC: U.S. Government Printing Office.

U.S. Office of Education. 1886. *Statistics of Public Libraries in the United States. From the Report of the Commissioner of Education for the Year 1884–85. With Additions*. Washington, DC: U.S. Government Printing Office.

Flint, Weston. 1893. *Statistics of Public Libraries in the United States and Canada*. Washington, DC: U.S. Government Printing Office.

U.S. Bureau of Education. 1897. *Public, Society and School Libraries in the United States, with Library Statistics and Legislation of the Various States*. Washington, DC: U.S. Government Printing Office.

Nongovernment Publications

Trübner, Nicholas, Benjamin Moore, and Edward Edwards. 1859. *Trübner's Bibliographical Guide to American Literature. A Classed List of Books Published in the United States of America during the Last Forty Years. With Bibliographical Introduction, Notes and Alphabetical Index*. Includes "Public Libraries in the United States." London: Trübner and Co.

1901–1950

Government Publications

U.S. Office of Education. 1901. *Public, Society, and School Libraries*. Washington, DC: U.S. Government Printing Office.

U.S. Office of Education. 1903. *Public, Society and School Libraries in the United States, with Library Statistics and Legislation of the Various States*. Washington, DC: U.S. Government Printing Office.

U.S. Bureau of Education. 1904. *Public, Society, and School Libraries*. Washington, DC: U.S. Government Printing Office.

U.S. Bureau of Education. 1909. *Statistics of Public, Society, and School Libraries Having 5,000 Volumes and Over in 1908*. Washington, DC: U.S. Government Printing Office.

U.S. Bureau of Education. 1913. *Public, Society, and School Libraries*. Washington, DC: U.S. Government Printing Office.

U.S. Bureau of Education. 1915. *Public, Society, and School Libraries*. Washington, DC: U.S. Government Printing Office.

U.S. Bureau of Education. 1926. *Statistics of Public, Society, and School Libraries, 1923*. Washington, DC: U.S. Government Printing Office.

U.S. Office of Education. 1931. *Statistics of Public, Society, and School Libraries, 1929*. Washington, DC: U.S. Government Printing Office.

U.S. Office of Education. 1939. *Public Library Statistics, 1938/39*. Washington, DC: U.S. Government Printing Office.

U.S. Office of Education. 1947. *Public Library Statistics, 1944–45*. Washington, DC: U.S. Government Printing Office.

U.S. Office of Education. 1947. *Statistics of Public Libraries in Cities with Populations of 100,000 or More*. Washington, DC: U.S. Government Printing Office.

Nongovernment Publications

American Library Association. 1916. *Statistics of Libraries*. Chicago: American Library Association.

1950–1988

Government Publications

Willhoite, Mary M. 1952. *Statistics of Public Libraries in Cities with Populations of 50,000 to 99,999, 1950*. Washington, DC: Education Office, Federal Security Agency.

Willhoite, Mary M. 1952. *Statistics of Public Libraries in Cities with Populations of 100,000 or More, 1951*. Washington, DC: Education Office, Federal Security Agency.

Willhoite, Mary M. 1953. *Statistics of 50 Large County and Regional Libraries for 1952*. Washington, DC: Education Office, Health, Education, and Welfare Dept.

Willhoite, Mary M. 1953. *Statistics of Public Libraries in Cities with Populations of 50,000 to 99,999, 1952.* Washington, DC: Education Office, Health, Education, and Welfare Dept.

Willhoite, Mary M. 1953. *Statistics of Public Libraries in Cities with Populations of 100,000 or More, 1952.* Washington, DC: Education Office, Health, Education, and Welfare Dept.

Dunbar, Ralph M. 1954. *Public Library Statistics, 1950.* Washington, DC: Education Office, Health, Education, and Welfare Dept.

Willhoite, Mary M. 1954. *Statistics of County and Regional Libraries Serving Populations of 50,000 or More, Fiscal Year 1953.* Washington, DC: Education Office, Health, Education, and Welfare Dept.

Willhoite, Mary M. 1954. *Statistics of Public Libraries in Cities with Populations of 100,000 or More, Fiscal Year 1953.* Washington, DC: Education Office, Health, Education, and Welfare Dept.

Willhoite, Mary M. 1954. *Statistics of Public Library Systems in Cities with Populations of 50,000 to 99,999, Fiscal Year 1953.* Washington, DC: Education Office, Health, Education, and Welfare Dept.

Willhoite, Mary M. 1955. *Statistics of County and Regional Libraries Serving Populations of 50,000 or More, Fiscal Year 1954.* Washington, DC: Education Office, Health, Education, and Welfare Dept.

Willhoite, Mary M. 1955. *Statistics of Public Libraries in Cities with Populations of 100,000 or More, Fiscal Year 1954.* Washington, DC: Education Office, Health, Education, and Welfare Dept.

Willhoite, Mary M. 1956. *Statistics of County and Regional Libraries Serving Populations of 50,000 or More, Fiscal Year 1955.* Washington, DC: Education Office, Health, Education, and Welfare Dept.

Willhoite, Mary M. 1956. *Statistics of Public Libraries in Cities with Populations of 50,000 to 99,999, Fiscal Year 1955.* Washington, DC: Education Office, Health, Education, and Welfare Dept.

Willhoite, Mary M. 1956. *Statistics of Public Libraries in Cities with Populations of 100,000 or More, Fiscal Year 1955.* Washington, DC: Education Office, Health, Education, and Welfare Dept.

Willhoite, Mary M. 1957. *Statistics of County and Regional Libraries Serving Populations of 50,000 or More, Fiscal Year 1956.* Washington, DC: Education Office, Health, Education, and Welfare Dept.

Willhoite, Mary M. 1957. *Statistics of Public Libraries in Cities with Populations of 50,000 to 99,999, Fiscal Year 1956.* Washington, DC: Education Office, Health, Education, and Welfare Dept.

Willhoite, Mary M. 1957. *Statistics of Public Libraries in Cities with Populations of 100,000 or More, Fiscal Year 1956.* Washington, DC: Education Office, Health, Education, and Welfare Dept.

Vainstein, Rose, and Mary M. Willhoite. 1958. *Statistics of Public Libraries in Cities with Populations of 50,000 to 99,999, Fiscal Year 1957.* Washington, DC: Education Office, Health, Education, and Welfare Dept.

Vainstein, Rose, and Mary M. Willhoite. 1958. *Statistics of Public Libraries in Cities with Populations of 100,000 or More, Fiscal Year 1957.* Washington, DC: Education Office, Health, Education, and Welfare Dept.

Vainstein, Rose, Mary M. Willhoite, and Doris C. Holladay. 1958. *Statistics of Public Libraries in Cities with Populations of 35,000 to 49,999, Fiscal Year 1957.* Washington, DC: U.S. Department of Health, Education, and Welfare.

Willhoite, Mary M. 1958. *Statistics of County and Regional Libraries Serving Populations of 50,000 or More, Fiscal Year 1957.* Washington, DC: Education Office, Health, Education, and Welfare Dept.

U.S. Office of Education. 1959. *Statistics of Public Libraries: 1955–56.* Washington, DC: U.S. Government Printing Office.

Vainstein, Rose. 1959. "Statistics of Public Libraries, 1955–56." In *Biennial Survey of Education in the United States, 1954–56.* Washington, DC: U.S. Office of Education.

Vainstein, Rose, and Doris C. Holladay. 1959. *Statistics of Public Libraries in Cities with Populations of 100,000 or More, Fiscal Year 1958.* Washington, DC: Education Office, Health, Education, and Welfare Dept.

Vainstein, Rose, and Doris C. Holladay. 1960. *Statistics of County and Regional Library Systems Serving Populations of 50,000 or More, Fiscal Year 1959.* Washington, DC: Education Office, Health, Education, and Welfare Dept.

Willhoite, Mary M. 1960. *Statistics of County and Regional Libraries Serving Populations of 50,000 or More, Fiscal Year 1959.* Washington, DC: Education Office, Health, Education, and Welfare Dept.

Rather, John Carson, and Nathan Marshall Cohen. 1961. *Statistics of Libraries, Annotated Bibliography of Recurring Surveys.* Washington, DC: Education Office, Health, Education, and Welfare Dept.

Schick, Frank Leopold, and Doris C. Holladay. 1961. *Statistics of Public Library Systems Serving Populations of 100,000 or More: Fiscal Year 1960.* Washington, DC: Education Office, Health, Education, and Welfare Dept.

Drennan, Henry T., and Doris C. Holladay. 1962. *Statistics of Public Library Systems Serving Populations of 35,000 to 49,999: Fiscal Year 1960.* Washington, DC: Education Office, Health, Education, and Welfare Dept.

Schick, Frank Leopold, Henry T. Drennan, and Doris C. Holladay. 1962. *Statistics of Public Library Systems Serving Populations of 50,000 to 99,999: Fiscal Year 1960.* Washington, DC: Education Office, Health, Education, and Welfare Dept.

Drennan, Henry T., Doris C. Holladay, and United States Office of Education. 1965. *Statistics of Public Libraries, 1962. Part I: Selected Statistics of Public Libraries Serving Populations of 35,000 and Above: Institutional Data.* Washington, DC: U.S. Government Printing Office.

U.S. Office of Education, Division of Library Services, and Educational Facilities and National Center for Educational Statistics. 1965. *Statistics of Public Libraries Serving Communities with at Least 25,000 Inhabitants.* Washington, DC: Education Office, Health, Education, and Welfare Dept.

U.S. Office of Education, Library Services Branch. 1966. *1962 Statistics of Public Libraries Serving Populations of Less Than 35,000*. Champaign, IL: Illini Union Book Store.

U.S. Office of Education, National Center for Educational Statistics. 1968. *Statistics of Public Libraries Serving Communities with at Least 25,000 Inhabitants, 1965*. Washington, DC: U.S. Government Printing Office.

Boaz, Ruth L., and National Center for Educational Statistics. 1970. *Statistics of Public Libraries Serving Areas with at Least 25,000 Inhabitants, 1968*. Washington, DC: U.S. Dept. of Health, Education, and Welfare, Office of Education, National Center for Educational Statistics.

Eckard, Helen M., and National Center for Educational Statistics. 1978. *Survey of Public Libraries: LIBGIS I, 1974*. Washington, DC: U.S. Dept. of Health, Education, and Welfare, Education Division.

National Center for Education Statistics. 1978. *Library Statistics Publications, 1960–1977*. Washington, DC: National Center for Education Statistics.

Eckard, Helen M., and National Center for Educational Statistics. 1982. *Statistics of Public Libraries, 1977–1978*. Washington, DC: National Center for Education Statistics.

U.S. Department of Education. 1986. *Patron Use of Computers in Public Libraries*. Washington, DC: U.S. Department of Education.

U.S. Office of Educational Research and Improvement Center for Statistics. 1986. *Statistics of Public Libraries, 1982*. Washington, DC: Center for Statistics, U.S. Department of Education.

U.S. Department of Education. 1988. *National Center for Education Statistics Survey Report: Services and Resources for Young Adults in Public Libraries*. Washington, DC: Office of Educational Research and Improvement, U.S. Department of Education.

Nongovernment Publications

Ulshafer, Anne. 1963. *Selected Statistics of Public Libraries in the United States and Canada Serving 100,000 Population or More*. Fort Wayne, IN: Fort Wayne Public Library.

Carpenter, Beth E., and Abla M. Shaheen. 1971. *Selected Statistics of Public Libraries in the United States and Canada Serving 100,000 Population or More*. Fort Wayne, IN: Fort Wayne Public Library.

Statistics of Public Libraries in the United States and Canada Serving 100,000 Population or More. 1977. Fort Wayne, IN: Fort Wayne Public Library.

Statistics of Public Libraries in the United States and Canada Serving 100,000 Population or More. 1979. Fort Wayne, IN: Fort Wayne Public Library.

Allen County Public Library. 1981. *Statistics of Public Libraries in the United States and Canada Serving 100,000 Population or More*. Fort Wayne, IN: Allen County Public Library.

Goldhor, Herbert. 1981. *Fact Book of the American Public Library*. Champaign: University of Illinois, Graduate School of Library and Information Science.

Allen County Public Library. 1983. *Statistics of Public Libraries in the United States and Canada Serving 100,000 Population or More*. Fort Wayne, IN: Allen County Public Library.

Public Library Association and American Library Association. 1985. *Statistics of Public Libraries, 1981–82: Data Gathered by the National Center for Education Statistics, U.S. Department of Education.* Chicago: Public Library Association.

Lynch, Mary Jo. 1987. *Libraries in an Information Society: A Statistical Summary.* Chicago: American Library Association.

1988–Present

Government Publications

Podolsky, Arthur. 1989. *FSCS: An NCES Working Paper: Public Libraries in Forty-Four States and the District of Columbia, 1988.* Washington, DC: U.S. Department of Education.

Lewis, Laurie, and Elizabeth Farris. 1990. *Services and Resources for Children in Public Libraries, 1988–89.* http://nces.ed.gov/pubs90/90098.pdf. Accessed November 25, 2002.

National Center for Education Statistics. 1991. *Public Library Data.* Washington, DC: U.S. Department of Education.

Podolsky, Arthur, and National Center for Education Statistics. 1991. *Public Libraries in 50 States and the District of Columbia, 1989.* Washington, DC: U.S. Department of Education.

Chute, Adrienne. 1992. *Public Libraries in the United States: 1990.* Washington, DC: U.S. Department of Education.

National Center for Education Statistics. 1992. *Public Library Data.* Washington, DC: U.S. Department of Education.

Chute, Adrienne. 1993. *Public Libraries in the United States: 1991.* Washington, DC: U.S. Department of Education.

Kindel, Carrol B. 1994. *Report on Coverage Evaluations of the Public Library Statistics Program.* E. D. TAB. NCES Number: 94430. Washington, DC: U.S. Department of Education.

Chute, Adrienne, and National Center for Education Statistics. 1994. *Public Libraries in the United States, 1992.* E.D. TAB. Washington, DC: U.S. Department of Education.

Data Comparability and Public Policy New Interest in Public Library Data: Papers Presented at Meetings of the American Statistical Association. 1994. Washington, DC: U.S. Department of Education.

U.S. Census Bureau, Governments Division. 1994. *Report on Coverage Evaluation of the Public Library Statistics Program: A Report.* Washington, DC: U.S. Department of Education.

U.S. Department of Education, National Center for Education Statistics. 1995. *Public Libraries in the United States: 1993.* E.D. TAB, edited by Adrienne Chute, et al. http://nces.ed.gov/pubsearch/pubsinfo.asp?pubid=95129.

National Center for Education Statistics. 1995. *Finance Data in the Public Library Statistics Program: Definitions, Internal Consistency, and Comparisons to Secondary Sources: A Report.* Washington, DC: National Center for Education Statistics.

Heaviside, Sheila, et al. 1995. "Services and Resources for Children and Young Adults in Public Libraries." http://nces.ed.gov/pubs95/95357.pdf.

Kindel, Carrol B. 1995. *Finance Data in the Public Library Statistics Program: Definitions, Internal Consistency, and Comparisons to Secondary Sources: A Report.* Washington, DC: National Center for Education Statistics.

Kindel, Carrol B. 1995. *Report on Evaluation of Definitions Used in the Public Library Statistics Program.* NCES 95430. Washington, DC: National Center for Education Statistics.

Kindel, Carrol B. 1995. *Staffing Data in the Public Library Statistics Program: Definitions, Internal Consistency, and Comparisons to Secondary Sources: A Report.* Washington, DC: U.S. Department of Education.

National Center for Education Statistics. 1995. *Public Libraries in the United States, 1993.* Washington, DC: U.S. Department of Education.

Kindel, Carrol B. 1996. *Public Library Structure and Organization in the United States.* http://nces.ed.gov/pubs/96229.pdf.

Collins, Mary A., and Kathryn Chandler. 1997. *Use of Public Library Services by Households in the United States: 1996.* http://nces.ed.gov/pubs/97446.pdf.

National Center for Education Statistics. 1997. *Public Libraries in the United States, 1994.* Washington, DC: U.S. Department of Education.

U.S. Census Bureau. 1997. *Public Libraries in the United States, FY 1994.* NCES 97-418. E.D. TAB. Washington, DC: U.S. Department of Education. http://nces.ed.gov/pubs97/97418.pdf.

Bassman, Keri, et al. 1998. *How Does Your Public Library Compare? Service Performance of Peer Groups.* Washington, DC: National Center for Education Statistics. http://nces.ed.gov/pubs98/98310.pdf.

National Center for Education Statistics. 1998. *Public Libraries in the United States, FY 1995.* Washington, DC: U.S. Department of Education.

Chute, Adrienne, and P. Elaine Kroe. 1999. *Public Libraries in the United States, FY 1996.* Washington, DC: U.S. Department of Education.

U.S. Department of Education. 1999. *Public Libraries in the United States: FY 1996.* E.D. TAB, edited by Adrienne Chute, et al. Washington, DC: U.S. Department of Education. http://nces.ed.gov/pubs99/1999306.pdf.

U.S. Department of Education. 2000. *Public Libraries in the United States: FY 1997.* E.D. TAB, edited by Adrienne Chute, et al. Washington, DC: U.S. Department of Education. http://nces.ed.gov/pubs2000/2000316.pdf.

Glover, Denise. 2001. *Public Library Trends Analysis Fiscal Years 1992–1996.* Washington, DC: U.S. Department of Education. http://nces.ed.gov/pubs2001/2001324.pdf.

U.S. Department of Education. 2001. *Public Libraries in the United States: Fiscal Year 1998.* E.D. TAB, edited by Adrienne Chute, et al. Washington, DC: U.S. Department of Education. http://nces.ed.gov/pubs2001/2001307.pdf.

National Center for Education Statistics. 2002. *Public Libraries in the United States, 1989–2000.* Washington, DC: U.S. Department of Education. http://purl.access.gpo.gov/GPO/LPS17333.

U.S. Department of Education. 2002. *Public Libraries in the United States: Fiscal Year 1999.* E.D. TAB, edited by Adrienne Chute, et al. Washington, DC: U.S. Department of Education. http://nces.ed.gov/pubs2002/2002308.pdf.

U.S. Department of Education. 2002. *Public Libraries in the United States, Fiscal Year 2000.* E.D. TAB, edited by Adrienne Chute, et al. Washington, DC: U.S. Department of Education. http://nces.ed.gov/pubs2002/2002344.pdf.

National Center for Education Statistics. *Public Libraries.* http://nces.ed.gov/pubsearch/pubsinfo.asp?pubid=2003398.

Kroe, Elaine. 2003. *Data File, Restricted Use: Public Libraries Survey: Fiscal Year 2001.* U.S. Department of Education. http://nces.ed.gov/pubsearch/pubsinfo.asp?pubid=2003397.

Chute, A., E. Kroe, P. O'Shea, T. Craig, M. Freeman, L. Hardesty, J. F. McLaughlin, and C. J. Ramsey. 2005. *Public Libraries in the United States: Fiscal Year 2002* (NCES 2005–356). U.S. Department of Education. Washington, DC: National Center for Education Statistics. http://harvester.census.gov/imls/pubs/Publications/2005356.pdf.

Chute, A., P. E. Kroe, P. O'Shea, T. Craig, M. Freeman, L. Hardesty, J. F. McLaughlin, and C. J. Ramsey. 2005. *Public Libraries in the United States: Fiscal Year 2003* (NCES 2005–363). U.S. Department of Education. Washington, DC: National Center for Education Statistics. http://nces.ed.gov/pubsearch/pubsinfo.asp?pubid=2005363.

Glander, M., and T. Dam. 2006. *Households' Use of Public and Other Types of Libraries: 2002* (NCES 2007-327). U.S. Department of Education. Washington, DC: National Center for Education Statistics. http://nces.ed.gov/pubsearch.

Chute, A., P. E. Kroe, P. O'Shea, T. Craig, M. Freeman, L. Hardesty, J. F. McLaughlin, and C. J. Ramsey. 2006. *Public Libraries in the United States: Fiscal Year 2004* (NCES 2006–349). U.S. Department of Education. Washington, DC: National Center for Education Statistics. http://harvester.census.gov/imls/pubs/Publications/2006349.pdf.

Chute, A., and P. E. Kroe. 2007. *Public Libraries in the United States: Fiscal Year 2005* (NCES 2008-301). Washington, DC: National Center for Education Statistics, Institute of Education Sciences, U.S. Department of Education. http://harvester.census.gov/imls/pubs/Publications/2008301.pdf.

Miller, K., C. Manjarrez, E. Henderson, T. Craig, S. Dorinski, M. Freeman, J. Keng, L. McKenzie, P. O'Shea, C. Ramsey, and C. Sheckells. 2008. *Public Libraries Survey: Fiscal Year 2006.* Washington, DC: Institute of Museum and Library Services. http://harvester.census.gov/imls/pubs/Publications/PLS2006.pdf.

Henderson, E., K. Miller, T. Craig, S. Dorinski, M. Freeman, N. Isaac, J. Keng, L. McKenzie, P. O'Shea, C. Ramsey, and C. Sheckells. 2009. *Public Libraries Survey: Fiscal Year 2007* (IMLS-2009–PLS-02). Washington, DC: Institute of Museum and Library Services. http://harvester.census.gov/imls/pubs/Publications/PLS2006.pdf.

Henderson, E., K. Miller, T. Craig, S. Dorinski, M. Freeman, N. Isaac, J. Keng, P. O'Shea, and P. Schilling. 2010. *Public Libraries Survey: Fiscal Year 2008* (IMLS-2010–PLS-02). Washington, DC: Institute of Museum and Library Services. http://harvester.census.gov/imls/pubs/Publications/pls2008.pdf.

Nongovernment Publications

Public Library Association Statistical Series. The *Public Library Data Service Statistical Report* is published annually. It presents exclusive, timely data from 1,000 public libraries across the country on finances, library resources, annual use figures, and technology. Some editions contain a special survey.

Public Library Association. 1988. *Public Library Data Service Statistical Report '88*. Chicago: American Library Association.

———. 1989. *Public Library Data Service Statistical Report '89*. Chicago: American Library Association.

———. 1990. *Public Library Data Service Statistical Report '90*. Chicago: American Library Association.

———. 1991. *Public Library Data Service Statistical Report '91*. Chicago: American Library Association.

———. 1992. *Public Library Data Service Statistical Report '92*. Chicago: American Library Association.

———. 1993. *Public Library Data Service Statistical Report '93*. Chicago: American Library Association.

———. 1994. *Public Library Data Service Statistical Report '94: Special Section—Children's Services Survey*. Chicago: American Library Association.

———. 1995. *Statistical Report '95: Public Library Data Service; Special Section, Technology Survey*. Chicago: American Library Association.

———. 1996. *Statistical Report '96: Public Library Data Service; Special Section, Business Services Survey*. Chicago: American Library Association.

———. 1997. *Statistical Report '97: Public Library Data Service; Special Section, Children's Services Survey*. Chicago: American Library Association.

———. 1998. *Statistical Report '98: Public Library Data Service. Special Section: Finance Survey*. Chicago: American Library Association.

———. 1999. *Statistical Report '99: Public Library Data Service; Special Section: Public Library Facilities Survey*. Chicago: American Library Association.

———. 2000. *Statistical Report 2000: Public Library Data Service; Special Section: Children's Services Survey*. Chicago: American Library Association.

———. 2001. *Statistical Report 2001: Public Library Data Service; Special Section: Finance Survey*. Chicago: American Library Association.

———. 2002. *Statistical Report 2002: Public Library Data Service; Special Section: Public Library Facilities Survey*. Chicago: American Library Association.

———. 2003. *Statistical Report 2003: Public Library Data Service; Special Section: Children's Services Survey*. Chicago: American Library Association.

———. 2004. *Statistical Report 2004: Public Library Data Service; Special Section: Internet Filtering Survey*. Chicago: American Library Association.

———. 2005. *Statistical Report 2005: Public Library Data Service; Special Section: Finance Survey*. Chicago: American Library Association.

———. 2006. *Statistical Report 2006: Public Library Data Service; Special Section: Children's Services Survey*. Chicago: American Library Association.

———. 2007. *Statistical Report 2007: Public Library Data Service; Special Section: Young Adult Services*. Chicago: American Library Association.

————. 2008. *Statistical Report 2008: Public Library Data Service; Special Section: Financial Practices*. Chicago: American Library Association.

————. 2009. *Statistical Report 2003: Public Library Data Service; Special Section: Public Library Facilities*. Chicago: American Library Association.

————. 2010. *Statistical Report 2010: Public Library Data Service; Special Section: Children's Services Survey*. Chicago: American Library Association.

Sources

Goldhor, Herbert. 1983. "U.S. Public Library Statistics in Series: A Bibliography and Subject Index." In *Bowker Annual of Library and Book Trade Information*. 28th ed, 327–335. New York: R.R. Bowker.

U.S. Institute of Museum and Library Services. http://www.imls.gov/.

U.S. National Center for Education Statistics. http://nces.ed.gov/.

Williams, Robert V. 1991. "The Making of Statistics of National Scope on American Libraries, 1836–1986: Purposes, Problems, and Issues." *Libraries and Culture* 26 (Spring): 464–485.

Williams, Robert V., and Mittie Kristina McLean. 2008. *A Bibliographical Guide to a Chronological Record of Statistics of National Scope on Libraries in the United States*. Columbia: University of South Carolina, School of Library and Information Science.

Index

Page numbers followed by the letter "f" indicate figures; "ch." followed by a number indicates the entry is relevant to the entire chapter.

About the Author and Contributors

Kathleen de la Peña McCook is Distinguished University Professor, School of Information, University of South Florida in Tampa. She was honored as the Dr. Jean E. Coleman Library Outreach Lecturer at the 2010 American Library Association conference. Her topic was "Librarians and Human Rights."

Kathleen is also a Visiting Scholar at Valdosta State University in Georgia working on the Laura Bush 21st Century Librarian Program, "Librarians Build Communities" (2009–2012). The Chicago Public Library honored Kathleen as its "Scholar in Residence" where she did a systemwide series of events on the role of the public library in building communities in 2003.

Kathleen received the Florida Library Association Lifetime Achievement Award in 2007; the Diversity Research Award from the ALA Office for Diversity in 2004; the Beta Phi Mu Award for distinguished service to education for librarianship in 2003; the ALA Elizabeth Futas Catalyst for Change Award in 1998; the ALA Margaret E. Monroe Adult Services Award in 1991; and the ALA Equality Award in 1987. She was the Lauretta McCusker Memorial Lecturer speaking on "Public Libraries and the Public Sphere" at Dominican University in 2003. She is past president of the Association for Library and Information Science Education and was 2002 REFORMA Latino Librarian of the Year (Trejo Award). She is a life member of REFORMA. In 1991 she was named Outstanding Alumna by the University of Wisconsin-Madison School of Library and Information Studies where she earned the PhD in 1980. She earned the MA in Library Science at the University of Chicago, Graduate Library School in 1974.

Other writing by Kathleen in the twenty-first century includes "Human Rights as a Framework for Reflection in Service Learning: 'Para que Otro Mundo es posible'" (in *Service Learning*, edited by Loriene Roy; ALA, 2009); "There Is Power in a Union" (*Progressive Librarian* 32, 2009; "Human Rights, Democracy and Librarians "(with Katharine J. Phenix; in *The Portable MLIS*; Libraries Unlimited, 2008; "Librarians as Advocates for the Human Rights of Immigrants" (*Progressive Librarian* 29, 2007); "Rebuilding Community in Louisiana after the Hurricanes of 2005" (with Alma Dawson; *RUSQ*, 2006); "Librarians and Social Movements" (with Elaine Harger and Isabel Espinal; in *Proceedings of the First National Joint Conference of Librarians of Color, 2006*); "Social Justice as a Context for a Career in Librarianship" (in *Perspectives, Insights and Priorities*, edited by Norman Horrocks; Scarecrow Press, 2005;

"Public Libraries and People in Jail" (*RUSQ*, 2004); "Public Policy as a Factor Influencing Adult Lifelong Learning, Adult Literacy and Public Libraries (with Peggy Barber; *RUSQ*, 2002); "Poverty, Democracy and Public Libraries" (in *Libraries & Democracy: The Cornerstones of Liberty*, edited by Nancy Kranich; ALA, 2001; *A Place at the Table: Participating in Community Building* (ALA, 2000); *Ethnic Diversity in Library and Information Science* (*Library Trends*, 2000); and *Library Services to Youth of Hispanic Heritage* (with Barbara Froling Immroth; McFarland, 2000).

Kathleen is a member of the editorial board of the journal *Progressive Librarian* and serves on the Coordinating Committee of the Progressive Librarians Guild. She coordinates the *Union Librarian* blog for the Guild. She is a member of AFT 7463.

***

Barbara J. Ford is Mortenson Distinguished Professor, Mortenson Center for International Library Programs, University of Illinois at Urbana-Champaign Library. She is a past president of the American Library Association (ALA) and former Assistant Commissioner of the Chicago Public Library.

Barbara began her international work as a Peace Corps volunteer in Panama and Nicaragua in the 1970s. As the 1997–1998 president of the ALA, Barbara's theme was "Libraries: Global Reach, Local Touch." In recent years the ALA and Chinese American Librarians Association have recognized her with awards for her significant contributions and dedication to international librarianship.

Barbara previously worked as assistant commissioner for central library services at the Chicago Public Library, executive director of the Virginia Commonwealth University libraries, and associate library director at Trinity University in San Antonio, Texas. She served in several capacities at the University of Illinois at Chicago, including documents librarian and audiovisual librarian. In addition, Barbara was director of the Soybean Insect Research Information Center at the Illinois Natural History Survey.

From 2005–2009 she served as an elected member of the International Federation of Library Associations and Institutions (IFLA) Governing Board. She previously served as the secretary for the IFLA Section on Government Information and Official Publications and on the IFLA Academic and Research Libraries Section. She was president of the Association of College and Research Libraries (ACRL), a division of ALA, from 1990 until 1991.

The author of many publications and presentations, Barbara has traveled around the world to address topics such as information literacy, government information, the future of libraries, the role of library associations, international cooperation among libraries, public libraries, among other topics. She serves on the editorial advisory boards of *Information Development*, *Libri*, and *World Libraries*.

In 1998 Barbara was named distinguished alumna by Illinois Wesleyan University where she earned a bachelor's degree in history and education. In 1997 she received the distinguished alumnus award from the Graduate School of Library and Information Science at the University of Illinois at Urbana-Champaign where she earned a master's degree in library science. Barbara also has a master's degree in international relations from the Fletcher School of Law and Diplomacy at Tufts University.

In 2010 Barbara visited and worked with library projects in China, Ghana, Korea, Latvia, the Philippines, Romania, Sweden, Taiwan, and Tanzania.

Alicia K. Long, ALA Spectrum Scholar 2009, is a graduate student in the Master of Library and Information Science program and research associate at the University of South Florida, School of Information. She also received the 2010 Florida Library Association's Bernadette Storck Scholarship and published in *Florida Libraries*. In her native Argentina, she was an elementary school teacher and literacy teacher working with teens and adults who needed to finish elementary school. She is currently a volunteer in several community organizations.

Katharine J. Phenix is the Adult Services Librarian (aka Experience Guide) at the Huron Street branch of the Rangeview Library District in Thornton, Colorado, which was one of the five library winners of the 2010 IMLS National Medal for Museum and Library Service. She has presented at state conferences on the "anythink revolution" at Rangeview, and on volunteer (aka Sidekick) programs in public libraries. She was formerly the Academic Collections Manager for netLibrary Inc. in Boulder, where she currently resides. She spent her undergraduate years in Montreal, Canada, where she worked for seven years as support staff at the Concordia University library. In her first professional position, after graduating with an MSLIS and a CAS at the University of Illinois, she created the first online bookmobile in 1986 for the Westminster Public Library in Westminster, Colorado. She was a Visiting Instructor at the Louisiana State University School of Library and Information Science in 1987–1988. Her publications include several years as the Software Columnist for *The Wilson Library Bulletin* and Events columnist for *Library Hi Tech News*. She is the author and co-author of several editions of *On Account of Sex: An Annotated Bibliography on the Status of Women in Librarianship*. She also compiled *The Subject Guide to Women of the World* for Scarecrow Press. She is currently researching, writing, and publishing books and articles about human rights and librarianship. She has served as Chair of the ALA Committee on the Status of Women in Librarianship and on the Editorial Advisory Board of *RQ*. She served on the ALA Sophie Brody Award committee from 2009–2011 and joined the Notable Books Council in 2011.